Anita E. Woolfolk

Rutgers University

Educational
Psychology

THIRD EDITION

Prentice-Hall, Inc.
Englewood Cliffs, New Jersey 07632

Library of Congress Cataloging-in-Publication Data

WOOLFOLK, ANITA.
  Educational psychology.

  Rev. ed. of: Educational psychology for teachers. 2nd ed. c1984.
  Bibliography: p.
  Includes indexes.
  1. Educational psychology. I. Woolfolk, Anita.
Educational psychology for teachers. II. Title.
LB1051.W74 1987   370.15   86-22723
ISBN 0-13-240607-1

To my first teachers,
Charles Goodwin Pratt and Marion Wieckert Pratt

And to all the others,
Bill Garber, Ouida Guthrie, Rachel Pearce, Julian Rush, Anita Wieckert
Leon Wilson, Mary Young . . .

Development Editor: Martha G. Wiseman
Cover and Interior Design: Judith A. Matz-Coniglio
Editorial Production/Supervision: Linda Benson
Photo Researcher: Ilene Cherna
Photo Editor: Lorinda Morris
Manufacturing Buyer: John Hall
Cover Photo: Kandinsky: In Alto 1929 Venezia, Guggenheim. Scala/Art Resource

© 1987, 1984, 1980 by Prentice-Hall, Inc.
A Division of Simon & Schuster
Englewood Cliffs, New Jersey 07632

Printed in the United States of America

10 9 8 7 6 5 4 3

Chapter Opener Photo Credits: (1) Jeffry Myers/FPG. (2) Taurus Photo. (3) L. Druskis/Taurus Photo (4) Four by Five. (5) Dan McCoy/Rainbow. (6) Lawrence Migdale/Photo Researchers. (7) Richard Hutchings/Photo Researchers. (8) Freda Leinwand/Monkmeyer Press. (9) Four by Five. (10) Lawrence Migdale/Photo Researchers. (11) Richard Hutchings. (12) Jeffry Myers/FPG. (13) Will McIntyre/Photo Researchers. (14) Stephen Collins/Photo Researchers. (15) Larry Voigt/Photo Researchers.

ISBN 0-13-240607-1   01

Prentice-Hall International (UK) Limited, *London*
Prentice-Hall of Australia Pty. Limited, *Sydney*
Prentice-Hall Canada Inc., *Toronto*
Editora Prentice-Hall Hispanoamericana, S.A., *Mexico*
Prentice-Hall of India Private Limited, *New Delhi*
Prentice-Hall of Japan, Inc., *Tokyo*
Prentice-Hall of Southeast Asia Pte. Ltd., *Singapore*
Editora Prentice-Hall do Brasil, Ltda., *Rio de Janeiro*

Contents

Preface   ix

AN INTRODUCTION TO EDUCATIONAL
PSYCHOLOGY

1   Teachers, Teaching, and Educational
Psychology   1

Overview   2
Teaching: An Art, a Science, and a Lot of Work   2
Social Issues Affecting Teachers Today   13
The Role of Educational Psychology   20
Major Areas of Study: The Contents of This Book   25
Summary/Key Terms   27
Suggestions for Further Reading and Study   28
Teachers' Forum   30

Appendix: Research in Educational
Psychology   33

Overview   34
Asking and Answering Questions   34
Is the Research Valid?   39
A Sample Study: The Effect of Student Expectations   41
Summary/Key Terms   44
Suggestions for Further Reading and Study   45

HUMAN DEVELOPMENT: A FRAMEWORK FOR TEACHERS

2 The Mind at Work: Cognitive Development and Language 47

Overview 48
Development: Toward a General Definition 48
A Comprehensive Theory about Thinking: The Work of Piaget 50
Piaget's Theory: Limitations and Implications 65
Another Perspective: Information Processing 71
The Development of Language 74
Summary/Key Terms 80
Suggestions for Further Reading and Study 81
Teachers' Forum 82

3 Personal, Social, and Moral Development 85

Overview 86
A Comprehensive Theory: The Work of Erikson 86
Issues in the Early Years 96
Issues Affecting Adolescents 101
Understanding Ourselves and Others 104
Education for Emotional Growth 114
Summary/Key Terms 118
Suggestions for Further Reading and Study 119
Teachers' Forum 120

4 Individual Variations 123

Overview 124
The Origin of Differences 124
Individual Differences in Intelligence 135
The Question of Creativity 149
Variations in Cognitive Styles 152
Summary/Key Terms 157
Suggestions for Further Reading and Study 158
Teachers' Forum 160

LEARNING THEORY AND PRACTICE

5 Learning: Behavioral Views 163

Overview 164
Learning: Toward a General Definition 164
Contiguity: Learning through Simple Associations 168

Classical Conditioning: Pairing Automatic Responses with New
Stimuli   169
Operant Conditioning: Trying New Responses   173
Learning by Observing Others   182
Applying the Principles: Behavioral Technology   187
Summary/Key Terms   192
Suggestions for Further Reading and Study   193
Teachers' Forum   194

6 Applications of Behavioral Approaches   197

Overview   198
Focusing on Positive Behavior   198
Developing New Behaviors   204
Coping with Undesirable Behavior   208
Special Programs for Classroom Management   213
Self-Management   221
Problems and Issues   225
Summary/Key Terms   228
Suggestions for Further Reading and Study   229
Teachers' Forum   230

7 Learning: Cognitive Views   233

Overview   234
Elements of the Cognitive Perspective   234
The Information Processing Model of Learning   236
Remembering and Forgetting   249
Learning about Learning: Metacognitive Abilities   258
Summary/Key Terms   264
Suggestions for Further Reading and Study   266
Teachers' Forum   268

8 The Cognitive Perspective and Teaching Practice   271

Overview   272
Learning Outcomes: Gagné   272
Learning through Discovery: Bruner   274
Reception Learning: Ausubel   276
Teaching and Learning about Concepts   280
Problem Solving   283
Study Skills   291
Teaching for Transfer   295
Teaching Thinking   302
Summary/Key Terms   305
Suggestions for Further Reading and Study   307
Teachers' Forum   308

MOTIVATION AND CLASSROOM MANAGEMENT

9 Motivation in the Classroom 310

Overview 312
What Is Motivation? 312
The Learning Process: Influences on Motivation 319
Teacher Expectations 331
Anxiety in the Classroom 339
Summary/Key Terms 343
Suggestions for Further Reading and Study 345
Teachers' Forum 346

10 Classroom Management and Communication 349

Overview 350
Classrooms Need Managers 350
Planning for Good Management 355
Maintaining Effective Management: Motivation and Prevention 363
The Need for Communication 368
Summary/Key Terms 376
Suggestions for Further Reading and Study 377
Teachers' Forum 378

PLANNING AND TEACHING

11 Setting Objectives and Planning 381

Overview 382
Teacher Planning 382
Objectives for Learning 383
Task Analysis 390
Taxonomies 392
Basic Formats for Teaching 398
Settings for Achieving Objectives 408
Summary/Key Terms 412
Suggestions for Further Reading and Study 413
Teachers' Forum 414

12 Effective Teaching 417

Overview 418
The Search for the Keys to Success 418
Meanwhile, What's Happening with the Students? 426
Effective Teaching for Different Subjects 429
Effective Teaching with Different Students 434

Integrating Ideas about Effective Teaching   440
Summary/Key Terms   445
Suggestions for Further Reading and Study   446
Teachers' Forum   448

13 Teaching Exceptional Students   451

Overview   452
What Does It Mean to Be Exceptional?   452
Students with Learning Problems   455
Mainstreaming   469
Students with Special Abilities: The Gifted   474
Multicultural and Bilingual Education   479
Summary/Key Terms   481
Suggestions for Further Reading and Study   483
Teachers' Forum   484

EVALUATING STUDENTS

14 Using Standardized Tests in Teaching   487

Overview   488
Measurement and Evaluation   488
What Do Test Scores Mean?   492
Types of Standardized Tests   502
Current Issues in Standardized Testing   510
Summary/Key Terms   518
Suggestions for Further Reading and Study   519
Teachers' Forum   520

15 Classroom Evaluation and Grading   523

Overview   524
Classroom Evaluation and Testing   524
Planning a Measurement Program   531
Effects of Grades and Grading on Students   535
Grading and Reporting: Nuts and Bolts   542
Beyond Grading: Communication   551
Summary/Key Terms   555
Suggestions for Further Reading and Study   556
Teachers' Forum   557

Epilogue: Teaching and Learning in the Computer Age   559

Overview   560
Computer Literacy: What Is It?   560
The Origins and Basics of Computer-Based Education   561

Putting Computers to Work in Today's Classrooms   564
Computers as Instructional Tools   571
Computers as Tutees: Programming   572
What the Future Holds   574
Summary/Key Terms   575
Suggestions for Further Reading and Study   576

Glossary   577

References   591

Name Index   605

Subject Index   613

Preface

Many of you reading this book will be enrolled in an educational psychology course as part of your professional preparation in teaching, counseling, speech therapy, or psychology. The material in this text should be of interest to all who are concerned about education and learning, from the nursery school volunteer to the instructor in a community program for handicapped adults. No background in psychology or education is necessary to understand this material. It is as free of jargon and technical language as possible.

Since the first edition of *Educational Psychology* appeared, there have been many exciting developments in the field. This edition has incorporated new insights and current trends and at the same time retained the focus and the best features of the previous work. The third edition continues to emphasize the educational implications of research on child development, learning, and teaching. Theories and applications are not separated but are considered together: the text shows how information and ideas drawn from research in educational psychology can be used to solve the everyday problems of teaching. To make the connections between knowledge and practice clear and interesting, many examples, case studies, guidelines, and practical tips from experienced teachers fill the upcoming pages. Professors and students who used the first two editions found these features very helpful. But what about the new developments?

This revision reflects the growing importance of cognitive perspectives for educational psychology. The old chapters on cognitive views of learning have been completely redone in collaboration with Professor Christine McCormick of the University of South Carolina. Topics include perception, attention, the structure of knowledge, schema theory, information processing, critical thinking, reading and comprehension, reciprocal teaching, metacognition, metacognitive strategy training, concept teaching, problem solving, and expertise.

Another area of critical importance to teachers is the growing body of research on classroom instruction. This research has been synthesized in the chapters on classroom management and effective teaching. Here you'll find up-to-date material on the ecology of the classroom, teacher planning, the influence of teacher and student perceptions, managing elementary and secondary classrooms (with a special focus on establishing procedures, setting rules, and getting started on the very first day of school), dealing with conflict, and encouraging communication. The chapter on effective teaching also includes a discussion of several models of effective instruction—Rosenshine's direct instruction, Hunter's Mastery Teaching, and Good and Grouws's Missouri Mathematics Program.

The Plan of the Book

Part One begins with you, the prospective teacher, and the questions you are probably asking yourself about a teaching career. What are the joys and conflicts teachers can expect? How can educational psychology increase the joys by helping to resolve the conflicts? Part Two, "Human Development: A Framework for Teachers," focuses on the students. How do they develop mentally, physically, emotionally, and socially, and how do all these aspects fit together? Where do individual differences come from, and what do they mean for teachers? The next three units are the heart of the book. Part Three, "Learning Theory and Practice," looks at learning from two major perspectives, the behavioral and the cognitive, with an emphasis on the latter. Learning theory has important implications for instruction at every level; cognitive research is particularly vital right now and promises a great fund of ideas for teaching in the immediate future. Part Four, "Motivation and Classroom Management," discusses the ever-present, linked issues of motivating and managing today's students. The information in these chapters is based on the most recent research in real classrooms. Part Five, "Planning and Teaching," has chapters on designing instruction, choosing and using effective teaching strategies, and working with exceptional students. Finally, Part Six, "Evaluating Students," looks at many types of testing and grading, providing a sound basis for determining how well students have learned.

Appendix and Epilogue

In addition to the 15 chapters, there are two "minichapters." The Appendix to Chapter 1, "Research in Educational Psychology," discusses basic vocabulary, concepts, and methods of psychological research. The Appendix takes you through the processes of planning and evaluating a study. The Epilogue, "Teaching and Learning in the Computer Age," is a very current introduction to computers and their educational applications. Designed for students who have no background in computers, it explains basic terms and concepts, indicates the ever-growing range of applications, and provides guidelines for selecting hardware and software to make the most of this revolutionary tool. Your instructor may or may not incorporate the Appendix and Epilogue into your regular class work. But even if they are not assigned, you will probably find both sections worthwhile reading.

Current Theory and Research

Over 300 new references have been added to this edition to bring prospective teachers the most current information. Topics include Vygotsky's theory of cognitive development, latchkey children, Bandura's social cognitive theory, critical thinking skills, teacher planning, the ecology of the classroom, self-worth theory, metacognition, schema theory, the psychology of instruction, studies of expert knowledge, studies of expert classroom managers, research on teacher effectiveness, holistic scoring, and current legal and social controversies in testing and grading.

Readability and Relevance

The responses of hundreds of students who read the first two editions were analyzed to make this edition clearer and more relevant and interesting. Jargon and technical language have been avoided. When a new term is introduced, it appears in **boldface** along with a brief definition in the margin. The concepts and principles discussed are related to life both inside and outside the classroom. Student teachers and master teachers around the country contributed many of the examples. Other case studies come from personal experience.

Aids to Understanding

At the beginning of each chapter you will find an *outline* of the key topics with page numbers for quick reference. An *overview* provides a chapter "orientation" along with a list of *learning objectives* (also useful for review later).

Within the chapter, *headings* and *margin notes* point out themes, questions, and problems as they arise, so you can look up information easily. These can also serve as a quick review of important points. As already noted, key terms are highlighted in boldface type. In addition to the brief *margin definitions*, more extended definitions can be found in the *Glossary* at the end of the book. Throughout the book, graphs, tables, photos, and cartoons have been chosen to clarify and summarize the text material—and make it all more enjoyable.

Each chapter ends with a *summary* of the main ideas and applications and a list of the *key terms* for review. *Suggestions for Further Reading and Study*, including nontechnical books, journal and magazine articles, and major texts in the field, are provided for further exploration of the chapter's topics.

Guidelines

An important reason for studying educational psychology is to gain skills in solving classroom problems. Often texts give pages of theory and research findings but little assistance in translating theory into practice. This text is different. Included in each chapter are several sets of *Guidelines*. These are teaching tips and practical suggestions based on the theory and research discussed in the chapter. Each suggestion is clarified by two or three specific examples. Although Guidelines cannot cover every possible situation, they do provide a needed bridge between knowledge and practice and should help you transfer the text's information to new situations.

Teachers' Forum

This highly acclaimed and popular feature from the first two editions is back in revised form. Here, master teachers from all over the country offer their own solutions to many of the diverse problems likely to be encountered in the classroom at every grade level. Their ideas truly show educational psychology at work in a range of everyday situations. The Teachers' Forum feature follows each chapter, bringing to life the topics and principles just discussed.

You are invited to criticize the solutions in the Teachers' Forum and suggest your own. Professors are encouraged to send case studies that they would like to see discussed in the next edition. Send letters to:

Woolfolk
EDUCATIONAL PSYCHOLOGY, 3/E
College Division
Prentice-Hall
Englewood Cliffs, NJ 07632

TO THE INSTRUCTOR

Supplements

Three printed supplements are available to make this textbook more useful. An *Instructor's Manual* includes expanded chapter objectives, outlines, discussion questions, student assignments, demonstrations, audiovisual aids, and class activities. A separate *Test Item File* has been completely revised based on class testings of the previous editions' items. There are three ways to use the *Test Item File:* you can simply use items as printed in a standard test item manual; if you have access to a microcomputer, you can create your own tests with the newly available test item computer disk; or you can take advantage of the telephone testing service, which provides typed or dittoed tests tailored to your own specifications. For more information, contact your local Prentice-Hall representative.

A *Student Guide* is available with chapter objectives and outlines, lists of key concepts, sample test questions, projects, and case studies to enrich your students' understanding of educational psychology and prepare them more thoroughly for in-class work. The *Student Guide* is also available on a computer disk.

New Computer Supplements

Four computer disks have been developed for this edition. As just noted, the *Test Item File* and *Student Guide* are both available in disk form. The third supplement is a class record system for instructors that serves as a *computerized grade book.* This system will store, print, average, and total scores; assign grades using norm-referenced or criterion-referenced methods; compute test statistics; and print graphs of class grades. Finally, for students there is an *instructional disk* of activities, experiments, and exercises keyed to

there is an *instructional disk* of activities, experiments, and exercises keyed to the text. Students have the chance to check their own formal operational thinking, analyze levels of moral reasoning, participate in a verbal learning experiment, practice communication skills, interpret standardized test scores, compare different grading approaches, and test their ability to recognize major theorists. Every time you see this symbol on the left of the text, it means that there is a related exercise on the instructional disk. The manual for the instructional disk describes how to use this unique supplement. A demonstration disk is also available to introduce you to these new computer supplements. For information about obtaining any of the disks, please contact Fay Dawson, College Correspondence Department, Prentice-Hall.

ACKNOWLEDGMENTS

During the years that I have worked on this book, from initial draft to this most recent revision, many people have supported the project. Without their help, this text simply could not have been written.

My writing was guided by extensive, thoughtful reviews from the following individuals: Hilda Borko, University of Maryland; Henry T. Clark, Pennsylvania State University; Eileen G. Cotton, California State University at Chico; Harold J. Fletcher, Florida State University; Virginia Koehler, University of Maryland; Joel R. Levin, University of Wisconsin; Michael Lindsay, University of Wisconsin-Eau Claire; Peter H. Nachtwey, Clarion University of Pennsylvania, Venango Campus; Thomas Oakland, University of Texas-Austin; Mary Rohrkemper, Bryn Mawr College; Barak Rosenshine, University of Illinois; Steven M. Ross, Memphis State University; Julie P. Sanford, University of Maryland; Sandra L. Stein, Rider College; and Peter H. Wood, Bowling Green State University.

Many classroom teachers across the country contributed their experience, creativity, and expertise to the Teachers' Forum. I have thoroughly enjoyed my association with these master teachers and am grateful for the perspective they brought to the book: Laura Atkinson, Chapel Hill, NC; Joan M. Bloom, Providence, RI; Kristine C. Bloom, Tonawanda, NY; Harriet Chipley, Lookout Mountain, TN; Carolyn R. Cook, Ramona, CA; Richard D. Courtright, Chapel Hill, NC; Jane C. Dusell, Medford, WI; Karen L. Eitreim, Richland, WA; Patricia Frank, South Brunswick, NJ; James C. Fulgham, Chattanooga, TN; Carol Gibbs, Rossville, GA; Nancy R. Gonzalez, Mount Prospect, IL; Leland J. Gritzner, Shoshone, CA; Dorothy Eve Hopkins, Homer, NY; Osborn Howes, Larkspur, CA; Larry A. Irwin, Greeley, CO; Sharon Klotz, Kiel, WI; J. D. Kraft, Wausau, WI; Harold Kreif, Fond du Lac, WI; Joan H. Lowe, Hazelwood, MO; Louise Harrold Melucci, Warwick, RI; Ida Pofahl, Denison, IA; Darline Reynolds, Spirit Lake, IA; Ruth Roberts, Rochester, NY; R. Chris Rohde, Chippewa Falls, WI; Charlotte Ross, Elmont, NY; Linda Stahl, Ponca City, OK; Katherine P. Stillerman, Fayetteville, NC; Jacqueline M. Walsh, Pawtucket, RI; and Arleen Wyatt, Rossville, GA.

The talented staff at Prentice-Hall deserves special mention. Bob Sickles, editor for the first edition, provided invaluable leadership. His faith in this project and his friendship will always be remembered. Shirley Chlopak, assistant to the editor, has been a participant in this work from the earliest days of the first edition. Her organization, dedication, and unfailing good humor were and are greatly appreciated. Mary Helen Fitzgerald worked diligently to obtain permissions for the material referenced in this text. Lorinda Morris and Ilene Cherna guided the new collection of photographs. The text and cover designer, Judith Matz-Coniglio, brought a fresh, colorful, clean look to the book. The production editor, Linda Benson, coordinated all the complex aspects of production with patience and humor. The supplements for the text were prepared under the able supervision of Audrey Marshall.

No person contributed more to this revision than the development editor, Martha Wiseman. She coordinated the entire project, but more important, her intelligent guidance, careful editing, good writing, and genuine commitment to the book made my difficult, day-to-day task of writing a professional and personal pleasure. I have worked with few colleagues anywhere who are her equal.

On this edition I was again privileged to work with Susan Willig, Executive Editor. Her good judgment, boundless energy, creativity, and strong leadership were essential in this project, from the first discussions about revisions to the last decisions about design. She is a valued friend.

Many colleagues contributed to this project. Chapters 7 and 8 were written in collaboration with Christine McCormick. Carol Weinstein wrote the section in Chapter 11 on the physical environment of the classroom. David Podell made helpful suggestions for the revision of Chapters 14 and 15. Steven Ross and Fran Doughty were responsible for the Epilogue, "Teaching and Learning in the Computer Age." Along with Jack Barnette and Gary Morrison, Steve Ross also designed and coordinated production of the instructional disk and computerized grade-book program that accompany this text. These clever, innovative materials make the significant concepts in the text come alive as students work with the simulations, activities, and exercises. These supplements set new standards for instructional software accompanying texts. Alison Gooding drew upon her experience as a gifted public school and college teacher to revise the *Instructor's Manual.* Jane Furr Davis and Todd M. Davis were responsible for the excellent revision of the *Student Guide,* and Katharine Cummings wrote the well-crafted test items to the test item file. And all the editions of this text have greatly benefited from the suggestions of my first educational psychology teacher, Ed Emmer, University of Texas at Austin, a gifted researcher and a good friend.

Several of my current and former students—Barbara Rosoff, Alison Gooding, and Fran Doughty—contributed in countless ways to the completion of this edition. Carolyn McNinch and Tony Larabina tirelessly typed the manuscript and supplements.

Finally, it is to my family, Rob and Elizabeth, that I owe inexpressible thanks for their kindness, understanding, and support during the long days and nights required to write this book. A very special thank you is due again to Jane Woolfolk, who dedicated many weeks to helping me care for my family during the hectic months of work. Without her selfless efforts, a third edition could not have been written.

A. E. W.
August 1986

Educational Psychology

1

Teachers, Teaching, and Educational Psychology

Overview
Teaching: An Art, a Science, and a Lot of Work   2
The Many Roles of a Teacher   4
Advantages and Disadvantages   8
Major Concerns of Beginning Teachers   12
Social Issues Affecting Teachers Today   13
Criticisms and Commissions   14
Teacher Quality   14
Accountability   17
Mainstreaming   18
New Technology/Old Curriculum   18
The Future of the Job Market   19
Changes in the Family   20
The Role of Educational Psychology   20
Definitions   21
The Need for a Scientific Approach   22
Major Areas of Study: The Contents of This Book   25
Putting the Book to Work   26
Summary/Key Terms
Suggestions for Further Reading and Study
Teachers' Forum

If you are like many students, you begin this course with a mixture of anticipation and wariness. Perhaps you are required to take educational psychology as part of a program in teacher education, speech therapy, nursing, or counseling. You may have chosen this class as an elective, simply because you are interested in education or psychology. No matter what your reason for enrolling, you probably have questions about teaching, schools, students, or even about yourself that you hope this course might answer. I have written *Educational Psychology* with questions such as these in mind.

In this first chapter we begin not with educational psychology but with education—more specifically, with the state of teaching today. Only a person who is aware of the problems teachers face can appreciate the contributions offered by educational psychology. For this reason, we will look first at the demands, challenges, and rewards of teaching, both in terms of day-to-day experience in the classroom and in terms of a broader view of education's role in our society. After introducing you briefly to the world of the teacher, we turn to a discussion of educational psychology itself. We will consider what educational psychology is and why you should study it. How can principles identified by educational psychologists benefit teachers, therapists, parents, and others interested in teaching and learning in our society? What exactly is the content of educational psychology, and where did this information come from? By the time you have finished this chapter, you will be in a much better position to answer these questions and many others:

- Would teaching be a good career for me?
- What are the greatest concerns of beginning teachers?
- What are the most important issues facing educators today?
- Will I be able to get a job in teaching?
- Why should I study educational psychology?
- What roles do theory and research play in this field?
- What specific kinds of problems will the study of educational psychology help me to solve?

We will start with the most basic and perhaps the most difficult question. What is teaching?

TEACHING: AN ART, A SCIENCE, AND A LOT OF WORK

It has been a favorite indoor sport of educators over the years to debate whether teaching is an art or a science. If it is an art, then teaching calls for inspiration, intuition, talent, and creativity—very little of which actually can be taught. If it is a science, however, teaching requires knowledge and skills

that can indeed be learned. Rules describing the effects of various teacher actions can be memorized and applied in the classroom. If we take the scientific argument to the extreme, teaching is merely selecting and applying the correct formula for each classroom situation.

Either or Both?

Some educators actually do take one or the other extreme position, believing that teaching is fully an art or that teaching is a science and nothing but a science. Most, however, agree that teaching has both artistic and scientific elements. Two decades ago, Charles Silberman had this to say:

> To be sure, teaching—like the practice of medicine—is very much an art, which is to say, it calls for the exercise of talent and creativity. But like medicine, it is also—or should be—a science, for it involves a repertoire of techniques, procedures, and skills that can be systematically studied and described, and therefore transmitted and improved. The great teacher, like the great doctor, is the one who adds creativity and inspiration to that basic repertoire. . . . (1966, p. 124)

Silberman's analogy to medicine is still a good one. The modern practice of medicine is based on scientific theory and research. But a doctor treating a patient also must use judgment, intuition, and creativity in solving the many medical problems for which there are no guaranteed answers. Still, the doctor cannot ignore the principles of biochemistry and, for example, give a patient a dose of medicine that is lethal at the person's body weight. Ignoring the principles that determine safe drug dosages would have results even the most creative doctor wants to avoid. The same is true in education. The teacher who does not know what scientists have discovered about learning and instruction is like the physician who does not understand the principles of biochemistry. Both could make decisions that would lead inevitably to failure.

Whether you work with youngsters or adults, in schools, hospitals, community agencies, or industry, teaching is complicated. It is essential to know a great deal about the subject matter, your students, and the processes of teaching and learning. You must also have or develop a certain flair for teaching—the artistic aspect of the role. Elliot Eisner describes this as the "willingness and ability to create new forms of teaching—new teaching moves—moves that were not part of one's existing repertoire" (1983, p. 8). However, much more should be included in a definition of teaching. Here we will look at several of these aspects.

The Many Roles of a Teacher

If a teaching job in a secondary school were described in the language of an employment ad, it might read like this:

WANTED

College graduate with academic major (master's degree preferred). Excellent communication and leadership skills required. Challenging opportunity to serve 150 clients daily, developing up to five different products each day to meet their needs. This diversified job also allows employee to exercise typing, clerical, law enforcement, and social work skills between assignments and after hours. Adaptability helpful, since suppliers cannot always deliver goods and support services on time. Typical work week 47 hours. Special nature of work precludes fringe benefits such as lunch and coffee breaks, but work has many intrinsic rewards. . . . (Darling-Hammond, 1984, p. 1)

As is evident from this simulated advertisement, teachers do more than explain, lecture, and drill. They also design materials, make assignments, evaluate student performance, organize activities, and maintain discipline. They must keep records, arrange the classroom, develop learning activities, talk to parents, and counsel students. A teacher assumes a multitude of roles. We will discuss the major ones here. As you read, you might consider how these roles relate to your own expectations, goals, and abilities.

Expertise

The Teacher as an Instructional Expert. Teachers must constantly make decisions about teaching materials and methods. These decisions are based on a number of factors, including the subject matter to be covered, the abilities and needs of the students, and the overall goals to be reached. What is the best way to teach subtraction to second graders? How can I teach creative writing to a seventh grader who has never mastered basic writing skills? What book should I use to teach reading to eleventh graders who read at a fifth-grade level but are insulted by fifth-grade readers? Should I let students cover the next assignment individually or in teams? Which would be best for this lesson: lecture, discussion, discovery learning, programmed instruction, recitation, or seatwork? Would a microcomputer be a worthwhile investment for the school, and how would I use it in my classes? Teachers make hundreds of these instructional decisions each week. In addition, they are expected to know the answers to a multitude of questions about the subject itself.

The Teacher as Motivator. Nothing the teacher does results automatically or magically in student learning. The students must act. One of the most important roles a teacher assumes is that of motivator. For today's media-saturated students, ordinary school activities may have little immediate appeal. Even having an exciting introduction to each lesson is not enough to spark and maintain interest and concentration.

Many decisions a teacher makes have an effect on student motivation. The grading method a teacher uses, for example, can motivate students to try harder or to give up. Any classroom materials chosen with student interest and ability in mind may help motivate students to learn. The question at the heart of effective teaching is, How can I keep my students actively involved in learning? It is something you will need to ask yourself every day.

The teacher's many roles are interdependent. One of the surest ways of motivating students, for example, is to be enthusiastic about the subject yourself. *(Richard Hutchings/ Photo Researchers)*

Juggling Time and Paper

classroom management: maintenance of a healthy learning environment, relatively free from behavior problems

The Teacher as Manager. Most elementary school teachers spend only an average of 20 to 30 percent of the day in direct verbal interaction with students (Rosenshine, 1977). Much of the remaining time is spent in some form of management. The figure for direct teaching in secondary schools is higher, but managing the class still takes up a large percentage of the teacher's time. Management includes supervising class activities, organizing lessons, completing forms, preparing tests, assigning grades, training aides, meeting with other teachers and parents, and keeping records. Given only 24 hours in the day, teachers must be skillful managers of time, projects, deadlines, and people if they hope to have any private life beyond working hours.

As a teacher you also will have to deal with another type of management: **classroom management,** which includes all the decisions and actions required to maintain order in the classroom (Doyle, 1985). You have met this concept many times under the more traditional heading of discipline. Actually, discipline and classroom management are not necessarily synonomous. One of the goals of this book is to provide teachers with understanding and skills that can minimize behavior problems and reduce the need for disciplinary action. Nevertheless, both major and minor behavior problems are likely to crop up at one time or another, and teachers need to develop a number of methods for dealing with them so the class can get on with the business of learning. Effective management and the problem of discipline are not only issues for individual teachers but are among the major societal concerns about our schools as well.

The Teacher as Leader.   Although teachers must be concerned with the needs of each student, in reality they seldom work with individuals for an extended period of time. Teaching, almost inevitably, is leading a group of students. An effective teacher is an effective leader, using the power of the group to promote individual growth. In the role of group leader, "the teacher is expected to be a referee, detective, limiter of anxiety, target for hostile feelings and frustrations, friend and confidant, substitute parent, object of affection and crushes, and ego supporter" (Ornstein & Miller, 1980, p. 226).

The Teacher as Counselor.   Although teachers cannot be expected to act as guidance counselors, they must be sensitive observers of human behavior. They must try to respond constructively when students' emotions get in the way of learning. They must know when a particular student needs to

Dealing with
Personal Problems

see a mental health specialist. In every class there are students who bring their personal problems to the teacher. In addition, teachers are expected to administer standardized intelligence, achievement, or interest tests and to interpret the results of these tests for the students and their parents. You should be aware of the opportunities and the dangers involved in all these situations. The feelings of parents, the standards of the community, and the needs of other teachers and students must all be considered.

The Teacher as Environmental Engineer.   The term *environmental engineer* may seem a bit far-fetched when you think about teaching. Yet the way the physical space of a classroom is used can either help or hinder learning. Changes made by a teacher may be minor (for example, hanging posters in the classroom or having students sit in a circle for a discussion), or they may involve major restructuring. School budgets usually do not allow for the purchase of extra bookshelves, room dividers, or learning carrels. Thus, in their role as environmental engineers, some teachers even build or adapt furniture for their classrooms. The instructor who spends a Saturday making a reading corner in a fifth-grade classroom is simply acting out one of the teacher's many roles.

The Teacher as Model.   No matter what you do as a teacher, you will be acting as a model for your students. Enthusiasm for a subject is more likely to be taught by an enthusiastic teacher giving a less than perfect demonstration than by a bored instructor lecturing brilliantly on the value of the sub-

Intentional and
Unintentional
Modeling

ject. At times, teachers use modeling intentionally. The demonstrations in physical education, chemistry, home economics, and industrial arts are examples of direct modeling. In many other cases, however, teachers are not so aware of their role as models. For example, teachers constantly act as models in demonstrating how to think about problems. If teachers can involve their students in thinking through various alternative solutions to problems, the students are more likely to learn that they themselves are capable of problem solving in all kinds of situations.

Having looked at just seven of the many different roles a teacher plays, you may feel overwhelmed. Many veteran teachers agree. Having to be so many things to so many people can create a deal of strain. And trying to meet all the often conflicting demands is time-consuming as well as stressful. Table 1–1 gives you an idea of what you can expect to do during a

Table 1–1 A Day in the Life of a Secondary School Teacher

Random Thoughts on the Way to Work	"My life happens in segments just like my eight-period day . . . lots of homework last night . . . hate grading essay papers, but really enjoyed working out today's lessons. I think they're going to work. . . . Hope I can keep Ralph quiet during fourth period. . . ."
Homeroom	"At least the flag salute quiets them down. Do I have all the attendance cards in order? Almost forgot to collect insurance forms. I figured those two would forget theirs again. 'Lost,' they say. I'll have to send a student to the office for extra forms."
Period 1: U.S. History (Standard)	"I really feel sharp today, but I think my students are half-asleep. Is it just that the lesson's not going as well as it could or that they're tired? Maybe the material isn't as good as I thought."
Period 2: Preparation Period	"I have a million things to do! I'd better beef up that U.S. history lesson before sixth period. I don't want to put another class to sleep. My turn to use the phone in the lounge—my only link with the outside world. Coffee! A few minutes to talk with friends and check the mail."
Period 3: Economics	"I love this course, partly because it's elective. All the kids want to be here. We can really tackle some difficult subjects. Great lesson today! The students are really getting excited. Madeline told me before class that she wants to major in economics in college. This kind of class makes it all worthwhile."
Period 4: U.S. History (Basics)	"Basics. They're rowdy but I love them. They've got character even though they don't give a damn about history. We have great lessons. . . . 'Get away from the window!' . . . 'Wait until the bell rings!' "
Period 5: Lunch Duty	"How demeaning to have to sit and watch kids eat!"
Period 6: U.S. History (Standard)	"Much better lesson than in first period. Maybe you really can learn from your mistakes. Or maybe these kids are just more awake."
Period 7: Library Duty	"It's remarkable how many students don't know the first thing about using a library. In the beginning I thought I would get some reading done during this period, but the interruptions make it impossible—a frustrating 40 minutes."
Period 8: Economics	"This lesson went so well this morning. What's different? I guess last period is a terrible time to have to talk about supply and demand. We all want to go home."
End of the Day	"I'm glad I got to speak to Jane after school. Intramurals is a great way to get to know the kids. It's easier to work with them in class now that I am learning more about them after school . . . but I'm exhausted . . . just don't want to face three new lessons tonight. Sometimes I wish I could leave my work at the office."

Adapted from the experiences of Howard Schober, high school social studies teacher in New Jersey.

typical day. The example is taken from the experiences of a high school teacher, but the variety of demands and the many roles played translate relatively easily to any teaching position.

You can probably tell from Table 1–1 that during much of the day the teacher is the only adult in a crowd of adolescents. For many people, this isolation from other adults is one of the major disadvantages of teaching. Will it be for you? What other disadvantages can you expect to find? Will the advantages of teaching outweigh the disadvantages?

Advantages and Disadvantages

Having so many roles to play brings a great deal of stress but also a number of rewards. Let us focus on the disadvantages first so we can end on a more cheerful note.

The Disadvantages of a Career in Teaching.

Results of a recent survey of 300 elementary school teachers found the following as the most disliked aspects of teaching: paperwork, nonteaching duties, administration, parents, low pay, lack of time to accomplish tasks, disruptive and apathetic students, and workload (Rasche, Dedrick, Strathe, & Hawkes, 1985). This list is confirmed by the experiences of many secondary school teachers as well.

Busywork for Teachers

Much of the teacher's time is filled with routine paperwork. Imagine for a moment that you have given an essay test to all five of your high school classes over a one-week period at the end of the semester. The following week you have to grade about 125 papers, turn in final grades for the semester, prepare 25 lessons, stand in line to use the mimeograph machine, prepare several transparencies for the lessons, sign up for the overhead projector, take attendance, answer memos from the administration, and perhaps meet with the photography club as their faculty adviser. In an elementary class you might have to prepare reading and math handouts and work sheets for students whose abilities span several grade levels; correct in-class ditto sheets, workbooks, and homework assignments; keep records on 25 students in six or seven different subjects; give achievement and placement tests; and keep track of PTA notices, T-shirt money (for the fund-raiser), lunch money, insurance forms, school picture forms, library notices, bus schedules, and weekly helper assignments. The idea that a teacher's day ends at 3 or 4 o'clock is definitely a misconception.

These busy teachers face the impossible challenge of encouraging maximum achievement in all their students. It is often difficult to see the results. Unlike the successful portrait painter, a teacher can seldom step back and admire the finished picture.

A teacher's work is never done. In this class, textbooks have just arrived (perhaps a week late) and must be distributed. The blackboard shows that monitors have been assigned, homework posted, and attendance taken. And it's probably only 9:00 A.M.! *(Richard Hutchings/Photo Researchers)*

Table 1–2 Average Salaries in Teaching

Region of the United States	Salaries for 1984–85[a] Salary	Projections for Average Salaries, 1987–90[b] Year	U.S. Average Salary
New England	$21,766	1987–88	$26,086
Mideast	24,958	1988–89	27,729
Southeast	18,429	1989–90	29,476
Great Lakes	23,525		
Plains	20,414		
Southwest	20,121		
Rocky Mountains	21,653		
Far West	23,816		
Alaska	37,807		
U.S. Average	21,935		

[a]*From National Education Association (1985),* Estimates of School Statistics, 1984–1985. *Washington, DC: NEA, p. 36.*
[b]*A. C. Ornstein (1980), Teacher salaries: Past, present, future.* Phi Delta Kappan, 61, *p. 678.*

Unlavish Salaries

For such potentially frustrating work, teachers are not lavishly paid. In terms of purchasing power, teachers' salaries have remained fairly constant over the years. In fact, from 1974–75 to 1984–85, the average salary dropped slightly in actual value (National Education Association, 1985). Teachers' salaries vary greatly from one part of the country to another and from one district to another, even in the same state. Salaries tend to be highest in the Far West and in the larger cities and suburbs, but the cost of living is often higher as well. In general, the average starting salary for teachers has lagged behind beginning salaries for most other college graduates. Once in the profession, the top figure teachers can expect to earn will be only about double their initial salary (Darling-Hammond, 1984). In addition, there is little opportunity for advancement, unless you return to school for further preparation to become a supervisor, principal, or educational specialist. Table 1–2 presents the average salaries for teachers across the United States and some predictions for the future.

Isolation

Teaching can be a very lonely endeavor, even though teachers are surrounded by people all day. A teacher's classroom is generally considered a solitary domain. Behind the classroom door, teachers are generally expected to solve their own problems. Even if help is available, teachers are given little time during the day to consult or plan with their colleagues.

It should be no surprise by now that teaching can be a very stressful profession. A quick rundown of sources of stress might include student mis-

"SURE, TEACHING IS AN ART AND A SCIENCE —BUT IT'S ALSO GUERRILLA WARFARE."

behavior, poor working conditions, unpleasant physical surroundings (rooms that are hot, cold, drafty, dark, dirty, noisy, or just plain ugly), lack of administrative and clerical support, little or no adult help, inadequate materials, large classes, few or no breaks, many nonteaching duties (hall patrol, bathroom monitoring), little chance for professional growth, low salaries, and overwork (Darling-Hammond, 1984; Schug, 1985).

Teacher Burnout

All these factors combine to produce "teacher burnout" (Schug, 1985). Around the country today there are more and more books and workshops designed to help teachers rekindle their enthusiasm and counteract the sense of being "burned out" on teaching. One school district in Washington has developed a plan that includes insurance coverage for teachers suffering long-term disabilities as a result of classroom burnout (Young, 1980).

The Advantages of a Career in Teaching. This would be a pretty grim picture if teaching did not offer some compensating advantages. An old joke quotes a university professor who said, "There are three good reasons for choosing teaching as a career: June, July, and August." This is probably the most widely held image of the advantages. However, there are other, more important reasons for becoming a teacher. Teachers surveyed in a recent study listed the following, in order of importance, as the best things about their job: the students, colleagues, summer vacations, student progress, job autonomy, professional satisfaction, variety, and helping others (Rasche, Dedrick, Strathe, & Hawkes, 1985).

Within limits that vary greatly from school to school, a teacher is autonomous in the classroom. Although a teacher may at times feel lonely and isolated as the only adult in the class, this very isolation has its advantages. With it comes the freedom to deal with instructional and behavioral problems as each teacher sees fit.

The Chance to
Make a Difference

But the major reward for teachers comes from the relationships with students and the chance to make a difference in the lives of these individuals. Each year I ask my students to interview teachers about the rewards and problems of the profession. The positive aspect mentioned most often is the chance to work closely with youngsters. When you return to visit teachers who were important to you and see their broad smiles, or when you hear teachers tell their own special success stories, you begin to understand how important these relationships can be.

So relationships with others, including colleagues and students, are more important to professional satisfaction than money or status (Chapman & Hutcheson, 1982; Roberson, Keith, & Page, 1983). Diane Ravitch has summed up the situation this way: "Teaching will never offer salaries that compare favorably with law or medicine, but it does offer satisfactions that are unique to the job. In every generation there are people born with a love of teaching. They want to open the minds of young people to literature, history, art, science, or something else that seized their imagination" (1985, p. 201).

Having looked at both the advantages and disadvantages of teaching, you may be asking yourself which are more important to you. No one can answer this question for you. You must consider how all the positives and negatives fit in with your own goals. If you decide to continue your preparation to enter the profession, you should be aware that you are likely to face various sorts of difficult situations at different stages in your career.

The main rewards of teaching come from having the chance to affect the lives of young people. You may be studying education today because you had one or two very influential teachers. *(Richard Hutchings/ Photo Researchers)*

Major Concerns of Beginning Teachers

It is impossible to talk about the concerns of teachers without taking the individual teacher's stage of development into consideration. At different points in their careers, teachers tend to be concerned about different issues. In fact, there appear to be at least three stages of psychological development for teachers: (1) a preteaching stage; (2) a beginning or early teaching stage; and (3) a mature or experienced stage (Fuller, 1969; Katz, 1972). Let us examine the stage that is probably of greatest interest to you—beginning teaching.

Stages of Teaching

In the first two years of "real" teaching, most people are concerned about their own competence. Young teachers tend to lack confidence in their teaching skills, and they worry about being liked by peers and students, making a good impression, and generally surviving from day to day and week to week (Evans, 1976). If you have had similar anxieties when you imagine your first day in front of a class, you are not alone.

Beginning teachers all over the world share many of the same concerns. A review of studies conducted around the world found that beginning teachers regard maintaining classroom discipline, motivating students, accommodating differences among students, evaluating student work, and dealing with parents as the most serious problems they faced (Veenman, 1984). Many teachers also experience what has been called "reality shock" when they take their first job and confront the "harsh and rude reality of everyday classroom life" (Veenman, 1984, p. 143). One of the sources of the shock may be that teachers cannot really ease into their responsibilities. On the first day of their first job, beginning teachers face the same tasks as teachers with years of experience. Student teaching, while it is a very useful experience, does not really prepare prospective teachers for starting off a school year with a new class. And schools usually offer little chance for contact with experienced teachers, so that their potential support and assistance may not be available. However, knowing that you are bound to have difficulties and worries when you start out may prepare you a little for that first phase of your career.

Reality Shock

Each year I ask my students, "Now that you've visited a classroom and observed things from the point of view of a prospective teacher, what do you expect to be the major problems you will encounter as a beginning teacher?" Here are some of the answers that have been collected over the years.

> Probably the most difficult problem I will encounter as a teacher is one of discipline. I found that quite often I would lose my temper and punish with threats of detention and the like. Then on occasion, after realizing that my anger was not warranted, I would revert back and overcompensate by kidding around. This whole issue of discipline and temper versus joking around and calm is definitely something I must learn to deal with!

> One problem I expect is becoming a believable authority figure. At the junior high level, the students are quite restless. They can't wait to grow up. Control is important and hard to come by. Finding enough material to vary the classes is another problem. You have to get their attention, and an interesting lesson plan is very important to both teacher and students.

> Frustration might be a major problem for me. In the course of observing my classes I found myself expecting a higher level of production than the students

Experience is a good teacher, but a hard one. Beginning teachers can learn from their more experienced colleagues and perhaps be spared some painful firsthand "learning experiences." *(Elaine Rebman/Photo Researchers)*

were able to give. But I also have feelings of inadequacy. Granted, what I give my students will be something more than what they'd have if I weren't there, but will I be able to give them as much as I'd like?

Both beginning and experienced teachers consider discipline a serious problem. For years, "lack of discipline" has been cited as the major problem facing the schools, according to the annual Gallup Poll of attitudes toward public education. Parents who move their children to private schools often give as their main reason the desire for better discipline (Frechling, Edwards, & Richardson, 1981). In light of these concerns, a large portion of three chapters (6, 9, and 10) has been devoted to managing classrooms and motivating students.

Of course, concerns don't disappear after the first few years. But most teachers do move beyond worries about adequacy to focus more on the needs of students. For this reason the experienced instructor, the one who has solved many of the initial problems of teaching, has a great deal to offer education students. I have polled a number of successful, experienced teachers for ideas about solving some of the problems of the early years. These common problems and possible solutions are found at the end of each chapter in the section called "Teachers' Forum." Although the vast majority of the material in this text is based on findings of educational psychologists, the ideas suggested by these experienced teachers offer a sound supplement.

The Voice of Experience

SOCIAL ISSUES AFFECTING TEACHERS TODAY

Now that we have examined the problems, joys, and concerns of teachers in their day-to-day classroom experience, let's step back and take a look at the profession from another vantage point. Our schools are part of our society and are at times rocked, swayed, and even improved by changes in the society itself. What issues in the larger society will affect teaching in the next few years?

Criticisms and Commissions

One of the important issues facing teachers today is public concern about the schools. Satisfaction with the public schools in America rises and falls with some regularity. In 1974, for example, 48 percent of the people responding to the Gallup Poll gave their local schools a grade of A or B for quality of education. By 1983, at the low point, only 31 percent of those polled were willing to give the schools such high grades. But by 1985 the figure had risen to 43 percent (Gallup, 1985). A closer examination of the 1985 survey shows that people in the Midwest, residents of towns with populations under 50,000, and parents whose children receive above-average grades were more satisfied than other groups.

What's Wrong with Our Schools?

Most people agree that schools could be improved, but they do not agree about what to do. During the 1960s and early 1970s, many solutions were suggested by such reformers as John Holt, Ivan Illich, Jonathan Kozol, and Neil Postman. A theme running through all of their criticisms and proposed solutions was that the schools were repressive and stifled real learning and creativity. A second important theme was that the schools discriminated against minorities and the socially and economically disadvantaged while favoring the white middle class. Conservative critics like Max Rafferty and Frank Armbruster, on the other hand, believed the schools were too permissive and lax in the enforcement of standards (Robinson, 1978).

By the early 1980s there was a growing concern that the quality of education, especially in America's high schools, was declining. Former Secretary of Education T. H. Bell established the National Commission on Excellence in Education (NCEE) to study the problem. *A Nation at Risk,* the report of this commission, made front-page national news when it concluded that "the educational foundations of our country are presently being eroded by a rising tide of mediocrity that threatens our very future as a nation and a people" (NCEE, 1983, p. 5).

Recommendations

During 1983, in answer to widespread public concern, a number of reports appeared, each with its own set of recommendations for improving the situation. Some reports suggested changes in the curriculum, such as stiffer requirements, more homework, a common core of courses, a longer school day and school year, and more work in both basic and higher-order skills. Other recommendations stressed attracting more talented, brighter teachers, giving them better preparation, and improving their salaries. Still other ideas included stronger roles for the federal government and for business in improving the schools, more aides for teachers, merit pay, and changes in the organization of schools (Howe, 1983). Many of the reports blamed poor teaching and low-quality teacher-education programs for the schools' severe problems.

Teacher Quality

The headline of the *New York Times 1985 Education Winter Survey* was "Improving Our Teachers." In the last several years, many national news magazines carried stories about the problem of teacher quality. As Diane Ravitch has said, "The most common response to the current crisis in education has been to assail public school teachers. Not only are they incompetent, goes the charge, but good people have abandoned or are shunning the teaching profession" (1985, p. 198). Let's look briefly at these two accusations.

Academic Abilities

There are certainly reasons to be concerned about the academic abilities of teachers. People intending to major in education appear to have lower scores on tests of academic aptitude, such as the SAT or GRE, than people who intend to pursue other careers (Schlechty & Vance, 1983; Weaver, 1979). Of course, this conclusion is based on comparing the average scores for various groups. A closer look shows that many individuals who choose teaching score as well as students in other majors (Savage, 1983).

Is the quality of teachers actually declining? There is no simple answer. There are, however, some clear and unfortunate recent trends. Fewer high-ability women and minorities are entering teaching today. Those who do become teachers are more likely to leave the profession than individuals who are less academically talented (Roberson, Keith, & Page, 1983; Schlechty & Vance, 1983). Able women and minorities simply have more career opportunities today than they did 30 years ago. This is good for the individuals involved but not so good for education.

The flight of the most academically talented teachers, male as well as female, may indeed be a general problem. One study found that after six years, only about one-third of the teachers who scored in the top 10 percent on tests of verbal ability remained in teaching, while almost two-thirds of the teachers in the bottom 10 percent were still in the classroom (Schlechty & Vance, 1981).

Quality of Teacher Training

The growing belief that teacher-education programs must become more selective and rigorous is already affecting program requirements at colleges and universities. From 1983 to 1984 about one-third of the teacher-education programs around the United States raised standards for certification (American Association of Colleges for Teacher Education, 1985). Recent reform efforts in education have also focused on making teaching more appealing to bright, talented people (Goldberg, 1985). Some states are considering substantial increases for teachers' starting salaries in order to attract highly qualified people to the profession. Such increases in beginning salaries would presumably shift all teaching salaries upward.

Another response to concerns about teacher quality has been competency testing for teachers. Almost 90 percent of the people surveyed in the 1985 Gallup Poll believed that teachers should have to pass a basic competency test before being hired. When teachers answered the same question the year before, 63 percent agreed that testing was a good idea (Gallup, 1984). By 1985, 30 states, mostly in the southern and western sections of the United States, reported that they had some kind of teacher-assessment program, and a dozen more states indicated that serious discussions were underway.

The assessment programs include testing in basic skills, professional skills, academic knowledge, or some combination of the three (Sandefur, 1985). These tests may be required for admission to teacher-education programs, for certification, or both. The trend is to use nationally standardized instead of locally developed tests. A few sample items from one of these tests, the National Teachers' Examination (NTE), are shown in Table 1–3. Besides passing paper-and-pencil tests, teachers in some states must suc-

Table 1–3   Sample Test Items

Professional Knowledge	General Knowledge

Professional Knowledge

1. Development of which of the following is likely to be furthered more in a classroom with a competitive atmosphere than in one with a cooperative atmosphere?
   (A) complex intellectual problem-solving
   (B) social problem-solving
   (C) interest in school and learning
   (D) affective development
   (E) drill- and speed-dependent skills

2. A policy of equal educational opportunity obligates the teacher in which of the following ways?
   (A) Every child must be taught the same things.
   (B) All children must be treated alike.
   (C) Instruction must exclude use of multicultural learning materials.
   (D) Every class must have a proportionate minority population.
   (E) Instructional strategies must be adapted to the individual.

3. A teacher with a grievance against the local school board would most likely obtain help and information about teacher rights and the available grievance or arbitration procedures from the
   (A) United States Department of Education
   (B) state education agency or department
   (C) local law-enforcement agency
   (D) local parent-teachers organization
   (E) local teachers' organization

General Knowledge

4. The process by which all people learn the rules according to which they are expected to behave is called
   (A) adaptation
   (B) institutionalization
   (C) normalization
   (D) socialization
   (E) naturalization

5. Which of these is NOT a correct way to find 75% of 40?
   (A) 75.0×40
   (B) $(75 \times 40) \div 100$
   (C) $75/100 \times 40$
   (D) $\frac{3}{4} \times 40$
   (E) 0.75×40

6. The growth of which of the following was LEAST stimulated by the growth of United States railroad lines during the 19th century?
   (A) wheat production
   (B) insurance companies
   (C) steel production
   (D) iron mining
   (E) tobacco production

7. Which of the following changes on Earth has taken place most recently?
   (A) appearance of humans
   (B) development of the atmosphere
   (C) formation of the seas
   (D) formation of the first fossils
   (E) appearance of reptiles

8. "They embrace. But they do not know the secret in the poet's heart." The stage direction above ends a play; the second sentence is not a typical stage direction for which of the following reasons?
   (A) Poets do not often appear in plays.
   (B) Plays are not often built around secrets.
   (C) The direction does not summarize the plot of the play.
   (D) The direction does not list the names of all the characters.
   (E) The direction cannot be acted out for the audience to see.

Question Number	Correct Answer	Percent Answering Correctly
1	E	73
2	E	59
3	E	56
4	D	73
5	A	76
6	E	15
7	A	73
8	E	73

cessfully demonstrate particular teaching skills on the job before they are given permanent certification. The skills they must master are based on studies of effective teaching. We will talk more about effective teaching in Chapter 12.

Accountability

Another kind of testing has changed teachers' lives in recent years. These are tests based on the notion that teachers should be held accountable for student learning.

Some educators and politicians believe teachers and schools should be held responsible for what the student does or does not learn. In several states **minimum competency tests** are now required for graduation from high school or for promotion from one grade to the next. All students are expected to learn at least enough to pass these tests. Advocates of **accountability** believe that teachers and schools are to blame when students fail to reach a minimum level of performance.

The position favoring accountability assumes that almost every student can learn the material taught in schools if given enough time and the right instruction. A second assumption is that teachers and schools play the major role in determining what students learn. Both assumptions have some validity, but there are problems with accepting them completely. Many other factors besides the teacher and the school influence what the student will learn. Students vary greatly in abilities and motivation. And some students are physically or psychologically absent from the classroom most of the time. No teacher can influence someone who is not there.

The call for accountability has both positive and negative aspects. On the positive side, it may encourage teachers to examine the results of their teaching more carefully and make improvements. The progress of each stu-

minimum competency tests: tests of basic information and skills students must pass

accountability: holding teachers responsible for what and how much students learn in school

To what extent can this teacher's clearly positive influence on her student be measured in quantitative terms? How much can she be held accountable for what the student learns or doesn't learn? *(National Education Association/ Joe Di Dio)*

dent may be more carefully watched. But should teachers' jobs and salaries depend on average achievement gains for each class?

One of the greatest problems with holding teachers responsible for student learning is the difficulty of measuring learning accurately. If standardized achievement or minimum competency tests are used to measure how well the student has learned (and thus how well the teacher has taught), will teachers be forced to teach just the material covered on the test to protect their jobs? Will students be robbed of the chance to view themselves as partly responsible for their own learning? Perhaps teachers, students, and parents should be held jointly accountable for student progress.

Mainstreaming

Recently, a new and perhaps even more difficult set of demands has been placed on teachers—the responsibility for teaching students who were formerly taught in separate, special classes.

mainstreaming:
teaching students
with special
learning needs in
regular classrooms

The movement of as many students as possible out of special education classes and into regular classrooms is generally called **mainstreaming.** For years, these students, if educated at all, were kept separate from others and given labels such as "retarded" or "physically handicapped." Landmark legislation passed in 1975, called Public Law 94-142, set the stage for bringing many of these young people into the mainstream of American schools. The new legislation compelled the public schools to provide an appropriate free education for every young person. The law recognized that many students with severe problems cannot function in a regular classroom, but other "special" students, given the needed support, can benefit greatly from spending at least part of their school day with their more "normal" peers.

Future of Recent
Laws

However, at this point the future of PL 94-142 is uncertain. The principle of a free public education for certain children like the profoundly retarded is being challenged in a few states. The mandate for an appropriate education for all has proved difficult to carry out. For one thing, schools seldom have been given enough money to support the program (Vitello & Soskin, 1984). The law may be rewritten or even repealed. But, even if the law is changed, regular classroom teachers will probably continue working with many "special" students, since separate classes and teachers for these children are expensive. In a time of budget cuts and inflation, it is often the regular teacher who is expected to do more. Because the demands on teachers dealing with mainstreamed students are significant, an entire chapter (Chapter 13) has been devoted to this topic.

New Technology/Old Curriculum

Almost everyone seems to agree with Alfred Bork that "one remarkable feature of education at all levels in the past few years has been the increasing importance of computers in the instructional process. All indicators suggest that the presence and influence of the computer in education will continue to grow" (1984, p. 239). Many people believe that the most dramatic changes in education involve the uses of new technologies. The number of computers in schools today is in fact growing so quickly that it is hard to get accurate estimates. In 1984 students in U.S. elementary and secondary schools

Technology has entered the classroom to stay. Teachers will need some knowledge of computer basics to make the wisest and most imaginative use of the new opportunities computers offer. *(Robert Isear/Photo Researchers)*

had approximately 350,000 computers available to them—that is, on average, about four computers per school. Since about 1980 that number has been doubling every year (Bork, 1984). Some colleges now require students to buy particular computers in the same way specific textbooks are required.

However, quantity and quality of educational software have not gone hand in hand in our computer age. Most experts also agree with Bork that "the *amount* of software—particularly commercially produced programs—available for use at all grade levels and in all content areas has increased greatly. But the *quality* of this software has remained consistently low" (1984, p. 240). Few programs take advantage of the real possibilities of the computer. Many are simply drill and practice workbooks in a new form. But the potential is great. The combination of computers and other technological advances like interactive video could reshape education. A few possibilities are the reproduction of scientific experiments; interviews with important people; simulations; learning tournaments with students across the country; and the relocation of schooling to homes, libraries, museums, shopping malls—anywhere with a telephone line. We will spend more time on this topic in the Epilogue, "Teaching and Learning in the Computer Age."

Quantity and Quality of Software

The Future of the Job Market

There is one question that affects everyone who wants to become a teacher: Will there be any jobs?

The first two editions of this book described the effects of declining birthrates on the job market for teachers. Twenty-eight percent fewer children were born in 1978 compared with 1959. This led to declining school enrollments until the mid-1980s. Today the picture has changed. A baby boom began in the early 1980s, and enrollments began to increase again in 1985. At the same time, the number of people preparing to teach has declined. The combined effect of these two factors has resulted in teacher shortages, present and projected, in many areas of the country. The supply of teachers is least adequate in mathematics, the natural and physical sciences, bilingual education, special education, computer programming, and vocational-technical subjects. It is most adequate in the social sciences, physical and health education, and art. Some states have teacher shortages in all subject areas; most states have too many applicants in some subjects and not enough in others (Akin, 1985).

Job Prospects

Even if job prospects are poor for the subject areas or the locations that interest you, you can begin now to improve your chances for finding a job. Check with your college's placement office to find out what qualities and skills local schools value in applicants. Build your credentials so that you have a good chance to fill one of the vacancies created by the resignations and retirements that occur in every school. Finally, if you are willing to relocate, you can usually find the position you want.

Changes in the Family

High divorce rates and a marked rise in teenage pregnancies have affected family life across the country. There has been a dramatic increase in the number of school-age children living with divorced or single parents and in the number of children born to mothers under the age of 15. It has been estimated, in fact, that 45 percent of the children born in 1976 will spend some part of their lives with a single parent before they turn 18 (Coates, 1978). The trauma of divorce, the strains of single parenthood, and the difficulties of teenage parenthood all take their toll on the children involved. These children often need extra support from their teachers and schools during times of crisis.

Social Trends

Out of necessity or by choice, the mothers of many students work outside the home. This has led to a decrease in the availability of volunteers to serve as teachers' aides, library workers, and club sponsors. But there has been an even more direct effect on children. One estimate indicates that 15 million children between the ages of 5 and 13 come home after school to an empty house because parents are at work (Rosenberger, 1985). Many communities are concerned about the growing number of these "latchkey" children. We will discuss the problems of latchkey children in Chapter 4.

I hope I have given you a balanced picture of the problems, concerns, rewards, and issues confronting teachers today. But this is an educational psychology book, and I have said very little so far about educational psychology. Let's turn now to the role educational psychology can play in helping teachers solve problems.

THE ROLE OF EDUCATIONAL PSYCHOLOGY

Before you began this book, the term *educational psychology* may or may not have had any meaning to you other than the obvious linking of two areas of study. We begin our consideration of the role of educational psychology with a closer look at what these words mean.

Definitions

education: transmission of knowledge, skills, and values within a society

Education itself has many definitions. One is "the process by which a society transmits to new members the values, beliefs, knowledge, and symbolic expressions to make communication within the society possible" (Roemer, 1978, p. 4). In our society, schools are the institutions formally responsible for educating new members. But not all education happens in schools, nor is every lesson that people learn intentionally taught. Education may be deliberate, as in classrooms and lecture halls, or it may be unintentional, as in the transmitting of prejudices from one generation to another within the family. Whenever education takes place, deliberately or unintentionally, it

psychology: study of human behavior and mental processes

educational psychology: discipline concerned with the teaching and learning processes; applies the methods and theories of psychology and has its own as well

is tied to **psychology,** since psychology is the study of human behavior, development, and learning. But as is often the case, the whole meaning of the term **educational psychology** is more than the sum of the two parts.

For as long as educational psychology has existed—about 80 years—there have been debates about what it really is. Some people believe educational psychology is simply the *knowledge* gained from psychology and applied to the activities of the classroom. Others believe it involves applying the *methods* of psychology to study classroom and school life (Clifford, 1984; Grinder, 1981). Many people argue that educational psychology is a distinct discipline, with its own theories, research methods, problems, and techniques. According to this view, which is generally accepted today, educational psychology is concerned primarily with (1) understanding the processes of teaching and learning and (2) developing ways of improving these processes.

Educational psychologists apply knowledge from other fields and also create knowledge. They employ general scientific methods and develop their own methods as well. They examine learning and teaching in the laboratory, in nursery, elementary, and secondary schools, in universities, in the military, in industry, and in many other settings. But no matter what the situation or subjects studied, educational psychologists are especially concerned with applying their knowledge to improve learning and instruction. Educational psychology is not something limited to the laboratory; it is intimately related to what is happening wherever people learn.

Educational psychologists make an important distinction between learning and teaching. Most of what we know about how people learn is based on controlled research in laboratories. But knowing how people learn in the controlled environment of a laboratory does not tell us how to teach those people in the often unpredictable environment of the classroom. Theories and methods of teaching, which are based on theories of learning, must be examined and tested outside the laboratory. Studying how people learn is only half of the equation. The other half is studying how to teach them. Educational psychologists do both.

The purpose of this text is to give you a large part of the most important knowledge that educational psychologists have gained over the years. Knowing what educational psychologists have learned will not automatically make you a great teacher. But not knowing this information can lead to failure in teaching or to the frustration of spending hours rediscovering what others already know. Findings from educational psychology are part of the scientific basis for becoming a teacher-artist.

The Need for a Scientific Approach

Does educational psychology really have anything new to say to future teachers? After all, most teaching is just common sense, isn't it? Let's take a few minutes to examine these questions.

No, It's Not Just Common Sense.   In many cases, the principles set forth by educational psychologists—after much thought, research, and money spent—sound pathetically obvious. People are tempted to say, and usually do say, "Everyone knows that!" Consider these examples:

TAKING TURNS
What method should a teacher use in selecting students to read in a primary-grade reading class?

Common-Sense Answer
Teachers should call on students randomly so that everyone will have to follow the lesson carefully. If a teacher were to use the same order every time, the students would know when their turn was coming up and would probably concentrate only on the line they were going to read. They would not have to pay attention during the rest of the lesson.

Answer Based on Research
Research by Ogden, Brophy, and Evertson (1977) indicates that the answer to this question is not so simple. In first-grade reading classes, for example, going around the circle in order and giving each child a chance to read led to better overall achievement. The system does let students figure out when their turn is coming, which gives them the opportunity to practice their own lines. This very practice, with teacher feedback, may be a more important aspect of learning to read than paying attention while others are reading, at least in the early grades. In addition, going around the circle means that teachers do not overlook certain students, perhaps those who need the most practice.

CLASSROOM MANAGEMENT
What should a teacher do when students are repeatedly out of their seats without permission?

Common-Sense Answer
The teacher should remind students to remain in their seats each time they get up. These repeated reminders will help them remember the rule. If the teacher does not remind them and lets them get away with breaking the rules, those students and the rest of the class might decide the teacher is not really serious about the rule.

Answer Based on Research
In a now-classic study, Madsen, Becker, Thomas, Koser, and Plager (1968) found that the more a teacher told students to sit down when they were out of their seats, the more often the students got out of their seats without permission. When the teacher ignored students who were out of their seats and praised students who were sitting down, the rate of out-of-seat behavior dropped greatly. When the teacher returned to the previous system of telling students to sit down, the rate of out-of-seat behavior increased once again. It seems that, at least under

some conditions, the more a teacher says, "Sit down!" the more the students stand up!

SKIPPING GRADES

Should a school encourage exceptionally bright students to skip grades or to enter college early?

Common-Sense Answer

No! Very intelligent students who are a year or two younger than their classmates are likely to be social misfits. They are neither physically nor emotionally ready for dealing with older students and would be miserable in the social situations that are so important in school, especially in the later grades.

Answer Based on Research

Maybe! According to Kirk and Gallagher (1983) "from early admissions to school . . . to early admissions to college . . . the research studies invariably report that those children who were accelerated made adjustments as good or better than did the comparison children of similar ability" (p. 105). Whether acceleration is the best solution for a student depends on many specific individual characteristics, including the intelligence and maturity of the student, and on the other available options. For some students, skipping grades is a very good idea.

You may have thought that educational psychologists spend their time discovering the obvious. The examples above point out the danger of this kind of thinking. When a principle is stated in simple terms, it can sound simplistic. A similar phenomenon takes place when we see a gifted dancer or athlete perform; the well-trained performer makes it look easy. But we see only the results of the training, not all the work that went into mastering the individual movements. And bear in mind that it is probably possible to make any research finding—or its opposite—*sound* like common sense. The issue is not what sounds sensible but what is demonstrated when the principle is put to the test.

Conducting research to test possible answers is one of two major tasks of educational psychology. The other is combining the results of various studies into theories that attempt to present a unified view of such things as teaching, learning, and development. In this book you will encounter both kinds of information: (1) the results of actual studies and experiments; and (2) descriptions of major theories about topics of importance to teachers. Here we will look briefly at each of these sources of information.

Principles to the Test

Using Research to Solve Classroom Problems. Educational psychologists design and conduct many different kinds of research studies in their attempt to achieve a better understanding of both teaching and learning. A number of studies are based on classroom **observation**. Generally, the results reported in these studies are **correlations**, which are findings that show the degree of relationship between two events or measurements.

The correlation indicates both the strength of the relationship and its direction. Correlations are expressed as numbers from 1.00 to −1.00. The closer the correlation is to either 1.00 or −1.00, the stronger the relationship. For example, the correlation between height and weight is about .70 (a fairly strong relationship); the correlation between height and number of languages spoken is about .00 (no relationship at all). The sign of the correlation tells the direction of the relationship. A positive correlation, such as the

observation: research method in which behavior is observed and recorded without any intervention

correlation: statistical description of how closely two variables are related

one between height and weight, indicates that the two factors increase or decrease together. As one gets larger, so does the other. A negative correlation means that increases in one factor are related to decreases in the other. For example, the correlation between outside temperature and the weight of clothing worn is negative, since people tend to wear clothing of decreasing weight as the temperature increases.

It is important to note that correlations do not prove cause and effect. Height and weight are correlated. Taller people tend to weigh more than shorter people. But gaining weight obviously does not cause you to grow taller. Knowing a person's weight simply allows you to make a general prediction about that person's height. Educational psychologists identify correlations so they can make predictions about important events in the classroom.

experimentation: research method in which variables are manipulated and the effects recorded

random: without any definite pattern; according to no rule

A second type of research allows educational psychologists to go beyond predictions and actually study cause and effect. **Experimentation** must be conducted to identify true cause-and-effect relationships. Instead of just observing an existing situation, the investigators introduce changes and note the results. First a number of comparable groups of subjects are created, usually by assigning subjects at **random** to the groups. Random means each subject has an equal chance to be in any group. In one or more of these groups, psychologists change some aspect of the situation to see if this change has an expected effect. The results in each group are then compared. A number of the studies we will examine attempt to identify cause-and-effect relationships by asking questions such as these: If teachers ignore students who are out of their seats without permission and praise students who are working hard at their desks (cause), will students spend more time working at their desks (effect)?

Correlations and Causes

In many cases, both kinds of research occur together. The study by Ogden, Brophy, and Evertson (1977) described at the beginning of this section is a good example. In order to answer questions about the selection of students to recite in a primary-grade reading class, these investigators first observed students and teachers in a number of classrooms and then measured the reading achievement of the students. They found that the teaching strategy of going around the circle asking each student to read was associated or correlated with gains in reading scores. With a simple correlation such as this, however, the researchers could not be sure that the strategy was actually causing the effect. In the second part of the study, Ogden and her colleagues asked several teachers to call on each student in turn. They then compared reading achievement in these groups with achievement in groups where teachers used other strategies. This second part of the research was thus an experimental study conducted to see whether a particular teaching strategy would actually improve reading scores. As we have already seen, a cause-and-effect relationship did appear to be involved, although the students had not been assigned randomly to the classes, so the results might have been due to other factors as well.

This has been a brief and simplified discussion of research methods. For a more complete description, see the Appendix that follows this chapter.

Theories for Teaching.   The major goal of educational psychology is understanding the teaching and learning processes, and research is a primary tool. If enough studies are completed in a certain area and findings repeatedly point to the same conclusions, we eventually arrive at a **principle.** This is the term for an established relationship between two or more factors—between a certain teaching strategy, for example, and student achievement. Principles that stand the test of time and repeated investigation become **laws** of human functioning.

Another tool for building a better understanding of the teaching and learning processes is **theory.** Given a number of established principles, educational psychologists have attempted to explain not just the relationship between two or more variables but much larger systems of relationships as well. Theories have been developed to explain how motivation works, how differences in intelligence occur, and, as noted earlier, how people learn.

Note that theories *attempt* to explain. In dealing with such broad areas, it would be impossible to have all the answers. In this book, you will see numerous examples of educational psychologists taking different theoretical positions and disagreeing on the overall explanations of such issues as learning and motivation. If any one theory offered all the answers, disagreement would clearly not exist.

So why, you may ask, is it necessary to deal with theories? Why not just stick to principles? The answer is that both are useful. Principles of classroom management, for example, will give you help with specific problems. A good theory of classroom management, on the other hand, will give you a new way of thinking about discipline problems; it will give you tools for creating solutions to a great many different problems. A major goal of this book is to provide you with the best and the most useful theories for teaching. Although you may like some of the theories better than others, each can be considered as a way of understanding the problems teachers face.

MAJOR AREAS OF STUDY: THE CONTENTS OF THIS BOOK

Now that we have explored the role of theory and research, let us turn to a consideration of the topics studied by educational psychologists.

In Part One, we have explored teaching from the teacher's point of view and presented an overview of the field of educational psychology.

In Part Two we turn to the students—or, more specifically, to the ways in which they develop. Human development is an important topic in educational psychology. As you will see, students of different ages bring a wide range of abilities and ways of thinking to the classroom. Besides having their own characteristic styles of thinking, students of different ages also face distinct challenges in social and emotional development. As a teacher, you will want to take into account the mental, physical, emotional, and social abilities and limitations of your students. To do this, you must know something about the general patterns of development in these areas and about the ways individuals differ within these patterns.

Having introduced the students themselves, we will move to one of the most important topics in both educational psychology and the classroom: human learning. In Part Three, I will describe the two approaches to the study of learning, the behavioral and the cognitive theories. We will also show how these theories can be applied in a number of very practical ways, including strategies for classroom management and instruction in various subject areas.

Yes, teachers *do* make a difference. (Camilla Smith/ Rainbow)

At that point we will have covered the dual foundations of teaching: the students and the processes of learning. Having dealt with the essentials, we can concentrate in Parts Four, Five, and Six on actual practice. Part Four examines theories of motivation and their applications to teaching and then takes a careful look at how to organize and manage a classroom. Since teachers deal with individuals as well as groups, we will spend some time discussing communication and interpersonal relationships. The focus is on creating conditions that keep students involved and learning.

In Part Five we look at instruction: how to set goals, select methods, plan activities, arrange the setting, group students, and teach effectively. We will draw heavily from research about how effective teachers actually operate. The last chapter of this section concentrates on designing instruction for special students—the handicapped, the gifted, and the bilingual child.

In Part Six, we evaluate what has been taught. Here we will look at standardized tests, teacher-made tests, grading systems, mastery learning, and various alternatives to the traditional systems of evaluation.

Putting the Book to Work

In Table 1–4 you will find a list of sample questions drawn from different parts of this book. The questions do not begin to cover the many topics that will be included in each part. However, they will give you a sense of the kind of information you will encounter.

As you continue through this book, you will not only encounter many questions but also discover a number of possible solutions. You will see, I think, that educational psychology has a great deal to offer teachers and all those interested in education.

Table 1–4   What Would You Like to Know? Educational Psychology Can Help

Questions	Source for Information
▪ What is it like to be a teacher? ▪ Why study educational psychology? ▪ How can a teacher use research and theory?	Part One: An Introduction to Educational Psychology
▪ How might my students' thinking processes differ from my own? ▪ What is the emotional and social world of my students like? ▪ How can I help my students develop a positive self-image? ▪ What is intelligence, and where does it come from? ▪ Are there inborn psychological differences between males and females?	Part Two: Human Development: A Framework for Teachers
▪ What causes some students to develop fears about school? ▪ Should I use punishment in my classes? ▪ Why do students remember some things and forget others? ▪ How should I teach difficult concepts to slower students? ▪ Will students use what I teach them?	Part Three: Learning Theory and Practice
▪ Can sine curves ever be as interesting to students as sex education? ▪ How can I deal with a really defiant student? ▪ What should I do when angry parents accuse me of treating their child unfairly?	Part Four: Motivation and Classroom Management
▪ Where do I start in planning my first class? ▪ Is lecture better than discussion or individualized instruction? ▪ What makes an effective teacher? ▪ What should I do if I'm assigned a student who is deaf?	Part Five: Planning and Teaching
▪ How can the results from standardized tests help me teach? ▪ Are grades really necessary? ▪ How should I test my students?	Part Six: Evaluating Students

SUMMARY

1. Teaching is both an art and a science. Effective teaching requires an understanding of research findings on learning and instruction. Teaching also calls for the creativity, talent, and judgment of an artist.

2. The disadvantages of teaching include isolation from other adults, the need to do a great deal of routine paperwork, the difficulty in actually seeing the re-

sults of the work done, the strain of many roles to play and many different people to please, and the often very modest salaries.

3. Balancing the disadvantages are the rewards of teaching: the satisfaction of performing a valuable service, autonomy in the classroom, and the chance to make a difference in the lives of students.

4. The concerns of teachers change as they progress through three stages: the preteaching years, the early teaching years, and the experienced teaching years. During the beginning years, concerns tend to be focused on survival. The experienced teacher can move on to concerns about professional growth and effectiveness with a wide range of students.

5. Many societal changes are having repercussions in today's classroom. While everyone today seems to agree that the schools could be improved, no one plan for change is acceptable to all. One challenge to our educational system is to attract and keep bright, talented teachers. There is a movement to hold schools and teachers accountable for student learning. Landmark federal legislation, passed in 1975, has called for an appropriate education for all students, regardless of ability or handicapping condition. There are teacher shortages in many subject areas. More and more students live in homes with just one parent, or in homes where both parents work, and many children undergo the crisis of divorce.

6. The goals of educational psychology are to understand and to improve the teaching and learning processes. Educational psychologists develop knowledge and methods; they also use the knowledge and methods of psychology and other related disciplines. Two very important aspects of educational psychology are its scientific approach and its concern with the practical application of research findings to the classroom.

7. Both observational studies and experimental research can provide valuable information for teachers. Correlations allow you to predict events that are likely to occur in the classroom; experimental studies can indicate cause-and-effect relationships and should help you implement useful changes.

8. The principles of educational psychology offer teachers a number of answers to specific problems. The theories offer perspectives for analyzing almost any situation that may arise.

KEY TERMS		
	classroom management	observation
	minimum competency tests	correlation
	accountability	experimentation
	mainstreaming	random
	education	principle
	psychology	law
	educational psychology	theory

SUGGESTIONS FOR FURTHER READING AND STUDY

FARLEY, F. H., & GORDON, N. J. (1981). *Psychology and education: The state of the union*. Berkeley, CA: McCutchan. This book has chapters written by authorities in different areas of educa-

tional psychology. Topics include individual differences, development, learning and instruction, and the future of the discipline.

GALLUP, A. M. Gallup Poll of the public's attitudes toward the public schools. *Phi Delta Kappan*. Each year the September issue of this journal reports results of the annual Gallup Poll on the public schools.

RASCHE, D. B., DEDRICK, C. V., STRATHE, M. I., & HAWKES, R. R. (1985). Teacher stress: The elementary teacher's perspective. *Elementary School Journal, 85,* 559–564. This article reports results of a study that asked teachers about sources of stress and the best and worst aspects of teaching.

ROBERSON, S. D., KEITH, T. Z., & PAGE, E. B. (1983). Now who aspires to teach? *Educational Researcher, 12,* 13–21. In this article we see some continuing trends and recent changes in the characteristics, background, and attitudes of teachers.

RUBIN, L. J. (1985). *Artistry in teaching.* New York: Random House. Rubin describes teaching as both art and theater, providing some specific ideas about how teachers can develop an artis-

tic flair in the classroom.

RYAN, K., NEWMAN, K., MAGER, G., APPLEGATE, J., LASHLEY, T., FLORA, R., & JOHNSON, J. (Eds.). (1980). *Biting the apple: Accounts of first-year teachers.* New York: Longman. This book is filled with real stories about the first year of teaching. The experiences are interesting, funny, inspiring, but, at times, depressing.

SLAVIN, R. (1981). A case study of psychological research affecting classroom practice: Student Team Learning. *Elementary School Journal, 82,* 5–17. Slavin traces the study of cooperative learning from its roots in psychological research laboratories to its application in methods and materials for teaching.

SOWELL, E., & CASEY, R. (1982). *Analyzing educational research.* Belmont, CA: Wadsworth. A book for people who need to read and understand educational research. Included are examples of complete reports and hands-on exercises in applying results.

Journals in the Field

Several professional journals have devoted special sections to articles on key issues in education. A few of the most recent are:

Educational Leadership (1985, November). This issue has a special section called "Making Teaching More Rewarding." In it are articles on teacher-development programs, career ladders in teaching, and the role of master teachers.

Educational Leadership (1985, March) and *Education and Urban Society* (1985, February). Both of these journals have special sections discussing the responses of schools to the calls for educational reform.

Phi Delta Kappan (1984, December). In a special section called "Visions of the Future in Educational Computing," six experts give their views about what computers can and cannot do for education.

Journal of Teacher Education (1984, March/April). In this professional journal for educators there are several articles on the history, current status, and likely effects of the movement to require competency testing for teachers.

Teachers' Forum

Becoming a Teacher

What led you to decide to become a teacher? Would you still choose to become a teacher if you were to make your career choice all over again? Why or why not?

A Late but Happy Choice

I was running a cattle ranch in the eastern Oregon desert and gradually losing my shirt as cattle prices fell, year after year. I loved the life, but food was necessary for my growing family. A college friend suggested that I apply for a teaching position. In the back of my mind, I had always envied a teacher's life—the long leisurely summer vacations and the genial camaraderie with students—but I had never seriously thought about teaching. I applied, and was accepted, and have been teaching nearly ever since.

I am really glad I stumbled into teaching. Even though it leaves a lot to be desired in monetary terms, it allows enough free time so that I have been able to compensate. The good fellowship has been all I expected; the ham in me is satisfied; and a latent desire to do some good has been, occasionally, fulfilled.

Osborn Howes, Eighth-Grade English, Economics, and History Teacher
Hall School, Larkspur, California

A Sense of Being Valued

The profile of a "typical" teacher frequently presents him or her as overworked, underpaid, frustrated, tired, and lacking recognition. All human beings, teachers included, need to feel valued, respected, fulfilled. As a human being, I sought a profession that would challenge and fulfill me at the same time. A summer as a counselor at a camp for handicapped boys convinced me that these youngsters had minds that needed healing as well as nurturing. That summer lead me to conclude that two important components of health are attitude and knowledge. Whereas medicine primarily addresses the physical element, teaching speaks to all three. The knowledge that I had the opportunity to influence the intellectual, emotional, physical, mental, and psychological development and well-being of my students, as well as their attitudes and values, challenged me to expand my own horizons. Perhaps teaching is not financially rewarding; but would I still make it my career choice if I had to choose again? You bet—in a heartbeat! Why? Because I anticipate tomorrow knowing that today I gave my students my best—knowing that I made a difference today—knowing that despite the fatigue and the frustration, I'm valued, I'm respected, I'm fulfilled.

Laura Atkinson, Special Education Teacher
Chapel Hill, North Carolina

Dedication and Frustration

I am not sure if I ever really made a conscious decision to become a teacher; it seems as though from about the fourth grade I just knew that I was going to be a teacher. The only conscious choice I made was about subject and grade level. In retrospect, I see that the inclination to teach was due to a relative degree of success in the educational environment and to a love of learning that continues even to this day.

I am not certain whether I would again choose teaching as a career. As a student during the 1960s, the career options open to a woman seemed much more limited than they are today, and seemed even more limited to a girl raised in a small Wisconsin town with little career counseling. As a teacher for the past 11 years, I have grown as an individual as well as a professional educator. Yet I grow daily more frustrated in that educational system. Part of that frustration is due to the students with whom I work. Perhaps because I love learning so intensely, I find the apathy, disinterest, and sometimes even resentment in today's students particularly disturbing. In addition, I tire of not being treated as a professional, whether by my administrators, the community, or the society that will not pay me the salary due a professional working in an extremely complex job. It is difficult to be serious about a career that no one outside the profession seems to take seriously.

Jane C. Dusell, High School English Teacher
Medford Senior High School, Medford, Wisconsin

Looking Back As a retired teacher, the time has now come for me to look back over my forty-three years in the classroom. How wonderful it is to see my goals, my values, and my influence as they are mirrored in the lives of the children with whom I have had contact. And these ideals and goals will in turn be mirrored in others. As a teacher, the choice, the challenge, and the responsibility were mine. Being a teacher was a most rewarding experience and career.

Leland J. Gritzner, Sixth-Grade Teacher
Death Valley Unified Schools, Shoshone, California

The Value of Teacher Training

Do you feel that the teaching methodology courses you took were useful? Which do you feel were more important to your success as a teacher, courses in teaching methods or courses in the content area in which you now teach?

The What and The courses I took in my content area were the most important college courses in
How regard to my teaching; they built the informational and knowledge background that I use daily in my classes. Without a sound background in my subject area, I would not be able to teach all that I should, at the appropriate depth.

However, I do see value in methods classes. My courses in teaching foreign languages, writing, and literature were very good and very valuable. They were informative, practical, and realistic. All three professors taught the courses to be useful to a beginning teacher.

My content area courses taught me what to teach; my methods courses gave me an idea of how to go about teaching it.

Karen L. Eitreim, High School German Teacher
Richland High School, Richland, Washington

The Effects of Family Life

Families have changed in many ways over the past few decades. Parents seem busier than ever. Life has become very full and complicated. What aspects of the family most affect a child's attitude, performance, and ability in school? As a liaison between the home and the school, how can a teacher deal with negative family influences? How can a teacher work with parents to create supportive home environments?

Attention and In most homes today, either both parents are working or there is only one parent.
Responsibility This means parents have little time to spend with their children, and the children yearn for attention. In school, they seek attention through negative behavior. Time after school is often filled with activities out of the home, allowing little time for home responsibilities. Because children have not had experience with responsibilities, they may show a lack of responsibility in school.

The teacher can try to recognize students in a positive manner whenever possible rather than pay attention to negative behavior. The teacher needs to give students continual encouragement to work up to their abilities. Classroom duties can make students feel important and help them learn to deal with responsibility. The parents can also be involved: if they are informed about what is expected of their child, they can reinforce the teacher. They should also be encouraged to work on projects with their child at home.

Harold Kreif, Fifth-Grade Teacher
Pier Elementary School, Fond du Lac, Wisconsin

Sensitivity The most important change in the family has to be the increasing number of single-parent families where the parent is unmarried, separated, divorced, or widowed. The teacher must be sensitive to changes in student performance or behavior and be familiar with the family situation. The teacher should *know* that it is the day one student's folks appear in court, or that another student is moving from one parent's home to the other's, or that a birthday or significant life event of a deceased parent is near. In addition, the teacher must accept the challenge of being a role model for the student, especially when both teacher and absent parent are the same gender.

Family economics—two working parents, latchkey children, parent's loss of a job—can bring stress that affects behavior and academic achievement. Job-related mobility, too, affects students whose families move frequently. A teacher must see that a new student who may have never been at *any* school more than one year is quickly integrated into the group and not allowed to flounder on the sidelines.

Richard D. Courtright, Gifted and Talented Elementary Teacher
Ephesus Road Elementary School, Chapel Hill, North Carolina

Testing Teachers

Many states are moving in the direction of basic skills and/or competency testing for teachers. In some states where this is already the practice, a disturbing percentage of current teachers have been found to be deficient. What do you think about testing teachers? What should be done about teachers and prospective teachers who do not perform well on the competency tests?

Strengths and Testing can be a threat to adults as well as children. Like kids, some of us take tests
Weaknesses well. Others of us do not. We also have our areas of strength as well as our areas of weakness. It is unrealistic to expect everyone to do well in all areas. However, if there is a deficiency in the area of expertise, or in many areas, then I would certainly question whether this person belongs in education or not. Perhaps a personal interview might help in the decision process.

Testing teachers may also be a good way to remind us how nervous some kids feel when taking a test. After all, testing isn't everything!

Carolyn R. Cook, Kindergarten Teacher
Ramona Elementary School, Ramona, California

New Opportunities

Many capable female and minority students are no longer considering teaching as a career but are looking at new alternatives. What advice would you offer to women and minorities about the attractions and rewards of a teaching career?

Career and Teaching is a career that offers many rewards. To me, these are the most notable: I
Family am contributing toward the education and development of our youth; teaching has given me the opportunity to continue my own intellectual growth; and it's a career where holidays and vacations many times coincide with my own children's school breaks, giving me the opportunity to spend additional time with them.

If we must work, and nowadays most of us must, teaching could be called a family-oriented career.

Nancy R. Gonzalez, Bilingual First-Grade Teacher
Robert Frost School, Mount Prospect, Illinois

APPENDIX
Research in Educational Psychology

Overview
Asking and Answering Questions 34
Forming a Research Question   34
Choosing Variables and Selecting Measurement Techniques   35
Stating a Hypothesis and Choosing an Approach   36
Is the Research Valid?   39
A Sample Study: The Effect of Student Expectations   41
Essential Data   42
Judging Validity   43
Summary/Key Terms
Suggestions for Further Reading and Study

The concepts, principles, laws, and theories of educational psychology come from somewhere. One step toward a better understanding of educational psychology is knowing how information in the field is created and how to judge the information you encounter. This appendix will explore the value and limitations of research, the major road to knowledge in educational psychology. Then we will examine a specific problem to determine how research might answer questions posed by teachers. Finally, we will describe how to judge a research study by evaluating a real experiment.

When you complete this appendix, you should be able to:

- Describe four methods for making measurements.
- Distinguish between correlational and experimental methods.
- Judge research to determine if it is valid.
- Propose a study to answer a question from your teaching.

ASKING AND ANSWERING QUESTIONS

A Sample Problem

To get a better understanding of a few of the basic methods for asking and answering questions in educational psychology, we can examine a question that might interest you: Do students' expectations about the competence of a new teacher influence the way the students behave toward the teacher? To be more specific, do students pay more attention to a teacher they expect to be good? Suppose, for our purposes here, that an educational psychologist decided to look for an answer to this question. What methods might be used to gather information?

Forming a Research Question

Make It Specific

The first step might be to frame a clear and specific question. In this case, we might begin with something like this: Do students' beliefs about a teacher's competence affect the amount of attention they pay to the teacher? Notice how specific the wording is. We will have problems if the question is too vague—for example, Do students' beliefs about a teacher affect the way they behave in class? There is too much territory to cover in answering the question. We need to be specific about what kinds of beliefs—beliefs about the teacher's competence, not age, intelligence, or marital status. And we need to be specific about what kind of behavior—attention to the teacher, not enthusiasm for the subject or anxiety about a new year.

Choosing Variables and Selecting Measurement Techniques

variable: any characteristic that can vary

At this point we are ready to identify the variables to be studied. A **variable** is any characteristic of a person or environment that can change under different conditions or differ from one person to the next. In our hypothetical study, we have decided to examine two variables—student beliefs about the teacher's competence and student attention to the teacher.

The next thing we must do is decide how we will define what we mean by *beliefs* and *attention*. This question leads to the issue of measurement, because our definitions will be useful only if they give us something we can measure.

To study any variable systematically, there must be a way to measure changes or compare different levels of the variable. To simplify matters, let us concentrate at this point on just one of the variables—student attention. We will need to find a way to measure the degree of attention shown by the students. The method chosen will depend in part on the design of the study and on the limitations imposed by the situation. Here we will look at four basic approaches to measurement: (1) self-report, (2) direct observation, (3) testing, and (4) teacher or peer ratings.

self-report: subjects responding directly to questions

Using the **self-report** method, we could ask the students questions about how attentive they thought they were being. Answers could be given in writing or face to face, in an interview with the students.

direct observation: watching and recording behavior without any intervention

If we decided instead to use **direct observation,** we could send researchers into the classroom to watch the students and assess their attention. These investigators might simply rate the students (on a scale of one to five, perhaps, from very attentive to very inattentive), or they could use a stopwatch to count the number of seconds each student watched the teacher. Observers could also work from a videotape recording of the class, replaying the tape several times so that each student could be observed and his or her

Quite a bit of our information about teaching comes from data gathered by trained observers in real classrooms. *(Wasyl Szkodzinsky/ Photo Researchers)*

level of attention rechecked. These are only a few of the systems that could be designed using observers to measure attention.

A **test** would be a little more difficult to construct in this case. Many variables are measured with tests, especially those involving learning or achievement. But since attention is a process rather than a product, it is hard to design a test to measure it. One approach, however, would be to use a "vigilance task." We could see if the students were paying attention by having the teacher give an unpredictable signal, such as "Stand up," during the lesson. The measure of attention in this case would be the number of people who stood up immediately (Woolfolk & Woolfolk, 1974).

Finally, we might decide to use **teacher ratings** or **peer ratings.** We could measure attention by asking the teacher or the students to rate the attention of every student in the class.

Clearly, each of these approaches has advantages and disadvantages. Using self-reports or ratings of teachers or peers means relying on the judgments of the participants themselves. Using observers or tests can be disruptive to the class, at least initially. Videotaping is difficult and expensive. Let us assume, however, that we have chosen direct observation from videotapes. We will train the observers to time student attention with a stopwatch to determine how many seconds each student looks at the teacher during a ten-minute lesson. Note that our system of measurement has given us our definition of attention: the number of seconds each student looks at the teacher during a ten-minute lesson. This seems to offer a reasonably good definition. If the measurement system did not offer a good definition, we would need to find another way of measuring.

To define and measure our first variable—students' beliefs about the teacher's competence—we could also choose from a number of methods. Let us assume, at least for the time being, that we have selected a rating system. Students' answers to the question "How competent do you think this teacher is?" should give us a good idea of student opinion.

One other definition may be in order here, although in this particular study it seems rather obvious. Since we will be studying student beliefs and student attentiveness, the subjects in our investigation will be students. As you probably know, **subjects** is the term for the people (or animals) whose behavior is being measured. We would want to specify the grade, sex, and type of student to be studied. For our hypothetical study, we will select male and female sixth-graders in a predominantly middle-class school.

Stating a Hypothesis and Choosing an Approach

At this point we have our research question, the variables to be studied, the definition of these variables, the system for measuring them, and the subjects to be studied. We are now ready to add two new details: a **hypothesis** or guess about the relationship between the two variables, and a decision about what kind of approach we will use in our study. To some extent, the hypothesis will dictate the approach.

At the most general level, there are two approaches to answering research questions. The first is to describe the events and relationships in a particular situation as they take place in real life. The second approach is to

test: series of questions or tasks for measuring a variable

teacher ratings: teachers evaluating students on a given variable

peer ratings: students evaluating one another on a given variable

subjects: people or animals studied

hypothesis: prediction or assumption that provides the basis for investigation

change one aspect of a situation and note the effects of the change. These two approaches are generally called *descriptive* and *experimental*.

A Descriptive Approach.   One hypothesis we might establish in our study of student beliefs and attention is that students pay more attention to a teacher they believe to be competent. To test this hypothesis, we could go into a number of sixth-grade classrooms and ask students to rate their teachers on competence. Ideally, we would conduct the study in a middle school where sixth-graders usually have more than one teacher each day. We could then observe the students and measure their level of attention to each teacher. At this point we could get some idea about whether believing that a teacher is competent and paying attention to that teacher go together.

correlation: statistical description of how closely two variables are related

Let's assume, for the sake of the argument, that the two variables do go together. What we have now is a **correlation.** If two variables tend to occur together, they are correlated. We have just assumed such a correlation between beliefs and attention. Other variables that are correlated are height and weight, income and education, and colder temperatures and falling leaves. A taller person, for example, is likely to weigh more than a shorter person. A richer person is likely to have completed more years of education than a poorer person. And, for the sake of the argument, we are now assuming that a student who believes a teacher to be competent is more likely to pay attention to that teacher.

But what does this correlation give us? If educational psychologists know that two variables are correlated, they can then make predictions about one of the variables based on knowledge of the other variable. For example, because the IQ scores of parents and children are correlated, educators can predict a child's IQ based on that of the mother or father. The prediction may not be correct every time, because the correlation between parents' IQs and children's IQs is not perfect. But the prediction is likely to be correct or nearly correct much more often than a prediction based on no information at all. Several studies have found a correlation between a teacher's enthusiasm and student learning (Rosenshine & Furst, 1973). If we have information about a teacher's enthusiasm, we can make a prediction about the achievement level of the students in his or her class.

Correlation v. Causation

But this last example brings us to a very important point about correlation and prediction, mentioned briefly in Chapter 1. Knowing that two variables tend to occur together does not tell us that one variable is actually *causing* the other. Although enthusiastic teachers may tend to have students who achieve more than the students of unenthusiastic teachers, we cannot say that teacher enthusiasm leads to or causes student achievement. We know only that teacher enthusiasm and student achievement tend to occur together. Perhaps teaching students who are achieving more makes a teacher more enthusiastic. Perhaps a third factor—the interesting materials a teacher has chosen to work with, for example—causes both teacher enthusiasm and student achievement. Knowing that two variables are correlated does not tell you that one variable is causing the other. You should not argue from correlation to cause, but you can make predictions.

Although being able to predict levels of one variable from information about levels of another is useful, teachers are often interested in finding out what factors actually *will* cause a desired change in behavior. For this, they would need a different kind of research—research based on experimental manipulation.

An Experimental Approach.   Returning to our original question about student beliefs and attention, suppose we made a different hypothesis. Rather than just hypothesizing that student attention and beliefs about teacher competence go together, we could hypothesize that one of the factors actually causing students to pay attention is the belief that a teacher is competent. In this case, the hypothesis states a causal relationship. To test this hypothesis, we must change one of the variables to see if this change actually causes changes in the other variable. In our study, this assumed cause—known as the **independent variable**—is the belief that the teacher is competent. The purpose of our experiment will be to see if changes in this variable really cause changes in the other variable—the **dependent variable** of student attention to the teacher.

Assume that we create three comparable groups of students by randomly assigning the students to the groups. Since the selection and assignment of students to groups is totally **random**—by chance, based on no particular plan—the three groups should be very similar.

We then tell one group of students that the teacher they are about to meet is a "very good" teacher; we tell the second group that the teacher they will have is "not a very good" teacher; and we tell the third group nothing about the teacher they are going to have. This final group serves as the **control group.** It will give us information about what happens when there is no experimental manipulation. At some point in the experiment we would ask the students what they believed about the teacher to make sure they had accepted the description they were given.

Next, the teacher, actually the same person in all three cases, teaches the same lesson to each group. Of course the teacher should not be told about the experimental manipulation. We videotape the students in each group as they listen to the teacher. Later, raters viewing the tapes measure the number of seconds each student in the three groups has looked at the teacher. (You may have noticed that although the definition and measurement of the attention variable remain the same as they were in the descriptive study, the definition and measurement of the belief variable have changed. As you can see, such a change is necessary to turn the study into an experiment.)

What kind of results can we expect? If we find that students who believed the teacher was competent paid attention most of the time, students who believed the teacher was not very good paid very little attention, and students who were given no information paid a moderate amount of attention, have we proved our hypothesis? No! It is assumed in educational psychology and in psychology that hypotheses are never really proved by one study because each study tests the hypothesis in only one specific situation. Hypotheses are "supported" but never proved by the positive results of a single study. So have we supported the hypothesis that student beliefs affect student attention? The answer to this question depends on how well we designed and carried out the study.

Since this is just a hypothetical study, we can assume, once again for the sake of the argument, that we did everything just right. If you read the following list of requirements for a "true experiment," set forth by Van Mon-

independent variable: variable changed to determine its effects on other variables

dependent variable: variable measured to determine if its changes are results of changes in the independent variable

random: without any definite pattern; following no rule

control group: subjects receiving no special treatment and serving as a basis for comparison

drans, Black, Keysor, Olsen, Shelley, and Williams, you will see that we were indeed on the right track:

A True Experiment

> The "true experiment" is usually defined as one in which the investigator can (a) manipulate at least one independent variable; (b) randomly select and assign subjects to experimental treatments; and (c) compare the treatment group(s) with one or more control groups on at least one dependent variable. (1977, p. 51)

However, with a real experiment, we would need to know more about exactly how every step of the investigation was conducted. And we would also want to know whether other researchers could come up with the same results if they did the same experiment.

IS THE RESEARCH VALID?

Being able to evaluate research studies has a dual payoff. The kind of thinking needed is in and of itself valuable. It is the same kind of thinking needed to evaluate any complex idea, plan, argument, or project. In all these cases, you need to search for errors, oversights, inconsistencies, or alternative explanations. The analytical ability necessary to evaluate research is useful in any occupation, from law to business to motorcycle maintenance. The second payoff is more specifically valuable for teachers. As an educator, you will have to evaluate research done in your school district or reported in professional journals to determine if the findings are relevant to your own situation.

To be valid, the results of an experiment must pass several tests. Changes in the dependent variable must be due solely to the manipulation of the independent variable. This means, for one thing, that the experimental and control groups must be exactly the same in every way except one—the differences in the independent variable. In the following pages, we will look at eight questions that can be asked in an evaluation of a research experiment.

Analyzing Validity

1. *Were the groups to be studied reasonably equal before the experiment began?* If the subjects vary greatly from group to group, any changes found at the end of the experiment may be the results of the original differences in the groups and not of changes in the independent variable. Random assignment of subjects to groups usually takes care of this problem. If instead of randomly selecting the subjects in our own study we had used three different sixth-grade classes, our results would be questionable. Maybe one class already had more generally attentive students, or maybe as a group these students had learned to be more generally attentive. If they had been given the teacher labeled "very good" in the experiment, their high degree of attention would have been relatively meaningless. With random selection from a number of sixth-grade classes, however, each group is likely to have gotten an equal share of the generally attentive and generally inattentive students.

2. *Were all the variables except the independent variable controlled so that the only real difference in the treatment of each group was the change in the independent variable?* We have just seen that the subjects in each group must be equivalent. This principle is equally true of everything else in the experiment. If

different procedures were used with each group, it would be difficult to determine which of the differences caused the results. In our study, for example, if we had used different teachers or different lessons in each group, we would have run into this problem in evaluating the results. The students' attention to the teacher could have been based on many things other than the initial statement given by the experimenter about the teacher's competence (the independent variable).

3. *Were the measurement procedures applied consistently to each group?* Unreliable results may at times be caused by an inconsistent measurement system. In our study, if we had used a different videotape rater for each group, we could not have trusted our results. Perhaps one rater would give credit for student attention when students had their faces pointed toward the teacher even if their bodies were turned away. Perhaps another rater would give credit only if the students' entire bodies were directed toward the teacher. Ideally, one rater should make all the measurements. If more are used, there must be some test of the raters' ability to agree on the results. One way to check this would be to see if they agreed when measuring the same students' behaviors.

4. *Are the results of the study due to the experimental procedures rather than to the novelty of the situation?* It is always possible that subjects will respond in some special way to any change, at least temporarily. This possibility was pointed out dramatically by studies conducted at the Western Electric Plant in Hawthorne, Illinois. Investigators were trying to determine which changes in the plant environment would lead to greater worker productivity. As it turned out, everything they tried, every change in the working conditions, seemed to lead to greater productivity, at least for a while (Roethlisberger & Dickson, 1939). In other words, the workers were reacting not to the actual changes but to something new happening. Because the experiment took place in Hawthorne, Illinois, such results are now said to be examples of the **Hawthorne effect.** Our control group helped us avoid this problem. Although the independent variable of a "good" or "bad" teacher label was not applied to the control group, these students were given the special attention of being in an experiment. If their attention ratings had been particularly high, we might have suspected the Hawthorne effect for all three groups.

Hawthorne effect: change resulting from subjects' knowledge that they are being studied

5. *Has the investigator who designed the study biased the results in any way?* There are a number of obvious and subtle ways in which an investigator can influence the participants in an experiment. The investigator may have no intention of doing so but may still communicate to the subjects what he or she expects them to do in a given situation (Rosenthal, 1976). In our study, for example, if the investigator had told the teacher involved what the purpose of the experiment was, the teacher might have expected less attention from one of the groups and unintentionally done something to increase or decrease the attention actually given. If the investigator had told the videotape raters the purpose of the experiment, the same thing might have happened. Without meaning to, they might have looked harder for attention in one of the groups. In order to eliminate these problems, both teacher and raters would have to be unaware of the independent variable that was being studied.

6. *Is it reasonably certain that the results did not occur simply by chance?* To answer this question, researchers use statistics. The general agreement is that differences among the groups can be considered "significant" if these differences could have occurred by chance only 5 times out of 100. In reading a research report, you might see the results stated in the following manner: "The difference between the groups was significant ($p < .05$)." Unless you are planning to do your own scientific research, the most important part of this is probably the word *significant*. The mathematical statement means that the probability *(p)* of such a difference occurring by chance factors alone is less than ($<$) 5 in 100 (.05).

7. *Will the findings in this particular study be likely to fit other, similar situations?* This is really a question of generalization. How similar does a new situation have to be to get the same results? Consider our own experiment. Would we get similar results (a) with much older or younger students? (b) with students who are more or less intelligent? (c) with students who already know the teacher? (d) with different teachers or different lessons? (e) with the removal of the videotape cameras? (f) with a lesson that lasts more than ten minutes?

We cannot answer these questions until the study has been repeated with many different subjects in many different situations. This brings us to the question of **replication.**

replication: repeating a research study to see if the same results are obtained

8. *Has the study been replicated?* A study has been replicated if it has been repeated and the same results are found. Replication may involve exactly the same study conditions or changes in conditions that will give us a better idea of the extent to which the findings can be applied to other situations. If results have been replicated in well-designed studies, the findings form the basis for principles and laws.

Since our own study was only hypothetical, we cannot get a replication of it. But we can look at a similar study done by Feldman and Prohaska (1979). Analyzing this study should be useful to you in two ways. First, it will provide a model for considering other research articles you will find in textbooks and in professional journals. Second, the results of the study itself will probably be of interest because they suggest ways in which student expectations may cause teachers to be more or less effective.

A SAMPLE STUDY: THE EFFECT OF STUDENT EXPECTATIONS

Feldman and Prohaska's 1979 study concerns student expectations about a teacher's competence and the effect of these expectations on the students' and the teacher's behavior. (Remember that we were looking only at student behavior in our hypothetical study.) You may want to read the study in the *Journal of Educational Psychology* (vol. 71, no. 4, 1979). At the beginning of the article you will find specific information: the names of the authors, the university where they work, the name of the article, the name of the journal, and the basic facts about the study. The basic facts describing the design and results of the study are usually included in a brief summary, called an **abstract,** found at the beginning of such an article.

abstract: brief summary of a study's key procedures and results

Essential Data

The subjects in Feldman and Prohaska's first experiment were undergraduate female volunteers from an introductory psychology class. They were randomly assigned to a positive-expectation group or a negative-expectation group.

Each subject arrived separately at the experimental center and was told she would have to wait a few minutes before she could see the teacher. While she waited, she met another student who had supposedly just been working with the teacher and was now completing a questionnaire evaluating the teacher. Actually, this student, a male, was a **confederate** of the experimenter—an assistant pretending to be one of the subjects. The confederate played one of two roles, depending on whether he was meeting a subject from the positive-expectation group or the negative-expectation group. (The subjects, of course, did not know what group they were in.) When the confederate met a subject from the positive group, he told her the teacher had been really good, effective, and friendly. He then gave her a completed questionnaire (which also said good things about the teacher) and asked her to turn it in for him, since he had to leave. When the confederate met a subject from the negative group, he said very uncomplimentary things about the teacher and gave the subject a questionnaire with very negative comments on it.

confederate:
assistant pretending
to be a subject in an
experiment

The subject then went into a room and met the teacher, who was the same person for both groups. The teacher did not know the subject had been given any expectations at all. While she taught two minilessons, she and the subject were secretly videotaped. After the two lessons, the subject took a short quiz on the material and filled out a questionnaire just like the one she had seen the confederate completing. The same procedure was repeated for each subject.

Measurement
System

Finally, the videotapes of all the subjects were shown to trained coders who were unaware of the actual experimental conditions. These coders measured three things: (1) percentage of time each subject looked at the teacher, (2) each subject's forward body lean toward the teacher, and (3) each subject's general body orientation toward the teacher. Taken together, these student behaviors could be called "paying attention." When the coders rated the same subject's videotape, their ratings of the three behaviors were highly correlated. Thus we can assume that the coders agreed about how to use the measurement technique.

Results

Results showed that the subjects who expected the teacher to be "bad" rated the lesson as significantly more difficult, less interesting, and less effective than the subjects who expected the teacher to be "good." They also found the teacher to be less competent, less intelligent, less likable, and less enthusiastic than the other subjects did. Furthermore, the subjects who expected the teacher to be "bad" learned significantly less from one of the two minilessons, as measured by the short quiz. They also leaned forward less often and looked at the teacher less than the subjects who expected the teacher to be good.

How would you evaluate this study? The full report (Feldman & Prohaska, 1979) gives many more details, but based on our summary alone, what can you tell about the validity of the findings?

Guidelines

Evaluating a Research Study

Ideally, each of these eight conditions should be met:

1. *Equality of the experimental groups before the experiment.*
2. *Equal treatment of the groups except for the independent variable.*
3. *Use of a consistent measurement process.*
4. *Control for the Hawthorne effect.*
5. *Nonbiased participation by experimenters and raters.*
6. *Results that are statistically significant.*
7. *Ability to generalize to other similar situations.*
8. *Replication.*

You will also want to consider these two questions:

1. *Are there alternative explanations for the results that were achieved?*
2. *Are the differences among the groups large enough to have educational as well as statistical significance?*

Judging Validity

Questions to Ask

If you look at the Guidelines for evaluating a research study, it appears that conditions 1, 3, 5, and 6 have been met. (Do you agree?) We cannot yet be certain about condition 2—equal treatment of the subjects—because in this first experiment we have no detailed information about the way the teacher behaved toward the subjects. We only know that the teacher was instructed to give the same lesson, in the same way, to each subject. But what if the differences in the subjects' behavior toward the teacher—the differences that were found in the study—caused the teacher to give the lesson in different ways to different students? Perhaps after the first minute or so, subjects were reacting to real differences in the way the teacher delivered the lesson.

Feldman and Prohaska looked at this very real possibility in their second experiment. They found that students' nonverbal behavior (leaning forward or looking at the teacher) actually could affect how well the teacher taught the lesson. Although this may, to some extent, lessen the validity of their first experiment, it is a worthy finding in and of itself.

You may have noticed that we have not yet discussed conditions 4, 7, and 8. Feldman and Prohaska did not include a control group. The fact that the two experimental groups reacted in significantly different ways, however, shows that they were not simply reacting to the novelty of the situation. If both groups had been particularly eager or bored, we might have had good reason to expect the Hawthorne effect.

We can't know anything about conditions 7 and 8, of course, until further research has been conducted. The evaluation of student expectations is a relatively new topic. Until now, research has placed more emphasis on the study of the effects of teacher expectations about students. In some ways, it is exciting to be in on a new type of experimentation. At the same time, it is frustrating not to have as much information as we would like to have about replication and the ability to generalize. We can say, however, that two respected educational psychologists have reported findings that seem to support our initial hypothesis. In some cases, at least, student expectations about a teacher's competence do have an effect, not only on the students' behavior but also on the teacher's behavior.

Judging Significance

The last two questions given in the Guidelines are equally difficult to answer. It is almost always possible to offer alternative explanations for the findings of any study. In a well-controlled study, an attempt is made to eliminate as many of these alternative explanations as possible. The question of educational versus statistical significance is also one on which reasonable people might easily differ. How large a difference between the test scores of the two groups is large enough to warrant a change in educational practice? This question must be answered in part by the individual teacher. Do the potential gains offered by the findings seem worthwhile enough to make whatever change is called for?

SUMMARY

1. Besides helping you answer questions about teaching, research can offer data to support your viewpoint and methods for carrying out your own studies.

2. There are two general approaches to research in educational psychology: (1) descriptive studies, in which correlational relationships are examined; and (2) experimental studies, where cause-and-effect relationships are found. An experimental study involves the carefully controlled manipulation of an independent variable (the presumed cause).

3. In evaluating research, just as in evaluating any complex idea, you must make judgments about how valid the results are. If a research study meets all or most of the validity conditions, you must still decide if the results will truly generalize to your situation and whether the change involved is worth making.

KEY TERMS

variable	independent variable
self-report	dependent variable
direct observation	random
test	control group
teacher ratings	Hawthorne effect
peer ratings	replication
subjects	abstract
hypothesis	confederate
correlation	

SUGGESTIONS FOR FURTHER READING AND STUDY

BORG, W. R., & GALL, M. D. (1983). *Educational research: An introduction* (4th ed.). New York: Longman. This latest version of a comprehensive text describes the entire research process from identifying the problem to writing the finished report.

SOWELL, E., & CASEY, R. (1982). *Analyzing educational research*. Belmont, CA: Wadsworth. A book for people who need to read and understand educational research. Included are examples of complete reports and hands-on exercises in applying results.

Journals in the Field

Professional education journals discuss current topics in education and often include information about research in educational psychology as well. Here are some examples:

American Journal of Education
Childhood Education
Contemporary Education Review
Educational Leadership
Educational Researcher
Harvard Educational Review

Journal of Education
Journal of Teacher Education
Phi Delta Kappan
The Review of Education
Teaching Exceptional Children
Theory into Practice

Other journals specialize in reports of research studies or reviews of several studies on one topic. Here are some examples:

Adolescence
American Educational Research Journal
Child Development
Cognitive Pschology
Contemporary Educational Psychology
Educational and Psychological Measurement
Elementary School Journal
Exceptional Children
Human Development
Journal of Applied Behavior Analysis
Journal of Applied Developmental Psychology
Journal of Educational Psychology

Journal of Educational Research
Journal of Experimental Child Psychology
Journal of Experimental Education
Journal of Learning Disabilities
Journal of Research and Development in Education
Journal of School Psychology
Monographs of the Society for Research in Child Development
Psychological Bulletin
Psychological Review
Psychology in the Schools
Sex Roles

The Mind at Work: Cognitive Development and Language

Overview
Development: Toward a General Definition   48
A Comprehensive Theory about Thinking: The Work of Piaget   50
Readiness and Thinking   51
Making Sense of the World   52
Four Stages of Cognitive Development   55
Piaget's Theory: Limitations and Implications   65
Understanding Thinking   67
Matching Strategies to Abilities   67
Speeding Up Cognitive Development: Pro and Con   70
Vygotsky's Zone of Proximal Development   70
Another Perspective: Information Processing   71
Attention   71
Memory and Metacognitive Abilities   72
The Development of Language   74
How Do We Learn Language?   74
Stages in the Process   75
Dialects: Variations within Languages   77
Teaching and Language   78
Summary/Key Terms
Suggestions for Further Reading and Study
Teachers' Forum

How does the mind of the average 8-year-old work? What about the mind of the average 14-year-old? Can you really explain geometry to second graders? Can you explain existentialism to seventh graders? The material in this chapter will help you answer these questions and many others about how young people think and how their thinking changes over time. These changes in thinking and understanding are called cognitive development.

In this chapter we will begin with a discussion of the general principles of human development. Then we will turn to what is perhaps the most influential of all modern theories of cognitive development, that of Jean Piaget. Piaget's ideas have implications about what to teach students and when to teach it. But Piaget's theory is not the only explanation of how cognitive development takes place. There are important criticisms of his ideas that we will examine as well.

When we consider the implications of Piaget's ideas, we will also look at what has been called the American question: Can cognitive development be speeded up? Should teachers try to help students move from one stage of cognitive development to the next as quickly as possible? Or is it better to let students proceed at their own pace? We turn next to the theorists who emphasize developmental changes in how children process information. Finally, we will explore language development and discuss the role of the school in developing and enriching language skills.

By the time you have completed this chapter, you should have a basic understanding of cognitive development. More specifically, you should be able to do the following:

- State three general principles of human development and give examples of each.
- List Piaget's four stages of cognitive development and explain how children's thinking differs at each stage of development.
- Argue for and against methods of accelerating cognitive development.
- Present alternative views about cognitive and metacognitive development.
- Discuss how children's attention and memory abilities change over time.
- Describe briefly the stages by which children learn language.
- Suggest ways a teacher can help children expand their language use and comprehension.

DEVELOPMENT: TOWARD A GENERAL DEFINITION

development:
orderly, adaptive changes we go through from conception to death

The term **development** in its most general psychological sense refers to certain changes that occur in human beings (or animals) between conception and death. The term is not applied to all changes, but rather to those that appear in orderly ways and remain for a reasonably long period of time. A temporary change due to a brief illness, for example, is not considered to be a part of development. There is also a value judgment made by psychologists in determining which changes qualify as development. The changes, at least those that occur early in life, are generally assumed to be for the better and to result in behavior that is more adaptive, more organized, more effective, more complex, and of a higher level (Mussen, Conger, & Kagan, 1984).

Human development can be divided into a number of different aspects. **Physical development,** as you might guess, deals with changes in the body. **Personal development** is the term generally used for changes in an individual's personality. **Social development** refers to changes in the way an individual relates to others. And as we've just seen, **cognitive development** refers to changes in thinking.

Many changes during development are simply matters of growth and maturation. **Maturation** refers to changes that occur naturally and spontaneously and that are, to a large extent, genetically programmed. Such changes emerge over time and are relatively unaffected by the environment, except in cases of malnutrition or severe illness. Much of a person's physical development falls into this category. Other changes are brought about through learning, as individuals interact with their environment. Such changes make up a large part of a person's social development. But what about the development of thinking and personality? Most psychologists agree that in these areas, both maturation and interaction with the environment (or nature and nurture, as they are sometimes called) are important but disagree about the amount of emphasis to place on each.

There is also a difference of opinion about the way development takes place. Does it follow certain predictable stages? Are later changes dependent on a number of very specific earlier changes? Or is development relatively flexible, with changes coming in different orders for different people? Again, we can find theorists who favor each of these views.

Although there is great disagreement about what is involved in development and about the way it takes place, there are a few general principles almost all theorists would support.

1. *People develop at different rates.* In your own classroom, you will have a whole range of examples of different developmental rates. Some students will be larger, better coordinated, or more mature in their thinking and social relationships. Others will be much slower to mature in these areas. Except in rare cases of very rapid or very slow development, such differences are normal and to be expected in any large group of students.

2. *Development is relatively orderly.* People tend to develop certain abilities before others. In infancy they crawl before they walk, babble before they talk, and see the world through their own eyes before they can begin to imagine how others see it. In school, they will master addition before algebra, *Bambi* before Shakespeare, and so on. Theorists may disagree on exactly what comes before what, but they all seem to find a relatively logical progression.

3. *Development takes place gradually.* Very rarely do changes appear overnight. A student who cannot manipulate a pencil or answer a hypothetical question may well develop this ability, but the change is likely to take time. Even Piaget, who believed that children do move from one specific stage to another, saw these changes as taking place slowly over time.

---

physical development: changes in body structure and function over time

personal development: changes in personality that take place as one grows

social development: changes over time in the ways we relate to others

cognitive development: gradual, orderly changes by which mental processes become more complex and sophisticated

maturation: genetically programmed, naturally occurring changes over time

A COMPREHENSIVE THEORY ABOUT THINKING: THE WORK OF PIAGET

During the past half-century, the Swiss psychologist Jean Piaget devised a model describing how humans go about making sense of their world by gathering and organizing information (Piaget, 1954, 1963, 1970). His theory emphasizes a number of distinct stages through which a person must go to develop the thinking processes of an adult.

Although Piaget's ideas about how thinking develops have been very influential, his methods have been criticized for being so vague that others could not replicate his procedures (Larsen, 1977). Piaget used the clinical method, approaching the study of children through extended, unstructured interviews. He also asked children to perform particular tasks, and he talked to them about their solutions. For obvious reasons, such methods are hard to reproduce in a scientifically controlled fashion. Piaget also has been criticized for drawing conclusions after studying only a few children. This second criticism is based on a misconception about how Piaget gathered his data. Although it is true that some of his early work focused on detailed observations of his own three children, his later research involved many more children (Elkind, 1981).

Swiss psychologist Jean Piaget taught us some very unexpected things about how children think and how their thinking changes over time. *(Jill Krementz)*

Critics have also questioned several of Piaget's conclusions. In recent years research has supported some of his basic ideas and cast doubt on others. Many psychologists disagree with his explanations about why thinking develops as it does. But even these critics tend to agree that Piaget's descriptions of children's logic and reasoning are accurate and insightful. Thanks to him we have a much richer understanding of the ways children think. For teachers, an appreciation of the child's mental world can be invaluable.

Readiness and Thinking

According to Piaget (1954), certain ways of thinking that are quite simple for an adult are not so simple for a child. There are specific limitations on the kinds of material that can be taught at a given time in a young person's life. Sometimes all you need to do to teach a new concept is to give a student a few basic facts as background. At other times, however, all the background facts in the world are useless. The student simply is not ready to learn the concept. With some students, you can discuss the general causes of civil wars and then ask why they think the American Civil War broke out in 1861. But suppose the students respond with "When is 1861?" Obviously their concepts of time are different from your own. They may think, for example, that they will someday catch up to a sibling in age, or they may confuse the past and the future (Sinclair, 1973). In order to experience some of these differences in thinking at first hand, try asking children of various ages the questions in Table 2–1.

Ability to learn a particular fact or idea is affected by the mental tools the student brings to the problem. For example, suppose you asked a young child who has not learned how to multiply, "How much is ten 6s?" The child might well give you the answer, after carefully adding $6+6+6+6+6+6+6+6+6+6=60$. The child has used current knowledge to solve the problem. An older child might multiply 6 by 10 or simply add a 0 to 6, depending on his or her understanding of how best to solve the problem—depending on the mental tools available.

In Piaget's view, each of us perceives and structures reality according to our available mental tools, or thinking processes. Thus, because the thinking processes of a child differ from those of an adult, the reality of the child is

Table 2–1 **Questions to Ask Children**

> What does it mean to be alive?
> Can you name some things that are alive?
> Is the moon alive?
> Where do dreams come from?
> Where do they go?
> Which is farther, to go from the bottom of the hill all the way to the top or go from the top of the hill all the way to the bottom?
> Can a person live in Chicago and in Illinois at the same time?
> Will you be just as old as your big brother some day?
> When is yesterday?
> Where does the sun go at night?

not necessarily the same as the adult's. Piaget attempted to identify a limited number of thinking processes for each stage of development. This part of Piaget's theory has been strongly questioned. But the idea that ways of thinking and seeing reality change as the child develops seems accurate.

Making Sense of the World

As you can see, cognitive development is much more than the addition of new facts and ideas to an existing fund of information. According to Piaget, our thinking processes change radically, though slowly, from birth to maturity. Why do these changes occur? Underlying Piaget's theory is the assumption that we constantly strive to make sense of the world. How do we do this? What principles might govern our efforts?

Influences on Development. In Piaget's theory, one of the most important influences on the changes in our thinking processes is *maturation,* the unfolding of the biological changes that are genetically programmed in each human being at conception. Of all the influences on cognitive development, this is clearly the least modifiable. We can think of maturation as providing the biological basis for all the other changes.

Another influence on changes in thinking processes is *activity*. With physical maturation comes the increasing ability to act on the environment and learn from it. When the coordination of a young child is reasonably developed, for example, the child may discover principles about balance by experimenting with a seesaw. So as we act on the environment—as we explore, test, observe, and eventually consolidate and organize information—we are likely to be altering our thinking processes at the same time.

And as we develop, we are also interacting with the people around us. According to Piaget, our cognitive development is influenced by *social transmission,* or learning from others. Without social transmission, we would need to reinvent all the knowledge already offered by our culture. The amount people can learn from social transmission varies according to their stage of cognitive development.

Maturation, activity, and social transmission all work together to influence cognitive development. How do we respond to these influences?

Basic Tendencies: Organization and Adaptation. As a result of his early research in biology, Piaget concluded that all species inherit two basic tendencies, or "invariant functions." The first of these tendencies is toward **organization**—the combining, arranging, recombining, and rearranging of behaviors and thoughts into coherent systems. The second tendency is toward **adaptation,** or adjusting to the environment.

Organizational Changes. Thus, according to Piaget, people are born with a tendency to organize their thinking processes into psychological structures. These psychological structures are our systems for understanding and interacting with the world. Simple structures are continually combined and coordinated to become more sophisticated and thus more effective. Very young infants, for example, can either look at an object or grasp it when it comes in contact with their hands. They cannot coordinate looking and

Biology,
Environment,
Society

organization:
ongoing process of arranging information and experience into mental systems or categories

adaptation:
adjustment to the environment

grasping at the same time. As they develop, however, the infants organize these two separate behavioral structures into a coordinated higher-level structure of looking at, reaching for, and grasping the object. Of course, they can still use each structure separately (Ginsburg & Opper, 1979).

schemes: mental systems or categories of perception and experience

Piaget gave a special name to these structures. In his theory, they are called **schemes.** Schemes are the basic building blocks of thinking. They are organized systems of actions or thoughts that allow us to represent mentally or "think about" the objects and events in our world. Schemes may be very small and specific—the sucking through a straw scheme or the recognizing a rose scheme, for example. Or they may be larger and more general—the drinking scheme or the categorizing plants scheme. As a person's thinking processes become more organized and new schemes develop, behavior also becomes more sophisticated and better suited to the environment.

Adaptive Changes.   In addition to the tendency to organize their psychological structures, people also inherit the tendency to adapt to their environment. Piaget believed that from the moment of birth, a person begins to look for ways to adapt more satisfactorily. Two basic processes are involved in adaptation: assimilation and accommodation.

assimilation: fitting new information into existing schemes

Assimilation takes place when people use their existing schemes to make sense of events in their world. Assimilation involves trying to understand something new by fitting it into what we already know. At times we may have to distort the new information to make it fit. For example, the first time many children see a skunk, they call it a kitty. They try to match the new experience with an existing scheme for identifying animals. A baby trying to suck on a new rattle is also attempting to assimilate the novel event by applying an existing scheme.

accommodation: altering existing schemes or creating new ones in response to new information

Accommodation occurs when a person must change existing schemes to respond to a new situation. If data cannot be made to fit any existing schemes, then more appropriate structures must be developed. We adjust our thinking to fit the new information, instead of adjusting the information to fit our thinking. Children demonstrate accommodation when they add the scheme for recognizing skunks to their other systems for identifying animals. The baby sucking the rattle soon develops new behaviors for dealing with the new object. With a little trial and error, the baby is likely to learn such appropriate rattle behavior as shaking or even throwing (less appropriate to parents but fine as far as the infant is concerned).

People adapt to their increasingly complex environments by using existing schemes whenever these schemes work (assimilation) and by modifying and adding to their schemes when something new is needed (accommodation). In fact, both processes are required most of the time. Even using an established pattern such as sucking to deal with an unfamiliar baby bottle may require some accommodation, since the new nipple may be slightly larger or smaller or have holes of a different size than the last bottle encountered. Whenever new experiences are assimilated into an existing scheme, the scheme is enlarged and changed somewhat, so assimilation involves some accommodation.

There are also times when neither assimilation nor accommodation is used. If people encounter something that is too unfamiliar, they may ignore it. Experience is filtered to fit the kind of thinking a person is doing at a given time. For example, if you overhear a conversation in a foreign lan-

The progression of development is relatively orderly. For example, this girl can work with concrete materials—strings of beads in this case—to understand the relation between symbols and quantity, before she can work with the symbols alone. *(Suzanne Szasz/Photo Researchers)*

guage, you probably will not try to make sense of the exchange unless you have some knowledge of the language.

Equilibration: Tying It All Together. Organizing, assimilating, and accommodating can be seen as a kind of complex balancing act. According to Piaget, that is an accurate description of what happens. In his theory, the actual changes in thinking take place through the process of **equilibration**—the act of searching for a balance. Piaget assumed that people continually test the adequacy of their thinking processes in order to achieve that balance.

equilibration: search for mental balance between cognitive schemes and information from the environment

Briefly, the process of equilibration works something like this. If we apply a particular scheme to an event or situation and the scheme works, then equilibrium exists. If the scheme does not produce a satisfying result, then disequilibrium exists, and we become uncomfortable. This motivates us to assimilate and/or accommodate, and thus thinking changes and moves ahead. In order to maintain a "fit" or a balance between our schemes for understanding the world and the data the world provides, we are continually assimilating new information using existing schemes and accommodating our thinking whenever necessary. Thus equilibration, the search for fit or balance, leads to changes in cognitive organization and the development of more effective systems for thinking.

The point that young people's thinking is not like that of adults has been made a number of times. Now we turn to the actual differences that Piaget hypothesized for children as they grow.

Four Stages of Cognitive Development

Piaget's four stages of cognitive development are sensorimotor, preoperational, concrete operational, and formal operational. Piaget believed that all people pass through the same four stages in exactly the same order. When these stages are discussed, they are generally associated with specific ages, as in Table 2–2. Before you read any further, however, please understand that these are only general guidelines. Knowing a student's age is never a guarantee that you know how the child will think in every situation. Even being 16 or 17 does not guarantee that someone has reached the final stage of formal operations (Ashton, 1978).

Ages and Stages: A Caution

Piaget was interested in the kinds of thinking abilities people are able to use. Often, people can use one level of thinking to solve one kind of problem and a different level to solve a different type. The stages, then, describe general ways of thinking, not labels than can be applied directly to individuals. Keep in mind that each stage of development brings new and more sophisticated thinking powers. Rather than focus on what children cannot understand, it is better to emphasize what they *can* understand.

As we examine the four stages, keep in mind too that there is a definite continuity in thinking. The stages in many ways are cumulative. As adaptation proceeds, each kind of thinking from the previous stage is incorporated and integrated into the stage that follows. We all continue to use the

Table 2–2 **Piaget's Stages of Cognitive Development**

Stage	Approximate Age	Characteristics
Sensorimotor	0 – 2 years	Begins to make use of imitation, memory, and thought. Begins to recognize that objects do not cease to exist when they are hidden. Moves from reflex actions to goal-directed activity.
Preoperational	2 – 7 years	Gradual language development and ability to think in symbolic form. Able to think operations through logically in one direction. Has difficulties seeing another person's point of view.
Concrete operational	7 – 11 years	Able to solve concrete (hands-on) problems in logical fashion. Understands laws of conservation and is able to classify and seriate. Understands reversibility.
Formal operational	11 – 15 years	Able to solve abstract problems in logical fashion. Thinking becomes more scientific. Develops concerns about social issues, identity.

From B. J. Wadsworth (1979), Piaget's theory of cognitive development: An introduction for students of psychology and education (2nd ed.). New York: Longman. Copyright © 1971, 1979, 1984 by Longman Inc. Reprinted with permission of Longman.

actions of infancy (such as grasping), although as we grow older we acquire other ways of dealing with the environment that we may wish to use instead. You, for example, may have developed very sophisticated abstract thinking abilities in your major area of study. But when someone asks you how many months are left until you finish school, you may count on your fingers, thus returning to a more primitive and concrete method of solving the problem.

sensorimotor: involving the senses and motor activity

Infancy: The Sensorimotor Stage. The earliest period is called the **sensorimotor** stage because the development at this stage is based upon information that is obtained from the senses (sensori) and from the actions or body movements (motor) of the infant.

The greatest conquest of infancy is the realization that objects in the environment exist whether the baby perceives them or not. This basic understanding, called **object permanence,** arises from many activities with and observations of objects and people appearing, disappearing, and reappearing. As most parents discover, before infants develop object permanence, it is relatively easy to take something away from them. The trick is to distract them and remove the object while they are not looking—"out of sight, out of mind." The older infant who searches for the ball that has rolled out of sight or cries for the toy sneakily removed by a parent is indicating an understanding that the objects still exist even though they can't be seen.

object permanence: understanding that objects have a separate, permanent existence

goal-directed actions: deliberate actions toward a goal

A second major accomplishment in the sensorimotor period is the beginning of logical, **goal-directed actions.** Think of the familiar dumping-bottle toy that babies like to play with. It is usually plastic and has a lid, and it contains several colorful plastic items that can be dumped out and replaced. If you give a bottle like this to a 6-month-old baby, the baby is likely to become frustrated trying to get to the toys inside. Shaking the bottle is not enough unless it is first inverted. Inverting it does no good unless the lid is removed. At this stage, the baby is not likely to have a sufficiently organized, systematic approach or scheme to get the items out.

But suppose you give the dumping bottle to an older child, one who has mastered the basics of the sensorimotor stage. This child, at age 2, will probably be able to deal with the bottle in a much more orderly fashion. Through trial and error the child will slowly build a "bottle dumping" scheme: (1) get the lid off; (2) turn the bottle upside down; (3) shake if the items jam; and (4) watch the items fall on the floor. Once this sequence is learned, the child will be able to deal with the dumping bottle efficiently on future occasions. Separate lower-level schemes have been organized into a higher-level scheme.

If you keep watching, you may notice that the child is soon able to reverse this action. The items can be picked up one by one and put in the bottle, which has been turned right side up, and the lid can be replaced. According to Case (1978a), learning to reverse actions is a basic accomplishment of the sensorimotor stage. As we will soon see, however, learning to reverse thinking—learning to *imagine* the reverse of a sequence of actions—takes much longer.

Early Childhood to the Early Elementary Years: The Preoperational Stage. Sensorimotor intelligence is not very effective for planning ahead or keeping track of information. For this children need what Piaget called **operations,** or actions that are mentally rather than physically carried out and reversed. The child at the second stage is only beginning to master operations. Thus the stage is called **preoperational.**

According to Piaget, the first step from action to thinking is the internalization of action. By the end of the sensorimotor stage the child can use many action schemes. However, as long as these schemes remain tied to action, they are of no use in recalling the past or predicting the future. The first type of thinking that is separate from action involves making these schemes symbolic. The ability to form and use symbols—words, images, signs, and so on—is a major accomplishment of the preoperational period.

The child's earliest use of symbols is generally in pretending or miming actions. Children who are not yet able to talk will often use action symbols—pretending to drink from an empty cup or touching a comb to their hair, showing that they know what each object is for. This behavior also shows that their schemes are becoming more general and less tied to specific actions. The eating scheme, for example, may be used in play as well as in asking for food. During the preoperational stage we also see the rapid development of that very important symbol system, language. Between the ages of 2 and 4, most children enlarge their vocabulary from about 200 to 2,000 words.

one-way logic: thinking through a task without being able to reverse the steps

As the child moves through the preoperational stage, the developing ability to think about objects in symbolic form remains somewhat limited to thinking in one direction only. A Piagetian road-building task provides a good example of this kind of **one-way logic.** Two sets of small objects and two strips of paper (roads) are needed. The child is given one road and one set of objects; the experimenter has the other road and the other object set. The experimenter then lines up the objects along the road and asks the child to make a road "just like mine." If the child has achieved the one-way logic of the preoperational stage, he or she will probably be able to do this.

reversible thinking: thinking backward, from the end to the beginning

To see if the child has moved beyond the preoperational stage, the experimenter may then ask the child to carry out a task calling for **reversible thinking.** Again, the experimenter builds a road but this time asks the child to "build one just like mine, but going the other way." As you can see in Figure 2–1, the preoperational child may begin just fine. Soon, however, the child is likely to start following the experimenter's original order rather than the reverse order. The child may then go back and forth in confusion between the two orders. Reversible thinking calls for the ability to keep the entire system in mind. The preoperational child has problems with this.

Figure 2–1   **Reversing the Objects at the Preoperational Stage**

Reversible thinking is involved in other tasks that are difficult for the preoperational child, such as the **conservation** of matter. Conservation is the principle that the amount or number of something remains the same even if the arrangement or appearance is changed, as long as nothing is added and nothing is taken away. You know that if you tear a piece of paper into several pieces, you will still have the same amount of paper. To prove this, you know that you can reverse the process by taping the pieces back together.

A classic example of difficulty with conservation is found in the preoperational child's response to the following Piagetian task. Leah, a 5-year-old, is shown two identical glasses, both short and fat in shape. Both have exactly the same amount of colored water in them. The experimenter asks Leah if each glass has the same amount of water, and she answers "Yes." The experimenter then pours the water from one of the glasses into a tall, thin glass, lines this glass up with the other short, fat glass, and asks Leah once again if each glass has the same amount of water. Now she is likely to insist that there is more water in the tall, thin glass because the water level is higher. Notice, by the way, that Leah shows a basic understanding of identity (it's the same water) but not an understanding that the *amounts* are identical (Ginsburg & Opper, 1979).

Which has more? Looks can be deceiving if you focus only on height. Actually, both have 500 ml. *(Mimi Forsyth/ Monkmeyer Press)*

Piaget's explanation for Leah's answer is that she is focusing, or centering, attention on the dimension of height. She has difficulty considering more than one aspect of the situation at a time, or **decentering.** The preoperational child cannot understand that increased diameter compensates for decreased height, since this would require taking two dimensions into account at once. Thus, children at the preoperational stage have trouble freeing themselves from their own perceptions of how the world appears. What looks like more must be more, even if logic says otherwise.

decentration: focusing on more than one aspect at a time

This brings us to another important characteristic of the preoperational stage. Preoperational children, according to Piaget, are very **egocentric;** they tend to see the world and the experiences of others from their own viewpoint. Egocentric, as Piaget intended it, does not mean selfish; it simply means children often assume that everyone else shares their feelings, reactions, and perspectives. For example, children at this stage may believe you see the same view as they do, even if you are facing another direction in the room. A child may see an animal through the window, ask you about it, and be very disappointed when you cannot answer, even though you have been sitting with your back to the window the entire time. During this period children are also likely to believe everyone feels the same way they do. These children center on their own perceptions and on the way the situation appears to them. This is one reason it is difficult for very young children to understand that your right hand is not on the same side as theirs when you are facing them.

egocentrism: assumption that others experience the world the way you do

Egocentrism is also evident in the child's language. You may have seen young children happily talking about what they are doing even though no one is listening. This can happen when the child is alone or, even more often, in a group of children—each child talks enthusiastically, without any real interaction or conversation. Piaget called this the **collective monologue.**

collective monologue: form of speech in which children in a group talk but do not really interact or communicate

Recent research has shown that young children are not totally egocentric in every situation, however. Children as young as 4 change the way they talk to 2-year-olds by speaking in simpler sentences, and even before age 2 children show toys to adults by turning the front of the toy to face the other person. So young children do seem quite able to take the needs and different perspectives of others into account, at least in certain situations (Gelman, 1979).

Dealing with preoperational children, at home or in school, has its problems and its rewards. Since you may well have students who use these ways of thinking, at least some of the time, a set of Guidelines is included on the next page.

Later Elementary to the Middle School Years: The Concrete Operational Stage. In any grade you teach, from kindergarten through twelfth, a knowledge of the thinking processes at the concrete operational stage will be helpful. In the early grades the students are moving toward this logical system of thought. In the middle grades it is in full flower, ready to be applied and extended by classroom work. In the high school years it is used often by students whose thinking may not have moved on to the higher stage of formal operations.

concrete operations: mental tasks tied to concrete objects and situations

Piaget coined the term **concrete operations** to describe this stage of "hands-on" thinking. The basic characteristics of the stage are (1) the recognition of the logical stability of the physical world; (2) the realization that

Guidelines

Teaching the Preoperational Child

Use concrete props and visual aids whenever possible.

Examples
1. When you discuss concepts such as "part," "whole," or "one-half," use shapes on a felt board or cardboard "pizzas" to demonstrate. Don't explain with words alone.
2. Let children add and subtract with counting sticks, rocks, or colored chips.

Make instructions relatively short, using actions as well as words.

Examples
1. When giving instructions about how to enter the room after recess and prepare for social studies, ask a student to demonstrate the procedure for the rest of the class by walking in quietly, going straight to her seat, and placing the social studies text, paper, and a pencil on her desk top.
2. Explain a game by acting out one of the parts.
3. Show students what their finished papers should look like. Use an overhead projector or display examples where students can see them easily.

Don't expect the students to be able consistently to see the world from someone else's point of view.

Examples
1. Avoid social studies lessons about worlds too far removed from the child's experience.
2. Avoid long lectures on sharing. Be clear with students on rules for sharing or use of materials, but avoid long explanations of the rationales for the rules.

Be sensitive to the possibility that students may have different meanings for the same word or different words for the same meaning. Students may also expect everyone to understand words they have invented.

Examples
1. If a student protests, "I won't take a nap. I'll just rest!" be aware that a nap may mean something like "changing into pajamas and being in my bed at home."
2. Ask children to explain the meanings of their invented words.

Give children a great deal of hands-on practice with the skills that serve as building blocks for more complex skills like reading comprehension.

Examples
1. Provide cut-out letters to build words.
2. Supplement workbooks and other strictly paper-and-pencil tasks in arithmetic with activities that require measuring and simple calculations—cooking, building a display area for class work, dividing a batch of popcorn equally.

Provide a wide range of experiences in order to build a foundation for concept learning and language.

Examples
1. Take field trips to zoos, gardens, theaters, and concerts; invite storytellers to the class.
2. Give students words to describe what they are doing, hearing, seeing, touching, tasting, and smelling.

---

elements can be changed or transformed and still conserve many of their original characteristics; and (3) the understanding that these changes can be reversed.

Conservation of quantity is probably the most basic of all concrete operations. We have already shown the difficulty the preoperational child has with conservation. Remember Leah's problem with judging the amount of water in the tall, thin glass? If Leah had been able to use concrete operations, she would have realized that the amount of water in the two glasses remained the same.

According to Piaget, a student's ability to solve conservation problems depends on understanding three basic aspects of reasoning: identity, compensation, and reversibility. With a complete mastery of **identity,** the student knows that if nothing is added or taken away, the material remains the same. With an understanding of **compensation,** the student knows that an apparent change in one direction can be compensated for by a change in another direction. That is, if the liquid rises higher in the glass, the glass must be narrower. And with an understanding of *reversibility,* the student can mentally cancel out the change that has been made. Note especially that a grasp of reversibility means the student at this stage has mastered two-way thinking.

Another important operation mastered at this stage is **classification.** Classification depends on a student's abilities to focus on a single characteristic of objects in a set and then to group the objects according to that single characteristic. Given 12 objects of assorted colors and shapes, the concrete operational student can invariably pick out the ones that are round.

More advanced classification at this stage involves recognizing that one class fits into another. While daisies and daffodils may each be in a class by themselves, both fit into the class of flowers, and flowers are members of the plant family. A city can be in a particular state or province and also in a particular country. As children apply this advanced classification to locations, they often become fascinated with "complete" addresses such as: Lee Donstein, 52 6th Street, Atlanta, Georgia, U.S.A., North America, Northern Hemisphere, Earth, Solar System, Milky Way, Universe.

Classification is also related to reversibility. The ability to reverse a process mentally now allows the concrete operational student to see that there is more than one way to classify a group of objects. The student understands that the objects can be classified in one way and then reclassified in another. Thus, big and small beads of two different shapes and two different colors can be classified and then reclassified in three different ways: by color, size, and shape.

Seriation is the process of making an orderly arrangement from large to small or vice versa. This understanding of sequential relationships permits a student to construct a logical series in which A < B < C (A is less than B is less than C) and so on. Before the stage of concrete operations, the student is likely to get stuck on the idea that both A and B are small, since A is smaller than C, and B is also smaller than C. The idea that B is larger than A is likely to get lost in the shuffle. But the concrete operational child can grasp the notion that B can be larger than A but smaller than C.

With the abilities to handle operations like conservation, classification, and seriation, the student at the concrete operational stage has finally developed a complete and very logical system of thinking. This system of thinking, however, is still tied to physical reality. The logic is based on concrete situations that can be organized, classified, or manipulated. Thus, these children can imagine several different arrangements for the furniture in their rooms or plan a layout for the electric train set before they act. They do not have to solve these problems strictly through trial and error by actually making the rearrangements.

identity: principle that a person or object remains the same over time

compensation: the principle that changes in one dimension can be offset by changes in another

classification: grouping objects into categories

seriation: arranging objects in sequential order according to one aspect like size, weight, or volume

Guidelines

Teaching the Concrete Operational Child

Continue to use concrete props and visual aids, especially when dealing with sophisticated material.

Examples
1. *Use time lines for history lessons and three-dimensional models in science.*
2. *Use diagrams to illustrate hierarchical relationships like branches of government and the agencies under each branch.*

Continue to give students a chance to manipulate and test objects.

Examples
1. *Set up simple scientific experiments like the following involving the relationship between fire and oxygen. What happens to a flame when you blow on it from a distance? (If you don't blow it out, the flame gets larger briefly, since it has more oxygen to burn.) What happens when you cover the flame with a jar? (It uses up all the oxygen and goes out.)*
2. *Have students make candles by dipping wicks in wax, weave cloth on a simple loom, bake bread, set type by hand, or do other craft work that illustrates the daily occupations of people in the colonial period.*

Make sure presentations and readings are brief and well organized.

Examples
1. *Assign stories or books with short, logical chapters, moving to longer reading assignments only when students are ready.*
2. *Break up a presentation with a chance to practice the first two steps before introducing the next steps.*

Use familiar examples to explain more complex ideas.

Examples
1. *Compare students' lives with those of characters in a story. After reading* Island of the Blue Dolphin *(the true story of a girl who grew up alone on a deserted island) ask, "Have you ever been really frightened by animals? Have you ever had to stay alone for a long time? How did you feel?"*
2. *Teach the concept of area by having students measure two rooms in the school that are different sizes.*

Give opportunities to classify and group objects and ideas on increasingly complex levels.

Examples
1. *Give students separate sentences on slips of paper to be grouped into paragraphs.*
2. *Use outlines, hierarchies, and analogies to show the relationship of new material to existing knowledge. Compare the systems of the human body to other kinds of systems: the brain to a computer, the heart to a pump, arteries and veins to roads with one-way traffic, nerves to a telephone system, digestive system to a factory. For classifying plants, list plants that humans can and cannot eat and plants that animals can and cannot eat. Break down stories into components, from the broad to the specific: author; story; characters, plot, theme; place, time; dialogue, description, actions.*

Present problems that require logical, analytical thinking.

Examples
1. *Use Mind Twisters, Brain Teasers, Master Mind, and riddles.*
2. *Discuss open-ended questions that stimulate thinking: "Are the brain and the mind the same thing?" "How should the city deal with stray animals?" "What is the largest number?"*

The concrete operational child is not yet able to think about thinking or to reason about hypothetical, abstract problems that involve the coordination of many factors at once. This kind of coordination is part of Piaget's next and final stage of cognitive development. But bear in mind that if you teach concrete operational students, part of your job will be to focus on what your students *can* do. A set of Guidelines is included to help you.

Junior High and High School Years: The Formal Operational Stage. As you will soon see, some students remain at the concrete operational stage throughout their school years, even throughout life. However, new experiences, usually those that take place in school, eventually present most students with problems that they cannot solve with concrete operations. It is fine to be able to pick out the red objects, to order items from large to small, but what happens when a number of variables interact, as in a laboratory experiment? Then a mental system for controlling sets of variables and working through a set of possibilities is needed. These are the abilities Piaget called **formal operations.**

formal operations: mental tasks involving abstract thinking and coordination of a number of variables

At the level of formal operations, all the earlier operations and abilities continue in force. Formal thinking is reversible, internal, and organized in a system of interdependent elements. The focus of thinking, however, shifts, so that the real, actually experienced situation is seen as only one of many possible situations. In order for this shift to occur, the students must be able to generate different possibilities for any given situation in a systematic way.

Formal operations include what we normally think of as scientific reasoning. Hypotheses can be made, and mental experiments can be set up to test them, with variables isolated or controlled. However, although formal operational students are able to use this type of thinking, they will not necessarily be able to describe it to you. It is the logician who describes systems for reasoning. The student simply makes use of the new mental tools.

The following experiment can help you identify students who can apply formal operations. The purpose is to test whether a person can determine, in an organized way, the number of different possibilities that exist within a reasonably limited framework. Ask your students: "How many different meals can be made if a shopper has bought the following for one week: (1) three meats—hamburger, chicken, and steak; (2) three vegetables—broccoli, spinach, and green beans; and (3) three starches—rice, noodles, and potatoes?" (Only balanced meals, please!) A student capable of formal operations would begin by laying out the possibilities systematically:

> Hamburger, broccoli, rice
> Hamburger, broccoli, noodles
> Hamburger, broccoli, potatoes
> Hamburger, spinach, rice
> Hamburger, spinach, noodles
> And so on

A student at the concrete operational stage, however, would be much less systematic; he or she might start with favorite foods and continue in the order of preference. It would not be unusual for the student to mention only three meals, using each food only once. The underlying system of combinations is not yet available.

Formal operational thinking is required in most advanced science courses. Without this capability, students have trouble systematically considering all the variables involved. *(Richard Wood/Taurus Photo)*

adolescent egocentrism: assumption that everyone else shares one's thoughts, feelings, and concerns

The ability to think hypothetically, consider alternatives, and analyze one's own thinking has some interesting consequences for adolescents. Since they can think about worlds that do not exist and create a set of "best" possibilities, these students can imagine ideal worlds (or ideal parents and teachers, for that matter). Adolescents can also imagine many possible futures for themselves and may try to decide which is the ideal. Feelings about any of these ideals may run quite strong.

Another characteristic of this stage is **adolescent egocentrism** (Elkind, 1968). Adolescents tend to be quite taken up with analyzing their own beliefs and attitudes. They reflect on others' thinking as well but often assume that everyone else shares their concerns and is as interested as they are in their thoughts, feelings, and behavior. Thus, they believe that others are analyzing them: "Everyone noticed that I wore this shirt twice this week." "The whole class thought my answer was dumb!" "Everybody is going to adore my new tape." You can see that imperfections in appearance or social blunders can be devastating if "everybody is watching."

Do We All Reach the Fourth Stage?   Most psychologists agree that there is a level of thinking more sophisticated than concrete operations. But the question of how universal formal thinking actually is, even among adults, is still under investigation. Accordng to Neimark (1975), the first three stages of Piaget's theory are forced on most people by physical realities. Objects really *are* permanent. The amount of water *doesn't* change when it is poured into another glass. Formal operations, however, are not so closely tied to the physical environment. Neimark has speculated that this last stage may be "a refinement of an advanced culture rather than a necessary condition for survival" (Neimark, 1975, p. 556).

Piaget himself (1974) suggested that most adults may be able to use formal operational thought only in a few areas, areas where they have the greatest experience or interest. De Lisi and Staudt (1980) found support for this idea. In their experiment, college students from three different majors (physics, political science, and English) were asked to solve several types of problems. Almost all the students were able to use formal operations when the problems were similar to the type encountered in their own major. However, when confronted with unfamiliar types of problems, only about half of the students applied formal thinking in finding solutions.

So do not expect every student in your junior high or high school class to be able to think hypothetically about all the problems you present. It is important to keep this in mind, since many of the tasks normally presented to high school and even junior high students require a good deal of formal thinking. Science and mathematics are especially likely to require formal operations; forming and mentally testing hypotheses are important aspects of both fields. Students who have not learned to go beyond the information that is presented to them are likely to fall by the wayside in these courses. Sometimes students find shortcuts for dealing with problems that are beyond their grasp; they may memorize formulas or lists of steps. These systems may be helpful for passing tests, but real understanding will take place only if students are able to go beyond this superficial use of memorization—only, in other words, if they learn to use formal operational thinking. The Guidelines on the next page should help you take all these possibilities into consideration.

Difficulties with
Abstractions

PIAGET'S THEORY: LIMITATIONS AND IMPLICATIONS

Piaget's influence on developmental psychology and education has been enormous, but his ideas have also been criticized, as we noted at the beginning of the chapter. Some psychologists have questioned the existence of four separate stages of thinking, even though they agree that children do go through the changes that Piaget described (Gelman & Baillargeon, 1983). One problem with the stage idea is the lack of consistency in children's thinking. Psychologists reason that if there are separate stages, and if the child's thinking at each stage is based on a particular set of operations, then once the child has mastered the operations, he or she should be able to be fairly consistent in solving *all* problems requiring those operations. In other words, once you can conserve, you ought to know that the number of blocks does not change when they are rearranged (conservation of number) *and* that the weight of a ball of clay does not change when you flatten it (conservation of weight). But it doesn't happen this way. Children can conserve number a year or two before they can conserve weight. One longitudinal study of 300 children found that most kindergarten students could

Lack of Consistency

Guidelines

Teaching Children Who Are Beginning to Use Formal Operations

Continue to use concrete operational teaching strategies and materials.

Examples
1. *Use visual aids such as charts and illustrations, as well as somewhat more sophisticated graphs and diagrams.*
2. *Compare the experiences of characters in stories to students' experiences.*

Give students the opportunity to explore many hypothetical questions.

Examples
1. *Have students write position papers, then exchange these papers with the opposing side and have debates about topical social issues—the environment, the economy, mandatory national service for all youth, disarmament.*
2. *Ask students to write about their personal vision of a utopia; write a description of a universe that has no sex differences; write a description of Earth after man is extinct.*

Give students opportunities to practice problem solving and scientific reasoning.

Examples
1. *Set up group discussions in which students design experiments to answer specific questions or criticize experimental designs provided by the teacher.*
2. *Encourage students to explain (think aloud) how they solve problems. This might be done with a whole class, in small groups, or in pairs.*
3. *Make sure at least some of the tests you give ask open-ended questions that require logical thinking.*
4. *Ask students to justify two different positions on abortion with logical arguments for each position.*

Whenever possible, teach broad concepts, not just facts, using materials and ideas relevant to the students' lives.

Examples
1. *When discussing the Civil War, consider what other issues have divided the United States since then.*
2. *Use lyrics from popular songs to teach poetic devices, to reflect on social problems, and to stimulate discussion on the place of popular music in our culture.*

perform some tasks involving concrete operations, but they could not perform other tasks supposedly requiring the same underlying operations until the fifth or sixth grade (Klausmeier & Sipple, 1982). If certain changes in thinking are based on mastering an underlying operation, then these changes in thinking should occur at the same time, not five or six years apart. Piagetian theorists have tried to deal with these inconsistencies, but not all psychologists are convinced by their explanations.

The Child's World

Even though research has not supported all his ideas, and even though his major purpose was to understand thinking, not to offer educational advice, Piaget still has much to say to teachers. First, he has taught us many surprising things about the child's world.

Piaget's main legacy may be his rich description of what it is we develop. . . . [He] revealed new developmental phenomena, many of which strike us as surprising or counter to common sense. Especially notable are the following: Infants apparently don't expect objects to be permanent. Preschoolers believe that rearranging objects can change their number. . . . More generally, most concepts not only take longer to develop than we might think, but also go through a number of interesting steps along the way. (Miller, 1983, p. 90)

Second, Piaget has taught us that we can learn a great deal about how children think by listening carefully—by paying close attention to the ways they try to solve problems. If we understand children's thinking, we will be better able to match teaching to children's abilities.

Understanding Thinking

The students in any class will vary greatly both in their level of cognitive development and in their academic knowledge. As a teacher, how can you determine if students are having trouble because they lack the necessary thinking abilities or because they simply have not learned the basic facts? To do this, Case (1978b) suggests you observe your students carefully as they try to solve the problems you have presented. What kind of logic do they use? Do they focus on only one aspect of the situation? Are they fooled by appearances? Do they suggest solutions systematically or by guessing and forgetting what they have already tried? Again, ask your students how they tried to solve the problem. Listen for their strategies. Try to understand the kind of thinking that is behind repeated mistakes or problems. The students are the best sources of information about their own thinking abilities. Of course, the difficulties you identify will not necessarily be related to Piagetian operations. There are many explanations for the mistakes students make in school, but understanding the thinking behind the mistakes should still be very valuable. You might check your ability to analyze children's thinking by completing the exercise in Table 2–3 on the next page.

Matching Strategies to Abilities

The Problem of the Match

Perhaps the most important implication of Piaget's theory for teaching is what Hunt (1961) has called "the problem of the match." Teachers must not underestimate or overestimate the current thinking abilities of their students. Students must be neither bored by work that is too simple nor left behind by teaching they cannot understand. According to Hunt, disequilibrium must be kept "just right" to encourage growth. Setting up situations that lead to errors can help create an appropriate level of disequilibrium. When students experience some conflict between what they think should happen (a piece of wood should sink because it is big) and what actually happens (it floats!), they may rethink their understanding, and new knowledge may develop.

It is worth pointing out, too, that many materials and lessons can be understood at several levels and can be "just right" for a range of cognitive abilities. Classics such as *Alice in Wonderland*, myths, and fairy tales can be enjoyed at both concrete and symbolic levels.

At every level of cognitive development, you will also want to see that students are actively engaged in the learning process. They must be able to incorporate the information you present into their own schemes. To do this,

Table 2–3   Different Thinking at Different Stages

Match the following examples with the appropriate stage and characteristic below:

1. Mary wants more cookies. Her mother breaks in half the ones she has already, and Mary is satisfied.
2. Jill is able to understand that some people say one thing but act in ways that are not congruent with their statements.
3. When given a set of cards picturing the steps in baking a cake, Don can put them in the proper order.
4. Johnny wants you to pick up his spoon and put it on his table so he can drop it again.
5. *Mother:* "How do you think Molly feels when you take her doll away?"
   Child: "She feels like I want to play with it."
6. Karen can predict the movement of a body, taking into account several influences simultaneously.

STAGES

a. Sensorimotor
b. Preoperational

c. Concrete operational
d. Formal operational

CHARACTERISTICS

A. Goal-directed activity: cause-and-effect relationship.
B. Hasn't achieved conservation.
C. Egocentrism.
D. Combinatorial logic.
E. Can hold more than one premise in mind at the same time.
F. Seriation of actions.

ANSWERS

1. (b, B).   2. (d, E).   3. (c, F).   4. (a, A).   5. (b, C).   6. (d, D).

they must act on the information in some way. Schooling must give the students a chance to experience the world. This active experience, even at the earliest school levels, should not be limited to the physical manipulation of objects. It should also include mental manipulation of ideas that arise out of class projects or experiments. Often this mental manipulation can even be turned into games (Farnham-Diggory, 1972; Ginsburg, 1985).

Thinking Games   Furth and Wachs (1975) describe many thinking games in their book *Piaget's Theory in Practice: Thinking Goes to School.* For example, after a social studies lesson on different jobs, a primary-grade teacher might show the students a picture of a woman and ask, "What could this person be?" After answers like "teacher," "doctor," "secretary," "lawyer," "saleswoman," and so on, the teacher could suggest, "How about a mother?" Answers like "sister," "daughter," "aunt," and "granddaughter" may follow. This should help the children switch dimensions in their classification and center on another aspect of the situation. Next the teacher might suggest "American," or "jogger," or "blonde." With older children, hierarchical classification might be involved: it is a picture of a woman, who is a human being; a human being is a primate, which is a mammal, which is an animal, which is a living thing.

Applying New Knowledge

Another important part of healthy cognitive development is the ability to apply and test the principles learned in one situation to new situations. Teachers should constantly be asking students to apply recently learned principles in a number of different situations. For example, the student who has learned how to form plurals by dropping the -y and adding -ies should be asked to form plurals of words like *party* and *pony* (where the rule fits) as well as words like *donkey* (where the rule does not work). If the principle applies, the student will gain practice in using it. If the principle does not fit, disequilibrium will occur, and new thinking abilities may develop.

All students also need to interact with teachers and peers in order to test their thinking, to be challenged, to receive feedback, and to watch how others work out problems. Disequilibrium is often set in motion quite naturally when the teacher or another student suggests a new way of thinking about something. As a general rule, students should act, manipulate, observe, and then talk and/or write (to the teacher and each other) about what they have experienced. Concrete experiences provide the raw materials for thinking. Communicating with others makes students use, test, and sometimes change their thinking abilities (Ashton, 1978).

In the early years, play is learning. Some psychologists believe that boys do better in math and science in later life because they have many more early experiences with manipulating objects and materials in their world. *(Rogers/ Monkmeyer Press)*

When the issue of changing or improving cognitive abilities is discussed, this question often arises: Is it possible to accelerate cognitive development? Piaget called this "the American question," which gives you a hint about his position on the matter.

Speeding Up Cognitive Development: Pro and Con

The position of Piaget and most psychologists who attempt to apply his theory to education is that development should not be speeded up. This traditional view has been well summarized by Wadsworth:

The Piagetian Position

> The function of the teacher is not to accelerate the development of the child or speed up the rate of movement from stage to stage. The function of the teacher is to insure that development within each stage is thoroughly integrated and complete. (1978a, p. 117)

According to Piaget, cognitive development is based on the self-directed actions and thoughts of the student, not on the teacher's actions. If you do try to teach a student something the student is not ready to learn, he or she may learn to give the "correct" answer. But this will not really affect the way the student thinks about this problem or any other problem. Therefore, from this perspective, acceleration is useless. A second Piagetian argument is that the acceleration is inefficient. Why spend a long time teaching something at one stage when students will learn it by themselves much more rapidly and thoroughly at another stage?

Some of the strongest arguments in favor of speeding up cognitive development are based on the results of cross-cultural studies of children (studies that compare children growing up in different cultures). These results suggest that certain cognitive abilities are indeed influenced by the environment and education. Children of pottery-making families in one area of Mexico, for example, learn conservation of substance earlier than their peers in families who do not make pottery (Ashton, 1978). Furthermore, children in non-Western cultures appear to acquire conservation operations later than children in Western cultures. These results may be due to the way the ability to conserve is measured in the studies. But it seems likely that some factors in the environment, not just the naturally evolving internal structures of the child, are involved.

Recently, many educators have become interested in the work of a Russian psychologist, Lev Vygotsky. His concept of the zone of proximal development provides an alternative to the two positions described in the preceding paragraphs.

Vygotsky's Zone of Proximal Development

Whereas Piaget described the child as a little scientist, constructing an understanding of the world largely alone, Vygotsky (1978) has suggested that cognitive development depends much more on other people. He believes that cognitive development occurs through the interaction of the child with adults and more capable peers. These people serve as guides and teachers for the child, providing the information and support necessary for the child to grow intellectually. Sometimes this assistance is called *scaffolding*. The term aptly suggests that children use this help for support while they build a firm understanding that will eventually allow them to solve the problems on their own.

According to Vygotsky, at any given point in development there are certain problems that children are on the verge of being able to solve. With these, the children just need some structure, clues, reminders, help with remembering details or steps, encouragement to keep trying, and so on. Some problems, of course, can already be solved independently. Others are beyond the child's capabilities, even if every step is explained clearly. The **zone of proximal development** is the middle point, the area where the child cannot solve a problem alone but can be successful under adult guidance or in collaboration with a more advanced peer (Wertsch, 1985; Wertsch & Rogoff, 1984). This is the area where instruction (and acceleration) can occur, because this is the area where real learning is possible.

zone of proximal development: phase at which a child can master a task if given appropriate help and support

Vygotsky's zone of proximal development fits well with Hunt's problem of the match. Both concepts suggest that students should be put in situations where they have to reach a bit to understand but where support and help, from other students or from the teacher, are also available. Sometimes the best teacher is another student who has just figured out the problem. This student is probably operating in the learner's zone of proximal development.

ANOTHER PERSPECTIVE: INFORMATION PROCESSING

information processing: human mind's activity of taking in, storing, and using information

Information processing is the study of how humans perceive, comprehend, and remember the information they gain from the world around them. The term *information processing* comes from computer science and its related theories. Recently, the principles of information processing have been used to explain cognitive development. According to Klahr (1978), cognitive development can be described as the ongoing improvement of a person's system for processing information. Over time, a person develops an increasingly complex, sophisticated, and powerful "computer" to solve the problems the world presents. This computer stores more and more knowledge about the world and develops better and better programs or strategies for processing information.

The information processing theorists have been less interested in creating a comprehensive description of cognitive development, like the ones offered by Piaget and Vygotsky, and more interested in studying specific cognitive processes like perception, attention, memory, and hypothesis testing. In Chapters 7 and 8, we will examine these processes in depth because they are central to an understanding of how cognitive theorists view human learning. Right now we will briefly consider how two important cognitive abilities, attention and memory, develop in children.

Attention

John Flavell (1977) has described four aspects of attention that seem to develop as children mature.

1. *Controlling Attention.* As they grow older, children are more able to control their attention. They not only have longer attention spans; they also become better at focusing on what is important and at ignoring irrelevant details. In addition, they can simultaneously pay attention to more than one dimension of a situation. How would you relate these improved abilities to better performance on a conservation task?

2. *Fitting Attention to the Task.* As they develop, children become better at fitting their attention to the task. Older children can focus on both height and width when determining if the tall, thin glass has more liquid than the short, fat glass, but if the glasses are the same size and shape, the children will focus only on height.

3. *Planning.* Children improve in their ability to plan how to direct their attention. They look for clues to tell them what is important and are ready to pay attention to those things. For example, older children may be able to tell from the teacher's gestures and tone of voice that the next part of the lesson is important. The children prepare themselves to pay full and concentrated attention.

4. *Monitoring.* Finally, children improve their abilities to monitor their attention, to decide if they are using the right strategy, and to change approaches when necessary to follow a complicated series of events. For example, when students realize that they are having trouble understanding the teacher and have been doodling in their notebooks while they are trying to listen, they can stop doodling and focus only on what the teacher is saying.

Memory and Metacognitive Abilities

The information processing theorists have been particularly interested in the development of memory, a topic that will require our extended attention in Chapter 7. Research indicates that young children have very limited short-term memory. In one study by Case (1978b), for example, children of 7 and

One important metacognitive ability is knowing when you don't understand and changing strategies to find a more effective approach. Improvements in this ability are part of cognitive development. *(Richard Hutchings/ Photo Researchers)*

8 could remember the number of items in only three small sets at a time. Case (1980) suggests that the total amount of "space" available for processing information is the same at each age, but young children must use quite a bit of this space to remember how to execute basic operations, like reaching for a toy, finding the right word for an object, or counting. Learning a new operation takes up quite a bit of the child's working memory. Once the operation is mastered, however, there is more working memory available for short-term storage of new information. In addition, as children grow older, they develop more effective strategies for remembering information and monitoring how well they are remembering.

Reasonable but Incorrect Strategies

According to Case (1978a), young children often use reasonable but incorrect strategies for solving problems because of their limited memories. They try to oversimplify the task by ignoring important information or skipping steps to reach a correct solution. They may consider only the height of the water in a glass, not the diameter of the glass, when comparing quantities, because this approach demands less of their memory. This would be Case's explanation for young children's inability to solve the classic Piagetian conservation problem. It may well be that students could handle more mature ways of thinking if they did not have to remember large amounts of information while using more sophisticated processes.

Case (1980) suggests the following procedures for instruction based on the information processing theory of cognitive development. First, observe the children who are failing at a particular task and determine how they are trying to oversimplify the task. Second, find some way to emphasize for the children what they are ignoring and why their oversimplified approach won't work. Then demonstrate a better strategy. Finally, have the students practice the new approach. Throughout this process, try to minimize the amount of information the students have to remember by reducing the number of items involved, using familiar terms, emphasizing what is really important, keeping the steps small, and giving lots of practice so each step will become as automatic as possible.

You may have noticed that one characteristic of cognitive development seems to be a growing ability to monitor and direct our own thinking—to keep track of how well we are paying attention and to select an effective strategy for solving a problem. The general term to describe this activity of monitoring our own cognitive processes is *metacognition*.

metacognition: knowledge about our own thinking processes

Metacognition literally means knowledge about thinking. Donald Meichenbaum and his colleagues have described metacognition as people's "awareness of their own cognitive machinery and how the machinery works" (Meichenbaum, Burland, Gruson, & Cameron, 1985, p. 5). Recently researchers have begun to study how people develop knowledge about their own thinking and the thinking of others. For example, as children grow older, they become more able to determine if they have understood instructions (Markman, 1977, 1979) or if they have studied enough to remember a set of items (Flavell, Friedrichs, & Hoyt, 1970). Older children automatically use more efficient techniques than younger children for memorizing information (Flavell & Wellman, 1977; Pressley, 1982). In fact, it is hard to tell if the improved memory skills of older children are due to increased capacity for remembering or to the use of more efficient strategies. Certainly, teaching younger children to use better strategies improves their memory. But even when you teach younger children to use more efficient strategies in

one situation, they often will not use them spontaneously when faced with a new problem (Brown, Bransford, Ferrara, & Campione, 1983).

Researchers still have much to learn about how metacognitive abilities develop, but many are enthusiastic about the possible implications for education. We will return to this issue in Chapters 7 and 8 when we discuss what teachers can do to help students use more effective cognitive learning strategies. Now we will turn to a topic that goes hand in hand with cognitive development—language.

THE DEVELOPMENT OF LANGUAGE

The language adults use is just as complicated as their thinking. In fact, if you try diagraming some of the sentences you hear in lecture classes, you may think language is even more complicated than the thoughts it expresses. As you may expect, there is much disagreement about how people develop this complex process of communication and about how it is related to their thinking processes.

How Do We Learn Language?

One of the most widely held views of language development assumes that children learn language just as they learn anything else, by repeating those behaviors that lead to some kind of positive result. The child makes a sound, the parent smiles and replies. The child says "Mmm" in the presence of milk, the parent says "Yes, milk, milk" and gives the child a drink. The child learns to say *milk* because it leads to a happy parent and a drink of milk. Children add new words by imitating the sounds they hear and improve their use of language when they are corrected by the adults around them.

Such a theory is in many ways convincing, but an important question remains. What originally induced the infant to make any sounds at all? Was the baby trying to make the sounds that an adult made? Research has shown that many of a child's earliest utterances are original. They are things the child has apparently never heard before. And they are unlikely to be rewarded, because they are "incorrect," even though they make sense to the people involved (R. Brown, 1973). Examples are such phrases as "paper find" and "car mosquito." In addition, researchers studying interactions between young children and their parents have discovered that parents rarely correct pronunciation and grammar during the early stages of language development. They are much more likely to respond to the content of the child's remarks (Brown & Hanlon, 1970). In fact, if parents spent all their time correcting the child's language and never "heard" what the child was trying to say, the child might give up trying to master a system as complicated as language.

Adults caring for children seem continually to adapt their language to stay just ahead of the child. Before children begin talking, adults may direct long, complicated sentences to them. But as soon as the child utters identifiable words, the language of adults becomes simplified. As the child progresses, adults tend to change their language to stay just a bit more ad-

Do Rewards Really Count?

Parents' Responses

vanced than the child's current level of development, thus encouraging new understanding (Moskowitz, 1978). It seems that in order to stretch the child's language development, adults give the kind of support, or scaffolding, that Vygotsky has recommended. Adults, by staying slightly more advanced in their language, may also create disequilibrium and encourage development as a result.

An Active Figuring Out

It is likely that many factors play a role in language development. Humans may be born with a special capacity for language (Chomsky, 1965). The important point is that children develop language as they develop other cognitive abilities, by actively trying to make sense of what they hear—by looking for patterns and making up rules to put together the jigsaw puzzle of language (Moskowitz, 1978). Reward and correction play a role in helping children learn correct language use, but the child's thinking and creativity in putting together the parts of this complicated system are very important. In the process they make some very logical "mistakes," as you will see.

Stages in the Process

Before they learn to speak, children communicate through crying, smiling, and body movements. But by the end of the first year, more or less, most children have spoken their first word. They have entered what psychologists imaginatively call the one-word stage. For the next three or four months they add slowly to their vocabulary until they have about ten words. After this, words are added rapidly. By about 20 months the vocabulary includes approximately 50 words (Nelson, 1981).

Even at this early stage, language is more complex than it might appear. One word can be used to communicate a variety of complex ideas. For example, my daughter's first word was *ite* (translated: light). Said loudly while reaching toward the light switch on the wall, "ITE!" meant "I want to flip the switch on and off (and on and off, and on and off)." When someone else flipped the switch while she was playing on the floor, Elizabeth might remark "Ite," meaning "I know what you just did. You turned on the light." When single words are used in this way, they are called **holophrases** because they express complex ideas or whole phrases.

holophrases: single words that express complex ideas

A second, related characteristic of this period is **overgeneralization.** Children may use one word to cover a range of concepts. For example, on a trip to the zoo, the 13-month-old son of a friend pointed excitedly at every animal, including peacocks and elephants, saying "Doug, doug" (translated: dog, dog). This was the only word he had that came close to being adequate. He wisely rejected his other possibilities: "bye-bye," "more," "Mama," and "Dada." He used the language tools available to him to make sense of his world and to communicate.

overgeneralization: defining a range of concepts according to only one dimension

At about 18 months many children enter the two-word stage. They begin to string words together in two-word sentences like "Daddy book," "Play car," "Allgone milk," and "More light." The speech is **telegraphic** (R. Brown, 1973). The nonessential details are left out and the words that carry the most meaning are included, as in a telegram: Arriving 8:35 P.M., track 12. Even though sentences are short, **semantics,** or meanings, can be complex. Children can express possession ("Daddy book"), recurrence ("More light"), action on an object ("Play car"), and even disappearance or nonexistence ("Allgone milk").

telegraphic speech: children's speech using only essential words, as in a telegram

semantics: meanings; the ways that meaning is organized in language

"WHEN I SAY 'RUNNED', YOU KNOW I MEAN 'RAN'. LET'S NOT QUIBBLE."

For about one year, children continue to focus on the essential words even as they lengthen their sentences. At a certain point that varies from child to child, new features are added. Children begin to elaborate their simple language by adding plurals, endings for verbs such as -ed and -ing, and small words like and, but, and in. In the process of figuring out the rules governing these aspects of language, children make some very interesting mistakes.

For a brief time children may use irregular forms of particular words properly, as if they simply are saying what they have heard. Then, as they begin to learn rules, they **overregularize** words by applying the rules to everything. Children who once said "Our car is broken" begin to insist "Our car is broked." Parents often wonder why their child seems to be regressing. Actually, these "mistakes" show how logical and rational children can be as they try to assimilate new words into existing schemes. Because most languages have so many irregular words, accommodation is necessary in mastering language.

overregularization: applying a learned rule to all situations, including inappropriate ones

Another aspect of overregularizing language involves the order of words in a sentence. Since the usual order in English is subject-verb-object, preschoolers just mastering the rules of language have trouble with sentences in any different order. For example, if they hear a statement in the passive voice like "The truck was bumped by the car," they usually think the truck did the bumping to the car (Berger, 1983). So in talking with young children, it is generally better to use direct language.

During the preschool years children learn new words very rapidly, doubling their vocabulary about every six months between ages 2 and 4. During this time they may enjoy making up words. Because their thinking is egocentric, they may assume you know exactly what they mean. They also tend to center on one meaning for a word, as the main character does in a popular children's book, *Cider with Rosie* by Laurie Lee:

> "What's the matter, Love? Didn't he like it at school, then?"
> "They never gave me the present."
> "Present? What present?"
> "They said they'd give me a present."
> "Well, now, I'm sure they didn't."
> "They did! They said: You're Laurie Lee, aren't you? Well you just sit there for the present. I sat there all day but I never got it. I ain't going back there again." (Donaldson, 1985, p. 69)

By about age 5 or 6, most children have mastered the basics of their native language. As noted earlier, the language of preschoolers can be quite egocentric. A few types of constructions, like passive voice, are still difficult at this age, but a remarkable amount has been accomplished. Children at this age enjoy playing with language. The young son of a friend wanted to name his new baby sister Brontosaurus because he "just liked to say it."

From ages 9 to 11, about 5,000 new words are added to the average child's vocabulary (Berger, 1983). As Moskowitz has noted: "Ten linguists working full time for 10 years to analyze the structure of the English language could not program a computer with the ability acquired by an average child in the first 10 or even 5 years of life" (1978, p. 92).

Thus far we have described general stages in language learning. In the next section we will consider differences within the languages themselves and ways a teacher can deal with these differences.

Dialects: Variations within Languages

dialect: rule-governed variation of a language spoken by a particular group

A **dialect** is a variation of a language spoken by a particular ethnic, social, or regional group. The rules for a language define how words should be pronounced, how meaning should be expressed, and the ways the basic parts of speech should be put together to form sentences. Dialects appear to differ in their rules in these areas, but it is important to remember that these differences are not errors. Each dialect within a language is just as logical, complex, and rule-governed as the standard form of the language (often called standard speech).

An example of this is the use of the double negative. In standard English the redundancy of the double negative is not allowed. But in many nonstandard dialects, like black English, just as in many other languages (for instance, Russian, French, Spanish, and Hungarian), the double negative is required by the grammatical rules. To say "I don't want anything" in Spanish, you must literally say "I don't want nothing," or *"No quiero nada."*

Another area in which nonstandard dialects differ from standard English is pronunciation, which can lead to spelling problems. In black English, for instance, there is less attention paid to pronouncing the ends of words than in standard English. A lack of attention to final consonants, such as *s*, can lead to failure to indicate possession, third-person singular verbs, and plurals in the standard way. So *John's book* might be *John book*, and words such as *thinks*, *wasps*, and *lists* may be difficult to pronounce. When endings are not pronounced, there are more homonyms (words that sound alike but have different meanings) in the student's language than the unknowing teacher could expect (*spent* and *spend* might sound alike, for example). Even without the confusions caused by dialect differences, there are many homonyms in English. Usually special attention is given to words such as these when they come up in the spelling lesson. If the teacher is aware of the special homonyms in student dialects, direct teaching of these spelling differences is also possible.

The Teacher's Dilemma

Now we turn to a very important issue. While the various dialects may be equally logical, complex, and rule-governed, should teachers make learning easier for children by teaching in the dialect of the majority of students? To do this would show respect for the child's language. But the child would be robbed of the opportunity to learn the standard speech of the culture. The best approach seems to be to focus on understanding the child and to accept the dialect as a valid and correct language system but to teach the standard form of language as an alternative. Like learning a second language, learning the standard speech is fairly easy for most children whose original language is a dialect. We will examine other issues related to first and second languages and dialects in Chapter 13 when we consider bilingual and multicultural education.

Teaching and Language

If the theorists who emphasize the role of thinking and logical rule-learning in language development are right, children are likely to continue generating "incorrect" language until they have reached a stage at which it is possible to remember all the correct patterns or schemes. In this case, certain things may be difficult, if not impossible, to teach young students. Students at different ages (or stages) have specifically limited abilities to benefit from corrective feedback. McNeill (1966) presents an example. A child said to his mother, "Nobody don't like me." The mother responded, "No, say 'Nobody likes me.'" The boy tried to correct himself but came out with the same sentence: "Nobody don't like me." The mother tried again, with the same results. After seven more identical statements and attempted corrections, the boy suddenly seemed to get the point and said, "Oh! Nobody don't *likes* me." Even though he was trying, the boy had difficulty discriminating between the two versions. He had a rule to follow, and he could not violate it. Children who come to school speaking a different dialect have similar problems.

Readiness and "Fixed" Rules

What does all this mean for teachers? How can they cope with such language diversity in the classroom? First, they can be sensitive to their own possible negative stereotypes about children who speak with a different dialect. Taylor (1983) found that teachers who held negative attitudes toward black English gave lower ratings for reading comprehension to students who spoke black English, even when the accuracy of the students' performance was the same as that of standard English speakers. Second, teachers can ensure comprehension by repeating instructions using different words and by asking students to paraphrase instructions or give examples. Throughout the school year, they can develop the language abilities and knowledge of their students in a variety of ways. Courtney Cazden (1968) suggests two possibilities. She proposes enriching the students' language environment by focusing not just on correct or incorrect usage but on the idea expressed. Probe and extend students' ideas. For example, if a student says, "I writed my name on my picture," the teacher could respond, "You wrote your name above the rocket. Where is your astronaut going?" In this way the teacher maintains the student's interest and at the same time introduces different grammatical constructions that the student can observe and perhaps adopt.

Cazden also suggests that word meanings are most easily learned through planned interactions and conversations with an adult in which the adult introduces new words. For example, when a student complains, "He does that on purpose, just to make me mad!" the teacher might respond, "So you think he is *intentionally* tripping by your desk just to *irritate* you. Why have you reached that conclusion?" Reading aloud is also a potent form of language stimulation. Reading to students often leads to conversations about the pictures or the ideas in the books. The importance of one-to-one interaction with an adult in developing language abilities has been stressed by many psychologists.

It is generally agreed that the first key to language development in school is to encourage students to use their language by talking, listening, reading, and writing. Help children communicate effectively. Around the age of 5 students begin to develop **metalinguistic awareness.** This means their understanding about language and how it works becomes explicit. They have knowledge about language itself. They are ready to study and extend the

Expanding Usage and Meanings

metalinguistic awareness: understanding about our own use of language

One of the best ways for children to learn language is in interaction with adults. Often a story provides the topic for discussion. *(Michael Heron/ Monkmeyer Press)*

rules that have been implicit—understood but not consciously expressed. This process continues throughout life, as we all become more able to manipulate and comprehend language in increasingly sophisticated ways.

SUMMARY

1. Theorists differ greatly in their approach to the study of development, especially in the emphasis they place on nature and nurture—on what is biologically determined and what results from interaction with the environment. Whether or not development proceeds in stages or in a set order is also a source of disagreement. All developmental theorists, however, tend to agree on three principles: (1) people develop at different rates; (2) development is relatively orderly; and (3) development takes place gradually.

2. Piaget's theory is based on the assumption that people seek to make sense of the world and actively create their own knowledge through direct experience with objects, people, and ideas. Maturation, activity, and social transmission all influence the way our thinking processes and knowledge develop.

3. Cognitive development occurs through adaptation (the complementary processes of assimilation and accommodation) and organizational changes (the development of schemes). The need for equilibrium plays a major role as well. Thinking grows when the equilibrium of a person's world view is threatened, and adaptation is used to restore this equilibrium. Equilibration is the search for this balance.

4. Piaget believed that young people pass through four stages as they develop: sensorimotor, preoperational, concrete operational, and formal operational.

5. In the sensorimotor stage, infants explore the world through their senses and motor activity and work toward mastering object permanence and goal-directed activities. In the preoperational stage, symbolic thinking and logical operations begin. Children in the stage of concrete operations can think logically about tangible situations; conservation, reversibility, classification, and seriation are mastered. The ability to think abstractly—to coordinate a number of variables, to form and test hypotheses, to imagine other worlds—marks the stage of formal operations.

6. Some theorists believe teachers should restrict their teaching to the current level of a student's cognitive development; others believe cognitive development should be encouraged or even stressed (accelerated). Still others emphasize that there are optimal points for any task at which a child can make use of help and support to gain full mastery.

7. Explanations of cognitive development based on information processing are concerned with specific cognitive skills like attention, memory, and the ability to monitor thinking processes. As children grow, they develop their abilities to focus attention, use strategies to remember information, and keep track of progress. These abilities in turn lead to more sophisticated thinking and reasoning capacities.

8. The development of language seems to be very closely related to cognitive development. Children try to understand and apply language rules; they attempt to coordinate their own capacity with what they hear. It may be that the capacity for language is inborn. Children use different approaches to solve the puzzle of language. But children everywhere generally move from holophrasic to telegraphic speech, through overgeneralization and overregularization, and finally complete most of their basic problem solving about language at around age 5 or 6.

9. Teachers may often have to deal with a number of different dialects in their

classes. A dialect is a variation of the standard speech. It is important to remember that dialects are rule-governed and logical.

10. Teachers can encourage children's language comprehension and use by reading aloud and in one-to-one interactions.

KEY TERMS

development
physical development
personal development
social development
cognitive development
maturation
organization
adaptation
schemes
assimilation
accommodation
equilibration
sensorimotor
object permanence

goal-directed actions
operations
preoperational
one-way logic
reversible thinking
conservation
decentration
egocentrism
collective monologue
concrete operations
identity
compensation
classification

seriation
formal operations
adolescent egocentrism
zone of proximal development
information processing
metacognition
holophrases
overgeneralization
telegraphic speech
semantics
overregularization
dialect
metalinguistic awareness

SUGGESTIONS FOR FURTHER READING AND STUDY

BYBEE, R. W., & SUND, R. B. (1982). *Piaget for educators* (2nd ed.). Columbus, OH: Charles E. Merrill. After describing Piaget's theory and discussing the characteristics of the four stages of cognitive development, the authors give many examples of how to extend this information to teaching situations.

FLAVELL, J. H. (1985). *Cognitive development* (2nd ed.). Englewood Cliffs, NJ: Prentice Hall. An excellent discussion of cognitive development by a person who has made many contributions in the area.

MILLER, P. H. (1983). *Theories of developmental psychology.* San Francisco: W. H. Freeman. A very thorough summary and analysis of the major schools of thought in developmental psychology including Piagetian, information processing, social learning, psychoanalytic, and others.

MOSOKOWITZ, B. A. (1978). The acquisition of language. *Scientific American, 239,* 92–108. A very readable overview of how language develops.

PIAGET, J. (1970). *The science of education and the psychology of the child.* New York: Orion Press. This volume presents Piaget's ideas about education and the problems that occur when teaching does not fit the child's thinking abilities.

ROHRKEMPER, M. M., & BERSHON, B. L. (1984). Elementary school students' reports of the causes and effects of problem difficulty in mathematics. *Elementary School Journal, 85,* 127–147. These researchers interviewed students to learn what the students believed about why math problems were hard and how the difficulties affected them. The authors relate their conclusions to Vygotsky's ideas about the teacher's role in helping students learn to solve problems.

YUSSEN, S. R. (Ed.). (1985). *The growth of reflection in children.* New York: Academic Press. This volume has chapters by top researchers in the areas of metacognition, Vygotsky's theory, and other very current topics in cognitive development.

Teachers' Forum

Seeing the Other's Point of View

Children in the later elementary grades still tend to be egocentric; they have a difficult time seeing the world from another person's point of view. This can cause difficulty when issues like sharing or following the rules of a game arise. When you notice children having a hard time taking each other into consideration, what do you do?

Considering Others

Children need to be given the opportunity to discuss feelings and emotions and to see how their actions can affect others. This is best done through puppet shows, plays, and stories that depict consideration of others. If a particular child showed insensitivity toward another, I would talk individually with the child about how the other might feel. This could be followed up with a short written assignment dealing with feelings and, if appropriate, an apology.

Harold Kreif, Fifth-Grade Teacher
Pier Elementary School, Fond du Lac, Wisconsin

Lessons from Piaget

What guidance have you found Piaget's theory really gives you as a teacher? Should we use Piaget's stages to determine what to teach and how to teach it?

Two Stages at Once

In a practical or applied sense, Piaget's theory provides very little direct benefit for me. However, his stages provide a framework or background to structure my teaching and to plan content presentation. I teach students who *should* all be at the formal operations stage. I'm not sure how complete the transition from concrete actually is. Much of the reasoning in my course involves second-order operations, and most students are able to handle this. In a course like chemistry, we continually work back and forth between the hypothetical and the real. What concerns me most is that most students be able to handle subject matter at the formal operations stage. However, when asked to do similar reasoning in daily situations outside of class, there seems to be more activity at the concrete operations stage.

R. Chris Rohde, High School Chemistry Teacher
Chippewa Falls Senior High School, Chippewa Falls, Wisconsin

Workbooks Overused?

Math workbooks and texts for all grades use pictures, numbers, graphs, and so on to present math concepts. While symbolic representation may be appropriate for some students at certain ages, it is not sufficient for all students in all grades. Also, the overuse of workbooks may make the students emphasize "getting the right answer" rather than understanding the process. What suggestions would you make to a beginning teacher who might rely heavily on the workbook in lesson plans?

Matching Teaching to the Student

A major goal of mathematics instruction should be to guide the learner from the concrete, to the semiconcrete, to the abstract stage of reasoning. It is imperative that the teacher determine at which stage each individual learner is presently functioning and build from there. As a general rule, math workbooks concentrate mainly on the semiconcrete stage. They tend to disregard students requiring more concrete explanations while limiting students capable of more abstract work. In addition, math workbooks by their very nature tend to stress product—the correct answer—as opposed to process, the how or the why. Once these limitations are understood, it is still possible to use workbooks in the math curriculum, but only as a supplement, never as the core. Depending upon need, workbooks could be augmented by the use of manipulative materials or high-level word problems. Regardless of the stage at which the learner is operating, however, explanations of how answers were arrived at should always be required.

Jacqueline M. Walsh, Sixth-Grade Teacher
Agnes E. Little Elementary School, Pawtucket, Rhode Island

The Value of Concrete Materials

As a primary-grade teacher for many years, I have found that it is of the utmost importance for young children to use concrete materials in order to understand math concepts. If I teach place value, then every child has sticks and rubber bands to create tens, ones, hundreds, and so on. There are so many commercial aids—flannel board materials, counting beads, toy clocks, play money, Cuisinaire rods. But you really don't have to buy anything—use the children themselves and relate math to materials and situations they are familiar with.

Charlotte Ross, Second-Grade Teacher
Covert Avenue School, Elmont, New York

The Problem of the Match

It is not unusual to find students with abilities ranging from the early concrete operational stage through formal operations in classes from the upper elementary grades through high school. This is especially true in smaller school districts, where enrollments are too small to allow ability grouping. How can you teach the same information to the entire class in such a way as to prevent either frustration or boredom?

Diversify Assignments

Present topics orally to the entire class with lively concrete illustrations and with some class discussion. Then in the follow-up time, diversify assignments. Extension and application of concepts will challenge those who have already gotten the message. A second explanation and provision for practice of drillable items will reinforce your presentation for those who need a second exposure. Even in testing, accommodation can be made. The first page of the test contains the basic information everyone must master. The second page has two versions. Each version tests the objectives of the study group.

Dorothy Eve Hopkins, Sixth-Grade Teacher
Homer Intermediate School, Homer, New York

A Full Range of Senses and Skills

There is no "quick fix" or easy answer to some of the problems that come with heterogeneous grouping. However, there are two approaches that *must* be employed if all of the students' needs are to be met. (1) Teaching methods and tactics should be varied to include activities that involve use of the various senses in every lesson. The more the student sees, says, hears, touches, becomes involved in a lesson, the more he or she learns. (2) Learning activities should cover a range of comprehension skills. Students need practice in all the different types of thinking, from perception to analysis.

Katherine P. Stillerman, Seventh-Grade Language Arts
and Social Studies Teacher
Pine Forest Junior High School, Fayetteville, North Carolina

3

Personal, Social, and Moral Development

Overview
A Comprehensive Theory: The Work of Erikson   86
Tasks and Stages throughout Life   87
Infancy: Trust v. Mistrust   88
The Toddler: Autonomy v. Shame and Doubt   90
Early Childhood: Initiative v. Guilt   91
Elementary and Middle School Years: Industry v. Inferiority   91
Adolescence: The Search for Identity   92
Beyond the School Years: Intimacy, Generativity, and Integrity   95
Issues in the Early Years   96
Sex-Role Development   97
The Impact of Day Care   98
Friendships in Childhood   100
Issues Affecting Adolescents   101
Physical Development in Adolescence   101
Sexual Maturity   103
Understanding Ourselves and Others   104
Self-Concept: Origins and Influences   104
The Self and Others   107
Moral Development   109
Education for Emotional Growth   114
What Do Teachers Think?   115
How Do Teachers Encourage Personal Growth?   115
Summary/Key Terms
Suggestions for Further Reading and Study
Teachers' Forum

OVERVIEW As we all know from experience, schooling involves more than cognitive development. In this chapter, we examine emotional, social, and moral development. We will look at the ways we learn to view ourselves and others, how we learn to relate to others, and the growth of moral reasoning.

We begin with the work of Erik Erikson, whose comprehensive theory provides a framework for studying personal and social development. We then consider several issues that are important in the early years—the development of sex roles, the effects of day care, and the child's changing relationships with friends. As the child enters adolescence, other issues become important—namely, physical and sexual maturing.

Next we explore ideas about how we come to understand ourselves and others. What is the meaning of the self-concept, and how is it shaped? How do our views of others change as we grow? What factors determine our views about morality? Do moral actions follow from moral beliefs? What can teachers do to foster such personal qualities as honesty, cooperation, empathy, and self-esteem? In the final section, we consider the somewhat controversial question of affective education—education for emotional growth—in the public schools.

By the time you have completed this chapter, you should have gained a number of new ways of looking at the students you will be teaching—and perhaps some new ways of looking at yourself. When you have studied the chapter, you should be able to do the following:

- Describe Erikson's stages of psychosocial development and list several implications of his theory for teaching.
- Discuss issues involved in the development of gender identity.
- Describe the child's changing view of friendship.
- Describe the problems of early and late maturers.
- Suggest how teachers can foster positive self-concepts in their students.
- Describe Kohlberg's stages of moral reasoning and give an example of each.
- Explain the factors that encourage cheating and aggression in classrooms and discuss possible responses to each.
- Take a stand on affective and moral education.

A COMPREHENSIVE THEORY: THE WORK OF ERIKSON

Like Piaget, Erik Erikson did not start out as a psychologist. In fact, Erikson never graduated from high school. He spent his early adult years studying art and traveling around Europe. A meeting with Sigmund Freud in Vienna led to an invitation from Freud to study psychoanalysis, which Erikson accepted. After completing his training, Erikson emigrated to America to practice his profession and to escape the threat of Hitler.

In his influential *Childhood and Society* (1950, 1963), Erikson offered a basic framework for understanding the needs of young people in relation to the society in which they grow, learn, and later make their contributions. Although Erikson's approach is not the only explanation of personal and social development, I have chosen it to organize our discussion for several reasons. Erikson emphasizes the emergence of the self, the search for identity, and the individual's relationships with others throughout life. Teachers must be concerned with both the personal and the social aspects of students' lives, and Erikson's theory gives us a means of linking these. Because children spend many important years in school as their sense of themselves and others is emerging, the social setting of the school is a major factor in development. And because Erikson describes development from infancy through old age, he provides essential insight into past and future influences on students. His comprehensive theory has implications for students and teachers at every grade level.

Tasks and Stages throughout Life

Erikson was particularly interested in the relationship between the culture in which a child is reared and the kind of adult the child becomes. He hypothesized that all humans have the same basic needs and that each society must provide in some way for those needs. After studying child-rearing practices in several societies, he concluded that despite differences, there were indeed recurrent themes in emotional and social development. Emotional changes and their relation to the social environment followed similar patterns.

This emphasis on the relationship of culture and the individual led Erikson to propose a **psychosocial** theory of development. His theory was based

psychosocial: describing the relation of the individual's emotional needs to the social environment

Erik Erikson formulated a comprehensive theory of emotional and social development involving a series of eight critical stages, each leading to a positive or a negative outcome. The successful resolution of each crisis contributes to the ability to meet future crises. *(Jill Krementz)*

in large part on Freud's work, but Erikson went beyond Freud's emphasis on early childhood and psychosexual development. Erikson also focused on parental and societal demands on the individual. An increasing responsibility for ourselves and for others and our methods of coping with this responsibility are very important aspects of identity according to Erikson's theory.

Like Piaget, and like Freud, Erikson sees development as a passage through a series of stages, each with its particular goals, concerns, accomplishments, and dangers. The stages are interdependent: accomplishments at later stages depend on how conflicts are resolved in the earlier years. At each stage, Erikson suggests, the individual faces a **developmental crisis.** Each crisis involves a conflict between a positive alternative and a potentially unhealthy alternative. The way in which the individual resolves each crisis will have a lasting effect on that person's self-image and view of society. An unhealthy resolution of problems in the early stages can have potential negative repercussions throughout life, although sometimes damage can be repaired at later stages. This is partly because none of the developmental crises is ever permanently resolved. However, if we are successful at resolving each crisis as it is encountered, we will have a reasonably solid foundation for our identity and for dealing with the next crisis. We will look briefly at all eight stages in Erikson's theory—or as he calls them, the "eight ages of man." Table 3–1 presents the stages in summary form.

developmental crisis: a specific conflict whose resolution prepares the way for the next stage

The Ages of Man

Infancy: Trust v. Mistrust

Erikson identifies *trust v. mistrust* as the basic conflict of infancy. In the first months of life, babies begin to find out whether they can depend on the world around them. According to Erikson, the infant will develop a sense of trust if needs for food and care are met with comforting regularity. Closeness and responsiveness on the part of the parents at this time contribute greatly to this sense of trust (Lamb, 1982).

Note that in this first year, infants are in the early part of Piaget's sensorimotor stage. They are just beginning to learn that they are separate from

Parents who are warm and responsive help their children develop the capacity to trust and the security to move beyond the family into the larger world. *(Betsy Lee/Taurus Photos)*

88

Table 3–1 Erikson's Theory: Stages of Psychosocial Development

Psychosocial Stage	Approximate Age	Elements for Positive Outcomes
Trust v. mistrust	Infancy 0–1 yr.	Infant's needs for nourishment, care, familiarity are met; parental responsiveness and consistency
Autonomy v. shame and doubt	Toddler period 1–2 yrs.	Greater control of self in environment—self-feeding, toileting, dressing; parental reassurance, availability, avoidance of overprotection
Initiative v. guilt	Early childhood 2–6 yrs.	Pursuing activity for its own sake; learning to accept without guilt that certain things are not allowed; imagination; play-acting adult roles
Industry v. inferiority	Elementary– middle school 6–12 yrs.	Discovery of pleasure in perseverance and productivity; neighborhood, school, and peer interaction become increasingly important
Identity v. role confusion	Adolescence	Conscious search for identity, built upon outcomes of previous crises
Intimacy v. isolation	Young adulthood	Openness and commitment to others in deepening relationships
Generativity v. stagnation	Young and middle adulthood	Having and nurturing children and/or involvement with future generations; productivity; creativity
Integrity v. despair	Later adulthood, old age	Consolidation of identity; sense of fulfillment; acceptance of death

Adaptation of material from Childhood and Society, 2nd ed. by Erik H. Erikson, is used with the permission of W. W. Norton & Company, Inc. Copyright © 1963, 1950 by W. W. Norton & Company, Inc. Erik H. Erikson's Literary Estate and Hogarth Press are also gratefully acknowledged.

the world around them and that other objects and people exist even when they cannot see them. This realization of separateness is part of what makes trust so important: infants must trust the aspects of their world that are beyond their control (Bretherton, 1985).

Trust and Attachment

Research on infant attachment supports Erikson's ideas about a baby's need to develop trust. Mary Ainsworth (1979) has studied the differences between babies who are "securely attached" to their mothers and those who are "anxiously attached." Babies in the first group have mothers who are more responsive to their needs. Ainsworth suggests that these babies come to see their mothers as accessible and available. They can use their mothers as a secure base for exploring their environment, knowing their mothers will respond when needed. These babies are more cooperative and less aggressive in their interactions with their mothers. As they grow older, they become more competent and sympathetic with peers and explore their environment with greater enthusiasm and persistence than the anxiously attached babies (Campos, Barrett, Lamb, Goldsmith, & Sternberg, 1983). By the preschool years, children who were securely attached as infants are rated by their teachers as more self-reliant and less dependent (Sroufe, Fox, & Pancake, 1983). Of course, these are correlations. We don't have (and wouldn't want to have) experimental tests of what happens when we manipulate levels of attachment.

The Toddler: Autonomy v. Shame and Doubt

Erikson's second stage, *autonomy v. shame and doubt,* marks the beginning of self-control and self-confidence. Young children are capable of doing more and more on their own. They are beginning to carry out the goal-directed activities of the later part of Piaget's sensorimotor stage. They are developing the physical and mental abilities that allow them some control over their own lives. They must begin to assume important responsibilities for self-care like feeding, toileting, and dressing. They are striving toward **autonomy.**

autonomy:
independence

During this period, parents must tread a fine line; they must be protective but not overprotective. Whether or not parents achieve this balance exerts a strong influence on the child's ability to achieve autonomy. If parents do not maintain a reassuring, confident attitude and do not reinforce the child's efforts to master basic motor and cognitive skills, children may begin to feel

Even though she would get dressed faster with adult help, this girl needs the opportunity to be responsible for the job herself. Her developing sense of autonomy is more important than efficiency.
(Pinney/Monkmeyer Press)

shame; they may learn to doubt their abilities to manage the world on their own terms. Erikson believes that children who experience too much doubt at this stage will lack confidence in their own powers throughout life.

Early Childhood: Initiative v. Guilt

According to Erikson, the child must now face the conflict of *initiative v. guilt*. For Erikson, "initiative adds to autonomy the quality of undertaking, planning, and attacking a task for the sake of being active and on the move" (Erikson, 1963, p. 255). But with **initiative** comes the realization that some activities are forbidden. At times children may feel torn between what they want to do and what should (or should not) be done. The challenge of this period is to maintain a zest for activity and at the same time to understand that every impulse cannot be acted upon.

initiative: willingness to begin new activities and explore new directions

Children in early childhood can imagine themselves playing various adult roles and begin to test their powers at "grown-up" tasks. The 4-year-old perched on a chair stirring cookie batter or solemnly passing tools to a parent who is fixing a broken bicycle is involved in important work. Children at this stage are often hero-worshipers; their heros tend to be easily recognizable, idealized adults like doctors, firefighters, and teachers. They are beginning to care about and to be able to imagine what the future might hold for them. Play is an important form of initiative; pretend games are common.

Children at this stage require confirmation from adults that their initiative is accepted and that their contributions, no matter how small, are truly valued. These children are eager for responsibility. Successful growth during this period rests upon the sense that they are accepted for themselves. Again, adults must tread a fine line, this time in providing supervision without interference. If children are not allowed to do things on their own, a sense of guilt may develop: they may come to believe that what they want to do is always "wrong."

Because you may be teaching children of this age, in preschool or kindergarten, the next set of Guidelines is directed toward the encouragement of initiative and the avoidance of guilt.

Elementary and Middle School Years: Industry v. Inferiority

In the early school years, students are developing what Erikson calls a sense of **industry**. They are beginning to see the relationship between perseverance and the pleasure of a job completed. This is also the period when students are beginning to conquer the physical environment with concrete operations. Play satisfied them before, but now they want to do productive work on their own and are physically and mentally ready for it. The crisis at this stage is *industry v. inferiority*.

industry: eagerness to engage in productive work

During this period the child must also conquer the world outside the home. In many societies, this period brings the child into direct involvement with the adult world of work. For children in modern societies, however, the school and the neighborhood offer a new set of challenges that must be balanced with those at home. Interaction with peers becomes increasingly

Guidelines

Encouraging Initiative in the Preschool Child

Encourage children to make and to act on choices.

Examples
1. *Have a free-choice time when children can select an educational game or activity.*
2. *As much as possible, avoid interrupting children who are very involved in what they are doing.*
3. *When children suggest an activity, try to follow their suggestions or incorporate their ideas into ongoing activities.*
4. *Offer positive choices: instead of saying, "You can't have the cookies now," ask, "Would you like the cookies after lunch or after naptime?"*

Make sure that each child has a chance to experience success.

Examples
1. *When introducing a new game or skill, teach it in small steps.*
2. *Avoid competitive games when the range of abilities in the class is great.*

Encourage make-believe with a wide variety of roles.

Examples
1. *Have costumes and props that go along with stories the children enjoy. Encourage the children to act out the stories or make up new adventures for favorite characters.*
2. *Monitor the children's play to be sure no one monopolizes playing "teacher," "Mommy," or "Daddy."*

Be tolerant of accidents and mistakes, especially when children are attempting to do something on their own.

Examples
1. *Use cups and pitchers that are easy to pour from and hard to knock over or spill.*
2. *Recognize the attempt, even if the product is unsatisfactory.*

important as well. The child's ability to move between these worlds and to cope with academics, group activities, and friends will lead to a growing sense of competence. Difficulty with these challenges can result in feelings of inferiority.

A recent study by George and Caroline Vaillant (1981) supports Erikson's notion of the importance of industry. These researchers followed 450 males for 35 years, beginning in early childhood. Their conclusion was that the men who had been the most industrious and willing to work as children were the best adjusted and best paid as adults. These men also had the most satisfying personal relationships. The ability and the willingness to work hard as a child seemed to be more important for success in later life than intelligence or family background. Again, these are only correlational data. We don't know for sure that being industrious *causes* success in later life. Still, industry is worth encouraging. The Guidelines offer some ideas.

Adolescence: The Search for Identity

identity: the complex answer to the question, Who am I?

The central issue for adolescents is the development of an **identity** that will provide a firm basis for adulthood. The individual has of course been developing a sense of self since infancy. But adolescence marks the first time that a conscious effort is made to answer the now-pressing question, Who am I? The conflict defining this stage is *identity v. role confusion*.

Erikson notes that the healthy resolution of earlier conflicts can now serve as a foundation for the search for identity. A basic sense of trust, if established, has prepared the young person to find people and ideas to have faith in. A firm sense of autonomy gives the adolescent courage to insist upon the chance to decide freely about her or his own career and life-style. The initiative that prompted the young child to play lawyer or painter can help the adolescent take steps toward assuming an adult role in reality. And out of a strong sense of industry can grow a feeling of competence, a belief in one's ability to make meaningful contributions to society.

Identity: Becoming Ourselves.   Exactly what do we mean by identity, and what does the crisis of this adolescent stage involve? Identity refers to the organization of the individual's drives, abilities, beliefs, and history into a consistent image of self. It involves deliberate choices and decisions, particularly about vocation, sexual orientation, and a "philosophy of life" (Marcia, 1982). If adolescents fail to integrate all these aspects and choices, or if they feel unable to choose at all, role confusion threatens.

identity achievement: strong sense of commitment to life choices after free consideration of alternatives

Elaborating on Erikson's work, James Marcia and his colleagues have suggested that there are four alternatives for adolescents as they confront themselves and their choices (Marcia, 1982; Schiedel & Marcia, 1985). The first is **identity achievement.** This means that after considering the realistic options, the individual has made choices and is pursuing them. It appears that few students achieve this status by the end of high school. Most are not

Guidelines

Encouraging Industry

Make sure that students have opportunities to set and work toward realistic goals.

Examples
1. *Begin with short assignments, then move on to longer ones. Monitor student progress by setting up progress checkpoints.*
2. *Teach students to set reasonable goals. Write down goals and have students keep a journal of progress toward goals.*

Let students have a chance to show their independence and responsibility.

Examples
1. *Tolerate honest mistakes.*
2. *Delegate to students tasks like watering class plants, collecting and distributing materials, monitoring the computer lab, grading homework, keeping records of forms returned, and so on.*

Provide support to students who seem discouraged.

Examples
1. *Use individual charts and contracts that show student progress.*
2. *Keep samples of earlier work so students can see their improvements.*
3. *Have awards for most improved, most helpful to other students, most hard-working.*

<!-- glossary margin -->**identity
foreclosure:**
accepting parental
life choices without
considering options

identity diffusion:
uncenteredness;
confusion about
who one is and
what one wants

moratorium:
identity crisis;
suspension of
choices because of
struggle

firm in their choices for several more years (Archer, 1982). **Identity foreclosure** describes the situation of adolescents who do not experiment with different identities or consider a range of options but simply commit themselves to the goals, values, and life-styles of their parents or of other significant authority figures. **Identity diffusion,** on the other hand, occurs when individuals reach no conclusions about who they are or what they want to do with their lives; they have no firm direction. Adolescents experiencing identity diffusion may have struggled unsuccessfully to make choices, or they may have avoided thinking seriously about the issues at all. Finally, adolescents in the midst of struggling with choices are experiencing a **moratorium.** This is what is really meant when we talk about an identity crisis. Marcia uses the term *moratorium* in a way that is slightly different from Erikson's original meaning. For Marcia, a moratorium involves actively dealing with the crisis of shaping an identity. For Erikson, the term refers to a delay in the adolescent's commitment to personal and occupational choices. This delay is very common, and probably healthy, for modern adolescents. Table 3–2 gives examples of each of these alternatives.

The Role of Teachers.　The teacher is often the most appropriate and available adult to help adolescents in their search for themselves as well as in their search for knowledge. When students are asked to list reasons for choosing a particular major, they often mention the importance of an effective, demanding, and warm teacher. Teachers can offer students ideas and people to have faith in. Teachers can support the students' need for free choice of careers. They can encourage aspirations and offer objective feedback on accomplishments in relevant subjects. But beware. As adolescents attempt to establish their own identities and see themselves as separate from their parents, they may also reject other authority figures—including teach-

Table 3–2　Marcia's Identity Statuses

James Marcia has suggested that there are four possible statuses for the adolescent identity. Here are examples of the types of responses he received from adolescents in each status to questions like, "How willing would you be to give up your current plans for your career if something better came along?"   **Identity achievement:** "It's hard to imagine anything really better for me. I might consider it, of course, if it was clearly better. But I've thought about my decision for a long time—it's the right one for me."   **Identity foreclosure:** "I wouldn't want to change my plans. My family and I have been working toward this ever since I can remember. Actually, I can't even imagine doing anything else; I just wouldn't feel comfortable."   **Identity diffusion:** "I don't really have any plans, so there must be something better than the last couple things I've been turning over in my mind. I don't really know what might work for me, anyway, or what I'd be able to do. . . ."   **Moratorium:** "Certainly, I might be willing to change. But I've been focusing on this one idea for a long time, looking at it from all kinds of angles. It's driving me crazy, but I'm almost to the point where I can say it looks like the best idea for me. But I couldn't say I'm sure yet."

Adapted from J. E. Marcia (1980), Identity formation in adolescence. In J. Adelson (Ed.), Handbook of adolescent psychology. *New York: Wiley.*

Guidelines

Encouraging Identity Formation

Give students many models for career choices and other adult roles.

Examples
1. *Point out models from literature and history. Have a calendar with the birthdays of eminent women, minority leaders, or people who made a little-known contribution to the subject you are teaching. Briefly discuss the person's accomplishments on his or her birthday.*
2. *Invite guest speakers to describe how and why they chose their professions. Make sure all kinds of work and workers are represented.*

Help students find resources for working out personal problems.

Examples
1. *Encourage them to talk to school counselors.*
2. *Discuss potential outside services.*

Be tolerant of teenage fads as long as they don't offend others or interfere with learning.

Examples
1. *Discuss the fads of earlier eras (neon hair, powdered wigs, men's pony tails).*
2. *Don't impose strict dress or hair codes.*

Give students realistic feedback about themselves.

Examples
1. *When students misbehave or perform poorly, make sure they understand the consequences of their behavior.*
2. *Give students model answers or show them other students' completed projects so they can compare their work to good examples.*
3. *Since students are "trying on" roles, keep the roles separate from the person. You can criticize a student's behavior without criticizing the student.*

ers. Don't take this questioning of authority too personally. It comes with the territory if you work with adolescents. The Guidelines offer a number of suggestions for helping students in their search for identity.

The school years may see only the beginning of identity formation. Like formal operations, identity formation may be an extended process for many people. But however the crisis of identity v. role confusion is resolved, we face new challenges and conflicts in adulthood. As we deal with these, our personalities continue to change and develop.

Beyond the School Years: Intimacy, Generativity, and Integrity

The crises of Erikson's stages of adulthood all involve the quality of human relations. The first of these stages is *intimacy v. isolation.* Intimacy in this sense refers to a willingness to relate to another person on a deep level, to have a relationship based on more than mutual need. It means giving and sharing without asking what will be received in return. Someone who has not achieved a sufficiently strong sense of identity tends to fear being overwhelmed or swallowed up by another person and may retreat into isolation.

Sexual relations do not necessarily indicate intimacy. People can be sexually intimate without establishing the personal commitment called for in true intimacy. However, within a truly intimate relationship, mutual sexual satisfaction increases the closeness of the people involved.

generativity: sense of concern for future generations

The conflict at the next stage is *generativity v. stagnation.* **Generativity** extends the ability to care for another person and involves caring and guidance for the next generation and for future generations. While generativity frequently refers to having and nurturing children, it has a broader meaning. Productivity and creativity are essential features. Erikson has compared generativity in its broad sense to the Hindu principle of the maintenance of the world. There is a time in the life cycle when death appears realistically certain, rather than as a far-off eventuality. A person does best at this time to put aside thoughts of death "and balance its certainty with the only happiness that is lasting: to increase, by whatever is yours to give, the good will and higher order in your sector of the world" (Erikson, 1974, p. 124).

This broad view of generativity may not only affect your view of yourself as a potential teacher but can also suggest issues that might be addressed in the classroom, particularly on the secondary level. Many students as well as teachers are concerned, for example, about the future of the environment and about fulfilling the American dream of equality for all citizens. What kind of world do we want to leave behind for the next generation, and what can we do to help create that world? These issues can provide important discussion and project material, enlarge students' frames of reference, and help them to appreciate the effect of today's decisions on tomorrow's quality of life. Dealing with such issues can also prepare them for the challenges of avoiding stagnation in later life.

integrity: sense of self-acceptance and fulfillment

The last of Erikson's stages is *integrity v. despair* and involves coming to terms with death. Achieving **integrity** (Erikson calls it ego integrity) means consolidating one's sense of self and fully accepting that self, its unique and now unalterable history, its responsible place in one's particular culture. Those unable to attain a feeling of fulfillment and completeness sink into despair and fear death.

The number of the aged is increasing in our society. More and more people are confronting these final challenges, and for longer and longer periods of time. What does it mean to be old? What are the needs of the elderly? What is society's responsibility toward them? These are all questions that students can profit from discussing. Several of the student teachers in my classes have designed social studies units on these themes, and the response has been excellent.

ISSUES IN THE EARLY YEARS

With Erikson's ideas about personal and social development as a background, let's now examine more closely several specific issues that are important in the years from infancy through elementary school. We will focus on three: sex-role development; the effects of day-care and preschool programs; and peer relations and friendships.

Sex-Role Development

Beliefs about what it means to be male or female are strongly influenced by the culture. Two important teachers in modern cultures are parents and schools.

The Role of Parents. We all may learn very early what it means to be male or female through the actions of our parents in the first years of our lives. It appears that mothers and fathers play and interact with their infants in qualitatively different ways. Fathers, for example, are more likely to play in physical or novel ways, whereas mothers tend to play traditional games such as peek-a-boo as well as provide most of the routine care (Lamb, 1978). Both ways of relating seem to be important to the child's development. Since there are such predictable differences in the ways mothers and fathers interact with their babies, Lamb (1979) believes that this is a main factor influencing the development of gender identity.

Mothers and Fathers Play Different Games

It is also possible that parents influence gender identity by behaving differently toward sons and daughters. Birns (1976) reports a number of studies indicating that both parents play more roughly and vigorously with sons than they do with daughters. Parents tend to touch male infants more at first; later, they keep male toddlers at a greater distance than females. Parents seem to spend more time interacting with sons, trying to get the babies to laugh or smile.

Different Treatment of the Sexes

Different treatment of the sexes seems to continue in early childhood. Boys are encouraged to be more physically active; girls are encouraged to be affectionate and tender. A number of researchers have found that boys are given more freedom to roam the neighborhood and are not protected as long as girls from potentially dangerous activities like playing with sharp scissors or crossing the street alone. Parents are quick to come to the aid of their daughters but are more likely to insist that their sons handle problems themselves (Block, 1979, 1983). Thus, independence and initiative seem to be more encouraged in boys than in girls. Lois Hoffman (1977) has suggested that girls are not so much trained in dependency as they are deprived of the independence training offered to boys.

The Schools and Sex Roles. Many of my student teachers are surprised when they hear young children talk about sex roles. Even in this era of great progress toward equality of the sexes, a preschool girl is more likely to tell you she wants to become a secretary than to say she wants to be an engineer. A colleague of mine brought her young daughter to her college class after she had given a lecture on the dangers of sex stereotyping in schools. The students asked the little girl, "What do you want to be when you grow up?" The child immediately replied, "A doctor," and her professor/mother beamed with pride. Then the girl whispered to the students in the front row, "I really want to be a nurse, but my Mommy won't let me." Actually, this is a normal reaction. Younger children tend to have more stereotyped notions of sex roles than older children, and all ages seem to have more rigid and traditional ideas about male occupations than about what females do.

Stereotypes in School

What is the role of the school in solidifying gender identity? Can teachers help students move beyond rigid notions about sex roles? Unfortunately, schools can foster stereotyped views of sex roles in a number of ways. Most of the textbooks produced for the early grades before 1970 portrayed both males and females in sexually stereotyped roles. Materials for the later grades often omitted women altogether from illustrations and text. In a study of 2,760 stories in 134 books by 16 publishers, a group called Women on Words and Images (1975) found the total number of stories dealing with males or male animals to be four times greater than the number of stories dealing with females or female animals. They also found that females tended to be shown in the home, behaving passively and expressing fear or incompetence. Males usually were more dominant and adventurous; they often rescued the females. Textbook publishers have recognized these problems to some extent in recent years. However, it still makes sense to check your teaching materials for such stereotypes.

Biases of Teachers The teacher's own attitude toward sex differences may be influential as well. When teachers want boxes carried to the basement, they may ask for male volunteers. When refreshments are needed or flowers must be arranged, they may again fall victim to stereotyped images and ask for female volunteers. When student teams are formed and the groups all choose boys as the leaders and girls as the secretaries, the teacher may accept these decisions. Guidance counselors, parents, and teachers often do not protest at all when a bright girl says she doesn't want to take any more math or science courses, but when a boy of the same ability wants to forget about math or science, they will object. In these subtle ways, students' stereotyped expectations for themselves can be reinforced (Jackson & Lahaderne, 1971; Levitan & Chananie, 1972; Sadker & Sadker, 1985). The Guidelines provide ideas for how to avoid sexism in your teaching.

The Impact of Day Care

With recent increases in two-career families and single-parent households, more and more children are spending part of their daily lives in group settings outside the family. In fact, over one-third of American children 3 to 4 years old are in school (*Harvard Education Letter*, June 1985). Many others are cared for by relatives or in private homes. What are the effects of these day-care arrangements on the millions of children involved? Researchers have been examining this question since the 1960s. Almost all of the studies have focused on children in formal day-care or preschool programs, so information on children cared for in private homes is very limited. This is true, in part, because data on private care arrangements are difficult to collect.

Effects on Personal and Social Development.   The effects of good day-care and preschool programs in this area seem generally positive. Children in these programs are more assertive, self-confident, socially mature, and outgoing. Evidence also suggests that day care is not disruptive to the child's emotional bonds with parents, even if it begins before the child's first birthday. (However, if day care begins before the child has developed a secure attachment, quality of attachment may be affected in some cases.) Children
Peer Interaction who attend preschool programs tend to interact more with their peers in both positive and negative ways. Some results indicate that these children may be more aggressive toward peers and adults (Clarke-Stewart & Fein,

1983). The effect of this aggression in later years has not yet been determined.

Effects on Intellectual Development. During the 1960s and 1970s, research on the effects of preschool experiences generally focused on compensatory programs—programs for children from low-income families, like Operation Head Start. Initial results showed that these programs raised intelligence and achievement test scores at first but that gains seemed to fade after a few years in elementary school. Recent evaluations, however, have painted a more optimistic picture. When we look at criteria of success other than test scores and follow the graduates of the programs through high school, we see definite differences. For example, two recent studies of 12 experimental preschool programs for poor children compared program participants to children of similar age and background who did not attend special preschools (Berrueta-Clement, Schweinhart, Barnett, Epstein, & Weikart, 1984; Lazar & Darlington, 1982). Children who attended the preschool programs had to repeat fewer grades, were less often assigned to special education classes and classified as mentally retarded, were arrested less frequently, had fewer illegitimate children, graduated from high school and went on to advanced schooling more often, depended less on welfare, and worked more.

Positive Effects
    The positive effects of good preschool programs apparently are not limited to low-income families. For example, by second grade the middle-class

children who participated in the intensive Brookline Early Education Project were reading better and had fewer problems learning basic skills than comparable children who did not attend the program (*Harvard Education Letter*, June 1985).

Friendships in Childhood

During their early school years, children move rather freely in and out of three overlapping worlds: the home, the school, and the neighborhood. Parents remain important, but children spend increasing amounts of time with other youngsters. Psychologists have found that as children mature, the meaning of friendship changes for them (Damon, 1977; Selman, 1981; Youniss, 1980).

Levels of Friendship

Damon has described three levels of friendship. At the first level, friends are the other children a child plays with often. Friends share food or toys and act "nice" toward each other. But friendships can begin and end quickly, based on acts of kindness or "meanness." There is little sense that friends have stable characteristics, so moment-to-moment actions define the friendship. Teachers working with young children should be aware that these rapidly changing allegiances are a normal part of development. Note, too, that a child's view of friends at this level may be related to the level of cognitive development: young children have difficulty seeing beyond the immediate situation.

Friendships at the next level are defined by a willingness to help when help is needed. Friends are playmates and companions. Children begin to base their choices for friends on fairly concrete but stable personal qualities

These two young girls are friends right now, sharing toys and being "nice" to each other. In a few hours, their friendship could end temporarily, if one grows tired of sharing. *(Suzanne Szasz/Photo Researchers)*

in another child, such as, "She always shares her lunch with me," or "He takes my side when people are mean to me." This level of friendship may be linked to concrete operational cognitive abilities.

At the highest level, as children move into adolescence, friends are seen as people who share common interests and values, faithfully keep one's most private revelations a secret, and provide psychological support when necessary. The personal qualities of a friend—loyalty, similar philosophy of life—are more abstract and less tied to behaviors (Furman & Bierman, 1984). The cognitive abilities to understand abstract concepts and to base judgments upon them may come into play here. Friendship is now a long-term proposition and usually cannot be destroyed by one or even several incidents. At this stage friendships can be very intense, especially for girls. At every stage, girls are more likely than boys to have one "best" friend and are more reluctant than boys to admit new members to a tight group of friends (Lever, 1978).

At every level, these friendships play a very significant role in healthy personal and social development. There is some evidence that adults who had close friends as children have higher self-esteem and are more capable of maintaining intimate relationships than adults who spent lonely childhoods (Liebert, Wicks-Nelson, & Kail, 1986). Life can be very difficult for a student whose social relationships are unsatisfying (or nonexistent).

Teachers sometimes forget just how central friendships are to their students' lives. When students are having problems with friends, when there has been a falling-out or an argument, when one child is not invited to a sleep-over, when rumors are started and pacts are made to ostracize someone, the results can be devastating to the children involved. Even when students begin to mature and know intellectually that rifts will soon be healed, they may still be emotionally crushed by temporary trouble in the friendship.

A teacher should also be aware of how each student gets along with the group. Are there outcasts? Do some students play the bully role? Careful adult intervention can often correct such problems, especially at the middle elementary school level. In these years, one of the teacher's jobs is to balance students' need to learn the curriculum with their need to establish healthy peer relationships.

ISSUES AFFECTING ADOLESCENTS

As students enter adolescence, they undergo dramatic changes. We will look at two interrelated kinds of development, physical and sexual, and the emotional, social, and academic repercussions of the changes in these areas.

Physical Development in Adolescence

Throughout elementary school, many of the girls are likely to be as large or larger than the boys in their classes. Between the ages of 11 and 14 girls are, on the average, taller and heavier than boys of the same age (Tanner, 1970). The size discrepancy can give the girls an advantage in physical activities, though some girls may feel conflict over this and, as a result, downplay their physical abilities. But the differences in growth rates are most pronounced (and perhaps most influential) at the beginning of puberty.

Puberty is not a single event, but a series of changes involving almost every part of the body. The final outcome of all these changes is the ability to reproduce. Generally, girls begin puberty about two years ahead of boys and reach their final height by age 16; most boys continue growing until about age 18. For the typical girl, the adolescent growth spurt begins with breast development between the ages of 10 and 11 and continues for about three years. While this is the average time frame for girls, the actual range is from 9 to 16 years. Eighty percent of American girls have their first menstrual period between the ages of 11½ and 14½. For the typical boy, the growth spurt begins between the ages of 12 and 13. In general, boys are more variable than girls when it comes to the physical changes of adolescence. The length of time that is required for all the changes of puberty to occur varies more with boys, and the range of differences in height and weight at the end of puberty is greater for boys than for girls (Rogers, 1985).

Early and Late Maturers.   The physical changes of adolescence have significant effects on the individual's identity. Psychologists have been particularly interested in the academic, social, and emotional differences they have found between adolescents who mature early and those who mature later.

First, there seems to be an academic advantage in early maturation. On the average, students who are physically mature tend to score higher on most tests of mental ability than less mature students of the same age (Fein, 1978). Second, early maturation seems to have certain special advantages for

boys. Early-maturing boys are more likely to enjoy high social status; they tend to be popular and to be leaders. Many of these advantages are sustained in later life. On the other hand, boys who mature late have an especially difficult time. Since girls mature well ahead of boys, even late-maturing girls have developed by the time the late-maturing boy finally has his chance. The last to leave childhood, he may have been surrounded by mature peers for years. These late-maturing boys tend to be less popular, more talkative, and hungrier for attention.

This situation seems very unfair, especially since there is little the individual can do to change the genetic timetable. But in later life there appear to be some compensations for the late-maturing boy. Some studies show that in adulthood, males who matured early are less flexible and less creative in their thinking, whereas men who matured later tend to be more creative, tolerant, and perceptive. Perhaps the trials and anxieties of maturing late teach some boys to be better problem solvers (Craig, 1986).

For girls, early physical maturity seems to be less important in determining social status. But maturing way ahead of classmates can be a definite disadvantage. Being larger than everyone else in the class is not a valued characteristic for girls in our culture. A girl who begins to mature early probably will be the first in her peer group to start the changes of puberty. This can be very upsetting to some girls, especially if they have not been prepared for the changes or if friends tease them. Later-maturing girls seem to have fewer problems, but they may worry that something is wrong with them. All students can benefit from knowing that the range of normal differences in rates of maturation is great.

Dramatic contrasts in size can occur during late childhood and early adolescence, due to varying rates of maturing and genetic differences in height. *(Alec Duncan/Taurus Photos)*

Sexual Maturity

Probably the most important aspect of development during these years is sexual maturation. Sexually mature adolescents become physically and hormonally equipped for sexual relationships but in modern cultures go through an extended period of continued education or other training before society considers them ready for marriage. The emotional impact of sexual experiences during this period may have repercussions in the school, both for the students involved and for fellow students who hear about the experiences. In previous decades, males were more likely than females to have sexual intercourse before marriage. Today about 60 percent of all unmarried American teenagers, girls as well as boys, have had sexual intercourse by age 19 (Rosen & Hall, 1983).

As their bodies become sexually mature, adolescents must make psychological and emotional adjustments. Their views of what it means to be male or female have been developing for years, probably since infancy. But now they must begin to solidify their sexual identity and feel comfortable with it.

Teachers are likely to have students who vary greatly in size, maturity, and sexual sophistication in almost every class. As we have seen, being very different from other students appears to be a plus only for boys who mature earlier than their peers. For everyone else, being very different can cause problems in emotional and social development. The Guidelines on the next page offer ideas for dealing with these problems.

Guidelines

Dealing with Physical Differences in the Classroom

Do not call unnecessary attention to physical differences among students.

Examples
1. *Avoid seating arrangements that are obviously based on height, but try to seat smaller students so they can see and participate in class activities easily.*
2. *Avoid games that call attention to differences in height, size, or strength.*
3. *Don't use or allow students to use nicknames based on physical traits.*

Help students obtain factual information on differences in physical development.

Examples
1. *Set up science projects on sex differences in growth rates.*
2. *Have readings and discussions that focus on differences between early and late maturers. Make sure that you present the positives and the negatives of each.*
3. *Find out the school policy on sex education and on informal guidance for students. Some schools, for example, encourage teachers to talk to girls who are upset about their first menstrual period, while other schools expect teachers to send the girls to talk to the school nurse.*
4. *Give students models in literature or in their community of high-achieving individuals who do not fit the ideal physical stereotypes.*

Accept that concerns about appearance and the opposite sex will occupy much time and energy for adolescents.

Examples
1. *Allow students a few moments at the end of class to socialize or to "adjust" their appearance.*
2. *Deal with some of these issues in curriculum-related materials.*

UNDERSTANDING OURSELVES AND OTHERS

In this section we examine several aspects of personal and social development that are issues throughout childhood and adolescence. What is self-concept? How do we come to understand ourselves and other people? How do we develop a sense of right and wrong, and do these beliefs affect our behavior? And how do the answers to all these questions affect teaching and learning?

Self-Concept: Origins and Influences

self-concept: our perceptions of ourselves

Self-concept, like many other psychological terms, is part of our everyday conversation. We talk about people who have a "low self-concept" or individuals whose self-concept is not "strong." In psychology, the term generally refers to "the composite of ideas, feelings, and attitudes people have about themselves" (Hilgard, Atkinson, & Atkinson, 1979, p. 605). We could also consider the self-concept to be our attempt to explain ourselves to ourselves, to build a scheme (in Piaget's terms) that organizes our impressions, feelings, and attitudes about ourselves. But this model or scheme is not permanent, unified, or unchanging. It is "a complex system of ideas, feelings, and desires, not necessarily well articulated or coherent" (Bromley, 1978, p. 164). Our self-perceptions vary from situation to situation and from one phase of our lives to another.

Young children see themselves in terms of their physical appearance, name, actions, and abilities but do not have a sense of their enduring characteristics or "personality." As they mature, children move from concrete and fragmented views of themselves to more abstract, organized, and objective views that include psychological characteristics. Here are three British children's descriptions of themselves (Bromley, 1978, pp. 151–152).

Examples:
Children's Self-
Perceptions

A 7-YEAR-OLD BOY

I am 7 and I have hazel brown hair and my hobby is stamp collecting. I am good at football and I am quite good at sums and my favourite game is football and I love school and I like reading books and my favourite car is an Austin.

A 9-YEAR-OLD BOY

I have dark brown hair, brown eyes and a fair face. I am a quick worker but am often lazy. I am good but often cheeky and naughty. My character is sometimes funny and sometimes serious. My behavior is sometimes silly and stupid and often good it is often funny my daddy thinks.

A 14-YEAR-OLD GIRL

I am a very temperamental person, sometimes, well most of the time, I am happy. Then now and again I just go moody for no reason at all. I enjoy being different from everybody else, and like to think of myself as being fairly modern. . . . When I am nervous I talk a lot, and this gives some important new acquaintances a bad impression when I am trying to make a good one. I worry a lot about getting married and having a family, because I am frightened that I will make a mess of it.

Children's self-concepts change as they develop. For young children concrete facts like physical appearance, name, or family membership are the important answers to the question, Who are you? *(Four by Five)*

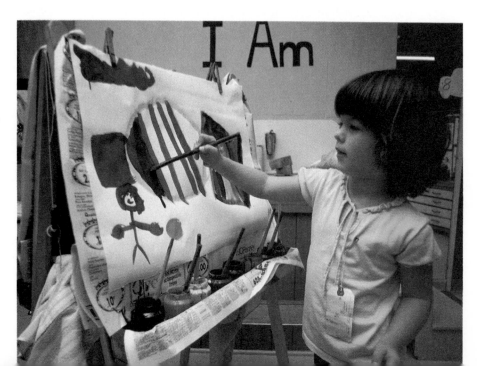

The developing self-concept of the child is influenced by parents and other family members in the early years and by friends, schoolmates, and teachers as the child grows. School clearly plays a major role. Shavelson and his colleagues have proposed that increasingly during the school years, a child's self-concept becomes organized along both academic and nonacademic lines. There are, in effect, at least two self-concepts (Marsh & Shavelson, 1985; Shavelson & Bolus, 1982; Shavelson, Hubner, & Stanton, 1976). The academic self-concept is based on how well the student performs in the various academic areas. The nonacademic self-concept is based on relationships with peers and other important people, on emotional states, and on physical qualities. The nonacademic self-concept could in fact be further subdivided into social, emotional, and physical self-concepts.

Multifaceted Self-Concepts

Recent research provides more evidence for the self-concept's multifaceted nature but suggests that its organization may be even more complicated. It appears that self-concept in mathematics and self-concept in English, for example, are not highly related and thus may not really fit into one general academic self-concept. It also seems that as students grow older, their self-concepts in different areas tend to become more and more separate (Marsh & Shavelson, 1985).

Shavelson has also suggested that the self-concept evolves through constant self-evaluation in different situations (Shavelson & Bolus, 1982). Children and adolescents are continually asking themselves, in effect, "How am I doing?" They compare their performance with their own standards and with the performances of peers. They also gauge the verbal and nonverbal reactions of significant people—parents, best friends, leaders, teachers. As you will see in the chapter on motivation, the way an individual explains success or failure in each situation is important, too. We must attribute our successes to our own actions, not to luck or to special assistance, in order to build a positive self-concept. Positive self-concept is the same as high self-esteem.

For teachers, there are at least two important, interrelated questions to ask about self-concept. The first is, How does self-concept affect a student's behavior in school? The second question is, How does life in school affect a student's self-concept?

School and Self-Concept

In answer to the first question, it appears that students with higher self-esteem are somewhat more likely to be successful in school (Purkey, 1970), although the strength of the relationship varies greatly depending on the characteristics of the students and the research methods used (Hansford & Hattie, 1982). In addition, a more positive self-concept is related to more favorable attitudes toward school (Metcalfe, 1981) and more positive behavior in the classroom (Reynolds, 1980). Of course, as we discussed in Chapter 1, knowing that two variables are related (correlated) does not tell us that one is causing the other. It may be that high achievement leads to positive self-concept, or vice versa. In fact, it probably works both ways (Shavelson & Bolus, 1982; West, Fish, & Stevens, 1980).

This leads us to the second question of how school affects self-concept. Bloom (1973) has said: "Successful experiences in school are no guarantee of a generally positive self-concept, but they increase the probabilities that such will be the case" (p. 142). Given this responsibility, what can teachers do? In their book *Teacher Behavior and Pupil Self-Concept*, Kash and Borich (1978) offer the suggestions listed in Table 3–3.

Table 3–3 Suggestions for Encouraging the Development of Positive Self-Concept

1. Value and accept all pupils, for their attempts as well as their accomplishments.
2. Create a climate that is physically and psychologically safe for students.
3. Become aware of your own personal biases (everyone has some biases).
4. Make sure that your procedures for teaching and grouping students are really necessary, not just a convenient way of handling problem students or avoiding contact with some students.
5. Make standards of evaluation clear.
6. Model appropriate methods of self-criticism and self-reward.
7. Avoid destructive competition and encourage students to compete with their own prior levels of achievement.
8. Accept a student even when you must reject a particular behavior.
9. Remember that positive self-concept grows from success in operating in the world *and* from being valued by important people in the environment. It takes both kinds of experiences to build a positive self-concept.

Adapted from M. M. Kash & G. Borich (1978), Teacher behavior and pupil self-concept. Reading, MA: Addison-Wesley, *pp. 217, 260. © 1978 by Addison-Wesley Publishing Company, Inc., Menlo Park, CA. Reprinted by permission.*

The Self and Others

You will recall that Erikson's theory was a psychosocial one: it focused on the search for identity within the context of the family and the larger culture. Erikson stressed the influence of the social environment. We have noted, too, how parents, family members, teachers, friends, and peers all affect our views of ourselves and our social roles—our self-concepts. As we search for our own identity and form images of ourselves in various social situations, we are also seeking and forming ways to understand the influential people around us. Children learn to see themselves as separate and thus to see others as separate people as well, with *their* own identities. We have seen how this change affects one kind of social relationship, friendship. What else can psychology tell us about how a child's view of others develops? How do we learn to interpret what others are thinking and feeling? How much do we take such interpretations into account? These questions will lead us to an examination of moral development—how children acquire a sense of right and wrong and learn to apply moral standards to behavior.

social cognition:
our conceptions of
other people

Social Cognition.   Psychologists interested in **social cognition** study questions about "how children conceptualize other people and how they come to understand the thoughts, emotions, intentions, and viewpoints of others" (Shantz, 1975, p. 1). Martin Hoffman (1979) describes four stages in the development of a child's concept of other people. During the first year or so, children do not distinguish between themselves and others in their world. Toward the end of the first year, along with object permanence, children develop "person permanence"—the awareness that other people are separate physical beings. But children at this stage still believe that everyone else has thoughts and feelings identical to their own. During the next two years children move toward an understanding that, in a particular situation, another person can have separate feelings and ideas. But children are 8 to 12 years old before they fully understand that other people have distinct, separate identities, life histories, and futures. You may remember being intrigued when you were that age with the idea that all the people passing you in cars on a busy street led separate lives filled with unique experiences—that they were all "heroes" in their own "movies."

empathy: ability to feel emotion as experienced by others

Empathy. Martin Hoffman (1978, 1979) has also suggested that **empathy** develops along with the understanding of others' separate identities. Empathy is the ability to feel an emotion as it is experienced by another person—to put yourself in another's shoes. Both adults and children respond emotionally to signs of distress in others. But the emotional reaction of a young child is not based on an understanding of how another feels, since the child cannot yet see the other's emotions as separate. Very young children may respond to seeing another child hurt as if they had been hurt themselves. A little later, children begin to be aware that others' feelings are separate but assume that those feelings must be the same as their own. Hoffman cites the example of a young boy who brought his own mother to comfort his crying friend, even though the friend's mother was available to help. The boy evidently assumed that his friend would want *exactly* the comfort he usually wanted in a time of trouble.

Children eventually become more and more able to imagine how other people would feel in a given situation. Older children usually can respond emotionally not only to the immediate distress of another person but also to a more abstract notion of another's life situation, even if the situation is quite removed from their own experience. Also, as children mature, they become more sophisticated in their descriptions of how others feel. Instead of categorizing the emotions of others with broad, general words like

Close friendships help us grow. As we share secrets, interests, and experiences, our ability to empathize deepens and our capacity for intimacy increases. *(Day Williams/Photo Researchers)*

"happy," "sad," or "mad," older children can recognize and discuss more specific and complex feelings like jealousy, disgust, or nervousness.

Empathy plays an important part in our ability to understand and get along with one another. Teachers can encourage the development of empathy by allowing students to work and talk together and discuss emotional reactions to various experiences. When disputes arise in the later elementary and the secondary grades, teachers can resist the temptation to quote rules or act as a judge and instead can help the combatants see one another's point of view.

Moral Development

If you have spent time with young children, you know that there is a period when you can say, "Eating in the living room is not allowed!" and get away with it. For young children, rules simply exist. Piaget (1962) called this the stage of moral realism. At this stage the child of 5 or 6 believes that rules about conduct or rules about how to play a game are absolute and can't be changed. If a rule is broken, the child believes that the punishment should be determined by how much damage is done, not by the intention of the child or by other circumstances. So accidently breaking three cups is worse than intentionally breaking one, and in the child's eyes, the punishment for the three-cup offense should be greater.

Shifts in Morality

As children interact with others and see that different people have different rules, there is a gradual shift to a morality of cooperation. Children come to understand that people make rules and people can change them. When rules are broken, both the damage done and the intention of the offender are taken into account. These developmental changes and others are reflected in Kohlberg's theory of moral development, based in part on Piaget's ideas.

Stages of Moral Development.   Lawrence Kohlberg (1963, 1975, 1981) has proposed a detailed sequence of stages of moral reasoning and has led the field in studying their evolution. He has divided moral development into three levels: (1) preconventional, where judgment is based solely on a person's own needs and perceptions; (2) conventional, where the expectations of society and law are taken into account; and (3) postconventional, where judgments are based on abstract, more personal principles that are not necessarily defined by society's laws. Each of these three levels is then subdivided into stages, as in Table 3–4.

moral dilemmas:
situations in which no choice is absolutely right

In numerous studies, Kohlberg has evaluated the moral reasoning of both children and adults by presenting them with **moral dilemmas,** or hypothetical situations in which a person must make a difficult decision. Subjects are asked what the person caught in the dilemma should do and why. In these situations there is no obvious answer; no action will provide a complete solution.

One of the most commonly used moral dilemmas can be summarized as follows: A man's wife is dying. There is one drug that could save her, but it is very expensive, and the druggist who invented it will not sell it at a price low enough for the man to buy it. Finally, the man becomes desperate and considers stealing the drug for his wife. What should he do, and why?

Table 3–4   **Kohlberg's Stage Theory of Moral Reasoning**

Level 1. Preconventional Moral Reasoning

Judgment is based on personal needs and others' rules.

Stage 1.   Punishment–Obedience Orientation
Rules are obeyed to avoid punishment. A good or bad action is determined by its physical consequences.

Stage 2.   Personal Reward Orientation
Personal needs determine right and wrong. Favors are returned along the lines of "You scratch my back, I'll scratch yours."

Level 2. Conventional Moral Reasoning

Judgment is based on others' approval, family expectations, traditional values, the laws of society, and loyalty to country.

Stage 3.   Good Boy–Nice Girl Orientation
Good means "nice." It is determined by what pleases, aids, and is approved by others.

Stage 4.   Law and Order Orientation
Laws are absolute. Authority must be respected and the social order maintained.

Level 3. Postconventional Moral Reasoning

Stage 5.   Social Contract Orientation
Good is determined by socially agreed-upon standards of individual rights. This is a morality similar to that of the U.S. Constitution.

Stage 6.   Universal Ethical Principle Orientation
Good and right are matters of individual conscience and involve abstract concepts of justice, human dignity, and equality.

Adapted from L. Kohlberg (1975), The cognitive–developmental approach to moral education, Phi Delta Kappan, 56, p. 671.

Presented with this story, subjects at three different levels are likely to give answers such as these:

Level 1:   "It's wrong to steal the drug because you might get caught."
Level 2:   "It's wrong to steal the drug because the law says it is wrong to steal," or "It's all right for the man to steal the drug because he means well—he is trying to help his wife."
Level 3:   "It's not wrong to steal the drug because human life must be preserved. But the man has to be willing to face the consequences of the theft and go to jail."

At level 1 (the preconventional level), the subject seems to be most swayed by the personal results of the action. This kind of answer may reflect the child's wondering, "What would happen to me if I stole something?" and concluding, "I might get caught and punished." The basic egocentrism of the child is evident in this reasoning.

At level 2 (the conventional level), the subject is able to look beyond the immediate personal consequences and consider the views, and especially the approval, of others. At this level, the child tends to uphold the traditional values of the family, the social group, or the country. Thus laws, religious or civil, are very important and are regarded as fairly absolute and unalterable. The child who says that stealing the drug is justified by the man's good intentions may place a high value on loyalty to family and loved ones.

At level 3 (the postconventional level), the subject is able to consider the underlying, individual values that might be involved in the decision. Abstract concepts are no longer rigid; as the name of this level implies, principles can be separated from conventional values. A person reasoning on this level understands that what is considered right by the majority may not be considered right by an individual in a particular situation. Rational, personal choice is stressed. When individuals at this level choose to break society's rules, they accept the consequences as dictated by the society. Part of Mahatma Gandhi's doctrine of nonviolent resistance, for example, was acceptance of imprisonment.

Links with Cognitive and Emotional Growth

The development of moral reasoning can be seen in relation to both cognitive and emotional development. Empathy and formal operations in particular play large roles in a progression through Kohlberg's stages and levels. As we have seen, abstract thinking becomes increasingly important in the higher stages, as children move from decisions based on absolute (though in some cases fairly abstract) rules to decisions based on principles such as justice and mercy. The abilities to see another's perspective and to imagine alternative bases for laws and rules also enter into judgments at the higher stages.

Stages of Morality: Problems and Criticisms. Kohlberg's stage theory has been criticized on several points. First, the stages do not seem in reality to be separate, sequenced, and consistent. People often give reasons for moral choices that reflect several different stages simultaneously. Or a person's

Perhaps to these boys it's OK to steal, as long as they don't get caught. If shoplifting is encouraged in the peer group, what can teachers do? (Rohn Engh/Photo Researchers)

choices in one instance might fit one stage and in a different situation reflect another stage. Second, the ordering of the stages indicates certain biases. More women than men are identified as being at stage 3 as opposed to stage 4, partly because women tend to value the approval of others and being merciful. But since these qualities are seen as representing a lower stage of moral development, the ordering of stages may reflect a bias in favor of males (Gilligan, 1977). Another criticism is that stage 6 reasoning is biased in favor of Western, libertarian values that emphasize individualism. In cultures that are more family-centered or group-oriented, the highest moral value might involve putting the opinions of the group before decisions based on individual conscience. (We will look at some of these cultural differences in values in the next chapter.) There has been much disagreement over the "highest" moral stage. In recent years, Kohlberg himself has questioned the inclusion of stage 6. Very few people other than trained philosophers reason naturally or easily at this level.

Critics of Kohlberg's theory have emphasized the importance of distinguishing between moral reasoning—what we say should be done—and moral behavior—actions based on ethical considerations. There is some question, too, about whether *ability* to reason at a particular level has much to do with actual reasoning in real situations or with actual behavior. In one study, for example, 15 percent of students judged to be capable of postconventional reasoning actually cheated on a task. Fifty-five percent of students at the conventional level and 70 percent of students at the preconventional level also cheated (Kohlberg, 1975). The fact that some students cheated in spite of their ability to reason at a principled, postconventional level suggests that a full understanding of moral (and immoral) actions requires more than knowledge about moral reasoning abilities.

Clearly, the ability to reason on a higher level does not mean people will always act consistently with their principles. The controversy over Kohlberg's theory and what it can tell us about moral judgments and moral behavior continues today (Reimer, Paolitto, & Hersh, 1983). These are thorny issues. How do they affect teachers? What can teachers actually do to deal with cheating, bullying, and the destruction of school property? First of all, knowledge about levels of moral development may help you to understand your students' positions. Knowing that students are likely to have different views about right and wrong and that their behavior may be influenced by emotional or social rather than purely moral considerations may be useful in sorting out these situations. Let's consider two common problem behaviors that raise moral issues in the classroom: cheating and aggression.

Cheating.   As we have just seen, cheating involves more than beliefs about right and wrong. Early research indicates that cheating seems to have more to do with the particular situation than with the general honesty or dishonesty of the individual (R. Burton, 1963). A student who cheats in math class is probably more likely to cheat in other classes but may never consider lying to a friend or taking candy from the local grocery store. But most students will cheat if the pressure to perform well is great and the chances of being caught are slim. When asked why students cheat, the 1,100 high school subjects in a study by Schab (1980) listed three reasons: (1) too lazy to study; (2) fear of failure; and (3) parental pressure for good grades. The students in this study were very pessimistic about the incidence of cheating.

Both boys and girls in the survey believed that over 97 percent of their peers had cheated at one time or another. However, this estimate may be high; figures depend partly on how cheating is defined.

The implications for teachers are fairly straightforward. To prevent cheating, try to avoid putting students in high-pressure situations. Make sure they are well prepared for tests and have some hope of doing reasonably well without cheating. Make extra help available for those who need it. Be clear about your policies in regard to cheating, and enforce them consistently. Help students resist temptation by monitoring carefully during testing. And don't get so engrossed in work that you can't keep track of what is happening in the room.

aggression: hostile behavior

Aggression. **Aggression** is not to be confused with assertiveness, which means affirming or maintaining a legitimate right. Helen Bee (1981) gives this example of the difference between the two types of behavior: "A child who says, 'That's my toy!' is showing assertiveness. If he bashes his playmate over the head to reclaim it, he has shown aggression" (p. 350). Learning by watching others plays an important role in the expression of aggression. Albert Bandura and his colleagues have demonstrated repeatedly that children will be generally more aggressive after watching others act aggressively (Bandura, Ross, & Ross, 1963). We will discuss the details of these studies in Chapter 5.

One very real source of aggressive models is found in almost every home in America—television. Most children spend more time watching television than they do in any other activity except sleep (Liebert, Sprafkin, & Davidson, 1982). Anyone who has watched television knows that violence is a common occurrence in many programs. The average dramatic show has about 8 acts of violence per hour, and children's cartoons may have anywhere from 20 to 30 incidents per hour (Gerber & Gross, 1974). In these programs the heroes are just as likely as the villains to use force for solving problems, and these solutions bring rewards. In cartoons, violent acts seem to have no real, permanent consequences. Wile E. Coyote in the *Roadrunner* cartoons returns no matter how many times he is squashed by boulders, flattened by trucks, incinerated, or hurled from cliffs (Bee, 1981).

Effects of TV Violence

How does all this violence affect children who are watching such programs? Many psychologists and parents believe that it has a strong and largely negative influence on children's behavior. Some research has shown that the more television children watch, the more violent they are in their play (Huesmann, Lagarspetz, & Eron, 1984; Liebert & Schwartzberg, 1977). But again, these correlations do not demonstrate that watching television *causes* children to be more violent. In one study that actually controlled the TV viewing of a large group of boys, ages 9 to 15, the researchers found that boys who watched the more violent programs were no more violent in their actions than boys who watched programs without violence (Fleshbach & Singer, 1971). But these researchers measured short-term effects. In fact, viewing violence on television may affect behavior in a more subtle way over a longer period of time. It is a complex issue. It is possible that TV violence has adverse effects on certain children under certain conditions. For example, children may "learn" that violent solutions to problems are appropriate by observing parents who applaud TV characters using such solutions.

The most obvious thing teachers can do to discourage aggression and to balance the possible adverse effects of TV viewing is to present a nonaggressive model. But there are a number of other factors to keep in mind, especially with young children. If the school environment provides too few favorite toys, students are likely to grab from each other, and verbal and physical fights may result. If there is too little play space, students are more likely to trip over one another or shove; again, this can easily lead to conflict (Bandura, 1973; Shantz & Voydanoff, 1973). Certain toys and activities, such as toy guns, plastic soldiers, and stories about cowboys and Indians, seem to encourage children to play more aggressively (Roedell, Slaby, & Robinson, 1976). When conflicts do arise and students are hurt, the best advice for teachers of young children is to comfort the victims and ignore the aggressors. You might step between the children as you console the child who has been hurt.

Encouraging Positive Social Behavior

Roedell, Slaby, and Robinson (1976) also suggest some useful ways to encourage positive social behavior in students. These include discussing the effects of certain actions (stealing, bullying, criticizing, and so on) on other people's feelings; emphasizing the similarities among people; setting up group projects that encourage cooperation; providing examples of sharing and cooperating from fiction, biography, newspapers, plays, and films; teaching students how to discuss and negotiate when there is no conflict so they can practice when they are not upset; and making sure students do not profit from aggressive behavior. Sometimes lessons about positive social behaviors can be incorporated into the class. One of my daughter's teachers became concerned that her sixth graders were too cruel and negative in criticizing each other. She chose as a reading assignment a book that emphasizes how such criticism makes others feel (*Felicia the Critic*, by Ellen Conford). Reading and discussing the book seemed to help the students become more constructive in their feedback to each other.

Throughout this chapter we have discussed specific ideas for helping individual teachers encourage personal and social development. Let's turn now to the somewhat controversial question about the role of the schools in promoting emotional growth.

EDUCATION FOR EMOTIONAL GROWTH

Educational goals have fluctuated greatly over the years. At times, the emphasis has been solely on cognitive outcomes. At other times, there has been an equal concern with social and affective, or emotional, outcomes (Shavelson, Hubner, & Stanton, 1976). Early in the century there was a strong emphasis on cognitive achievement, which Callahan (1962) has called the "cult of efficiency." Emphasis shifted in the 1930s to a concern with social and affective learning (Aiken, 1942). Then came Sputnik (1957) and a flurry of interest in teaching the basics, especially mathematics and science (Bruner, 1960).

During the 1960s schools were criticized for teaching only the intellect and ignoring the "whole person." As a result, personal and social development were once again considered as part of the curriculum. Then in the late 1970s, reports of declining achievement-test scores and high school graduates unable to read, write, or calculate brought the cry "back to basics"

(Armbruster, 1977). Nevertheless, the majority of Americans have seemed to agree that moral education belongs in the classroom in some form. In 1975, four out of five Americans polled in the annual Gallup Poll of attitudes toward public schools believed that schools should teach something about morals and moral behavior. Of course, there has seldom been agreement as to what constitutes moral behavior: conservatives are generally concerned with respect for authority, while liberals tend to focus on human rights.

affective education: education focusing on emotional growth

Critics of **affective education** believe that schools should stick to cognitive goals and leave the rest to the family. They also emphasize that the most significant values schools can teach, such as the importance of knowledge and academic achievement, are already built into the traditional curriculum. Where do today's teachers stand on these issues?

What Do Teachers Think?

A recent study by Richard Prawat and his colleagues asked this question (Prawat, Anderson, Diamond, McKeague, & Whitmer, 1981). The researchers interviewed 40 elementary school teachers from 24 schools to determine what teachers really believed about encouraging personal and social development in schools and how their thinking influenced their behavior. By asking the teachers a series of indirect and probing questions and then analyzing the 3,600 pages of interview transcripts, Prawat reached the following conclusions. First, over twice as many teachers emphasized affective as opposed to cognitive goals. Affective goals included interpersonal skills, independence, self-discipline, responsibility, self-worth, self-understanding, enthusiasm for learning, and "manners." Second, most teachers judged the success of a school day based upon affective accomplishments, such as getting everyone to cooperate and participate enthusiastically in activities. Third, when teachers described their ideal student, they stressed personal qualities like eagerness, self-motivation, high standards, and pleasant, well-mannered (but not conforming) behavior as much as they emphasized academic abilities. Fourth, the teachers' views about the importance of personal and social development were related to their own behavior. Teachers who emphasized independence, for example, had fewer class rules about when and how to move around the room; teachers most concerned about self-worth had fewer quietness rules.

Emphasizing
Affective Goals

How Do Teachers Encourage Personal Growth?

A second goal of Prawat's study was to identify the strategies most often used to encourage personal development. The most frequently used approach involved group discussions of ideas, feelings, or problems. Next, teachers relied on rewards and praise to encourage interpersonal skills, cooperation, independence, and so on. Many teachers tried to foster feelings of self-worth in small ways, such as meeting students at the door at the beginning of class. Some commercially prepared materials were used to teach lessons on affective goals directly, and these goals were also incorporated into academic lessons.

The Small Things
Count, Too

The teachers in Prawat's study worked with elementary school children and may naturally have been more focused on emotional and social development than subject specialists in high schools tend to be. The important point is the elementary teachers' belief that both psychosocial and cognitive development should receive attention in schools. In practice, it is very difficult to separate emotions from thinking.

The Whole Person

> In psychological works the distinction often made between cognitive and social-emotional processes is a simplistic convenience not in accord with actual psychological functioning. . . . This point was noted by Piaget (1967) as he discussed the inseparability of cognition and affectivity. He suggested that affectivity provides the energetic component to cognitive processes. The message behind this material is clear: the prudent educator is interested not only in cognitive processes but also in affectivity. (N. Gordon, 1981, pp. 136–137)

This argument may be a strong rationale for affective education programs, whether formal or informal. Let's now consider one of the most common formal programs for affective education, one based on Kohlberg's work.

A Formal Program: Moral Dilemmas.   Some educators believe schools should help students develop higher levels of moral reasoning. Classroom discussion of moral dilemmas similar to those Kohlberg used to analyze moral reasoning is one method for achieving this goal. The best dilemmas to discuss are those that have already come up or that are likely to arise in the class. What should be done about stealing, fist fights, or the abuse of privileges? The following is an example of how one teacher used the events of the week for discussion:

A Basis for
Discussion

> [The teacher] decided that at the end of each week the children would discuss a slice of moral life from their classroom. During the week, they were invited to complete a sentence written on a chart at the front of the room: "This was the week when _____." On Friday, the class eagerly discussed the chart's various entries: e.g., "There were fights on the morning bus," "Someone had money taken," "Mrs. _____ kept the projector too long and we couldn't see the movie because you had to send it back." . . . Talking about in-school problems led children to raise dilemmas from their lives outside school. . . . (Reimer, Paolitto, & Hersh, 1983, pp. 122–123)

During the discussion of moral dilemmas, students are likely to encounter challenges from other students that will create disequilibrium and cause them to examine their own moral reasoning. Students can certainly be helped in this way to see many sides of an issue. A broader perspective on a particular issue may help make their moral reasoning more sophisticated. Plus-One Matching A technique called "plus-one matching" is useful for encouraging more advanced reasoning by creating disequilibrium (Lockwood, 1978). With this technique, the teacher establishes the students' current level of reasoning according to Kohlberg's scheme and then presents conflicting arguments based on reasoning one stage above that of the students. Generally, however, the teacher's role is to lead the discussion. It is the students who should talk, give reasons, and respond to one another. Discussion groups should be kept small. To keep the discussion organized, you can list student opinions and reasons on the board (Lickona, 1977).

In summarizing the research on the use of moral dilemmas in the classroom, Lockwood (1978) has drawn two conclusions. First, the direct discussion approach (with or without plus-one matching) can produce significant development in moral reasoning, at least in some students. The success of

Guidelines

Affective Education Programs

Help students examine the kinds of dilemmas they are currently facing or will face in the near future.

Examples
1. *In elementary school, discuss sibling rivalries, teasing, stealing, prejudice, treatment of new students in the class, behavior toward handicapped classmates.*
2. *In high school, discuss cheating, letting friends drive when they are intoxicated, conforming to be more popular, protecting a friend who has broken a rule.*

Help students see the perspectives of others.

Examples
1. *Ask students to describe their understanding of the views of another, then have the other person confirm or correct the perception.*
2. *Have students exchange roles and try to "become" the other person in a discussion.*

Help students make connections between expressed values and actions.

Examples
1. *Follow a discussion of "What should be done?" with "How would you act? What would be your first step? What problems might arise?"*
2. *Help students see inconsistencies between their values and their own actions. Ask them to identify inconsistencies, first in others, then in themselves.*

Safeguard the privacy of all participants.

Examples
1. *Remind students that they can "pass" and not answer questions in a discussion.*
2. *Intervene if peer pressure is forcing a student to say more than he or she wants to.*
3. *Don't reinforce a pattern of telling "secrets."*

Make sure students are really listening to each other.

Examples
1. *Keep groups small.*
2. *Be a good listener yourself.*
3. *Recognize students who pay careful attention to each other.*

Make sure that as much as possible your class reflects concern for moral issues and values.

Examples
1. *Make clear distinctions between rules based on administrative convenience (keeping the room orderly) and rules based on moral issues (respecting the privacy of others).*
2. *Enforce standards uniformly. Be careful about showing favoritism.*

Adapted from J. W. Eiseman (1981), What criteria should public school moral education programs meet? The Review of Education, 7, pp. 226 – 227.

the approach seems to vary greatly from student to student. Second, changes seem most likely at Kohlberg's second and third stages. It is difficult to help students already at stage 4 or above advance further.

Where do you stand? Should moral behavior be taught in classrooms, or should it be primarily the responsibility of parents and others outside the school? Is affective education a frill or an inseparable part of all learning? If you decide to include specific lessons on personal and social development in your teaching, there are many factors to keep in mind. Several are listed in the Guidelines.

1. The work of Erik Erikson offers a comprehensive theory of emotional development from infancy through old age. According to Erikson, people go through eight stages, each of which involves a central crisis that must be resolved. Adequate resolution of the crisis leads to increased personal and social competence and a stronger foundation for resolving future crises.

2. In the first two developmental stages, according to Erikson, an infant must develop both a sense of trust and a sense of autonomy. Without these, feelings of mistrust and of shame and doubt can prevail. Research confirms the importance of trust. Secure parent-infant attachments help children become more self-reliant and better adjusted.

3. In Erikson's theory, the focus in early childhood is on development of initiative and avoidance of guilt. The elementary years bring the child to Erikson's fourth stage and are devoted to achieving a sense of industry. The danger in this stage is development of a pervasive sense of inferiority.

4. Erikson's fifth stage, identity v. role confusion, involves the adolescent's conscious attempt to solidify the identity. Adolescents have four alternatives for dealing with their search for identity: achievement, foreclosure, diffusion, and a moratorium.

5. According to Erikson, the three stages of adulthood involve struggles to achieve intimacy, generativity, and integrity.

6. Fathers and mothers interact differently with their babies. Both parents treat sons and daughters differently. Both these patterns help explain sex-role development. Since their attitudes can be influential, teachers should be careful not to reinforce sex-role stereotypes.

7. Quality day-care and preschool programs seem to have generally positive effects on emotional and intellectual development.

8. Friendships progress from play relationships based on immediate situations, through companionships based on a growing understanding of stable personal qualities, to close and psychologically supportive relationships that can be long-lasting and are tied to more abstract values.

9. In adolescence, both sexes experience a growth spurt and become sexually mature. Adolescents often face emotional struggles to cope with all these changes. Females mature about two years ahead of males. Research indicates that maturing more quickly than others in the same grade is a social advantage for boys but a social disadvantage for girls.

10. Our self-concept—our view of ourselves—becomes increasingly complex and abstract as we mature. It is not necessarily unified or stable but has many dimensions, based upon different roles in different situations.

11. Social cognition deals with our conceptions of other people. These conceptions change as we grow. Young children believe that everyone has the same thoughts and feelings they do. Later, they learn that others have separate identities and therefore separate feelings; they develop empathy, the ability to feel emotions as experienced by others.

12. Lawrence Kohlberg's theory of moral development includes three levels: (1) a preconventional level, where judgments are based on self-interest; (2) a conventional level, where judgments are based on traditional family values and social expectations; and (3) a postconventional level, where judgments are based on more abstract and personal ethical principles. One of the objections to the theory is that it may not deal adequately with the difference between moral reasoning and moral action.

13. Cheating seems widespread in schools, but it may not reflect any particular student's tendency toward dishonesty or general ability to reason or act mor-

ally. Aggression is probably learned through observation of others' behavior. Television is a prime source of aggressive models, but it is not clear to what extent TV viewing actually affects children's aggressive behavior.

14. Over the years, the focus in education has shifted back and forth. Sometimes the greater emphasis has been on cognitive goals and at other times on fostering emotional, social, and moral development (affective goals). Today's teachers, at least at the elementary school level, believe affective goals should be a part of schooling. It is difficult, if not impossible, to separate students' socioemotional development from their intellectual development.

KEY TERMS

psychosocial	identity achievement	self-concept
developmental crisis	identity foreclosure	social cognition
autonomy	identity diffusion	empathy
initiative	moratorium	moral dilemmas
industry	generativity	aggression
identity	integrity	affective education

SUGGESTIONS FOR FURTHER READING AND STUDY

ERIKSON, E. (1963). *Childhood and society* (2nd ed.). New York: W. W. Norton. In this book, which is not at all dry or "theoretical," you will find a complete description of Erikson's ideas about personal and social development.

ERIKSON, E. (1968). *Identity, youth, and crisis.* New York: W. W. Norton. If you are teaching any of the secondary grades, you may find this book on the adolescent's search for a personal identity especially rewarding.

KASH, M. M., & BORICH, G. (1978). *Teacher behavior and pupil self-concept.* Reading, MA: Addison-Wesley. This book offers a thorough look at research on how teachers can influence the self-concepts of their students. Each chapter has a list of recommendations for teachers.

MARSH, H. W., & SHAVELSON, R. (1985). Self-concept: Its multifaceted, hierarchical structure. *Educational Psychologist, 20,* 107–123. This is the latest statement of Shavelson's theory. A full understanding of the article requires a knowledge of statistics, but even without this knowledge, you can gain an appreciation of the complexity of self-concept and of one approach used to study it.

PRAWAT, R. S. (1980). Teacher perceptions of student affect. *American Educational Research Journal, 17,* 61–73. This article reports results of interviews with 84 elementary teachers who describe the role of students' emotions in significant classroom situations.

REIMER J., PAOLITTO, D. P., & HERSH, R. H. (1983). *Promoting moral development: From Piaget to Kohlberg* (2nd ed.). New York: Longman. This book has a full explanation of both Piaget's and Kohlberg's theories, plus several chapters on how to apply the theories in teaching.

RUBIN, A. (1980). *Children's friendships.* Cambridge, MA: Harvard University Press. This book is a combination of current theoretical perspectives on the development of friendships and lively examples, often in the words of the children themselves.

SADKER, M., & SADKER, D. (1985, March). Sexism in the schoolroom of the '80s. *Psychology Today,* pp. 54–57. This very readable article demonstrates that sexism is still alive and well in classrooms around America, despite the strides made by and for women during the past two decades.

THORNBURG, H. (1979). *The bubblegum years: Sticking with kids from 9–13.* Tuscon, AZ: HELP Books. This delightful book will give you a good feel for the difficult times that children face.

Teachers' Forum

Grown-up Children

Although older adolescents may appear adultlike, they sometimes lose their composure and act impulsively and childishly. What have you found to be the best ways to respond to the "no-longer-a-child, not-yet-an-adult" characteristics of high school students?

A Challenge

Honesty. Humor. Forgiveness. And by admitting to the mistakes I make. Teenagers are a challenge to work with, but they are also a lot of fun, simply because there is so much growth and change going on in their lives. It is exciting to be a part of that growth and discovery.

If an outburst disrupts class or turns ugly, I remove the student from class until the two of us can sit down together and talk about it. Once you can get beyond the anger or emotion, teenagers are usually quite reasonable.

Karen L. Eitreim, High School German Teacher
Richland High School, Richland, Washington

Knowing When to Draw the Line

Although older adolescents, even seniors, may sometimes act like children, they still want to be regarded as adults. My treatment of these grown-up children often depends on the individual and the situation. I believe that it is important to remember that sometimes even the most responsible adults may behave in a silly, childish manner. At a time like that, no one enjoys having that behavior receive full public attention in a belittling manner. Often, a few quiet words will remind the student that his or her behavior is inappropriate in a senior high classroom and should be saved for a more suitable time. On the other hand, if it seems as though the entire class is headed toward mass insurrection, a few quiet words with an individual will not work. A group of grown-up children acting like 6-year-olds can be a nonproductive situation, and the entire class must be compelled to see it as such.

Jane C. Dusell, High School English Teacher
Medford Senior High School, Medford, Wisconsin

Identity and Sex Roles

Students often have very stereotypical ideas about appropriate roles—both occupational and social—for males and females. What, if anything, do you do in your classroom to help students broaden their ideas about sex roles?

Science Is for Everyone

Although our text uses both sexes as role models for depicting careers in chemistry (which is sometimes perceived as a male profession), I have found it is very effective to use previous students as examples. During various units, topics are raised that allow me to point out how a former student has excelled in college or in a science-related career. Very often, these are relatives or neighbors of students currently taking my class. This seems to bring home the idea that in science, at least, there are no assumptions to be made on the basis of sex.

R. Chris Rohde, High School Chemistry Teacher
Chippewa Falls Senior High School, Chippewa Falls, Wisconsin

Queen Kong

Imagine that one of the students in your class is very large. In fact, she's obese. The other students are merciless in their teasing, calling her Queen Kong among many other clever but heartless names. The girl is miserable but doesn't seem to know how to make friends or cope with the teasing. She is, however, a very good student and seems very eager to please you, the teacher. What would you do to help this student? What, if anything, would you say to the rest of the class?

A Step-by-Step Approach

I would first try to help this girl gain some self-confidence by asking her to help me correct some papers or do a bulletin board display in my classroom during her free time. I would then ask her to help another student in the class who is not doing very well (peer tutoring), perhaps a girl who I know would be nice to her and who might strike up a friendship with her on the basis of mutual need. I would then plan a few small group activities in the class in which it would be advantageous to have someone who is a good student in the group. I would only say something to the class if on a given day the girl was not in class. I might point out that everyone has strong and weak points and that we should make an effort to overlook the weak points of a person, whether they be physical or personal, and admire that person for his or her strong points.

Kristine C. Bloom, High School French Teacher
Tonawanda High School, Tonawanda, New York

Tolerance and Guidance

There are two basic problems that need attention—the class's attitude and the girl's inability to cope. Class discussion and/or human relations experiments on tolerance of individual differences might be helpful. Included in this could be self-inventories and positive reactions to other individuals. Queen Kong herself needs individual guidance in coping skills. During class it might improve self-image and peer relationships if the teacher would put this student in a leadership role and provide verbal reinforcement when appropriate. A conference with the school nurse and parents might help set the scene for proper diet and weight loss over a period of time.

Darline Reynolds, Junior High School Teacher
Spirit Lake Junior High School, Spirit Lake, Iowa

Clarifying Values

You have been working with a unit on values clarification. After school one day a small group of students comes by and asks to speak with you. They seem very concerned about an issue, so you agree to take time to talk with them. They ask very directly, "Is abortion wrong? We've heard a lot about that. But we hear a lot of conflicting opinions. Who is right?"

No Absolutes

The worst thing a teacher can do is dictate values. The most effective procedure is to get the students to figure out both sides of the issue. With luck, this group will disagree within itself, giving the teacher the opening to point out that people of good will can see an issue from different viewpoints and that there is no absolute answer to the question.

I am not against giving my own opinion, but I make sure students know that it is *only* my opinion and not a direct message from Above.

Osborn Howes, Eighth-Grade English, Economics, and History Teacher
Hall School, Larkspur, California

Encouraging Personal Reflection

I would point out that on all major issues there is a divergence of opinion and that one can usually find intelligent, thoughtful, and moral people who support with conviction their positions on either side of the issue. For this reason, I would advise the students to be independent thinkers on controversial issues and encourage them to have confidence in any decision that is reached through the process of nonbiased fact-finding and careful personal reflection.

Katherine P. Stillerman, Seventh-Grade Language Arts
and Social Studies Teacher
Pine Forest Junior High School, Fayetteville, North Carolina

4

Individual
Variations

Overview
The Origin of Differences   124
Hereditary Factors   125
The Role of the Environment   126
Current Views: A Complicated Interaction   134
Individual Differences in Intelligence   135
What Does Intelligence Mean?   135
How Is Intelligence Measured?   138
What Does an IQ Score Mean?   140
Intelligence: Nature or Nurture?   142
Improving Intelligence   143
Gender and Mental Abilities   145
Age and Mental Abilities   147
Ability Grouping   148
The Question of Creativity   149
Assessing Creativity   149
Creativity in the Classroom   151
Variations in Cognitive Styles   152
Field Dependence and Independence   152
Impulsive and Reflective Styles   155
Summary/Key Terms
Suggestions for Further Reading and Study
Teachers' Forum

Every child is unique. This is a statement all educators and psychologists would affirm. But so far we have talked little about individuals. We have discussed principles of development that apply to everyone—stages, processes, conflicts, and tasks. Our development as human beings is similar in many ways—but not in every way. Even among members of the same family, there are marked contrasts in appearance, interests, abilities, and temperament. Some people learn very quickly in school. Others learn slowly or do not seem at all interested in learning. How do such wide-ranging differences originate, and what do they mean for teachers? These are the questions we will consider now.

In this chapter we will examine a controversial and unresolved issue—the roles of heredity and environment in creating differences among individuals. We will look briefly at the concept of heritability and then at the influences of social class, culture, and the family on the child, as well as the possible effects of individual children on the adults around them. Then we will focus on intellectual abilities, which vary so greatly from individual to individual and have proved so difficult to define and measure. Finally, we'll consider two other types of differences—creativity and the relatively new area of cognitive styles. Many other categories of variation exist, but these are particularly significant in classrooms.

In discussing the many ways individuals vary, I hope to communicate two important messages. First, for each individual, the combined influences of heredity and environment create a unique pattern of characteristics. The range of abilities, styles, behaviors, and characteristics that qualify as normal is enormous. Adults, particularly teachers, are often too quick to label a child as "abnormal" in some way. But most of the differences among individuals are quite normal, even though they may appear great at times. Second, not all differences in students' school performance are due to differences in intelligence or effort. Many other factors, such as cultural differences and cognitive styles, play significant roles in shaping classroom behavior and achievement.

When you complete this chapter, you should be able to do the following:

- Discuss the concept of heritability in human development.
- Discuss the roles of social class and culture in shaping similarities and differences among individuals.
- Give examples of the possible effects of different child-rearing practices.
- Begin to develop a personal concept of intelligence to aid you in your teaching.
- List five specific teaching strategies for encouraging creativity.
- Discuss the educational implications of differences in students' cognitive styles.

THE ORIGIN OF DIFFERENCES

If you look across the room in any class, you will see a host of individual differences. Even children of approximately the same age vary greatly in appearance, abilities, temperament, interests, and attitudes—to name only a few possibilities. Where do these differences come from? For centuries, there has been debate over the relative importance of nature versus nurture (or heredity versus environment) in creating human variation. Until fairly recently, it was difficult even to consider this question scientifically; little was known about *behavior genetics,* the study of genetic factors involved in characteristics such as intelligence, musical abilities, or moods. Even with modern scientific techniques, we are far from determining definite answers. The more we learn, the more complex these abilities and characteristics— and their origins—appear to be.

Hereditary Factors

heritability ratio: the proportion of a characteristic's variability attributable to genetic causes

Scientists and psychologists use the term *heritability* to discuss how much of a certain characteristic is due purely to genetic makeup. A **heritability ratio** thus expresses the proportion of a particular characteristic's variability that can be attributed to genetic causes. Heritability can vary from 0.0 (none of the variance is due to heredity) to 1.0 (all of the variance is due to heredity). As you might expect, there is seldom complete agreement on heritability ratios for humans. For example, you might see the heritability of intelligence given as .8, .7, .5, .4, or even .3, depending on who did the calculating. The size and meaning of heritability ratios for intelligence have been major controversies in psychology and education.

There are several other things to bear in mind when you encounter heritability figures (Buss & Poley, 1976). First, the figures themselves refer to the relative contribution of heredity to differences among individuals in a given population, and *not* to the specific contribution of heredity to a particular individual. To produce a given characteristic in an individual, both heredity and environment are 100 percent necessary. Second, even behavior that is 100 percent heritable may be modifiable by changes in the environment. For example, the genetic disorder commonly called PKU disease (discussed in Chapter 13) causes severe mental retardation. This retardation is completely genetic in origin, but the effects can be minimized or even eliminated if the disorder is detected early enough. So heritable does not mean unchangeable. By the same token, some learned behaviors, like regional ac-

The forces of nature and nurture can both be seen at work in that all-important influence on all of us—the family. *(Pam Hasegawa/Taurus Photos)*

cents, are sometimes almost impossible to change, so learned does not always mean changeable, either. Third, heritability is a relative concept. The ratio determined applies only to the particular population and conditions being studied. This means that comparisons across different races or very different environmental conditions may not be appropriate.

The Role of the Environment

Many environmental factors, including family income, status, cultural group, education, and the mother's health during pregnancy, influence an individual's characteristics and abilities, sometimes even before birth. In addition, every family creates a distinct environment for its members—to which they each may react quite differently.

socioeconomic status (SES): relative standing in the society based on income, power, background, and prestige

Socioeconomic Differences. The term used by sociologists for variations in wealth, power, and prestige is **socioeconomic status,** or **SES.** Most researchers identify three levels of SES—upper, middle, and lower. No single variable, not even income, is an effective measure of SES. Backman (1972) has described an index of SES that reflects father's education and occupation, mother's education, family income, the value of the home, and the specific facilities and economic goods in the home, such as televisions, radios, and typewriters. Probably the most important SES variable with regard to a child's performance in school is the level of education attained by the child's parents. This is because the more education the parents have, the more they tend to hold positive attitudes toward schooling, which they pass on to their children. That is, a high level of parental education correlates with positive attitudes toward education (Laosa, 1982, 1984).

Parents' Education

As you will see, there are many relationships between SES and individual variations. For example, it is well documented that high-SES students of all ethnic groups show higher average levels of achievement on test scores, receive better grades, and stay in school longer than low-SES students (Alwin & Thornton, 1984; Backman, 1972; White, 1982). The correlation between socioeconomic status and achievement in sixth grade is about .50 (Loehlin, Lindzey, & Spuhler, 1979).

Why might this be so? What are the effects of low status that might explain the lower school achievement of many low-SES students, aside from the obvious problems imposed by limited income? For one thing, being labeled lower-class makes life more difficult. Children of poverty often see that they cannot easily attain the advantages of their middle-class peers. Others may respond to them in terms of class rather than individual worth, and their self-esteem is likely to be affected adversely. Adjustment to school may be more difficult for these children, since schools tend to value and expect the behaviors more often taught in middle-class homes. And as we will see shortly, differences in the child-rearing styles of low-SES and high-SES parents may put these children at a disadvantage when they attempt to learn the verbal skills so necessary for success in school.

culture: the values, beliefs, attitudes, and rules that define regional, ethnic, religious, or other groups

Cultural Differences. There are many definitions of **culture.** Most include the rules, expectations, attitudes, beliefs, and values that guide behavior in a particular group of people. Groups can be defined along regional, ethnic, religious, or other lines. Culture involves a total life-style. There are many cultures, of course, in the United States. Students growing up in a small rural town in the Deep South can in many ways be considered part of a different cultural group from students in a large urban center or students in a West Coast suburb. All these individuals share many common experiences and values—this is especially true because of the influence of the mass media; but other aspects of their lives are shaped by their different cultural backgrounds.

Cultural Values in Conflict

Within cultures, similarity among members tends to be encouraged. This then reinforces the differences among cultural groups and the cultural diversity of the overall population. Each cultural group teaches its members certain "lessons" about living. Cultures differ in (1) rules for conducting interpersonal relationships; (2) orientations toward the past, present, and future and beliefs about how best to use time; (3) images of the ideal personality; (4) ideas about the relationship between humans and nature—whether humans should dominate or live in cooperation with nature; and (5) the most cherished value (Kagan, 1983; Maehr, 1974). Because of your cultural background, your views on these subjects are likely to be quite different from the views of other individuals who are also Americans.

In addition, because of these basic cultural differences, the behaviors and values a child learns at home and in the community may not fit the expectations of the school and its teachers. In general, schools expect and reward the behaviors, attitudes, and abilities fostered by white, middle-class America—the culture of most teachers. Table 4–1 presents a few examples of potential conflict. But the generalities offered here do not hold for every group

Table 4–1 **Values and Attitudes: Potential Cultural Conflicts in the Schools**

Significant Areas for All Cultures	Majority Cultural Values: The School's Expectations	Minority Cultural Values: Student Expectations
Interpersonal relationships	Competition among individuals; emphasis on individual accomplishment	Many Native American and Hispanic cultures: Mutual assistance; emphasis on group accomplishment
Orientation toward time	Planning for future; individual works for own future	Some Native American groups: Focus on present; cultural group provides for individuals' future
		Some Oriental cultures: Significance of past, tradition, ancestors
Valued personality type	Busy, occupied, efficient	Some Oriental and Hispanic cultures: Methodical, relaxed, meditative
Relationship of humanity to nature	Humans control and improve nature; focus on technology	Native American cultures: Humans at one with nature; mutual support of nature and humanity
Most cherished value	Individual freedom	Some Oriental cultures: Tradition; group loyalty

Adapted from M. L. Maehr (1974), Sociocultural origins of achievement. Monterey, CA: Brooks/Cole.

or for every individual within a group. What these comparisons should do is give you some idea of the role of culture in creating variations among individuals. As you will see in Chapter 13, there is increasing interest in valuing and preserving these differences instead of trying to create one national culture—the old idea of the "melting pot."

In discussing the effects of growing up in particular SES or cultural groups, we have actually been focusing on the variations among groups, not between individuals. But in every group there are vast differences among the individuals. Think about your own neighbors. Even though they may share your cultural and socioeconomic background, they probably differ from you in important ways. Another possible source of these differences is that smaller but very powerful group, the family.

Child-Rearing Practices. In 1965, Burton White and his colleagues at Harvard University began studying the effects of early experiences on the development of "competence" in young children (White, Kaban, Attanucci, & Shapiro, 1978). In White's definition, competence involves both social and cognitive skills, especially communication and language abilities. Competent children can secure and maintain adults' attention in reasonable, acceptable ways and can seek the right help when they recognize that a task is too difficult. They lead, follow, and compete with peers easily and are able to express both affection and annoyance with adults and peers. They tend to play make-believe games about adult roles and take pride in their accomplishments.

What kind of influence do parents have on the development of these important abilities? Potentially, a great deal, according to White, who has found that certain child-rearing practices tend to encourage competence in children. These include structuring the home environment so the child can explore freely and safely without restrictions; being sensitive to the child's needs and interests; recognizing achievement; encouraging curiosity and competitiveness; and talking to the child about topics of immediate interest (B. White, 1975; White, Kaban, Attanucci, & Shapiro, 1978). These child-rearing practices are in keeping with Erikson's descriptions of ways to encourage trust, initiative, and industry in young children.

Are there child-rearing differences among SES groups? Studies have shown that middle-class mothers talk more, give more verbal guidance, help their children understand the causes of events, make plans and anticipate consequences, direct their children's attention to the relevant details of a problem, and, rather than impose solutions, encourage children to solve problems themselves (Hess & Shipman, 1965; Willerman, 1979). By assisting their children in these ways, mothers are actually following Vygotsky's advice to provide intellectual support, or scaffolding, in the children's zone of proximal development, as we discussed in Chapter 2. Recently, Hess and McDevitt (1984) studied mothers and children over an eight-year period and found more evidence that this "teaching as opposed to telling" style often used by middle-class mothers is related to higher achievement-test scores for children from ages 4 through 12. These differences in parental interaction styles may account for some of the differences among children from various SES groups.

One of the most extensive studies of child-rearing practices has been directed by Diana Baumrind, who for two decades has studied parental disci-

Development of Competence

SES Child-Rearing Differences

Parents who help by explaining, probing, calling attention to important information, and helping their children reason are more effective than parents who simply tell them what to do. Through their help and encouragement, parents can also communicate a love of learning to their children. *(B. I. Ullmann/Taurus Photos)*

Parental Discipline Styles

pline styles. Her research has identified three parental styles—authoritative, authoritarian, and permissive. Authoritative parents are firm, demanding, and controlling but also consistent, loving, and communicative. They are willing to listen and to explain reasons for their rules. They may at times inflict punishment, but they tend to reward a child's good behavior rather than punish misbehavior. Their children tend to be content, self-reliant, and assertive, with high self-esteem. These high-achieving children cooperate well with others.

Authoritarian parents are also controlling but by contrast do not listen to their children; they are less involved, sometimes removed and cold. Punishments and orders are routine. Their children, as you might guess, are generally withdrawn and unhappy; they have trouble trusting others and are low achievers.

Permissive parents contrast with the other types by being undemanding and warm, having few rules, and avoiding punishments. They also distrust their own abilities as parents and are inconsistent as a result. Their children do not seem to learn self-reliance and tend to be unhappy; boys in particular may be low achievers (Baumrind, 1973).

Birth Order. Even within a particular family, the experiences of one child will not be like those of siblings. Research has found that quite a few of these differences are associated with birth order. For example, first-born children tend to be more adult-oriented, self-controlled, conforming, anxious, fearful of failure, studious, and passive than later-born children (Hetherington & Parke, 1979). But before you decide that first-borns are cursed by their position in the family, you should know that first-borns also tend to be high achievers. They are more likely to earn high scores on intelligence tests, receive good grades in college, be National Merit scholars, or be cited in *Who's Who* (Hilgard, Atkinson, & Atkinson, 1979).

Only Children

There are many stereotypes about only children. It is often assumed that "onlies" are more selfish, egotistical, lonely, and unsociable than children with brothers and sisters. But there is little evidence that these assumptions are true. Only children seem to have all the benefits of first-born children. In fact, as a group they are more secure, are better adjusted socially, and are higher achievers than children with siblings, even first-born children (Polit, Nuttall, & Nuttall, 1980).

The picture is less clear for later-born children. Their experiences may vary greatly, depending on the number of older and younger children and the family situation. There are tendencies for middle children to be more extroverted and less achievement-oriented than first-borns. It seems that the often-indulged "baby" of the family has many of the advantages of first-borns with few of the problems; they are high achievers, popular, and more optimistic, secure, and confident than first-borns (Hetherington & Parke, 1979). Again, of course, all these characteristics are true for large-group comparisons only; many individuals do not fit these descriptions.

Middles and Babies

Children of Divorce. Lately there has been a great deal of interest in studying the effects on children of two aspects of modern family life—divorce and the single-parent home. It is now estimated that 40 percent of current marriages of young adults will end in divorce. As noted in Chapter 1, almost 50 percent of the children born in 1970 will spend some time living in a single-parent household (Hetherington, 1979). In any given year, about 1 million children are living in families going through a divorce (Craig, 1986).

Separation and divorce are stressful events for all participants, even under the best circumstances. The actual separation of the parents may have been preceded by years of conflict in the home or may come as a shock to all, including friends and children. During the divorce itself, conflict may increase as property and custody rights are being decided. Children may have to cope with angry, tired, anxious parents.

After the divorce, more changes may disrupt the children's lives. The parent who has custody (today, as in the past, usually the mother) may have to move to a less expensive home, find new sources of income, go to work for the first time, or work longer hours. For the child, this can mean leaving behind important friendships in the old neighborhood or school, just when support is needed the most. It may mean not only having just one parent but one who has less time than ever to be with the children. Money shortages lead to fewer toys and trips and less recreation in general. To add to all these adjustments, the children may be asked to accept their parent's lover or even a new stepparent (Guerney, 1981). Not every situation is the same, of course. In some divorces there are few conflicts, ample resources, and the continuing support of friends and extended family. But divorce is never easy for anyone.

Stress of Divorce

Just as no two divorces are the same, the effects of divorce on children vary from one situation to the next. The first two years after the divorce seem to be the hardest for both boys and girls. During this time children may have problems in school, lose or gain an unusual amount of weight, develop difficulties sleeping, and so on. They may blame themselves for the breakup of their family or hold unrealistic hopes for a reconciliation (Pfeffer, 1981). Long-term adjustment appears to be more difficult for boys. They

Guidelines

Helping Children of Divorce

Take note of any sudden changes in behavior that might indicate problems at home.

Examples
1. *Be alert to physical symptoms like repeated headaches or stomach pains, rapid weight gain or loss, fatigue or excess energy.*
2. *Be aware of signs of emotional distress, like moodiness, temper tantrums, difficulty in paying attention or concentrating.*
3. *If necessary, let parents know about the student's signs of stress. They may be unaware of the effects the divorce is having on their child. Be ready to suggest sources of help (see the fifth guideline).*

Talk individually to students about their attitude or behavior changes. This may give you an opportunity to find out about unusual stresses, including divorce.

Examples
1. *Be a good listener. Students may have no other adult willing to hear their concerns.*
2. *Let students know you are available to talk. Some children, however, may be very sensitive about their personal life and resent excessive probing. Let the student set the agenda for discussions.*

Watch your language to make sure you avoid stereotypes about "happy" (two-parent) homes.

Examples
1. *You might simply say "your families" instead of "your mothers and fathers" when addressing the class.*
2. *Statements such as "We need volunteers for room mother," "Your father can help you fix it," or "Get your father to throw you some long passes" may be hard for some children to take.*

Help students maintain self-esteem.

Examples
1. *Recognize a job well done.*
2. *Make sure the student understands the assignment and can handle the workload. This is not the time to pile on new and very difficult work.*
3. *The student may be very angry at his or her parents but may direct the anger at teachers. Don't take the student's anger personally. If there is an angry outburst, let the student save face—avoid public reprimands, and don't force a public apology.*

Find out what resources are available at your school.

Examples
1. *Talk to the school psychologist, guidance counselor, social worker, or principal about students who seem to need outside help in coping with the situation.*
2. *Consider establishing a discussion group, led by a trained adult, for students going through a divorce. Often each child thinks his or her problems are unique.*

Be sensitive to both parents' rights to information.

Examples
1. *When parents have joint custody, both are entitled to receive information and attend parent-teacher conferences.*
2. *Even if one parent has custody, the noncustodial parent may still be concerned about the child's school progress. Check with your principal about state laws regarding the noncustodial parent's rights.*

tend to show a higher rate of behavior and interpersonal problems at home and in school than girls in general or boys from intact families (Hethering-ton, 1979). But living with one fairly content, if harried, parent may be better than living in a conflict-filled situation with two unhappy parents. The Guidelines on the previous page offer suggestions for helping students through this difficult time.

Mothers at Work.   More and more mothers are joining the work force. What is known about the general effects on a child of having a working mother? Research has been focusing on this question for several years. The effects seem to be more positive for daughters than for sons, especially when the mothers serve as models of independent, achieving individuals.

Mothers as Models

Reviewing the research, Lois Hoffman (1979) concluded, "Daughters of working mothers are more outgoing, independent, active, highly motivated, score higher on a variety of indices of academic achievement, and appear better adjusted on social and personality measures" (p. 864). The sons also are more independent but have slightly lower scores on intelligence tests than the sons of women who do not work. The reasons for these differences are not known.

Clearly, not every situation involving a working mother is the same. Recent studies have looked at the factors that lead to successful adjustment for children with working mothers. It appears that problems can be avoided if parents are sensitive to the special needs of their children and compensate for time away by having more high-quality direct interaction with their children when at home (L. Hoffman, 1979). But allowing for this "quality time" often proves difficult for families with many children and few financial resources. It also requires great energy.

Latchkey Children.   Another phenomenon associated with the societal trends we've been discussing is the growing number of **latchkey children.** In 1983 there were about 7 million in the United States. These children are left without adult supervision to care for themselves for some part of the workday. They are called latchkey children because they must let them-selves in when they get home from school—no adult is at home. In urban areas, self-care is second only to care by parents as an arrangement for youngsters under 14 (Strother, 1984).

latchkey children: children without adult supervision for some part of the day

We know little about the emotional or academic effects of being a latchkey child, since research in this area is just beginning. It does seem clear that children left to care for themselves, especially in urban areas, are more fear-ful than children who have adult supervision (Long & Long, 1981; National Survey of Children, 1976). Common fears involve being hurt by intruders or by siblings. Of course, much depends on the age and maturity of the child, the neighborhood, the resources available, and the child's relationship with parents.

In many areas the public schools are providing before- and after-school care for students whose parents work. Other help for latchkey children, sometimes sponsored by schools, includes seminars for parents or students about self-care skills, discussion groups for latchkey children, and telephone hotlines for children home alone who need emergency help, advice, assis-tance with homework, or just an adult's listening ear. Teachers can help by identifying the students in their classes who have to care for themselves before or after school. Then it is a good idea to explain homework assignments clearly and carefully—latchkey children will have no adult around later to help out when they get stuck on a problem. Also, you can be sensitive to the children's special needs to talk with an adult. You might ask the latchkey children in your class to help on special projects so that they each have a few minutes alone with you (Strother, 1984).

Child Abuse.   All teachers must be alert to another situation that develops in many families—child abuse. Accurate information about the number of abused children in the United States is hard to find; estimates range from 1.5 to 2 million children per year (Straus, Gelles, & Steinmetz, 1980). But most experts agree that an enormous number of cases go unreported. Children under the age of 3 and boys seem to be at greatest risk. About half of all abusive parents could change their destructive behavior patterns if they received help. But without assistance, probably only about 5 percent of abusing parents improve (Starr, 1979). Of course, parents are not the only people who have been known to abuse children. Siblings, other relatives, and even teachers have been responsible for the physical and sexual abuse of children.

Teachers'
Responsibilities

As a teacher, you must alert your principal, school psychologist, or social worker if you suspect abuse. In all 50 states of America, the District of Columbia, and the U.S. territories, the law *requires* certain professionals, often including teachers, to report suspected cases of child abuse. The legal definition of abuse has been broadened in many states to include neglect and failure to provide proper care and supervision. Most laws also protect teachers who report suspected neglect in good faith (Beezer, 1985). Be sure to understand the laws in your state on this important issue—as well as your own moral responsibility. Approximately 2,000 children die each year, in many cases because no one would "get involved."

Causes of Abuse

The causes of child abuse are complex. The child may be disappointing to the parents (the wrong sex, unattractive, unhealthy, or slow to develop). Parents with unrealistic expectations about how children should behave and people who were disciplined harshly themselves are most likely to lash out against their own children (Berger, 1980). Parents who are inconsistent or unable to agree about how to manage their children may create more discipline problems and then punish the children far too harshly or inappropriately. Too often parents attribute adult motivations to the child's behavior, assuming the child is intentionally being difficult, when in fact the child simply does not understand what is expected.

However, the child's behavior may play a role, too, even though he or she does not mean to be irritating. Often parents who abuse their child say the child drove them to the beatings by being annoying or persistent, crying loudly or otherwise "misbehaving." There is evidence that certain abused children may in fact be especially difficult: even when these children are placed in foster homes, they tend to be abused by foster parents who have not treated children improperly before (Bell, 1979).

We have discussed the effects of many hereditary and environmental factors on children. Now let's try to put these influences together in a more integrated view of the origin of individual differences.

Current Views: A Complicated Interaction

Methods of studying individual differences have been problematic. Heredity and environment are correlated; it is difficult to separate these closely interwoven strands. High-ability parents tend to give their children a richer, more stimulating environment. Musically talented parents, for example, often provide an environment filled with opportunities to hear and learn about music. Low-ability parents, on the other hand, tend to create less intellectually stimulating environments for their children.

Can We Really Separate the Strands?

To put it simply, human beings are complicated. They are influenced by their environment but also create and shape that environment. The effects of experiences depend on how long the experiences last, what happens afterward, and the meaning of the events to the individual. Timing is a key factor as well. A current burning interest will cause one child to make the most of a particular experience when others remain unaffected. A book about the stars for my daughter, bought after a trip to a planetarium, was read with excitement. A similar book received earlier was never opened.

The temperament of each child (which we know to be biologically determined to a great extent) may influence not only how parents treat the child but also how much this treatment will affect the child. Parents of passive children, for example, may become very protective, particularly with young boys who appear more vulnerable in the rough world of other preschool boys. Thus, a largely biologically determined characteristic (passive temperament) helps create a particular environment (protective parenting) that can have lasting effects (Kagan, 1979). And these effects may be even stronger because of the original temperament.

Children can have effects on teachers as well as on parents. For example, students who express positive attitudes nonverbally—by smiling, nodding at the teacher, and paying attention—are more likely to be seen by the teacher as interested and intelligent. The teacher may feel and act more positively toward them and see them as more "teachable" (Woolfolk & Brooks, 1983, in press). These students help to create warm, supportive environments for themselves in school.

Children Affect Adults, Too

The research on the effects of children on adults has several implications. First, it shows one way heredity and environment interact to produce individual differences. Second, it removes from parents and teachers some of the pressure to create perfect children by always implementing the "right" child-rearing or teaching strategy. Parents and teachers are not sculptors working with a lump of clay; they are not solely responsible for the product. Many factors influence each child's development—friends, the media, culture, nutrition, health or illness, to name just a few. Parent and child are two powerful human beings, negotiating their relationship day-to-day. Their goals are seldom the same.

Parents and teachers must be sensitive to the differences among children and their needs, as well as the differences between the needs of children and adults. But adults must also have the courage to face conflict and set limits. Baumrind's years of research on child-rearing demonstrate that adult guidance and control are necessary; recall that the firm, consistent approach of the authoritative parents tended to produce happier children. This is because, as Bell (1979) has written, "friction and conflict characterize optimal child-rearing situations" (p. 825). Consistent rules help steer us

In every class there is likely to be a wide range of values, abilities, interests, and temperaments. Teachers must be sensitive to all the differences—and to each individual's potential. *(Laimute E. Druskis)*

through. Great affection is also necessary. Teachers, like parents, must have the energy and courage to face different and developing individuals.

INDIVIDUAL DIFFERENCES IN INTELLIGENCE

intelligence:
ability or abilities to acquire and use knowledge for solving problems and adapting to the world

Because the concept of **intelligence** is so important in education, so controversial, and so often misunderstood, we will spend quite a few pages discussing it. We begin with a basic question.

What Does Intelligence Mean?

The idea that people vary in what we call intelligence has been with us for a long time. Plato discussed similar variations over 2,000 years ago. Most early theories about the basic nature of intelligence involved one or all of the following three themes: (1) the capacity to learn; (2) the total knowledge a person has acquired; and (3) the ability to adapt successfully to new situations and to the environment in general (Robinson & Robinson, 1976).

In this century, there has been considerable controversy over the meaning of intelligence. In 1921, 14 psychologists offered 14 different views about the nature of intelligence in a symposium on the subject, reported in the *Journal of Educational Psychology* (Neiser, 1979). Today opinion is still divided. A few psychologists believe that intelligence is nothing more than a label used to describe the skills measured by intelligence tests. In other words, intelligence is what intelligence tests measure. Other psychologists believe intelligence is much more than simply what it takes to do well on IQ tests.

They link intelligence to successful coping in the world. David Wechsler, who was responsible for three of the most frequently used individual intelligence tests, defined intelligence as "the aggregate or global capacity of the individual to act purposefully, to think rationally, and to deal effectively with his environment" (Wechsler, 1958, p. 7). This brings us to a central question about intelligence. Is it a general quality or a collection of many specific abilities?

Intelligence: One Ability or Many? Wechsler's use of the phrase "aggregate or global capacity" reflects an important and unresolved issue concerning the nature of intelligence. Some theorists believe intelligence is a basic ability that affects performance on all cognitively oriented tasks. An "intelligent" person will do well in computing mathematical problems, in analyzing poetry, in taking history essay examinations, and in solving riddles. Evidence for this position comes from correlational evaluations of intelligence tests. In study after study, moderate to high positive correlations are found among all the different tests that are designed to measure separate intellectual abilities (McNemar, 1964). But the correlations are not perfect. For example, the correlation between children's scores on one particular vocabulary test and scores on a test of facts and knowledge is .69. Scores on the same vocabulary test correlate only .38 with performance on a test of memory for a series of numbers. The vocabulary and memory scores are still related, but the relationship is not as strong (Wechsler, 1974). What could explain these results?

Correlations among Abilities

Several approaches have been taken to explain the persistent but less than perfect relationships among abilities to perform various types of mental tasks. Charles Spearman (1927) suggested there was one factor or mental attribute, which he called *g* or general intelligence, that was used to perform any mental test. But the *g* factor alone could not explain performance on *all* mental tests because the correlation among test scores was not perfect. So Spearman suggested that each test required some specific abilities in addition to *g* or the general ability. For example, performance on a test of memory for numbers probably involves both *g* and some specific ability for immediate recall of what is heard. Spearman assumed that individuals varied in both general intelligence and specific abilities and that together these factors determined performance on mental tasks.

Critics of Spearman's position insisted that there were several "primary mental abilities," not just one. Thurstone (1938) listed verbal comprehension, memory, reasoning, ability to visualize spatial relationships, numerical ability, word fluency, and perceptual speed as the major mental abilities underlying intellectual tasks. But tests of these "separate" factors showed that ability in one area was correlated with ability in the others. Even though people tended to perform better on some tests than on others, in general those who received high scores on the reasoning test did pretty well on the test of spatial relations, while low scores on the verbal test tended to go along with low scores in numerical ability, word fluency, and so on.

faces of intellect: in Guilford's theory, the three basic categories of thinking— operations, contents, and products

J. P. Guilford (1967) and Howard Gardner (1983) are the most prominent modern proponents of multiple cognitive abilities. Guilford has suggested that there are three basic categories, or **faces of intellect:** *mental operations,* or the processes of thinking; *contents,* or what we think about; and *products,* or the end results of our thinking. Mental operations are divided into five different subcategories: cognition (recognizing old information and discovering new), convergent thinking (where there is only one answer or solution), divergent thinking (used when many answers may be appropriate), evaluation (decisions about how good, accurate, or suitable something is), and finally, memory. The contents on which people operate are divided into four subcategories: visual figures, word meanings, symbols, and behaviors. The different products that may result are divided into six subcategories: units, classes, relations, systems, transformations, and implications. (Are you still there?)

120 Different Abilities

Think for a minute about how many combinations of operations, contents, and products there are. As you may have calculated, there are 120, or $5 \times 4 \times 6$. Guilford contends that each of us varies in our competence in each of the 120 abilities. Tests have been developed for many of the 120 areas, but some of the abilities still exist only in theory.

According to this view, carrying out a cognitive task is essentially performing a mental operation with some specific content to achieve a product. For example, listing the next number in the sequence 3, 6, 12, 24, . . . requires a convergent operation (there is only one right answer) with symbolic content (numbers) to achieve a relationship product (each number is double the one before).

Guilford's model of intelligence has several advantages as well as one major drawback. The model broadens our view of the nature of intelligence by adding such factors as those related to social judgment (the evaluation of others' behavior) and creativity (divergent thinking) (Gleitman, 1986). We will discuss the latter contribution later in this chapter. Certainly human mental abilities must be complex, but Guilford's model may be too complex to serve as a guide for predicting behavior in real situations or for planning instruction. In addition, the problem of explaining the persistent correlations among all these "separate" mental abilities remains.

Howard Gardner (1983) has proposed a "theory of multiple intelligences." According to Gardner, there are at least seven separate kinds of intelligence: linguistic (verbal), musical, spatial, logical-mathematical, bodily, knowledge of self, and understanding of others. Gardner has based his notion of separate abilities in part on evidence that brain damage, from a stroke for example, often interferes with functioning in one area like language but does not affect functioning in other areas. Gardner has also noted that individuals often excel in one of these seven areas but have no remarkable abilities in the other six.

A Components View of Intelligence.   In the past few years, psychologists have looked to research on cognitive development and information processing for guidance in understanding intelligence. Some psychologists have focused on the mental processes that people use to solve problems, both on intelligence tests and in life. Based on this work, a new way of looking at intelligence is emerging. One approach describes the mental processes that are involved in intelligent performance in terms of **components.** A component is "an elementary information process that operates upon internal representations of objects or symbols" (Sternberg, 1985, p. 97). Components are classified by the functions they serve and by how general they are. There are at least three different functions served. The first function—higher-order planning, strategy selection, and monitoring—is performed by *metacompo-*

components: in an information processing view, basic problem-solving processes underlying intelligence

nents. Examples of metacomponents are identifying the problem, allocating attention, and monitoring how well a particular strategy is working. Another name for the function served by metacomponents is metacognition, as you saw in Chapter 2. A second function served by components—executing the strategies selected—is handled by *performance components*. One performance component allows us to perceive and store new information. The third function—gaining new knowledge—is performed by *knowledge-acquisition components,* such as separating relevant from irrelevant information as you try to understand a new concept (Sternberg, 1985).

Some components are specific; they are necessary for one kind of task but not for others. For example, to solve verbal analogies you must be able to infer the relationship between the words involved, but no inference is required to do arithmetic computations. Other components are very general and may be necessary in almost every cognitive task. For example, metacomponents are always operating to select strategies and keep track of progress. This may help to explain the persistent correlations among all types of mental tests. People who are effective in selecting good problem-solving strategies, monitoring progress, and moving to a new approach when the first one fails are more likely to be successful on all types of tests. Individuals who are weaker in these metacomponents will have trouble with a wide range of tasks, from verbal analogies to arithmetic computations. Metacomponents may be the modern-day version of Spearman's *g.* We will discuss information processing and the development of metacognitive strategies further in Chapters 7 and 8.

General and Specific Components

Although the components view of intelligence is controversial, it does suggest a way to relate mental abilities to one another and to the thinking processes underlying these abilities. Research in the next decade should provide exciting clues to our understanding of what may be involved in intelligence and intelligent actions. By understanding exactly what people do when they solve problems well or creatively, we should be able to help all students behave in more "intelligent" ways.

Even though psychologists do not agree about what intelligence is, they do agree that intelligence, as measured by standard tests, is related to learning in school. In fact, scores on intelligence tests predict school achievement quite well. What do these tests involve?

How Is Intelligence Measured?

A brief history of intelligence testing should give you some insight into the reasons intelligence is measured as it is today.

Binet's Dilemma.   In 1904, Alfred Binet was confronted with the following problem by the minister of public instruction in Paris: How can students who will need special teaching and extra help be identified early in their school careers, before they fail in regular classes? At the time, many of these students, who are now called mentally retarded, were likely to spend several years in regular classes, falling farther and farther behind, when they might have been in classes designed to meet their needs. Binet's task was to devise some way to identify these students. Binet was also very concerned with the rights of children. He believed that having an objective measure of learning ability might protect other students, particularly those from poor families, who might be forced to leave school because they were the victims of discrimination and assumed to be slow learners.

Binet and his collaborator Théophile Simon wanted to measure the intellectual skills students needed to do well in school, not merely school achievement. They searched first for test items that could discriminate between students who were doing well and students of the same age who were doing poorly. They tested students in regular schools and students of the same age in institutions for the retarded and then compared the results. After trying many different types of test items, Binet and Simon finally identified 58, several for each age group from 3 to 13.

Binet and Simon devised an ingenious system for clustering the tests by age group. They based this system on the straightforward idea that children's mental abilities increase with age. If an item was successfully completed by 60 to 90 percent of all 6-year-old children tested, for example, that item was placed at the 6-year level. A child who succeeded on all the 6-year items was considered to have a **mental age** of 6, whether the child was actually 5, 6, or 7 years old. A child who succeeded on some of the items for 5-year-olds, some for 6-year-olds, and some for 7-year-olds might also earn a mental age of 6 overall.

The concept of **intelligence quotient** or **IQ** was added after the test was brought to the United States and revised at Stanford University to give us the Stanford-Binet test. An IQ score was computed by comparing the mental-age score to the person's actual chronological age. The formula was

$$\text{intelligence quotient} = \frac{\text{mental age}}{\text{chronological age}} \times 100$$

The early Stanford-Binet has been revised four times, most recently in 1986 (Thorndike, Hagan, & Sattler, 1986). The practice of computing a mental age proved problematic. As children grow older, the range and variability of mental ages increase. By ages 13 or 14, the variability of mental ages in a large sample of students is much greater than it was when the same children were 3 or 4. For this reason, IQ scores calculated based on mental age do not have the same meaning at every age. To cope with this problem, the concept of **deviation IQ** was introduced. The deviation IQ score is a number that tells exactly how much above or below the average a person scored on the test, compared to others in the age group. The different rates of growth at different ages, the changes in the variabilities in mental age, and individual differences in development are taken into account by basing the score on the standard deviation for each age group. We will discuss this idea more fully in Chapter 14.

The Wechsler Scales. A second series of intelligence tests has been developed by David Wechsler. Like the Stanford-Binet, the Wechsler Scales must be given individually by a trained professional. Each takes one to two hours to complete. Wechsler devised three scales: the Wechsler Adult Intelligence Scale (WAIS-R, the revised version), the Wechsler Intelligence Scale for Children (WISC-R, the revised version), and the Wechsler Preschool and Primary Scale of Intelligence (WPPSI).

All three of these tests are designed to measure both verbal and perfor-

mental age: in intelligence testing, a score based on average abilities for that age group

intelligence quotient (IQ): score comparing mental and chronological ages

deviation IQ: score based on statistical comparison of individual's performance with the performance of others in that age group

mance (or visual-conceptual) intelligence. The verbal tests ask you to define words, answer factual questions, solve arithmetic problems without pencil and paper, and perform several other tasks that require you to understand and use words. The performance tests involve identifying the missing part in a picture, assembling puzzles, copying symbols quickly, arranging pictures to tell a story, and completing other tasks that require no verbal response. But the separation into the verbal and performance categories is not perfect. Verbal skills are needed to understand the directions for the performance items and to complete the test successfully.

Verbal and Conceptual Abilities

Higher scores on both scales also depend, in part, on the ability to work quickly. Many of the tests on both the performance and verbal scales are timed. Students' scores suffer if they do not work well under time pressure or if poor motor coordination slows them down when working with the performance scale materials. In a later section we will discuss some additional reasons why some students, especially nonnative English speakers and minority students, may have difficulties with the questions on intelligence tests.

Items from Intelligence Tests.   In order to get a better feel for what intelligence tests measure, let's examine some questions you might be asked on these tests. Figure 4–1 shows several examples taken from Morris (1985).

Group vs. Individual IQ Tests.   Some of you may have taken an individual intelligence test like the Stanford-Binet or one of the Wechsler Scales. Probably, however, you were given a group intelligence test with many other students. A group test is much less likely to yield an accurate picture of any individual's abilities. When students take tests in a group, they may do poorly because they do not understand the instructions, because their pencil breaks, because they are distracted by other students, or because they do not shine on paper-and-pencil tests. Most of the questions on an individual test are asked orally and do not require reading or writing. On an individual test, a student can usually pay closer attention, be less distracted, and be more motivated to do well, since an adult is working directly with the student. As a teacher, you should be very wary of IQ scores based upon group tests.

Unreliability of Group Tests

Now, let's turn to a brief look at how test scores are interpreted. (We will discuss the meaning of scores on standardized tests in detail in Chapter 14.)

What Does an IQ Score Mean?

Individual intelligence tests are designed so that they have certain statistical characteristics. Like the college entrance examinations, intelligence tests have a standard average score. For IQ tests, the average score is 100. Fifty percent of the people from the general population who take the tests will score 100 or below and 50 percent will score above. About 68 percent of the general population will earn IQ scores between 85 and 115. Only about 16 percent of the population will receive scores below 85, and only 16 percent will score above 115. Note, however, that these figures hold true for white, native-born Americans whose first language was standard English. As you will see later, the numbers may not be appropriate guides for evaluating scores of other groups of students.

Figure 4–1 **Items from Intelligence Tests**

1. Describe the difference between laziness and idleness.

2. Which direction would you have to face so your right hand would be toward the north?

3. In what way are an *hour* and a *week* alike?

4. Select the item that completes the series of four figures below:

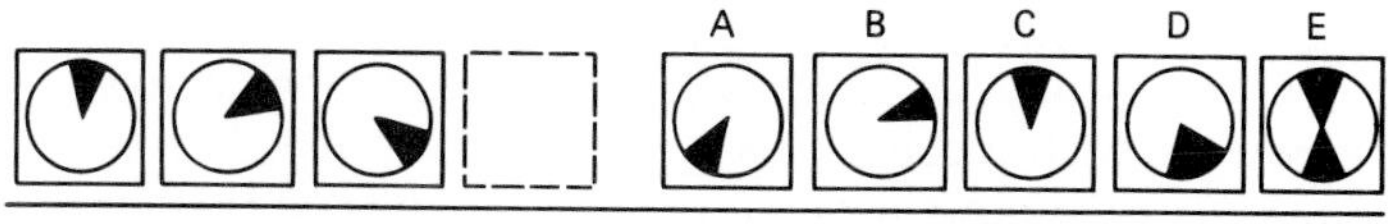

5. Choose the lettered block that best completes the pattern in Figure 1.

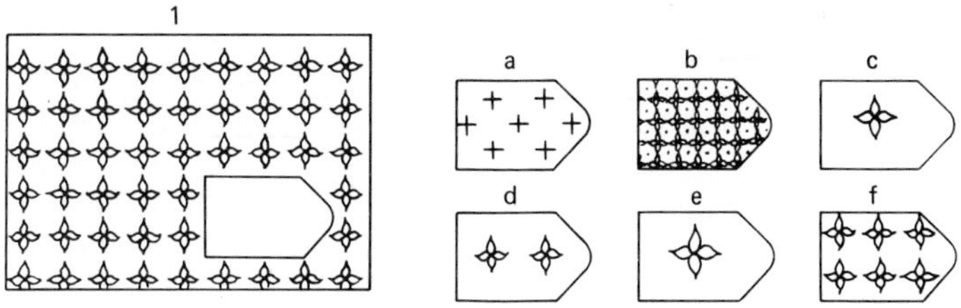

6. The opposite of hate is:
   (a) enemy (b) fear (c) love (d) friend (e) joy

7. If 3 pencils cost 25 cents, how many pencils can be bought for 75 cents?

8. Choose the set of words that, when inserted in the sentence, *best* fits in with the meaning of the sentence as a whole:

   From the first, the islanders, despite an outward ____ , did what they could to ____ the ruthless occupying power.
   (a) harmony . . . assist (b) enmity . . . embarrass (c) rebellion . . . foil
   (d) resistance . . . destroy (e) acquiescence . . . thwart

9. Select the lettered pair that best expresses a relationship similar to that expressed in the original pair:

   CRUTCH: LOCOMOTION   (a) paddle: canoe
   (b) hero: worship (c) horse: carriage (d) spectacles: vision
   (e) statement: contention

10. The first three figures are alike in some way. Find the figure at the right that goes with the first three.

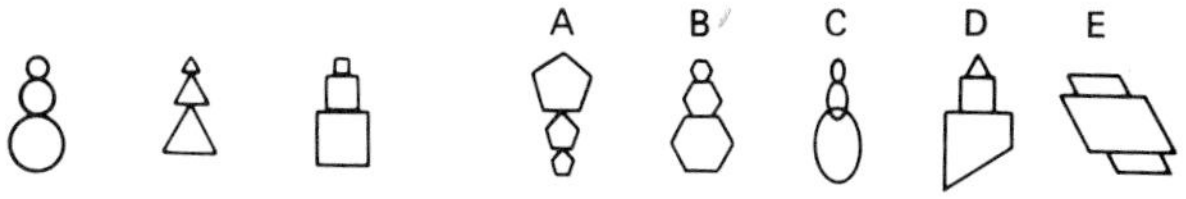

11. For each figure, decide whether or not it can be completely covered by using all the given blue pieces without any overlapping.

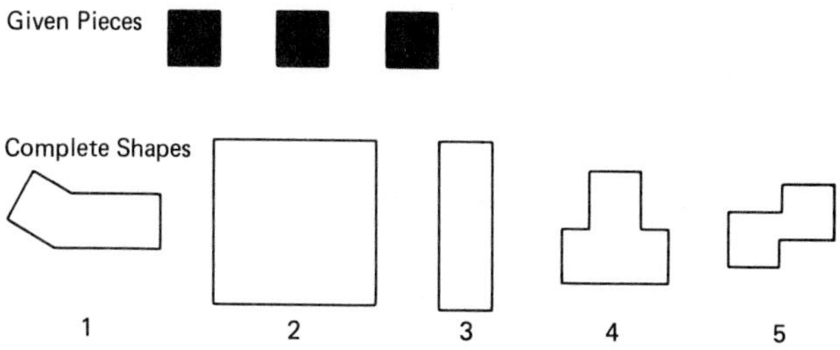

Charles G. Morris, Psychology: An Introduction. © *1985, pp. 273, 274. Adapted by permission of Prentice-Hall, Englewood Cliffs, New Jersey.*

People often wonder what IQ scores mean in terms of future achievement. Intelligence test scores predict achievement in schools quite well, at least for large groups. The correlation between performance on the WISC-R and on school achievement tests, for example, is about .65 (Sattler, 1982). But do people who score high on IQ tests achieve more in life? Here the answer is less clear. It appears that when the number of years of education is held constant, IQ scores and school achievement are not highly correlated with income and success in later life. If you complete college, your chances of doing well in your career in comparison to your classmates cannot be predicted accurately from your scores on IQ tests (McClelland, 1973). Within a given type of job, success does not seem to be related to measured intelligence (Jencks et al., 1972). Other factors like motivation, social skills, and luck may make the difference. However, the average IQ scores of members of different occupations vary quite a bit. The highest average scores are found among top civil servants, professors, and research scientists and the lowest average scores in occupations such as unskilled labor. But within every group there are individuals with higher and lower scores (Sattler, 1982).

IQ Scores and Success in Life?

This brings us to a very important question. How much can intelligence be influenced by education and other aspects of the environment?

Intelligence: Nature or Nurture?

Nowhere, perhaps, has the nature versus nurture debate raged so hard as in the area of intelligence. The main topic of controversy is whether intelligence should be seen as innately limited or as an ever-improvable, ever-expandable achievement. In other words, is intelligence a potential, limited by our genetic makeup, that once fulfilled cannot be exceeded? Or does it simply refer to an individual's current level of intellectual functioning, as fed and influenced by experience and education?

As with any issue of heritability in people, it is almost impossible to separate intelligence "in the genes" from intelligence "due to experience." Intelligence, in fact, seems even more complicated than other variable characteristics. Mental abilities, to the extent that they are determined by heredity, are **polygenetic,** or influenced by many sets of genes. There is no simple relationship like that found with some physical traits like eye color or blood type. Despite much debate, however, most experts would agree that the heritability of human intelligence in modern, industrialized countries is somewhere between .4 to .8 (Gleitman, 1986).

polygenetic:
influenced by more than one set of genes

So what can we conclude about intellectual abilities? Abilities as measured by standard IQ tests seem to be strongly influenced by heredity, but what people do with these abilities, their level of achievement, seems very much influenced by environment. As a teacher, it is especially important for you to realize that cognitive skills, like any other skills, are always improvable. Intelligence is a current state of affairs, affected by past experiences and open to future changes—probably within limits, but limits that are not yet fully understood. Even if intelligence is a limited potential, that potential is still quite large, and a challenge to all teachers.

There is another problem with IQ testing that has added considerably to the controversy. Students from lower socioeconomic classes tend to score lower on mental abilities tests than middle- and upper-class students do, regardless of ethnicity. But black students, on the average, score below Hispanics, who score below whites, who score below Orientals. The average difference between blacks and whites on most measures of intelligence is around 15 points (Loehlin, Lindzey, & Spuhler, 1979). Few psychologists dispute the existence of these differences in performance, but there is great disagreement about the cause of the differences and what they really mean.

Effects of Genetic Differences

Because there is evidence that intellectual abilities are determined, in part, by heredity, some psychologists have suggested that these differences among groups on average test scores indicate genetic differences. Other psychologists point out that an estimate of the heritability of any characteristic *within* a particular group does not tell us anything about differences *between* groups unless environmental conditions have been identical for both groups. Given the very different economic, social, and educational conditions that historically have affected many racial and ethnic groups, the influence of genetic differences is probably small compared to the influence of culture and experience (Scarr & Carter-Saltzman, 1982; Vernon, 1979).

A third explanation for the differences among various groups in measured intelligence is that the tests themselves are biased against minorities. We will examine this last suggestion more thoroughly in Chapter 14 when we discuss factors that influence standardized test results.

Focus on the Individual

No matter what the explanation for differences in IQ scores, there is extensive overlap in the distribution of scores for blacks and whites. Many black students will have IQ scores above the mean for white students, and many white students will have IQ scores below the mean for black students. Since you will teach individual students and not the whole population, you should avoid making predictions about the abilities of any one student based on social class, race, or ethnicity. The range of abilities is much greater within each racial or ethnic group than between groups. In the end, since the goal of education is to help students move forward no matter what the state or level of their intellectual abilities, it really does not matter what proportion of those abilities is determined by heredity or environment or both. The crucial question is how you help your students learn. The Guidelines on the next page should be of help not only in dealing with this particular issue but also in interpreting IQ scores in general.

Improving Intelligence

In light of the differences in test scores among ethnic groups, several educators and psychologists have attempted to design educational programs that would eliminate these discrepancies. Have they been successful? The answer appears to depend on how you define success.

Raising IQs of Poor Children

Craig Ramey and Ron Haskins (1981a, 1981b) examined the possibility of improving IQ scores for children from very poor homes whose mothers' average IQ was around 82. Given the home conditions and the mothers' IQ, chances were considered good that the measured intelligence of these children would be below normal. The project began when the infants were 4 months old or younger. All children in the study received improved nutrition, health care, and social services. Half the children, chosen at random, also attended a specially designed, intensive educational program every day. At ages 2, 3, 4, and 5 years, the average IQ score of the children in the

Guidelines

Interpreting IQ Scores

Check to see if the score is based on an individual or a group test. Be wary of group test scores.

Examples
1. *Individual tests include the Wechsler Scales (WPPSI, WISC-R, WAIS-R), the Stanford-Binet, the McCarthy Scales of Children's Abilities, the Woodcock-Johnson Psycho-Educational Battery, and the Kaufman Assessment Battery for Children.*
2. *Group tests include the Lorge-Thorndike Intelligence Tests, the Analysis of Learning Potential, the Kuhlman-Anderson Intelligence Tests, the Otis-Lennon Mental Abilities Tests, and the School and College Ability Tests (SCAT).*

Remember that IQ tests are only estimates of general aptitude for learning.

Examples
1. *Ignore small differences in scores among students.*
2. *Bear in mind that even an individual student's scores may change over time due to many causes, including measurement error.*
3. *Be aware that a total score is usually an average of scores on several kinds of questions. A score in the middle or average range may mean that the student performed at the average on every kind of question, or that the student did quite well in some areas (for example, on verbal tasks) and rather poorly in other areas (for example, on quantitative tasks).*

Remember that IQ scores reflect a student's past experiences and learning.

Examples
1. *Consider these scores as predictors of school abilities, not measures of innate intellectual abilities.*
2. *If a student is doing well in your class, do not change your opinion or lower your expectations just because one score seems low.*
3. *Be wary of IQ scores for minority students and for students whose first language was not English. Even scores on "culture-free" tests are lower for disadvantaged students.*

---

educational program was significantly higher than the average score of the children who were reared at home.

Other studies have shown dramatic improvements of 30 to 40 IQ points for children from orphanages and other deprived situations (Hunt, 1981). But these differences seem to fade as the children progress through school. By the time they reach junior or senior high and often earlier, the children who participated in the early educational programs have the same average IQ scores as peers who had no special teaching (Jensen, 1981). However, the children who completed many of the programs have shown some long-term gains. They have tended to make better grades, to be held back less often, and to need fewer remedial services (Berrueta-Clement et al., 1984; Lazar & Darlington, 1982; Ramey & Haskins, 1981b).

Here again, we can draw a few conclusions. In the normal course of development, intelligence, as measured by IQ tests, can be changed and often is. Without participating in any special program, one out of seven middle-class children in a 15-year study changed 40 points or more in IQ between ages 2 1/2 and 17 (McCall, 1981). Even if the heritability of intelligence is .8, as some suggest, IQ changes of up to 45 points could follow from alterations in environmental conditions (Jensen, 1981). Changes this great may be possible only if children are moved from very deprived to very enriched environments. If special teaching methods and enrichment do not continue throughout school, the IQ gains of high-risk children probably will not hold up. Other types of gains do seem to last.

There is another question about group differences in intelligence that has been debated recently—are there gender differences in mental abilities?

Gender and Mental Abilities

From infancy through the preschool years, most studies find few differences between boys and girls in mental and motor development generally or in specific abilities. When any differences are noted, they usually favor girls but are quite small (Willerman, 1979). For example, girls in these early years may have an edge in verbal skills.

During the school years and beyond, psychologists find no differences in general intelligence on the standard measures, but these tests have been designed and standardized to minimize sex differences. Usually items that favor one sex are eliminated or balanced by adding an equal number of items that favor the other sex. But even though the overall IQ scores of males and females are not significantly different on the average, scores on several subtests show sex differences. For example, on the WAIS, Matarazzo

In some schools there are no differences in mathematics or science achievement between males and females. Teachers in these schools have a strong background in both areas and emphasize abstract reasoning in all their classes and with all their students. *(Alec Duncan/Taurus Photos)*

(1972) found that men performed significantly better on the arithmetic test, whereas women were superior on a test requiring them to copy symbols quickly and accurately. Maccoby and Jacklin (1974) have also reported the following well-documented differences in school-aged children: (1) girls excel in verbal ability, particularly after the onset of adolescence; (2) boys show better performance on visual and spatial tasks; (3) boys are superior in mathematical performance.

It is important to realize that the differences between the average scores of boys and girls on tests of verbal, spatial, and mathematical ability, though significant statistically, appear to be rather small in size (Hyde, 1981). And not all psychologists agree that these differences have been conclusively demonstrated. The contention of male superiority in mathematical ability has been a frequent target for debate. Some researchers have found girls to be better than boys on some kinds of problems—for example, on computational problems and logical, abstract problems—while boys do better than girls on other kinds of problems—for example, story problems and spatial relations problems (Marshall, 1984; Pattison & Grieve, 1984).

Do More Math Courses Make the Difference?

One controversial question is whether boys are better in mathematics because they take more math courses than girls. There appear to be few or no differences between boys and girls in math achievement at the beginning of high school. But during high school, girls take fewer math courses (Pallas & Alexander, 1983). As soon as mathematics courses become optional, many girls avoid them. Thus, girls tend not to develop their abilities in this area and in the process limit their college and career choices, since colleges require applicants to possess some proficiency in mathematics and many jobs demand abilities in this area as well. There is mounting evidence that the differences between boys and girls in math achievement decrease substantially or disappear altogether when the actual number of previous math courses taken by each student is considered (Fennema & Sherman, 1977; Pallas & Alexander, 1983). But other researchers have reported that high-ability boys are superior in mathematics reasoning to high-ability girls, even when participation in previous math courses is taken into account (Benbow & Stanley, 1980, 1983; Kolata, 1980).

We don't know what the situation would be like if all students, boys and girls, received appropriate instruction and encouragement in math. For example, Patricia Casserly of the Educational Testing Service has studied 20 high schools where no sex differences are found in mathematics performance. Even though the schools are not alike in all ways, they share several common features. The teachers have strong backgrounds in mathematics, engineering, or science, not just in general education. They are enthusiastic about mathematics. The brightest students, male and female, are grouped together for instruction in math, and there is heavy emphasis on reasoning in the classes (Kolata, 1980). The activities used to teach math may make a difference as well. Elementary-aged girls may do better in math if they learn in cooperative as opposed to competitive activities; boys may do a bit better in competitive activities. Certainly it makes sense to balance both kinds of approaches so that students who learn better each way have equal opportunities (Peterson & Fennema, 1985).

Emphasizing Reasoning, Balancing Approaches

It is possible that there are biologically based sex differences in specific mental abilities. But a wide range of abilities occurs in both groups. Even if boys did have an edge in mathematics as a group, this wouldn't mean that

© 1986 Joel Pett in the
Kappan.

"So according to the stereotype, you *can put two and two together, but* I *can read
the handwriting on the wall."*

all boys would be superior to all girls. In every class there will be many girls
with excellent potential for mathematics and many boys who have great
difficulty.

Age and Mental Abilities

As the number of older people in our society increases, interest grows in
studying the changing pattern of mental abilities across the life span. There
are many myths about the effects of aging on intellectual performance. As a
result of early research, most psychologists assumed that intelligence increased throughout childhood, peaked in adolescence or early adulthood,
and declined from then on (Papalia & Olds, 1981). This conclusion has been
criticized because it is based on comparisons of the test performances of
younger and older people. Since these groups may have had very different
experiences, the lower IQ scores found for the older group may not represent any decline with age. For example, the older group probably had less
education, on the average, and poorer health care in childhood. Critics suggest that the same people must be tested from childhood through old age to
see if a decline in intelligence actually occurs for most people. Studies of this
type, called **longitudinal studies,** often have found no decrease in IQ. But
the issue is more complicated than the question of decline versus no decline.
It is likely that different types of abilities are affected in different ways by
aging.

    One concept that may be helpful in understanding the changes in intelli-
gence that come with age is the distinction between fluid and crystallized
intelligence (Cattell, 1963). **Fluid intelligence** involves many basic processes
such as reasoning, forming concepts, drawing inferences, and dealing with
abstractions. The main characteristic of fluid intelligence is that it is not dependent on formal education; it is sometimes considered the basic ability to
solve new or unpracticed problems without formal training. Development

longitudinal study:
study of people over
a period of time

fluid intelligence:
basic thinking
abilities that
develop without
formal training and
decline with age

of fluid abilities seems closely allied to the development of the brain and nervous system and is influenced by experiences that directly affect this system, such as early nutrition and disease (Horn & Donaldson, 1980). Injury to the system and deterioration in later life result in deterioration in fluid abilities (Havighurst, 1981).

Crystallized intelligence is made up of those abilities that are highly valued and directly taught by the culture. Reading comprehension, a command of vocabulary, general knowledge, making change, balancing a checkbook, taking tests, and appropriate behavior in a religious service are examples of crystallized abilities in our culture (Horn & Donaldson, 1980). As people grow older, crystallized abilities do not decrease and may improve if the individuals stay intellectually active. Even though the neurological deterioration that comes with age may hurt fluid abilities, we can continue to add to our store of knowledge and increase our technical proficiency throughout life (Horn & Donaldson, 1980).

We have spent quite a bit of time considering individual differences in intelligence. When we discuss effective teaching in Chapter 12, we will explore ways of adapting instruction to the needs and abilities of individual students. But before we leave this section, let's examine one common practice that attempts to deal with differences in student intelligence—ability grouping.

crystallized intelligence: those mental abilities valued by one's culture and not affected by aging

Ability Grouping

The expressed goal of ability grouping is to make teaching more appropriate for students. As we will see, this does not always happen. There are two main ways to group students by ability. The first is to assign students to classes or tracks based on their ability. The second is to form small groups within a given class based on ability.

The first method, forming whole classes based on ability, is a very common practice in secondary schools. Most high schools have "college prep" courses and "general" courses or, for example, high-, middle-, and low-ability classes in a particular subject. Although this seems on the surface to be an efficient way to teach, research has consistently shown that segregation by ability is a very ineffective arrangement for low-ability students (Good & Marshall, 1984; Persell, 1977).

Problems with Ability-Grouped Classes

There are several problems with segregated ability classes. Low-ability classes seem to receive lower-quality instruction in general. Teachers tend to focus on lower-level objectives and routine procedures. There are more management problems. Teacher enthusiasm and enjoyment are less in the low-ability classes. These differences in instruction and the teachers' negative attitudes may mean that low expectations are communicated to the students. Student self-esteem suffers almost as soon as the assignment to "dummy" English or math is made. Attendance may drop along with self-esteem. Many times the lower tracks have a disproportionate number of minority and low-SES students, so ability grouping, in effect, becomes re-segregation in school. Possibilities for friendships become limited to students in the same ability range. Often, assignments to classes are made on the basis of group IQ tests instead of tests in the subject area itself. Group IQ tests are not good guides for what someone is ready to learn in a particular subject area. All in all, the only people to benefit from ability-grouped classes seem to be the high-ability students assigned to honors classes (Corno & Snow, 1986; Good & Brophy, 1984; Kulik & Kulik, 1982; Slavin & Karweit, 1984).

The second method of ability grouping, clustering students by ability within the same class, is another story. Almost all elementary school classes are grouped for reading, and many are grouped for math. This allows students to learn and practice material at their own level. The results are generally positive for students at all ability levels, if the following conditions are met (Good & Brophy, 1984; Slavin & Karweit, 1984).

Conditions for Within-Class Grouping

1. The groups should be formed and reformed on the basis of students' current performance in the subject being taught. This means students grouped on the basis of current reading level for reading instruction and on the basis of current math achievement for math instruction. This also means frequent changes in group placement when students' achievement changes.

2. The teacher should discourage comparisons between groups and encourage students to develop a whole-class spirit. Make sure there are many lessons and projects that mix members from the groups. Experiment with learning strategies in which cooperation is stressed (described in Chapter 9).

3. The number of groups should be kept small (two or three at the most) so that the teacher can provide as much direct teaching as possible. When we discuss effective management and teaching in Chapters 10 and 12, you will see that leaving students on their own for too long leads to less learning.

We now turn to another characteristic that concerns teachers—one that is as complex and hard to define as intelligence.

THE QUESTION OF CREATIVITY

creativity: imaginative, original thinking or problem solving

To some psychologists, **creativity** is a personal quality or trait. We often talk about creative people. But what is it that makes a person creative? According to Davis, "the single most important characteristic of the highly creative individual is creative attitudes. The concept of creative attitudes is broadly defined to include purposes, values, and a number of personality traits that together predispose an individual to think in an independent, flexible, and imaginative way" (Davis, 1976, p. 219). Other psychologists suggest that creativity is not a personality trait but a skill or process that produces a "creative" product, such as a painting, invention, computer program, or solution to a personal problem.

At the heart of all concepts of creativity we find the notion of newness. Creativity results in new, original, independent, and imaginative ways of thinking about or doing something. Although we frequently associate the arts with creativity, any subject can be approached in a creative manner.

Assessing Creativity

Psychologists confront all the usual research problems when they attempt to study creativity. "How shall we define creativity?" becomes "How shall we measure creativity?" Several answers have been proposed. One answer has been to equate creativity with **divergent thinking.** As we saw when we discussed Guilford's faces of intelligence, this is the ability to come up with many different ideas or answers. **Convergent thinking** is the more common ability to come up with one answer. This solution for measuring creativity is not perfect, but certain divergent thinking tests, given under certain conditions, do seem to predict actual creative behavior fairly well (Barron & Harrington, 1981).

E. P. Torrance has developed two types of creativity tests, verbal and graphic (Torrance, 1972; Torrance & Hall, 1980). In the verbal test, you might be instructed to think up as many uses as possible for a tin can or asked how a particular toy might be changed to make it more fun to play with. On the graphic test, you might be given 30 pairs of parallel vertical lines and asked to create 30 different drawings, each drawing including one pair of lines (Hudgins, 1977).

Responses to all these tasks are scored for originality, fluency, and flexibility, three aspects of divergent thinking. *Originality* is usually determined statistically. To be original, a response must be given by fewer than 5 or 10 people out of every 100 who take the test. *Fluency* is simply the number of different responses. *Flexibility* is generally measured by counting the number of different categories of responses. For instance, if you listed 100 uses for a tin can but each use was as some type of container, your fluency score might be high, but your flexibility score would be quite low.

In general, it appears that at least average intelligence is required to be

Creativity often involves seeing familiar forms in new ways. This student is expressing her own vision in her sculpture—and transforming the human body in the process. *(Richard Hutchings/Photo Researchers)*

creative, but beyond this, IQ and creativity are not related. Very intelligent people can be quite creative, very conventional, or anything in between. People of average intelligence can also be more or less creative. In fact, it is likely that creativity is a bit like intelligence. We all have intelligence and creativity, but some people seem to have more of one or of both qualities.

Creativity in the Classroom

Should teachers promote creative thinking? If so, how can this be done? Teachers are not always the best judges of creativity. In fact, Torrance (1972) reports data from a 12-year follow-up study indicating no relationship between teachers' judgments of their students' creative abilities and the actual creativity these students revealed in their adult lives. But even though creative students may be difficult to identify, creativity is worth fostering. Certainly the many economic, social, and environmental problems now facing our society will require creative solutions.

Perhaps the most important step teachers can take to encourage creativity is to make sure students know their creativity will be appreciated. All too often teachers stifle creative ideas without realizing the effects of their actions. Teachers are in an excellent position to encourage or discourage creativity through their acceptance or rejection of the unusual and imaginative. Rejection may be fatal to creativity.

brainstorming:
generating ideas without stopping to evaluate them

The Brainstorming Strategy. In addition to encouraging creativity through everyday interactions with students, teachers can try **brainstorming.** The basic tenet is to separate the *generation* of ideas (thinking up or originating ideas) from the *evaluation* of ideas (Osborn, 1963). You probably are quite familiar with the usual sequence of events when a group is trying to solve a problem:

LEADER: We have to decide on a senior project.

PARTICIPANT 1: How about cleaning up the river by the park?

PARTICIPANT 2: No, that won't work. Someone's bound to get hurt.

PARTICIPANT 1: Not necessarily. Five years ago the senior class did it and everything went fine.

PARTICIPANT 2: Yes, but . . . .

In discussions such as this, the attempt to have creative ideas about solving a problem often turns into a debate about the merits of one idea. Many participants become bored and tune out. The principle of brainstorming is to generate as many ideas as possible, no matter how impractical they seem at first. Evaluation, discussion, or criticism of the ideas is left until all possible suggestions have been made. In this way, one idea may inspire others. Perhaps more important, people do not withhold what could be creative solutions out of fear of criticism. After all the ideas are in, they can be evaluated, modified, or combined to produce a creative answer to the original problem.

Individuals as well as groups may benefit from brainstorming. In writing this book, for example, it has sometimes been helpful simply to list all the different topics that could be covered in a chapter, then leave the list and return to it later to evaluate the ideas. Individual brainstorming can be especially helpful when you or your students do not know where to begin on a large project.

Take Your Time.   In addition to recognizing and valuing creativity and helping students examine a range of possibilities, teachers can encourage students to be more reflective, to take time for ideas to grow and develop. Other ideas for encouraging creativity, some taken from Frederiksen (1984), are described in the Guidelines.

VARIATIONS IN COGNITIVE STYLES

cognitive styles: different ways of perceiving and organizing information

The notion of **cognitive styles** is fairly new. It grew out of research on how people perceive and organize information from the world around them. Results from these studies suggest that individuals differ in how they approach the experimental tasks, but these variations do not reflect levels of intelligence or patterns of special abilities (Tyler, 1974). Instead, they have to do with "preferred ways that different individuals have for processing and organizing information and for responding to environmental stimuli" (Shuell, 1981a, p. 46). For example, certain individuals tend to respond very quickly in most situations. Others are more reflective and slower to respond, even though both types of people are equally knowledgeable about the task at hand.

Cognitive styles are often described as falling on the borderline between mental abilities and personality traits (Shuell, 1981a). They are styles of "thinking" and thus are probably influenced by and in turn influence cognitive abilities (Brodzinsky, 1982). But these preferred ways of dealing with the world also affect social relationships and personal qualities.

Field Dependence and Independence

field-dependent: cognitive style in which patterns are perceived as wholes

field-independent: cognitive style in which separate parts of a pattern are perceived and analyzed

In the early 1940s Herman Witkin became intrigued by the observation that certain airline pilots would fly into a bank of clouds and fly out upside down, without realizing that they had changed position. His interest led to a great deal of research on how people separate one factor—for example, true upright position—from the total visual field (Willerman, 1979). Based on this research, Witkin identified the cognitive styles of field-dependence and field-independence. People who are **field-dependent** tend to perceive a pattern as a whole. They have difficulty focusing on one aspect of a situation or analyzing a pattern into different parts. **Field-independent** people are more likely to perceive separate parts of a total pattern and to be able to analyze a pattern according to its components (Wittrock, 1978). In addition, field-dependent individuals tend to be more oriented toward people and social relationships, whereas field-independent individuals are more likely to be task-oriented (Sigel & Brodzinsky, 1977).

There are some clear developmental trends in cognitive styles. As children grow older, they generally become more field-independent, at least until the middle teenage years. Then development levels off until later adult life, when there is a tendency to become more field-dependent. Even with

Guidelines

Encouraging Creativity

Accept and encourage divergent thinking.

Examples
1. During class discussion, ask: "Can anyone suggest a different way of looking at this question?"
2. Reinforce attempts at unusual solutions to problems, even if the final product is not perfect.

Tolerate dissent.

Examples
1. Ask students to support dissenting opinions.
2. Make sure nonconforming students receive an equal share of classroom privileges and rewards.

Encourage students to trust their own judgment.

Examples
1. When students ask questions you think they can answer, rephrase or clarify the questions and direct them back to the students.
2. Give ungraded assignments from time to time.

Emphasize that everyone is capable of creativity in some form.

Examples
1. Avoid describing the feats of great artists or inventors as if they were superhuman accomplishments.
2. Recognize creative efforts in each student's work. Have a separate grade for originality on some assignments.

Be a stimulus for creative thinking.

Examples
1. Use a class brainstorming session whenever possible.
2. Model creative problem solving by suggesting unusual solutions for class problems.
3. Encourage students to delay judging a particular suggestion for solving a problem until all the possibilities have been considered.

these changes, over the years people remain fairly stable in comparison with others their age. So a person who tends to be field-dependent as a child may become more independent with age but may still be less independent than peers who have also changed with age. Some studies show that boys tend to be more field-independent than girls. This could be related to the way girls are socialized in our culture or to the testing situation itself. Confident parents who encourage self-reliance and curiosity and do not stress conformity or obedience tend to foster field-independence in their children (Sigel & Brodzinsky, 1977). These conditions are more likely to occur for boys than for girls in our society. In Eskimo society, in contrast, girls are given considerable independence, and no sex differences are found in this cognitive style (Willerman, 1979).

This discussion may seem to imply that it is "better" to be more field-independent. But each style has advantages and disadvantages. For example, field-dependent individuals are superior in remembering social information such as conversations or interpersonal interactions, probably because they are more attuned to social relationships. They are often better in subjects like history, literature, and the social sciences. They may work well in groups because they are sensitive to the feelings of other members. Field-independent people are better at analyzing complex, unstructured material and organizing it to solve problems. Science and mathematics may be their stronger subjects, and as you might expect, they often work well on their own (Shuell, 1981a, 1981b).

Although you will not necessarily be able to determine all the variations in your students' cognitive styles, you should be aware that the students approach problems in different ways. Some may need help in learning to pick out important features and to ignore irrelevant details. This does not mean that they are less intelligent but simply that they tend to perceive patterns as wholes and have trouble analyzing. They may seem lost in less structured situations and need clear, step-by-step instructions. They may work best in social situations and be less motivated by individual contracts or projects. Other students may be great at organizing but less sensitive to the feelings of others and not as effective in social situations. Table 4–2 presents some of the other learning characteristics of field-dependent and field-independent individuals.

Teachers also have their own cognitive styles, which affect their approaches to teaching. Field-dependent teachers often have a more interpersonal style in teaching, and they may be less critical of wrong answers. Field-independent teachers may prefer to organize the classroom and mate-

The task of organizing information from many different sources can be difficult for students who have a field-dependent cognitive style. They have trouble breaking information down into units and recombining the parts into new patterns. *(Zimbel/ Monkmeyer Press)*

Table 4–2   Learning Characteristics of Field-Dependent and Field-Independent Students

Field-Dependent	Field-Independent
■ Are better at learning material with social content	■ May need help in focusing attention on material with social content
■ Have better memory for social information	■ May have to be taught how to use context in understanding social information
■ Require externally defined structure, goals, and reinforcement	■ Tend to have self-defined goals and reinforcement
■ Are more affected by criticism	■ Are less affected by criticism
■ Have greater difficulty learning unstructured material	■ Can impose their own structure on unstructured situations
■ May need to be taught to use memory aids	■ Can analyze a situation and reorganize it
■ Tend to accept the organization given and be unable to reorganize	■ Are more likely to be able to solve problems without explicit instructions and guidance
■ May need more explicit instruction on how to solve problems	

Adapted from H. A. Witkin, C. A. Moore, D. R. Goodenough, & R. W. Cox (1977), Field dependent and field independent cognitive styles and their educational implications. Review of Educational Research, 47, pp. 17–27. © 1977. AERA, Washington, D.C.

rials themselves, with less input from students. They also may be more focused on wrong answers (Gordon & Gross, 1978).

Impulsive and Reflective Styles

impulsive:
cognitive style of responding quickly but often inaccurately

reflective:
cognitive style of responding slowly, carefully, and accurately

You may be the type of individual who responds very quickly; you finish multiple-choice tests long before your friends. Or you may still be checking your answers when the instructor is collecting the papers. If you fit the first description, you could be a true **impulsive** individual. But not everyone who works fast is impulsive. Some people are simply very bright and quick to understand. These individuals are called "fast-accurate" in the jargon of psychology. The true impulsive individual is one who responds very quickly but also makes quite a few errors in the process. If you are the last to finish the test, you may be a truly **reflective** individual; or you may have just studied the wrong material for the test. The true reflective person is one who is slow and careful to respond but also tends to answer correctly. Those who are slow and make many errors are called "slow-inaccurate."

The most common method for measuring impulsive-reflective styles is the Matching Familiar Figures test. An item from one version of this test is shown in Figure 4–2. The goal is to find the teddy bear from the bottom group that is exactly the same as the one on top. Impulsive children tend to select the first match that looks right without scanning all the examples and comparing each with the top bear. You can see how the tendency to go with the first reasonable choice could result in a low score on this test. The same thing often happens in college classes when some students hurry through a multiple-choice test, selecting the first good answer they find and never even reading the better (correct) answer listed after their selection.

As with field-dependence, impulsive and reflective cognitive styles are not highly related to intelligence within the normal range. However, as children grow older, they generally become more reflective, and for school-age

Figure 4–2 **Measuring Reflective Impulsive Styles**

J. Kagan, B. L. Rosman, D. Day, J. Albert, & W. Phillips (1964), *Information processing in the child: Significance of analytic and reflective attitudes. Psychological Monographs, 78, 1(Whole 578). Copyright © 1964 by the American Psychological Association and reproduced with permission.*

children being more reflective does seem to improve performance on school tasks like reading (Messer, 1976). In addition, reflective children are less likely to fail one of the early grades (Messer, 1970). It is not clear what influences the early development of this cognitive style, although genetic factors may play a role (Sigel & Brodzinsky, 1977).

However, students can learn to be more reflective if they are taught specific strategies. One that has proved successful in many situations is **self-instruction.** Students learn to give themselves reminders to go slowly and

self-instruction: talking yourself through the steps of a task

carefully. They "talk themselves through" the tasks, saying such things as, "Okay, what is it I have to do? . . . copy the picture with the different lines. I have to go slowly and carefully. Okay, draw the line down, down, good; then to the right, that's it; now . . ." (Meichenbaum, 1977, p. 32). Another possibility is learning scanning strategies. For example, students might be encouraged to cross off each alternative as they consider it, so no possibilities will be ignored. They might work in pairs and talk about why each possibility is right or wrong. In math classes, impulsive children need to be given specific strategies for checking their work. Just slowing down is not enough. These students must be taught effective strategies for solving the problem at hand by considering each reasonable alternative.

I have also encountered several bright students who seem *too* reflective. They turn 30 minutes of homework into an all-night project. These children may be afraid of failure, or they may be bored with the assignment; they may be revealing a thoroughness of analysis or a creativity better spent on something else. They need help in learning to work steadily through a project. They sometimes need help in being selective about when to analyze each alternative carefully and when to move quickly to a few reasonable choices. For example, at times my daughter has to be encouraged to *stop* taking notes for a research report, especially when she has read several times the number of sources required for the assignment.

The message for teachers in the work on cognitive styles is that not all differences in class performance are due to differences in ability or effort. We all probably have preferred ways of processing new information, as well as blind spots in our approaches to new tasks. Flexibility and willingness to experiment with different methods for different students are the keys.

SUMMARY

1. The relative contributions of heredity and environment to individual variations are difficult to determine. The nature versus nurture debate is an old one in psychology.

2. Heritability measures the proportion of variability of a given characteristic in a particular population that is attributed to genetic factors. A heritability ratio of 0.0 indicates that none of the variance is due to heredity; a ratio of 1.0 indicates that all variance is due to heredity.

3. Significant environmental influences on individuals include socioeconomic status (SES) and cultural background. A family's SES may limit available experiences and resources. Cultural groups generally teach their members different values, attitudes, and expectations.

4. The family also exerts a powerful influence on each individual. Child-rearing styles and birth order may account for many differences. Divorce, abuse, two-career and single-parent households, and lack of supervision for latchkey children are experiences that significantly affect children in different ways and to different degrees.

5. The temperament of each child may also partially determine the reactions of parents and teachers. Day-to-day life is a constant interchange between the child and the environment, with each influencing the other.

6. There is little agreement about what intelligence is. Some psychologists have theorized that intelligence is a collection of separate abilities; according to oth-

ers, it is a general mental ability to learn new information and cope with the world. More recently, psychologists have proposed that mental abilities have to do with the use of strategies for problem solving.

7. As IQ is measured today, with individually administered tests such as the Stanford-Binet and the Wechsler Scales, it is closely related to success in school. IQ as measured by the original Stanford-Binet was based on a comparison of mental age with chronological age. Now these tests compare the individual's performance with average scores for the same age group. The Wechsler Scales measure both verbal and visual-conceptual performance.

8. IQ scores must be interpreted with caution, particularly for minority students. Different groups tend to have different patterns of performance on measures of certain general and specific abilities.

9. There has been great controversy over the contributions of heredity and environment to intelligence, particularly in the area of ethnic and gender differences. A practical conclusion is that though both heredity and environment probably play a part, intelligence is always open to change over time; it is not fixed. Opportunity to learn is likely to be the key.

10. Creativity involves originality, imagination, and new ways of thinking about or doing something. Divergent thinking patterns help individuals arrive at creative solutions.

11. There are characteristic differences among people in the ways they organize and process information. These different cognitive styles are not related to intelligence or effort, but they do affect school performance.

12. A field-dependent style involves seeing a pattern or a situation as a whole; a field-independent style involves analyzing a pattern into separate components. Impulsive people respond quickly but often make mistakes. Reflective people respond slowly, carefully, and usually correctly.

KEY TERMS

heritability ratio	intelligence quotient (IQ)	convergent thinking
socioeconomic status (SES)	deviation IQ	brainstorming
culture	polygenetic	cognitive styles
latchkey children	longitudinal study	field-dependent
intelligence	fluid intelligence	field-independent
faces of intellect _Guilford_	crystallized intelligence	impulsive
components	creativity	reflective
mental age	divergent thinking	self-instruction

SUGGESTIONS FOR FURTHER READING AND STUDY

ALLERS, R. D. (1982). *Divorce, children, and the schools*. Princeton, NJ: Princeton Book Company. This book discusses the child's experience of divorce as well as suggestions for teachers and other school personnel.

BEEZER, B. (1985). Reporting child abuse and neglect: Your responsibilities and your protections. *Phi Delta Kappan, 66*, 434–436. This ar-ticle gives a brief summary of the teacher's legal standing in responding to suspected cases of child abuse.

BELL, R. Q. (1979). Parent, child, and reciprocal influences. *American Psychologist, 34*, 821–826. A brief summary of the more recent views on how children help to create the environments that influence them.

CORNO, L., & SNOW, R. E. (1986). Adapting teaching to individual differences in learners. In M. Wittrock (Ed.), *Handbook of research on teaching* (3rd ed.). New York: Macmillan. In this chapter, the research related to individual differences and teaching is analyzed—not light reading, but a very thorough discussion.

GARDNER, H. (1983). *Frames of mind: The theory of multiple intelligences.* New York: Basic Books. Gardner outlines his theory and the basis for his ideas; very worthwhile and interesting reading.

Phi Delta Kappan. (1986, March). This issue has a special section on "Women in Education." There are articles on sexism in the classroom, mathematics teaching, teaching as a career for women, and other timely topics.

SHUELL, T. J. (1981). Dimensions of individual differences. In F. H. Farley & N. J. Gordon (Eds.), *Psychology and education: The state of the union.* Berkeley, CA: McCutchan. An overview of several important ways that individuals differ, with examples of recent research in each area.

STERNBERG, R. J. (1986). *Intelligence applied: Understanding and increasing your own intellectual skills.* New York: Harcourt Brace Jovanovich. This book provides a clear statement of Sternberg's theory of intelligence. As the title indicates, the emphasis is on how to use this approach to improve your own intellectual performance.

VERNON, P. E. (1979). *Intelligence: Heredity and environment.* San Francisco: Freeman. Here you will find a very thorough evaluation of the roles of heredity and environment in the development of intelligence. Vernon synthesizes an extensive number of older and more recent studies.

Teachers' Forum

Coping with Differentness

Suppose you have a student in your class who is very different from you. He is from a different culture and has different values, and his temperament is different from your own. There is a strain between the two of you, and you tend to avoid him. The students, following your example, also shy away from him. How could you establish a relationship with him and reverse the trend toward estrangement and isolation?

Understanding and Communication

As I have some responsibility for the alienation occurring here, I need to take the initiative in working to alleviate the estrangement. I find that in most cases of this nature, a better understanding of each other and improved communication are essential. I would make a point of determining this student's interests in and out of class and talk to him about one of these. I would tell him about the discomfort I was feeling and let him know that I would like to work on the problem. I would ask for his help in planning classroom activities around individual and cultural differences, giving him and other class members the opportunity to share information about their views and ways of life. By enlisting his support in the project, I would also make him responsible for its outcome.

Linda Stahl, High School Psychology Teacher
Ponca City Senior High School, Ponca City, Oklahoma

Getting to Know You . . .

As the adult in this situation, it is up to me, the teacher, to increase interaction with this child. Getting to know the child better would be my first goal. Having the children write autobiographies is a good way to do this. Inviting parents in for a conference or making a home visit is sure to increase my understanding of this child and his culture. Beginning a Child-of-the-Week activity with this child scheduled early would be good. My next goal would be to let the child know that I accept him as an individual and to encourage his particular contributions to our class. I would purposely find at least one time each day I could interact with him personally and positively. Children readily see through deception, so these interactions must be realistic. Soon the other students will follow the model of increased interaction.

Arleen Wyatt, Third-Grade Teacher
Happy Valley School, Rossville, Georgia

Does the Average Student Count?

How can a beginning teacher keep from overlooking the average, quiet students, when so much emphasis is placed on students who have special learning limitations and needs or who are identified as gifted and talented?

Positive Involvement

It's certainly easy to overlook the average child—especially if he's quiet! We must make every effort to involve each child positively in our lessons, every day. If these children do not volunteer information or ideas, we can ask them what they think of John's or Mary's idea. Do you agree/disagree with him or her, and why? Accept all the responses they can justify. When they can't justify their answers, help them, in as nonthreatening a manner as possible, to understand why they responded that way. You can also have them work in heterogeneous groups and encourage interaction within the groups. Try to make each child feel comfortable in the class.

Carolyn R. Cook, Kindergarten Teacher
Ramona Elementary School, Ramona, California

Original Thinking

Imagine that you have just finished grading the essay questions on your unit examination. Many of the answers were straight from the book and terribly uncreative. How would you handle this problem? How might you encourage more creativity in your students?

Analyzing the Situation When students parrot back information from lectures or from the textbook, it is usually because they know what the teacher requires for an answer. As a teacher, this is a time for self-evaluation. The teacher may feel a need to control the students; or the students may be seeking the approval of the teacher. It might be best to avoid written tests for a while and concentrate on discussions requiring students to look at things from more than one perspective.

Leland J. Gritzner, Sixth-Grade Teacher
Death Valley Unified Schools, Shoshone, California

Creative Twists

What do you do with students who rewrite questions on tests, then give wonderful, creative answers that are not directly related to your original questions? Should you try to curb this kind of creativity in the interests of making sure specific skills are learned?

A Wildcard for Creativity No matter how carefully teachers construct assignments, some students will intentionally or unintentionally find unique ways of interpreting them. To keep my teaching flexible enough to handle good student writing that does not relate to my assignments, I use what I call the Wildcard System. Students must, of course, redo the work to meet my standards. However, their quality creative work is encouraged and rewarded with an automatic wildcard having one of three values: (1) grade-raising wildcards that can be used to raise an existing grade; (2) add-on wildcards that add an extra-credit grade; and (3) replacement wildcards that replace the lowest existing grade with an A. I have found that this system both ensures that students do the intended work and encourages free thinking.

J. D. Kraft, Twelfth-Grade Sociology Teacher
Wausau West High School, Wausau, Wisconsin

No More Moron Stuff?

You are concerned about one of your students. Although she seems bright, she isn't performing well on tests and acts uninterested in class. When you ask her about it, she tells you that she has an IQ of 130 and shouldn't have to deal with this "moron" stuff. You agree to give her an achievement test, and if she scores well enough, you will help her find other challenging material to work on. But her scores on the test reveal a number of basic areas in which she needs work.

Balance Strengths and Weaknesses The student must realize that although certain areas need to be addressed, other areas in which she is well versed can be expanded upon with more challenging material. The teacher should provide this student with meaningful experiences in *all* areas by using games, puzzles, computers, projects, etc., instead of memorization. The basic areas in which the student is weak can be addressed by utilizing her strong areas. It also may be helpful to enter into an agreement with the student regarding the goals to be accomplished.

Harold Kreif, Fifth-Grade Teacher
Pier Elementary School, Fond du Lac, Wisconsin

5

Learning: Behavioral Views

Overview
Learning: Toward a General Definition   164
Behavioral and Cognitive Views   165
Learning Is Not Always What It Seems   167
Contiguity: Learning through Simple Associations   168
Classical Conditioning: Pairing Automatic Responses with New Stimuli   169
Pavlov's Dilemma and Discovery   169
Examples of Classical Conditioning: Desirable and Undesirable   171
Generalization, Discrimination, and Extinction   171
Classroom Applications   172
Operant Conditioning: Trying New Responses   173
The Work of Thorndike and Skinner   174
The ABCs of Operant Conditioning   176
Controlling the Consequences   176
Reinforcement Schedules   178
Controlling the Antecedents   181
Learning by Observing Others   182
Elements of Observational Learning   184
Classroom Applications of Observational Learning   185
Applying the Principles: Behavioral Technology   187
Programmed Instruction   188
The Keller Plan   191
Summary/Key Terms
Suggestions for Further Reading and Study
Teachers' Forum

If you were asked to give 10 to 20 different examples of learning, what would your response be? You might begin by listing school subjects or certain activities you had set about mastering at some point in your life. You might also list different emotional reactions or insights you have had. But unless you've already had a few courses in psychology, it is likely that the examples you would choose would cover only a few of the aspects included in the psychological definition of learning. We will spend the next four chapters looking at learning and its many classroom applications.

We begin this chapter with a very general definition. It is a definition that takes into account the opposing views of different theoretical groups. We will then highlight one of these groups, the behavioral theorists, in this chapter and the next. The other major group, the cognitivists, will be highlighted in Chapters 7 and 8.

Our discussion in this chapter will focus on four different behavioral learning processes. Then we will look at two of the teaching aids behavioral theorists offer classroom teachers—programmed instruction and the Keller Plan. By the time you have completed this chapter, you should have a much better idea of what is involved in learning. More specifically, you should be able to do the following:

- Offer a reasonably precise definition of learning.
- Give positive and negative examples of learning through the principle of contiguity.
- Compare classical and operant conditioning, giving examples of each.
- Give examples of four different kinds of consequences that may follow any behavior and the effect each is likely to have on future behavior.
- Describe situations in which a teacher may wish to use modeling.
- Give three specific examples of the ways in which you might use behavioral principles to solve problems that could arise in your own classroom.

LEARNING: TOWARD A GENERAL DEFINITION

One way to understand the psychological meaning of learning is to note what it is *not*. First, learning is not something found only in the classroom. *Learning Is Constant* It takes place constantly, every day of our lives. Second, it does not only involve what is "correct." If a student misspells a word on a test, we cannot say that the student did not learn to spell the word, only that the student learned the wrong spelling. Third, learning does not have to be deliberate or conscious. A tennis player may have learned a bad method of tossing the ball before serving, but the player may be completely unaware of the pattern until the instructor points it out. Finally, learning does not always involve knowledge or skills, such as spelling and tennis. Attitudes and emotions can also be learned (W. Hill, 1985).

Encouraged by their teacher, these students are learning more than reading. They are developing positive attitudes toward school and a sense of personal competence as well. Attitudes and emotions are an important part of learning in classrooms. *(Conklin/ Monkmeyer Press)*

The Basic Elements: Change and Experience

What, then, does learning involve? Learning always involves a change in the person who is learning. The change may be deliberate or unintentional, for the better or for the worse. To qualify as learning, this change must be brought about by experience—by the interaction of a person with his or her environment. Changes due simply to maturation, such as a toddler's beginning to walk, do not really qualify as learning. Temporary changes due to illness, fatigue, or hunger are also excluded from a general definition of learning. A person who has gone without food for two days does not learn to be hungry, and a person who is ill does not learn to run more slowly.

With these two factors—change and experience—we can begin to develop a definition. Learning is a change in a person that comes about as a result of experience. But you might well ask, "A change in what aspect of the person?" It is the way this question is answered that has traditionally separated the behavioral definition of learning from the cognitive definition.

Behavioral and Cognitive Views

behavioral learning theories: theories that focus on observable behavior

Most of the psychologists discussed in this chapter and the following one hold the **behavioral** view of learning. According to this view, learning is a change in behavior, in the way a person acts in a particular situation. Theorists such as J. B. Watson, E. L. Thorndike, and B. F. Skinner are considered behavioral psychologists because they have focused almost solely on observable behavior and behavioral changes. In fact, many behaviorists have refused even to discuss the concepts of thinking or emotion, since thoughts and emotions cannot be observed directly. Today, behaviorism's primary champion is B. F. Skinner.

cognitive learning theories: theories that focus on mental processes

In contrast, **cognitive** psychologists, such as Jean Piaget, Robert Glaser, John Anderson, Jerome Bruner, and David Ausubel, would say that learning itself is an internal process that cannot be observed directly. The change occurs in a person's *ability* to respond in a particular situation. According to the cognitive view, the change in behavior that strict behaviorists call learning is only a reflection of the internal change. So in contrast to the behaviorists, cognitive psychologists studying learning are interested in such unobservable factors as knowledge, meaning, intention, feeling, creativity, expectations, and thought.

Differences in
Methods

Behavioral and cognitive views differ in many other important ways, and the differences are apparent in the methods each group has used to study learning. A great deal of the work on behavioral learning principles has been done with animals in controlled laboratory settings. These studies have been an attempt to identify a few general laws of learning that would apply to all higher organisms (including humans) regardless of age, intelligence, or other individual differences. The behaviorists have hoped that these laws could then be used to predict and control changes in the behavior of any organism (Estes, 1975). Cognitive psychologists, on the other hand, have been more interested in explaining how the many types of human learning actually take place. They have attempted to find out how different people solve problems, learn concepts, perceive and remember information, and accomplish many other complex mental tasks.

The most important thing for teachers is that both cognitive and behavioral psychologists offer helpful information. Teachers must, after all, be concerned with observable student behavior—that is, the actual work done on assignments or behavior in class—as well as with less observable qualities, like abstract thinking and attitudes.

neobehaviorists:
behavioral
psychologists whose
view of learning
includes mental
states and events

**social cognitive
theory:** theory that
emphasizes learning
through observing
others

In recent years, the behavioral psychologists known as **neobehaviorists** have expanded the behavioral view of learning to include such internal, unobservable events as expectations, intentions, beliefs, and thoughts. A prime example of this expanded behavioral view is Albert Bandura's (1986) **social cognitive theory,** which equates learning with much more than observable behavior. Bandura suggests that people may "know" more than their behavior indicates. Learning is seen as the *acquisition* of knowledge and behavior as the observable *performance* based on that knowledge; this is an important distinction for Bandura and others. In describing the cognitive-behavioral position, Bandura (1971) has written:

> Man is a thinking organism possessing capabilities that provide him with some power of self-direction. To the extent that traditional behavioral theories could be faulted, it was for providing an incomplete rather than an inaccurate account of human behavior. The social learning theory places special emphasis on the important roles played by vicarious, symbolic, and self-regulatory processes. (p. 2)

Social cognitive theory can in many ways be considered a link between behaviorism and cognitive approaches.

learning: change
in capabilities as a
result of experience

Taking into account the traditional behavioral and cognitive views and the more recent work of the social learning theorists, we can now suggest this general definition of learning. **Learning** is an internal change in a person—the formation of new associations—or the potential for new responses. Learning is thus a relatively permanent change in a person's capabilities. This definition acknowledges that learning is a process taking place within a person (the cognitive view), but it also emphasizes the importance of changes in observable behavior as indications that learning has taken place (the behavioral view). Although this definition might not be acceptable to psychologists who hold extreme behavioral or cognitive views of learning, it is a reasonable beginning.

Because this chapter focuses on behavioral views of learning, we will be more concerned, for the time being, with the changes in observable behavior. These changes can take place through four different learning processes: contiguity, classical conditioning, operant conditioning, and observational learning. Let's step into an actual classroom and see some of these processes at work. Don't worry about identifying the various processes at this point; it should all become very clear as you read the rest of the chapter.

Learning Is Not Always What It Seems

Elizabeth was beginning her first day of solo teaching. After weeks of working with her cooperating teacher in an eighth-grade social studies class, she was ready to take over. As she moved from behind the desk to the front of the room, she saw another adult approach the classroom door. It was Mr. Ross, her supervisor from college. Elizabeth's neck and facial muscles suddenly became very tense.

"I've stopped by to observe your teaching," Mr. Ross said. "This will be my first of six visits. I tried to reach you last night to tell you."

Elizabeth was beginning to feel weak and nauseated. Her worst fear was confirmed: he was going to observe her on her first solo day. She tried to hide her reaction, but without much success. Her hand trembled as she gathered the notes for the lesson. Elizabeth had planned a slightly unorthodox introduction, and she now found herself wishing she had chosen something a bit less risky. After a few seconds of reflection, she decided to stick to her original plan.

"Let's start today with a kind of game. I will say some words. I want you to tell me the first words that you can think of when you hear my words. Don't bother to raise your hands. Just say the words out loud, and I will write them on the board. Don't all speak at once, though. Wait until someone else has finished to say your word. Okay, here is the first word: slavery."

"Civil War." "Lincoln." "Freedom." "Emancipation Proclamation." The answers came very quickly and Elizabeth was relieved to see that the students understood the game.

"All right, very good," she said. "Now try another one: South."

"Carolina." "Pacific." "No, the Confederacy, you dummy." *"Gone with the Wind."* "Clark Gable." With this last answer, a ripple of laughter moved across the room.

"Clark Gable!" Elizabeth sighed dreamily, looking "star-struck" for a moment. Then she laughed too. Soon all the students were laughing. "Okay, settle down," Elizabeth said. "Here is another word: North."

"Bluebellies." (The students continued to laugh.) "Yellowbellies." "Belly-dancers." (More laughter and a few appropriate gestures.)

"Just a minute," Elizabeth pleaded. "These ideas are getting a little off base!"

"Off base? Baseball," shouted the boy who had first mentioned Clark Gable.

"Popcorn." "Hotdogs." "Drive-in movies." *"Gone with the Wind."* "Clark Gable." The responses now came too fast for Elizabeth to stop them.

For some reason, the Clark Gable line got an even bigger laugh the second time around, and Elizabeth realized she had lost the class. At this point, her cooperating teacher would have sent "Clark Gable" and a few others in the fan club to the principal's office. But Elizabeth feared her college supervisor would see that approach as a failure to handle the situation constructively. She looked to the back of the room and saw Mr. Ross writing in a notebook and shaking his head.

It appears, on the surface at least, that very little learning of any sort was taking place in Elizabeth's classroom. If you consider the psychological definition of learning, however, you can see evidence of a good deal of learning. Four events can be singled out for our purposes here, each related to a different learning process. First, the students were able to associate the words *Carolina* and *Pacific* with the word *South*. Second, Elizabeth's hands trembled and she became nauseated when her college supervisor entered the room. Third, one student continued to disrupt the class with inappropriate responses. And fourth, after Elizabeth had laughed at a student comment, the class joined in her laughter. In the next four sections we will examine these four different kinds of learning, with special attention to the third type.

CONTIGUITY: LEARNING THROUGH SIMPLE ASSOCIATIONS

contiguity:
association of two events because of repeated pairing

stimulus: event that activates behavior

response:
observable reaction to a stimulus

Simply phrased, the principle of **contiguity** states that whenever two sensations occur together over and over again, they will become associated. Later, when only one of these sensations (a **stimulus**) occurs, the other will be remembered too (a **response**). Some early twentieth-century psychologists claimed that this principle explained most learning. Edwin Guthrie, for example, believed that "if you do something in a given situation, the next time you are in that situation you will tend to do the same thing again" (W. Hill, 1985, p. 34).

Many of us learned quite a few basic facts in school through the repetitive pairing of a stimulus and a correct response. For example, a student repeats "The capital of Texas is Austin" over and over until seeing the stimulus "The capital of Texas is _____" on a test brings to mind the response "Austin." Spelling drills in the earlier grades and the memorizing of vocabulary words in foreign-language classes are other examples of the positive use of contiguity. Some results of contiguous learning were also evident in Elizabeth's class. When she said "South," students associated the word with *Carolina* and *Pacific*. They had heard these words together many times.

Stereotypes

As I mentioned earlier, not all learning is deliberate, and of course, not all learning leads to positive results. Through contiguous learning, children sometimes develop stereotypes about the way people are or should be. The media frequently present the image of a mother of young children as a young, attractive, full-time homemaker. We may tend to associate the idea of "mother" with this picture. Yet a large number of women in this country with children under 5 are employed full time. And many of these women are in their 30s or 40s.

The principle of contiguity can certainly be used positively to help students learn, even though, as we will see, there is also more to learning than contiguity. Contiguity actually plays a major role in another, more complex learning process. It has been called by various names: classical conditioning, respondent conditioning, and signal learning, among others. Here we will use the first name.

CLASSICAL CONDITIONING: PAIRING AUTOMATIC RESPONSES WITH NEW STIMULI

classical conditioning: association of automatic responses with new stimuli

Through the process of **classical conditioning,** humans and animals can learn to respond automatically to a stimulus that once had no effect or a very different effect on them. The learned response might be an emotional reaction, such as fear or pleasure, or a physiological response, such as muscle tension. These normally involuntary responses can be conditioned, or learned, so that they will occur automatically in particular situations. Looking at the way in which classical conditioning was discovered should help make this learning process clearer.

Pavlov's Dilemma and Discovery

In a Russian laboratory in the 1920s, physiologist Ivan Pavlov was plagued by a series of setbacks. He was trying to answer questions about the digestive system of dogs, including how long it took a dog to secrete digestive juices after it had been fed. But this time period kept changing. At first, the dogs salivated in the expected manner while they were being fed. Then the

Pavlov's apparatus for classical conditioning of a dog's salivation. The experimenter sits behind a two-way mirror and controls the presentation of the conditioned simulus (tone) and the unconditioned stimulus (food). A tube runs from the dog's salivary glands to a vial, where the drops of saliva are collected as a way of measuring the strength of the dog's response. *(C. G. Morris, Psychology: An Introduction, 5/e. Prentice-Hall, 1985, p. 186. Used with permission of Prentice-Hall, Inc.)*

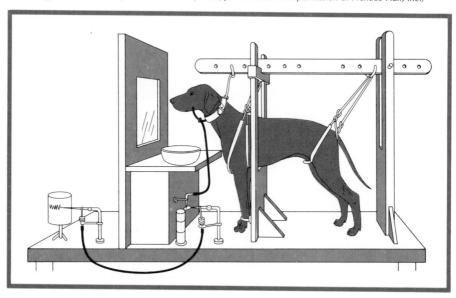

dogs began to salivate as soon as they saw the food. Finally, they salivated as soon as they saw the scientist enter the room. Because Pavlov decided to make a detour from his original experiments and examine these unexpected interferences in his work, we now have a better understanding of an important form of learning—classical conditioning.

In one of his first experiments investigating the phenomenon he had stumbled onto, Pavlov began by sounding a tuning fork and recording the dog's response. As expected, there was no salivation. Then he fed the dog. The response was salivation. The food in this case was an **unconditioned stimulus (US),** since it brought forth an automatic response of salivation. The salivation was an **unconditioned response (UR),** again because it occurred automatically. No prior learning or "conditioning" was needed to establish the natural connection between food and salivation. The sound of the tuning fork, on the other hand, was at this point a neutral stimulus (NS) because it brought forth no response.

Using these three elements—the food, the salivation, and the tuning fork—Pavlov demonstrated that a dog could be conditioned to salivate after hearing the tuning fork. He did this by contiguous pairing of the sound with food. At the beginning of the experiment, he sounded the fork and then quickly fed the dog. After repeating this several times, the dog began to salivate after hearing the sound but before receiving the food. Now the tone had become a **conditioned stimulus (CS)** that could bring forth salivation by itself. The response of salivating after the tone, now a **conditioned response (CR),** was very similar to the original response to the food. Table 5–1 is a schematic diagram of what happened in Pavlov's laboratory.

Pavlov's findings and those of others who have studied classical conditioning have at least two implications for teachers. First, it is possible that many of our emotional reactions to various situations are learned in part through classical conditioning. It is important to remember that emotions and attitudes as well as facts and ideas are more than likely learned in classrooms, and sometimes this emotional learning can interfere with academic learning. By the same token, procedures based on classical conditioning can be used to help people learn more adaptive emotional responses.

unconditioned stimulus (US): stimulus that automatically produces an emotional or physiological response

unconditioned response (UR): naturally occurring emotional or physiological response

conditioned stimulus (CS): stimulus that evokes an emotional or physiological response after conditioning

conditioned response (CR): learned response to a previously neutral stimulus

Table 5–1   **Classical Conditioning in Pavlov's Laboratory**

Before Conditioning	Conditioning	After Conditioning
US = food (unconditioned stimulus)	Present NS = tone	CS = tone (conditioned stimulus)
↓		
UR = salivation (unconditioned response)	Present US = food	
	↓	
–BUT–	UR = salivation	
NS = tone (neutral stimulus)	Repeat	
↓		CR = salivation (conditioned response)
No response	Repeat	

Examples of Classical Conditioning: Desirable and Undesirable

Fear and Anxiety

There is actually no definite proof that we learn to be fearful and anxious in school through classical conditioning (Brewer, 1974), but consider these possibilities. A young child who is initially fearless on the playground may be involved in a painful accident on a swing. Later, the child may refuse to get on the swing again and may seem fearful of other playground equipment and even of recess itself. A previously neutral stimulus, the swing, now automatically brings the response of fear. Other examples include learning to fear or hate school after several embarrassing or frightening experiences. A student may also learn to be very anxious or even physically sick during tests, because tests have been associated with failure and possibly with punishment or ridicule at home. Finally, a student may learn the very common fear of speaking before a group.

Confidence and Relaxation

Of course, positive emotional responses can be learned as well. If students frequently experience success in school, they will probably respond to new learning tasks with confidence rather than anxiety. Students who have been relatively successful in algebra will be more likely to face a new subject like geometry with a relaxed attitude. In contrast, students who have found algebra a source of failure or even humiliation may face the first day of geometry with sweaty palms.

Generalization, Discrimination, and Extinction

Do you remember Elizabeth's response to the arrival of her supervisor? It is very possible that she had previously had bad experiences speaking publicly, especially when her performance was being evaluated. It is also possible that she had had unpleasant experiences in her college supervisor's class. Her trembling hands and nausea could have been conditioned responses brought forth by people or situations associated with unpleasant, frightening, or embarrassing events in the past. These emotional responses might have spread to other similar situations, such as the new one she was facing.

generalization: responding to similar stimuli in the same way

This spreading of responses is called **generalization.** Pavlov demonstrated this phenomenon with his dogs. After the dogs learned to salivate in response to one particular tone, they would also salivate after hearing other tones. The response of salivating generalized to stimuli that were similar to the original conditioned stimulus. Perhaps Elizabeth had been ridiculed by one college professor, and her conditioned response of anxiety had generalized to similar stimuli—that is, to other college professors.

discrimination: responding differently to similar stimuli

Does this mean that Elizabeth fears *all* speaking experiences? No. Elizabeth was not anxious about speaking to her class when her supervisor was not present. What she was doing is called **discrimination**—that is, responding differently to similar but not identical situations. Pavlov's dogs were also capable of discriminating when they learned that the food always followed one of the tones and not the others. Thus, it is possible that only adults (or only college professors, or only this particular professor) are capable of eliciting Elizabeth's anxiety reaction.

"PERHAPS, DR. PAVLOV, HE COULD BE
TAUGHT TO SEAL ENVELOPES."

extinction: gradual
disappearance of a
learned response

Discrimination occurs in part because of another process called **extinction.** If a conditioned stimulus is presented repeatedly but is not followed by the unconditioned stimulus (the tone but no food), the conditioned response (salivating after the tone) will finally go away, or extinguish. So Pavlov's dogs could be conditioned to discriminate between two similar tones if the food was consistently withheld after one tone and given after another, because the conditioned response to one of the tones would be extinguished. Similarly, if Elizabeth had initially been afraid of lecturing to her class but then never actually experienced anything unpleasant in doing so, her fear of speaking before the class would probably become extinguished. In other words, she would learn to discriminate between her class and other similar anxiety-arousing public-speaking situations. Of course, not all fears are so easily extinguished, as most psychotherapists know from experience.

Classroom Applications

The examples we have given so far have illustrated a number of different ways in which emotional responses can be conditioned in humans. Generally, the conditioning involved in these examples has been haphazard, with no Pavlovian scientist pulling strings. However, classical conditioning can also be used directly for positive changes in the classroom. In every class, most teachers meet several students who are overly concerned about their performance, who are fearful and withdrawn, who avoid new activities rather than risk failure. Techniques based on classical conditioning can help these students learn more positive responses to frightening situations.

Prevention.   To prevent the development of negative emotional reactions to school situations, teachers can attempt to associate positive stimuli with experiences in school. This could mean preparing students in the early grades for potentially frightening experiences like physical examinations or fire drills by telling them what is about to happen and encouraging the children to talk about their concerns. It could also mean making the classroom a pleasant and comfortable physical environment. Finally, at every grade level students sometimes need to be protected from embarrassment, especially in a public situation, through well-timed interventions by the teacher.

Preparation

Cures.   Once a student has developed a fearful or anxious reaction to some aspect of school, one of the least complicated approaches is to use the principle of extinction. Encourage students to put themselves in the problem situation and then make sure unpleasant events do *not* follow. If a student is mildly fearful of the guinea pig in your classroom, you could encourage the student to touch the animal if you are certain no negative results will follow. After several uneventful contacts with the animal, the student's fear of it should be extinguished.

Gradual Extinction.   But often students will not put themselves in the problem situation. If a student absolutely refuses to take part in gym class, he or she will never learn that the embarrassment or pain of the past will not occur again. And even if the student is willing to take part, it is possible that the anxiety the student feels will actually interfere with performance, and failure or other unpleasant experiences will continue. The learned response of anxiety may be perpetuated. This is a definite possibility in cases of severe test anxiety.

Anxiety Perpetuated

One approach for coping with these more difficult situations is gradual extinction. If a student is too fearful to participate in gym class, he or she can gradually work out the problem by taking small steps toward the goal. Clarizio (1971) suggests that such a student first read exciting stories about sports figures, then watch others play at recess, then keep score, and then slowly get more and more involved in the activities in gym. A student who is anxious about tests can also be asked to take small steps—perhaps a number of short quizzes of varying difficulty in a noncompetitive situation. The Guidelines on the next page offer some other ideas for using classical conditioning in the classroom.

OPERANT CONDITIONING: TRYING NEW RESPONSES

So far, we have concentrated on the relatively automatic learning of emotional responses, such as fear, anxiety, and relaxation. Clearly, not all human learning is of this type. Learners are often quite actively involved in the learning process. People constantly take deliberate action; they "operate" on their environment. Operant conditioning is the behavioral learning process that involves these deliberate actions.

Guidelines

Using Classical Conditioning

Try to associate positive, pleasant events with learning tasks.

Examples
1. *Use more group competition and less competition between individuals, since many students have negative emotional reactions to competition. These negative emotions might generalize to many school tasks.*
2. *Make voluntary reading appealing by creating a comfortable reading corner with pillows, colorful displays of books, and reading "props" like puppets (see Morrow & Weinstein, 1986, for ideas).*
3. *Make division drills fun by letting students decide how to divide refreshments equally, then let them eat the results.*

Encourage students to put themselves into feared situations voluntarily, as long as you are fairly certain that there will be no negative results.

Examples
1. *Assign a shy student the responsibility of teaching two other students how to distribute and collect materials for map study.*
2. *Encourage students to make a brief presentation to the class about a hobby or interest they know well. Make sure that there is no pressure for a polished performance.*

If a student's fears are too strong for immediate participation, devise small steps toward the goal.

Examples
1. *If a student "freezes" on tests, give ungraded daily tests for practice, then a weekly ungraded practice test. If performance on a practice test is much better than on a real test, count the practice test as part of the weekly grade.*
2. *If a student is afraid of speaking before the class, let the student read a report to a small group while sitting down, then while standing. The next steps can be to give a report from notes and then to read a report to the whole class while seated. When the student feels comfortable with that, he or she can give a report using notes while seated and, finally, can stand alone before the whole class to give the report.*

Help students recognize differences and similarities among situations so they can discriminate and generalize appropriately.

Examples
1. *Emphasize that it is appropriate to be suspicious of strangers who offer gifts or rides but safe to accept favors from adults when you are with parents.*
2. *If good students are anxious about taking college entrance exams, assure them that this test is like all other achievement tests they have taken. If they usually do well, they probably will again.*

The Work of Thorndike and Skinner

Thorndike and Skinner both played major roles in developing the knowledge we now have of operant conditioning. Edward Thorndike's (1913) early work was with cats he placed in problem boxes. To escape from the box and reach food outside, the cats had to pull out a bolt or perform some other task. They had to act on their environment. During the frenzied movements that followed the closing of the box, the cats eventually made the correct movement to escape, usually by accident. After repeating the process several times, the cats learned to make the correct response almost immediately. Thorndike decided, on the basis of these experiments, that one important law of learning was the **law of effect:** any act that produces a satisfying effect in a given situation will tend to be repeated in that situation. Because pulling out a bolt produced satisfaction (access to food), that movement was repeated when the cats found themselves in the box again.

Thorndike thus established the basis for operant conditioning, but the person generally thought to be responsible for developing the concept is B. F. Skinner (1953). Skinner began with the belief that the principles of classical conditioning account for only a small portion of the behaviors that are learned. Classical conditioning describes how existing behaviors might be paired with new stimuli but not how *new* behaviors are acquired. Many behaviors are not simple responses to stimuli, but deliberate actions or *operants.* According to Skinner, these operants are affected by what happens after them. Thus, **operant conditioning,** or operant learning, involves control of the consequences of behavior.

To study the effects of consequences on behavior under carefully controlled conditions, Skinner designed a special cagelike apparatus. The subjects of Skinner's studies were usually rats or pigeons placed in the cages, which soon came to be called **Skinner boxes.** A typical Skinner box is a small enclosure containing only a food tray and a lever or bar (for rats) or a disk (for pigeons). The lever or disk is connected to a food hopper. Modifications of this basic box include lights close to the lever or disk and electrified floors used to shock the animals.

You can probably imagine how such a box might be used to study the effects of positive consequences (food) or unpleasant consequences (shocks). A hungry pigeon is placed in the box and proceeds to explore it. Since pigeons tend to peck, the animal will eventually get around to pecking the disk. At that point, a small food pellet will drop into the food tray. The hungry animal eats the pellet, moves around the box, and soon pecks the disk again. There is more food, and before long the pigeon is pecking and eating continuously. The next time the pigeon is placed in the box, it will go directly to the disk and begin pecking.

Using this approach, Skinner has been able to study many questions

B. F. Skinner was a pioneer in the study of operant conditioning and remains today a major voice in the field. *(Sam Falk/ Monkmeyer Press)*

about the effects of consequences on behavior. For example, how is the rate of pecking affected if the pigeons do not get food every time they peck? How long will the pigeon continue to peck if no food follows at all? How does the negative effect of a shock compare with the positive effect of food?

The ABCs of Operant Conditioning

Behavior, like *response* or *action,* is simply a word for what a person does in a particular situation. Conceptually, we may think of a behavior as sandwiched between two sets of environmental influences: those that precede it (its **antecedents**) and those that follow it (its **consequences**) (Mahoney & Thoresen, 1974). This relationship can be shown very simply as antecedent → behavior → consequence, or A → B → C.

antecedents: events that precede an action

consequences: events that follow an action

Thus, behavior can be changed by a change in the antecedents, the consequences, or both. Let us first consider the alteration of consequences. Much more research has been conducted on the effects of consequences. As we've indicated, Skinner's work—the basis of operant conditioning—has focused largely on controlling consequences. According to the behavioral view, the consequences determine to a great extent whether a person (or animal) will repeat an action in the future.

Controlling the Consequences

The consequences brought about by a particular behavior can be pleasant or unpleasant for the person involved. Variations in the timing of the consequences may also have an effect on the person.

Reinforcement. Reinforcement is a common word in everyday conversation. When most people use the term, they mean something like "reward." But *reinforcement* has a particular meaning in psychology. It is one type of consequence. The effect of a consequence determines whether the consequence is reinforcing. Any consequence is a reinforcer if it strengthens the behavior it follows. Using the ABC notion of behavior, we can say that behaviors followed by reinforcement are likely to be repeated in the future. **Reinforcement** strengthens behavior. Whenever you see a behavior persisting or increasing over time, you can assume something is reinforcing that behavior.

reinforcement: consequence that strengthens behavior

It is important to remember that the event reinforcing the behavior may not seem pleasant or desirable to you. Reinforcers are defined by their effect of strengthening behavior. Students who are sent to the principal's office repeatedly for the same offense may be indicating that the trip is in some way reinforcing for them, even if it hardly seems reinforcing to you. Whether the consequences of any action are reinforcing probably depends on the individual's perception of the event and the meaning it holds for her or him. The chance to give an oral report to the entire class may be a very enjoyable event for one student and a task to be avoided at all costs for another. Another way of defining reinforcer is to say that a reinforcer is an event a person will work to attain.

positive reinforcement: strengthening behavior by presenting a desired stimulus after the behavior

There are two types of reinforcement. The first, called **positive reinforcement,** occurs when a (usually pleasant) stimulus is presented following a particular behavior. Examples include money and praise presented to students when they bring home A's on their report cards, or cheers and laughter presented by other students following the class clown's silly answers during reading group. Notice that positive reinforcement can occur even when the behavior being reinforced (shouting out silly answers) is not "positive" from the teacher's point of view. The expert on old movies in Elizabeth's class continued to shout "Clark Gable," so the consequences—teacher attention and laughter from other students—must have been reinforcing for him. Positive reinforcement of inappropriate behaviors occurs unintentionally in many classrooms. Many teachers help maintain problem behaviors by inadvertently reinforcing these behaviors—for example, by smiling when one student makes a clever but inappropriate remark about another teacher.

Whereas positive reinforcement involves the *presentation* of a desired stimulus, the second kind of reinforcement, called **negative reinforcement**, involves the *removal* or avoidance of an aversive (unpleasant) stimulus. A stimulus is aversive if you would do something in order to escape or avoid it. If a particular action allows you to avoid or escape something that is aversive, you are likely to repeat the action when you are again faced with a similar situation. Consider the students who are repeatedly sent to the principal's office. Their rule breaking is probably being reinforced in some way, because they continue to do it. The misbehavior may be getting them out of "bad" situations such as a test or a class that causes anxiety. If so, the misbehavior is being maintained through negative reinforcement.

Negative reinforcement operates in many everyday situations. One example is a policy allowing cars with more than one passenger to bypass the toll at the Oakland Bay Bridge in San Francisco. Here the behavior of car pooling is reinforced (strengthened). The consequence that leads to the

negative reinforcement: strengthening behavior by removing an aversive stimulus

Reinforcement can be deceptive. Though intended as punishment, this trip to the principal's office may actually be reinforcement in disguise for the student seeking attention or diversion. If the unwanted behavior persists or even increases after the visit, what is the teacher's next resort? *(Richard Hutchings/Photo Researchers)*

strengthening is the avoidance of an aversive situation—waiting in line and having to pay—so the reinforcement is negative (Baldwin & Baldwin, 1986).

Punishment.   Negative reinforcement is often confused with punishment. The process of reinforcement (positive or negative) always involves strengthening behavior. **Punishment,** on the other hand, involves a decrease in or a suppression of behavior. A behavior followed by punishment is less likely to be repeated in similar situations in the future. Again, the effect defines a consequence as punishment. In the hope of increasing good writing, a teacher may try to use reinforcement ("You did such good work on those written reports that I'm going to let you present them to the entire class!") only to find the students behave as if they have been punished. They stop working hard on written reports.

Like reinforcement, punishment may take one of two forms. The first type has been called punishment I or positive punishment, but these names seem misleading. I have chosen the name **presentation punishment.** It occurs when the *appearance* of a stimulus following the behavior suppresses or decreases the behavior. When teachers use demerits, extra work, running laps, and so on, they are attempting to use this kind of punishment. The other type of punishment, **removal punishment,** involves the *disappearance* or removal of a stimulus. When teachers or parents take away privileges after a young person has behaved inappropriately, they are applying this second kind of punishment. With both types, the effect is to decrease the behavior that led to the punishment. Figure 5–1 summarizes the four different processes we have just discussed: the two kinds of reinforcement and the two kinds of punishment.

punishment:
anything that weakens or suppresses behavior

presentation punishment:
presenting an aversive stimulus

removal punishment:
removing something pleasant or desired

Reinforcement Schedules

continuous reinforcement:
reinforcing a behavior each time it occurs

When people are learning a new behavior, they will learn it faster if they are reinforced for every correct response. This is a **continuous reinforcement** schedule. Once the response has been mastered, however, it is generally

Figure 5–1   **Reinforcement and Punishment**

		EFFECT	
		Behavior Is Increased	Behavior Is Suppressed
STIMULUS	Presented	Positive reinforcement Example: good grades	Presentation punishment Example: spanking
	Removed	Negative reinforcement Example: excused from homework	Removal punishment Example: no TV for a week

Table 5–2 Reinforcement Schedules

Schedule	Definition	Example	Response Pattern
Fixed-interval	Predictable reinforcement, based on set time intervals	Reinforcing the first correct response occurring after each 5-minute interval	Increased rate of responding as time for reinforcement approaches; pause after reinforcement
Variable-interval	Unpredictable reinforcement, based on varying time intervals	Reinforcing the correct response after 5 minutes, then after 7 minutes, then 3, then 9	Slow, steady rate of responding; very little pause after reinforcement
Fixed-ratio	Predictable reinforcement, based on set number of responses	Reinforcing every 10th correct response	High rate of responding; pause after reinforcement
Variable-ratio	Unpredictable reinforcement, based on varying number of responses	Reinforcing the 10th correct response, then the 7th response, then the 9th, then the 12th	Very high rate of responding; little pause after reinforcement

intermittent reinforcement: reinforcing a behavior frequently, but not each time

better to reinforce on an **intermittent** schedule—that is, reinforcing often but not every time. There are several reasons for using intermittent schedules to maintain established skills. One is simply that reinforcing every correct response would be time-consuming and practically impossible for the classroom teacher. Another is that intermittent reinforcement helps the student learn not to expect reinforcement every time.

There are four basic types of intermittent reinforcement schedules. Two are based on the amount of time that passes between reinforcers, and these are called *interval schedules.* The other two are based on the number of responses given between reinforcers, and these are called *ratio schedules.* Table 5–2 offers a summary of the four different schedules. Not much research has been done in the classroom to test the effects of different reinforcement schedules on students. However, we can make some good guesses based on studies in other areas (Ferster & Skinner, 1957).

fixed-interval schedule: reinforcement is given at set intervals

Response Patterns.   First, let's look at the effects different schedules have on the timing of responses. When reinforcement is based on a **fixed-interval** standard (every 5 minutes, for example), the reward is predictable. Reinforcement will always be given for the first correct response that occurs after a certain time period. Because the reinforcement is so predictable, there tends to be increased response as the expected time for reinforcement approaches and then a pause right after the reinforcement is given. Assume, for example, that you know your teacher will stop by the library every 15 minutes to praise those who are working. No one in the library has a watch. Still, after about 12 minutes you all begin to focus on your reading so the teacher will not catch you talking. Just after the teacher completes one of the visits and praises you for working, however, you can relax and take a break, knowing that your chance for reinforcement (or punishment) will not come around again for several minutes.

variable-interval schedule: reinforcement is given after varying amounts of time

fixed-ratio schedule: reinforcement is given after a fixed number of responses

variable-ratio schedule: reinforcement is given after varying numbers of responses

Under a **variable-interval** reinforcement schedule, however, the pattern of responding is quite different. If the teacher described above stopped by on a highly unpredictable basis, sometimes returning just 45 seconds after the last visit, there would probably be fewer breaks or pauses after each visit. A teacher who wanted some serious studying to take place would be happier with a variable-interval schedule.

This same principle holds for **fixed-ratio** and **variable-ratio** schedules. If you know a teacher is only interested in completed papers (a fixed-ratio schedule), you would be likely to pause after each paper and take a few days off before beginning the large job involved in writing a new paper. If you are like many other students, you might even take a week or two off and end up tackling it all the last night. However, if the teacher asked for partial results at unpredictable stages and graded you on progress (a variable-ratio schedule), you would be more likely to do a little work each day. Again, a teacher who wanted students to spend two weeks on a project, not just one or two days, might be happier with a variable-ratio schedule.

Speed of Performance. Different reinforcement schedules can also have an effect on the speed at which a person performs. If reinforcement is based on the number of responses a person gives—a ratio rather than an interval schedule—the person has more control over the timing of the reinforcement. The faster the person accumulates the correct number of responses, the faster the reinforcement will come. A teacher who says, "As soon as you complete these ten problems correctly, you may go to the student lounge," can thus expect higher rates of performance than a teacher who says, "Work on these ten problems for the next 20 minutes. Then I will check your papers and those with ten correct may go to the lounge."

Persistence. The third aspect of performance affected by different schedules is persistence. If reinforcement is withdrawn completely, the person is likely to slow down and finally stop giving a particular response. In other words, the behavior will probably be extinguished. The rate of extinction

Why are young people so persistent in their pursuit of videogame mastery? What reinforcement schedule do these games provide? *(L.T. Rhodes/Taurus Photos)*

will depend in large part on the schedule of reinforcement before the reinforcement stops.

If the reinforcement follows every response (continuous reinforcement), the person will quickly stop responding when the reinforcement stops. Fixed schedules (interval or ratio) also lead to relatively quick extinction. If people are reinforced every five minutes or after five responses, they will soon stop responding when reinforcement does not follow the expected pattern. Both continuous and fixed patterns of reinforcement are quite predictable: we come to expect reinforcement at certain points and generally are quick to give up when the reinforcement does not meet our expectations. To encourage persistence of responding, variable schedules are most appropriate.

Controlling the Antecedents

Antecedents provide information about which behaviors are appropriate in a given situation—that is, which behaviors will lead to positive consequences and which to negative. Quite often a kind of antecedent cue is involved. The antecedent cue of a principal standing in the hall provides information to students about the probable consequences of running or attempting to break into a locker. We often respond to such antecedent cues without fully realizing that they are influencing our behavior. But cues can be used deliberately in teaching.

cueing: providing a stimulus that "sets up" a desired behavior

By definition, **cueing** is the act of providing an antecedent stimulus just before a particular behavior is to take place. Cueing is particularly useful in setting the stage for behaviors that must occur at a specific time but are easily forgotten. In working with young people, teachers (and parents, for that matter) often find themselves correcting behaviors after the fact. For example, they may remind children to do better next time or ask students, "When are you going to start remembering to. . . ?" Such reminders often lead to irritation. The mistake is already made, and the young person is left with only two choices, to promise to try harder or to say, "Why don't you leave me alone?" Neither response is very satisfying.

Establishing a nonjudgmental cue can help avoid these negative confrontations. When a student performs the appropriate behavior after a cue, the teacher can reinforce the student's accomplishment instead of punishing the student's failure. Without cueing teachers might never have a chance to reinforce appropriate behaviors, since students might not remember to perform them (Knapczyk & Livingston, 1974).

An Example

Cueing might have worked in Elizabeth's classroom. To begin her game, Elizabeth might have said something like this: "When you play this game, it is sometimes hard to resist the temptation to make silly remarks. You can all help by not laughing if someone makes a remark that is just a joke." After the first few serious remarks, she could have then said: "You are doing a good job of sticking to the subject. Since you are coming up with such good words, we can play the game for a few more minutes before I begin the lesson."

The uses of operant conditioning in the classroom are numerous. To help you summarize the many points made here, a set of Guidelines on this subject is included.

Guidelines

Using Operant Conditioning

Make sure that positive behavior in class is reinforced.

Examples
1. *When presenting class rules, set up positive consequences for following rules as well as negative consequences for breaking rules: "If everyone turns in the homework tomorrow, there will be no homework for the following day."*
2. *Recognize honest admission of mistakes by giving a second chance: "Bill, since you admitted that you copied from Ann's paper, I'm going to give you another test tomorrow. If this happens again, I'll have to give you an F for the test."*

Make sure reinforcement is truly reinforcing.

Examples
1. *Offer meaningful rewards for academic efforts, such as free time at the end of class, extra recess time, exemptions from homework or tests, the chance to tutor younger children, opportunities to work in the computer lab, time in the class "listening booth," extra credit on major projects.*
2. *Discuss appropriate rewards for especially good work with the class.*

When students are tackling new material or trying new skills, give plenty of reinforcement.

Examples
1. *Find and comment on something right in every student's first life drawing.*
2. *Reinforce students for encouraging each other: "French pronunciation is difficult and awkward at first. Let's help each other by eliminating all giggles when someone is brave enough to attempt a new word."*

After new behaviors are established, give reinforcement on an unpredictable schedule to encourage persistence.

Examples
1. *Offer surprise rewards for good participation in class.*
2. *Start classes with a short, written extra-credit question. Students don't have to answer, but a good answer will add points to their total for the semester.*
3. *Make sure the good students get compliments for their work from time to time. Don't take them for granted.*

Use cueing to help establish new behaviors.

Examples
1. *Put up humorous signs in the classroom to remind students of rules.*
2. *At the beginning of the year, as students enter class, call their attention to a list on the board of the materials they should have with them when they come to class.*

LEARNING BY OBSERVING OTHERS

When Elizabeth laughed at "Clark Gable's" comments in class, she communicated that laughing was appropriate in this situation. Soon all the students were laughing along with her, and she did not try to stop them until it was too late. They were learning through observation—even though this was not the type of learning Elizabeth had intended. Elizabeth, through her behavior, provided a model for her students to imitate.

There are two main ways of learning through observation. First, **observational learning** can take place through *vicarious conditioning.* This happens when we see others rewarded or punished for particular actions, and then we increase or decrease our behavior as if we had received the consequences ourselves. For example, after two people in my department were promoted, almost everyone coming up for tenure in the next few years used the same format for promotion materials as the reinforced models had used. This illustrates vicarious reinforcement. Punishment can also be vicarious: you may slow down on a particular street after having seen several people get speeding tickets on that street.

In the second kind of observational learning, the observer imitates the behavior of a model even though the model receives no reinforcement or punishment while the observer is watching. Often, the model is demonstrating something the observer wants to learn and expects to be reinforced for mastering—for example, the proper way to position hands while playing a piano or the correct pronunciation of *bonjour.* But imitation can also occur when the observer simply wants to become more like an admired, high-status model. Models need not be real people. We may use fictional characters as models too and try to behave as we imagine the character would (W. Hill, 1985).

Albert Bandura (1971, 1977) is responsible for much of what we know today about observational learning. This type of learning is a major element of social cognitive theory. In the early 1960s Bandura was already at work on this theory, showing ways in which cognitive processes could be important in learning new behaviors. In a classic study, he demonstrated that children were more aggressive after watching an aggressive model, a film of an aggressive model, or a cartoon depicting violence than they were after viewing a nonaggressive model or no model at all (Bandura, 1963). It seems, in fact, that both hostile behavior and moral standards are readily imitated by observers (Bower & Hilgard, 1981).

The repeated demonstration that people and animals can learn merely by observing another person or animal learn has offered a challenge to the behaviorist idea that cognitive factors are unnecessary in an explanation of

Modeling can occur even if the reinforcement isn't observed directly. Just hearing about the positive consequences of behavior can lead to imitation if you, like Nancy's friends, expect to be reinforced, too. (© United Features Syndicate)

learning. Observation can be a very efficient learning process. The first time children hold hairbrushes, cups, tennis rackets, or steering wheels, they usually brush, drink, swing, or steer as well as they can, given their current muscle development and coordination. Through modeling, we learn not only how to perform a behavior but also what will happen to us in specific situations if we do perform it. For example, you may be more careful about reading the newspaper in certain classes because you have seen what happened to other students in those classes who were caught reading the paper. Let's take a closer look at how observational learning occurs.

Elements of Observational Learning

Bandura (1986) notes that there are four important elements to be considered in observational learning. They are attention, retention, production, and motivation or reinforcement.

Attention. In order to learn through observation, we have to pay attention. Whether students pay attention to a particular model will depend on many things. As we've noted, people who are attractive, popular, competent, respected, or admired tend to get our attention (Sulzer-Azaroff & Mayer, 1986). For younger children this could mean parents, older brothers or sisters, or teachers. For older students, it may mean popular peers, rock stars, or TV idols. (At the time of this writing, for example, it seems many men are trying new styles of dress and grooming by imitating the stars of "Miami Vice.") Often, behaviors that have little or nothing to do with the high status of very prestigious models may be imitated. For example, students may be popular because they have excellent interpersonal skills or are considered very attractive. If these students happen to adopt a particular style of dress or manner of speech, others may imitate the dress or speech, even though these behaviors are not the main reasons for the students' popularity.

In teaching, you will have to ensure students' attention to the critical features of the lesson by making clear presentations and highlighting important points (more about this in Chapters 7 and 8). In demonstrating a skill (for example, threading a sewing machine or operating a lathe), you may need to have students look over your shoulder as you work. Seeing your hands from the same perspective as they see their own directs attention to the right features of the situation and makes imitation easier.

Retention. In order to imitate the behavior of a model, you have to remember it. This involves mentally representing the model's actions in some way, probably as verbal steps ("Hwa-Rang, the eighth form in Tae Kwan Do is a palm-heel block, then a middle riding stance punch, then . . ."), or as visual images, or both. Retention can be improved by mental rehearsal (imagining yourself imitating the behavior) or by actual practice. In the retention phase, practice helps you remember the sequence of steps.

Production. Once we "know" how a behavior should look and remember the steps, we still may not perform it smoothly. Sometimes a great deal of practice, feedback, and coaching about subtle points is needed before we

High-Status Models

can reproduce the behavior of the model. In the production phrase, practice makes the behaviors smoother and more expert.

Motivation or Reinforcement.   As I mentioned earlier, social cognitive theory distinguishes between acquisition and performance. We may acquire a new skill or behavior through observation, but we may not perform that behavior until there is some incentive to do so.

Anticipating Rewards

Reinforcement can play several roles in observational learning. If we anticipate being reinforced for imitating the actions of a model, we may be more motivated to pay attention, remember, and reproduce the behaviors. In addition, reinforcement is important in maintaining learning. Even if modeling causes you to try a new behavior, you are unlikely to persist if you receive little reinforcement (Barton, 1981; Ollendick, Dailey, & Shapiro, 1983). For example, if an unpopular student adopted the dress of the in-group but was greeted with teasing and ridicule, it is unlikely that the imitation would continue.

Classroom Applications of Observational Learning

A dramatic example of the impact of modeling is found in a study by O'Connor (1969). He began by identifying a group of preschool children who were very isolated from their peers and seemed unable to play normally. Half of this group were shown a film in which a child gradually moved from playing alone to playing with peers; positive consequences followed the child's increased social interaction in the film. The other half of the preschool group saw a film with no human characters. The children who saw the first film increased their own interactions with their peers dramatically.

Effects of Observational Learning

Although such dramatic results are not always possible, observational learning deserves considerable attention. This learning process can have five different effects.

Teaching New Behaviors.   A wide range of new behaviors, such as speaking a foreign language, developing skills in sports, and tasting wine properly, are acquired through observing others. The appropriate if often embarrassing use of colorful language by children is another example. Throughout the school years, but particularly during adolescence, students often learn how to dress, talk, and behave by observing the interactions of popular peers (Baldwin & Baldwin, 1986).

Given all this, consider the role of the classroom teacher. Teachers serve as models for the acquisition of a tremendous range of new behaviors, from pronouncing vocabulary words to enthusiasm about learning. According to Bandura (1986), learning new behavior through observation of someone else may well be more efficient than learning the behavior through direct reinforcement. For teachers, this fact presents endless opportunities, as well as some obvious need for care.

Encouraging Already Learned Behaviors.   The preschool students viewing O'Connor's film were probably already able to interact with their peers. They simply didn't do it very often. The effect of viewing the film was to

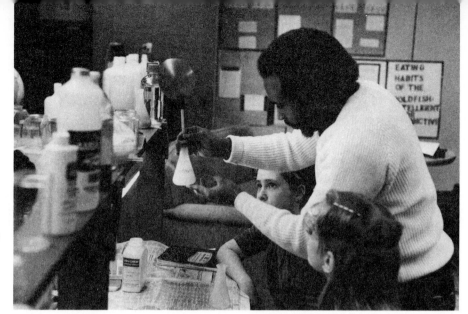

This teacher's role as model pervades everything he does. Not only is he showing his students how to do something, but he is conveying enthusiasm, interest, and commitment to learning. *(Ken Karp)*

draw forth behaviors already in the students' repertoire. All of us have had the experience of looking for cues from other people when we find ourselves in unfamiliar situations. Observing the behavior of others tells us which of our already learned behaviors to use: the proper fork for eating the salad, when to leave a gathering, what kind of language is appropriate, and so on. Adopting the dress and grooming styles of TV idols is another example of this kind of effect.

Strengthening or Weakening Inhibitions. If a class witnesses one student breaking a class rule and getting away with it, they may learn that undesirable consequences do not follow rule breaking. Members of the class may be less inhibited in the future about breaking this rule. If the rule breaker is a well-liked, high-status class leader, the effect of the modeling may be even more pronounced. One psychologist has called this phenomenon the **ripple effect** (Kounin, 1970). You saw an example in Elizabeth's class. When she laughed and did not stop the first few students from giggling, she encouraged more laughter.

ripple effect: "contagious" spreading of behaviors through imitation

The ripple effect can also work for the teacher's benefit. When the teacher deals effectively with a rule breaker, especially a class leader, the idea of breaking this rule may be suppressed in the other students viewing the transaction. This does not mean that teachers must reprimand each student who breaks a rule. As we will see in Chapter 6, praising appropriate behavior while ignoring inappropriate behavior is sometimes much more effective. But once a teacher has called for a particular action, following through is an important part of capitalizing on the ripple effect.

The ripple effect could have been used to great advantage in Elizabeth's class. Remember the problems she had with the game? If all else had failed, she could have dealt with the situation by calling the game to a halt early and saying, "Linda, Carol, David, and Steven, you gave some thoughtful answers. You may hand out these papers (or leave for lunch early, or lead the small discussion groups today)." Although this strategy might not have salvaged the game for the day, it could have had a positive effect on the other students. They could have learned through observation how to conduct themselves. And the next time Elizabeth introduced a game, students might be ready to participate more appropriately, since they had already seen that appropriate participation produced desirable consequences.

Directing Attention.   By observing others, we may not only learn about what they do, we may also learn about aspects of the situation, either about specific objects that are involved or about the setting in general. In the future, we may notice those aspects and make greater use of them. For example, children who watched a doll being pounded with a mallet not only imitated the pounding but also started using the mallet for many other purposes (Bandura, 1986). In a preschool class, when one child plays enthusiastically with a toy that has been ignored for days, many other children may want to have the toy, even if they play with it in different ways or simply carry it around without really playing with it at all. This happens, in part, because the children's attention has been drawn to that particular toy.

Arousing Emotion.   Finally, through observational learning, people may develop emotional reactions to situations they themselves have never experienced, such as flying or driving. A child who watches a friend fall from a swing and break an arm may become fearful of swings. Students may be anxious when they are assigned to a certain teacher just because they've heard frightening stories about how "mean" that teacher is. Note that hearing or reading can be considered observation as well.

A set of Guidelines on observational learning appears on the next page.

APPLYING THE PRINCIPLES: BEHAVIORAL TECHNOLOGY

In a recent article in the *American Psychologist*, B. F. Skinner (1984) gave these four general guidelines for improving teaching based on behavioral principles:

Skinner's Guidelines

1. *Be clear about what is to be taught.* Make sure both you and your students are aware of what they are supposed to learn. It is important for you to know exactly what achievements you will reinforce. And as we will see in Chapter 11, it is much easier for students to learn something if they know what it is. This is especially true with basic skills and factual material.

2. *Teach first things first.* Many times students have trouble learning because they have not mastered the basic skills necessary for understanding a more complex concept. Children who cannot read many of the words on a work sheet will have trouble matching words and definitions. Before students can write creatively, they must be able to write. Many failures occur because we expect students to use several skills together when they cannot even use each skill separately.

3. *Stop making all students advance at essentially the same rate.* This procedure makes some students move too fast and holds others back. Many people have wrestled with this problem in education. We will look at a number of solutions in Chapter 11.

Guidelines

Using Observational Learning

Model those behaviors you want your students to learn.

Examples
1. *Show enthusiasm for the subject you teach.*
2. *Be willing to demonstrate both the physical and mental tasks you expect the students to perform. I once saw a teacher sit down in the sandbox while her 4-year-old students watched her demonstrate the difference between "playing with sand" and "throwing sand."*
3. *When you read to students, model good problem solving about the reading. Stop and say, "Now let me see if I remember what happened so far" or "That was a hard sentence. I'm going to read it again."*

Use peers as models.

Examples
1. *In group work, pair students who do well with those who are having difficulties.*
2. *Ask students to demonstrate the difference between "whispering" and "silence—no talking."*

Make sure students see that positive behaviors lead to reinforcement for others.

Examples
1. *Point out the connections between positive behavior and positive consequences in stories.*
2. *Be fair in giving reinforcement. The same rules for rewards should apply to the problem students as well as to the good students.*

Enlist the help of popular students in modeling behaviors for the entire class.

Examples
1. *Ask a well-liked student to be friendly to an isolated, fearful student.*
2. *Let high-status students lead an activity when you need class cooperation or when students are likely to be reluctant at first. Popular students can model dialogues in foreign-language classes or dissection procedures when first introduced in biology.*

4. *Program the subject matter.* Skinner believes programmed instruction is a valuable teaching tool. Let's take a closer look.

Programmed Instruction

programmed instruction: self-instructional materials with small steps and immediate feedback

As with many other concepts in educational psychology, no one definition of **programmed instruction** would satisfy everyone. The safest definition is that it is a set of instructional materials students can use to teach themselves about a particular topic. Furthermore, it is a set of materials that has been developed in keeping with several key principles, many of them behavioral in origin. According to O'Day, Kulhavy, Anderson, and Malczynski (1971), these principles include:

1. Specification of the goal to be mastered by the learner.
2. Careful pilot testing of the material.
3. Self-pacing to allow learners to move through the material at their own rate.
4. The need for definite responses from the learner.
5. Immediate feedback so the learner will know if a response is correct.
6. A division into small steps.

frames: small steps in programmed instruction

The small steps used in programmed instruction are generally called **frames.** Most contain some text or information and at least one question requiring a student response. Students read the material, answer the question(s) immediately, check to see if the response is correct, and then move on to the next frame. The step from one frame to the next is so small that students can expect to be correct most of the time. But of course, they are not always correct. There are two different kinds of programmed instruction, each with a different way of handling wrong answers.

Linear Programs.   The linear approach is often called Skinnerian programming, because Skinner was its founder and has been its prime advocate. One of its most distinctive features is that students must create an answer, not just select one from a multiple-choice format. In **linear programs** students move through a fixed sequence of frames designed to lead them from one concept to the next with as few errors as possible. If students do make a wrong response, they learn of their error immediately, see the correct answer, and move on to the next frame.

linear program: fixed sequence of frames requiring created answers

Linear programmers believe students should make errors on no more than 5 to 10 percent of the frames. To keep errors at this low level, many of the frames contain some kind of prompt or clue to help students create the correct answer. For example, students may be given four-letter lines to fill in when the correct answer has exactly four letters. Figure 5–2 presents other examples of prompts.

The linear programmers' emphasis on error-free learning goes back to Skinner's belief that wrong answers strengthen unwanted responses (Skinner, 1954). Advocates of branching programs are less concerned about eliminating wrong answers and, in fact, use wrong answers as part of the teaching approach.

Branching Programs.   This second approach to programmed instruction is often called multiple-choice programming because students are given several choices for each response. After each choice, students are told to go to a particular frame for more information. If they choose the correct answer, they will be directed to a frame that says, in effect, "You're right. Congratulations! Here's another problem." If they choose the wrong answer, they are sent to a frame telling them they are wrong, giving a remedial explanation, and then sending them back to try again. Crowder (1960) is the person usually credited with establishing this approach to programmed instruction.

branching program: multiple-choice format with multiple sequences of frames

The primary advantage of a **branching program** is that the developer can first test a frame to find the most common student errors and misconceptions. Then remedial frames can be designed to correct these common errors. A second potential advantage of branching programs is that very bright or well-prepared students can move through the material quickly, skipping

Figure 5–2   Prompts for Programmed Instruction

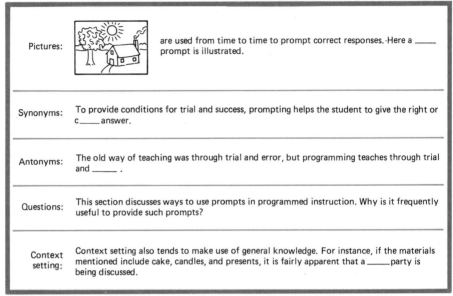

Pictures:	are used from time to time to prompt correct responses. Here a _____ prompt is illustrated.
Synonyms:	To provide conditions for trial and success, prompting helps the student to give the right or c____ answer.
Antonyms:	The old way of teaching was through trial and error, but programming teaches through trial and _____ .
Questions:	This section discusses ways to use prompts in programmed instruction. Why is it frequently useful to provide such prompts?
Context setting:	Context setting also tends to make use of general knowledge. For instance, if the materials mentioned include cake, candles, and presents, it is fairly apparent that a _____party is being discussed.

Adapted from B. Sulzer-Azaroff & G. R. Mayer (1986), Achieving educational excellence using behavioral strategies. *New York: Holt, Rinehart and Winston, p. 272. Copyright © 1986 by CBS College Publishing. Used by permission of CBS College Publishing.*

the remedial frames, while slower students receive all the help they need. The disadvantage of branching programs is that they do not lend themselves very well to materials such as handouts or books. Turning back and forth to find the next frame can get very confusing. Once you lose your place in a branching-program book, it is very difficult to find it again (O'Day, Kulhavy, Anderson, & Malczynski, 1971).

The Usefulness of Programmed Instruction.   Research comparing the effectiveness of linear and branching programs has failed to demonstrate that one type is better than the other (Silberman, Melaragno, Coulson, & Estevan, 1961; O'Day, Kulhavy, Anderson, & Malczynski, 1971). Similarly, research has not demonstrated that programmed instruction is any better or any worse than other forms of teaching (Bangert, Kulik, & Kulik, 1983), although Langer's review of 112 studies indicated that programmed instruction has led to significantly more student learning in about 40 percent of the studies examined (Langer, 1972). As we will continue to discover throughout this text, no one method is best all the time for every subject and student.

My experience with programmed instruction is that the process of designing a program for students can be very enlightening in and of itself. Trying to break material down into small steps helps teachers realize how much they often take for granted in their teaching. We all frequently take large steps in our explanations, leaving many students behind. In addition, seeing the students' wrong answers can help you improve your teaching by pinpointing key misunderstandings.

There are a number of cases in which programmed instruction may prove valuable. Having these materials available to reteach concepts can be very helpful if only a few students need extra help. Low-achieving students and very anxious students often benefit from programmed instruction, probably because it is clear, well organized, and allows the students to repeat parts they do not understand the first time through (Cronbach & Snow, 1977; S. Tobias, 1981, 1982). Finally, you might consider asking students to write programs themselves. This activity not only helps the students learn the material, but it also provides you with programs that might be appropriate for slower students.

As a teacher, you probably would write linear rather than branching programs for your students. A really sophisticated branching program is difficult to create and even more difficult to put on paper. For this reason, branching programs are often presented by computers. This is just one of the many uses of the computer in the classroom. Computers are becoming so important in education that I have included an epilogue on their role, "Teaching and Learning in the Computer Age." The advent of the computer has added new possibilities for designing instruction in the 1980s; but more on this later. Let's end this chapter with a look at a system that does not require any special equipment, the Keller Plan.

The Keller Plan

In the mid-1960s, Fred Keller developed an approach to individualizing instruction that does not rely on any special materials or machines. The system makes use of several behavioral principles (specific goals, small steps, and immediate feedback) as well as lectures, demonstrations, and tutoring (Keller, 1966). It has been used mostly for college teaching and has been very carefully researched.

Keller Plan/PSI:
program with small
units, specific goals,
self-pacing, and
feedback

The **Keller Plan,** also called the **Personalized System of Instruction (PSI),** has a number of basic components (Robin, 1976). First, course readings are broken down into small units, each with specific goals and study guides. Students move at their own pace through the units and then come to class for testing. Proctors, usually students who have successfully completed the course, administer an oral or written test for the unit in class and give immediate feedback. If students have mastered the unit (generally with a score of 80 percent or better), they can go on to the next. If not, they must repeat the unit and take another test. Grades depend on the number of units successfully completed and perhaps to a small extent on a midterm and a final examination. Lectures and demonstrations are used more to motivate students than to present information.

Evaluations of PSI have been very positive. In a review of 39 studies comparing the Keller approach with other teaching methods, Robin (1976) found significantly higher student achievement in 30 of the 39 studies. Using sophisticated statistical procedures to analyze the results of 75 studies with college students, Kulik, Kulik, and Cohen (1979) found that students in Keller Plan courses scored higher on final exams and on tests given several months after the course and made higher final grades as well. Students found the Keller Plan courses more enjoyable and demanding and higher in overall quality than regular classes.

A number of studies have examined the Keller Plan to determine which components are the most important for student learning. The most important elements appear to be (1) specific goals; (2) frequent testing; (3) proctoring; (4) having to master one unit before moving on to the next; and (5) a relatively high level for mastery. Self-pacing and lectures do not seem necessary, and tests can be either oral or written. Even if you do not use the entire Keller Plan, you might consider incorporating some of the effective features into your teaching, especially if you work with high school students.

SUMMARY

1. In defining learning, theorists disagree about the role of thinking, although most would agree that learning is demonstrated when a person responds to a situation in a new way and the new response continues to occur in similar situations.

2. Behavioral theorists place special emphasis on environmental stimuli and observable responses.

3. In contiguity learning, if two events occur together repeatedly, they will become associated. Later, when only one event is present, the other will also be remembered.

4. In classical conditioning, a previously neutral stimulus is repeatedly paired with a stimulus (the unconditioned stimulus) that is already capable of bringing forth an emotional or physiological response. After several pairings, the (previously neutral) conditioned stimulus alone will bring forth a similar response (the conditioned response).

5. In classical conditioning, responses are subject to the processes of generalization, discrimination, and extinction.

6. Operant conditioning is concerned with the deliberate responses of people to their environment. A response can be influenced by its antecedents and its consequences.

7. The consequences following an action may become reinforcement or punishment for the person involved. The effects of a consequence define it as reinforcement or punishment. Positive and negative reinforcement strengthen behavior. Punishment decreases or suppresses behavior.

8. The scheduling of reinforcement can have a major influence on the speed and persistence of responses. The highest rates of responding are found with ratio schedules. The greatest persistence occurs with variable schedules.

9. Antecedent cues can be used to let students know which behaviors will be followed by positive consequences and which will be followed by negative consequences.

10. Observational learning can take place in two ways: vicarious conditioning and imitation of high-status models. This type of learning involves four elements: attention, retention, production, and motivation or reinforcement.

11. Observational learning can teach new behaviors, encourage learned behaviors, strengthen or weaken inhibitions, direct attention, and arouse emotion.

12. Programmed instruction offers a systematic application of behavioral learning principles, allows for self-pacing, and breaks lessons into small steps. There are two basic types of programs—linear and branching.

13. Another method based on behavioral principles is the Keller Plan, or the Personalized System of Instruction (PSI).

KEY TERMS

behavioral learning theories	reinforcement
cognitive learning theories	positive reinforcement
neobehaviorists	negative reinforcement
social cognitive theory	punishment
learning	presentation punishment
contiguity	removal punishment
stimulus	continuous reinforcement
response	intermittent reinforcement
classical conditioning	fixed-interval schedule
unconditioned stimulus (US)	variable-interval schedule
unconditioned response (UR)	fixed-ratio schedule
conditioned stimulus (CS)	variable-ratio schedule
conditioned response (CR)	cueing
generalization	observational learning
discrimination	ripple effect
extinction	programmed instruction
law of effect	frames
operant conditioning	linear program
Skinner box	branching program
antecedents	Keller Plan/PSI
consequences	

SUGGESTIONS FOR FURTHER READING AND STUDY

BALDWIN, J. D., & BALDWIN, J. I. (1986). *Behavioral principles in everyday life* (2nd ed.). Englewood Cliffs, NJ: Prentice-Hall. The focus here is on using behavioral principles in a variety of real-life situations, not just the classroom.

BANDURA, A. (1986). *Social foundations of thought and action: A social cognitive theory.* Englewood Cliffs, NJ: Prentice-Hall. This is the latest elaboration of Bandura's ideas. The book is not light reading, but it is an important integration of behavioral and cognitive perspectives.

BOWER, G. H., & HILGARD, E. R. (1981). *Theories of learning* (5th ed.). Englewood Cliffs, NJ: Prentice-Hall. This is a classic reference on the range of learning theories, from behavioral to cognitive.

HILL, W. F. (1985). *Principles of learning: A handbook of application* (4th ed.). Sherman Oaks, CA: Alfred Publishers. While this book emphasizes applications of behavioral views, it goes on to discuss language, memory, thinking, and moral development.

MORROW, L., & WEINSTEIN, C. (1986). Encouraging voluntary reading: The impact of a literature. *Reading Research Quarterly, 21,* 330–346. This article has some very imaginative, research-based suggestions for boosting young children's interest in reading and literature.

Teachers' Forum

Being Comfortable with Being Positive

According to one of the principles of operant conditioning, if you want to increase a child's desirable behavior, positively reinforce that behavior when it occurs. Teachers are told, "Catch the child being good." However, in the course of a busy school day it is often difficult, especially for beginning teachers, to act on this advice and to feel natural and comfortable about it. How did you get yourself into the habit of noticing desirable behaviors? Did you feel awkward at first?

The Importance of Practice

After ten years of teaching, I still make every effort to catch *each* child being good. Yes, I did feel awkward the first few months of my first year. However, now it's part of my philosophy of teaching as well as of daily living—to reward, compliment, and praise. I got myself in the habit of noticing students' desirable behavior by rewarding appropriate actions, good work habits, and acceptable social skills. When I make a request, I reward those who comply immediately. When I wish to change a student's undesirable behavior, I seat that student by another who exhibits the desired behavior—so it can be rewarded and reinforced.

Patricia Frank, Fourth- and Fifth-Grade Teacher
Cambridge School, South Brunswick, New Jersey

A Variety of Rewards

During class and study time, I walk around the room and tell students quietly at their desks how well they are doing. At the end of each week I have an Award Day. I hand out awards to the child with the best spelling sentences or the neatest penmanship, to the most improved student, to the student who's had all work completed on time to the best of his or her abilities, and so on. At the end of each month, one student is chosen as Student of the Month. The student's picture is taken and posted in the hallway with the other sixth-grade students chosen. The student's name is announced over the public address, and he or she receives an award signed by the principal and the appropriate teachers.

Sharon Klotz, Sixth-Grade Language Arts Teacher
Kiel Middle School, Kiel, Wisconsin

Make It Unpredictable

Studies of operant conditioning indicate that there are advantages to variable reinforcement schedules—reinforcing at unpredictable intervals or at unpredictable stages in a task. How do you go about making rewards unpredictable? Have you found that unpredictable rewards work in your classroom?

On Our Toes

Children, like adults, like to receive "strokes" when deserved. The element of surprise is often effective. I will sometimes give children a sticker, star, or a verbal compliment on the spur of the moment. This tends to keep children "on their toes," since they don't know when I will do this. Also, it gives me a chance to recognize the child who seldom gets a reward (verbal or otherwise), in the rare moment that she or he truly deserves the positive recognition. That child needs this too—perhaps more than anyone else in the classroom! But the praise must be honest and earned. If we observe carefully, we *can* recognize all children at some time or other.

Carolyn R. Cook, Kindergarten Teacher
Ramona Elementary School, Ramona, California

Shaping Patience

How do you keep your patience while trying to shape skill behaviors in students who just don't seem to make any progress?

Variety and Support

Vary materials and techniques you are using with these students (at least it will be refreshing for *you*). Take a step or two away from the situation and analyze why your methods are not working. Share your frustrations with a teacher who has experienced the same difficulty; he or she just might have a solution that would work well for you.

Carol Gibbs, Sixth-Grade Teacher
Happy Valley School, Rossville, Georgia

Break Down the Task

If students do not understand or are having difficulty acquiring a new skill, I look for alternate explanations, analogies, or different teaching methods to use, instead of losing my patience. One very helpful technique is to fragmentize the problem or skill into smaller, more manageable or more easily solved parts. The greater the difficulty, the smaller the fragments. As a teacher, this keeps you focused on student learning, rather than on your own frustration.

R. Chris Rohde, High School Chemistry Teacher
Chippewa Falls Senior High School, Chippewa Falls, Wisconsin

Sick of Oral Assignments

One of your students asks to see the school nurse at least twice a week. According to the nurse, most but not all of the complaints have been groundless. Once he did have severe stomach cramps. Another time he was coming down with the flu. On the average, though, there has been nothing wrong at all. Recently you have noticed that he tends to get sick during oral assignments. What steps would you take in this situation?

Unthreatening Practice

Many students dread oral assignments; for that matter, so do many adults. Informal rehearsals, in which the student can practice his presentation before one or two of his peers, works wonders for this type of "stage fright." For the exceptionally reluctant student, a tape recorder can be provided for practice. In addition to being a nonthreatening activity for the shy student, practicing in small groups will improve the overall quality of the class in oral presentations.

Katherine Stillerman, Seventh-Grade Language Arts
and Social Studies Teacher
Pine Forest Junior High School, Fayetteville, North Carolina

How Serious Is the Problem?

In this case, my job is to discover how serious the problem is. First, (1) establish the pattern of the student's behavior by observation; (2) suggest he stay with the class but allow him to go to the nurse if he feels worse in ten minutes; (3) suggest he go to the nurse after he's given his speech; (4) include him in a panel presentation rather than ask him to give a solo presentation; (5) suggest he write and then simply read his assignment. If these attempts do not seem to solve the problem, I would then (1) alert his adviser that a discussion of this problem is urgent; (2) have a class discussion on how all students view oral assignments; (3) assure the student privately that this is a normal fear and try to work with him on a possible solution.

Shirley Wilson Roby, Sixth-Grade Reading Teacher
Lakeland Middle School, Shrub Oak, New York

6

Applications of Behavioral Approaches

Overview
Focusing on Positive Behavior   198
Reinforcing with Teacher Attention   199
Alternatives to Problem Behaviors   200
Selecting the Best Reinforcers   202
Developing New Behaviors   204
Cueing and Prompting   204
Modeling   207
Shaping   207
Coping with Undesirable Behavior   208
Negative Reinforcement   209
Satiation   210
Punishment   211
Special Programs for Classroom Management   213
Group Consequences   214
Token Reinforcement Programs   216
Contingency Contract Programs   218
Self-Management   221
Approaches to Self-Management   221
Teaching Self-Management   223
Problems and Issues   225
Ethical Issues   225
Criticisms of Behavioral Methods   226
Summary/Key Terms
Suggestions for Further Reading and Study
Teachers' Forum

In this chapter we will look at the classroom application of the behavioral learning principles covered in the last chapter. These principles have proved particularly helpful in classroom management, partly because they focus directly on changes in behavior. Thoughtful use of behavioral methods can make a difference to teachers trying to set up a healthy classroom environment with a minimum of disruptions.

We look first at methods that focus on positive behaviors; then we turn to strategies for helping students develop new skills and abilities. Since there are times when teachers must deal directly with undesirable behaviors, we also present methods for coping with these problems. Then we turn to several more formalized programs that have proved effective in situations where other reinforcement systems have failed—group responsibility programs, token reinforcement, and contingency contracts. Next we discuss involving students in their own learning through self-management. Finally, we explore some of the ethical issues involved in the application of behavioral techniques.

By the time you have finished this chapter, you should be able to do the following:

- Describe how teachers use and misuse attention and praise to reinforce student behavior.
- List criteria for selecting appropriate reinforcers.
- Plan strategies for offering alternative behaviors and using cueing, modeling, and shaping.
- Suggest effective techniques for stopping problem behavior.
- Describe and give examples of formal programs for classroom reinforcement.
- Discuss aspects of self-management and suggest steps by which students can learn greater responsibility for their own behavior.
- Discuss potential dangers and some of the ethical issues involved in the use of any behavioral management technique.

FOCUSING ON POSITIVE BEHAVIOR

To reinforce a behavior is to strengthen it, whether the behavior is spelling words correctly or hitting baseballs. As we noted in Chapter 5, actions followed by reinforcers will be repeated in similar situations in the future. The classroom teacher can capitalize on this principle simply by reinforcing positive behaviors.

What's Right?

This technique seems easy enough to apply—but in truth it takes substantial effort. Misbehavior is easy to recognize. Positive behavior, on the other hand, is often overlooked. We all tend to be good critics. It is usually easier to point out what is wrong than what is right.

Reinforcing with Teacher Attention

Few psychologists would argue with the notion that teachers should recognize and acknowledge the accomplishments of students. And certainly the teacher's attention and recognition seem to be among the least expensive and most readily available reinforcers for students. But does teacher attention really act as a reinforcer for most students? To answer this question, we need results from an experimental study like the classic one conducted by Madsen, Becker, and Thomas (1968).

A Classic Study

This study focused on two problem students in a second-grade class who spent about half their time in school hitting, fighting, destroying school property, running around the room, and disturbing other pupils. Several approaches were tested systematically to see if improvements followed. Setting explicit class rules and repeatedly reminding the students of the rules did nothing to stop the problems. Ignoring the inappropriate behavior and emphasizing the rules also had little effect. If anything, the disruptive behavior increased.

Next the teacher began to give praise and attention to the two students when they were working or playing constructively. The teacher said such things as, "I like the way you are working so quietly!" The teacher also continued to make the rules explicit and to ignore any infractions. This combination of setting and holding to explicit rules, ignoring problem behavior, and praising positive behavior seemed to work. For the first time, there was a significant decrease in the disruptive behavior.

Then the teacher returned to the original classroom procedures used before the study began. The rate of disruption returned to the earlier level, making it clear that the combination of rules, praise, and ignoring was the effective ingredient. When the teacher resumed these procedures, the two students immediately became less disruptive. This gave even more evidence of a definite cause-and-effect relationship. The treatment led to changes. The changes disappeared when the treatment was removed but reappeared when the treatment was again applied.

How would you deal with this student? Should his inattentiveness simply be ignored and his involvement reinforced? What if there is never any attention to reinforce? *(Richard Hutchings/Photo Researchers)*

Praise-and-Ignore as a Cure-all. Based on results of studies like these, some psychologists have encouraged teachers to "accentuate the positive"— to make liberal use of praise for good behavior while ignoring mistakes and misbehavior. This praise-and-ignore approach can be helpful, but we should not expect it to solve all management problems. Remember, the strategy led to *improvements* in the studies listed above, not to a total elimination of problems. Several studies have shown that disruptive behaviors persist when teachers use positive consequences (mostly praise) as their *only* classroom management strategy (Phiffner, Rosen, & O'Leary, 1985; Rosen, O'Leary, Joyce, Conway, & Phiffner, 1984). For example, when a teacher working with eight problem students eliminated all negative consequences (reprimands, loss of privileges, and so on) and tried using only positive responses to manage the class, the students became more disruptive and less involved in their work. The only way that the teacher was able to keep students engaged without using any negative consequences was to establish an individual reinforcement program with new and highly appealing rewards (Phiffner et. al., 1985). The praise-and-ignore approach might be best thought of as a method for dealing with minor misbehaviors or an option to be used along with other strategies.

There is a second consideration in using praise. The positive results found in research are based on situations in which teachers carefully and systematically praised their students. Unfortunately, praise is not always given appropriately and effectively. Simply "handing out compliments" will not improve behavior. To be effective, praise must (1) be contingent on the behavior to be reinforced, (2) specify clearly the behavior being reinforced, and (3) be believable (O'Leary & O'Leary, 1977). In other words, the praise should be sincere recognition of a well-defined behavior, so students understand what they did to warrant the recognition.

Teachers who have not received special training often violate these conditions (Brophy, 1981). Research indicates that teachers seldom specify clearly the behaviors they are praising. In one study, this specification occurred only 5 percent of the time (Anderson, Evertson, & Brophy, 1979). Of course, students may understand the connection without a clear statement from the teacher, but often they understand less than the teacher assumes. At times, teachers fail to make praise contingent on appropriate behavior and may even praise wrong answers. Finally, teachers make praise seem insincere by saying positive things with facial expressions or voice tones that do not fit. Ideas for using praise effectively, based on Brophy's (1981) extensive review of the subject, are presented in the Guidelines.

Some psychologists have suggested that teachers' use of praise tends to focus students on learning to win approval rather than on learning for its own sake. Perhaps the best advice is to be aware of the potential dangers of the overuse or misuse of praise and to navigate accordingly. What other tools and approaches are available to teachers?

Alternatives to Problem Behaviors

Any negative behavior (hitting or forgetting homework, for example) can be viewed as an absence of positive behavior (cooperative play or turning in homework on time). In other words, if students are playing cooperatively,

Effects of Praise Alone

Specificity and Sincerity

Overuse or Misuse

Guidelines

Using Praise Appropriately

Be clear and systematic in giving praise.

Examples
1. *Make sure praise is tied directly to appropriate behavior and doesn't happen randomly.*
2. *Make sure the student understands the specific action or accomplishment that is being praised. You could say, "You brought the materials I lent you back on time and in excellent condition. Well done!" instead of saying, "You were very responsible."*

Recognize genuine accomplishments.

Examples
1. *Reward the attainment of specified goals, not just participation, unless participation is the major goal of the activity.*
2. *Be especially careful not to reward uninvolved students just for being quiet and not disrupting class.*
3. *Tie praise to students' improving competence or to the value of their accomplishment. You might say, "You are working more carefully now. I noticed that you double-checked all your problems. That is a very important habit to develop. Your score reflects your careful work," instead of simply, "Good for you. You have the top grade in your group."*

Set standards for praise based on the individual abilities and limitations of the student involved.

Examples
1. *Praise progress or accomplishment in relation to the individual student's past efforts.*
2. *Focus the student's attention on his or her own progress, not on comparisons with others.*

Attribute the student's success to effort and ability, so the student will gain confidence that success is possible again.

Examples
1. *Avoid implying that the success may be based on luck, extra help, or easy material.*
2. *Ask students to describe the problems they encountered and how they solved them.*

Make praise really reinforcing.

Examples
1. *Avoid singling out students for praise in an obvious attempt to influence the rest of the class. This tactic often backfires, since students know what's really going on. In addition, if you say, "I like the way Ken is . . . ." too many times, Ken will be embarrassed and may be seen as the teacher's pet.*
2. *Don't give undeserved praise to students simply to balance failures. (Brophy calls this "praise as a consolation prize.") It is seldom consoling and calls attention to the student's inability to earn genuine recognition.*

they cannot be hitting one another at the same time. One aspect of dealing with any problem behavior should be reinforcing more desirable behaviors when they do occur. If you simply try to stop negative behaviors without providing alternatives, students are likely to find their own replacements. The new situation may be as bad as or worse than the original.

positive practice:
practicing correct
responses
immediately after
errors

Positive practice is a strategy for helping students replace one behavior with another. This approach is especially appropriate for dealing with academic errors. When students make a mistake, they must correct it as soon as possible and practice the correct response. Foxx and Jones (1978) and Ollendick, Matson, Esveldt-Dawson, and Shapiro (1980) used this procedure, combined with positive reinforcement, to improve spelling. Students were rewarded for the words they spelled correctly and had to practice their misspelled words in a variety of ways (using correctly in sentences, spelling phonetically, writing a full dictionary definition, and so on). The combination of positive reinforcement and practice led to 100 percent accuracy in spelling and was preferred by the students to more traditional systems for studying misspelled words. The same principle could be applied when students break classroom rules. Instead of being punished, the student might be required to practice the correct alternative action.

Using Negative Reinforcement

Another approach for decreasing undesirable behavior by offering an alternative involves negative reinforcement. Basically, this means saying to students, if you stop doing x and start doing y, you can get out of an unpleasant situation. For example, my daughter's second-grade teacher used negative reinforcement to help the class learn math facts. As soon as a student answered every problem correctly two weeks in a row on Friday's timed test of addition and subtraction, he or she did not have to take the test anymore. Successful students got to watch their classmates endure the weekly unpleasantness of "Take out your pencil . . . ." A system like this one is appropriate when all the students have the ability to master the material but may simply need some incentive to do so.

Selecting the Best Reinforcers

There are many reinforcers other than teacher attention already available in most classes. In fact, teachers often grant privileges and tangible rewards,

What would students do with free time in school? Many would read, if the materials available and the space provided were appealing and engaging. The best reinforcers are educational as well as entertaining. *(Will McIntyre/Photo Researchers)*

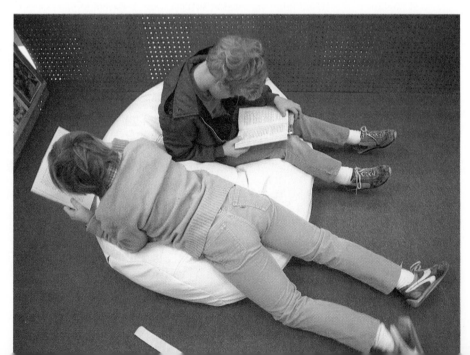

202

Table 6–1 **What Do You Like? Reinforcement Ideas from Students**

NAME _____ Grade _____ Date _____

Please answer all the questions as completely as you can.

1. The school subjects I like best are:
2. Three things I like most to do in school are:
3. If I had 30 minutes free time at school each day to do what I really liked, it would be:
4. My two favorite candies are:
5. At recess I like most to (three things):
6. If I had $1 to spend on anything, I would buy:
7. Three jobs I would enjoy in the class are:
8. The two people I most like to work with in school are:
9. At home I really enjoy (three things):

Adapted from G. Blackham & A. Silberman (1975), Modification of child and adolescent behavior (2nd ed.). Belmont, CA: Wadsworth, pp. 281–83. © 1975 by Wadsworth Publishing Co, Inc. Reprinted by permission of publisher.

such as the chance to talk to other students or feed the class animals. But many teachers tend to offer these rewards in a rather haphazard way. Just as with praise, by making privileges and rewards directly contingent upon learning and positive behavior, the teacher may greatly increase both learning and desired behavior.

Premack principle: states that a more preferred activity can serve as reinforcer for a less preferred activity

A very helpful guide to choosing the most effective reinforcers is the **Premack principle,** named for David Premack (1965). According to the Premack principle, a high-frequency behavior (a preferred activity) can be an especially effective reinforcer for a low-frequency behavior (a less preferred activity). This is sometimes referred to as "Grandma's rule": First do what I want you to do, then you may do what you want to do.

If no work demands were placed on students, what would they do? The answers to this question can suggest many possible reinforcers. For most students, talking, moving around the room, sitting near a friend, being exempt from assignments or tests, reading magazines, or playing games are preferred activities. The best way to determine appropriate reinforcers for your students may be to watch what they do in their free time. If you find yourself saying to a student, "Stop doing that and pay attention!" or "Please put that away until the end of class!" you have probably found a perfect reinforcer for that student.

Another good method is to ask the class for ideas. Questionnaires like the one in Table 6–1 can elicit suggestions. Remember that what works for one student may not be right for another. Serralde de Scholz and McDougall (1978), for example, found that average and fast learners tended to value approval, praise, and being correct much more than slow learners. For students with learning problems, tangible rewards, activities, and privileges may be most effective.

In applying the Premack principle, it is important to remember that the low-frequency behavior must happen first. Consider the Premack principle, and note what is wrong with the following conversation:

STUDENTS:	Oh, no! Do we have to diagram sentences again today? The other classes got to discuss the film we saw in the auditorium this morning.
TEACHER:	But the other classes finished the lesson on sentences yesterday. We're almost finished too. If we don't finish the lesson, I'm afraid you'll forget the rules we reviewed yesterday.
STUDENTS:	Why don't we finish the sentences at the end of the period and talk about the film now?
TEACHER:	Okay, if you promise to complete the sentences later.

The teacher in this example had a perfect opportunity to use the Premack principle. Discussing the film could have served as a reinforcer for completing the lesson on sentences first. As it is, the class could easily spend the entire period discussing the film. But just as the discussion becomes fascinating, the teacher will have to play the role of police officer and insist that the class return to the sentences.

This is not to suggest that a teacher should follow a lesson plan as if it were carved in stone. But in this situation the teacher seemed to have a good reason for continuing with the lesson. Instead of letting the students discuss the film first, she might have said: "I promise you that if we all concentrate, we can finish the sentences in 20 minutes. Then that will be that—you'll understand the lesson and be done with it. *Then* we can spend the rest of the period discussing the film. That way, if the discussion becomes interesting I won't have to stop it in the middle to finish the sentence lesson." In this case, both teacher and students would have achieved their goals.

No matter what reinforcers are best in your classroom, you will benefit from stressing the positive. The Guidelines should help summarize the many methods of reinforcing positive behavior.

DEVELOPING NEW BEHAVIORS

What if the behavior you want to encourage never occurs? A teacher cannot provide a positive consequence for an action that never takes place. In this section we will discuss three approaches to helping students learn new behaviors: cueing, modeling, and shaping. Cueing and modeling are usually considered first, since shaping is a much more time-consuming strategy.

Cueing and Prompting

As we saw in Chapter 5, a cue is a stimulus that provides information about what behavior is appropriate and will be reinforced in a particular situation. Cues are useful in helping students demonstrate behaviors they are physically capable of performing but seldom or never perform on their own. Every student in the room, for example, may be able to get his or her materials ready and begin working immediately after the class bell rings, but few will do so automatically. The bell could serve as a cue, but many students have learned to ignore the bell—possibly because they have not been reinforced for paying attention to it.

The problem in this situation is to teach the students to respond in a positive way (by working) to an antecedent stimulus in their environment (the bell). One approach would be to provide an additional cue—a prompt—just after the first cue occurs. So the strategy for teaching students to get ready for work after hearing the bell might be this:

A Cue/Prompt Strategy

1. On the first day, the teacher begins by saying, "We have been wasting quite a bit of time settling down to work after the bell rings. I have a new system to help us get going more quickly. When the bell rings, I am going to turn on this buzzer. As soon as every person has his or her work started, I will turn off the buzzer."

2. The teacher implements the procedure, upon hearing the class bell.

3. During the first week, the teacher continues the process and praises the students who begin working as soon as the bell rings.

4. During the second week, the teacher begins to wait longer before turning the buzzer on, but she continues to reinforce students for beginning work promptly.

5. By the end of the week, she does not use the buzzer at all but continues to praise the students who respond appropriately to the bell.

 Wesley Becker and his associates have offered two principles for using a cue and a prompt to teach a new behavior (Becker, Engelmann, & Thomas, 1975). First, make sure the environmental stimulus that you want to become a cue occurs right before the prompt you are using, so students will learn to respond to the cue and not just rely on the prompt. Second, fade the prompt as soon as possible so students do not become dependent upon it.

The strategy for teaching students to respond to the bell follows this pattern: first the cue (the bell), then the prompt (the buzzer), and then the gradual fading of the prompt. This strategy also uses negative reinforcement—escape from an unpleasant situation. As soon as the students start working, the teacher removes the unpleasant stimulus of the buzzer.

Another example of cueing is providing students with a checklist or reminder sheet. Figure 6–1 is a checklist for the steps in peer tutoring. After

Figure 6–1   **Written Cues: A Peer-Tutoring Checklist**

Adapted from B. Sulzer-Azaroff & G. R. Mayer (1986), Achieving educational excellence using behavioral strategies. *New York: Holt, Rinehart & Winston, p. 89. Copyright © 1986 by CBS College Publishing. Reprinted by permission of CBS College Publishing.*

students learn the procedures, the checklist may no longer be needed, but the teacher should continue to monitor the process, recognize good work, and correct mistakes.

Modeling

Modeling has long been used, of course, to teach dance, sports, and crafts, as well as the skills in such subjects as home economics, chemistry, and shop. Modeling can also be applied deliberately in the classroom to teach mental skills and to broaden horizons—to teach new ways of thinking, in other words. For example, a teacher might model sound critical thinking skills by thinking "out loud" about a student's question. Or a teacher concerned about girls in a high school class who seem to have stereotyped ideas about the careers available to women might invite women with nontraditional jobs to speak to the class. We have also seen that teachers inadvertently model behaviors that students pick up.

Applying Modeling

Modeling, when applied deliberately, can be an effective and efficient means of teaching new behavior. Research in this area, though still not extensive, offers encouraging results. Studies indicate that modeling can be most effective when all the elements of observational learning, as we noted in Chapter 5, are taken into account—especially reinforcement and practice. Modeling can also reinforce reinforcement—it can make praise more effective. Zimmerman and Pike (1972), for example, found that modeling plus praise was much more effective than praise alone in helping second-grade students learn to ask questions in a small group. Swanson and Henderson (1977) found that the most effective strategy for teaching preschool children to ask questions was to show a videotaped model of children asking questions and then give the children a chance to practice the skill along with appropriate feedback.

In some situations, however, a good cue or even a good model will not help students learn to behave in new ways. Shaping may be appropriate in these cases.

Shaping

What happens when students continually fail to gain reinforcement because they simply cannot perform a skill or behavior in the first place? Consider these examples:

When Shaping Can Help

A fourth-grade student looks at the results of the latest mathematics test. "No credit on almost half of the problems again because I made one dumb mistake in each problem. I hate math!"

A tenth-grade student tries each day to find some excuse for not participating in the softball game in gym class. The student cannot catch a ball and now refuses to try.

In both situations the students are receiving no reinforcement for their work because the end product of their efforts is not good enough—not close enough to the skill or behavior required. A safe prediction is that the students will soon learn to hate the class, the subject, and perhaps the teacher and school in general.

shaping:
reinforcing each
small step of
progress toward a
desired goal or
behavior

One way to prevent this problem and help the students learn the needed behaviors is the strategy of **shaping,** also called successive approximations. Shaping involves reinforcing progress instead of waiting for perfection. In order to use shaping, the teacher must break down the final complex behavior the student is expected to master into a number of small steps, just as in programmed learning a complex lesson or task is broken down into steps. Krumboltz and Krumboltz (1972) have described the following four methods of using shaping.

Methods

1. *Reinforce each subskill.* A complete skill can be broken down into all its subskills, and the student can be reinforced for mastering each subskill. A research paper, for example, can be broken down into outlining skills, using indexes and tables of contents, summarizing information from several sources, drawing conclusions, writing footnotes, and so on.

2. *Reinforce improvements in accuracy.* Sometimes a student can perform the desired behavior, but the results are not very accurate. The teacher in this case might want to emphasize improvements in accuracy. A language teacher, for example, might first reinforce a vague approximation of the correct pronunciation of *Monsieur,* then continue to raise standards gradually until pronunciation is close to that of a native.

3. *Reinforce longer and longer periods of performance.* Students often can perform in a desirable fashion, but only for a few minutes at a time. They can be encouraged to extend this period of time with reinforcement at longer and longer intervals. For example, a student who frequently talks to others during class may be reinforced for remaining quiet for 5 minutes, then 8 minutes, then 12, and so on.

4. *Reinforce longer and longer periods of participation.* Students are sometimes reluctant to participate because they have been embarrassed in the past. In this case, a teacher could begin by reinforcing even the smallest contributions of a student who seldom participates in class. This should probably be done in a matter-of-fact way, since extravagant praise may be embarrassing to a shy student.

Many behaviors can be improved through shaping, especially skills that involve persistence, endurance, increased accuracy, greater speed, or extensive practice to master. Because shaping is a time-consuming process, however, it should not be used if success can be attained through cueing or modeling. The Guidelines for all three procedures—cueing, modeling, and shaping—help clarify these distinctions.

COPING WITH UNDESIRABLE BEHAVIOR

There Will Be
Times. . . .

Up to this point, we have emphasized strategies with a positive focus. I have deliberately begun with these strategies because these approaches should be considered first, before more negative methods are tried. But no matter how successful you are at accentuating the positive, there are times when you must cope with undesirable behavior, either because other methods do not seem sufficient or because the behavior itself is dangerous or calls for direct action. For this purpose, negative reinforcement, satiation, and punishment all offer possible solutions.

Guidelines

Developing New Behaviors

If students are already capable of performing a behavior but often forget to perform it, provide a cue to remind them.

Examples
1. Before changing activities and getting out new materials, remind students of the procedure. You can refer to a list of steps posted on the board or walls.
2. When the due date for a long-term assignment is approaching, put a note on the board: "Book reports due next Monday," or, "Final outlines due in one week!"

If students must learn a new behavior, you may want to provide a model.

Examples
1. When the assignment is to combine collage and watercolor, show several examples of previous students' work.
2. If a new form is required for references, post several examples of correct bibliographies on the bulletin board.

If the goal is far beyond the present ability of the student, try shaping.

Examples
1. When a new procedure is introduced in arithmetic, give partial credit for each step done correctly. Later, require all steps to be correct before students get any credit.
2. If a student never participates in class discussions, begin by asking the student questions that can be answered very briefly and easily. Gradually ask questions that require longer and more complex answers.

Negative Reinforcement

Recall the basic principle of negative reinforcement presented in Chapter 5: if an action stops something unpleasant, then the action is likely to occur again in similar situations. An example is the use of seat-belt buzzers in cars. Fastening the seat belt stops the buzzer. After fastening the seat belt for several weeks, you may continue to do so, for a while at least, even if your buzzer breaks down. Negative reinforcement operates in a number of other everyday situations. Parents, for example, learn to rock their babies in certain ways when the rocking stops the baby's crying. (A crying baby definitely makes for an unpleasant situation.)

Negative reinforcement may also be used to enhance learning. To do this, you must place students in mildly unpleasant situations so they can "escape" when their behavior improves. Consider these examples:

Classroom Examples
A teacher says to a third-grade class, "When the art supplies are put back in the cabinet and each of you is sitting quietly, we will go outside. Until then, we will miss our recess."

A high school teacher says to a student who seldom finishes in-class assignments, "As soon as you complete the assignment, you may join the class in the auditorium. But until you finish, you must work in the study hall."

You may wonder why these examples are not considered punishment. Surely, staying in during recess or not accompanying the class to a special program is punishing. But the focus in each case is on *strengthening* specific behaviors by removing something aversive as soon as the desired behaviors occur. When behavior is strengthened, reinforcement has occurred. Since the consequence involves removing or "subtracting" a stimulus, the reinforcement is negative.

Contrasts to Punishment

There is also the issue of control. Missing recess and staying behind in study hall are unpleasant situations, but in each case the students retain control. As soon as they perform the appropriate behavior, the unpleasant situation ends. In contrast, punishment occurs after the fact, and a student cannot so easily control or terminate it. Sometimes the line between punishment and negative reinforcement is easily crossed. For instance, the third-grade teacher could have used punishment by saying, "Since you are so noisy and haven't put away your art supplies, we will miss 15 minutes of recess!" The high school teacher could have used punishment by saying, "Because you haven't completed your assignment again, I want you to go to the study hall and work instead of attending the special program." In these situations, the students would have had no options. Control of the unpleasant condition would have remained in the hands of the teacher. Only by defying or outwitting the teacher could the students have had an impact.

An equally important difference between negative reinforcement and punishment is found in the potential effect each is likely to have. The ultimate effect of negative reinforcement, when used successfully, is to strengthen some positive behavior. The effect of punishment is to suppress behavior. Negative reinforcement contains a means for ending a certain behavior by increasing a more positive alternative, as we have discussed. At best, punishment will simply help you stop or suppress an undesirable behavior.

Rules

Krumboltz and Krumboltz (1972) offer several rules for negative reinforcement. First, describe the desired change in a positive way. Second, don't bluff. Make sure you can enforce your unpleasant situation. Third, follow through despite complaints. And fourth, insist on action, not promises. If the unpleasant situation terminates when students promise to be better next time, you have reinforced making promises, but not making changes.

Satiation

Another way to stop problem behavior is to insist that students continue the behavior until they are tired of doing it. This procedure should be applied with care. Continuing some behaviors may be very dangerous. For example, a command to smoke every cigarette in a pack would not make sense.

satiation: repeating a problem behavior past the point of interest or motivation

An example of a more appropriate use of **satiation** is related by Krumboltz and Krumboltz (1972). In the middle of a ninth-grade algebra class, the teacher suddenly noticed that four students were making all sorts of unusual motions. When the teacher asked them what they were doing, they initially said it was nothing. When encouraged, they finally admitted they were bouncing imaginary balls. The teacher pretended to greet this idea with enthusiasm and suggested the whole class do it. At first, there was a great deal of laughing and joking. After a minute this stopped, and one student even quit. The teacher, however, insisted that all the students continue. After five minutes and a number of exhausted sighs, the teacher allowed the students to stop. No one bounced an imaginary ball in that class again.

Teachers also may allow students to continue some action until they stop by themselves, if the behavior is not interfering with the rest of the class. This can be done by simply ignoring the behavior. Remember that responding to an ignorable behavior may actually reinforce it.

In using satiation, a teacher must take care not to give in before the students do. It is also important that the repeated behavior is the one you are trying to end. If the algebra teacher above had insisted that the students write, "I will never bounce imaginary balls in class again" 500 times, the students would have become satiated with writing rather than with bouncing balls.

Punishment

As we have already noted, punishment is at best a means of suppressing behavior, either by the presentation of something negative or by the removal of something positive. It does not, in and of itself, lead to any positive behavior. Thus, whenever you consider the use of punishment, you should make it part of a two-pronged attack. The first prong is to carry out the punishment and suppress the undesirable behavior. The second prong of the attack is to make clear what the student should be doing instead and provide reinforcement for those alternative actions. Thus, while the problem behaviors are being suppressed, positive alternative responses are being strengthened.

Punishment is a very popular method for influencing behavior in schools. However, the approach has not eliminated problems. This lack of impact may be due to our lack of knowledge about what constitutes effective punishment. Many methods may stop misbehavior for a few minutes, but punishment should have a more lasting effect. Three strategies—reprimands, response cost, and social isolation—have proved successful in some situations (O'Leary & O'Leary, 1976a).

The Benefits of Reprimands. In an issue of the *Junction Journal,* my daughter's school newspaper, I read the following lines in a story called "Why I Like School," written by a fourth grader: "I also like my teacher. She helps me understand and learn. She is nice to everyone. . . . I like it when she gets mad at somebody, but she doesn't yell at him or her in front of the class, but speaks to them privately."

A study by O'Leary and his associates examined the effects of soft, private **reprimands** versus loud, public reprimands on decreasing disruptive behavior (O'Leary, Kaufman, Kass, & Drabman, 1970). Reprimanding a problem student quietly so that only the student can hear seems to be much more effective. When the teacher in the study spoke to the offenders loudly enough for the entire class to hear, the disruptions increased or continued at a constant level. Perhaps the students enjoyed the public recognition ("You really got the teacher going today, didn't you?"). Perhaps public condemnation encourages a student to save face by having the last word. At any rate, the additional initial effort required to use soft reprimands seems to be a good investment in making lasting improvements.

Part of a Two-Pronged Attack

reprimands: criticisms for misbehavior; rebukes

Response Cost.   The concept of **response cost** is familiar to anyone who has ever paid a fine. For certain infractions of the rules, people must lose some reinforcer (money, time, privileges, pleasures). In a class, the concept of response cost may be applied in the following way. Five problem talkers in a sixth-grade classroom begin each day with 15 marks beside their names on the blackboard. Each time one of the students talks without permission, she or he erases one mark from the board. For each mark remaining at the end of the day, the student gets two minutes of free time. As the students improve, they begin the day with fewer marks. But each mark is now worth more minutes of free time, so the potential reward is still 30 minutes. Later, the number of minutes of available free time is decreased as well.

Social Isolation.   One of the most controversial behavioral methods for decreasing undesirable behavior is the strategy of **social isolation,** often called timeout from reinforcement. The process involves removing a highly disruptive student for five to ten minutes. The student is placed in an empty, uninteresting room alone. It seems likely that the factor that actually decreases behavior is the punishment of brief isolation from other people (Drabman & Spitalnik, 1973; O'Leary & O'Leary, 1976a). It should also be borne in mind that a trip to the principal's office or confinement to a chair in the corner of the regular classroom does not have the same effect as sitting alone in an empty room.

There are several problems with using social isolation. With limited facilities, it is usually impractical or impossible for schools to set aside a separate timeout room or cubicle for each classroom or to coordinate the use of such a room among a number of classes. For these reasons, social isolation is used most often just with problem students in special education classes. When there is an available timeout room, teachers must be able to ensure that a sometimes reluctant student stays in it. With older students, this be-

Social isolation, often called timeout from reinforcement, can be an effective punishment if administered carefully. But is this chair outside the principal's office really "isolated"? It may serve as a reward—all your friends can see "you got the teacher again." *(Richard Hutchings/Photo Researchers)*

comes increasingly difficult. For very resistant problems, however, social isolation can be quite effective. Simply removing a student from the room temporarily (never for more than 15 minutes) is a kinder way to cope with misbehavior than harsh words or hard punishment.

Use with Care

Great care should be exercised with social isolation. Consultation with a school psychologist or specially trained teacher is recommended before attempting this procedure, unless it is a regular part of school policy. Social isolation is easily abused and often misunderstood. Some schools believe social isolation means sending a student to a detention room. But since other people are usually in the room, there is little or no isolation. Also, the average stay in a detention room is longer than 15 minutes.

Some Cautions.   It bears repeating that any procedure that involves unpleasant events should be handled with caution. Punishment can have several negative side effects. Most of us have strong emotional reactions to being punished. The people or situations involved in the punishment tend to become associated with these negative feelings, possibly through a process similar to classical conditioning. We all tend to avoid people and situations associated with pain or unpleasantness in the past. Students may learn to fear or hate teachers, subjects, and events that have been punishing, especially if the students have received little reinforcement in those situations to offset the punishment.

Attempting to escape or avoid unpleasant situations is also a predictable human response. If the consequences of failing are too severe, students may learn to cheat. If the consequences of attending school are too unpleasant, students may cut class or drop out altogether.

A Model for Aggression

Finally, we have seen how students learn behavior and responses through modeling, intentional or otherwise. The adult's response to the misbehavior of a student can become a model for dealing with problems. If you listen to the conversation or watch the play of young students, you often see problems solved through aggression. Some part of that aggression may be learned by observing adults trying to discipline students.

Of course, despite the potentially harmful side effects of negative control, punishment may sometimes be necessary. If a student consistently misbehaves, rarely acts in any positive way that can be reinforced, and shows no desire to change, the problem behavior must be stopped or at least slowed down so that other responses can occur and be reinforced. In such a case, punishment may indeed be called for. In addition, actions that are genuinely dangerous to the student, to others, or to school property at times must also be punished.

It is obvious that effective punishment requires hard work and careful management. The teacher who chooses to use punishment may profit from the Guidelines on the following pages, adapted from the work of Becker, Engelmann, and Thomas (1975).

SPECIAL PROGRAMS FOR CLASSROOM MANAGEMENT

In some situations, you may want to consider using a much more formal system of reinforcers. Three possibilities, all based on behavioral principles, are group consequences, token programs, and contingency contracts.

Guidelines

Punishment

Try to structure the situation so you can use negative reinforcement rather than punishment.

Examples
1. *Allow students to escape unpleasant situations (completing additional workbook assignments, writing a sentence with every spelling word, weekly tests of math facts) when they reach a certain level of competence (85 percent on the unit test, defining each word correctly, 100 percent on the math test three weeks in a row).*
2. *Insist on actions, not promises. Don't let students convince you to change the terms of the agreement.*

Be consistent in your application of punishment.

Examples
1. *Avoid inadvertently reinforcing the behavior you are trying to punish. Don't laugh at the misbehavior and then try to enforce punishment. Keep confrontations private, so that the students involved won't become heroes for standing up to the teacher in a public showdown.*
2. *Let students know in advance the consequence for breaking the rules by posting major class rules for younger students or listing rules and consequences in a course syllabus for older students.*
3. *Tell students they will receive one and only one warning before punishment is given. Give the warning in a calm way, then follow through.*
4. *Make punishment unavoidable and as immediate as is reasonably possible.*

Group Consequences

The Good Behavior Game

Reinforcement for the class can be based on the cumulative behavior of all members of the class, usually by adding each student's points to a class or a team total. The Good Behavior Game is an example of this approach. A class is divided into two teams. Specific rules for good behavior are established. Each time a student breaks one of the rules, that student's team is given a mark. The team with the fewest marks at the end of the period receives a special reward or privilege (longer recess, first to lunch, and so on). If both teams earn fewer than a preestablished number of marks, both teams receive the reward. Harris and Sherman (1973) found that a criterion of as few as four marks worked effectively in maintaining good behavior. Most studies indicate that while the game produces only small improvements in academic achievement, it can produce definite improvements in the behaviors listed in the good behavior rules.

A variation of this game was effective in improving the behavior of an extremely disruptive group while they were in the library. The librarian worked with the students to set rules, divided the class into teams, and gave points to one or both teams several times during the period, as long as everyone on the team followed the rules. The winning team members, or both teams if each received the necessary number of points, collected their reward in the regular classroom once each week (Fishbein & Wasik, 1981).

Focus on the students' actions, not on the students' personal qualities.

Examples
1. *Reprimand in a calm but firm voice.*
2. *Avoid vindictive or sarcastic words or tones of voice. You might hear your own angry words later when students model your sarcasm.*
3. *Stress the need to end the problem behavior instead of expressing any dislike you might feel for the student.*

Adapt the punishment to the infraction.

Examples
1. *Ignore minor misbehaviors that do not disrupt class, or stop these misbehaviors with a disapproving glance or a move toward the student.*
2. *Don't use homework as a punishment for misbehaviors like talking in class.*
3. *When a student misbehaves to gain peer acceptance, removal from the group of friends can be effective, since this is really timeout from a reinforcing situation.*
4. *If the problem behaviors continue, analyze the situation and try a new approach. Your punishment may not be very punishing, or you may be inadvertently reinforcing the misbehavior. I once worked with a teacher who wondered why a boy continued to disrupt her math class every day even though she promptly sent him to the principal each time. It turned out that the boy hated math and really liked the principal, who felt sorry for the boy and always talked sports with him after giving him a brief scolding.*

Whole-Class Rewards

You can also use group consequences without dividing the class into teams. Reinforcement can be based on the behavior of the whole class. Wilson and Hopkins (1973) conducted a study using group responsibility to reduce noise levels. Radio music served as the reinforcer for students in a home economics class. Whenever noise in the class was below a predetermined level, students could listen to the radio; when the noise exceeded the level, the radio was turned off. Given the success of this simple method, such a procedure might be considered in any class where music or similar reinforcers do not interfere with the task at hand. Another example is a method developed by Switzer, Deal, and Bailey (1977) to eliminate stealing in three second-grade classrooms. Each day the teachers said, "If I don't notice anything missing this morning, you will have ten minutes of free time after you have had your snack." Whenever anything was taken, the teacher left the room for a few seconds. If the articles were returned, the free time was still given.

Cautions. In many ways, programs using group consequences have been just as successful as those based on individual consequences. However, caution is needed in applying group approaches. Some systems require individual students to earn points for the whole group. In such situations there is likely to be pressure on these students from the rest of the class. If the students are genuinely unable to perform the required behavior, then failure is probable. The consequences of failure may be great, especially for students who have difficulties making friends.

Pressures on
Students

Even with procedures involving all students, peer pressure may be heavy on students who are not contributing sufficiently to the class or team point total or who are responsible for the loss of points. This peer pressure is not always easy for the teacher to monitor. Recently I saw an entire class break into cheers when the teacher announced that one boy was transferring to another school. The chant "No more points! No more points!" filled the room. The points referred to a system of giving one point to the whole class each time anyone broke a rule. Every point meant five minutes of recess lost. The boy who was transferring had been responsible for many losses. He was not very popular to begin with, and the point system, though quite effective in maintaining order, had led to rejection and even greater unpopularity.

Peer pressure in the form of support and encouragement, however, can be a positive influence. Teachers might show students how to give support and constructive feedback to classmates. If a few students seem to enjoy sabotaging the system, those students may need separate arrangements.

Token Reinforcement Programs

token
reinforcement:
reinforcing behavior
with points, chips,
etc., that can be
exchanged for
rewards

Often it is difficult to recognize and reinforce all the students who deserve it. A **token reinforcement** system can help solve this problem by allowing all students to earn tokens for both academic work and positive classroom behavior. The tokens may be points, checks, holes punched in a card, chips, play money, or anything else that is easily identified as the student's property. Periodically the students exchange the tokens they have earned for some desired reward.

A good example of the application of a token program can be found in Project Success Environment, conducted in a very difficult inner-city school system (Rollins, McCandless, Thompson, & Brassell, 1974). Sixteen teachers were trained in a summer workshop to use praise-and-ignore techniques and token reinforcement. The following year they implemented this combination of methods in their classes in the first, second, third, sixth, and eighth grades. The performance of the students in all these classes (the experimental group) was compared with that of similar students in 14 comparable classes (the control group).

Procedures in an
Inner-City Program

Throughout the year, all the project teachers used the praise-and-ignore techniques for reinforcing appropriate behaviors. In addition, students were given tokens for positive behaviors—in this case, checks on reward cards. During the first three weeks, the reinforcement was given mainly for following conduct rules. After the third week, reinforcement was shifted to academic achievement. All along, students were told what they would be reinforced for. Checks were at first given fairly continuously and predictably; later they were dispensed more intermittently and unpredictably. During the third and fourth months, the rewards that could be purchased with the tokens were changed from candy and toys to activities and school supplies. By the fourth month, students could earn time in a supervised activity room. Toys, games, and comic books were provided in the elementary school activity rooms. Games, magazines, radios, and records were available

Music, stories, and plays on records or tapes can be excellent additions to a reinforcement menu. If students wear headphones, they won't disturb others and won't be distracted themselves by noise in the room. *(Richard Hutchings/Photo Researchers)*

in the middle school activity room. Over the course of the year, the number of checks needed to earn the rewards increased.

Substantial Results

With such an elaborate project, one would hope that the results were substantial. They were. The 16 project classes and the 14 comparison classes were observed during the entire year, and a number of major differences were noted. First, the project teachers reinforced students about twice as often and punished students much less than the teachers in the comparison classes. Second, the students in the project classes exhibited dramatically lower levels of disruptive behavior. Third, the project students also spent a much greater amount of time working on their assignments. Perhaps the most exciting result of the program, however, was the fourth finding. The project students improved greatly in both academic aptitude and achievement. Their gains on the California Test of Mental Maturity and the California Reading Achievement Test were twice as large as the gains made by the comparison students.

Variations

Several variations are possible in designing a token program. In some programs students have been trained to be managers, dispensing tokens and freeing the teacher to focus on other activities. Winett, Krasner, and Krasner (1971), for example, developed a system that used a rotating student monitor to reinforce class members for reading independently while the teacher worked with other students. Another variation is to allow students to earn tokens in the classroom and exchange them for rewards at home. These plans are very successful when parents are willing to cooperate. Usually a note or report form is sent home daily or twice a week. The note indicates the number of points earned in the preceding time period. The points may be exchanged for minutes of television viewing, access to special toys, or private time with parents. Points can also be saved up for larger rewards such as trips.

Whatever the variation, a number of basic steps should be taken in setting up a token reinforcement program. The Guidelines on the next page on the token reinforcement programs list the essential ones.

Guidelines

Token Reinforcement Programs

Before presenting the program to students, make sure you have all the details worked out.

Examples
1. *Establish rules that clearly specify requirements, such as how many problems done correctly will earn a point.*
2. *Make sure your system is workable and not too complicated. You might discuss it with another teacher to identify possible sources of problems.*

You may want to have different goals for different groups of students.

Examples
1. *Focus on cooperative behaviors for students who are disruptive.*
2. *For high-achieving students, give tokens for enrichment work, peer tutoring, or special projects.*
3. *Match the token to the age of the student—colored chips for younger children, points for older students.*

Offer a variety of rewards at different prices.

Examples
1. *Offer rewards that can be purchased for only two or three tokens, so that all students will be motivated to try.*
2. *Offer rewards that make more extensive efforts or saving up tokens worthwhile.*

Gradually increase the requirements for each token.

Examples
1. *Begin with one token for each correct answer, then give a token for every three correct answers, and so on.*
2. *Offer tokens for five minutes of attention to assignments, then eventually for a whole day of attentive work.*

Gradually change from tangible rewards and privileges to time focused on enjoyable learning experiences.

Examples
1. *With young students start with candy or small toys, but move to assisting the teacher and free reading time.*
2. *With older students, start with such things as magazines and move toward free time to spend on special projects, the chance to tutor younger children, or the opportunity to work in the computer lab.*

Contingency Contract Programs

contingency contract: agreement between teacher and student specifying what the student must do to earn rewards

In a **contingency contract** program, the teacher draws up an individual contract with each student describing exactly what the student must do to earn a particular privilege or reward. In some programs, students participate in deciding on the behaviors to be reinforced and the rewards that can be gained. The negotiating process itself can be an educational experience, as students learn to set reasonable goals and abide by the terms of a contract.

A sample blank form for a contract is shown in Figure 6–2. This would be appropriate for younger students and could be used for specifying work

Figure 6–2   A Contingency Contract Form

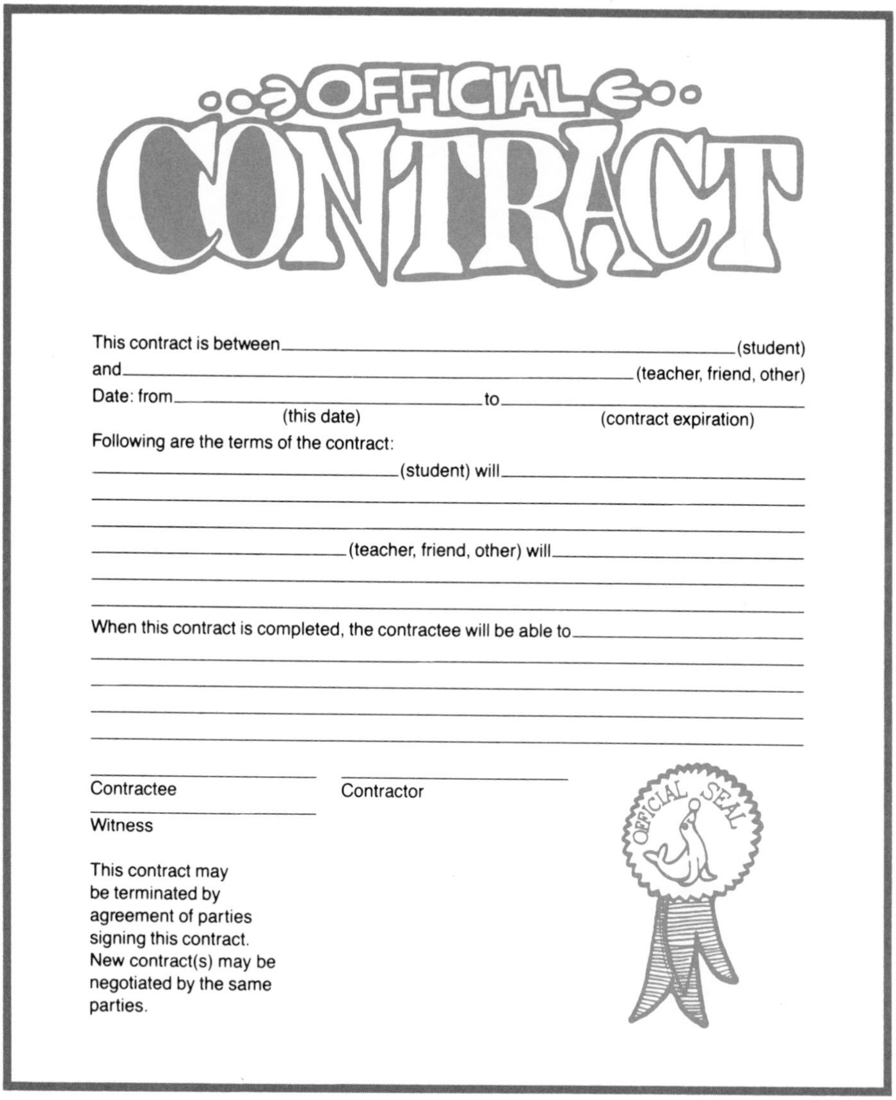

···OFFICIAL··· CONTRACT

This contract is between_____(student)

and_____(teacher, friend, other)

Date: from_____to_____
                              (this date)   (contract expiration)

Following are the terms of the contract:

_____(student) will_____

_____

_____

_____(teacher, friend, other) will_____

_____

When this contract is completed, the contractee will be able to_____

_____

_____

_____

_____

_____   _____
Contractee   Contractor

_____
Witness

This contract may
be terminated by
agreement of parties
signing this contract.
New contract(s) may be
negotiated by the same
parties.

Adapted from B. Sulzer-Azaroff & G. R. Mayer (1986), Achieving educational excellence using behavioral strategies. *New York: Holt, Rinehart & Winston, p 322. Copyright © 1986 by CBS College Publishing. Reprinted by permission of CBS College Publishing.*

to be completed, improvements in behavior or attendance, or any other goal. An example of a contract for completing assignments that is appropriate for intermediate and upper-grade students is presented in Figure 6–3. This chart serves as a contract, assignment sheet, and progress record. Something like this might even be useful for planning work in college.

The few pages devoted to token reinforcement and contingency contracts here can offer only an introduction to these programs. Suggested readings

Figure 6–3 A Contingency Contract for Completing Assignments

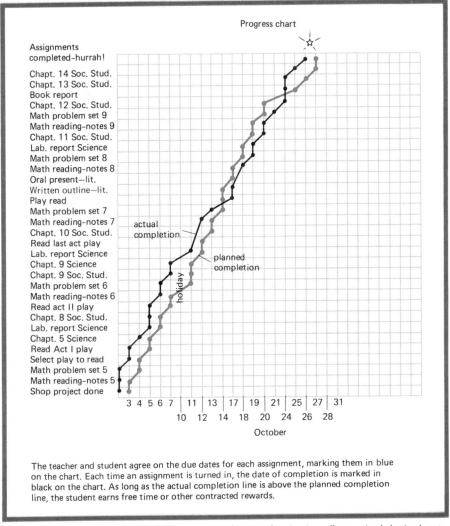

The teacher and student agree on the due dates for each assignment, marking them in blue on the chart. Each time an assignment is turned in, the date of completion is marked in black on the chart. As long as the actual completion line is above the planned completion line, the student earns free time or other contracted rewards.

Adapted from B. Sulzer-Azaroff & G. R. Mayer (1986), Achieving educational excellence using behavioral strategies. *New York: Holt, Rinehart & Winston, p. 277. Copyright © 1986 by CBS College Publishing. Reprinted by permission of CBS College Publishing.*

at the end of the chapter provide greater detail. If you want to set up a large-scale reward program in your classroom, you should probably seek professional advice. Often the school psychologist, counselor, or principal can help. In addition, you should consider the cautions about using reward systems discussed at the end of this chapter. Applied inappropriately, methods that provide external rewards can undermine the students' motivation to learn (Deci, 1975; Lepper & Greene, 1978).

The goal of most teaching is to help students become independent learners. In the next section we look at some management techniques students can use in or out of school.

Advice and Cautions

SELF-MANAGEMENT

If one goal of education is to produce people capable of educating themselves, students must learn to regulate and manage their own lives, set their own goals, and provide their own reinforcement. In adult life, rewards are sometimes vague and goals often take a long time to reach. For example, I began writing this text several years before I received the final reinforcement of seeing the completed book. Along the way I had to set small objectives and reinforce myself for the completion of each chapter. Life is filled with tasks that call for this sort of **self-management.** Yet psychologists have only recently begun to understand the process (Coates & Thoresen, 1979).

self-management:
using behavioral
principles to change
one's own behavior

Approaches to Self-Management

Students may be involved in any or all of the steps in implementing a behavior-change program. They may help set goals, observe their own work, keep records of it, and evaluate their own performance. Finally, they can select and deliver reinforcement. This kind of involvement can help students learn to perform all the steps on their own in the future.

It appears that the goal-setting phase is a very important one in self-management. In fact, some recent research suggests that setting specific goals and making them public may be the critical elements of self-management programs. For example, Hayes and his colleagues identified college students who had serious problems with studying and taught them how to set specific study goals. Students who set goals and turned them in to the experimenter performed significantly better on tests covering the material they were studying than students who set goals privately and never showed them to anyone (Hayes, Rosenfarb, Wulfert, Munt, Korn, & Zettle, 1985). Other studies have shown that, in general, students work as hard under self-imposed standards as they do under standards imposed by adults (Felixbrod, 1974).

High Standards,
High Performance

No matter who sets the goals, higher standards tend to lead to higher performance (McLaughlin & Gnagey, 1981). Unfortunately, student-set goals have a tendency to become lower and lower. Teachers can help students maintain high standards by monitoring the goals set and reinforcing high standards (O'Leary & O'Leary, 1976a). In one study, a teacher helped first-grade students raise the number of math problems they set for themselves to work on each day by praising them whenever they increased their objective by 10 percent. The students maintained their new, higher work standards, and the improvements even generalized to other subjects (Price & O'Leary, 1974).

Students may also participate in the recording and evaluation phases of a reinforcement program. Some examples of behaviors that are appropriate for self-recording are the number of assignments completed, time spent practicing a skill, number of books read, and number of times out of seat without permission. Tasks that must be accomplished without teacher supervision, like homework or private study, are also good candidates for self-monitoring. Students keep a chart, diary, or checklist recording the frequency or duration of the behaviors in question. Table 6–2 is a self-monitoring log for students who have trouble remembering all the steps in completing homework properly. Because cheating on records is a potential problem, espe-

Table 6–2 A Self-Monitoring Log for Homework

Categories	Days of Week																			
	Mon		Tues		Wed		Thurs		Fri		Mon		Tues		Wed		Thurs		Fri	
	yes	no	yes	no	yes	no	yes	no	yes	no	yes	no	yes	no	yes	no	yes	no	yes	no
1. Are you ready to start at 7:00?																				
2. Is your assignment written down?																				
3. Did you bring all materials home?																				
4. Is your work done on looseleaf paper?																				
5. Is the paper unfolded and neat?																				
6. Is the proper heading on the paper?																				
7. Is your penmanship neat?																				
8. Is your work done in ink?																				
9. Is the assignment complete?																				
10. Did you pack everything to return to school?																				
Number of points scored																				
Total points for the week																				

Adapted from D. P. Fromberg & M. Driscoll (1985), The successful classroom: Management strategies for regular and special education teachers. New York: Teachers College Press, p. 148.

cially when students are rewarded for improvements, intermittent checking by the teacher plus bonus points for accurate recording may be helpful (Hundert & Bucher, 1978).

Qualitative Judgments

Self-evaluation is somewhat more difficult than simple self-recording because it involves making a judgment about quality. Very few studies have been conducted in this area, but it appears that students can learn to evaluate their behavior with reasonable accuracy (Santogrossi, O'Leary, Romanczyk, & Kaufman, 1973). One key seems to be periodically checking students' self-evaluations and reinforcing them for making accurate judgments. Older students may learn this more readily than younger students.

You may be interested in the results of a study conducted by Mark Morgan (1985) that combined goal setting, self-recording, and self-evaluation. Morgan taught self-monitoring strategies to all the education students in the required educational psychology course at his college. The students who set specific, short-term objectives for each study unit and monitored their progress toward the objectives outperformed the students who simply monitored study time, even though the students who monitored their time actually spent *more* hours studying! So the combination of setting specific objectives, like those we will discuss in Chapter 11, and keeping track of progress seems to be an important aspect of self-management.

Rewarding
Ourselves

The last step in self-management is self-reinforcement. There is some disagreement, however, as to whether this step is actually necessary. Some psychologists believe that setting goals and monitoring progress alone are sufficient and that self-reinforcement adds nothing to the effects (Hayes et al., 1985). Other people believe that rewarding yourself for a job well done can lead to higher levels of performance than simply setting goals and keeping track of progress (Bandura, 1978). If you are willing to be tough and really deny yourself something you want until your goals are reached, then perhaps the promise of a reward can provide extra incentive for work. With that in mind, you may want to think of some creative way to reinforce yourself when you finish this chapter. As I've noted, a similar approach helped me write this chapter in the first place.

Teaching Self-Management

Creative Writing

Ballard and Glynn (1975) describe one program in which a third-grade teacher used self-management to encourage the development of creative writing abilities. At 1 P.M. each day, the 37 students in the class were given a creative writing period. They were encouraged to write about anything that interested them and to use as many action words and describing words as possible. After a while, the teacher asked the students to record on special sheets the number of sentences, action words, and describing words in their stories each day. The students did this, but no increase in sentences, action words, or describing words followed. Then the teacher allowed the students to earn free activity time based on some aspect of their writing. This time was self-monitored, with periodic checks by the teacher. At this point, radical improvements were seen in all aspects of student writing. Not only did the number of sentences, action words, and describing words increase, but the overall quality improved, as judged by independent raters at a university.

Sports

A second example of self-management is found in a study by McKenzie and Rushall (1974). The coaches of a competitive swim team with members from ages 9 to 16 were having difficulty persuading swimmers to maintain high work rates. Then the coaches drew up four charts indicating the training program to be followed by each member and posted the charts near the pool. The swimmers were given the responsibility of recording number of laps and completion of each training unit. Because the recording was public, swimmers could see their own progress and that of others, give and receive congratulations, and keep accurate track of the work units completed. This seemed to offer a good deal of reinforcement. Work output increased by 27 percent when the charts were introduced. The coaches liked the system because swimmers could begin to work immediately without waiting for instructions. The coaches could then devote their time to training individuals.

Self-Management for
Impulsive Students

The third example involves teaching students to give themselves silent instructions about the task at hand. At first the teacher may have students say the instructions out loud, to make sure they understand the system. Later the instructions may be whispered, and finally just "thought." This approach has helped impulsive students slow down and consider each alternative more carefully. Poor readers have been taught a set of self-instructions to guide reading. They learn to ask themselves questions about the content as they go along, outline each passage in their heads, relate the ideas in the reading to other information, and so on (Bornstein, 1985; Kendall, 1981; Meichenbaum, 1977).

Appropriate Goals

One important aspect of the self-instructional approach is to give students something concrete to do that focuses their attention. But the instructions must involve a task that fits the goals of the particular situation. Asking questions as you read not only helps maintain attention but also helps you understand what you are reading. Some other system, like imagining painful punishment every time your mind wanders, might keep you focused on the words in the book, but it probably would not improve comprehension.

The Guidelines may prove helpful if you decide to introduce self-management techniques in your classroom.

Guidelines

Self-Management Programs

Introduce the system in a positive way.

Examples
1. *Emphasize the lifelong value of developing habits of self-management.*
2. *Consider starting the program just with volunteers.*
3. *Describe how you use self-management programs yourself.*

Help students learn to set appropriate goals.

Examples
1. *Monitor goals frequently at first and praise reasonably high standards.*
2. *Make goals public by having students tell you or members of their work group what they want to accomplish.*

Provide a way for students to record and evaluate their progress.

Examples
1. *Divide the work into easily measured steps.*
2. *Provide models of good work where judgments are more difficult, such as in creative writing.*
3. *Give students a record form or checklist to keep track of progress.*

Check the accuracy of student records from time to time.

Examples
1. *Have many checkups when students are first learning, fewer later.*
2. *Have students check one another's records.*
3. *Where appropriate, test the skills that students are supposed to be developing and reward students whose self-evaluations match their test performances.*

PROBLEMS AND ISSUES

The preceding sections have provided an overview of several strategies for changing classroom behavior. These strategies are tools that may be used responsibly or irresponsibly.

Ethical Issues

The ethical questions related to the use of the strategies described in this chapter are similar to those raised by any process that seeks to influence people. What are the strategies to be used for? How do these goals fit in with those of the school as a whole? Might students be rewarded for the "wrong" thing, though it seems "right" at first? By what criteria should the strategies be chosen? What effect will a strategy have on the individuals involved? Is too much control being given to the teacher or to a majority?

Selecting Goals. In selecting goals, the question that seems to arise most often is whether to focus on classroom conduct or on academic behavior. According to the *Preliminary Report of the Commission on Behavior Modification* (American Psychological Association, 1976), "there appears to be a wide consensus that simply improving classroom conduct does not necessarily result in academic change" (p. 6).

What Is the Real Goal?

This leads us to one of the most obvious potential abuses of behavior modification. The strategies described in this chapter could be applied exclusively to teach students to sit still, raise their hands before speaking, and remain silent at all other times (Winett & Winkler, 1972). This certainly would be an unethical use of the techniques. It is true that a teacher may need to establish some organization and order, but stopping with improvements in conduct will not ensure academic learning.

On the other hand, in some situations, reinforcing academic skills may lead to improvements in conduct (Ayllon & Roberts, 1974). Emphasis should be placed, whenever possible, on academic behaviors. Academic improvements generalize to other situations more successfully than changes in classroom conduct, which often are exhibited in the classroom where they are learned but nowhere else (O'Leary & O'Leary, 1976b). Of course, academic and social behaviors may be improved simultaneously.

Selecting Strategies. As noted earlier, punishment can have negative side effects; it can serve as a model for aggressive responses, and it can encourage negative emotional reactions. Punishment is unnecessary and even unethical when positive approaches, which have fewer potential dangers, might work as well.

Start with the Least Restrictive

A set of guidelines originally prepared to select programs for retarded students offers a logical progression of strategies that may be applied in any classroom setting. These guidelines recommend that the first procedures should be those that are "the least intrusive and restrictive, the most benign, practical, and economical (in the long run) in implementation, but yet optimally effective" (APA, 1976). When simpler, less restrictive procedures fail, then more complicated procedures should be tried. In Table 6–3, a general hierarchy has been created based on these guidelines.

Table 6–3	Choosing Strategies for Classroom Management
First try:	Praising positive behaviors and ignoring undesirable behaviors.
If that doesn't work, try:	Praise-and-ignore techniques with prompting and cueing, soft reprimands, modeling, or shaping.
If that doesn't work, try:	Praise-and-ignore techniques with negative reinforcement, satiation, response cost, or social isolation.

Fit the Strategy to the Student

A second consideration in the selection of a strategy is the impact of the strategy on the individual student. For some students, even a soft reprimand might be overkill. Simply reinforcing the appropriate behavior of a nearby student might work better. If a student has a history of being severely punished at home for bad reports from school, a home-based reward program might be very harmful to that student. Reports of unsatisfactory progress at school could lead to increased abuse at home. The responsibility of fitting the strategy to the special needs of each student calls for some expenditure of time to gather information. This will be especially true of the more elaborate programs.

Before introducing a program such as token reinforcement, a teacher must examine all the possible consequences for all the students. To gather information about the students and the possible results of such a program, teachers ideally should consult psychologists, administrators, counselors, and the parents involved.

Criticism of Behavioral Methods

Properly used, the strategies in this chapter can help students learn academically and grow in self-sufficiency. However, effective tools do not automatically produce excellent work. The indiscriminate use of even the best tools can lead to difficulties. Critics of behavioral methods point to two basic problems that may arise.

Decreased Interest in Learning. Some psychologists stand firmly behind the belief that token programs lead to token learning. They fear that rewarding students for all learning will cause the students to lose interest in learning for its own sake (Deci, 1975; Lepper & Greene, 1978; Lepper, Greene, & Nisbett, 1973). Recent studies have suggested that using reward programs with students who are already interested in the subject matter may, in fact, cause students to be less interested in the subject when the reward program ends. But for students who are not initially interested in the subject, being in a reward program not only increases achievement but also appears to increase interest in the subject itself.

Token Learning?

The lesson here is straightforward. Fit rewards to the individual. If a student is already being reinforced in a subject (by interest in the subject, parental or teacher approval, or some other factor), there is no need to add reinforcers. If, however, the student does not find a subject reinforcing, then reward programs may help kindle an interest (O'Leary & O'Leary, 1976b).

Another factor that may be critical in determining whether rewards enhance or undermine interest and motivation is the student's perception of the function of the reward. If the reward is seen as an indication that the student is becoming more competent and skillful at the task being rewarded, then reinforcement can spur interest and increase motivation to learn. In this case the reward is a symbol of task mastery. If, however, the activity being rewarded is simply seen as a means to the reward and the student gathers that improved competence really doesn't matter, then using rewards is more likely to decrease interest in the task itself. So when reinforcing students, whether with praise, privileges, or rewards, it is best to emphasize that the reinforcement is a symbol of how much the student is learning and progressing (Morgan, 1984).

Student Perceptions

In most situations, reward programs can be gradually phased out and learning maintained by teacher attention and student success. If the reward system cannot be removed successfully, perhaps the material is not appropriate for the student.

Impact on Other Students. Just as you must take into account the effects on the individual, you must also consider the impact of a reward system on other students. Using a reward program or giving one student increased attention may have a detrimental effect on the other students in the classroom. Is it possible that other students will learn to be "bad" in order to be included in the reward program? Most of the evidence on this question suggests that reward programs do not have any adverse effects on students who are not participating in the program *if* the teacher believes in the program and explains the reasons for using it to the nonparticipating students (Christy, 1975).

*Drawing by Lorenz; ©
1986 The New Yorker
Magazine, Inc.*

"*That is the correct answer, Billy, but I'm afraid
you don't win anything for it.*"

Whatever was maintaining the "good" behavior of the nonparticipating students (teacher approval, interest in the subject) will probably continue maintaining good behavior. If the conduct of some students does seem to deteriorate when their peers are involved in special programs, many of the same procedures discussed in this chapter should help them return to previous levels of appropriate behavior.

SUMMARY

1. Teachers can stress and reinforce positive, appropriate student behavior with attention, recognition, and praise.

2. The combination of praising positive and ignoring undesirable behavior can sometimes be an effective management tool. But this approach is not a cure-all. Teachers must apply it with care and thoughtfulness.

3. An important aspect of dealing with undesirable or inappropriate behavior is providing alternative behaviors for students. Negative reinforcement and positive practice can help students adopt these alternatives to replace the inappropriate responses.

4. The Premack principle can help teachers choose appropriate reinforcers for both the class as a whole and for individuals. According to the principle, a preferred or frequently performed activity can serve as a reinforcer for a less preferred or less frequent activity.

5. If students are already able to act in certain ways but seldom do, a teacher may want to use cues to encourage the behavior.

6. If students do not know how to perform the behavior, a model may help. Modeling combined with reinforcement and practice has proved effective in teaching new skills.

7. The most time-consuming process for developing a new behavior is shaping. This involves breaking down the behavior to be learned into small steps, then reinforcing gradual step-by-step progress (successive approximations of the behavior) toward the final goal.

8. Using negative reinforcement, a teacher can put students in a mildly unpleasant situation and allow them to leave only when their behavior improves. This keeps students in control—*their* behavior is the determining factor.

9. With satiation, a teacher can insist that students continue problem behavior until they grow tired of it.

10. When all else fails, some form of punishment such as a private reprimand, the loss of privileges (response cost), or social isolation may be necessary.

11. Because students are influenced by their peers, it sometimes is productive to enlist the help of the whole class. Group-consequence techniques can be applied by rewarding the class teams for points achieved or by making rewards contingent on the behavior of the class as a whole. A teacher must be aware of the dangers of too much peer pressure on the individual, however.

12. Token reinforcement programs allow all students to earn tokens for academic work and positive behavior. Tokens are periodically exchanged for desired rewards. Contingency contracts focus on what an individual student must accomplish in order to win a reward.

13. Many of the methods described in this chapter can be applied by students to manage their own behavior. Students can participate in setting goals, keeping track of progress, evaluating accomplishments, and selecting and giving reinforcement. In addition, students can learn to internalize specific instructions that can help focus their attention on the task at hand.

14. Whenever possible, teachers should focus on academic improvement, not just on how well class rules are followed, and use positive reinforcement before trying negative reinforcement, satiation, or punishment. They should generally seek professional help before implementing a large-scale program.

15. Critics of behavioral methods suggest that reinforcing a student for accomplishments may put too much emphasis on the system for receiving rewards and undermine the student's natural interest in learning for its own sake. Critics also have pointed out potential adverse effects on students not participating in the program.

KEY TERMS   positive practice   response cost

             Premack principle   social isolation

             shaping   token reinforcement

             satiation   contingency contract

             reprimands   self-management

SUGGESTIONS FOR FURTHER READING AND STUDY

BUCKLEY, N. K., & WALKER, H. M. (1978). *Modifying classroom behavior: A manual of procedures for classroom teachers* (rev. ed.). Champaign, IL: Research Press. Here you will find a basic guide for teachers who wish to use behavioral methods of classroom management. The revised edition describes ways of involving parents in school-based programs.

KRUMBOLTZ, J. D., & KRUMBOLTZ, H. D. (1972). *Changing children's behavior.* Englewood Cliffs, NJ: Prentice-Hall. This very readable and practical book presents 13 principles for teaching students along with a number of examples and case studies.

MEICHENBAUM, D. (1977). *Cognitive behavior modification: An integrative approach.* New York: Plenum. Meichenbaum's text describes his work with impulsive children and the basic principles of cognitive behavior modification.

O'LEARY, K. D., & O'LEARY, S. G. (Eds.). (1977). *Classroom management: The successful use of behavior modification* (2nd ed.). New York: Pergamon. A classic collection of articles on behavioral methods for classroom management by experts in the field.

SULZER-AZAROFF, B., & MAYER, G. R. (1986). *Achieving educational excellence using behavioral strategies.* New York: Holt, Rinehart & Winston. This is a book for teachers about how to use behavioral strategies. There are chapters on general principles as well as chapters on teaching specific subjects such as math.

WOOLFOLK, A. E., & WOOLFOLK, R. L. (in press). Time-management: An experimental investigation. *Journal of School Psychology.* This article describes the results of a program to teach time-management strategies to student teachers, with an emphasis on setting goals and monitoring progress.

H & H Enterprises publishes a series of booklets called *How to be a better behavior manager*. The series editors are N. Azrin, V. Besalel, R. V. Hall, and M. C. Hall. The address for the series is: Box 1070-BT, Lawrence, Kansas 66044. Some of the booklets are:

How to use positive practice   *How to select reinforcers*
How to plan for generalization   *How to use reprimands*
How to maintain behavior   *How to use shaping*
How to teach through modeling and imitation   *How to use overcorrecting*
How to use planned ignoring

Teachers' Forum

Putting Teachers to the Test

Students are likely to "test" beginning teachers, student teachers, and substitute teachers. What have you found to be the best ways to handle student "testing" behaviors?

Laying the Groundwork

My first year teaching public school was a bearcat. Those kids ran me ragged. I just endured. The second year there was no problem; I was the established element and the students were new.

When I know I will need a substitute, I lay the groundwork the day before, informing the classes about what I expect them to cover and attempting to predispose their minds to work with the substitute, not against him. I have not hit on a foolproof system for "testing" a substitute, but I do not have the problem myself.

Osborn Howes, Eighth-Grade English, Economics, and History Teacher
Hall School, Larkspur, California

Acceptance, Flexibility, and Much More

As a beginning teacher who has experienced the inevitable "testing" of new teachers and as a supervisor of new teachers, I have found that the best approach to handling the situation is eightfold:

1. Recognize that the "testing" behavior is normal, and don't take it personally. Maintain your sense of perspective, and remember, a sense of humor is a valuable asset. Watch students closely during this period.
2. Always be prepared. Know your material and any special characteristics of your students, particularly what is motivating and reinforcing to them.
3. Project confidence; be fair, consistent, respectful, purposeful, and positive; friendly, but *professional*.
4. Predetermine goals and the vehicles for achieving them. Communicate these to your students.
5. Make each student a partner in sharing the responsibility for his or her success. Ask for student input—and really listen to what is offered.
6. Plan carefully and continually. Be flexible and recognize that not all great plans work. Try to anticipate, but have alternatives in mind.
7. Recognize that one style of teaching, one topic, etc., will not suit everyone. Vary your approaches and use different teaching strategies. Be enthusiastic. Enthusiasm is contagious. Be creative.
8. Have fun. If you are enjoying yourself, you will communicate this to your students and get more mileage out of yourself and them as a result.

Laura Atkinson, Special Education Teacher
Chapel Hill, North Carolina

Staying Busy

I think all teachers, including student, beginning, and substitute teachers, need to know that some "testing behavior" could very well be ignorable; however, the best way to handle testing behavior that is not ignorable is to deal with it quickly and firmly by removing the student from the class. Often he or she can stand outside the classroom; in some instances the student may have to be sent to the principal's office. In all cases, an ounce of prevention is worth a pound of cure. I try to keep students too busy to act out.

Louise Harrold Melucci, Fourth-Grade Teacher
Greenwood School, Warwick, Rhode Island

A "Poor-Me" Student

You have a capable, attractive student in your class who is continually running herself down. She makes statements like "I'm not smart enough to do this," "Nobody wants to work with me," "I always do so badly," "I don't have any friends," and so on. How might a behavioral approach help this student develop a more positive attitude toward herself and school?

Keeping Track with a Contract

This often requires a type of behavior modification contract. I would begin by keeping a record of her self-put-downs and discuss them with her in terms of what she *really* believes about herself and the image she would like to project. Together, we would construct a list of simple self-buildup statements that she could begin using— "I'd like to try that," instead of "I'm not smart enough to do that." The two lists would be used to chart the decrease in the negative comments and the increase in the positive ones.

Issues such as rewards, who keeps the records, and at what point the process should end would also need to be discussed and recorded.

J. D. Kraft, Twelfth-Grade Sociology Teacher
Wausau West High School, Wausau, Wisconsin

Solving the Homework Problem

There are several students in your class who consistently fail to turn in homework assignments. You are fairly certain that they are capable of doing the work. Their problem seems to be a lack of interest, motivation, or good work habits. What would you do to change their behavior patterns?

Family Involvement

Parental involvement is essential in developing good work habits. Introduce a homework assignment schedule that parents as well as students are aware of. This may include a plan for an entire month at a time, perhaps written on a calendar page. Vary traditional written homework with activities or projects that involve the parents or other family members.

Carol Gibbs, Sixth-Grade Teacher
Happy Valley School, Rossville, Georgia

Some Negative Reinforcement and the Teacher's Homework

I always provide catch-up time, usually once a week, for those who are behind in their work. During this time, those who are caught up get involved with me in a fun activity; anyone not caught up must complete assignments and can join us when the work is finished.

Also, if any of my students consistently failed to turn in work because they lacked interest, motivation, or good work habits, I would first double-check achievement tests and IQ scores from the previous year to make sure they were capable of the work. I would also check with their former teachers to see what instructional methods were most successful with each student. Next, I would have an individual conference with each child to discuss the problem. I would also call the parents to discuss what was happening in the classroom. I would send home a weekly report sheet showing what assignments were completed with the percentage scores and also any missing assignments. Parents would be expected to sign the form, including any comments they want to make, and return it with the child on Monday.

Sharon Klotz, Sixth-Grade Teacher
Kiel Middle School, Kiel, Wisconsin

7

Learning: Cognitive Views

Overview
Elements of the Cognitive Perspective   234
The Information Processing Model of Learning   236
The Sensory Register   236
Influence of Perception   238
The Role of Attention   241
Short-Term Memory   242
Long-Term Memory   244
Schemata   247
Remembering and Forgetting   249
Why Do People Forget?   249
How Do People Remember?   250
Strategies for Helping Students Remember   253
Make It Meaningful   254
Learning about Learning: Metacognitive Abilities   258
Strategy Instruction   259
Metacognition and Reading   260
Summary/Key Terms
Suggestions for Further Reading and Study
Teachers' Forum

OVERVIEW   In this chapter we turn from the behavioral views of learning to a different perspective, the cognitive orientation. Essentially, this means a shift from "viewing the learners and their behaviors as products of incoming environmental stimuli" to seeing the learners as "sources of plans, intentions, goals, ideas, memories, and emotions actively used to attend to, select, and construct meaning from stimuli and knowledge from experience" (Wittrock, 1982, pp. 1–2).

We will begin with a discussion of the general cognitive approach to learning and memory. Then we will introduce a widely accepted cognitive model—information processing. This model provides a framework for organizing many ideas from the cognitive perspective. Within this framework we will consider how facts, concepts, rules, and other forms of knowledge are organized and represented so they can be stored and used. Next we will examine explanations of how and why people forget some information but remember other information. We will also look at ways memory can be improved. Finally, we will explore a promising new field of study—metacognition—that may provide insights into individual and developmental differences in memory skills. Of course, all these facets of human learning and memory have implications for teaching.

By the time you have completed this chapter, you should have a number of new ideas about how learning takes place and how you can improve your own learning. More specifically, you should be able to do the following:

- Describe a cognitive model of human learning—information processing.
- Give examples of the role of perception in learning.
- Discuss how the representation of knowledge influences learning.
- Describe the role of schemata in learning and remembering.
- Use memory strategies and study skills derived from cognitive theory to prepare for the test you may have to take on this chapter.
- Develop a plan for teaching learning strategies and study skills to your students.

ELEMENTS OF THE COGNITIVE PERSPECTIVE

The cognitive perspective is not a unified theory. It can best be described as a generally agreed upon philosophical orientation. This means that cognitive theorists share basic notions about learning and memory but by no means agree upon a single model of learning. In contrast, you remember that behaviorists *do* fundamentally agree upon a specific learning model, as described in Chapters 5 and 6.

Cognitive theorists believe that learning is the result of our attempts to make sense of the world. To do this, we use all the mental tools at our

This chapter written in collaboration with Christine McCormick.

disposal. The ways in which we think about situations, along with our beliefs, expectations, and feelings, influence how and what we learn.

Internal Events

The behavioral approach argues that since mental events, like thoughts, images, and consciousness, cannot be observed, they are not legitimate objects for study. Cognitive theorists view this argument as too limiting. Their concern with mental events is reflected in the topics studied by cognitive psychologists—memory, attention, perception, problem solving, and concept learning. Cognitive research techniques also depend upon internal events; the researchers themselves must often make inferences about the subjects' mental processes. Investigators in the behavioral tradition prefer simple observation of behaviors.

Reinforcement

Both behavioral and cognitive theorists believe reinforcement is important in learning, but for different reasons. The strict behaviorist maintains that reinforcement strengthens responses; cognitive theorists see reinforcement as a source of feedback. This feedback provides information about what is likely to happen if the behaviors are repeated. In the cognitive view, reinforcement serves to reduce uncertainty and thus leads to a sense of understanding and mastery.

The cognitive view of learning sees people as active processors of information. They initiate experiences that lead to learning, seek out information to solve problems, and reorganize what they already know to achieve new learning. Instead of being passively influenced by environmental events, people actively choose, practice, pay attention, ignore, and make many other responses as they pursue goals (Miller, Galanter, & Pribram 1960).

The cognitive approach also suggests that one of the most important in-

Cognitive theories emphasize the human mind as an active and individual processor of information. Certainly, active thinking is going on here, influenced by feelings, beliefs, and existing knowledge and bound in turn to influence the structure of new thoughts. *(Alex Von Koschembahr/Photo Researchers)*

fluences in the learning process is what the *individual* brings to the learning situation. Cognitive psychologists are becoming more and more interested in the role of prior knowledge in learning. What we already know determines to a great extent what we will learn, remember, and forget (Peeck, van den Bosch, & Kreupeling, 1982; Resnick, 1981).

Cognitivists study a wide range of learning situations. Because of their focus on individual and developmental differences in cognition, they, unlike the behaviorists, have not sought general laws of learning that apply to both animals and humans in all situations. This is one of the reasons that there is no single cognitive model or theory of learning representative of the entire field. In order to organize and examine some of the major findings from cognitive research, we will use one of the most influential and thoroughly studied models—that of information processing.

THE INFORMATION PROCESSING MODEL OF LEARNING

The Computer Analogy

The information processing approach relies on the computer as a model for human learning. Like the computer, the human mind takes in information, performs operations on it to change its form and content, stores and locates it, and generates responses to it. Thus, processing involves gathering and representing information, or *encoding*; holding information, or *retention*; and getting at the information when needed, or *retrieval*. Information processing theorists approach learning primarily through a study of memory.

Figure 7–1 is a schematic representation of a typical information processing model, derived from the ideas of several theorists (Atkinson & Shiffrin, 1968; R. Gagné, 1985). Other models have been suggested that include some combination of the features of this model, along with other components. All of the models, despite their variations, resemble the flow charts used to represent computer programs. In Figure 7–1, the three boxes depict cognitive structures where information may be held and transformed. The arrows indicate the flow of information. The large oval shape at the top of the figure represents control processes that affect the flow of information throughout the system. Let's look at this model more carefully—first, the sensory register.

The Sensory Register

receptors: parts of the human body that receive sensory information

sensory register: system of receptors holding sensory information very briefly

Stimuli from the environment (sights, sounds, smells, and so on) constantly bombard our receptors. **Receptors** are the components of the sensory system for seeing, hearing, tasting, smelling, and feeling. The whole system of receptors is called the **sensory register.**

The patterns of neural activity produced when stimuli reach the receptors last only a very brief time (one to two seconds). But in these moments, we have a chance to select information for further processing. There are several activities you can use to experience this brief holding of sensory information in your own sensory register. Tap your fingers against your arm. Feel the immediate sensations. Then stop tapping and note how the sensations fade away. At first you retain the actual feeling of the tapping, but later you only

Figure 7–1   **Information Processing Model**

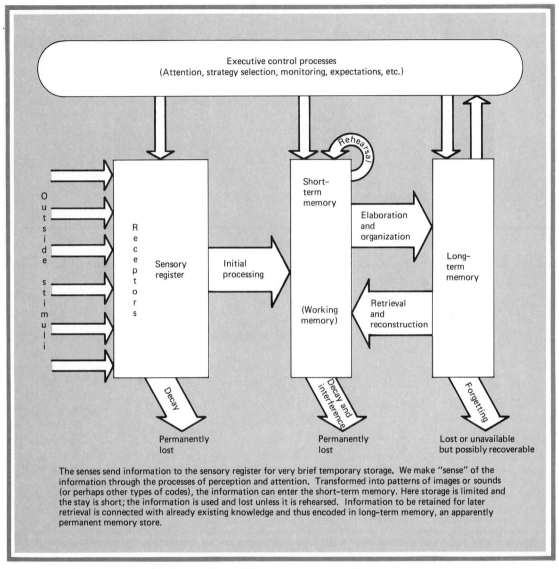

The senses send information to the sensory register for very brief temporary storage. We make "sense" of the information through the processes of perception and attention. Transformed into patterns of images or sounds (or perhaps other types of codes), the information can enter the short-term memory. Here storage is limited and the stay is short; the information is used and lost unless it is rehearsed. Information to be retained for later retrieval is connected with already existing knowledge and thus encoded in long-term memory, an apparently permanent memory store.

Adapted from R. Gagné (1985), The conditions of learning and theory of instruction (4th ed.). New York: Holt, Rinehart & Winston, p. 71; and M. Hunt (1982, Jan. 24), How the mind works, The New York Times Magazine, p. 32.

recollect that your arm was tapped. Wave a pencil (or your finger) back and forth in front of your eyes while you stare straight ahead. See the shadowy image that trails behind the object (Lindsay & Norman, 1977).

In each of these cases, the sensory input remains very briefly after the stimulus has left. You can feel a trace of the tap and see a trace of the pencil after the actual stimulus has been removed. Thus, for a second or two, the data from a sensory experience remain intact. It seems that sensory information is held by the sensory register in a form that resembles the sensation from the original stimulus. Visual sensations are coded briefly by the sensory register as images, and auditory sensations as sound patterns. It may be that the other senses also have their own codes.

Because the sensory register holds everything briefly, we have a chance to make sense of it—to organize it (Lindsay & Norman, 1977). Organization is necessary because there is much more information available in the sensory register than can possibly enter the next system—the short-term memory. Instead of perceiving everything, we pay attention to certain features of the total content in the sensory register and look for patterns. The processes of perception and attention are critical at this stage.

Influence of Perception

perception:
interpretation of sensory information

Perception refers to the meaning we attach to the information received through our senses. This meaning is constructed partly from objective reality and partly from the way we organize the information. Smith (1975) has summarized these points as follows:

> It is important to grasp that the eyes merely look and the brain sees. And what the brain sees may be determined as much by cognitive structure as by the information from the world outside. We perceive what the brain decides is in front of our eyes. (pp. 26–27)

Smith illustrated this phenomenon with the following exercise. Look at the marks below:

$$\mathsf{I3}$$

If asked what the letter is, you would say "B." If asked what the number is, you would say "13." The actual marks remain the same; the perception, their meaning, changes based on your expectation of recognizing a number or a letter. To a child without the appropriate cognitive structures to perceive either a number or a letter, the marks would probably be meaningless.

Gestalt: German for pattern or whole

Gestalt theory: holds that people organize their perceptions into coherent wholes

Prägnanz: Gestalt principle—we reorganize perceptions to make them simpler and more regular

Early Views of Perception. Some of our present-day understanding of perception is based on studies conducted in Germany early in this century by psychologists called **Gestalt** theorists. *Gestalt*, which means pattern or configuration in German, refers to people's tendency to organize sensory information into patterns or relationships in order to make sense of the world. The basic principle of Gestalt psychology is called *Prägnanz* and states that we recognize patterns by reorganizing stimuli to make them simpler, more complete, and more regular than they actually are. Consider, for example, the following marks:

$$\mathsf{BOOK}$$

These marks are likely to be perceived as the word *book* because such a perception is simpler, more complete, and more regular than a series of unrelated marks of varying sizes and shapes.

figure-ground:
Gestalt principle—
tendency to focus
on certain elements
as standing out
against a
background

Figure-ground is another key concept of Gestalt psychology. Viewing any scene—whether in reality or in a painting, photograph, or film—a person tends to focus attention on a basic figure and note that figure's details. The rest of the scene becomes less important and is forced into a vaguer, undifferentiated background (Travers, 1982). An example can be found in Figure 7–2. What do you see at first glance? If you see devils, you are seeing black figures against a white background. If you see angels, you have made white the figure and black the ground. Which perception is correct? Neither? Both? It all depends on your perception.

As a teacher, you may notice that a particular behavior of one student has become "figure" to you, while the same behavior in other students is "ground." It may seem that one student is constantly turning in papers late,

Figure 7–2   **A Matter of Perception**

BEELDRECHT, Amsterdam/V. A. G. A., New York, Collection Haags Gemeentemuseum—The Hague.

or losing a pencil, or giving excellent answers when, in fact, a number of students are behaving in the same way. If this happens, it may be good to check your perceptions by making an objective assessment of the behavior of all the students. Why are you noticing the good or bad behavior of one student? Are you letting your attitudes and expectations concerning one student color your perceptions?

Current Ideas about Perception. The Gestalt principles are valid explanations of certain aspects of perception, but they are not the whole story. For example, you would not have seen the marks earlier as the word *book* if you were not familiar with English. There are two current explanations for how we recognize patterns and give meaning to sensory events. The first is called **feature analysis** or **bottom-up processing.** This suggests that we search a new stimulus for basic elements or features in order to recognize it. Anderson (1980) gives the following example. A capital letter *A* consists of two relatively straight lines at a 45-degree angle (/\) and a horizontal line (—) combined in a particular way. Whenever we see these features, or anything close enough, we recognize an *A*. Thus Λ , А , д , ᴀ , ʎ , A might be perceived as *A*'s. This explains how we are able to read words written in other people's handwriting. Feature analysis is often called bottom-up processing because the stimulus must be analyzed into specific features or building blocks and assembled into a meaningful pattern "from the bottom up."

> **feature analysis:**
> recognizing a new
> stimulus by
> identifying elements
>
> **bottom-up
> processing:**
> analyzing basic
> elements and
> combining them
> into meaningful
> patterns

If all perception relied on feature analysis, learning would be very slow. In fact, if reading were based entirely on this bottom-up processing, we would have to analyze and combine about 15,000 features to read just one page, since each letter has about 5 features (Anderson, 1980). Luckily, humans are capable of another type of perception based on context, often called **top-down processing.** We do not need to analyze every feature in a particular stimulus to make sense of it. Much of the information is redundant anyway. To recognize patterns rapidly, in addition to noting features, we use the context of the situation—what we know about words or pictures or the way the world generally operates. If you catch only a fleeting glimpse of a medium-sized, four-legged animal being led down a city street, you are likely to perceive a dog, based on the context and what you know about the situation. Of course you may be wrong, but not very often.

> **top-down
> processing:**
> understanding by
> inference

In everyday life we use both bottom-up and top-down processing, usually in tandem. For example, if you heard the sentence "For dinner I had fried tr____," but missed the last word, you would use feature analysis to identify a set of possible words (those beginning with *tr*, thus eliminating *chicken* and *shrimp*). You would also be aware of the context, since items like *trash* and *tractor* are usually not on the menu for dinner. Combining what you know about features of words (bottom-up processing) with what you know about the context (top-down processing), you would be able to complete the sentence with the word *trout* (Anderson, 1980).

The patterns people perceive are based on their prior knowledge, what they expect to see, the concepts they understand, and many other factors as well. For example, a neighbor had never seen me in my college office and was used to seeing me only in our community. When the young woman decided to take some courses at the college and encountered me in my office, she had a hard time placing my face. She finally remarked, "Mrs. Woolfolk, what are *you* doing here?" Her expectations had interfered with her ability to use pattern recognition to identify a familiar face.

The Role of Attention

Attention Is
Selective

Our senses are bombarded with sights and sounds every second. If every variation in color, movement, sound, smell, temperature, and so on had to be perceived, life would be impossible. By paying attention to certain stimuli and ignoring others, we select from all the possibilities what will be processed. But attention is limited. Unless you are very accomplished at two demanding tasks, you probably cannot do both at once. When you were learning to drive, knit, or type, you had to concentrate. However, if you are now accomplished at any of these tasks, you may be able to drive, knit, or type and at the same time talk, listen to music, or compose a letter. This is because many processes that require attention and concentration at first become automatic with practice. Thus, the first-grade reader who must sound out each word and pay attention to almost every letter becomes a fast, fluent reader in time. It is important to note that students can vary greatly in their ability to attend selectively to information in their environment. In fact, many students diagnosed as being learning disabled actually seem to have attentional disorders (Keogh & Margolis, 1976), particularly with relatively long tasks (Pelham, 1981). We will discuss these problems in Chapter 13.

Implications for Teachers. Many factors influence student attention. Eye-catching or startling displays or actions can draw attention at the beginning of a lesson. A teacher might begin a science lesson on pressure by blowing up a balloon until it pops. Bright colors, unusual placement of words, underlining, highlighting written or spoken words, surprise events, and changes in voice level, lighting, or pacing can all be used to gain attention. There is some evidence that students learn more when the teacher is ani-

Storytellers use emotions, animated gestures, inflection, and voice levels and often ask the kids to join in. The result? As you can see, an involved, attentive, happy group of children, who need no reminders to "pay attention." *(Will McIntyre/Photo Researchers)*

Table 7–1 Suggestions for Focusing Attention

1. Tell students the purpose of the lesson. Indicate how learning the material will be useful or important to them.
2. Ask students why they think learning the material will be important.
3. Arouse curiosity with questions such as "What would happen if . . .?"
4. Create shock by staging an unexpected event such as a loud argument just before a lesson on communication.
5. Alter the physical environment by changing the arrangement of the room or moving to a different setting.
6. Shift sensory channels by giving a lesson that requires students to touch, smell, or taste.
7. Use movements, gestures, and voice inflection—walk around the room, point, speak softly and then more emphatically.
8. Avoid distracting behaviors such as tapping a pencil or touching your hair.

Adapted from E. Emmer & G. Millett (1970), Improving teaching through experimentation: A laboratory approach. *Englewood Cliffs, NJ: Prentice-Hall. © 1970. Adapted by permission of Prentice-Hall.*

mated in delivering a lecture and uses nonverbal material along with the verbal (Kaufman, 1976). Table 7–1 offers additional ideas for capturing students' attention. We will return to this issue when we discuss stimulating student interests in Chapter 9.

So people make sense of the vast amount of sensory stimuli around them by paying attention to certain aspects of the situation and by using Gestalt principles, feature detection, the context of the situation, and prior knowledge about similar situations to recognize patterns. This describes how the processes of perception and attention affect information in the sensory register. The next step in information processing is the move to short-term memory.

Short-Term Memory

short-term memory: working memory, holding a limited amount of information briefly

rehearse: repeat; practice

Once transformed into patterns of images or sounds (or perhaps other types of sensory codes), the information in the sensory register can enter the **short-term memory** system. The stay here, like that in the sensory register, is short, probably about 20 seconds. Information can be held for a longer period of time only if you do something with it. To prevent forgetting, most people **rehearse** the information mentally until it is no longer needed. As long as you focus on and repeat the information in the short-term memory, it is available. In fact, information can be maintained in short-term memory indefinitely through rehearsal. Rehearsal is thus a control process (see the model in Figure 7–1) that affects the flow of information through the information processing system. Most children discover rehearsal on their own at around age 10, as we noted in Chapter 2.

Short-term memory is limited not only by the length of time unrehearsed information can be retained but also by the number of items that can be held at one time. In experimental situations, it appears that only about five to nine separate new items can be held in short-term memory at one time (Miller, 1956). This limitation seems to hold true to some degree in everyday life. It is quite common to rehearse a phone number after looking it up, as you walk across the room to make the call. But if you have two friends to call in succession, would it occur to you to keep both numbers in mind? Probably not. Experience tells us that two phone numbers (14 digits) probably cannot be stored simultaneously. And in any event, the time required to complete the first conversation would result in the loss of the second number from short-term memory.

Remember—put in your short-term memory—that we are discussing the recall of *new* information. There is an important distinction that should be made here. In daily life, we certainly can hold more than that five to nine units of information in our short-term memories at once. While you are dialing that seven-digit phone number you just looked up, you are bound to have other things "on your mind"—in your memory—such as how to use a telephone, whom you are calling, and why. You don't have to rehearse these things; they are not new knowledge. They stay with you as you perform this particular task. However, because of the short-term memory's limitations, if you were in a foreign country and were attempting to use an unfamiliar telephone system, you might very well have trouble remembering the phone number because you were trying to figure out the phone system at the same time. You might have to rehearse the relevant information in order to save it a bit longer.

What's on Your Mind?

The short-term memory is sometimes known as the *working memory*, since it seems to hold the information that we are thinking about at any given moment (or more specifically, during any given 20 seconds). In other words, if we want to use any information, it must be in our short-term memory. For this reason, some psychologists have also considered the short-term memory to be synonymous with "consciousness."

The limited capacity of short-term memory can also be somewhat circumvented by the control process of **chunking**. Since the *number* of bits of information, not the size of each bit, is the problem for short-term memory, individual bits of information can be combined in some meaningful way, so that the capacity is not exceeded and more information can be retained. For example, if the six digits 3, 5, 4, 8, 7, and 0 have to be remembered, it is easier to put them together into three chunks of two digits each (35, 48, 70) or two chunks of three digits each (354, 870). With these changes, there would be only two or three bits of information to hold at one time. We use chunking frequently when trying to remember a telephone number (exchange number–rest of number) or a social security number (group of three numbers–two numbers–four numbers).

chunking: grouping individual bits of data into meaningful larger units

It may seem to you that a memory system with a 20-second time limit is not very useful. But without this system you would already have forgotten what you read in the first part of this sentence, before you came to these last few words. This would clearly make understanding sentences very difficult. It would also be a disadvantage to remember permanently every sentence you ever read. Finding a particular bit of information in all that sea of knowledge would be impossible. So it is helpful to have a system that provides temporary storage.

We have been discussing short-term memory as if it were a set capacity in all people. As you might expect, however, individuals differ in this area as well. You may remember from Chapter 2 that as children grow older, their short-term memory capacities appear to increase. Of course, this increased capacity may be due to the use of more effective strategies like chunking. But at every developmental level there appear to be individual variations in short-term memory. Some people are simply better than others at this kind of task (Dempster, 1981).

Of course, all of us know a great deal—for example, most people know more than two telephone numbers. But these have been learned over a long period of time and are not as accessible as a number you have just looked up and are about to dial. They are part of long-term memory and require a bit of effort to retrieve.

Long-Term Memory

long-term memory: permanent store of knowledge

There are a number of differences between short-term and **long-term memory,** as you can see in Table 7–2. Information enters short-term memory very quickly. More time and a bit of effort are required to move information into long-term storage. Whereas the capacity of short-term memory is limited, the capacity of long-term memory appears to be unlimited for all practical purposes. In addition, once information is securely stored in long-term memory, it apparently remains there permanently. Theoretically, we should be able to remember as much as we want for as long as we want. Of course, the problem is to find the right information when it is needed. Our access to information in short-term memory is immediate: one way to define the information in short-term memory is what we are thinking about at that very moment. But access to information in long-term memory requires time and effort.

Here again, we see the analogy to computers. Information in short-term memory is like information in the work space of a computer. It is what you are dealing with at the moment. If you wish to "save" the information, you have to do something with it to place it in permanent storage. If you want to work with information previously stored, you have to retrieve it from storage and bring it into the current work space.

Representation and Organization

Just what is done to "save" information permanently? How can we make the most effective use of our practically unlimited capacity to learn and remember? One important requirement is that we integrate new material with information already stored in long-term memory. When we talk about how information is stored, we are talking about how the information is represented and how it is organized. Representation and organization have been described in a variety of ways. In the following pages we will examine several of these descriptions. The ideas, though somewhat different, are not mutually exclusive.

Table 7–2   **Short-Term and Long-Term Memory**

Type of Memory	Input	Capacity	Maintenance	Retrieval
Short-term	Very fast	Limited	Very brief	Immediate
Long-term	Relatively slow	Practically unlimited	Practically unlimited	Depends on organization

Adapted from F. Smith (1975), Comprehension and learning: A conceptual framework for teachers. *© 1975 Holt, Rinehart, and Winston. Reprinted by permission of publisher and CBS College Publishing.*

Semantic and Episodic Memory. Endel Tulving (1972) drew a distinction between two kinds of information stored in long-term memory—**episodic** and **semantic.** Episodic information is associated with a particular time and place. Thus, episodic memories are often memories of personal experiences—the Thanksgiving vacation you spent at your roommate's house or the meat loaf you had for dinner last night. In contrast, semantic memory involves knowledge of general facts and concepts that are *not* tied to a particular time or place. Recalling the nutritional value of a meat loaf dinner would be drawing on your semantic memory. Most material learned in school is stored in semantic memory. Of course, this distinction between episodic and semantic memory is not always evident, since our general knowledge of concepts is typically gained through experiences specific to a certain time and place. It is best to think of episodic and semantic memory as two often overlapping kinds of information stored in long-term memory.

The Structure of Knowledge in Long-Term Memory. Another important question concerns the form or structure in which knowledge is stored in long-term memory. Allan Paivio (1971) has suggested that information is stored either as visual images or verbal units, or both. Psychologists who agree with this point of view suggest that information that can be coded both visually *and* verbally is easiest to remember. (This may be one reason that explaining an idea with words *and* representing it visually in a figure, as we do in textbooks, have proved helpful to students.) It is also possible that episodic information tends to be stored as visual imagery and semantic information as verbal units in the form of networks of ideas.

A **propositional network** is an interconnected set of bits of information.

Coding information both visually and verbally may make it easier to retain and retrieve. Building a model of a molecule allows these students to connect the verbal information—a sugar molecule, for example, has carbon, hydrogen, and oxygen atoms in a certain ratio—with a visual image. *(Paul Conklin/ Monkmeyer Press)*

A proposition is the smallest unit of information that can be judged true or false. The statement *Ida borrowed the antique tablecloth* has two propositions:

1. Ida borrowed the tablecloth.
2. The tablecloth is an antique.

The sentence can be represented by the network in Figure 7–3. The diagram shows the simple relationship in which Ida does the borrowing (or is the *agent*) and the *object* of the borrowing is the tablecloth. Since the verb is in the past tense, the time of action is in the past. The same propositional network would apply to these sentences: *The antique tablecloth was borrowed by Ida*, or *Ida borrowed the tablecloth, which was an antique*. The meaning is the same, and this is what is stored in memory.

Even though they may have slightly different methods of diagramming the networks, many cognitive psychologists believe certain types of knowledge are organized and represented in propositional networks like the one in Figure 7–3. It is possible that all or most information is stored and represented in propositional networks (rather than as either visual images or verbal codes, as Paivio suggested). When we want to recall a bit of information, we may translate its meaning (as represented in the propositional

Networks and Codes (margin note)

Figure 7–3   A Propositional Network

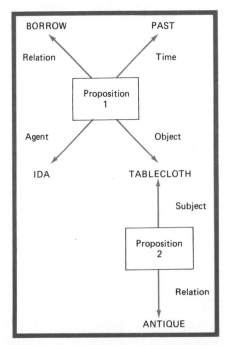

Developed from material in J. Anderson (1985), Cognitive psychology and its implications (2nd ed.). San Francisco: W. H. Freeman; and D. Gentner (1975), Evidence for the psychological reality of semantic components: The verbs of possession. In D. Norman & D. Rumelhart (Eds.), Explorations in cognition. San Francisco: W. H. Freeman.

network) into familiar phrases and sentences, or mental pictures. Also, because of the network, recall of one bit of information can trigger recall of another. We are not aware of these networks; they are not part of our conscious memory (Anderson, 1985). In much the same way, we are not aware of underlying grammatical structure when we form a sentence in our own language; we don't have to diagram a sentence in order to say it.

When you hear the sentence *Ida borrowed the antique tablecloth*, you probably know even more about it than the propositions in Figure 7–3. This is because you have *schemata* about borrowing, tablecloths, antiques, and maybe even Ida herself.

Schemata

schemata (sing., schema): basic structures for organizing information; concepts

As Anderson (1985) has noted, "Propositions are fine for representing small units of meaning, but they fail when it comes to representing the larger sets of organized information that we know about particular concepts" (p. 124). For this larger, more complex task we need data structures that organize vast amounts of information into a meaningful system. These data structures are called *schemata*. A **schema** (the singular form) thus becomes a pattern or guide for understanding an event. The schema tells you what specific information to look for in a particular situation, what to expect. The schema is like a stereotype, specifying the "standard" relationships and sequence of events involved with an object or situation (Rumelhart & Ortony, 1977). You encountered the very similar concept of "scheme" when we discussed Piaget's theory of cognitive development in Chapter 2.

Reading *Ida borrowed the antique tablecloth,* most of us know without being told that the lender does not have the tablecloth now because it is in Ida's possession and that Ida has an obligation to return the cloth to the lender (Gentner, 1975). None of this information is explicitly stated in the original sentence but instead is part of our schema for understanding the meaning of *borrow.* Other schemata allow us to be fairly certain that the cloth is not plastic (if it is a real antique) and that Ida has probably invited guests for a meal. Our schema about Ida may even allow us to predict how promptly the cloth will be returned and in what condition.

The Key to Comprehension

Many cognitive psychologists believe schemata are the "key units of the comprehension process" (Rumelhart & Ortony, 1977, p. 111). To comprehend a story, we select a schema that seems appropriate. Then we use this framework to decide which details are important, what information to seek, and what to remember. It is as though the schema is a theory about what *should* occur in the story. The schema guides us in "interrogating" the text, filling in the specific information we expect to find so that the story makes sense (Resnick, 1981). Without the appropriate schema, trying to understand a story, textbook, or classroom lesson is a very slow and difficult process, something like finding your way through a new town without a map.

Storing knowledge of the world in schemata has advantages and disadvantages. Having a well-developed schema about Ida lets us recognize her (even as her appearance changes), remember many of her characteristics, and make predictions about her behavior. But it also allows us to be wrong. We may have incorporated incorrect or biased information into our schema of Ida. For example, if Ida is a member of an ethnic group and we believe that group is dishonest, we may assume that Ida will keep the tablecloth. In this way, racial and ethnic stereotypes can function as schemata for understanding (or misunderstanding) and responding to individuals.

Not all cognitive psychologists believe that human memory can be completely explained by the multistore (sensory/short-term/long-term) view of memory. Craik and Lockhart (1972) first proposed their **levels of processing theory** as an alternative to the multistore models. They suggested that what determines how long information is remembered is not *where* it is stored but how completely the information is analyzed and connected with other information. The more completely information is processed, the better our chances of remembering it.

More recently, Craik (1979) has suggested that the multistore model and the levels of processing view are not entirely incompatible. There may be different structural components or memory stores similar to the sensory register, short-term, and long-term distinctions, as well as different strategies or levels of processing that "move" information from one stage to the next (Reed, 1982). At any rate, both explanations agree that humans have a re-

levels of processing theory: holds that recall of information is based on how deeply it is processed

Guidelines

Applying the Ideas of the Information Processing Theorists

Make sure you have the students' attention.

Examples
1. *Develop a signal that tells students to stop what they are doing and focus on you. Some teachers move to a particular spot in the room, flick the lights, or play a chord on the class piano.*
2. *Move around the room, use gestures, avoid speaking in a monotone.*
3. *Begin a lesson by asking a question that stimulates interest in the topic.*
4. *Regain the attention of individual students if necessary by walking closer to them, using their names, or asking them a question that they can answer.*

Help students separate essential from nonessential details and focus on the most important information.

Examples
1. *Summarize instructional objectives to provide an indication of what students should be learning. Relate the material you are presenting to the objectives as you teach: "Now I'm going to explain exactly how you can find the information you need to meet Objective One on the board—determining the tone of the story."*
2. *When you make an important point, pause, repeat, ask a student to paraphrase, note the information on the board in colored chalk, or tell students to highlight the point in their notes or readings.*

Help students make connections between new information and what they already know.

Examples
1. *Review prerequisites to help students bring to mind the information they will need to understand new material: "Who can tell us the definition of a quadrilateral? Now, what is a rhombus? Is a square a quadrilateral? Is a square a rhombus? What did we say yesterday about how you can tell? Today we are going to look at some other quadrilaterals."*

markable capacity to process, organize, and remember vast amounts of information. The Guidelines should help you apply these theories.

REMEMBERING AND FORGETTING

All of us remember some things and forget others. Some might even call this the basic pattern of our mental lives. With the information processing model as a framework, we are ready to examine some of the hows and whys of remembering and forgetting. First, we'll ask . . .

Why Do People Forget?

With such an amazing capacity to store information, why do we forget so much? Actually, there are several trouble spots along the road from short-term memory to long-term memory to recall.

---

2. *Use an outline or diagram to show how new information fits with the framework you have been developing. For example, "Now that you know the duties of the FBI, where would you expect to find it in this diagram of the branches of the U.S. government?"*
3. *Give an assignment that specifically calls for the use of new information along with information already learned. After learning how to determine calorie intake and expenditure, have students keep track of everything they do and everything they eat for a week, then decide if they are eating more or less than they need. (Be careful of this assignment with students who seem to have tendencies toward anorexia.)*

Provide for repetition and review of information.

Examples
1. *Begin the class with a quick review of the homework assignment.*
2. *Give frequent, short tests.*
3. *Build practice and repetition into games, or have students work with partners to quiz each other.*

Present material in a clear, organized way.

Examples
1. *Make the purpose of the lesson very clear.*
2. *Give students a brief outline to follow. Put the same outline on an overhead so you can keep yourself on track. When students ask questions or make comments, relate these back to the appropriate section of the outline.*
3. *Use summaries in the middle and at the end of the lesson.*

Focus on meaning, not memorization.

Examples
1. *In teaching new words, help students associate the new word to a related word they already understand: "Enmity is from the same base as enemy. . . ."*
2. *In teaching about remainders, have students group 12 objects into sets of 2, 3, 4, 5, 6, and 7. Ask them to count the "leftovers" in each case.*

Forgetting and Short-Term Memory. Information is thought to be lost from short-term memory by two basic means. Interference is fairly straight-forward. Remembering new things interferes with remembering old things. At a certain point, the limited capacity of short-term memory is simply filled, and the old information is lost.

Interference and Decay

Information is also lost from short-term memory by time decay. The longer information is held in short-term memory, the weaker it becomes until it simply disappears. As discussed earlier in this chapter, forgetting can be very useful. Without it, people would quickly overload their short-term memories and learning would cease.

Forgetting and Long-Term Memory. Information lost from short-term memory truly disappears. No amount of effort will bring it back. But it seems that information stored in long-term memory is never lost and can always be retrieved, given the appropriate conditions. Freud suggested that we sometimes intentionally forget or *repress* certain information or experiences we do not really want to remember. But this cannot explain why some painful experiences are remembered vividly while others that are pleasant or neutral are forgotten. What else causes problems in long-term memory?

Repression

The idea that interference causes forgetting in long-term as well as short-term memory seems to be supported by evidence from research. Newer memories may interfere with or obscure older memories by becoming confused with them. When new verbal associations make it difficult for a person to remember older information, the interference is called **retroactive interference.** If older memories associations make it difficult to remember new information, the interference is called **proactive interference** (Crouse, 1971).

retroactive interference: new information interferes with old

proactive interference: old information interferes with new

The interference explanation of forgetting does not contradict the notion that we never really forget anything stored in long-term memory. The interference is not necessarily occurring in the long-term memory itself; it probably occurs when the information is retrieved and brought back to short-term memory. So the problem lies in the retrieval process. This brings us to a very important issue for teachers. How do people retrieve the information they need when they need it? In other words . . .

How Do People Remember?

Cultural Reconstructions

Successful retrieval is really a problem-solving process that makes use of logic, cues, and other knowledge to reconstruct information and fill in any missing parts (Lindsay & Norman, 1977). Sometimes these reconstructed recollections are incorrect, as early work on remembering stories demonstrated. In 1932, Bartlett conducted a series of famous studies. He read a complex, unfamiliar story about a tribe of North American Indians to students at England's Cambridge University. He then asked the students to recall the story after various lengths of time. The students' recalled stories were generally shorter than the original and were translated into the concepts and language of the Cambridge students. The story told of a seal hunt, but many students remembered a "fishing trip," an activity closer to their experience. Instead of remembering the exact words of the story, the students remembered the meaning, but the meaning they remembered was generally somewhat altered to fit their cultural expectations and stereo-types—in other words, their schemata.

Another example of reconstruction occurs when we retrieve information that is only partially correct. You probably have had an experience like this: you are looking for a book and saying, "I know it's blue with white letters on the cover." When you finally find the book, it does turn out to have white letters, but the cover is really orange. Maybe you had not paid atten-tion to the color; maybe the color of the object was encoded incorrectly in the first place; maybe you confused it with another book you were reading at the time (you forgot because of interference); or perhaps you encoded the right color, but it never reached your long-term memory (it was not pro-cessed deeply enough). You did, however, retrieve *part* of the information. The parts you couldn't remember, you reconstructed.

Not all reconstructed memories are distorted. In fact, reconstruction strat-egies often lead to remarkable successes. Consider this question: "What were you doing on Monday afternoon in the third week of September two years ago?" (Lindsay & Norman, 1977, p. 372). One subject solved this seemingly impossible retrieval problem this way:

> Come on. How should I know? . . . OK. Let's see: Two years ago . . . I would be in high school in Pittsburgh. . . . That would be my senior year. . . . Third week in September—that's just after summer—that would be the fall term. . . . Let me see. I think I had chemistry lab on Mondays. . . . I don't know. I was probably in the chemistry lab. . . . Wait a minute—that would be the second week of school. I remember he started off with the atomic table—a big, fancy chart. I thought he was crazy, trying to make us memorize that thing. You know, I think I can remember sitting. . . .

Sometimes we attempt to retrieve information from our long-term mem-ory and feel as if we're "about to remember" but cannot quite grasp what we're looking for. You might run into an acquaintance whose name seems to be "on the tip of your tongue"—you might even recall the sound of the name or the first letter. Or you might be sure you know the word that fits the definition for 27 Down on the crossword puzzle—but you just can't come up with it. This near-retrieval is known, not surprisingly, as the **tip-of-the tongue phenomenon** (Brown & McNeill, 1966).

Even though our long-term memory system is theoretically unlimited in capacity and duration, it is probably becoming clear to you that successful recall is no simple matter. What are the primary influences on successful recall? The way we learn information in the first place—the way we process it at the outset—seems to affect its recall later. What are the important ele-ments of this processing?

Elaboration.   When confronted with the sentence about Ida and the table-cloth, we tend to "fill in," or elaborate, the new information with what we already know. **Elaboration** is the addition of meaning to new information through its connection with already existing knowledge. In other words, we apply our schemata and draw on already existing knowledge to make sense of new information. We often elaborate automatically. Much as with Ida's sentence, a paragraph we read about a historical figure in the seventeenth century tends to activate our already existing knowledge about that period; we use the old knowledge to understand the new.

Material that is elaborated when first learned will be easier to recall later. The more one bit of information or knowledge is associated with other bits, the more routes there are to follow to get to the original bit. Or put another way, you have several handles, or *retrieval cues,* by which you can recognize or "pick up" the information you might be seeking. If you were asked to memorize the sentence *Ida borrowed the antique tablecloth,* you could elaborate it by picturing Ida setting the table, or by adding to the sentence *and she sold it to buy booze,* or by focusing on the old lace tablecloth your mother used for special occasions, or by completing the story with a big dinner party. In these ways, you would have a much better chance of remembering the original sentence (or at least its essence) at a later time. You would have given yourself several possible cues that could lead you back to the original information. Psychologists have also found that the more precise and sensible the elaborations, the easier recall will be (Bransford, Stein, Vye, Franks, Auble, Mezynski, & Perfetto, 1982; Stein, Littlefield, Bransford, & Persampieri, 1984).

Elaborating Ida

Organization. A second element of processing that improves retrieval, particularly of complex or of large amounts of information, is *organization.* Material that is well organized is easier to learn and to remember than bits and pieces of information. Placing a concept in a hierarchical structure will help you learn and remember either general definitions or specific examples.

Figure 7–4 **Organizing the Concept of *Consequence***

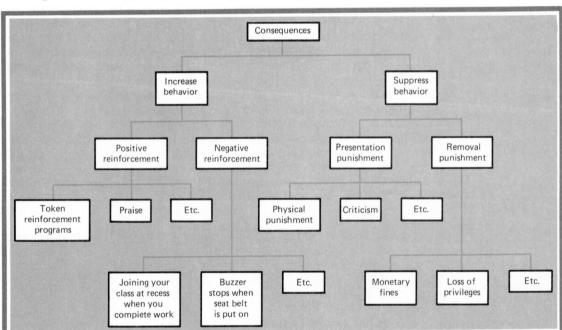

The look and layout of their chemistry lab, the time of day, their partner, and even what they say to one another will probably be coded in long-term memory along with the steps of the experiment these students are working on. All these aspects of context may help them remember the essential scientific information when they need it. *(Will/ Deni McIntyre/Photo Researchers)*

The structure serves as a guide back to the information when you need it. Figure 7–4 shows how the concept of consequences in a behavioral view of learning could be placed in a hierarchy.

Context.   A third element of processing that influences retrieval is *context*. Aspects of physical and emotional contexts—places, rooms, how we are feeling on a particular day, who is with us—are learned along with other information. Later, if you try to remember the information, it will be easier if the current context is similar to the original one. This has been demonstrated in the laboratory. Students who learned material in one type of room performed better on tests taken in a similar room than on tests taken in a very different-looking room (Smith, Glenberg, & Bjork, 1978). So studying for a test under "testlike" conditions might result in improved performance. Taking a psychology exam in the same room where the course is held will also improve your chances of remembering the material. Of course, you can't always go back to the same or a similar place in order to recall something. But you can picture the setting, the time of day, and your companions, and you may eventually reach the information you seek.

Reproducing the Scene

Strategies for Helping Students Remember

How can teachers help their students learn and remember information? There are two general categories of strategies. The first category includes techniques for rote memorization. These strategies are limited to learning material that has no inherent meaning—the populations of the ten largest cities in the world, for example. The second group of strategies applies to meaningful material.

Rote Memorization.   Some things need to be learned by rote, but not very many. We all probably learned the names of the numbers one to ten by rote memorization. After ten, the whole procedure became a lot easier because prior knowledge of the first ten numbers helped us crack the system. The learning became meaningful because of this prior knowledge.

Let's look at another example of rote memorization. How might a student go about memorizing the abbreviations of the chemical elements by rote in a single weekend? One possibility is to break the list of elements into a number of separate lists and practice each one intermittently throughout the weekend. The student might also ask a friend to hear recitations of the short lists and later ask the friend to pick elements at random and give a test.

part learning: breaking a list of rote items into shorter lists

Breaking the list into segments is an example of **part learning.** Moving information into long-term memory takes effort; only a few items can make it into long-term memory at any given time. So it makes sense to concentrate on a limited number of items. From a reinforcement point of view, the immediate success of learning each partial list can encourage the student to continue.

serial-position effect: remembering beginning and end but not middle of a list

If you have tried to memorize a list of items that are all similar to one another, you may have found that you tended to remember items at the beginning and at the end of the list but forgot those in the middle. This is called the **serial-position effect.** Part learning can help prevent this effect. Breaking a list into several short lists means there will be fewer middle items to cause problems.

distributed practice: practice in brief periods with rest intervals

massed practice: practice for a single extended period

A final strategy for making the memorization of a long list easier is the use of **distributed practice.** A student who studies the abbreviations of the chemical elements intermittently throughout the weekend will probably do much better than a student who tries to memorize the entire list on Sunday night. Studying for an extended period rather than for briefer periods with rest time in between is called **massed practice.** There are several reasons why distributed practice is more effective. Too long a study session leads to fatigue, and motivation lags. In addition, forgetting begins promptly at the end of the learning session. If several sessions are used, what is forgotten from one session can be relearned in the next. The **relearning** will be faster than starting from scratch because forgetting is only partial; some items will be familiar.

relearning: filling in the gaps and encoding more completely material that is not totally unfamiliar

Make It Meaningful

Perhaps the best single method for helping students remember what they learn is to make each lesson as meaningful as possible. Meaningful lessons are presented in vocabulary that makes sense to the students. New terms are clarified through the use of more familiar words and ideas. Meaningful lessons are also well organized, with clear connections between the different elements of the lesson. Finally, meaningful lessons make natural use of old information to help students understand new information by giving examples or analogies.

The importance of meaningful lessons is emphasized in an example presented by Smith (1975). Consider the three lines below:

1.   KBVODUWGPJMSQTXNOGMCTRSO
2.   READ JUMP WHEAT POOR BUT SEEK
3.   KNIGHTS RODE HORSES INTO WAR

Begin by covering all but the first line. Look at it for a second, close the book, and write down all the letters you remember. Then repeat this procedure with the second and third lines. Each line has the same number of letters, but the chances are great that you remembered all the letters in the third line, a good number of letters in the second line, and very few in the first line.

Sense and Nonsense

The first line makes no sense. There is no way to organize it in a brief glance. The second line is more meaningful. You do not have to see each letter because you bring prior knowledge of spelling rules and vocabulary to the task. The third line is the most meaningful. Just a glance and you can probably remember all of it because you bring to this task prior knowledge not only of spelling and vocabulary but also of rules about syntax and probably some historical information about knights (they didn't ride in tanks). This sentence is meaningful because you have existing schemata for assimilating it. It is fairly easy to associate the words and meaning with other information already in long-term memory.

The challenge for teachers is to make lessons less like learning the first line and more like learning the third line. Although this may seem obvious, think about the times when you yourself have read a sentence in a text or heard an explanation from a professor that might just as well have been KBVODUWGPJMSQTXNOGMCTRSO.

mnemonics: art of memory; also, techniques for remembering

In recent years, educators have become more interested in exploring the effectiveness of mnemonic aids in classroom contexts. **Mnemonics** are systematic procedures for improving one's memory. The term can also refer to the art of memory, which had an important place in ancient Greek culture. Mnemonic techniques have recently been demonstrated to be effective for students of all ages, from preschool to college (Levin, 1985; McCormick & Levin, in press).

Among the several useful systems are peg systems such as loci, pegwords, and first letters; chaining systems such as stories; and systems based on word meanings, such as the keyword method. As you will see, many of these strategies use imagery.

Peg-Type Mnemonics. Peg-type methods require that you memorize a standard list of places or words. Then, whenever you want to learn a list of items, you associate this information with the "pegs" already in memory.

PEANUTS ®   **By Charles M. Schulz**

Lucy develops a new strategy for helping her brother remember. Did the ancient Greeks know about this one? (© 1969 United Features Syndicate)

One peg-type approach, the **loci method,** derives its name from the plural form of the Latin word *locus,* meaning "place."

To use the loci method, you must first imagine a very familiar place, such as your own house or apartment. Now pick out particular locations that you might notice in a walk through your house. For instance, the entry hall leads into the formal living room. Off to the right-hand side of the living room is the dining room. Through the french doors is the kitchen. Whenever you have a list to remember, simply place each item from the list in one of these locations in the house. For instance, let's say you want to remember to buy milk, bread, butter, and cereal at the store. Imagine a giant bottle of milk blocking the entry hall, a lazy loaf of bread sleeping on the living room couch, someone sliding on a stick of butter and knocking over the dining room table set with the best china, and finally, dry cereal covering the entire kitchen floor. When you want to remember the items, all you have to do is take an imaginary walk through the house and see what is in the entry hall, the living room, the dining room, and the kitchen. The same locations serve as pegs every time you have a list to remember.

The **pegword method** has often been used by entertainers to dazzle the public with feats of memory. In the most formal variation of the method, you begin by learning a set of pegwords. Lindsay and Norman (1977) suggest ten simple words that incorporate rhymes to make the list easier to learn:

One is bun.	Six is sticks.
Two is shoe.	Seven is heaven.
Three is tree.	Eight is gate.
Four is door.	Nine is line.
Five is hive.	Ten is hen.

When you know the pegwords, new lists of items to be learned can be associated with these words through an image. For example, if you have to stop at the cleaners, the bank, the post office, and the supermarket on your way home from school, you might imagine your clothes that need cleaning because someone threw hamburger *buns* covered with mayonnaise and ketchup at you. Next, you could see money stuffed into a pair of *shoes.* Then you could envision letters hanging like leaves on a *tree.* Finally, you might imagine smashing down a *door* with a shopping cart.

The pegs we have discussed thus far are used to learn new material, generally material that will be needed for only a short period of time. Other types of peg approaches work better if you need to remember information for long periods of time. One common type is the *acronym*—a word formed from the first letters of the words of a phrase. Examples include NATO (North American Treaty Organization), UNESCO (United Nations Educational, Scientific and Cultural Organization), and even laser (light amplification by stimulated emission of radiation). An acronym is a kind of abbreviation. Another method involves forming phrases or sentences out of the first letters of each word or item in a list. You may be familiar with a sentence known by all young music students—Every Good Boy Does Fine. The first letter of each word stands for the name of a line of the G clef: E, G, B, D, F. The first letter of each word in the sentence provides the peg. Since the words must make sense as a sentence, this approach also has some characteristics of the chain methods—one item is linked to the next in order.

Chain Methods.   Chain mnemonics (or linking mnemonics, as they are sometimes called) connect the first item to be memorized with the second, the second with the third, the third with the fourth, and so on. In one type of chain method each item on a list is linked to the next through some visual association. If you have to stop at the cleaners, the bank, the post office, and the supermarket, you might begin by imagining the cleaner cleaning the money that is going to be sent to the bank. Then you might imagine the money stuffed in envelopes. Finally, you might imagine these envelopes in a shopping cart. In each case, one visual cue leads you to the next.

Another chain-type approach is to incorporate all the items to be memorized into a jingle with rhymes, like "*i* before *e* except after *c*" and "Thirty days hath September." These approaches do stick in our memories. Most of us still repeat the "Thirty days" rhyme to determine the length of a given month.

Visual Cues

Rhymes

The Keyword Method.   The mnemonic system that has been most extensively applied in teaching is the **keyword method.** Although the idea has a long history, research by Atkinson and his colleagues in the mid-1970s sparked serious interest, especially in foreign-language teaching (Atkinson, 1975; Atkinson & Raugh, 1975). This research has demonstrated impressive results.

keyword method: associating new words or concepts with similar-sounding cue words

The approach has two stages. To remember a foreign word, you must first choose an English word, preferably a concrete noun, that sounds like the foreign word or a part of it. Next, you associate the meaning of the foreign word with the English word through an image or sentence. For example, the Spanish word *carta* (meaning "letter") sounds like the English word *cart*. *Cart* becomes the keyword: you imagine a shopping cart filled with letters on its way to the post office, or you make up a sentence, such as *The cart full of letters tipped over* (Pressley, Levin, & Delaney, 1982). Figure 7–5 offers another example of this method in teaching Spanish vocabulary.

Applications

Other possible applications of the method include learning the names and the order of the U.S. presidents, concrete biographical information, relatively abstract statistical information, and relatively complex scientific concepts (Levin, Dretzke, McCormick, Scruggs, McGivern, & Mastropieri, 1983; McCormick & Levin, in press). The keyword method has also been used successfully with poor readers and learning disabled students (Goin, Peters, & Levin, 1986; Peters & Levin, 1986; Scruggs, Mastropieri, McLoone, Levin, & Morrison, 1985).

In general, the techniques we've been describing that require self-generated imagery are more appropriate for students in the later elementary and secondary grades. Younger students have some difficulty forming their own images. For them, memory aids that rely on auditory cues—rhymes like "*i* before *e* except after *c*" and "Thirty days hath September"—seem to work better. If you want to use aids requiring imagery with younger or less able students, you'll probably need to help them find appropriate images or keywords (Pressley, Levin, & Delaney, 1982).

Figure 7–5   **Using Keywords to Learn Spanish**

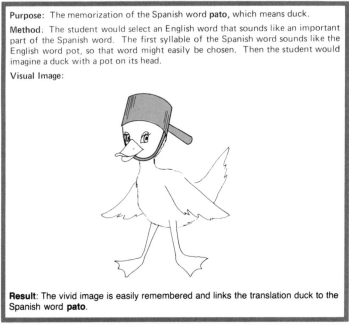

Purpose: The memorization of the Spanish word **pato**, which means duck.

Method: The student would select an English word that sounds like an important part of the Spanish word. The first syllable of the Spanish word sounds like the English word pot, so that word might easily be chosen. Then the student would imagine a duck with a pot on its head.

Visual Image:

Result: The vivid image is easily remembered and links the translation duck to the Spanish word **pato**.

Adapted from Images are a Key to Learning. Wisconsin Research and Development Center News (1979, Spring), pp. 1–2.

LEARNING ABOUT LEARNING: METACOGNITIVE ABILITIES

Thus far we have discussed general cognitive learning principles—principles that seem to apply to most people. But experience tells us that individuals differ in how well or how quickly they learn. One question that intrigues many cognitive psychologists is why some people learn and remember more than others. Researchers have looked for answers by studying differences between younger and older learners as well as differences between more and less able learners. Results of both types of comparisons point to the importance of metacognitive abilities (Pressley, Borkowski, & Schneider, in press).

metacognition: knowledge and monitoring of thinking and learning strategies

The term **metacognition,** as you saw in Chapter 2, was introduced by psychologists to refer to knowledge about and control over thinking and learning activities (Flavell, 1976). Metacognition involves at least two separate components: (1) an awareness of the skills, strategies, and resources needed to perform a task effectively—knowing *what* to do; and (2) the ability to use self-regulatory mechanisms to ensure the successful completion of the task—knowing *how* and *when* to do the *what.*

The strategies in the first component—knowing what to do—include identifying the main idea, rehearsing information, forming associations and images, using mnemonics, organizing new material to make it easier to remember, applying test-taking techniques, outlining, and note taking. The regulatory mechanisms—the second component, knowing how and when— include checking to see if you understand, predicting outcomes, evaluating the effectiveness of an attempt at a task, planning the next move, testing strategies, deciding how to apportion time and effort, and revising or switching to other strategies to overcome any difficulties encountered (Baker & Brown, 1984a). The use of these regulatory mechanisms is known as cognitive monitoring (Flavell, in press). Notice that these cognitive monitoring processes can be thought of as part of the executive control processes operating on the flow of information through memory systems in the information processing model (see Figure 7–1).

Metacognitive Development

In general, metacognitive abilities begin to develop around ages 5 to 7 and improve throughout school. But there is great variability even among students of the same age. Most children go through a transitional period during which they can apply a particular strategy if reminded but will not apply it on their own (Brown, Campione, & Day, 1981).

Strategy Instruction

One goal of education, according to many experts, should be to help students learn to use effective metacognitive strategies. Fortunately, studying *how* to teach these executive control skills has become a high priority in education, and several important principles have been identified.

The "simple" acts of reading and studying are really very complex. As this student works, he must identify main ideas, organize and elaborate information, form images, and take notes. He must also monitor his comprehension, constantly planning and adjusting. If he's stuck, will he know he needs to switch gears? Direct teaching of metacognitive strategies—a promising new area of education—may help. *(Donald Dietz/ Stock, Boston)*

First, students must be exposed to a number of different strategies—not only general thinking strategies but very specific strategies, such as the mnemonic techniques described earlier in this chapter.

Second, providing instruction in the *when, where,* and *why* of strategy use seems very important (Pressley, Borkowski, O'Sullivan, 1984). Although this may seem obvious, teachers often neglect this information, either because they do not realize its significance or because they assume students will make inferences on their own. We do know that a strategy is more likely to be maintained and employed if this information is provided about the when, where, and why.

Third, we cannot forget the relationship between performance and attitude. Students may know when and how to use a strategy, but unless they also develop the desire to employ these skills, general learning ability will not improve. Those who use strategies effectively believe that they can affect their own performance by using a strategy; other students must be given the opportunity to develop feelings of effectiveness in applying strategies. Several learning strategy programs (Borkowski, Johnston, & Reid, in press; Dansereau, 1985) include a motivational training component. In Chapter 9 we will look more closely at this important issue of motivation.

Fourth, direct instruction in schematic knowledge is often an important component of strategy training. In order to identify main ideas—a critical skill for a number of learning strategies—you must have an appropriate schema for making sense of the material. The effectiveness of specific schema training has been repeatedly demonstrated. For instance, awareness of the typical form of narratives enhances story recall (Rumelhart, 1977). These typical forms are called **story grammars.** A story grammar is something like this: Boy meets girl, boy and girl fall in love, misunderstanding occurs, boy loses girl, reconciliation (music fades). In other words, it is a typical general structure—a schema or stereotype—that could fit many specific stories. If you know what to expect next as you are reading a story, you will probably find it easier to understand and remember the story.

story grammars:
typical structures or
organizations for
stories

Metacognition and Reading

In order to illustrate the practical significance of metacognition, let's focus on a common school task—reading comprehension. Clearly, a good deal of the knowledge available to students in schools is packaged in the form of written materials. Reading comprehension is important to all school subjects. In recent years, metacognitive research has made significant contributions to our understanding of that process.

If you were asked to describe what you did as you were reading the previous paragraph, you'd probably say, "What do you mean, what did I do? I just read the words." But reading comprehension is a much more complicated process than just "reading the words." Comprehension is the result of an interaction between the text itself and the cognitive structures (story grammars, other schemata, propositional networks, strategies) that the reader draws on and applies during the reading process. To get a feel for this interaction, we can examine differences in metacognitive skills between expert (older or better) readers and novice or unskilled (younger or poorer) readers.

A Complex
Interaction

This student seems at least to have grasped the importance of monitoring his own comprehension—"listening" to see if he is understanding what he reads. *(Bob McCullough)*

"I can't explain what I just read. Because I wasn't listening."

decoding: translating the printed word into speech

Younger and poorer readers treat reading as a decoding process (they try to understand each separate word) rather than as a meaning-getting process (understanding what the text as a whole means) (Garner & Kraus, 1982). **Decoding** is the translation of the printed word to speech. Children are taught to read by decoding, so for young readers it is generally the only activity involved in reading. The reading rate of both younger and poorer readers tends to be unvarying, no matter what their purpose in reading is (Forrest & Waller, 1980). In other words, it doesn't matter whether they are reading to study, for fun, or to skim; these readers make no adjustment in the *way* they read. They also have difficulty selecting the important ideas in the text (Brown & Smiley, 1977) and detecting gross violations of logical structure in a text (Danner, 1976). For example, if two sentences in the same paragraph contradict each other, a less able reader might not notice the contradiction. Moreover, poorer and younger readers have difficulties bringing to mind related knowledge and using the context to help them interpret what they are reading (Winograd & Johnston, 1982). In fact, these readers lack the awareness that they should even do these things. Finally, younger and poorer readers have few strategies at their disposal for dealing with any failures to understand the text, even if they become aware of problems (Baker & Brown, 1984b).

The first part of Table 7–3 lists the difficulties younger or less able students might have as they try to comprehend written material. As you can

Table 7–3   Comprehension Failures and Remedies

POSSIBLE COMPREHENSION FAILURES

1. Failure to understand a word
   a. Novel word
   b. Known word that doesn't make sense in the context
2. Failure to understand a sentence
   a. Can find no interpretation
   b. Can find only vague, abstract interpretation
   c. Can find several possible interpretations (ambiguous sentence)
   d. Interpretation conflicts with prior knowledge
3. Failure to understand how one sentence relates to another
   a. Interpretation of one sentence conflicts with another
   b. Can find no connection between the sentences
   c. Can find several possible connections between the sentences
4. Failure to understand how the whole text fits together
   a. Can find no point to whole or part of the text
   b. Cannot understand why certain episodes or sections occurred
   c. Cannot understand the motivations of certain characters

POSSIBLE REMEDIES

1. *Ignore and read on,* because this information is relatively unimportant.
2. *Suspend judgment,* because it is likely to be cleared up later.
3. *Form a tentative hypothesis* to be tested as reading continues.
4. *Reread the current sentence(s)* or look for a tentative hypothesis.
5. *Reread the previous context* to resolve the contradiction.
6. *Go to an expert source,* because it simply doesn't make sense.

Adapted from A. Collins & E. Smith (1980), Teaching the process of reading comprehension (Technical report no. 182). Urbana-Champaign: Center for the Study of Reading, University of Illinois.

students can fail to understand a word, a sentence, a group of sentences, or the whole passage. The second part of the table offers some remedies that students might use to resolve these failures (Collins & Smith, 1980). Notice that these remedies are presented from the least disruptive to the most disruptive and should probably be tried in this order. For instance, ignoring and reading on is less disruptive than rereading the previous material. The strategies farther down on the list should be attempted only when the earlier strategies prove inadequate.

reciprocal teaching: a method, based on modeling, to teach reading comprehension strategies

Training in Reading Comprehension Strategies.   Collins and Smith (1982) have demonstrated the effectiveness of modeling as a technique for teaching reading comprehension strategies. One very successful method for this use of modeling is called **reciprocal teaching** (Palincsar & Brown, 1984). This approach teaches students four strategies: summarizing the content of a passage; asking a question about the central point; clarifying the difficult parts of the material; and predicting what will come next. First the teacher and group of students read a short passage silently. Then the teacher provides a model by summarizing, questioning, clarifying, and predicting based on the reading. Next, everyone reads another passage, and the students begin to assume the teacher's role. Often the students' first attempts are halting and incorrect. But the teacher gives clues, guidance, and encouragement (what Vygotsky might call scaffolding) to help the students master these strategies.

Let's look at some examples of reciprocal teaching in action. The first example is an early lesson. Here the teacher is guiding a student as he tries to formulate a question about the central point in a passage on spiders (*Harvard Education Letter*, March 1986, p. 6):

Example: An Early Lesson

TEXT:	Spinner's mate is much smaller than she, and his body is dull brown. He spends most of his time sitting at one side of her web.
CHARLES:	(No question)
TEACHER:	What's this paragraph about?
CHARLES:	Spinner's mate. How do spinner's mate . . .
TEACHER:	That's good. Keep going.
CHARLES:	How do spinner's mate is smaller than . . . How am I going to say that?
TEACHER:	Take your time with it. You want to ask a question about spinner's mate and what he does, beginning with the word "how."
CHARLES:	How do they spend most of his time sitting?
TEACHER:	You're very close. The question would be, "How does spinner's mate spend most of his time?" Now, you ask it.
CHARLES:	How does spinner's mate spend most of his time?

After a while, students are usually able to take more and more responsibility for the teaching. In the following example, Laura shows how much progress she has made after about 12 lessons (*Harvard Education Letter*, March 1986, p. 6):

Example: The Lessons Pay Off

TEXT:	The second oldest form of salt production is mining. Unlike early methods that made the work extremely dangerous and difficult, today's methods use special machinery, and salt mining is easier and safer. The old expression "back to the salt mine" no longer applies.
LAURA:	Name two words that often describe mining salt in the old days.
KIM:	Back to the salt mines?
LAURA:	No. Angela?
ANGELA:	Dangerous and difficult.
LAURA:	Correct. This paragraph is all about comparing the old mining of salt and today's mining of salt.
TEACHER:	Beautiful!
LAURA:	I have a prediction to make.
TEACHER:	Good.
LAURA:	I think it might tell when salt was first discovered, well, it might tell what salt is made of and how it's made.
TEACHER:	O.K. Can we have another teacher?

Research on reciprocal teaching has shown some dramatic results. Most of the work has been done with young adolescents who can read aloud fairly accurately but are far below average in reading comprehension. After 20 hours of practice with this approach, many students who were in the bottom quarter of their class moved up to the average level or above on tests of reading comprehension. Based on the results of several studies, Palincsar has identified three guidelines for effective reciprocal teaching (*Harvard Education Letter*, March 1986; Palincsar & Brown, 1984):

<table>
<tr><td>Reciprocal Teaching
Guidelines</td><td>1.</td><td>*Shift gradually.* The shift from teacher control to student responsibility must be gradual.</td></tr>
<tr><td></td><td>2.</td><td>*Match demands to abilities.* The difficulty of the task and the responsibility must match the abilities of each student and grow as these abilities develop.</td></tr>
<tr><td></td><td>3.</td><td>*Diagnose thinking.* Teachers should carefully observe the ''teaching'' of each student for clues about how the student is thinking and what kind of instruction the student needs.</td></tr>
</table>

This has been a necessarily brief introduction to the concept of metacognition. You will need to retrieve some of this knowledge from long-term memory when we discuss problem-solving skills, study skills, and thinking skills in the next chapter.

SUMMARY

1. Cognitive learning theorists focus on the human mind's active attempts to make sense of the world. Prior knowledge, context, feelings, beliefs, and expectations all influence what and how we learn.

2. One influential cognitive model, which is based on the analogy of the mind to the computer, is the information processing model. One version of this model consists of several storage systems: sensory, short-term, and long-term. Information processing involves encoding, retention, and retrieval.

3. The sensory register takes in sensory stimuli and holds the information very briefly.

4. Perception refers to the meaning we attach to data received through our senses. Our understanding of perception is based in part on the work of the Gestalt psychologists early in this century. They formulated basic principles by which we organize our perceptions into meaningful wholes, including *Prägnanz* and figure-ground.

5. Bottom-up processing allows us to understand stimuli by recognizing familiar elements. In top-down processing, we apply previous knowledge to fill out and understand patterns. We often use both types together. Attention is also an important aspect of perception.

6. Short-term memory, or our working memory, contains a limited amount of readily accessible information. It can generally hold about five to nine separate items for a maximum of 20 seconds. However, this limitation can be extended through rehearsal and chunking.

7. Long-term memory appears to hold an unlimited amount of information permanently.

8. Information in long-term memory may be coded verbally or both verbally and visually. It is thought that bits of information are stored and interrelated in propositional networks. Larger data structures known as schemata allow us to represent large amounts of complex information, make inferences, and understand new information.

9. A view of memory that does not depend on the short-term/long-term distinction is the levels of processing theory. According to this view, recall of information is determined by how completely information is processed.

10. Forgetting in short-term memory can result from interference or time decay. Interference, either retroactive or proactive, also occurs in long-term memory.

11. Remembering seems to be a reconstruction process, sometimes accurate, sometimes only partly accurate. A sense of "almost remembering" (the tip-of-the-tongue phenomenon) can also occur.

12. The more information is elaborated, the more likely and the more accurate retrieval will be. Organization and context also aid retrieval.

13. Rote memorization can be improved by part learning, which combats the serial-position effect, and by distributed practice.

14. Effective mnemonics include the loci and pegword methods, acronyms, making meaningful sentences or phrases out of items, combining items into rhymes or stories, and keyword methods.

15. Metacognition, or knowledge of and control over thinking, involves an awareness of what thinking strategies to use and the monitoring of these strategies—knowing when, how, and why to apply them.

16. Students can be taught effective thinking strategies. In particular, students can be helped to draw on and apply the cognitive structures and processes discussed as part of long-term memory.

17. Metacognitive instruction has proved especially helpful in improving reading comprehension. Reciprocal teaching involves the modeling of summarizing, questioning, clarifying, and predicting strategies while reading.

KEY TERMS

receptors	chunking
sensory register	long-term memory
perception	episodic memory
Gestalt	semantic memory
Gestalt theory	propositional network
Prägnanz	schemata, schema
figure-ground	levels of processing theory
feature analysis	retroactive interference
bottom-up processing	proactive interference
top-down processing	tip-of-the-tongue phenomenon
short-term memory	elaboration
rehearse	part learning

serial-position effect

distributed practice

massed practice

relearning

mnemonics

loci method

pegword method

keyword method

metacognition

story grammars

decoding

reciprocal teaching

SUGGESTIONS FOR FURTHER READING AND STUDY

ANDERSON, J. R. (1985). *Cognitive psychology and its implications* (2nd ed.). San Francisco: W. H. Freeman. A very well-written text with excellent explanations and many examples.

BIGGE, M. L. (1982). *Learning theories for teachers* (4th ed.). New York: Harper and Row. This latest edition of a classic text discusses both behavioral and cognitive views of learning, with an emphasis on the latter.

BRANSFORD, J. D. (1979). *Human cognition: Learning, understanding, and remembering.* Belmont, CA: Wadsworth. A very readable but thorough introduction to the field of cognitive psychology.

BROWN, A. (1980). Metacognitive development and reading. In R. Spiro, B. Bruce, & W. Brewer (Eds.), *Theoretical issues in reading comprehension.* Hillsdale, NJ: Lawrence Erlbaum. Ann Brown is one of the leading authorities on metacognition in learning. This chapter is an excellent explanation of the relationship between metacognition and learning tasks in school.

CRAIK, F. I., & LOCKHART, R. S. (1972). Levels of processing: A framework for memory research. *Journal of Verbal Learning and Verbal Behavior, 11,* 671–684. This article presents Craik's and Lockhart's criticisms of the "stages" of memory theories (short-term, long-term) and proposes an alternative view, suggesting that how well something is remembered is determined by how deeply the information is processed.

DERRY, S. J., & MURPHY, D. A. (1986). Designing systems that train learning abilities. *Review of Educational Research, 56,* 1–39. This article covers a very wide range of topics, from metacognition to memory training to problem solving—an excellent overview of the research,

problems, and possibilities involved in teaching people how to learn.

HALL, J. F. (1982). *An invitation to learning and memory.* Boston: Allyn and Bacon. This text covers both behavioral and cognitive views but clearly emphasizes the cognitive perspective.

HART, L. A. (1983). *Human brain and human learning.* New York: Longman. Hart proposes a new approach to teaching and learning based on research on the human brain—an interesting contrast to more traditional views.

HIGBEE, K. L. (1977). *Your memory: How it works and how to improve it.* Englewood Cliffs, NJ: Prentice-Hall. A very interesting and useful guide—not just for teaching but for anyone who wants to "remember better."

IRWIN, J. W. (1986). *Teaching reading comprehension processes.* Englewood Cliffs, NJ: Prentice-Hall. This is a very current discussion of reading comprehension from a cognitive perspective—complete with many teaching ideas.

KLATZKY, R. L. (1980). *Human memory: Structures and processes* (2nd ed.). San Francisco: W. H. Freeman. A classic text that presents the information processing approach clearly and completely.

NEISSER, W. (1976). *Cognition and reality: Principles and implications of cognitive psychology.* San Francisco: W. H. Freeman. A short but thorough discussion of perception, attention, schemata, and memory by a major figure in cognitive psychology.

NORMAN, D. A. (1982). *Learning and memory.* San Francisco: W. H. Freeman. A concise and intriguing statement from one of the most important researchers in the field of cognitive psychology.

PRESSLEY, M. (1982). Elaboration and memory development. *Child Development, 53,* 296–309. A review of research on how children use elaboration, spontaneously or with instruction, to improve memory. Educational applications such as the keyword method are discussed as well.

PRESSLEY, M., FORREST-PRESSLEY, D. L., ELLIOT-FAUST, D., & MILLER, G. (1985). Children's use of cognitive strategies, how to teach strategies, and what to do if they can't be taught. In M. Pressley & C. Brainerd (Eds.), *Verbal processes in children: Progress in cognitive development research* (pp. 125–148). New York: Springer-Verlag. The title pretty much says it all. This is a very useful discussion by experts in the field.

PRESSLEY, M., LEVIN, J., & DELANEY, H. D. (1982). The mnemonic keyword method. *Review of Research in Education, 52,* 61–91. A thoughtful review of research on the keyword method by educational psychologists who have been instrumental in developing the approach.

RUMELHART, D. E., & ORTONY, A. (1977). The representation of knowledge in memory. In R. Anderson, R. Spiro, & W. Montague (Eds.), *Schooling and the acquisition of knowledge.* Hillsdale, NJ: Lawrence Erlbaum. A carefully written explanation of the role of schemata in learning and remembering.

Teachers' Forum

How Will They Remember?

How do you help students with those basic skills, retaining and retrieving information? Do you have special techniques for preventing boredom in the unavoidable rote memorization tasks? What about teaching vocabulary, facts, or concepts?

Act It Out

I use mnemonic devices and spelling tricks to help students do rote memory work. Also, acting out situations can help students personalize and thus retain information. An example: Laurie is the sun, Steve is the earth, Susie is the moon. Steve is the one who most needs to understand what the earth does. Laurie stands in the center, Steve rotates around her, Susie revolves around Steve. After repeating this a few times on subsequent days, Steve will understand.

Bonnie Hettman, High School Teacher
Lima Central Catholic High School, Lima, Ohio

Games at Work

For all subject areas requiring immediate recall, drill can take many exciting forms. Flashcards can be used in countless game-type settings, in which teams of students oppose one another. For those who learn best through auditory techniques, teacher-made tapes are valuable tools. Variations on well-known games are also very effective in reinforcing information—Beat the Clock, Tic-Tac-Toe, Concentration, and Jeopardy are only a few that can provide structure for drill activities. Timed tests and peer-tutoring sessions have also proved effective.

Jacqueline M. Walsh, Sixth Grade Teacher
Agnes E. Little Elementary School, Pawtucket, Rhode Island

Student-Made Quizzes

One method I use to provide interest and variety in the necessary repetition of material is to have students make miniquizzes, play teacher, and give their quizzes to the rest of the class. I also allow students to create games with various subjects and then teach them to and play them with the rest of the class.

Sharon Klotz, Sixth-Grade Teacher
Kiel Middle School, Kiel, Wisconsin

Make It Meaningful

Cognitive psychology has taught us that the material we remember best is the most meaningful to us—it makes sense in terms of our existing knowledge, it's organized, clear, and full of detail and examples, and it has some personal connection to us. What does making lessons meaningful mean to you?

The Interrelatedness of Things

Generally, meaningful learning seems to occur most frequently when students have the opportunity to manipulate materials—either physically or mentally. Teachers can also help students retain and transfer learning by making clear the connections between old and new material and by stressing both similarities and dissimilarities. Students need specific categories for organizing information as well as overviews that help them see the interrelatedness of knowledge.

Jane C. Dusell, High School English Teacher
Medford Senior High School, Medford, Wisconsin

One Project,
Many Skills

In my years of teaching, I found it best to use innovative, special activities that drew on the children's creativity and self-expression. My most successful project was having my sixth graders collect information on the flowers and animals of our valley, which we later incorporated into a booklet for publication. The children did the research and illustrated the book. They all had an opportunity to contribute intellectually, emotionally, and physically. This gave us an ongoing project for many weeks that used knowledge and skills from all subjects. It was a very special learning experience that also proved to be a great public relations effort.

Leland J. Gritzner, Sixth-Grade Teacher
Death Valley Unified Schools, Shoshone, California

Making It
Personal

Obviously the best way to make something meaningful is to apply it to one's own set of circumstances. One of my favorite classroom projects comes after the lesson on operant conditioning. Each student designs his own behavior modification project, establishes a baseline, determines reinforcers and contingencies, and starts to work on the selected behavior. After three weeks of modification, the student outlines his project and discusses the outcomes. I find that each student winds up displaying a thorough understanding of the material.

Linda Stahl, High School Psychology Teacher
Ponca City Senior High School, Ponca City, Oklahoma

Knowledge as
Cumulative—and
Relevant

Day-to-day survival tends to make us forget the most elementary teaching/learning strategies. It is crucial that both students and teachers view knowledge as cumulative and in need of continual reinforcement. I design assignments and tests for each new unit that require application of previous knowledge. In addition, I encourage students to ask the question teachers fear most: What does this have to do with me? Of course, students must ask it, not of teachers, but of themselves.

J. D. Kraft, Twelfth-Grade Sociology Teacher
Wausau West High School, Wausau, Wisconsin

But I Read It Three Times!

Many students don't realize that they haven't fully understood what they've read. How do you help them learn to monitor their own reading comprehension and get the most out of their reading?

Bring the Texts to
Life

There are several ways to deepen students' reading and self-monitoring abilities—and to develop a greater appreciation of reading in the process. They can pick out the three main points of a text or themes of a story and do three drawings to illustrate each. They can make up their own tests based on the text to give to one another. Sometimes checklists of who, what, where, and when are useful for younger students to refer to as they read. Older students often enjoy reversals—let them pick out three minor details or characters and rewrite the text using these as the main points or characters. Set up a talk show around several texts: some students play the authors and are interviewed by student-hosts about their work. Or have a trial based on a novel or play, with the main action as the crime and each character interrogated about his role. Students not taking active roles can be journalists covering the trial.

Simone Wharton, High School English Teacher
New York, New York

8

Doing Words:
write   play
draw   listen
paint   talk
fix   read
build
plo
he
as

Asking Words:
when? _____
where? _____
how? _____
who? _____
why? _____
        ?
        ?

The Cognitive Perspective and Teaching Practice

Overview
Learning Outcomes: Gagné   272
Learning through Discovery: Bruner   274
Discovery in Action   275
Reception Learning: Ausubel   276
Advance Organizers   278
Making the Most of Expository Teaching   279
Teaching and Learning about Concepts   280
How We Understand Our World   281
Views of Concept Learning   282
Strategies for Teaching   282
Problem Solving   283
Understanding and Representing the Problem   283
Selecting the Approach   288
Executing the Plan   289
Evaluating the Results   289
Effective Problem Solving: What Do the Experts Do?   290
Study Skills   291
PQ4R   292
Underlining and Note Taking   294
Teaching for Transfer   295
Positive and Negative Transfer   295
Specific and General Transfer   296
Teaching for Positive Transfer: Principles   301
Teaching Thinking   302
Improving Thinking   304
Summary/Key Terms
Suggestions for Further Reading and Study
Teachers' Forum

As you saw in the previous chapter, the cognitive approach to learning emphasizes how people perceive, understand, and remember information. The focus of this chapter is on instructional approaches that have evolved from the cognitive orientation. We will be concerned with the implications of cognitive theories for the day-to-day practice of teaching.

Since the cognitive perspective is a philosophical orientation and not a unified theoretical model, teaching methods derived from it are necessarily varied. In this chapter, we will examine the instructional theories of three cognitive psychologists—Robert Gagné's categorization of learning outcomes, Jerome Bruner's discovery learning, and David Ausubel's expository teaching. In addition, we will consider concept learning, problem solving, study skills, and critical thinking. In the last section of this chapter, we will discuss how to encourage the transfer of learning from one situation to another.

By the time you finish this chapter, you should be able to do the following:

- Develop lessons using Gagné's categorization of learning outcomes, Bruner's discovery approach, and Ausubel's expository approach.
- Describe the steps in solving complex problems.
- Discuss the implications of cognitive theories for teaching study and thinking skills.
- List three ways a teacher might encourage positive transfer of learning.

LEARNING OUTCOMES: GAGNÉ

Humans are remarkably versatile. We learn a wide variety of skills and possess a great deal of knowledge about the world. If we hope to teach (and continue to learn) so many kinds of skills, we must have some organized way of considering them. Cognitive psychologist Robert Gagné has categorized the skills people can learn—what are called *outcomes* of learning—under five headings: attitudes, motor skills, verbal information, intellectual skills, and cognitive strategies (Gagné, 1974, 1977). Let's look at each category.

Attitudes

Attitudes are probably learned through positive and negative experiences and modeling. For example, if you are a member of the basketball team and receive a great deal of recognition for your performance on the team, you are likely to have a positive attitude toward basketball. If a respected friend, teacher, coach, parent, or sibling has a positive view of basketball, this can also encourage a favorable attitude. The relationship between attitude and performance is very strong.

Motor Skills

The acquisition of *motor skills* involves learning to coordinate movements. Motor skills have two components: knowledge of what to do (the steps in-

This chapter written in collaboration with Christine McCormick.

Positive attitudes are often learned through modeling. Few young performers would endure the practice required to excel without the positive example, interest, and encouragement of a parent, teacher, or mentor. *(Sybil Shackman/Monkmeyer Press)*

volved) and the actual physical practice that makes the movements fluid. Much of the learning of young children falls into this category. Children learn to walk, tie their shoes, "pump" on the swing, throw and catch a ball, run, skip, and print. Older students must master skilled movements for sports and learn to use a scale or centrifuge in chemistry lab, dissect a frog in a biology class, type in a business or journalism class, work with a potter's wheel in art, or thread a sewing machine in home economics.

Verbal Data

Verbal information could be described as knowing *what*. Included in this category is the content of most lessons—facts, names, descriptions, dates, and characteristics.

Intellectual Skills

Intellectual skills have been characterized as knowing *how*. These skills make it possible for people to use symbols and communicate. Through symbols we interact with the environment indirectly, using mental manipulations and calculations to solve problems.

There are several different types of intellectual skills. Gagné has arranged them in a hierarchy, with mastery of each skill a prerequisite for mastery of the next. *Discrimination*, or making distinctions among symbols, is a prerequisite for the next skill, forming *concepts*. This is because in order to learn a concept, students must be able first to discriminate among separate elements; then they can classify and sort the elements into groups. The next step in the hierarchy is relating different concepts through *rules*. For example, the rule about calculating area is based on the relation of the concepts of length, width, and area to one another. Finally, rules can be combined into more complex, *higher-order rules*. To design an experiment comparing teaching methods, we must combine learned rules into new, more complex rules about selecting subjects, designing strategies, and evaluating results.

cognitive strategies: in Gagné's hierarchy, strategies for retrieval, processing, and monitoring

The final category in Gagné's hierarchy is **cognitive strategies.** These are the skills involved in processing information—directing attention, selecting patterns from the sensory register, deciding which information in short-term memory will be rehearsed, elaborating and organizing information, and selecting a retrieval strategy. Do these skills sound familiar? Deliberate use of

Table 8–1   Gagné's Types of Learning Outcomes

Types of Learning Outcomes	Examples
Attitudes	Choosing to join the backpacking club, listening to Bruce Springsteen, or electing to take German
Motor skills	Mastering a front walkover, throwing a straight pot on a potter's wheel
Verbal information	Stating an author's works, publication dates, and so on

Intellectual skills
  Discriminations
  Concepts
  Rules
  Higher-order rules
	Using symbols to communicate and solve problems
	  Distinguishing between p and q or a circle and oval
	  Categorizing paintings by artist, style, period, subject
	  Demonstrating that water freezes at 32°F or 0°C
	  Predicting the amount of growth of a plant based upon available water, fertilizer, and sunlight

Cognitive strategies	Using the loci method to remember points in a speech, using analogies to solve a problem

From Robert M. Gagné (1984), Essentials of learning for instruction. Copyright © 1984 by the Dryden Press. Adapted by permission of CBS College Publishing.

these strategies involves the metacognitive abilities discussed in the last chapter. Table 8–1 is a summary of the five possible learning outcomes described by Gagné, along with examples of each.

LEARNING THROUGH DISCOVERY: BRUNER

According to Jerome Bruner, teachers should provide problem situations that stimulate students to discover the structure of the subject matter for themselves. **Structure** refers to the fundamental ideas, relationships, or patterns of the subject—that is, the essential information. Specific facts and details are not part of the structure. Bruner believes that classroom learning should take place *inductively*. **Inductive reasoning** means moving from details and examples to the formulation of a general principle. In discovery learning, the teacher presents specific examples, and the students work with the examples until they discover the interrelationships and thus the subject's structure.

For instance, if you learned the terms *figure, plane, simple, closed, quadrilateral, triangle, isosceles, scalene, equilateral,* and *right,* you would be on your way to understanding one aspect of geometry. But how do these terms relate to one another? If you can place the terms into a **coding system** such as the one in Figure 8–1, you will have a better understanding of the basic structure of this part of geometry. A coding system is a hierarchy of related concepts. (You encountered this kind of hierarchy in Chapter 7's discussion of organization in long-term memory.) At the top of the coding system is the most general concept, in this case *plane, simple, closed figure.* More spe-

structure: according to Bruner, the fundamental framework of ideas

inductive reasoning: formulating general principles based on knowledge of examples and details

coding system: a hierarchy of ideas or concepts

Figure 8–1   A Coding System for Triangles

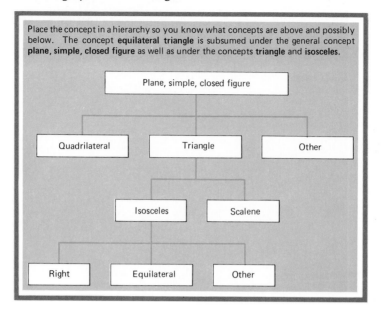

Place the concept in a hierarchy so you know what concepts are above and possibly below. The concept **equilateral triangle** is subsumed under the general concept **plane, simple, closed figure** as well as under the concepts **triangle** and **isosceles**.

eg-rule method:
teaching or learning by moving from specific examples to general rules

cific concepts are arranged under the general concept. According to Bruner, if students are presented with enough examples of triangles and nontriangles, they will eventually discover what the basic properties of any triangle must be. Encouraging inductive thinking in this way is sometimes called the **eg-rule method** (*e.g.* is from the Latin meaning "for example").

Discovery in Action

intuitive thinking:
making imaginative leaps to correct perceptions or workable solutions

An inductive approach requires **intuitive thinking** on the part of students. Bruner suggests that teachers can nurture this type of thinking by encouraging students to make guesses based on incomplete evidence and then to confirm or disprove the guesses systematically (Bruner, 1960). After learning about ocean currents and the shipping industry, students might be shown old maps of three harbors and asked to guess which one became a major port. Then students could check their guesses through systematic research. The research might prove more interesting than usual for students, since it is their own guesses that would be at stake. Unfortunately, educational practices often discourage intuitive thinking by punishing wrong guesses and rewarding safe but uncreative answers.

discovery learning:
Bruner's approach, in which students work on their own to discover basic principles

guided discovery:
an adaptation of discovery learning, in which the teacher provides some direction

Thus, in Bruner's **discovery learning,** a teacher organizes the class so that the students learn through their own active involvement. A distinction is usually made between discovery learning, in which the students work on their own to a very great extent, and **guided discovery,** in which the teacher provides some direction. For most situations, guided discovery is preferable. Students are presented with intriguing questions, baffling situations, or interesting problems: Why does the fire go out when we cover it with a jar? What are those black specks in the bottom of the fish tank, and where did

What kind of soil do seeds need to grow? How much light and water do seedlings need? Why do they need light and water? What happens when they are deprived of these things? What is the effect of atificial light? What happens when daytime and nighttime are reversed? With a little guidance, young students can discover many principles of botany on their own—and have fun into the bargain. *(Four by Five)*

they come from? Why does this heavy piece of wood float? Why does this pencil seem to bend when you put it in water? What is the rule for grouping these words together? Instead of explaining how to solve the problem, the teacher provides the appropriate materials, encourages students to make observations, form hypotheses, and test solutions. For example, to answer the question about the fire, students might note the size of the jar, how long it takes for the fire to go out, and what happens if the jar has holes or if someone blows into the jar with a straw. To solve the problem, students must use both intuitive and analytical thinking. The teacher *guides* the discovery by asking leading questions: What occurs in larger quantities inside an empty jar? Why does a fire go out when you put dirt on it? The teacher also provides feedback about the direction activities take. Feedback must be given at the optimal moment, when students can either use it to revise their approach or take it as encouragement to continue in the direction they've chosen.

Questions, Encouragement, Feedback

The Guidelines should help you apply Bruner's suggestions to various classroom situations.

RECEPTION LEARNING: AUSUBEL

David Ausubel's (1963, 1977) view of learning offers an interesting contrast to that of Bruner. According to Ausubel, people acquire knowledge primarily through reception rather than through discovery. Concepts, principles, and ideas are presented to them and received by them, not discovered by them. The more organized and focused the presentation, the more thoroughly the person will learn, as you saw in the previous chapter.

276

Applying Bruner's Ideas in the Classroom

Present both examples and nonexamples of the concepts you are teaching.

Examples
1. *In teaching about mammals, include people, kangaroos, whales, cats, dolphins, and camels as examples and chickens, fish, alligators, frogs, and penguins as nonexamples.*
2. *Ask students for additional examples and nonexamples.*

Help students see connections among concepts.

Examples
1. *Ask questions such as these: What else could you call this apple? (fruit) What do we do with fruit? (eat) What do we call things we eat? (food)*
2. *Use diagrams, outlines, and summaries to point out connections.*

Pose a question and let students try to find the answer.

Examples
1. *How could the human hand be improved?*
2. *Are bacteria plants or animals?*
3. *What is the relation between the area of one tile and the area of the whole floor?*

Encourage students to make intuitive guesses.

Examples
1. *Instead of giving a definition for a word, say, "Let's guess what it might mean by looking at the words around it."*
2. *Give students a map of ancient Greece and ask where they think the major cities were.*
3. *Don't comment after the first few guesses. Wait for several suggestions before giving the right answer.*

---

meaningful verbal learning: verbal information, ideas, and relationships among ideas

expository teaching: Ausubel's method—teachers present material in complete, organized form, moving from broadest to more specific concepts

subsumer: the most general concept in a coding system

rule-eg method: teaching or learning by moving from general principles to specific examples

Ausubel stresses what is known as **meaningful verbal learning**—verbal information, ideas, and relationships among ideas, taken together. Rote memorization is *not* considered meaningful learning, since material learned by rote is not connected with existing knowledge. Unfortunately, despite the ineffectiveness of rote learning, of many lessons seem to rely on little else (Ausubel, 1977). Ausubel has proposed his model of **expository teaching** to encourage meaningful rather than rote reception learning. (*Exposition* means explanation, or the setting forth of facts and ideas.) In this approach, teachers present materials in a carefully organized, sequenced, and somewhat finished form, and students thus receive the most usable material in the most efficient way. Ausubel does agree with Bruner that people learn by organizing new information into hierarchies or coding systems. Ausubel calls the general concept at the top of the system the **subsumer** because all other concepts are subsumed under it, as in Figure 8–1. Ausubel believes that learning should progress, not inductively as Bruner recommends, but *deductively*—from the general to the specific, or from the rule or principle to examples. The deductive approach is sometimes called the **rule-eg method.**

Ausubel's expository teaching model has four major characteristics. First, it calls for a great deal of interaction between teacher and students. Although the teacher makes the initial presentation, students' ideas and responses are solicited throughout each lesson. Second, expository teaching makes great use of examples. Although the stress is on verbal learning, examples may include drawings, diagrams, or pictures. (We'll discuss the importance of examples in greater depth later in the chapter.) Third, expository teaching is deductive, as you've seen. The most general and inclusive concepts are presented first, and the more specific concepts are derived from them. Finally, it is sequential. Certain steps must be followed.

Advance Organizers

advance organizer:
statement of inclusive concepts to introduce and sum up material that follows

Meaningful learning generally occurs when there is a potential fit between the student's schemata and the material to be learned. To make this fit more likely, a lesson following Ausubel's strategy always begins with an **advance organizer.** This is an introductory statement of a relationship or a high-level concept broad enough to encompass the information that will follow.

The function of advance organizers is to provide scaffolding for new information. You can also see the organizer as a kind of conceptual bridge between the new material and students' current knowledge (Faw & Waller, 1976). Textbooks often contain such advance organizers—the chapter overviews in this book are examples. The organizers can serve three purposes: they can direct your attention to what is important in the upcoming material; they can highlight relationships among ideas that will be presented; and they can remind you of relevant information you already have. In teaching a lesson on the caste system in India, the organizer might deal with the concept of classes and stratification in societies (Joyce & Weil, 1986). A teacher introducing a unit on poetry might ask, What *is* poetry? and provide a poetic quote defining poetry, as well as examples of rhymed, unrhymed, and free verse.

activate: bring from long-term memory into working memory

In general, advance organizers fall into one of two categories, *comparative* and *expository* (Mayer, 1979). Each fulfills an important function. Comparative organizers **activate** (bring into working memory) already existing schemata. They remind you of what you already know but may not realize is relevant. A comparative advance organizer for long division might point out the differences and similarities between division and multiplication (Joyce & Weil, 1986). You might begin a history lesson on revolutions with a statement that compared military uprisings with the physical and social changes involved in the Industrial Revolution; you could also make a statement linking the common aspects of the French, English, Russian, and American revolutions. Expository organizers provide *new* knowledge that students will need to understand the upcoming information. An expository organizer is thus a statement of a subsumer, a definition of a general concept. In an

Example

English class, you might begin a large thematic unit on rites of passage in literature with a very broad statement of the theme and why it has been so central in literature—something like, "A central character coming of age must learn to know himself or herself, often makes some kind of journey of self-discovery, and must decide what in the society is to be accepted, what rejected. . . ."

The next step in an expository lesson is to present subordinate content in terms of basic similarities and differences, with the use of specific examples. If you began with a comparative organizer, now you can expand on these comparisons. Ausubel's emphasis on both similarities and differences reflects one of his basic ideas, the importance of the schemata-fit notion. To learn any new material, students must not only see the similarities between the material presented and what they already know; they must also see the differences, so that interference, the confusion of old and new material, can be avoided.

Comparing and Contrasting

It is often helpful in an expository lesson to ask students to supply similarities and differences themselves. In a grammar lesson, you might ask, What are the differences between a comma and a semicolon? Suppose in teaching the coming of age theme in literature, you choose *The Diary of Anne Frank* and *The Adventures of Huckleberry Finn* as the basic material for the unit. As the students read the first book, you might ask them to compare the central character's growth, state of mind, and position in society with characters from other novels, plays, and films. When the class moves on to the second book, you can start asking students to compare Anne Frank's inner journey with Huck Finn's trip down the Mississippi. As comparisons are made, whether within a single class lesson or an entire unit, it is useful to underscore the goal of the lesson—to repeat the advance organizer with amendments and elaborations—from time to time.

Using Specific Examples

Along with the comparisons, specific examples must come into play. You can see that the best way to point out similarities and differences is with examples. There must be specific examples of comma and semicolon usage; the specific elements of Huck Finn's and Anne Frank's dilemmas must be clear. This may seem obvious, but it's important to stress specificity. Finally, when all the material has been presented, students can be asked to discuss how the examples can be used to expand on the original advance organizer.

Making the Most of Expository Teaching

As with any teaching approach, expository teaching works better in some situations than in others. First, this approach is most appropriate when you want to teach about the relationships among several concepts. Students must have some knowledge of the actual concepts first. What if students in a history class had never heard of the French Revolution or the Industrial Revolution? How could they compare these specific events to get a better understanding of elements that characterize revolutions? They might resort to memorizing definitions and lists—"A revolution has five characteristics: (1) . . . ." Even in a lesson on what poetry is, students who don't have a basic understanding of the concept of literature—why people write and why they read—will be at a loss.

Prior Knowledge

Age as a Factor

Another consideration with expository teaching is the age of the students. This approach requires students to manipulate ideas mentally, even if the ideas are fairly simple and based on physical realities such as rocks and minerals. This means that expository teaching is generally more appropriate for students at or above the late elementary school level (Luiten, Ames, & Ackerson, 1980).

The most thoroughly studied aspect of expository teaching is the use of advance organizers. The general conclusion of this research is that advance organizers *do* help students learn, especially when the material is quite unfamiliar, complex, or difficult (Faw & Waller, 1976; Shuell, 1981b). Of course, the effects of advance organizers depend on how good they are and

Guidelines

Applying Ausubel's Ideas in the Classroom

Use advance organizers.

Examples
1. *English: Shakespeare used the social ideas of his time as a framework for his plays—*Julius Caesar, Hamlet, *and* Macbeth *dealt with concepts of natural order, a nation as the human body, the place of man between the angels and beasts, etc.*
2. *Social Studies: Geography dictates economy in preindustrialized regions or nations.*
3. *History: Important concepts during the Renaissance were symmetry, admiration of the classical world, the centrality of the mind of man.*

Use a number of examples.

Examples
1. *In mathematics class, ask students to point out all the examples of right angles that they can find in the room.*
2. *In teaching about islands and peninsulas, have maps, slides, models, postcards.*

Focus on both similarities and differences.

Examples
1. *In a history class, ask students to list the ways in which the North and South were alike and different before the Civil War.*
2. *In a biology class, ask students how they would transform spiders into insects or an amphibian into a reptile.*

Effective Organizers   how students actually use them. First, to be effective, the organizer must be processed and understood by the students. This was demonstrated dramatically in a study by Dinnel and Glover (1985). They found that instructing students to paraphrase an advance organizer—which, of course, requires them to understand its meaning—increased the effectiveness of the organizer. Second, the organizer must really *be* an organizer—it must encompass all the material that will follow and indicate relations among the basic concepts and terms that will be used. In other words, a true organizer isn't just a statement of historical or background information. No amount of student processing can make a bad organizer more effective.

The Guidelines should help you use advance organizers and Ausubel's other ideas in the classroom.

TEACHING AND LEARNING ABOUT CONCEPTS

The word *concept* has appeared repeatedly throughout this text. It is common in everyday conversation as well. In fact, most of what we know about the world involves concepts and relations among concepts (Bourne, Dominowski, Loftus, & Healy, 1986). In this chapter we have discussed concept formation as one of the intellectual skills in Gagné's hierarchy of learning outcomes. As you have seen, concepts also figure prominently in Bruner's and Ausubel's ideas. But what exactly is the concept of *concept*? Do you have to understand it before you can define it?

concepts: general categories of ideas, objects, people, or experiences whose members share certain properties

Concepts are categories used to group similar events, ideas, objects, or people. When we talk about a particular concept like *student* or *war*, we refer to a category of people or events that are similar to one another. The concept *student*, for example, refers to all people who study a subject. The people may be old or young, in school or not; they may be studying baseball or Bach, but they can all be categorized as students. Concepts are abstractions. The pure concept *student* does not exist in the real world. Only individual examples of the concept exist.

Concepts help us organize vast amounts of information into meaningful units. For instance, there are about 7.5 million distinguishable differences in colors. By categorizing these colors into some dozen or so groups, we manage to deal with this diversity fairly well (Bruner, 1973). The previous chapter stressed the importance of organization in the storage and retrieval of information in long-term memory. You may recall that Piaget also emphasized organization in his theory of cognitive development. Without the ability to form concepts, we would find life a confusing series of unrelated experiences. Every new object encountered would require a new name, a new set of rules for recognition, and a new response. The load on long-term memory would be unbearable. There would be no way of grouping things together, no symbols or shorthand for talking and thinking about similar objects and events. Nothing would be like anything else, and communication would be impossible.

Learning Chinese provides a concise lesson in concepts. Much of the Chinese language consists of ideograms—symbols that represent things or ideas rather than particular words or sounds. This student is learning to manipulate increasingly complex ideas as his Chinese improves. He is probably also absorbing some of the concepts that underlie a very different culture. *(Joseph Nettis/Photo Researchers)*

Views of Concept Learning

defining attributes:
distinctive features
shared by members
of a category

Traditionally, psychologists have assumed that members of a category share a set of **defining attributes,** or distinctive features. Students all study; books all contain pages of printed, drawn, or photographed material and are bound along one edge. You can see the similarity between the distinctive features notion of concepts and the feature analysis (bottom-up processing) involved in perception. Both theories suggest that we recognize specific examples of a concept by noting key features.

Recently these long-popular views about the nature of concepts and category systems have been challenged. While some concepts such as *equilateral triangle* have clear-cut defining attributes, most concepts do not. Take the concept of *party*. What are the defining attributes? We might have difficulty listing these attributes, but we certainly know a party when we see (or hear) one. What about the concept of *bird?* Your first thought might be that birds are animals that fly. But is an ostrich a bird? What about a penguin?

prototype: best
representative of a
category

According to critics of the traditional view of concept learning, we have in our minds a **prototype** of a party and a bird—an image that captures the essence of each concept. A prototype is the best representative of its category. The best representative of the category of birds might be a robin (Rosch, 1973). Potential members of the category may be very similar to the prototype (sparrow) or similar in some ways but different in others (chicken, ostrich). Thus, whether something fits into a category or not is a matter of *degree.* Some events, objects, or ideas are simply better examples of the concept than others (Rosch, 1975). It is likely that children first learn concepts in the real world from best examples or prototypes pointed out by adults (Tennyson, 1981).

Most of the current approaches to teaching concepts still rely heavily on the traditional analysis of defining attributes. But it should be pointed out that the defining attributes and the prototype views of concept learning are not totally incompatible. The teaching of concepts can combine both distinctive features and prototypes, and new approaches that do so are promising (Tennyson, 1981).

Strategies for Teaching

Four Components
for Teaching

No matter what strategy you use for teaching concepts, you will need to have four components in any lesson: (1) the name of the concept, (2) a definition, (3) relevant and irrelevant attributes, and (4) examples and nonexamples (Eggen, Kauchak, & Harder, 1979).

The verbal label that identifies the concept is not the same as the concept itself. The label is important for communicating but is somewhat arbitrary. Simply learning a label does not mean the person understands the concept, although the label is necessary for the understanding.

A definition makes the nature of the concept clear. A good definition has two elements: a reference to any more general category or concept that the new concept falls under, and a statement of the new concept's defining attributes (Klausmeier, 1976). For example, an equilateral triangle is defined as a plane, simple, closed figure (general category), with three equal sides and three equal angles (defining attributes).

The identification of relevant and irrelevant attributes is another aspect of teaching concepts. The ability to fly, as we've seen, is not a relevant attribute for classifying animals as birds. Even though many birds fly, some birds do not (ostrich, penguin) and some nonbirds do (bats, flying squirrels).

Examples are essential in teaching concepts. More examples are needed in teaching complicated concepts and in working with younger or less able students. Both examples and nonexamples (sometimes called *positive* and *negative instances*) are necessary to make the boundaries of the category clear. The *examples* should be chosen to show the wide range of possibilities the category includes. In other words, they should point out the variety of irrelevant attributes within the category, so that students will not focus on an irrelevant attribute as a distinguishing feature. In teaching the concept of bird, examples should include ostriches and penguins, since these birds vary on an irrelevant dimension for the category, the ability to fly. Since size is also an irrelevant attribute, birds of many sizes should be used as examples. This will prevent **undergeneralization,** or excluding some animals from their rightful place in the category of *bird*.

Nonexamples should be very close to the concept but miss by one or just a few critical attributes. For instance, the figure $\bigwedge$ is not an example of an equilateral triangle because it is not closed (it could also be said to have four instead of three sides). Including nonexamples will prevent **overgeneralization,** or the inclusion of figures that are not equilateral triangles.

Once we have learned a concept, what do we do with it? Another goal of teachers is to help students manipulate concepts in order to solve problems.

undergeneralization: exclusion of some true members from a category; limiting a concept

overgeneralization: inclusion of nonmembers in a category; overextending a concept

PROBLEM SOLVING

"Educational programs," Gagné has written, "have the important ultimate purpose of teaching students to solve problems—mathematical and physical problems, health problems, social problems, and problems of personal adjustment" (1977, p. 177). **Problem solving** is usually defined as formulating new answers, going beyond the simple application of previously learned rules to create a solution. Problem solving is what happens when routine or automatic responses do not fit the current situation.

In general, there are four stages in problem solving: understanding and representing the problem; selecting or planning the solution; executing the plan; and evaluating the results (Wessells, 1972).

problem solving: creating new solutions for problems

Understanding and Representing the Problem

The first step in problem solving is to decide exactly what the problem is. This often means finding the relevant information in the problem and ignoring the irrelevant details. In other words, we must use our information processing skill of selective attention to perceive patterns. For example, consider the following problem:

> If you have black socks and brown socks in your drawer, mixed in the ratio of four to five, how many socks will you have to take out to make sure of having a pair the same color? (Sternberg & Davidson, 1982)

What information is relevant to solving this problem? Did you realize that the information about the four-to-five ratio of black socks to brown socks is irrelevant? As long as you have only two different colors of socks in the drawer, you will have to remove only three socks before two of them are bound to match.

In addition to identifying the relevant information in a problem, you must develop an accurate representation of the situation involved. Let's assume we are dealing with problems that are stated orally or written out, like the socks problem above—"story" problems very familiar to you after years of schooling. There are two major tasks required in order to represent these problems successfully (Mayer, 1983). The first is **linguistic comprehension,** or understanding the meaning of each sentence in the problem. Take, for example, the following sentence from an algebra story problem:

linguistic comprehension: understanding the meaning of sentences

The river boat's rate in still water is 12 miles per hour more than the rate of the current.

This is a *relational proposition*. It describes the relationship between two rates, that of the river boat and that of the current. Here is another sentence from a story problem:

The cost of the candy is $1.75 per pound.

This is an *assignment proposition*. It simply assigns a value to something; in this case, the cost of one unit of candy.

Understanding Propositions

To solve problems containing either of these two sentences, you must understand what the sentence is telling you. But some propositions are more difficult than others to figure out. Research shows that relational propositions are harder to understand and remember than assignment propositions. In one study, when students had to recall relational and assignment propositions like those above, the error rate for recalling relational propositions was about three times higher than the error rate for assignment propositions. Some students even turned relational propositions into assignment propositions, remembering, for example, "The river boat's rate in still water is 12 miles per hour more than the rate of the current" simply as "The riverboat's speed in still water is 12 miles per hour" (Mayer, 1982). If you misunderstand the meaning of individual statements in a problem, you will have a hard time representing the whole problem correctly.

Assembling the Parts

The second task in representing a problem is to assemble all the sentences into an accurate understanding of the total problem. Even if you understand every sentence, you may still misunderstand the problem as a whole. Consider this example:

Two train stations are 50 miles apart. At 2 P.M. one Saturday afternoon two trains start toward each other, one from each station. Just as the trains pull out of the stations, a bird springs into the air in front of the first train and flies ahead to the front of the second train. When the bird reaches the second train it turns back and flies toward the first train. The bird continues to do this until the trains meet. If both trains travel at the rate of 25 miles per hour and the bird flies at 100 miles per hour, how many miles will the bird have flown before the trains meet? (Posner, 1973)

If you interpret this as a distance problem ("I have to figure out how far the bird travels before it meets the oncoming train and turns around, then how far it travels before it has to turn again, and finally add up all the trips back and forth. . ."), then you have a very difficult problem on your hands. But there is a better way to structure the problem. You can represent it as a question of time and focus on the time the bird is in the air. If you know how long the bird is in the air, then you can easily determine the distance it will cover, since you know exactly how fast it flies. The solution could be stated like this:

> Since the stations are 50 miles apart and the trains are moving toward each other at the same speed, the trains will meet in the middle—25 miles from each station. Because they are traveling 25 mph, it will take the trains one hour to reach the meeting point. In the one hour it takes the trains to meet, the bird will cover 100 miles because it is flying at 100 miles per hour. Easy!

Research shows that students can be too quick to decide what a problem is asking, perhaps assuming too readily that they are experts. After reading only the first few sentences of standard algebra problems, the subjects in one study made their decisions and categorized the problems (Hinsley, Hayes, & Simon, 1977). Once a problem is categorized ("Aha, it's a distance problem!"), a particular schema is activated. The schema used directs attention to relevant information and sets up expectations for what the right answer should look like (Hayes & Robinson, 1977; Robinson & Hayes, 1978).

Correct and
Incorrect Schemata

When students use the proper schema for representing a problem, they are less likely to be confused by irrelevant information or tricky wording, like *more* in a problem that really requires subtraction or *fewer* in an addition problem (Resnick, 1981). But as you've seen, when students use the wrong schema, critical information is overlooked, irrelevant information is used, and some information may even be misread or remembered incorrectly so that it fits the schema. Errors in representing the problem and difficulties in solving it are the results.

Translation and Schema Training.   How can students be trained to improve translation and schema selection? Mayer (1983) has recommended giving students practice in the following:

1.   Recognizing and categorizing a variety of problem types
2.   Representing problems—either concretely, in pictures, symbols, or graphs, or in words
3.   Selecting relevant and irrelevant information in problems

Practice with
Representation

At least some research suggests that Mayer's ideas are on target. It may be quite helpful to have students practice representing story problems with diagrams. Table 8–2 shows diagrams for representing the eight types of simple addition and subtraction story problems. When these procedures were taught to primary-grade students, their performance on story problems did improve significantly (Lindvall, Tamburino, & Robinson, 1982). The researchers stressed that these diagramming methods should *not* be taught as just another computation procedure. Students should be encouraged to create their own ways of diagramming.

Table 8–2 **Representing Addition and Subtraction Story Problems**

Type of Problem	Example	Diagram Taught
1. Combining (putting sets together)	Ann had 3 apples. Jill had 4 apples. How many apples did they have all together?	
2. Separating (taking sets apart)	Together Bob and Tony had 8 toy cars. Bob owned 3 of the cars. How many did Tony have?	
3. Changing increase (getting more things)	Sue had 5 pencils. She got 4 more pencils. How many did she have then?	
4. Changing decrease (losing some things)	May had 7 cookies. She then ate 3 of them. How many did she have left?	
5. Comparing—more (how many more)	Rick had 6 kites. Dan had 8 kites. How many more kites did Dan have than Rick?	
6. Comparing—less (how many less)	Len had 5 books. Rita had 9 books. How many less books did Len have than Rita?	
7. Equalizing—taking away (making same size—taking away)	Jim had 4 cookies. Al had 7 cookies. How many cookies would Al have to eat to have as many as Jim?	
8. Equalizing—adding on (making same size—adding on)	Sally had 8 rings. Jan had 5 rings. How many more would Jan have to get to have as many as Sally?	

Adapted from C. M. Lindvall, J. L. Tamburino, & L. Robinson (1982), An exploratory investigation of the effect of teaching primary-grade children to use specific problem-solving strategies in solving simple arithmetic story problems. Paper presented at annual meeting of the American Educational Research Association.

Factors That Hinder Understanding. Consider the following situation:

You enter a room. There are two ropes suspended from the ceiling. You are asked by the experimenter to tie the two ends of the ropes together and assured that the task is possible. On a nearby table are a few tools, including a hammer and pliers. You grab the end of one of the ropes and walk toward the other rope. You immediately realize that you cannot possibly reach the end of the other rope. You try to extend your reach using the pliers but still cannot grasp the other rope. What can you do? (Maier, 1933)

This problem can be solved by using an object in an unconventional way. If you tie the hammer or the pliers to the end of one rope and start swinging it like a pendulum, you will be able to catch it while you are standing across the room holding the other rope. You can use the weight of the tool to make the rope come to you instead of trying to stretch the rope. People often fail to solve this problem because they seldom consider unconventional uses for materials that have a specific function. This difficulty is called **functional fixedness** (Duncker, 1945). Problem solving requires seeing things in new ways. In your everyday life, you may often exhibit functional fixedness. Suppose a screw on a dresser-drawer handle is loose. Will you spend 20 minutes searching for a screwdriver? Or will you think to use another object not necessarily designed for this function, like a knife or a dime?

functional fixedness: inability to use objects or tools in a new way

A related block to effective problem solving is rigidity or set, sometimes called **response set.** Consider the following problem:

response set: rigidity; tendency to respond in the most familiar way

In each of the four examples below, move only one match and change the equation to represent a true equality.

$$\text{V} = \text{VII} \qquad \text{VI} = \text{XI} \qquad \text{XII} = \text{VII} \qquad \text{VII} = \text{I}$$

You probably figured out how to solve the first example quite quickly. You simply move one match from the right side over to the left to make $\text{VI} = \text{VI}$. Examples two and three can also be solved without too much difficulty by changing the V to an $\times$, or vice versa. But the fourth example (taken from Raudsepp & Haugh, 1977) probably has you stumped. To solve this problem, you must change sets, or switch schemata. What has worked before will not work this time. The answer here lies in using both an Arabic number and a square root, changing $\text{VII} = \text{I}$ to $\sqrt{1} = 1$, which is simply the symbolic way of saying that the square root of 1 equals 1.

The Importance of Flexibility. Functional fixedness and response set interfere with accurate representation of problems. What factors might speed up representation and lead to a solution? The Gestalt psychologists believed that insight is a key to problem solving. **Insight** is the sudden reorganization or reconceptualization of a problem that clarifies the problem and suggests a feasible solution.

insight: sudden realization of a solution

Functional fixedness, response set, and insight all point to the importance of flexibility in understanding problems. If you get started with an inaccurate or inefficient representation of the true problem, it will be difficult or at least very time-consuming to reach a solution (Wessels, 1982). Sometimes it is helpful to "play" with the problem. Ask yourself: What do I know? What do I need to know to answer this question? Can I look at this problem in other ways? As you no doubt recall from Chapter 4, fluency and flexibility of ideas are important components of creativity.

Aha! I understand! Sometimes you can actually see a student make a breakthrough in solving a problem or understanding a difficult idea.
(Richard Hutchings/ Photo Researchers)

Selecting the Approach

Once you have developed an accurate representation of the problem, you are on the right track, but success is not guaranteed. Other steps remain and difficulties could still arise. It is useful to make a distinction between two types of procedures for solving problems. One of these types of procedures, called an **algorithm,** is a step-by-step prescription for achieving a particular goal. An algorithm, if implemented correctly, is guaranteed to accomplish what it is intended to accomplish. In contrast, a **heuristic** is only a good bet, a strategy that has a reasonable chance of succeeding. In math class, you probably experienced a certain amount of success applying algorithms to solve problems. As long as you were careful in your computations, you were able to solve problems such as "What is 1678 divided by 38?" by using the rules for long division, a basic mathematical algorithm. Later you were given geometry proofs to verify or equations to differentiate, and there weren't any algorithms guaranteeing a solution. If you did not develop or learn some simple heuristics, you probably bailed out of math classes as soon as possible. Since many of life's problems are fuzzy, with ill-defined problem statements and no apparent algorithms, the discovery or development of effective heuristics is important. Let's examine a few.

In **means-ends analysis,** the problem is divided into a number of subproblems and then a means of solving each is figured out. For example, writing a 20-page term paper can be an insurmountable problem for some students. They would be better off breaking this task down into several subproblems, such as selecting a topic, locating sources of information, reading and organizing the information, making an outline, and so on. Keep in

algorithm: step-by-step procedure for solving a problem; prescription for solutions

heuristic: general strategy used in attempting to solve problems

means-ends analysis: heuristic in which goal is divided into subgoals

mind that psychologists have yet to discover an effective heuristic for students who are just starting their term paper the night before it is due. No heuristic will solve the problem of not having enough time.

Working Backward

Some problems lend themselves to a *working-backward* strategy, in which you begin at the goal and move back to the unsolved initial problem. Working backward is sometimes an effective heuristic for solving geometry proofs. It can also be a good way to set intermediate deadlines ("Let's see, if I have to submit this chapter in three weeks, then it has to be in the mail by the 28th, so I have to get it to the typist by . . .").

Using Analogies

Another useful heuristic is *analogical thinking* (Copi, 1961). This limits your search for solutions to situations that bear some resemblance to the one you currently face. When submarines were first designed, engineers had to figure out how battleships could determine the presence and location of vessels hidden in the depths of the sea. Studying how bats solve an analogous problem of navigating in their environment led to the invention of sonar.

Verbalization

Trying to put your plan for solving a problem into words and giving reasons for selecting the plan can lead to successful problem solving. You may have discovered the effectiveness of this *verbalization* process accidentally when a new plan popped into your head as you were explaining the problem to someone else. Gagné and Smith (1962) found that when ninth- and tenth-grade students were instructed to state a reason for each step they were taking, they were much more successful in solving the problem than students who did not state reasons.

Executing the Plan

After representing the problem and selecting the approach, the next step is to execute the plan. If the plan primarily involves the use of algorithms, it is important to keep in mind that systematic "bugs,"or erroneous algorithms, may have developed in the procedures used. Brown and Burton (1979) developed computer programs that located bugs used by students in solving subtraction problems. Their research indicated that there are many more bugs in children's algorithms than teachers are aware of. One buggy algorithm they found, for example, was the consistent subtraction of the smaller from the larger number, regardless of which one was on top. Once teachers discover a bug, they can give specific tips for reworking problems. This is much more helpful than merely advising the child to try again and be more careful. We will see how teachers can help students get rid of "bugs" in Chapter 15.

Evaluating the Results

After you choose a solution and implement it, you should evaluate the results. This involves checking for evidence that confirms or contradicts your solution. Many people tend to stop working before reaching the *best* solution and simply accept an answer that works in some cases. I once tested a high school student with the following problem:

$$8x + 4y = 28$$
$$4x - 2y = 10$$

The student quickly wrote: $x = 2$, $y = 3$. This solution works for the first equation, but not for the second. The student found evidence to confirm the solution but did not keep checking to see if the solution fit all aspects of the problem. As we saw in Chapter 4, students with an impulsive cognitive style may need extra help in this area.

Checking Answers

In solving other mathematical problems, evaluating the answer also might mean applying a checking routine such as adding to check the result of a subtraction problem or, in a long addition problem, adding the column from bottom to top instead of top to bottom. Another possibility is estimating the answer. For example, if the computation was 11×21, the answer should be around 200, since 10×20 is 200. A student who reaches an answer of 2,311 or 23 or 562 should quickly realize these cannot be correct. Estimating an answer is particularly important when students rely on calculators, since they cannot go back and spot an error in the figures.

Effective Problem Solving: What Do the Experts Do?

Most psychologists agree that effective problem solving is based on an ample store of knowledge about the problem area. Remember the matchstick problem? In order to solve it, you had to understand Roman and Arabic numbers as well as the concept of square root. You also had to know that the square root of 1 is 1. Experts in any given field have a good supply of knowledge, facts, concepts, and procedures. This rich store of knowledge must be elaborated and organized so that it is easy to retrieve from long-term memory when needed.

Expert problem solvers are also persistent. Motivation plays an important role as well: "Successful problem solvers are often those who simply are willing to put in the necessary effort" (Sternberg & Davidson, 1982, p. 44).

declarative knowledge: verbal information; knowledge of facts, concepts, and principles

procedural knowledge: knowing how; knowledge of strategies

As you can see, experts not only have a wealth of **declarative knowledge**—facts, concepts, and principles; they also have at their command considerable **procedural knowledge**—an understanding of how to perform various cognitive activities. In other words, they can readily manipulate their declarative knowledge to solve problems. Not surprisingly, the processes experts apply to solve problems seem to be quite different from those of beginners.

Experts' Pattern Recognition. The modern study of expertise began with investigations of chess masters (Simon & Chase, 1973). Results indicated that masters can quickly recognize about 50,000 different arrangements of chess pieces. They can look at one of these patterns for a few seconds and remember where every piece on the board was placed. It is as though they have a "vocabulary" of 50,000 patterns. For the masters, patterns of pieces are like words. If you were shown any word from your vocabulary store for just a few seconds, you would be able to remember every letter in the word in the right order (assuming you could spell the word).

But a series of letters arranged randomly is hard to remember, as you saw in Chapter 7. An analogous situation holds for chess masters. When chess pieces are placed on a board randomly, masters are no better than the average individual at remembering the positions of the pieces. The master's memory is for patterns that make sense or could occur in a game. Thus, "high-level competence in this case does not appear to reside in conscious analytical thinking processes. The chess master is a superior recognizer rather than a deep thinker" (Glaser, 1981, p. 931).

A similar phenomenon occurs in other fields. There may be a kind of intuition about how to solve a problem based on recognizing patterns and knowing the "right moves" for those patterns. Experts in physics, for example, organize their knowledge around central principles, whereas beginners organize their (smaller amounts) of physics knowledge around the specific details stated in the problems. The experts can find the patterns needed to solve a particular problem very quickly without putting a heavy strain on working memory. They use less bottom-up processing of details. So experts literally don't have to think as hard (Glaser, 1981).

Less Work for the Experts

In addition to representing a problem very quickly, experts know what to do next. They have a large store of *condition-action schemata*—knowledge about what action to take in each situation. So the steps of understanding the problem and choosing a solution happen together and fairly automatically (Norman, 1982).

Novice Knowledge. Studies of the differences between experts and novices in particular areas have revealed some surprising things about how novices understand and *misunderstand* a subject. Physics again provides many examples. Most beginners approach physics with a great deal of misinformation and apprehension. Many of our intuitive ideas about the physical world are wrong. For example, most elementary school children believe that light helps us see by brightening the area around objects. They do not realize that we see an object because the light is reflected off the object to our eyes. This concept does not fit with the everyday experience of turning on a light and "brightening" the dark area. Researchers from the Elementary Science Project at Michigan State University found that even after completing a unit on light in which materials explicitly stated the idea of reflected light and vision, most fifth-grade students—about 78 percent—continued to cling to their intuitive notions. But when new materials were designed that directly confronted the students' misconceptions, only about 20 percent of the students failed to understand (Eaton, Anderson, & Smith, 1984).

Unlearning Common Sense

It seems quite important for science teachers to understand their students' intuitive models of basic concepts. This again goes back to adequate and accurate representation of a problem. In order to learn new information, students must sometimes "unlearn" common-sense ideas. A set of Guidelines is included on the next page for helping students in any subject learn efficient and useful problem-solving strategies.

Let's turn now to specific help in solving a very common problem for students—how to study.

STUDY SKILLS

Teachers typically do not provide much deliberate instruction in study skills. After over 45 hours of observation in fourth-grade classrooms, Durkin (1978) reported that on the average, only 1 percent of each social studies period was spent on explicit instruction in study strategies. Yet it is clear that study skills and learning strategies are important and improvable aspects of learning. One of the most thoroughly researched study skills is reading.

Guidelines

Problem Solving

Ask students if they are sure they understand the problem.

Examples
1. *Can they separate relevant from irrelevant information?*
2. *Are they aware of the assumptions they are making?*
3. *Encourage them to visualize the problem by diagramming or drawing it.*
4. *Ask them to explain the problem to someone else. What would a good solution look like?*

Encourage attempts to see the problem from different angles.

Examples
1. *Suggest several different possibilities yourself and then ask students to offer some.*
2. *Develop unconventional uses for common objects—use empty tin cans to support a grill over a fire; use a long metal fingernail file to roast marshmallows.*

Help students develop systematic ways of considering alternatives.

Examples
1. *Think out loud as you solve problems.*
2. *Ask, "What would happen if . . . ?"*
3. *Keep a list of suggestions.*

Teach heuristics.

Examples
1. *Ask students to explain the steps they take as they solve problems.*
2. *Use analogies to solve the problem of limited parking in the downtown area. How are other "storage" problems solved?*
3. *Use working backwards to plan a party.*

Let students do the thinking; don't simply provide solutions.

Examples
1. *Offer individual problems as well as group problems, so that each student has the chance to practice.*
2. *Give partial credit if students have good reasons for "wrong" solutions to problems.*
3. *If students are stuck, resist the temptation to give too many clues. Let them think about the problem overnight.*

PQ4R

Over the years there have been many suggestions about how to understand and remember what you read. One of the most enduring systems is the SQ3R (survey, question, read, recite, review) approach developed by F. P. Robinson (1961). You may have been exposed to this study strategy at some point during your academic career. A more recent variation is called PQ4R (Thomas & Robinson, 1972). In this system the extra R is for reflection, and the P stands for preview; so the acronym means Preview, Question, Read, Reflect, Recite, and Review. Here is how you would apply the PQ4R method to study this text.

Preview. Introduce yourself to the chapter you are about to read by surveying the major topics and sections. Read the overview, the objectives, the section headings and subheadings, the summary, and perhaps the initial sentences of the major sections. If you have the *Study Guide* for this book, you might look over the chapter objectives and outlines. All of these procedures will help activate schemata so you can interpret and remember the text that follows. Previewing also allows you to formulate your own general purpose for reading each section, whether it is to identify the main idea or note the general biases of the author.

Question. For each major section, generate questions that are related to your reading purposes. One way is to turn the headings and subheadings into questions. For example, in this chapter you might ask: "How can I help students improve their study skills?" "What are some effective problem-solving strategies?" If you are beginning to use this method of reading, it often is helpful to write down brief questions as they come to mind.

Read. At last! The questions you have formulated can be answered through reading. You should pay attention to the main ideas, supporting details, and other data in keeping with your purposes. You may have to adjust your reading speed to suit the difficulty of the material and your purpose in reading.

Reflect. While you are reading, try to think of examples or create images of the material. Elaborate and try to make connections between what you are reading and what you already know.

Recite. After reading each section, sit back and think about your initial purposes and questions. Can you answer the questions without looking at the book? In doing this, your mind has a second chance to connect what you have read with what you already know. If your mind is blank after reading the section, it may have been too difficult to read comfortably, or you may have been daydreaming. Reciting helps you to monitor your understanding and tells you when to reread before moving on to the next section. Reciting should take place after each headed section but might be required more often in reading difficult material.

Review. Effective review incorporates new material more thoroughly into your long-term memory. As study progresses, review should be cumulative, including the sections and chapters you read previously. Rereading is one form of review, but trying to answer key questions without referring to the book is the best way. Wrong answers can direct you to areas that need more study, especially before an exam.

Effectiveness of PQ4R. In a study by Adams, Carnine, and Gersten (1982), fifth-grade students given systematic instruction in the technique recalled more information than other students on both immediate and delayed tests. Why might this be so? Anderson (1980) suggests several reasons for PQ4R's effectiveness. First, following the steps makes students more aware of the organization of a given chapter. How often have you skipped reading headings entirely and thus missed major clues to the way the information was organized? Readers who use the author's organization to organize their own memory of material actually recall more than those who do not follow the texts' organization (Meyer, Brandt, & Bluth, 1980). Next, these steps require the student to study the chapter in sections instead of trying to learn all the information at once. This makes use of distributed practice. Creating and answering questions about the material force the student to process the information more deeply and with greater elaboration. Student-generated questions, as well as questions in the text, have been shown to improve retention of information (Doctorow, Wittrock, & Marks, 1978; Hamilton, 1985). Reviewing with questions in mind encourages more connections to be made between new and old information. In general, it is likely that using the PQ4R method means investing greater time and effort in studying.

Age Levels

As you might have guessed, the PQ4R method is most appropriate for older children. Very little is known about teaching study skills to students before about fifth grade. The effective application of study skills probably requires metacognitive development beyond the range of most very young children. And of course, young children are still focusing much of their attention on learning the basics of word recognition and decoding.

Underlining and Note Taking

Do you underline or highlight key phrases in textbooks? Are my words turning yellow or pink at this very moment? What about outlining or taking notes? Underlining and note taking are probably two of the most commonly used strategies among college students. Yet few students have ever received any direct instruction in the best ways to underline and take notes. So it is not surprising that many students use ineffective strategies.

Many students take notes, but not all take useful notes. Good notes are concise and well organized; they highlight connections between new ideas and existing knowledge. *(Owen Franken/Stock, Boston)*

One common problem is that students underline or highlight too much. It is better to be selective. In studies that limit how much students could underline—for example, only one sentence per paragraph—learning has improved (Snowman, 1984). In addition to being selective, you also should actively transform the information into your own words as you underline or take notes. Don't rely on the words of the book or lecturer. Finally, look for organizational patterns in the material and use them to guide your underlining or note taking (Irwin, 1986).

Fortunately, there are a number of study-strategy books that provide excellent guidelines. The suggestions in Table 8–3 on the following pages are taken from one of these books, *How to Study in College,* by Walter Pauk. Your college may have a study-skills center that can provide extra help.

Mapping
Relationships
Effective use of PQ4R, underlining and note taking all rely on understanding the organization of the text. Recently, some study strategies have been developed to help students with this key element. Armbruster and Anderson (1980) taught students specific techniques for diagramming relationships among ideas presented in a text. "Mapping" these relationships by noting causal and comparison/contrast connections and examples improved recall. Davidson (1982) has suggested that students compare their maps with one another's and discuss the differences. Two mapping methods are shown in Figure 8–2 on page 298. As you can see, Map A uses a main-idea/detail structure to organize information about the Puritans, and Map B stresses a causal relationship between religious beliefs and other activities.

TEACHING FOR TRANSFER

Think back for a moment to one of your high school classes you did not go on to study in college. Imagine the teacher, the room, the textbook. If you can do all this, you are using your information processing strategies for search and retrieval very well. Now remember what you actually studied in class. If it was a science class, what were some of the formulas you learned? How about chemical reactions? Oxidation reduction? If you are like most of us, you may remember that you learned these things, but you will not be quite sure exactly *what* you learned. Were those hours wasted? These are essentially questions about the transfer of learning.

The Guidelines for study skills on page 299 apply not just to prospective teachers but to all of you who want to become expert learners. Note that these suggestions essentially involve the metacognitive abilities discussed in the last chapter.

Positive and Negative Transfer

transfer: influence of previously learned material on new material
Whenever something learned previously influences current learning, **transfer** has occurred. If students learn a mathematical principle in first period and use it to solve a physics problem in fifth period, then positive transfer has taken place. Even more rewarding for teachers is the positive transfer that takes place when a math principle learned in October is applied to a physics problem in March.

However, the effect of past learning on present learning is not always so positive. Both proactive interference (old learning interferes with new) and

Table 8–3 Suggestions for Marking Textbooks

Explanation and Description	Symbols, Markings, and Notations
1. Double lines under words or phrases signify the main ideas.	<u><u>Radiation can produce mutations</u></u> . . .
2. Single lines under words or phrases signify supporting material.	<u>comes from cosmic rays</u> . . .
3. Small circled numbers above the initial word of an underlined group of words indicate a series of arguments, facts, ideas, either main or supporting.	Conditions change . . . ①<u>rocks rise</u> . . . ②<u>some sink</u> . . . ③<u>the sea dashes</u> . . . ④<u>strong winds</u> . . .
4. Rather than underlining a group of three or more important lines, you may use a vertical bracket in the outer margin.	⌈had known . . . |who gave . . . |the time . . . ⌊of time . . .
5. One asterisk in the margin indicates ideas of special importance; two, ideas of unusual importance; and three, ideas of outstanding importance: reserved for principles and high level generalizations.	*When a <u>nuclear blast</u> is . . . **people <u>quite close</u> to the . . . ***The main <u>cause of mutations</u> . . .
6. Circle key words and terms.	The ⟨genes⟩ are the . . .
7. Box in the words of enumeration and transition.	⟦fourth,⟧ the lack of supplies . . . ⟦furthermore,⟧ the shortage . . .

retroactive interference (new learning wipes out old) are examples of negative transfer. So are functional fixedness and response set, since they involve the attempt to apply familiar but inappropriate strategies to a new situation.

Specific and General Transfer

Specific transfer occurs when a rule, fact, or skill learned in one situation is applied in another very similar situation. Examples of specific transfer include applying rules of punctuation to write a job application letter and using knowledge of the alphabet to find a word in the dictionary. *General transfer* involves dealing with new problems based on principles and attitudes learned in other, often dissimilar situations. Thus, general transfer might mean using problem-solving heuristics to solve issues in your personal life—

Explanation and Description	Symbols, Markings, and Notations
8. A question mark in the margin, opposite lines you do not understand, is an excellent reminder to ask the instructor for clarification.	? The latest . . . cold period . . . about 1,000,000 . . . Even today . . .
9. If you disagree with a statement, indicate that in the margin.	*Disagree* Life became . . . on land only . . . 340 million years . . .
10. Use the top and bottom margins of a page to record any ideas of your own that are prompted by what you have read.	*Why not use carbon dating?* *Check on reference of fossil found in Tennessee stone quarry.*
11. On sheets of paper that are smaller than the pages of the book, write longer thoughts or summaries, then insert them between the pages.	*Fossils* Plants = 500,000,000 years old Insects = 260,000,000 " " Bees = 100,000,000 " " True fish = 330,000,000 " " Amphibians = 300,000,000 " " Reptiles = 300,000,000 " " Birds = 150,000,000 " "
12. Even though you have underlined the important ideas and supporting materials, still jot brief summaries in the side margins.	*Adapt* - - - - - - - - - *fossil* - - - - - - - - - *layer* - - - - - - - - -

From W. Pauk (1974), How to Study in College (3rd ed.). Boston: Houghton Mifflin, p. 155. Copyright © 1974 by Houghton Mifflin Company. Used by permission.

for example, applying working backwards to decide when you have to order your new car so that it will be delivered in time to be past the break-in period and first servicing for your trip through Canada.

The Breakdown of Mental Discipline

Studies of transfer undertaken in the early twentieth century have probably had more impact on education than any other research conducted by psychologists (Travers, 1977). Before that, it was assumed that learning certain subjects, like Latin and mathematics, provided a kind of mental discipline. By studying these subjects, the theory went, students learned powers of thinking and reasoning that could be applied to all subjects. Thorndike and his colleagues conducted research to determine if studying Latin, Greek, and mathematics actually did lead to increased intellectual achievement in other subjects (Brolyer, Thorndike, & Woodyard, 1927). They found no general transfer to other areas. Learning Latin, for example, seemed to transfer primarily to learning more Latin (and perhaps to learning some English vocabulary). In other words, transfer was specific, not general.

Figure 8–2   **Mapping a Social Studies Chapter**

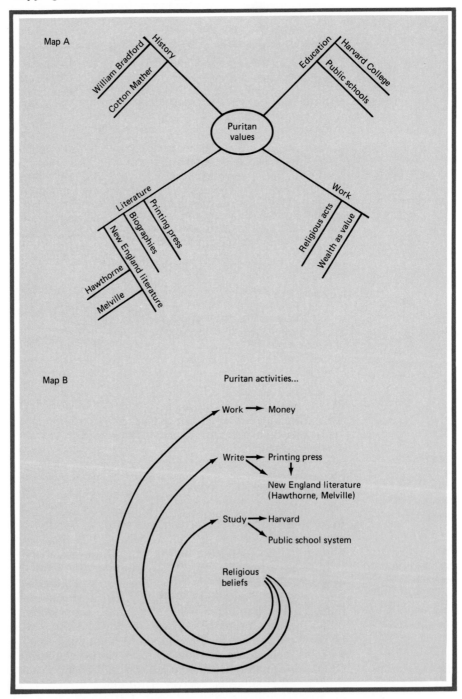

From J. W. Irwin (1986), Teaching reading comprehension processes. © 1986, p. 55. Reprinted by permission of Prentice-Hall, Inc. Englewood Cliffs, N.J.

Guidelines

Study Skills and Learning Strategies

Make sure you have the necessary declarative knowledge (facts, concepts, ideas) to understand new information.

Examples
1. *Keep definitions of key vocabulary available as you study.*
2. *Review required facts and concepts before attempting new material.*

Find out what type of test the teacher will give (essay, short answer), and study the material with that in mind.

Examples
1. *For a test with detailed questions, practice writing answers to possible questions.*
2. *For a multiple-choice test, use mnemonics to remember definitions of key terms.*

Make sure you are familiar with the organization of the materials to be learned.

Examples
1. *Preview the headings, introductions, topic sentences, and summaries of the text.*
2. *Be alert for words and phrases that signal relationships, such as on the other hand, because, first, second, however, since.*

Know your own cognitive skills and use them deliberately.

Examples
1. *Use examples and analogies to relate new material to something you care about and understand well, such as sports, hobbies, or films.*
2. *If one study technique is not working, try another—the goal is to stay involved, not to use any particular strategy.*

Study the right information in the right way.

Examples
1. *Be sure you know exactly what topics and readings the test will cover.*
2. *Spend your time on the important, difficult, and unfamiliar material that will be required for the test or assignment.*
3. *Keep a list of the parts of the text that give you trouble and spend more time on those pages.*
4. *Process the important information thoroughly by using mnemonics, forming images, creating examples, answering questions, making notes in your own words, and elaborating on the text. Do not try to memorize the author's words—use your own.*

Monitor your own comprehension.

Examples
1. *Use questioning to check your understanding.*
2. *When reading speed slows down, decide if the information in the passage is important. If it is, note the problem so you can reread or get help to understand. If it is not important, ignore it.*
3. *Check your understanding by working with a friend and quizzing one another.*

Adapted from B. B. Armbruster & T. H. Anderson (1981), Research synthesis on study skills. Educational Leadership, 39, pp. 154–156. Reprinted with permission of the Association for Supervision and Curriculum Development and the authors. Copyright © 1981 by the Association for Supervision and Curriculum Development. All rights reserved.

I REMEMBER **NOTHING** THAT I LEARNED IN HIGH SCHOOL.

THE DEATH OF GEOMETRY

*Drawing by Ziegler; ©
1983 The New Yorker
Magazine, Inc.*

Once the findings of Thorndike's research were publicized, the notion of mental discipline began to fade, and curricula and graduation requirements were altered. Thanks to educational psychology (at least indirectly), you did not have to study Greek and Latin throughout your school years.

Thorndike's own theory of transfer states that learning one particular skill is likely to improve the learning of another skill only to the extent that the two skills overlap or have common elements. The more similar two particular skills are, the more likely it is that transfer will occur from one to the other. The stress is on specific transfer. Learning to drive one automatic-shift car prepares you quite well for driving another automatic-shift car, somewhat for driving a standard shift, and not very well for driving a motorcycle. But some specific transfer does take place in each case, since each type of vehicle has elements in common.

Both Types Have Value

Both specific and general transfer are important in the classroom. In learning the basic skills, students must acquire a great deal of information that they will apply directly every day. But beyond this, it is difficult to predict the specific knowledge students will need in the future. As a child growing up in Texas in the 1950s and 1960s, I learned little about ecology, conservation, nuclear power, or how to deal with the high cost of energy. With gasoline selling for 27 cents a gallon, the politics of oil supply and demand and concerns for ecology and conservation were not a part of the high school curriculum. But learning to use a slide rule was taught. Now calculators have made this skill obsolete. Word processors and spelling checkers may soon make typing and spelling correction obsolete as well. Undoubtedly changes as extreme and unpredictable as these await the students you will teach. For this reason, the general transfer of principles, attitudes, and problem-solving strategies will be just as important to these students as the specific transfer of basic skills.

Teaching for Positive Transfer: Principles

Many of the principles you have already encountered in this and in the previous chapter will help you teach for positive transfer. First, you must answer the question, "What *is* worth learning?"

Basic Skills

The first part of the answer is obvious. The learning of basic skills like reading, writing, computing, and speaking will definitely transfer to other situations because these skills are necessary for later work both in and out of school. All later learning depends on positive transfer of these basics to new situations. Certainly in the early grades this content is critical.

Preparing for the Future

Teachers must also be aware of what the future is *likely* (teachers are not fortunetellers, after all) to hold for their students, both as a group and as individuals. Will they go on with their education? What will society require of them as adults? What will their careers require of them? Some of the answers to these questions involve applied basic skills like writing job applications; reading government forms; calculating insurance needs; figuring income tax; locating and evaluating needed services; household budgeting; borrowing money for college, car, or house payments; computer literacy; and evaluating advertisement claims. These important skills will transfer to other situations because they are necessary for survival in the modern world.

Thoroughness

Another principle is that material must be presented *thoroughly*. Thorough understanding involves incorporating the new information into existing schemata, elaborating it and organizing it as much as possible—in other words, encoding it for storage in long-term memory in easily retrievable form. Making learning meaningful really implies teaching for transfer—teaching for permanent storage, deep processing, and easy retrieval.

In our consumer society, you can be assured that these students will remember and use what they are learning here.
(David S. Strickler/Monkmeyer Press)

DO YOU UNDERSTAND MONEY MATTERS?

What did you buy?

How much does it cost?

How much change should you receive?

DO YOU NEED PRACTICE?

Students will be more likely to transfer information to new situations if they have been actively involved in the learning process. Of course, active involvement does not refer to any one particular method, such as discovery learning. Involvement can take the form of discussion, independent library research, group experiments, or just mental activity during lectures. Student engagement with the material is the essential point.

Newly mastered concepts, principles, and strategies must be practiced in a wide variety of situations. Some of these applications should involve complex, unstructured problems, since many of the problems to be faced in later life, both in school and out, will not come to students complete with instructions. Practice solving this kind of problem can be enormously helpful.

Remember the discussion in Chapter 7 of the importance of similar context in memory retrieval? The same principle applies for positive transfer. New skills practiced under conditions similar to those students will have to cope with later have a good chance of transferring. Your student teaching, for example, will take place under conditions very similar to those in a real assignment and should help you when your first job begins. This is the reason that simulations have proved so successful in training pilots, physicians, and drivers (Bower & Hilgard, 1981).

overlearning:
practicing a task past the point of mastery to combat forgetting

Finally, greater transfer can be ensured by **overlearning.** This simply means practicing a skill past the point at which the desired goal has been attained. Many of the basic facts students learn in elementary school, such as the multiplication tables, are traditionally overlearned. Overlearning helps students retrieve the information quickly and accurately when it is needed.

TEACHING THINKING

In schools, we tend to emphasize teaching children *what* to think rather than *how* to think. Recently, the teaching of thinking has become a national issue. Years ago the cry was "Johnny can't read!" Today the educational and business communities fear that "Johnny can't think—and neither can Joanna!" Even if we are successful in teaching reading and the other basics, can we be sure that our students will be able to analyze and evaluate what they read? Will they be able to go beyond the information they are given to generate new ideas?

From our discussion of transfer, it is easy to see why the teaching of thinking is an important issue. Well-developed thinking skills can transfer positively to almost every life situation—even evaluating the media ads that constantly bombard us. For example, to evaluate the claim that 99 out of 100 dentists prefer a particular brand of toothpaste, you must consider such questions as: Which dentists were polled? How were they chosen? Was the toothpaste company involved in the polling process? If so, how could this bias the results of the poll? Or when you see a group of gorgeous people extolling the virtues of a particular brand of orange juice as they frolic in minuscule bathing suits, you must decide if sex appeal is a relevant factor in choosing a fruit drink.

But psychologists have not been able to agree on the skills that constitute critical thinking. Perkins (1986) emphasizes the capacities to identify the problem, to detect and avoid bias in reasoning, and to see knowledge as an invention of people for a particular purpose, not as information that is set or unchanging. Other psychologists have different ideas. Table 8–4, taken from Kneedler (1985), provides a fairly representative list.

Table 8–4 **Essential Critical Thinking Skills**

Defining and Clarifying the Problem

1. **Identify central issues or problems.**
   The ability to identify the main idea of a passage, an argument, or a political cartoon, or the reasons and conclusions in an argument.
2. **Compare similarities and differences.**
   The ability to compare similarities and differences among two or more people, objects, ideas, or situations at the same or different points in time.
3. **Determine which information is relevant.**
   The ability to make distinctions between verifiable and unverifiable and relevant and nonrelevant information.
4. **Formulate appropriate questions.**
   The ability to formulate questions that will lead to a deeper and clearer understanding of an issue or situation.

Judging Information Related to the Problem

5. **Distinguish among fact, opinion, and reasoned judgment.**
   The ability to apply criteria for judging the quality of observation and inference.
6. **Check consistency.**
   The ability to determine whether given statements or symbols are consistent with each other and their context—for example, whether the different points in a political argument are logically connected and agree with the central issue.
7. **Identify unstated assumptions.**
   The ability to identify what is taken for granted, but not explicitly stated.
8. **Recognize stereotypes and clichés.**
   The ability to identify fixed or conventional notions about a person, group, or idea.
9. **Recognize bias, emotional factors, propaganda, and semantic slanting.**
   The ability to identify bias in written and graphic materials and to determine the credibility of sources.
10. **Recognize different value systems and ideologies.**
    The ability to recognize the similarities and differences among different value systems and ideologies.

Solving Problems/Drawing Conclusions

11. **Recognize the adequacy of data.**
    The ability to decide whether the information provided is sufficient in quality and quantity to justify a conclusion, decision, generalization, or plausible hypothesis.
12. **Predict probable consequences.**
    The ability to predict probable consequences of an event or series of events.

Adapted from P. Kneedler (1985), California assesses critical thinking. In A. Costa (Ed.), Developing minds: A resource book for teaching thinking. Alexandria, VA: Association for Supervision and Curriculum Development, p. 277. Reprinted with permission of the Association for Supervision and Curriculum Development and the author.

Improving Thinking

Many educational psychologists believe that thinking skills can and should be taught. But clearly, the teaching of critical thinking entails much more than the standard classroom practice of completing work sheets, answering "thought" questions at the end of the chapter, and participating in teacher-led discussions. One possibility is to use special programs designed to teach thinking skills. There are many choices. A recent resource book for educators (Costa, 1985) lists over 15 different programs, including de Bono's CoRT system, *Odyssey: A Curriculum for Thinking,* Winocur's Project Impact, Lipman's Philosophy for Children, and Meeker's SOI.

A second possibility is to emphasize thinking as part of your regular lessons. Beyer (1985) describes two ways of doing this. One is an inductive approach, much like guided discovery learning. The other is a deductive lesson, similar to expository teaching. Let's assume you teach history and have decided to focus on detecting bias, a skill many experts list as an important component of critical thinking. Exactly how would you go about using these two methods?

Discovering Bias: An Inductive Lesson. In this approach the steps are introduction, experimentation, reflection, application, and review. First the teacher gives a brief and general *introduction,* stating the purpose of the lesson (to learn how to detect bias in historical documents) and perhaps giving a definition and a few examples of bias in written materials. This introduction is very much like an advance organizer, though quite general. Without any other explanation, the students are given the following passage so they can *experiment:*

EXCERPT A
Some of these lords of the loom . . . employ thousands of miserable creatures . . . [who are] kept, fourteen hours in each day, locked up, summer and winter, in a heat of from *eighty to eighty-four degrees.* . . . What then must be the situation of these poor creatures who are doomed to toil day after day . . . ? Can any man, with a heart in his body . . ., refrain from cursing a system that produces such slavery and cruelty? [T]hese poor creatures have no cool room to retreat to . . . [and] are not allowed to send for water to drink; . . . even the rain water is locked up, by the master's order. . . . [A]ny spinner found with his window open . . . is to pay a fine. . . . (Cobbett, 1824)

Experimenting simply means attempting to identify bias in the passage as best you can. Students might work alone, in pairs, or in small groups.

Next, students *reflect* on what they have just done. Is the passage biased Most students will answer a resounding "Yes!" As evidence of bias, they may list emotionally charged words and phrases like "miserable creatures" or "doomed to toil." They may notice overgeneralization ("Any spinner") or rhetorical questions ("Can any man, with a heart"). After identifying a number of examples, the student can begin to notice similarities. What could we call phrases like "miserable creatures" or "doomed to toil"? The general category of emotionally charged language should emerge from this discussion.

Now the students are ready to *apply* the categories they have just identified to a new passage. They are given the following:

I have visited many factories . . . and I never saw . . . children in ill-humor. They seemed to be always cheerful and alert, taking pleasure in the light play of their muscles—enjoying the mobility natural to their age. The scene of industry . . . was exhilarating. It was delightful to observe the nimbleness with which they pieced the broken ends as the mule carriage began to recede from the fixed roller-beam and to see them at leisure after a few seconds' exercise of their tiny fingers, to amuse themselves in any attitude they chose. . . . The work of these lively elves seemed to resemble a sport. . . . [T]hey evidenced no trace of exhaustion on emerging from the mill in the evening; for they . . . skip about any neighborhood playground. . . .(Ure, 1861)

The last step is to *review* what has been learned. What kinds of clues do you look for in detecting bias? What general procedures should you follow?

Specifying Bias: A Deductive Lesson.   The steps in a deductive lesson are introduction, explanation, demonstration, application, and reflection. The *introduction* or advance organizer is similar to the one used for the previous lesson—purpose, definition of the skill, examples. Next, the teacher *explains* the main procedures, especially the use of clues for detecting bias. Clues would be emotionally loaded language, one-sided presentation, rhetorical questions, and so on. Procedures might include searching each line for clues; looking for patterns to see if the general tone created is positive, negative, or neutral; and keeping track of all evidence of bias.

Now the teacher uses Excerpt A to *demonstrate* the skill. Students are led step by step to identify clues and use procedures for detecting bias. Then they are ready to *apply* the skill themselves by analyzing Excerpt B. Finally, the students should *reflect* on what they did in executing the skill. What was hard? What was easy? What helped? Can they summarize the general procedures and kinds of clues?

No matter what approach the teacher chooses, it is important to follow up with additional guided practice. One lesson is not enough. Analyzing other written historical documents, contemporary advertisements, or news stories would give needed practice. Until thinking skills become overlearned and relatively automatic, they are not likely to be transferred to new situations. Instead, these skills will be used only to complete the lesson in social studies but not to evaluate the claims made by friends, politicians, toy manufacturers, or diet plans.

SUMMARY

1. Gagné has suggested five basic categories of learning outcomes: (1) attitudes; (2) motor skills; (3) verbal information; (4) intellectual skills (discriminations, concepts, rules, and higher-order rules); and (5) cognitive strategies.

2. Bruner's work has focused on learning through discovery. According to Bruner, students learn best when they themselves discover the structure of a subject by inductive means. In guided discovery, the teachers ask leading questions and give directive feedback.

3. According to Ausubel, learning should be primarily deductive. Students must understand the more general concepts, or subsumers, before mastering details and subconcepts.

4. Ausubel's expository teaching makes use of advance organizers to introduce basic concepts. Subordinate content is presented in terms of similarities and differences, with ample use of specific examples.

5. Concepts are categories used to group similar events, ideas, people, or objects. We probably learn concepts from prototypes of the category, then refine them through increased experience of relevant and irrelevant features.

6. Lessons about concepts include four basic components: concept name, definition, attributes, and examples.

7. The four stages of problem solving are understanding and representing the problem, selecting the solution, executing the plan, and evaluating the results. A critical element in solving problems in school is representing the problem accurately. Translation and schema training may improve this ability. Correct representation can lead to a sudden insight into the solution.

8. Students often find it difficult to represent problems because of functional fixedness or rigidity (response set). The application of algorithms and of heuristics such as means-ends analysis, analogical thinking, working backward, and verbalization may help students solve problems.

9. Research indicates that experts organize their knowledge around general principles that apply to large classes of problems.

10. Instruction in study skills like the PQ4R method, note taking, and underlining can be very valuable to students.

11. The transfer of learning from one situation to another may be either positive (the use of a math formula in physics class) or negative (the problem of functional fixedness or interference). It may also be specific (the use of language skills in writing letters) or general (the use of learned problem-solving strategies to solve new problems).

12. Critical thinking skills are among the most valuable and positively transferable skills schools can teach students.

KEY TERMS

cognitive strategies

structure

inductive reasoning

coding system

eg-rule method

intuitive thinking

discovery learning

guided discovery

meaningful verbal learning

expository teaching

subsumer

rule-eg method

advance organizer

activate

concepts

defining attributes

prototype

undergeneralization

overgeneralization

problem solving

linguistic comprehension

functional fixedness

response set

insight

algorithm

heuristic

means-end analysis

declarative knowledge

procedural knowledge

transfer

overlearning

SUGGESTIONS FOR FURTHER READING AND STUDY

BROWN, A. L., CAMPIONE, J. C., & DAY, J. D. (1981). Learning to learn: On training students to learn from text. *Educational Researcher, 9,* 14–21. A very helpful review of research on different learning strategies for reading and studying prose.

COSTA, A. L. (Ed.). (1985). *Developing minds: A resource book for teaching thinking.* Alexandria, VA: Association for Supervision and Curriculum Development. This is an extensive guide for teachers and administrators. There are many articles on teaching strategies, special programs, computers and thinking skills, and assessing thinking.

Educational Leadership. (1986, May). This issue has a special section called "Frameworks for Teaching Thinking." There are articles on the direct teaching of thinking, decision making, and even how to do homework.

EGGEN, P. D., KAVCHAK, D. P., & HARDER, R. J. (1979). *Strategies for teachers: Information processing models in the classroom.* Englewood Cliffs, NJ: Prentice-Hall. This very practical book describes five different models for teaching, including approaches based on the work of Bruner and Ausubel.

FENKER, R. (1981). *Stop studying—start learning: Or how to jump start your brain.* Fort Worth, TX: Tangram. A highly readable and humorous guide for becoming an "expert" student.

FREDERIKSEN, N. (1984). Implications for cognitive theory for instruction in problem solving. *Review of Educational Research, 54,* 363–408. This is a very up-to-date look at what cognitive science can tell educators about instruction in problem solving.

LARKIN, J., McDERMOTT, J., SIMON, D. P., & SIMON, H. A. (1980). Expert and novice performance in solving physics problems. *Science, 208,* 1335–1342. Intriguing ideas about the factors that influence expert performance, especially the role of representing and organizing knowledge.

LUITEN, J., AMES, W., & ACKERSON, G. (1980). A metaanalysis of the effects of advance organizers on learning and retention. *American Educational Research Journal, 17,* 211–218. This article summarizes many studies on the effectiveness of advance organizers.

MAYER, R. E. (1983). *Thinking, problem solving, cognition.* San Francisco: W. H. Freeman. This new book by the author of *Thinking and Problem Solving* is an interesting text with many visual aids. There are sections on historical perspectives, basic thinking tasks, information processing, and implications of the cognitive approach for learning and teaching.

PAUK, W. (1974). *How to study in college.* Boston: Houghton Mifflin. A classic book—this has helped many college students and can give ideas for secondary students as well.

STERNBERG, R., & DAVIDSON, J. (1982). The mind of the puzzler. *Psychology Today, 16,* 37–144. In this fascinating article the authors describe differences between good and bad problem solvers.

TENNYSON, R. D., & COCCHIARELLA, M. J. (1986). An empirically based instructional design theory for teaching concepts. *Review of Educational Research, 56,* 40–71. This is a very current theory merging critical features and prototype approaches to teaching concepts.

Teachers' Forum

Discovery for Everyone?

One problem with discovery techniques is that the brightest students often "discover" the points quickly and are bursting to share their new-found wisdom with the rest of the class. This can spoil the lesson for those who are not as quick—and can also lead to feelings of ineffectiveness. How do you deal with this?

Journals of Discovery

One very effective technique is to have students log their findings in a notebook and then share portions of their discoveries with the class. Everyone can work at her or his own pace. Some students will have more to read than others, but each will have the chance to share her or his best work.

Katherine P. Stillerman, Seventh-Grade Language Arts
and Social Studies Teacher
Pine Forest Junior High School, Fayetteville, North Carolina

Balancing the Energy

It's difficult to restrain children who are overflowing with energy and ideas. They can take over a classroom if you let them. What can teachers do? We can talk to the whole class about respecting the rights of all and giving everyone an opportunity to respond. Perhaps we can allow the advanced children to lead the discussions, at least in part, after we have modeled this behavior. Another thing to do is encourage all the children to come up with many different ideas, avoid acknowledging any correct response, and have each child back up his or her answers. We can also have children draw pictures or write out their discoveries before verbalizing them. Some discovery activities have no right or wrong answers, and these can be used to encourage all children to respond without feeling threatened.

Carolyn R. Cook, Kindergarten Teacher
Ramona Elementary School, Ramona, California

Representing Story Problems

When students have difficulty with story problems in math, it is often because they are not representing the problems so that they can "see" the appropriate solution strategies. What are some techniques you use to help students represent problems?

Act It Out

Role playing is an excellent way to help children visualize and understand the process of solving story problems. For instance, if a story problem involves two characters, I select two students for the roles. I set the scene by reading the story. To personalize it, each student plays himself and decides what lines he would say in that particular situation. (In the beginning, students may require some prompting.) Then I write the story on the chalkboard in equation form and explain it. A second story problem is presented, and new volunteers are selected for role playing. A volunteer is also selected to write the story on the board as an equation. The students soon learn to write their own story problems in this form. Should a student fail to understand the process, he can draw a picture or retell the story to me. Invariably, the child will "see" the solution.

Nancy R. Gonzalez, Bilingual First-Grade Teacher
Robert Frost School, Mount Prospect, Illinois

Effective Problem Solving

How do you help students in your class to become effective problem solvers, particularly when dealing with the complex, "fuzzy" problems of daily life?

Brainstorming Solves Problems

The first steps are to have students state the problem clearly and then to list all possible solutions on the board. After all solutions are in, the process of elimination begins. Solutions shouldn't be eliminated unless everyone agrees. Students can consolidate, delete, and add to solutions until an acceptable final list is arrived at. Then duties are assigned and materials distributed in order to carry out the solutions. Finally, the process is evaluated: have the goals actually been reached?

Other useful problem-solving activities include simulations and cause-and-effect games—"What would happen if . . .?" For these games, the students can write stories or draw or paint pictures showing what they think the outcome would be.

Ida Pofahl, Second-Grade Teacher
Denison Elementary School, Denison, Iowa

Transfer: The Classroom and Beyond

What kinds of in-class activities have you found aid students' transfer of learning? How do you make connections between lessons and the "real life'" beyond the school walls?

"Out of School" Experiences—in School

I feel students transfer learning best if they actually get involved in their work. In math, we have a week of following the stock market. We keep a chart in the room to see if we make money. We also write checks and balance a family budget for a month. In spelling, we play games like the Great American Giveaway, which reinforces learning so students can retain and transfer it. If students spell three unit words correctly, they can choose one of two doors. Behind each door is a picture from a magazine of something the children enjoy or want—for example, Oreo-cookie ice cream. The child who opens that door wins an imaginary month's supply of the ice cream.

Sharon Klotz, Sixth-Grade Teacher
Kiel Middle School, Kiel, Wisconsin

Turning to the Broader Community

To make learning more applicable to life outside the classroom, I have days when students bring in calculators for math. I also try to utilize the resource people of the neighborhood—artists or nurses, for example—who speak to the class about relevant topics. For each of the seven social studies units, we have a guest speaker who has lived or traveled in the area being studied. I think children want to feel connected to the outside world. They appreciate knowing that classroom lessons are not restricted to teachers and students, that the broader community also uses the same knowledge.

Louise Harrold Melucci, Fourth-Grade Teacher
Greenwood School, Warwick, Rhode Island

9

Motivation in the Classroom

Overview 312
What Is Motivation? 312
Behavioral Views of Motivation 313
Cognitive Views of Motivation 315
Humanistic Approaches to Motivation 318
The Learning Process: Influences on Motivation 319
Attitudes toward Learning 321
Meeting Students' Needs 321
What Does Achievement Theory Mean for Teachers? 323
Tapping Interests and Arousing Curiosity 324
Maintaining a Positive Emotional Climate 326
Reinforcement and Fostering a Sense of Competence 328
Teacher Expectations 331
Two Kinds of Expectation Effects 332
Sources of Expectations 334
Teacher Behavior and Student Reactions 335
Anxiety in the Classroom 339
Individual Differences in Anxiety 339
Coping with Anxiety 342
Summary/KeyTerms
Suggestions for Further Reading and Study
Teachers' Forum

"Why don't the students pay attention?" "Kids today don't seem to care about school." "The trouble is these students have no motivation!" If you have spent much time in schools, you have heard these laments before. Most educators have made similar comments at one time or another. Is lack of motivation really at the heart of school failure? We will examine this question and several others here.

We begin with a discussion of the meaning of the term *motivation* and a consideration of three basic orientations: behavioral, cognitive, and humanistic. Many theories have been offered to explain just why people are moved to behave as they do, and in the next section we will explore some of the most influential of these. Using the framework of the learning process, we will examine three questions: (1) What factors influence motivation before a lesson begins? (2) What can the teacher do during the lesson to encourage motivation? (3) How can the outcome of the learning experience foster continuing motivation? We will discuss student attitudes, needs, interests, and curiosity; different goal structures and team learning; and competence and reinforcement. Teachers themselves often unintentionally influence motivation: in the next section, we will focus on the role of teacher expectations. Finally, we will look at the effects of varying levels of student anxiety, a problem that is often overlooked.

By the time you have completed this chapter, you should have a relatively good idea of both the theoretical and the practical roles of motivation in the classroom. More specifically, you should be able to do the following:

- Define the concept of motivation from the behavioral, cognitive, and humanistic points of view, and describe a representative theory from each perspective.
- Give examples of intrinsic and extrinsic motivation.
- List Maslow's seven levels of needs and give a classroom example of each.
- Discuss possible motivational effects that success and failure may have on different students.
- Describe several potential effects of a teacher's expectations of failure and success on the students involved.
- Devise a strategy for teaching a basic subject to an uninterested student and to an anxious student.

WHAT IS MOTIVATION?

motivation:
general process by which behavior is initiated and directed toward a goal

Motivation is usually defined as something that energizes and directs behavior. Obviously, this is a very general definition. How can we be more specific? We all know what it feels like to move energetically toward a chosen goal. What else is involved? Psychologists studying motivation have generally focused on three basic questions. First, what is it that originally causes a person to initiate some action? Second, what causes a person to move toward a particular goal? And third, what causes a person to persist in attempts to reach that goal?

Many activities, interests, and needs compete for students' attention today. During adolescence there is strong competition from extracurricular activities like dating and socializing and from the growing need to develop intimate relationships. *(Dave Schaeffer/Monkmeyer Press)*

Many different answers have been suggested, involving instincts, drives, needs, incentives, goals, social pressure, and more. However, the major explanations of motivation tend to fall into three fairly clear categories: cognitive, behavioral, and humanistic.

Three Views

No matter what their specific explanations for the causes of motivation, psychologists agree that no one can ever be said to be completely unmotivated. Thus, all student behavior is motivated, even staring out the window and avoiding schoolwork. What teachers usually mean when they say students lack motivation is that students are not motivated to do what the teacher has in mind. Psychologists also agree about the significance of motivation in the classroom. Both teachers (Lufler, 1978) and researchers (Walberg & Uguroglu, 1980) maintain that motivating students toward appropriate goals is one of the critical tasks of teaching.

Behavioral Views of Motivation

As we saw in Chapters 5 and 6, behavioral psychologists have developed concepts such as contiguity, reinforcement, punishment, and modeling to explain learning. Those principles also explain motivation: within the strict behavioral framework, to motivate students is really to apply the principles described in Chapter 5 and 6 for strengthening, maintaining, or suppressing behaviors. Behaviorists assume that we have basic physiological needs that motivate us—hunger, thirst, sex, and so on. These needs are met by primary reinforcers such as food. When these needs are met, certain events and experiences are associated with the primary reinforcers, probably through classical conditioning. These associated events become secondary reinforcers. For example, affection becomes associated with food as we are fed and nurtured by our parents. You may remember that one definition of a reinforcer given in Chapter 5 is something you will work to attain. Thus, according to the behavioral view, we are motivated to behave as we do to gain primary and secondary reinforcers and avoid punishment.

If we are consistently reinforced for certain behaviors, we may develop habits or tendencies to act in certain ways. For example, if a student is repeatedly rewarded with affection, money, praise, or privileges for earning letters in baseball but receives little recognition for studying, the student will probably work longer and harder on perfecting her fastball than on understanding geometry. Of course, in any individual case, many other factors affect how a person would behave.

extrinsic motivation: motivation created by external rewards

Motivation based on gaining external rewards that have nothing to do with the learning situation itself is generally called **extrinsic motivation.** Providing grades, points, and other rewards for learning is an attempt to motivate students by extrinsic (external) means.

This is not to imply that behavioral approaches to motivation focus only on reinforcement and punishment. That would be an inaccurate representation of current trends in the area. The recent work of Bandura (1977, 1986) and the social learning theorists has extended the traditional behavioral view of motivation to include cognitive factors such as expectancies ("What will I get out of doing this?"), intentions ("I want to finish this so I can do something else"), anticipations ("This will take too long, so I won't do it"), and self-evaluations ("I am not very good at that, so I'll avoid it"). In fact, Bandura's theory is sometimes classified as a cognitive approach (Bower & Hilgard, 1981). It is discussed with the behavioral theories because it provides an effective bridge to the cognitive approaches.

self-efficacy: beliefs about personal competence in a particular situation

Social Cognitive Theory. Bandura (1977, 1986) suggests several basic sources of motivation. One source consists of thoughts and projections about possible outcomes of behavior: Will I succeed or fail? Will I be liked or laughed at? We imagine future consequences based upon past experiences, the consequences of those experiences, and our observations of others. These projections are also affected by our sense of **self-efficacy.** This is an important aspect of Bandura's theory and refers to our beliefs about our personal competence in a given area. Clearly, our ability to imagine ourselves succeeding at a particular task will be determined by our sense of self-efficacy in that area.

According to Bandura, another source of motivation is the active setting of goals. The goals we set become our standards for evaluating performance. Our sense of self-efficacy comes into play here as well, influencing the goals we will attempt to reach. As we work toward those goals, we imagine the possible positive outcomes of succeeding and the negative outcomes of failing. We tend to persist in our efforts until we meet the standards we have set. Upon reaching our goals, we may be satisfied for a short time but then tend to raise our standards and set new goals.

The *types* of goals we set will also influence the amount of motivation we have to reach them. Goals that are specific, moderately difficult, and likely to be reached in the near future tend to enhance motivation and persistence. Specific goals provide clear standards for judging performance. Moderate difficulty provides a challenge, but not an unreasonable one. Finally, good intentions for distant goals are often overshadowed by more immediate con-

Figure 9–1   Goal-Completion Award

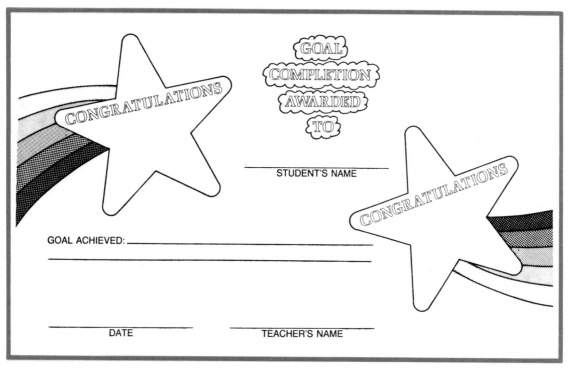

GOAL COMPLETION AWARDED TO

CONGRATULATIONS

CONGRATULATIONS

STUDENT'S NAME

GOAL ACHIEVED: _____

_____

DATE

TEACHER'S NAME

From V. F. & L. S. Jones (1986), Comprehensive classroom management: Creating positive learning environments, *2/e. Copyright © 1986 by Allyn and Bacon, Inc. Reprinted with permission.*

cerns. But goals that can be reached fairly soon are less likely to be abandoned or pushed aside in the day-to-day business of coping. Thus, students are more likely to work toward goals that are clear, specific, reasonable, moderately challenging, and attainable within a relatively short period of time. An award like the one shown in Figure 9–1 may help spur students to set achievable goals.

Cognitive Views of Motivation

One of the central assumptions in cognitive views of motivation is that people do not respond only to external events or to physical conditions like hunger; they also respond to their perceptions of these events. You may have had the experience of being so interested or involved in a project that you missed a meal. You did not even realize you were hungry until you noticed the time. In contrast to the behavioral view, the cognitive view emphasizes **intrinsic** (internal) sources of motivation, such as curiosity, interest in the task for its own sake, the satisfaction of learning, and a sense of accomplishment.

intrinsic motivation: motivation associated with activities that are their own reward

Some cognitive theories assume that humans have a basic need to understand their environment and to be competent, active, and effective in coping with the world (R. W. White, 1959). This is similar to Piaget's notion of equilibration, the active search for mental balance. Equilibration is based on the need to assimilate new information and make it fit cognitive schemes—in other words, the need to understand. So in the cognitive theories, people are seen as active and curious, searching for information to solve personally relevant problems, ignoring even hunger or enduring discomfort to focus on self-selected goals. People work hard because they enjoy the work and because they want to understand.

Attribution Theory.   In the classroom, the quest for understanding often leads to questions about success and failure. Students may ask themselves: "Why did I flunk my midterm?" "What's wrong with my essay?" "Why did I do so well this grading period?" They attempt to explain why things happened as they did, to make *attributions* about causes. Students may attempt to explain their successes and failures by focusing on ability, effort, mood, luck, help, interest, or clarity of instructions. **Attribution theories** of motivation describe how the individual's explanations, justifications, and excuses influence motivation.

attribution theories: cognitive theories concerning how we explain behavior and outcomes, especially successes and failures

Bernard Weiner is one of the main educational psychologists responsible for relating attribution theory to school learning (Weiner, 1979, 1984). According to Weiner, most of the causes to which students attribute their successes or failures can be characterized in three different ways, or as psychologists say, along three different dimensions: as internal or external (inside or outside the person), as stable or unstable, and as controllable or uncontrollable. For example, for older students and adults, ability is an internal, stable, and uncontrollable cause. It is a quality of the individual (internal); it is fairly unchanging—at least over the short term (stable); and it is not controllable—you may be able to change your achievement in an area, but not your basic ability. It seems, however, that younger students tend to view ability as more unstable and controllable (Dweck, 1983). Luck and mood are considered external, unstable, and uncontrollable causes. Effort is internal and unstable (it can be more or less) but controllable, whereas a particular task's difficulty is external, stable, and uncontrollable.

Weiner (1979, 1984) believes that each of these dimensions has important implications for motivation. The internal/external dimension, for example, seems to be closely related to feelings of confidence, self-esteem, pride, guilt, or shame (Weiner, 1980). If success or failure is attributed to internal factors, success will lead to pride and increased motivation, whereas failure leads to shame. If the causes are seen as external, gratitude might follow success, and anger could follow failure. This dimension is closely related to Rotter's (1954) idea of **locus of control.** Rotter suggested that some people have an internal locus of control. They believe they are responsible for their own fate and like to work in situations where skill and effort can lead to success. Other people tend to have an external locus of control, generally believing that people and forces outside themselves control their lives. These individuals prefer to work in situations where luck determines the outcome (Lefcourt, 1966).

locus of control: "where" people locate responsibility for successes and failures—inside or outside themselves

The stability dimension seems to be closely related to expectations about the future. If, for example, students attribute their success (or failure) to stable factors such as ability or the difficulty of the test, they are likely to expect to succeed (or fail) on similar tasks in the future. But if they attribute the outcome to unstable factors such as mood or luck, they are likely to expect changes in the future when confronted with similar tasks.

The control dimension is probably related to both confidence and future expectations, although more research is needed to confirm this. A student who attributes a high grade on a history exam to controllable factors takes pride in the grade and expects to achieve a similar grade on future tests. But if the student thinks the grade had very little or nothing to do with controllable factors—"It was a fluke"; "I just happened to feel sharp that day"—he or she is likely only to feel grateful and perhaps to hope that the good luck will continue.

Attributions and Student Motivation. Students usually try to explain their failures to themselves. Generally successful students may make external attributions, deciding, for example, that the test was unfair or the teacher was biased. They may also make internal attributions—they misunderstood the directions or simply did not study hard enough. When students see themselves as capable and attribute failure to lack of effort (an internal, controllable cause), they usually focus on strategies for succeeding next time. This is a positive, adaptive response, one likely to lead to achievement, pride, and a greater sense of control (Ames, 1985).

But the greatest problems of motivation arise when students attribute failures to internal, stable, and uncontrollable causes such as ability. They may seem resigned to failure, depressed, helpless—what we generally call "unmotivated" (Weiner, Russell, & Lerman, 1978). These students respond to failure by focusing even more on their own inadequacy; their attitudes toward schoolwork may deteriorate even further (Ames, 1985). Apathy is a logical reaction to failure if students believe the causes are their own doing (internal), are unlikely to change (stable), and are beyond their control anyway. In addition, students who view their failures in this light are less likely to seek help—they believe nothing and no one *could* help (Ames & Lau, 1982). They may even develop what has been called **learned helplessness,** the sense that nothing they do will matter, that they are doomed to fail (Maier, Seligman, & Solomon, 1969).

Just telling students that 'trying harder" will lead to future achievement is not particularly effective. They don't think any amount of trying will change things. The students need real evidence that effort will pay off in order to believe the situation could change. One promising approach is to emphasize the progress the student has made in a particular area and stress the connection between past efforts and past accomplishments (Schunk, 1982, 1985). You might return work with very specific suggestions for improvements, then revise the student's grade when improvements are made. Another possibility is to keep a portfolio for each student with examples of particularly good work. During individual conferences you can discuss with students how they accomplished these assignments. There is no substitute for continuing success. In order to keep trying, students must be successful a good portion of the time, and they must attribute some of that success to their own efforts.

At the heart of attribution theory is the notion of individual perception. If students believe they lack the ability to deal with higher mathematics, they probably will act on this belief even if their actual abilities are well

Control and Confidence

learned helplessness: sense that one is doomed to fail, based on past experiences

above average. These students are likely to have little motivation to tackle trigonometry or calculus, since they expect to do poorly in these areas.

Humanistic Approaches to Motivation

Humanistic psychology emphasizes personal freedom, choice, self-determination, and striving for personal growth. This means, of course, that like the cognitive approaches, humanistic views stress intrinsic motivation.

In many humanistic theories, the role of needs is central. According to Kolesnik (1978), a **need** can be defined as "any type of deficiency in the human organism or the absence of anything the person requires, or thinks he requires, for his overall well-being" (p. 149). But our needs are seldom if ever satisfied completely and perfectly; improvement is always possible. People are thus motivated primarily by their needs, or by the tensions the needs create. Their behavior can be seen as movement toward goals they believe will help satisfy their needs. Let's look at how one very influential humanistic theory of motivation deals with this central concept.

Maslow's Hierarchy. Abraham Maslow has had a great impact on psychology in general and on the psychology of motivation in particular. Maslow (1970) has suggested that human needs function as a hierarchy. Lower-level needs for survival and safety are the most essential. We all require food, air, water, and shelter; we all seek freedom from danger. These needs determine our behavior until they are met. But once we are physically comfortable and secure, we are stimulated to fulfill needs on the next levels—social needs for belonging and love and needs for self-esteem. And when these needs are more or less satisfied, we turn to the higher-level needs for intellectual achievement, aesthetic appreciation, and finally self-actualization. **Self-actualization** is Maslow's term for self-fulfillment, the realization of personal potential. Figure 9–2 is a graph of Maslow's hierarchy.

Maslow (1968) has called the four lower-level needs—for survival, safety, belonging, and self-esteem—**deficiency needs.** When these needs are not met, motivation increases to find ways of satisfying them. When they are satisfied, the motivation for fulfilling them decreases. Maslow has labeled the three higher-level needs—intellectual achievement, aesthetic appreciation, and self-actualization—**being needs.** When they are met, a person's motivation does not cease; instead, it increases to seek further fulfillment. For example, the more successful you are in your efforts to know and understand, the harder you are likely to strive for even greater knowledge and understanding. So unlike the deficiency needs, these being needs can never be completely filled. The motivation to achieve them is endlessly renewed.

Maslow's theory has been criticized for the very obvious reason that people do not always appear to behave as the theory would predict. Most of us move back and forth among different types of needs and may even be motivated by many different needs at the same time. Some people deny themselves safety or friendship in order to achieve knowledge, understanding, or greater self-esteem. But Maslow's theory remains one of the most complete explanations of needs and motivation thus far formulated. Also, it gives us a way of looking at the full person, whose physical, emotional, and intellectual needs are all interrelated.

Figure 9–2 **Maslow's Hierarchy of Needs**

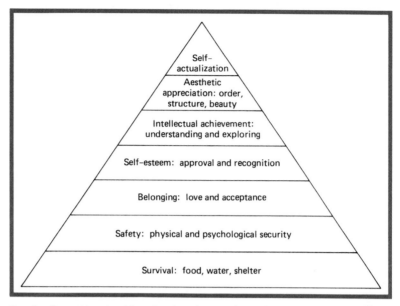

Data (for diagram) based on Hierarchy of Needs in ''A Theory of Human Motivation'' in Motivation and Personality, 2/e by Abraham Maslow. Copyright © 1970 by Abraham H. Maslow. Reprinted by permission of Harper & Row, Publishers, Inc.

Educational
Implications

This has important implications for education. Students who come to school hungry, sick, or hurt are unlikely to be motivated to seek knowledge and understanding. A child whose feelings of safety and sense of belonging are threatened by divorce may have little interest in learning to divide fractions. If the classroom is a fearful, unpredictable place and students seldom know where they stand, they are likely to be more concerned with security and less with learning. Also, Maslow's hierarchy can provide insight into students' behavior. Their desires to fill lower-level needs may at times conflict with a teacher's desire to have them achieve higher-level goals. Belonging to a social group and maintaining self-esteem within that group, for example, are important to students. If doing what the teacher says conflicts with group rules, students may choose to ignore the teacher's wishes or even defy the teacher. We will look at more specific implications and applications of Maslow's theory in the next section when we discuss considering students' needs before the lesson begins.

THE LEARNING PROCESS: INFLUENCES ON MOTIVATION

One way to organize the vast amount of information on motivation is to consider the factors that influence motivation at different times in the learning process itself (Wlodkowski, 1981). As students begin a lesson or class, they bring with them particular attitudes and needs. Both influence moti-

Figure 9–3   Motivation in the Learning Cycle

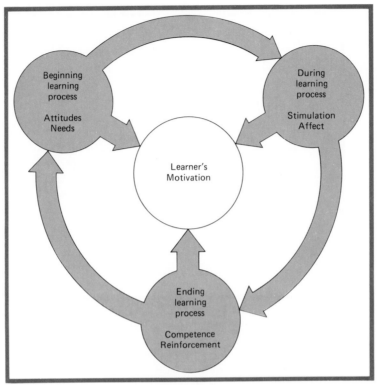

From R. J. Wlodkowski (1982), Motivation and teaching: A practical guide. *Washington, DC: National Education Assoc. Press. Copyright 1978 by R. J. Wlodkowski. Used with permission.*

vation to participate, as Maslow might point out. During the lesson, the immediate stimulation of the activities and the students' feelings about the experience itself have powerful effects on motivation. At the end of the lesson, if the students are left with a sense of competence from their own accomplishments or their efforts are reinforced in other ways, they will be more motivated to pursue similar tasks in the future. Figure 9–3 shows how all these elements act together to influence the learner's motivation.

Interrelated Influences

As you can see in the figure, the different influences on motivation are all related. Obviously it is artificial to separate needs and attitudes from interests or reinforcement. One reason to approach motivation in this way is simply to provide a structure for organizing and remembering the information. Then, in the future, when you think about motivating students, you can remember many possible strategies by thinking about what factors might be considered before, during, and after a lesson.

Wlodkowski (1981) has suggested that teachers ask themselves two questions related to motivation before beginning an activity: (1) What can I do to guarantee a positive attitude toward the upcoming activity? (2) How can I best meet my students' needs through this activity?

Attitudes toward Learning

Positive Attitudes

To answer the first question about guaranteeing positive attitudes, you must know what influences students' attitudes toward the topic or subject at the outset. We discussed the formation of positive and negative attitudes about school when we considered the applications of classical conditioning in Chapter 5. Applying these principles would mean making the conditions surrounding the topic or lesson as positive as possible. In addition to associating pleasant experiences with learning, teachers can also confront negative attitudes directly. In math classes, teachers might ask how many students believe the material is too hard. What is the basis for those impressions? What would make the material easier? As you can see in Figure 9–3, prior experiences with similar lessons and situations greatly influence attitudes. This means that today's math lesson will in turn affect attitudes toward math tomorrow. The development of positive attitudes is an ongoing challenge to teachers.

Meeting Students' Needs

Maslow's theory can suggest ways to plan activities that meet students' needs and increase motivation. Remember that lower-level needs must be met before higher-level needs can become motivating. To make students feel safer and more secure with difficult material, you might organize extra tutoring sessions (Wlodkowski, 1981). You can also create a psychologically safer class environment: wrong answers and mistakes can become occasions for learning, for probing the thinking behind the answers, instead of simply occasions for criticism (Fetterman & Rohrkemper, 1986). Needs for belonging and self-esteem might be met in part by allowing students to work in teams. We will discuss this possibility more fully later in the chapter.

A great deal has been written about needs and motivation. For teaching, the most fully developed and relevant work involves the need to achieve.

Achievement Needs. David McClelland and John Atkinson were among the first to concentrate on the study of **achievement motivation** (McClelland, Atkinson, Clark, & Lowell, 1953). People who strive for excellence in a field for the sake of achieving and not for some reward are considered to have a high need for achievement. This need has been labeled n-Ach for convenience.

achievement motivation: desire to excel; striving for excellence and success

The origins of high achievement motivation are assumed to be in the family and cultural group of the child. As you might guess from our discussions of parenting styles and cultures in Chapter 3, if achievement, initiative, and competitiveness are encouraged and reinforced in the home, and if parents let children solve problems on their own without becoming irritated by the children's initial failures, children are more likely to develop a high need for achievement (Kolesnik, 1978; McClelland & Pilon, 1983). Children who see that their actions can have an impact on their environment and who are taught how to recognize a good performance are more likely to grow up with the desire to excel (Morris, 1985).

Atkinson (1964) added a new consideration to the theory of achievement

Fear of failure can cause some students to avoid activities that require public performances. But coping successfully with this fear can help students take more risks in the future. A student who is very concerned about failure needs especially gentle direction during play rehearsal. *(Pam Hasegawa/Taurus Photos)*

resultant motivation: whichever is the stronger tendency—the need to achieve or the need to avoid failure

need when he noted that all people have a need to avoid failure as well as a need to achieve. If our need to achieve in a particular situation is greater than the need to avoid failure, the overall tendency, or **resultant motivation,** will be to take the risk and try to achieve. On the other hand, if the need to avoid failure is greater, the risk will be threatening rather than challenging. An extended example should help clarify Atkinson's views.

A coach wants the school team to try a new routine at the gymnastic meet coming up in two months. The routine involves several new and very difficult movements. If the movements are executed well, the team is certain to win the meet. If the team tries but fails, it is sure to lose.

Jennifer is one of the best gymnasts on the team and could probably master the movements with ease. But she insists on perfecting the old routine instead of learning a new one. She is immobilized by her fear of embarrassing herself in front of so many people. For Jennifer, the fear of failure is greater than the need for achievement in this particular situation.

Another member of the team, Kelly, is very eager to try the new routine. While she and Jennifer are similar in ability, Kelly is less afraid of embarrassment and is willing to work at mastering the new movements. She is generally the last to leave every practice session and seems to look forward to new challenges. Kelly's need for achievement overcomes any fear of failure.

Effects on Students

If students' motivation to achieve is greater than their motivation to avoid failure, a moderate amount of failure can often enhance their desire to pursue a problem. They are determined to achieve, so they try again. If Kelly, for example, were to fall off the balance beam (uninjured!), she would be likely to try even harder to master the balance beam movements. On the other hand, success gained too easily can actually decrease motivation for those with high achievement needs. Kelly probably realizes this. Just relying on the old routine is not particularly challenging or motivating for her.

In contrast, students motivated by the need to avoid failure are usually discouraged by failure and encouraged by success. Jennifer, for example, might quit the team if she were embarrassed publicly by her mistakes. If the old routine won the meet, however, she probably would experience unqualified pleasure as well as relief.

Achievement Motivation and Self-Worth. Covington and his colleagues have attempted to specify the connections between the attributions we make, our need for achievement, and our self-worth (Covington, 1984; Covington & Beery, 1976; Covington & Olemich, 1979, 1984). They suggest that there are three kinds of students: mastery-oriented, failure-avoiding, and failure-accepting.

Mastery-oriented students are generally successful and see themselves as capable. They are high in achievement motivation and tend to take risks and to select moderately challenging problems. They perform best in competitive situations, learn fast, assume responsibility readily, are more persistent in the face of failure, have more self-confidence and energy, are more tense, welcome concrete feedback, and are eager to learn "the rules of the game" so they can succeed (Alderman, 1985; McClelland, 1985; Morris, 1985).

Failure-avoiding students have experienced some successes and a good bit of failure but still have not formed a firm sense of their own competence and self-worth. In other words, the question of their own general competence is still open in their minds. In order to protect themselves (and their self-images) from failure, they may procrastinate—a form of avoidance. This allows them to justify a low grade by saying, "I did OK considering I didn't start the assignment until last night." Or they may set very low or very high goals. Setting unrealistically high goals that are almost impossible to reach provides some protection from failure, because "no one could have succeeded at that!" Finally, they may exert very little effort, since to try hard and fail would be a sure sign of low ability.

Unfortunately, failure-avoiding strategies are self-defeating, generally leading to the very failure the students try to avoid. If failures continue and excuses wear thin, the students may finally decide that they are incompetent. This is what they fear in the first place, but they come to accept it. Their sense of self-worth deteriorates. They give up and thus become failure-accepting students. They are convinced that their problems are due to low ability and that there is little hope for change. They can no longer protect themselves from this conclusion. As we saw earlier, students who attribute failure to low ability are likely to become depressed, apathetic, and helpless.

Teachers may be able to prevent some failure-avoiding students from becoming failure-accepting by helping them to find new and more realistic goals. Also, some students may need support in aspiring to higher levels in the face of sexual or ethnic stereotypes about what they "should" want or what they "should not" be able to do well. This kind of support could make all the difference.

What Does Achievement Theory Mean for Teachers?

Since needs for achievement vary from one individual to another, it may help in planning activities to know where students stand—which students, for instance, have high achievement needs, which are low in achievement

Table 9–1   Achievement Motivation: Restructuring a High School Phys. Ed. Class

First day
Individual goal-setting: Students do self-evaluations of physical fitness, competence, interests; set yearly goals for themselves.

Weekly
Concrete feedback: Weekly self-tests in flexibility, strength, posture; individual scores recorded in team notebook.

Three times a week
Practicing skills: Students set their own specific schedules to practice three times a week; practices recorded on individual cards.

End of first grading period
Checking for realistic goals: Based on scores from self-tests, students set final exam goals for themselves, compare goals to original yearly goals. Variety of ways available to reach each type of goal; for aerobic goals, students can jog, walk, jump rope. Instructor meets with each student to discuss goals.

After final exam
Self-evaluation: Students evaluate what they have learned.

Adapted from M. Alderman & M. Cohen, Eds. (1985), Motivation theory and practice for preservice teachers. Washington, DC: Eric Clearinghouse on Teacher Education, pp. 50–51.

needs, and which seem primarily motivated by a need to avoid failure. Those who are more highly motivated to achieve are likely to respond well to challenging assignments, strict grading, corrective feedback, new or unusual problems, and the chance to try again. But less challenging assignments, ample reinforcement for success, small steps for each task, lenient grading, and protection from embarrassment are probably more successful strategies for those students who are very eager to avoid failure.

An example of a high school girls' physical education class designed to develop achievement motivation is shown in Table 9–1.

Tapping Interests and Arousing Curiosity

It seems logical that learning experiences should be related to the interests of the students. But this is not always an easy or even a desirable strategy; there are times when students must master basic skills that hold no intrinsic interest for them. Nevertheless, if a teacher knows what students' interests are, these can be part of many teaching strategies. Sylvia Ashton-Warner (1963), for example, has described a system for teaching reading by using students' own stories about topics of interest to them.

Discovering Interests   There are a number of ways to determine students' interests (Rust, 1977). The most direct is to ask the students themselves, either in a discussion or through a questionnaire. You can also observe students during their free time. How do they spend it? Attentiveness during classroom lessons is another key. Once you have an understanding of your students' interests, you can apply this knowledge in your teaching. Three examples should show some of the many ways student interests can encourage classroom motivation.

One high school teacher used students' interest in popular and rock music to make the science laboratory a more pleasant place to work.

A music teacher encouraged an interest in Bach by helping students see how certain popular music used a similar style.

A history teacher discovered that some students were interested in historical novels. "What was the truth about Anne Boleyn?" one student asked. A brief argument ensued, with the other historical-novel fans giving their opinions. The library assignment that followed was geared to help students see how historical novels rely on (and bend) history. The students were also given a chance to learn about historical documents and to debate the questions about Anne Boleyn.

In this last example, the teacher is also modeling an inquiring approach, a willingness to follow the threads of student interest.

What's This?!

Curiosity is another important aspect of motivation that teachers can stimulate and encourage. How? The old saying "Variety is the spice of life" holds true for school. The classroom should be an interesting, provocative (though of course safe) place. In an unchanging environment, students are bound to get bored (Vidler, 1977). One teacher I know has an "interesting table," a rotating exhibit of strange, beautiful, or hard-to-identify items that students bring in.

Displays or activities designed to arouse curiosity can be built into the lesson or unit. These should be matched to the cognitive abilities of the students. For younger students, the chance to manipulate and explore objects relevant to what is being studied may be the most effective way to keep curiosity stimulated. For older students, well-constructed questions or abstract, logical puzzles designed as part of the lesson can have the same effect. Other possibilities for older students and adults are the presentation of problems involving paradoxes and contradictions (Vidler, 1977) or role playing and simulations (Stewart, 1980). One example is a NASA simulation experiment that asks students the most important items to take on a space trip. This exercise might be a good opener or midpoint activity for a unit about the solar system or space travel.

Many students are interested in dinosaurs. If a trip to a museum is followed by reading, science, writing, or mathematics lessons that build on the museum experience, motivation for the lessons may be high. *(Mike Kagan/ Monkmeyer Press)*

Table 9–2 **Different Goal Structures**

Cooperative	Students believe their goal is attainable if and only if other students will also reach the goal.
Competitive	Students believe they will reach their goal if and only if other students do *not* reach the goal.
Individualistic	Students believe their own attempt to reach a goal is not related to other students' attempts to reach goals.

Adapted from D. Johnson & R. Johnson (1975), Learning together and alone: Cooperation, competition, and indi-vidualization. *Englewood Cliffs, NJ: Prentice-Hall, pp. 7 and 32.*

Maintaining a Positive Emotional Climate

Students in the classroom function as part of a large group. Johnson and Johnson (1975, 1978) have given considerable attention to this in their work on motivation. They have found that motivation can be greatly influenced by the ways in which we relate to the other people who are also involved in the accomplishment of a particular goal. Johnson and Johnson have la-beled this interpersonal factor the **goal structure** of the task. There are three such structures: cooperative, competitive, and individualistic, as shown in Table 9–2.

goal structure: the way students strive toward a goal in relation to others

Johnson and Johnson have stressed that a cooperative goal structure works best for most school situations and learning tasks. Other psycholo-gists have disagreed with this emphasis on the grounds that individual dif-ferences in abilities require more individualistic approaches to the learning of concepts, principles, and so on. But Johnson and Johnson have based their belief in the appropriateness of cooperative goal structures on a num-ber of research studies. Several studies have shown, for example, that when the task involves complex learning and problem-solving skills, cooperation leads to higher achievement than competition, especially for low-ability stu-dents (Davis, Laughlin, & Komorita, 1976; Edwards & DeVries, 1974; Slavin, 1977). In another study, achievement for all students was increased when the group was rewarded based on the average learning of the group mem-bers (Slavin, 1983). In addition, cooperative learning seems to result in im-proved ability to see the world from another person's point of view (Bridge-man, 1977), in better relations among different ethnic groups in schools and classrooms, in increased self-esteem, and in greater acceptance of handi-capped and low-achieving students (Slavin, 1986).

Benefits of Cooperative Structures

Thus, in the cooperative goal structure, each person's individual efforts contribute to the benefit of both the individual and the group. All the people in the group are working toward a single outcome. Materials and responsi-bilities can be shared. Students can learn to negotiate and to be more toler-ant of others. The interaction with peers that students seem to enjoy so much becomes a part of the learning process. The need for belonging de-scribed by Maslow is more likely to be met.

Using Cooperative Techniques.   Many activities can be approached coop-eratively. Here are a few examples:

Students can work together in conducting local surveys. How do people feel about the plan to build a new mall that will bring more shopping *and* more traffic? Would the community support or oppose the building of a nuclear power plant?

All the students in a class may gain a better understanding of the difference between an acre and a hectare if they work together to mark out and measure the two different areas.

What kind of assistance should underdeveloped countries be given? What should be done about terrorism? The class as a whole can discuss and make decisions about this type of social question.

But cooperative learning is not limited to specific or elaborate activities like these. Many of the most ordinary assignments can be enhanced by cooperation. If students must learn ten new definitions in a biology class, why not let students divide up the terms and definitions and teach one another? Be sure, however, that everyone in the group can handle the task; sometimes a cooperative effort ends with one or two students doing the work of the entire group. Work groups should be monitored to make sure that each person is contributing and that hostilities, if they develop, are resolved in some positive way.

Potential Problems

However, even if the group as a whole is successful in reaching the goal, there is still no guarantee that every student has benefited equally. In practice, the effects of learning in a group vary, depending on what actually happens in the group and who is in it. If only a few people take responsibility for the work, these people will learn, but the nonparticipating members probably will not. Students who ask questions, get answers, and attempt explanations are more likely to learn than students whose questions go unasked or unanswered. In setting up the groups, it often makes sense to balance the number of boys and girls. Some research indicates that when there are just a few girls in a group, they tend to be left out of the discussions unless they are the most able or assertive members. When there are only one or two boys in the group, they tend to dominate and be "interviewed" by the girls unless these boys are less able than the girls or very shy. In general, for very shy and introverted students, individual learning may be a better approach (Webb, 1980, 1985). No matter what, teachers must monitor groups to make sure everyone is contributing and learning.

Robert Slavin and his associates have developed a system for overcoming the disadvantages of the cooperative goal structure while maintaining its advantages. The system is called **Student Teams-Achievement Divisions,** or **STAD** (Slavin, 1978, 1980a, 1980b, 1986). Each team has about five members, with a mix of abilities, ethnic backgrounds, and sexes. The teacher calculates an **individual learning expectation** score, or base score, for each team member. This score is based on previous work and represents the student's average level of performance. Details about how to determine the base scores are given in Table 9–3.

Student Teams-Achievement Divisions (STAD): cooperative learning with heterogeneous groups and elements of competition and reward

individual learning expectation: constantly recomputed average score in a subject

Students work in their teams to study and prepare for twice-weekly quizzes, but they take the quizzes individually, just as in a regular class. Based on test performance, each team member can earn from one to three points for the group. Table 9–3 shows how points are awarded by comparing each student's current test score to his or her base score (Slavin, 1980b). As you can see from the table, every student has an equal chance to contribute the maximum number of points to the team total. Thus, every student, not just the most able or motivated, has reason to work hard. This way, the

Table 9–3 Using Individual Learning Expectations

The idea behind individual learning expectations, or ILEs, is that students ought to be judged in relation to their own abilities and not compared to others. The focus is on improvement, not on comparisons among students.

To calculate an ILE score, the teacher simply averages the student's grades or test scores from previous work. These scores are usually on a 100-point scale. Letter grades can be converted to points based on the school's system—for example, A = 90 points, B = 80 points, and so on. The student's average score is her or his initial base score. The ILE score becomes the standard for judging each student's work.

If the teacher is using the STAD system of cooperative learning, then students earn points for their group based on the following system:

Test Score	Points Earned for Group
A perfect score	3
10 or more points above base score	3
5 to 9 points above base score	2
4 points below to 4 points above base (ILE) score	1
5 or more points below base score	0

problem of students' unequal contributions to a group project is avoided. Every week, the group earning the greatest number of points is declared the winner. Team accomplishments should be recognized in a class newsletter like the one in Figure 9–4 or on a bulletin board display. Every few weeks the teams can be changed so that students have a chance to work with many different class members.

Every two weeks or so the teacher must recompute the base score by averaging the old base score with grades on the recent tests. With this system, improvement pays off for all students. Those with less ability can still earn the maximum for their team by scoring ten or more points above their own base score. Those with greater ability are still challenged because they must score well above their own average or make a perfect score to contribute the maximum to the group total.

Individualistic Structures

In an individualistic goal structure, students work independently and are evaluated only on their own achievements, regardless of how others do in the class. But there has been little research on individualistic structures. Most studies have focused on competition and cooperation.

Reinforcement and Fostering a Sense of Competence

If you look back at Figure 9–3, you see that competence and reinforcement influence motivation at the end of the learning experience. What can teachers do to increase student feelings of competence?

First, a teacher can help students see the connections between their actions and the outcome of the lesson. What did students do to overcome problems they encountered? If they made mistakes and did not correct them, how might they monitor their work more effectively next time? In raising these questions, the teacher is attempting to nurture a sense of re-

Figure 9–4   Sample STAD Newsletter

SPOTSYLVANIA ELEMENTARY SCHOOL

Issue No. 5
March 21, 198—

CALCULATORS OUTFIGURE CLASS!

The Calculators (Charlene, Alfredo, Laura, and Carl) calculated their way into first place this week, with big three-point scores by Charlene, Alfredo, and Carl, and a near-perfect team score of 11! Their score jumped them from sixth to third in cumulative rank. Way to go Calcs! The Fantastic Four (Frank, Otis, Ursula, and Rebecca) also did a fantastic job, with Ursula and Rebecca turning in three-pointers, but the Tigers (Cissy, Lindsay, Arthur, and Willy) clawed their way from last place last week to a tie with the red-hot Four, who were second the first week and first last week. The Fantastic Four stayed in first place in cumulative rank. The Tigers were helped out by three-point scores from Lindsay and Arthur. The Math Monsters (Helen, Octavia, Ulysses, and Luis) held on to fourth place this week, but due to their big first-place score in the first week they're still in second place in overall rank. Helen and Luis got three points to help the M.M.'s. Just behind the Math Monsters were the Live Wires (Carlos, Irene, Nancy, Charles, and Oliver), with three-point scores by Carlos and Charles, and then in order the Little Professors, Fractions, and Brains. Susan turned in three points for the L.P.'s as did Linda for the Brains.

This Week's Rank	This Week's Score	Overall Score	Overall Rank
1st–Calculators	11	61	3
2nd–Fantastic Four	9	64	1
2nd–Tigers	9	50	6
4th–Math Monsters	8	62	2
5th–Live Wires	7	56	5
6th–Little Professors	6	46	8
7th–Fractions	5	58	4
8th–Brains	4	48	7

THREE-POINT SCORES

Charlene	(Calculators)	Helen	(Math Monsters)
Alfredo	(Calculators)	Luis	(Math Monsters)
Carl	(Calculators)	Carlos	(Live Wires)
Ursula	(Fantastic Four)	Charles	(Live Wires)
Rebecca	(Fantastic Four)	Susan	(Little Professors)
Lindsay	(Tigers)	Linda	(Brains)
Arthur	(Tigers)		

* * * * *

Adapted from R. Slavin (1980), Using student team learning (rev. ed.). Baltimore: Center for Social Organization of Schools, The John Hopkins University.

sponsibility, which is an important element of competence. Several psychologists have suggested that this sense of personal causation is the key to motivation, and they have designed a special program to teach it.

Origins and Pawns: A Special Program to Enhance Competence. In 1976, Richard de Charms published a book called *Enhancing Motivation: Change in the Classroom,* describing the results of a four-year effort to enhance motivation in several elementary and junior high classrooms. The program was based on de Charms's (1968) study of classroom motivation and the characterization of students as "origins" and "pawns." We will look first at the results of his earlier work and then at the program itself.

origins: those who take responsibility for setting and reaching their own goals

pawns: those who feel helpless and out of control of their fate

According to de Charms (1968), **origins** are people who are in control of their own achievement. They have developed goal-setting skills and can plan strategies to reach these goals, and they are willing to take responsibility for their own actions. In contrast, **pawns** are people who are at the mercy of the environment and feel helpless in the face of its forces. Some situations seem to encourage pawnlike behavior; others seem to encourage people to be achievement-oriented origins. De Charms believes that schools should create environments in which students have as many chances as possible to act as origins, although not all students are able to do so immediately.

As a result of these earlier studies, de Charms became involved in a special program to enhance motivation in the schools. The elementary and junior high teachers in the program were asked to introduce their students to a number of the concepts we have been discussing in this chapter: (1) self-worth, (2) achievement motivation, (3) realistic goal setting, and (4) the origin/pawn distinction. Games, exercises, creative writing, journals, artwork, and other techniques were used to help students understand these ideas. Table 9–4 shows one of the methods for teaching the origin/pawn concept to sixth and seventh graders.

In this exercise and in others used in the program, students were asked to set reasonable goals, make concrete plans to reach those goals, devise ways of evaluating their progress, and assume personal responsibility. These are all steps toward becoming self-motivated. They are also in many ways reminiscent of the social cognitive and achievement motivation theories as well as of the research on metacognitive skills and self-management. De Charms has brought all these ideas together in his program. Attribution theory, too, is applied: by helping students to see themselves as origins, this

Table 9–4   Training Students to Be Origins

Approach: Introduce a set of words describing origin behavior, along with a gimmick—the use of the letter *p*—to hold student attention.

Origins are people who:
- (a) take *personal* responsibility
- (b) *prepare* their work carefully
- (c) *plan* their lives to help them reach their goals
- (d) *practice* their skills
- (e) *persist* in their work
- (f) have *patience*—they know that some goals take time to reach
- (g) *perform*—they know they have to do certain things to reach their goals
- (h) check their *progress* (use feedback)
- (i) move toward *perfecting* their skills, paying special attention to improvement.

Activity: Students are asked to set personal goals and construct checklists to keep track of the number of times they act in accordance with their goals.

Adapted from Richard de Charms (1976), Enhancing motivation: Change in the classroom. © 1976 by Irvington Publishers, Inc., New York. Used with permission.

type of program encourages them to view their successes and failures as the outgrowth of internal, controllable causes. All these factors contribute to a sense of personal competence.

Incentives for Learning.   Not every lesson successfully completed will enhance a sense of competence. Some activities necessarily involve drill and repetition. Students may feel "competent enough," so they have no intrinsic interest in working on the task to improve their competence. In this case, the teacher may decide to provide extrinsic reinforcement for successful completion of the work. Practicing math facts, doing your 30 daily sit-ups, repeating the French dialogue for the fifteenth time, or memorizing the symbols for the chemical elements are all tasks that might be completed more readily with the incentive of a reward at the end.

Some students—those with less ability, a low need for achievement, inadequate preparation, a history of failing in a particular subject, or a poor academic self-concept—may need extra incentives at the outset in order to tackle what for them is a difficult task. In these situations, the teacher may plan the lesson to include systematic reinforcement. Chapters 5 and 6 described many approaches for applying the principles of reinforcement to enhance motivation and pointed out instances when using these principles is not advisable. Although we noted this before, it bears repeating, since external rewards used inappropriately can undermine students' natural interest in a subject (Cohen, 1985; Deci, 1975).

Up to this point we have considered the deliberate process of planning lessons. The Guidelines on the following pages summarize the main principles we have discussed. In the next sections, we will examine subtle and often unplanned factors that might affect student motivation.

Margin note: Providing Extrinsic Reinforcement

TEACHER EXPECTATIONS

Almost 20 years ago, a study by Rosenthal and Jacobson (1968) captured the attention of the national media in a way that few studies by psychologists have since. Articles in newspapers across the country reported the seemingly remarkable effects of *Pygmalion in the classroom*, which was the title of the book written about the experiment. The study also caused great controversy within the professional community. Debate about the meaning of the results continues, and so does research (Braun, 1976; Brophy, 1982; Mendels & Flanders, 1973; Snow, 1969; Wilkins & Glock, 1973).

What did Rosenthal and Jacobson do that caused such a stir? They chose several students at random in a number of elementary school classrooms, then told the teachers that these students probably would make significant intellectual gains during the year. The students did indeed make larger gains than normal that year. The researchers presented data suggesting the existence of a self-fulfilling prophecy in the classroom. A **self-fulfilling prophecy** is essentially a false or groundless expectation that comes true simply because it has been expected. In the classroom this means that a teacher's incorrect beliefs about students' abilities or behaviors in some way bring about the very behaviors the teacher expects.

The original study was heavily criticized for the experimental and statistical methods used (Elashoff & Snow, 1971; Snow, 1969); several researchers

Margin note: **self-fulfilling prophecy:** an incorrect expectation that is confirmed because it has been expected

Guidelines

Applying the Theories of Motivation

Make the classroom and the lesson inviting and interesting.

Examples
1. *Use puzzles, games, and simulations that demonstrate the concepts you are teaching.*
2. *Try new desk arrangements or room arrangements.*
3. *Introduce a lesson with music or put up posters related to the material.*
4. *Relate class work to field trips, guest speakers, news events.*

Make sure that students have a sufficient chance to fulfill their needs for affiliation and belonging.

Examples
1. *Provide some time for interaction with friends, possibly as a reinforcement for positive academic and social behavior.*
2. *After teaching a difficult concept, ask students to check their understanding by explaining the material to the student beside them.*
3. *When work is particularly anxiety-provoking (oral reports, major tests), have students work in groups to prepare.*

Make the classroom a pleasant and safe place.

Examples
1. *Provide tutors for students who are falling behind.*
2. *Choose assignments to ensure that each student experiences success more often than failure. If students are having trouble, break the work into smaller steps and teach the steps.*
3. *Do not permit ridicule or public criticisms of a student by other students.*

Recognize the possibility that students come to school with different patterns of needs based on past experiences.

Examples
1. *Students who are overly concerned with achievement may need help in relaxing. Give some ungraded assignments, or let the students redo or revise work to improve it.*

such as Claiborn (1969) and Wilkins and Glock (1973) tried but were unable to replicate the findings. However, other researchers have found results supporting the idea that teachers' expectations can influence student performance (Cornbleth, Davis, & Button, 1974; Good, 1970; Pippert, 1969). Let's look first at the kinds of effects that can occur and then at how they might come about.

Two Kinds of Expectation Effects

Actually, two kinds of expectation effects can occur in classrooms. The first is the self-fulfilling prophecy described above. In this situation the teacher's beliefs about the student's abilities are actually incorrect, but student behavior comes to match the initially inaccurate expectation. The second kind of expectation effect occurs when teachers are fairly accurate in their initial

2. *Students who have a great need to avoid failure may need ways of working that protect them from public embarrassment or criticism. Have individual conferences to discuss progress. Consider using the individual learning expectations system (ILE) to recognize improvement.*

Help students take appropriate responsibility for successes and failures.

Examples
1. *When you make a mistake or when your work is less than perfect, discuss it with your students. Be appropriately critical of yourself, and take responsibility for your mistakes.*
2. *Invite guest speakers who are willing to speak about their own successes and failures.*
3. *See the humor in situations. Failure should not be grim defeat. Sometimes mistakes are funny.*

Encourage students to see the connections between their own efforts and accomplishments.

Examples
1. *After completing a complex assignment, ask students to discuss what was especially hard about the assignment and how they conquered it.*
2. *Discuss reasons for particular successes as well as failures.*
3. *Avoid making quick judgments about the reasons for a student's success or failure. When things don't work out as expected, take the time to discuss what might be done to avoid the problems next time. Reinforce good problem diagnosis and planning.*

Help students set reasonable short-term goals.

Examples
1. *Encourage students who set low goals to raise them a little at a time.*
2. *When students set unrealistically high goals, suggest alternatives.*
3. *Have students write goals for the day or week in a notebook, then share the goals with their work group. Ask the students to indicate when and where they will work on the goal, what materials they will need, and when they expect to finish.*

sustaining expectation effect: student performance maintained at a certain level because teachers don't recognize improvements

reading of students' abilities and respond to students based on those readings. So far, so good. There is nothing wrong with forming and acting on accurate estimates of student ability. Indeed, many teachers do this almost automatically. The problems arise when students show some improvement but teachers do not alter their expectations to take account of the improvement. This is called a **sustaining expectation effect** because the teacher's unchanging expectation sustains the student's achievement at the expected level. The chance to raise expectations, provide more appropriate teaching, and thus encourage greater student achievement is lost. In practice, sustaining effects are more common than self-fulfilling prophecy effects (Cooper & Good, 1983).

Good and Brophy (1984) suggest that teacher expectations may affect students in the following manner. Teachers begin by forming expectations about how individual students will behave or how well each will do in the class. The teachers then treat each student according to these expectations.

If they expect a student to do well, that student may be given more encouragement or more time to answer a question. Because the students are treated differently from one another, they respond differently, often in ways that complement the teachers' expectations. Students given more time and more encouragement answer correctly more often. If this pattern is repeated daily for months, the students given more time and encouragement will do better academically and score better on achievement tests. Over time, the students' behavior moves closer and closer to the kind of performance originally expected by the teachers.

Vicious Cycles

The same cycle of expectation, teacher behavior, and student response can occur with whole classes. A teacher who expects the lower-track mathematics class to have difficulties may assign easier work, move at a slower pace, accept poorer answers, make fewer demands, and generally be less enthusiastic about working with the group. Some of these responses may be appropriate, but many are not. As we saw in Chapter 4, whole-class ability grouping is not a useful approach for the low-ability student. Some of the problems may be traced to teachers' lower expectations for these classes. We will return to these problems when we discuss how instructional strategies can communicate expectations.

Expectations, Motivation, and Self-Concept. A student's achievement motivation, aspiration level, and self-concept may all be affected by a teacher's expectations. If you remember the discussion of self-concept in Chapter 3, you should be able to make a connection between a teacher's communication of low expectations and the student's self-esteem. Many students use the teacher's behavior as a mirror in which to see themselves. If the reflection they see says, "You probably won't be able to do this," their self-esteem is likely to suffer. Of course, students differ. Some are more sensitive than others to the teacher's opinions. The teacher's evaluation may be very significant to one student and be disregarded by another. In general, students who are young, dependent, conforming, or who really like the teacher are most likely to have their self-esteem affected by the teacher's views (Brophy, 1982).

The Teacher as Mirror

Sources of Expectations

Braun (1976) has developed a model based on research findings to explain the origins of teacher expectations and the ways in which these expectations are communicated to students and then perpetuated by student behavior. Figure 9–5 shows the basic elements of this model.

Braun lists ten possible sources of teacher expectations. Intelligence test scores are an obvious source, especially if teachers do not interpret the scores appropriately (see Chapter 4 for a discussion of this issue). Sex also influences teachers; most teachers expect more behavior problems from boys than from girls. Oddly enough, names may also be influential. The notes from previous teachers and the medical or psychological reports found in cumulative folders (permanent record files) are another obvious source of expectations. Knowledge of ethnic background also seems to have an influence, as does knowledge of older brothers and sisters. The influence of students' physical characteristics is shown in several studies, indicating that

Figure 9–5   Teacher Expectations and Changes in Student Behavior

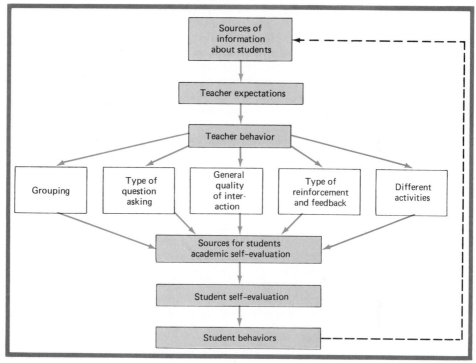

Adapted from C. Braun (1976), Teacher expectations: Sociopsychological dynamics. Review of Educational Research, 46, 185–213. Copyright © 1976 American Educational Research Association, Washington, D.C.

teachers hold higher expectations for attractive students. Previous achievement, socioeconomic class, and the actual behaviors of the student are also often used as sources of information.

Given these and other sources of information, teachers form expectations about students' probable classroom behavior and academic achievement. These expectations may be accurate or inaccurate. Even accurate predictions can lead to problems if teachers are inflexible or use inappropriate methods. Let's look more closely at these types of situations.

Teacher Behavior and Student Reactions

In Figure 9–5, you see five areas in which teachers may behave differently toward students. The first and last of these, grouping and different activities, involve instructional strategies.

Instructional Strategies.   As we have seen, different grouping processes may well have a marked effect on students. It appears that even very young students assigned to low reading groups are aware of their grouping and tend to prefer friends from higher-ability groups. Teachers also seem to prefer students in the higher reading groups (McGinley & McGinley, 1970). Rist (1970) described a teacher in a kindergarten class who assigned students to three separate worktables after just a few days, based on guesses about intellectual ability. The lowest-ability table was the one farthest from the teacher's desk. Students at that table had difficulty hearing the teacher and received less attention. These students had reason to believe the teacher expected less of them and in turn may have expected less of themselves.

Once teachers assign students to ability groups, they usually assign different learning activities. To the extent that teachers choose activities that challenge students and increase achievement, these differences are probably

Keeping Activities
Appropriate

necessary. Activities become inappropriate when students who are ready for more challenging work are not given the opportunity to try it because teachers believe they cannot handle it. This is an example of a sustaining expectation effect. It may be appropriate to teach at a slower pace and to cover less material with certain students, but the pace and quantity should increase as soon as the students are ready. Setting higher standards leads to greater achievement for all students (Doyle, Hancock, & Kifer, 1971; Pidgeon, 1970).

Other problems occur when teachers make accurate predictions about students' abilities but at the outset select inappropriate teaching methods. For example, a teacher may be correct in predicting that one group of students will have great difficulty with a particular lesson and another group will learn the new material easily. The teacher may decide against spending much time with either group, since one group "can't benefit from help" and the other "doesn't need help." But in this way, both groups are robbed of the chance to do their best (Brophy, 1982).

Teacher-Student Interactions. However the class is grouped and whatever activities are assigned, the amount and the quality of student-teacher interactions are likely to affect the students. These are in fact central aspects of students' experiences in the classroom. Researchers have examined the three specific factors in Braun's model—kinds of questions asked, quality of interaction, and reinforcement—in an attempt to pinpoint the effects of interactions on student motivation.

Differential
Treatment of
Students

Students who are expected to achieve tend to be asked more and harder questions, to be given more chances and a longer time to respond, and to be interrupted less often than students who are expected to do poorly (Allington, 1980; Cornbleth, Davis, & Button, 1974; Good & Brophy, 1984; Rosenthal, 1973).

Teachers also give these high-expectation students clues and prompts, communicating their belief that the students can answer the question (Rosenthal, 1973). Teachers tend to be more encouraging in general toward those students for whom they have high expectations. They smile at these students more often and show greater warmth through such nonverbal responses as leaning toward the students and nodding their heads as the students speak (Woolfolk & Brooks, 1983, 1985). In contrast, with students for whom expectations are low, teachers ask easier questions, allow less time for answering, and are much less likely to give prompts. Teachers can use a questionnaire like the one shown in Table 9–5 to assess their treatment of students and what it may be communicating.

If you think about all this from the teacher's perspective, it is somewhat understandable. Calling on high-expectation students is a much easier and

Table 9–5   Questionnaire: Teacher-Student Interactions

Check the appropriate box	Home run	3rd base	2nd base	1st base	Strike-out!
1. Am I courteous?					
2. Do I treat students fairly?					
3. Do I touch you?					
4. Do I talk over problems with you?					
5. Are you praised for your work?					
6. Am I patient and understanding?					
7. Do I keep my temper?					
8. Do you think that I like you?					
9. Can you trust me?					
10. Do I embarrass you?					
11. Do I listen to you?					
12. Do I smile at you?					
13. Am I friendly?					
14. Do I have a sense of humor?					
15. Do I show appreciation for special things you do?					
16. Do I encourage you?					
17. Do I give you helpful feedback?					
18. Do I look at you when I talk to you?					
19. Do I think you can do your work?					

Thank you for completing this questionnaire. Your responses help me evaluate my teaching.

COMMENTS

Adapted from V. F. & L. S. Jones (1986), Comprehensive classroom management: Creating positive learning, *2/e. Copyright © 1986 by Allyn and Bacon, Inc. Used with permission.*

more rewarding way to have a class discussion. Very often these are the students who will have the best answers. Think about this, too: the more practice in class participation these students get, the more skilled at discussion they become, thus increasing their chances of being called on. The teacher might even come to depend on these students whenever a discussion is planned.

Feedback and Expectations

It appears that feedback and reinforcement are also somewhat dependent on teacher expectations. Good and Brophy (1984) have noted that teachers demand better performance from high-achieving students, are less likely to accept a poor answer from them, and praise them more for good answers. Teachers are more likely, on the one hand, to accept or even reinforce inadequate answers from low-achieving students or, on the other, to criticize the students for wrong answers. Even more disturbing is the finding that low-achieving students receive less praise than high-achieving students for similar correct answers. On tests when an answer is "almost right," the teacher is more likely to give the benefit of the doubt (and thus the better grade) to high-achieving students (Finn, 1972).

This inconsistent feedback can be very confusing for low-ability students. Imagine how hard it would be to learn if your wrong answers were sometimes praised, sometimes ignored, and sometimes criticized and your right answers received little recognition (Good, 1983).

In Summary: The Effects on Students.   Teacher behaviors from all five categories taken together can communicate to students just how they are viewed by a very significant person, their teacher. Think about students' attributions. If youngsters see the inevitable mistakes that accompany learning as a consequence of their own lack of ability, they are likely to lower their level of aspiration. Decreased motivation follows lowered expectations. The student and the teacher set lower standards, persistence is discouraged, and poorer performance results. Students start saying "I don't know" or nothing at all rather than risk failure again. Here the teachers' attributions enter the picture: teachers accept the poor performance and attribute it to lack of ability. The lower expectation for the student thus seems to be confirmed, and as the dotted line in Figure 9–5 shows, the cycle continues.

Teacher expectations can sustain student performance at a particular level, even when students are ready to move on to more challenging work. If the materials chosen are too easy, if the ability groups are never changed, or if the teacher's nonverbal messages are negative, students may not reach their potential. *(Richard Hutchings/Photo Researchers)*

Even when student performance does not fit expectations, the teacher may rationalize and attribute the performance to external causes outside of the students' control. For example, a teacher may assume that the low-ability student who did well on a test must have cheated and that the high-ability student who failed must have been upset that day. In both cases, behavior that seems "out of character" is dismissed. It may take many instances of supposedly uncharacteristic behavior to change the teacher's beliefs about a particular student's abilities. Thus, expectations often remain in the face of contradictory evidence (Brophy, 1982; Darley & Fazio, 1980).

You may be promising yourself that you will never communicate low expectations to your students, especially now that you know about the dangers involved. Of course, not all teachers form inappropriate expectations or act on their expectations in unconstructive ways (Babad, Inbar, & Rosenthal, 1982). But avoiding the problem may be more difficult than it seems. In general, low-expectation students tend also to be the most disruptive students. (Of course, low expectations can reinforce their desire to disrupt or misbehave.) Teachers may call on these students less, wait a shorter time for their answers, and give them less praise for right answers in part to avoid the wrong, careless, or silly answers that can cause disruptions, delays, and digressions (Cooper, 1979). The challenge is to deal with these very real threats to classroom management without communicating low expectations to some students or fostering their own low expectations of themselves. The Guidelines may help you avoid some of these problems.

ANXIETY IN THE CLASSROOM

Students who worry that they will not be able to complete a task satisfactorily often end up with a feeling of **anxiety,** or "an experience of general uneasiness, a sense of foreboding, a feeling of tension" in situations where the cause of these feelings is not apparent (Hansen, 1977, p. 91). These feelings may be more or less intense, but they do seem to have significant effects on behavior. In fact, one researcher found that very anxious students are much more likely than less anxious students to drop out of school if they get failing grades (Spielberger, 1966).

Individual Differences in Anxiety

Researchers have found a number of relationships between anxiety and academic performance. People who are highly anxious tend to score lower on tests of intellectual aptitude than people who are less anxious (Sarason, Davidson, Lightall, Waite, & Ruebush, 1960). Although we do not know for certain, it appears that high anxiety is the cause of the poor performance instead of the poor performance causing the anxiety. Anxiety appears to improve performance on simple tasks or on skills that have been practiced at length but to interfere with the accomplishment of more complex tasks or skills that are not thoroughly practiced (Ball, 1977). Perhaps simple practiced tasks are boring, and a bit of anxiety provides some incentive to finish. But if a task is difficult, we need to focus all our attention on it, and anxiety is distracting. A more difficult task may even raise our anxiety levels if we try but fail initially.

Guidelines

Avoiding the Negative Effects of Teacher Expectations

Use information from tests, cumulative folders, and other teachers very carefully.

Examples
1. *Some teachers avoid reading cumulative folders for several weeks at the beginning of the year.*
2. *Be critical and objective about the reports you hear from other teachers, especially "horror stories" told in the teachers' lounge.*

Be flexible in your use of grouping strategies.

Examples
1. *Review work of students in different groups often and experiment with new groupings.*
2. *Use different groupings for different subjects.*
3. *Use mixed-ability groups in cooperative exercises when all students can handle the same material.*

Make sure all the students are challenged.

Examples
1. *Avoid saying, "This is easy, I know you can do it."*
2. *Offer a wide range of problems, and encourage all students to try a few of the harder ones for extra credit. Try to find something positive about these attempts.*

Be especially careful about how you respond to low-achieving students during class discussions.

Examples
1. *Give them prompts, clues, and time to answer.*
2. *Give ample praise for good answers.*
3. *Call on low achievers as often as high achievers.*

Use materials that show a wide range of ethnic groups.

Examples
1. *Check readers and library books. Is there ethnic diversity?*

In the classroom the conditions surrounding a test can influence how well a highly anxious individual performs. For example, Hill and Eaton (1977) found that very anxious fifth and sixth graders worked as quickly and accurately as their less anxious classmates when there was no time limit for solving arithmetic problems. However, with a time limit the very anxious students made three times as many errors as their classmates, spent about twice as much time on each problem, and cheated twice as often as the less anxious group. Conditions that arouse fears about losing in a competitive situation or failing to complete work may bring out the worst in highly anxious students. In fact, Williams (1976) found that very anxious students outperformed all other groups when they did not have to put their names on test papers, which seemed to remove some of the personal cost of failing.

2. *Ask your librarian to find multiethnic stories, filmstrips, etc.*
3. *If few materials are available, ask students to research and create their own, based on community or family resources.*

Be fair in evaluation and disciplinary procedures.

Examples
1. *Make sure equal offenses merit equal punishment. Find out from students in an anonymous questionnaire whether you seem to be favoring certain individuals.*
2. *Try to grade student work without knowing the identity of the student. Ask another teacher to give you a "second opinion" from time to time.*

Communicate to all students that you believe they can learn—and mean it.

Examples
1. *Return papers that do not meet standards with specific suggestions for improvements.*
2. *If students do not have the answers immediately, wait, probe, and then help them think through an answer.*

Involve all students in learning tasks and in privileges.

Examples
1. *Use some system for calling on or contacting students to make sure you give each student practice in reading, speaking, and answering questions.*
2. *Keep track of who gets to do what job. Are some students always on the list while others seldom make it?*

Monitor your nonverbal behavior.

Examples
1. *Do you lean away or stand farther away from some students? Do some students get smiles when they approach your desk while others get only frowns?*
2. *Do you avoid touching some students?*
3. *Does your tone of voice vary with different students?*

Recently, Sigmund Tobias (1979) has suggested a model to explain how anxiety interferes with learning and test performance. When students are learning new material, attention is very important. To learn something, you must pay attention to it. Highly anxious students evidently divide their attention between the new material and their preoccupation with concerns about how nervous they are feeling. So instead of concentrating on a lecture or on what they are reading, they keep noticing the tight feelings in their chest, thinking, "I'm so tense, I'll never understand this stuff!" Much of their attention is taken up with negative thoughts about performing poorly, being criticized, and feeling embarrassed. From the beginning, the anxious students may miss much of the information they are supposed to learn because their thoughts are focused on their own worries (Hill & Wigfield, 1984; Paulman & Kennelly, 1984).

But the problems do not end here. Even if they are paying attention, many anxious students have trouble learning material that is somewhat disorganized and difficult—material that requires them to rely on their memory. Unfortunately, much material in school could be described this way. Anxious students may be more easily distracted by irrelevant or incidental aspects of the task at hand. They seem to have trouble focusing on the significant details (Hill & Wigfield, 1984). In addition, many highly anxious students have poor study habits. Simply learning to be more relaxed will not automatically improve student performance unless the learning strategies and study skills described in Chapter 8 are improved as well (Paulman & Kennelly, 1984). Finally, as we've seen, anxious students often know more than they can demonstrate on a test. Again, highly anxious students often lack critical test-taking skills. So anxiety interferes at several points in the learning and testing cycle.

Anxiety, Distractibility, and Study

Coping with Anxiety

Teachers should help highly anxious students to set realistic goals, since these individuals often have difficulty making wise choices. They tend to select either extremely difficult or extremely easy tasks. In the first case, they are likely to fail, which will increase their sense of hopelessness and feelings of foreboding associated with school. In the second case, they probably will succeed, but they will miss the sense of satisfaction that could encourage greater effort and ease their fears about schoolwork. They may need a good deal of guidance in choosing both short-term and long-term goals. They may also need help working at a moderate pace, especially when taking tests. These students often work either too quickly and make many careless errors or too slowly and are never able to finish the task.

Need for Structure

Since anxiety appears to interfere with both attention and retention (Wittrock, 1978), highly anxious students (at least those of average or high ability) benefit most from instruction that is very structured and allows for repetition of parts of the lesson that are missed or forgotten (Seiber, O'Neil, & Tobias, 1977). Programmed instruction is one solution that fits these requirements and minimizes the failure that anxious students dread. Other possibilities are audio tapes or videotapes that can be rewound to repeat missed sections. Oosthoek and Ackers (1973) found that being able to rewind a tape helped anxious students learn; these students took advantage of the rewinding possibility more than nonanxious students using the same materials.

Test Anxiety

The greatest anxiety-arousing situation in schools at every level is the test. Students know that test results will influence decisions about their future education and employment, so it is natural that testing tends to arouse their anxiety. In many states today, graduation may depend on passing one final minimum competency test. As we already have seen, highly anxious students do not shine on standardized and timed tests or on any important classroom test. Their test scores are not likely to be valid measures of their abilities. In these cases, you can develop other, more informal methods for evaluation. The Guidelines give some ideas for dealing with anxiety, both in classroom lessons and in testing.

Guidelines

Dealing with Anxiety

Use competition carefully.

Examples
1. Monitor activities to make sure no students are being put under undue pressure.
2. During competitive games, make sure all students involved have a reasonable chance of succeeding.

Avoid situations in which highly anxious students will have to perform in front of large groups.

Examples
1. Ask anxious students questions that can be answered with a simple yes or no, or some other brief reply.
2. Give anxious students practice in speaking before smaller groups.

Make sure all instructions are clear.

Examples
1. Write test instructions on the board or on the test itself instead of giving them orally.
2. Check with students to make sure they understand. Ask several students how they would do the first question of an exercise or the sample question on a test. Correct any misconceptions.
3. If you are using a new format or starting a new type of task, give students examples or models to show how it is done.

Avoid unnecessary time pressures.

Examples
1. Give occasional take-home tests.
2. Make sure all students can complete classroom tests within the period given.

Remove some of the pressures from major tests and exams.

Examples
1. Teach test-taking skills; give practice tests; provide study guides.
2. Avoid basing most of a report-card grade on one test.
3. Make extra-credit work available to add points to course grades.
4. Use a variety of different types of items in testing, since some students have difficulty with certain types.

SUMMARY

1. The study of motivation is essentially a study of how and why people initiate actions directed toward specific goals and persist in their attempts to reach these goals.

2. Behaviorists tend to stress extrinsic motivation caused by external stimuli and reinforcement. Physical conditions and physical needs such as hunger may be involved.

3. According to social cognitive theory, sources of motivation include our beliefs about our own competence (self-efficacy), our projections about future successes and failures, and the goals we set for ourselves.

4. Cognitive psychologists stress a person's active search for meaning, understanding, and competence. The attribution theory of motivation suggests that the explanations people give for behavior, particularly their own successes and failures, have a strong influence on future goals and performance. One of the important features of an attribution is whether it is internal (within a person's control) or external (outside a person's control).

5. Like the cognitivists, humanists stress intrinsic motivation. Humanists also emphasize the need for personal growth and fulfillment. Maslow has suggested that people are motivated by a hierarchy of needs, beginning with basic physical requirements and moving upward toward self-actualization.

6. Students' needs and attitudes toward learning must be taken into account when planning activities and lessons.

7. The need for achievement is balanced by the need to avoid failure. Together these are strong motivating forces. A low sense of self-worth seems to be linked with failure-avoiding and failure-accepting strategies.

8. Teachers can enhance motivation by stimulating students' curiosity, taking students' current interests into account, maintaining a positive emotional climate with cooperative techniques, and helping students to take responsibility for their own goals and actions.

9. Ideally, a classroom lesson should enhance a student's sense of competence. Competence will increase motivation for the next lesson. If the lesson is routine, the teacher may have to build reinforcement into the activity.

10. Several studies have pointed to the important role teacher expectations and resultant strategies may play in motivating students. Teachers tend to treat students differently depending on their own views of how well the students are likely to do. Students may behave accordingly, fulfilling teachers' predictions or staying at an expected level of achievement.

11. In the classroom, anxiety seems to interfere with performance on complex assignments and tests and thus may hamper motivation.

KEY TERMS		
motivation	being needs
extrinsic motivation	achievement motivation
self-efficacy	resultant motivation
intrinsic motivation	goal structure
attribution theories	Student Teams-Achievement Divisions (STAD)
locus of control	individual learning expectation
learned helplessness	origins
humanistic psychology	pawns
need	self-fulfilling prophecy
self-actualization	sustaining expectation effect
deficiency needs	anxiety

SUGGESTIONS FOR FURTHER READING AND STUDY

ALDERMAN, M., & Cohen, M. (Eds.). (1985). *Motivation theory and practice for preservice teachers.* Washington, DC: Eric Clearinghouse on Teacher Education. This is a collection of very brief articles on intrinsic and extrinsic motivation, achievement motivation, self-worth theory, attribution theory, and other topics that are particularly relevant for teachers.

AMES, R., & AMES, C. (Eds.). (1984). *Research on motivation in education* (Vol. 1). Orlando, FL: Academic Press. Volume 2 is in press. These two volumes provide a basic and very current reference on classroom motivation.

CLIFFORD, M. M. (1984). Thoughts on a theory of constructive failure. *Educational Psychologist, 19,* 108–120. This article gives a different and very "constructive" perspective on failure.

ELEMENTARY SCHOOL JOURNAL (1984, September). Special issue on motivation. There are articles on teacher expectations, cooperative learning, test anxiety, student and teacher attributions, self-worth theory, and many other relevant topics, all written by experts in their fields.

SLAVIN, R. (1980). *Using student team learning* (rev. ed.). Baltimore: Center for Social Organization of Schools, The Johns Hopkins University. This is a manual for teachers describing step by step how to use several forms of cooperative learning—STAD, Jigsaw, and Teams-Games-Tournament.

WEBB, N. (1985). Verbal interaction and learning in peer-directed groups. *Theory into Practice, 24,* 32–39. Webb summarizes her research on small-group learning and gives guidelines for how to set up good learning groups.

Teachers' Forum

A Sense of Control

Students are most likely to be motivated in school when they attribute their performance (both successes and failures) to controllable personal causes like their own effort. Suppose a student in your class gives up easily and is not highly motivated. When his performance is poor, he tends to blame it either on the assignments you give or on his own lack of ability. How can you help this student to be more highly motivated in class? What can you do to help him see his own effort as an important determinant of success or failure?

Tasting Success

Nothing succeeds like success, and anybody can succeed at *some* level. I try to introduce reluctant students to material which is within their grasp, to let them taste success. Sometimes the satisfaction of doing things right is enough to motivate. If it isn't, I try again.

There are always a few I can't reach on an academic level. Sometimes, I can make contact on a personal or athletic basis and thus win their confidence, which carries over into class.

Osborn Howes, Eighth-Grade English, Economics, and History Teacher
Hall School, Larkspur, California

A Personal Approach

All students need to be individually motivated to do their best. Students often need more of a personal relationship with the teacher, to want to please someone besides themselves. This personal interest can be shown through individual conversations, giving praise and encouragement, and so on. When an honest and open relationship has been established, the teacher can convey to the student that he must do his best and that nothing less will be accepted. Because students are often *not* expected to do their best, they don't even realize their own potential.

Harold Kreif, Fifth-Grade Teacher
Pier Elementary School, Fond du Lac, Wisconsin

Guarantees and Rewards

The child needs to feel self-worth. If failure seems imminent, effort will be lacking. At first, the child should be given assignments in which success is guaranteed. Successful effort and achievement should be rewarded promptly. Small-group work is also a way to involve the child. Placement is very important, so that the child will be accepted and not allowed to be a nonparticipant. Another suggestion is to talk to the child and set up a behavior modification program. A chart can be used to list acceptable performances, the rewards, the consequences for unacceptable performances, and time limits. This chart can be posted on the child's desk or in a folder. The child could be responsible for marking the chart. When using a device like this, consistency is very important.

Ida Pofahl, Second-Grade Teacher
Denison Elementary School, Denison, Iowa

Cumulative Records

What is the role of cumulative records? Preconceptions (and perhaps misconceptions) based on cumulative records may lead to expectations, which in turn influence how the teachers behave toward the students. How can you use information from cumulative records in a positive way?

Read Selectively

Cumulative records contain essential health information, like clinically diagnosed conditions, of which a teacher must be aware. At the beginning of each year, I examine the records for this information alone. The records also contain each previous teacher's assessment of a child's performance and behavior. I purposely ignore these observations, as a child's developmental processes and environmental circumstances may cause dramatic differences in performance and behavior from one year to the next. Since children do react differently to each teacher's personality and method of teaching, I use caution at the end of the year in preparing the cumulative record for the next teacher. Each child needs a fresh start each year.

Arleen Wyatt, Third-Grade Teacher
Happy Valley School, Rossville, Georgia

Form Your Own Opinions First

I feel the cumulative record is definitely an asset to the classroom teacher. However, I seldom refer to the records until I have given myself a couple of weeks with the children in order to form my own opinions.

Once I have made a generalization about a child, I refer to the records. If my feelings are confirmed, I carry on. If I have formed a different opinion from previous teachers, I usually approach them to find out why this might be.

Joan M. Bloom, First-Grade Teacher
Henry Barnard Lab School for Rhode Island College, Providence, Rhode Island

Different Information for Different Problems

Cumulative records should be used as a reference tool. I like to check achievement test scores and IQ scores prior to instruction so I know if the materials I am using are at the child's instructional level. I also like to check the health records to see if there are any physical problems I should be aware of. After the first-quarter grading period, I like to check last year's grades for a comparison. I generally use the remainder of the information after I myself see a problem.

Sharon Klotz, Sixth-Grade Teacher
Kiel Middle School, Kiel, Wisconsin

Controlling Biases

It is inevitable for teachers, like others, to form impressions about people. How do you control your biases both toward "teacher's pets" and toward students for whom you have little regard or low expectations?

Focus on the Individual

I have always regarded controlling my biases toward "high-expectation" vs. "low-expectation" students as a personal challenge. The high-expectation students are generally "together" personalities—they hold themselves in high esteem and have a sense of purpose, belonging, contributing, and accomplishment. Problematic students generally have poorly defined selves in these categories. However, both groups need to be valued and encouraged as individuals—the former, in order to maintain their levels of accomplishment and to grow, and the latter, to foster these same qualities in the first place. My challenge, then, is to find the key to stimulate each individual to "make the effort" and then to structure the learning experience so that the student and I become partners in a positive interaction that will, hopefully, become self-reinforcing.

Laura Atkinson, Special Education Teacher
Chapel Hill, North Carolina

10

Classroom Management and Communication

Overview
Classrooms Need Managers   350
The Ecology of Classrooms   351
The Goals of Classroom Management   353
Planning for Good Management   355
A Look Back   355
Some Research Results   356
Rules and Procedures Required!   356
Getting Started: The First Weeks of Class   361
Maintaining Effective Management: Motivation and
    Prevention   363
Encouraging Engagement   363
Prevention Is the Best Medicine   364
Special Problems with Secondary Students   367
The Need for Communication   368
Communication and Metacommunication   368
Diagnosis: Whose Problem Is It?   370
Counseling: The Student's Problem   371
Confrontation and Assertive Discipline   372
Summary/Key Terms
Suggestions for Further Reading and Study
Teachers' Forum

OVERVIEW Although we have been talking about classroom management throughout this book, we are now ready to examine several key aspects of this issue in depth. Few topics in educational psychology are as important for teaching. Classroom management is certainly one of the main concerns of teachers, particularly beginning teachers, as well as administrators and parents. Even students expect teachers to be effective managers. When class time is consumed by management problems, students are uncomfortable, and little real learning takes place. In other words, good classroom management is one of the strongest influences on academic learning (Good, 1979).

The very nature of classes, teaching, and students makes good management a critical ingredient of success; we will look at why this is true. Next we will turn to the goals of classroom management. Successful managers create more time for learning, involve more students, and help those students to become self-managing.

To accomplish these goals, teachers must establish a good working atmosphere. The first step in this process is planning rules, procedures, routines, and activities. The next step is teaching students how to follow the rules and procedures so activities can flow smoothly. This must begin on the first day of class.

Once established, a positive working environment must be maintained throughout the year. One of the best ways to do this is to try to prevent problems from occurring at all. But when problems arise—as they always do—an effective response is important. What will you do when students challenge you openly in class, when one student asks your advice on a difficult personal problem, or when another withdraws from all participation? We will examine the ways that teachers can communicate effectively with their students in these and many other situations.

By the time you have finished this chapter, you should be able to do the following:

- Describe the special managerial demands of classrooms and relate these demands to students of different ages.
- Create a list of rules and procedures for a class.
- Develop a plan for organizing your first week of teaching.
- Explain Kounin's suggestions for preventing management problems.
- Describe how you might respond to a student who seldom completes work.
- Suggest two different approaches for dealing with a conflict between teacher and student or between two students.

CLASSROOMS NEED MANAGERS

For the sixteenth time in 17 years, "lack of discipline" was listed as the number-one problem facing the public schools in the annual Gallup Poll of attitudes toward public schools (Gallup, 1985). In a survey of teachers, chronic student misbehavior was noted as the main source of job stress by 58 percent of respondents (Feitler & Tokar, 1982). The behaviors that most teachers find troubling are not acts of violence but the more common problems of class disruption, incomplete work, nonparticipation, cheating, repeated tardiness, and absences. In order to understand the causes and consequences of these problems, let's take a closer look at the classroom itself.

The Ecology of Classrooms

The word *ecology* is usually associated with nature. But classrooms are ecological systems, too. The environment of the classroom and the inhabitants of that environment—students and teachers—are constantly interacting. Each aspect of the system affects all others. The characteristics of classrooms, the tasks of teaching, and the needs of students all influence classroom management.

Beyond the Fifth Dimension

Characteristics of Classrooms. Classes are particular kinds of environments. They have "distinctive properties affecting participants regardless of how students are organized for learning or what educational philosophy the teacher espouses" (Doyle, 1986, p. 394). Let's look at six of these features described by Doyle (1986).

Classrooms are *multidimensional*. They are crowded with people, tasks, and time pressures. Many individuals, all with differing goals, preferences, and abilities, must share resources, accomplish a number of tasks, use and reuse materials without losing them, move in and out of the room, keep track of what is happening, and so on. In addition, actions can have multiple effects. Calling on low-ability students may encourage their participation and thinking but may slow the discussion and lead to management problems if the students can't answer.

A related feature is *simultaneity*. Everything happens at once. A teacher explaining a concept must also notice if students are following the explanation, decide whether two whispering boys should be ignored or stopped,

Classrooms are busy places, filled with people, activities, materials, and conversations. Skillful management is required to gain and maintain the cooperation of students in this complex environment. *(Freda Leinwand/Photo Researchers)*

determine if there is enough time to start the next topic, and decide who should answer the question that Jill just asked.

The next characteristic, *immediacy*, has to do with the fast pace of classroom life. Teachers have literally hundreds of exchanges with students during a single day.

In this rapid-fire existence, events are quite *unpredictable*. Even when plans are carefully made, the overhead projector is in place, and the handouts are ready, the lesson can still be interrupted by a burned-out bulb in the projector, a child who suddenly becomes ill, or a loud, angry discussion right outside the classroom window.

The way the teacher handles these unexpected intrusions is seen and judged by all, because classrooms are *public*. Students are always noticing if the teacher is being "fair." Is there favoritism? What happens when a rule is broken?

Finally, classrooms have *histories*. The meaning of a particular teacher's or student's actions depends in part on what has happened before. The fifteenth time a student arrives late requires a different response from the teacher than the first late arrival. In addition, the history of the first few weeks of school affects life in the class all year.

The Need for Cooperation.   No productive activity can take place in a group without the cooperation of all members. This obviously applies to classrooms. Even if some students don't participate, they must allow others to do so. You have probably seen one or two students bring an entire class to a halt. So the basic management task for teachers is to achieve order by gaining and maintaining student cooperation in class activities (Doyle, 1979). Given the multidimensional, simultaneous, immediate, unpredictable, public, and historical nature of classrooms, this is quite a challenge.

Gaining student cooperation means much more than dealing effectively with misbehavior. It means planning activities, having materials ready, making appropriate behavioral and academic demands on students, giving clear signals to students, accomplishing transitions smoothly, foreseeing problems and stopping them before they start, selecting and sequencing activities so that order and flow are maintained—and much more. Also, remember that different activities require different managerial skills. For example, a new or complicated activity may be a greater threat to classroom order than a familiar or simple activity. We will look at many of these skills in the upcoming pages.

Gaining Cooperation: What's Involved?

Age-Related Needs.   Another necessary consideration is the age-related needs of students. Obviously, gaining the cooperation of kindergarteners is not the same task as gaining the cooperation of high school seniors. Jere Brophy and Carolyn Evertson (1978) have identified four general stages of classroom management, defined by age-related needs. Let's look briefly at each.

Four Stages of Management

During kindergarten and the first few years of elementary school, children are learning how to go to school. They are being socialized into a new role. Direct teaching of classroom rules and procedures is important during this stage. Little learning will take place until the children master these basics. Luckily, most children this age are willing to accept adults as authority figures—to follow instructions and try to please.

Children in the middle elementary years are usually familiar with the student role, even if they are not always perfect examples of it. Many school and classroom routines have become relatively automatic. Specific new rules and procedures for a particular activity may have to be taught directly, however. And you may hear the familiar refrain, "My teacher last year didn't do it that way!" Still, at this stage you will spend more time monitoring and maintaining the management system than teaching it directly.

Toward the end of elementary school and the beginning of high school, as you saw in Chapter 3, friendships and status within peer groups take on tremendous importance. Pleasing the teacher may be replaced by pleasing peers. Some students begin to test and defy authority. The management challenges at this stage are to deal productively with these disruptions and to motivate students who are becoming less concerned with teachers' opinions and more interested in their social lives.

By the end of high school, the focus of most students returns to academics. Many of the truly alienated have dropped out. Classroom management at this stage involves managing the curriculum, fitting academic material to students' interests and abilities, and helping students become more self-managing in their learning. The first few classes each semester may be devoted to teaching particular procedures for using materials and equipment or for keeping track of and submitting assignments. But most students know what is expected.

The Goals of Classroom Management

Three Reasons for Management

Order for its own sake is an empty goal. As we discussed in Chapter 6, it is unethical to use class management techniques simply to keep students docile and quiet. What, then, is the point of working so hard to manage classrooms? There are at least three reasons why management is so important.

More Time for Learning. As a child, I once used a stopwatch to time the commercials during a TV quiz show. I was amazed to find that half of the program was devoted to commercials. Actually, very little quizzing took place. If you used a similar approach in classrooms, timing all the different activities throughout the day, you might be surprised by how little actual teaching takes place. Many minutes each day are lost through interruptions, disruptions, late starts, and rough transitions. The time actually spent on academic tasks varies greatly from class to class, but easily 25 percent of the available time in a school year disappears. Sometimes the causes are unavoidable, as with fire drills, but often they could be prevented (Karweit, 1981; Karweit & Slavin, 1981).

Obviously, students will learn only the material they have a chance to learn. If a class does not reach the last three chapters in a textbook, you can't expect the students to learn the information in those chapters. Almost every study examining opportunity to learn has found a significant relationship between content covered and student learning (Armento, 1977; Good & Beckerman, 1978). In fact, the correlations between content covered and student learning are usually larger than the correlations between specific teacher behaviors and student learning (Rosenshine, 1979). So one important goal of classroom management is to expand the sheer number of minutes available for learning. This is sometimes called **allocated time.**

allocated time: time set aside for learning

But simply making more time for learning will not automatically lead to achievement. Students may have the opportunity to learn but let that opportunity slip through their fingers. To be valuable, time must be used effectively. As you saw in the chapters on cognitive learning, the way students process information is a central factor in what they learn and remember. Basically, students will learn what they practice and what they pay attention to (Doyle, 1983). Bloom (1976) reviewed 15 studies of student attention and found a very high correlation between student attention and learning. Even higher correlations have been reported in studies that measured attention only to academic tasks (Rosenshine, 1979). Time spent actively attending to specific learning tasks is often called **engaged time,** or sometimes *time on task.* So a second goal of class management is to improve the quality of time use by keeping students actively engaged in worthwhile learning activities.

engaged time: time spent actively learning

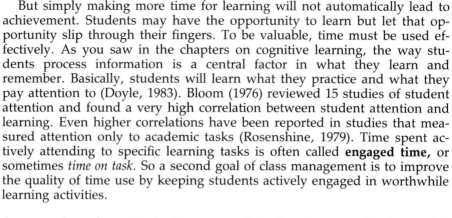

participation structures: rules defining how to participate in different activities

Access to Learning.   Each classroom activity has its own rules for participation. Sometimes these rules are clearly stated by the teacher, but often they are implicit and unstated. Teacher and students may not even be aware that they are following different rules for different activities (Berliner, 1983). And the differences are sometimes quite subtle. For example, in a reading group students may have to raise their hands to make a comment, but in a show-and-tell circle in the same class they may simply have to catch the teacher's eye. The rules defining who can talk, what they can talk about, and when, to whom, and how long they can talk are often called **participation structures** (Erickson & Shultz, 1977). In order to participate successfully in a given activity, students must understand the participation structures. However, understanding is not always easy, since, as we noted, participation rules often go unstated.

This can create conflicts. Some students seem to come to school better able to participate than others. The participation structures they learn at home in interactions with siblings, parents, and other adults match the participation structures of school activities fairly well. For other children, what works at home does not match what is expected in school. But teachers are not necessarily aware of this conflict. Instead they see that a child simply doesn't fit in, always seems to say the wrong thing at the wrong time, or is very reluctant to participate, and they are not sure why.

Example: Participation Conflict

An excellent example of the effects of such conflicts can be seen in the Kamehameha Early Education Project, or KEEP (Au, 1980). Researchers discovered that interactions in Hawaiian families involved much overlapping in conversation, with people chiming in whenever they had something to add. In school, this style of interacting was seen as interrupting. But when reading lessons were changed to allow this overlapping style, reading achievement improved for the Hawaiian children in the project (Au & Mason, 1981). Access to learning was increased for these children when the rules for participation were changed to fit their experiences.

Teachers' unspoken assumptions about participation rules can also lead to problems. As you have seen, some students learn these unstated, often subtle rules easily, but others may have trouble. Teachers are also not always consistent in their behavior: sometimes they give students mixed messages and assume, usually unconsciously, that students know what is going on. This can be especially confusing when students have more than one teacher's rules to follow. Green and Weade (1985) described the management problems created when a student teacher unwittingly changed the groundrules for show and tell. The cooperating teacher always sat up straight, asked one student at a time to speak, and used a formal, public-speaking voice. When the student teacher led the group, she leaned forward, spoke in a very intimate tone, and encouraged many comments. Soon the students moved out of the circle and crowded around the student teacher. The discussion became very chaotic. The student teacher had signaled a change in the rules by her behavior. The students didn't know which rules to follow, or exactly what the new rules were.

Awareness, Adaptability, and Clarity

What can we conclude? In order to involve all your students in smoothly run activities, you must make sure that everyone knows how to participate in each specific activity. When necessary, you must adapt participation structures to match students' home experiences. The key is awareness. What are your rules and expectations? Do they fit those of your students and their other authority figures? What unspoken rules or values may be operating? Are you clear and consistent in signaling your students about how to participate?

Management for Self-Management.   One goal of any management system ought to be to help students become better able to manage themselves. We discussed self-management in Chapter 6 and self-efficacy in Chapter 9. I won't add much here, except to note that encouraging self-management may require some extra time. Teaching students how to take responsibility instead of taking care of everything yourself may seem inefficient, but the investment can be well worth the effort.

PLANNING FOR GOOD MANAGEMENT

In making plans for your class, much of what you have already learned in this book should prove helpful.

A Look Back

Taking Development and Differences into Account

Problems are prevented when individual variations, such as those discussed in Chapters 2, 3, and 4, are taken into account in instructional planning. Sometimes students become disruptive because the work assigned is not at their level. A student who reads at fourth-grade level but is told to read silently ten pages of a text written at eighth-grade level will be restless, distractible, and discouraged—in short, a prime candidate for trouble. Students who are bored by lessons well below their ability levels may also be interested in finding more exciting activities to fill their time. Over the summer, before you start teaching, you might find out about the range of achievement levels in your class so you can plan to have appropriate materials. To avoid forming expectations about the abilities of particular students before you see their work in your own class, you might ask for a list of scores without names.

Motivation

In one sense, teachers are preventing discipline problems whenever they make an effort to motivate students. A student involved in mastering course objectives is usually not involved in a clash with the teacher or other students at the same time. All plans for motivating students are steps toward preventing problems.

Attention and Consequences

In Chapters 5 and 6 you learned that teachers often perpetuate inappropriate behavior by reinforcing it with attention. You can prevent some classroom problems by making rules clear and specific and establishing consequences for breaking them. The first week of school is too late to make these plans. As you will see, effective teachers have these rules and consequences worked out before the students arrive.

Some Research Results

What else can teachers do to be good managers? Over the past several years, educational psychologists at the Research and Development Center for Teacher Education at the University of Texas at Austin studied classroom management quite thoroughly (Emmer, Evertson, & Anderson, 1980; Emmer, Evertson, Clements, Sanford, & Worsham, 1984; Evertson, Emmer, Clements, Sanford, Worsham, & Williams, 1984). Their general approach was to observe and videotape a large number of classrooms, making intensive observations the first weeks of school and less frequent visits later in the year. After several months there were dramatic differences among the classes. Some had very few management problems, while others had many. The most and least effective teachers were identified on the basis of the behavior of their classes later in the year.

Development of Management Principles

At the end of the year, the researchers looked at the videotapes of the first weeks of class to see how the effective teachers got started. Other comparisons were made between the teachers who ultimately had well-behaved, high-achieving classes and those whose classes were fraught with problems. On the basis of these comparisons, management principles were developed. The researchers then taught these principles to a new group of teachers to see if their application would in fact lead to good classroom management. The results were quite positive. Teachers who applied the principles had fewer problems; their students spent more time working and less time disrupting; and achievement was higher.

The findings of these studies formed the basis for two books on classroom management (Emmer et al., 1984; Evertson et al., 1984). Many of the ideas in the following pages are taken from these manuals.

Rules and Procedures Required!

At the elementary school level, teachers must lead 20 to 30 students of varying abilities through many different activities each day. Without efficient rules and procedures, a great deal of time is wasted answering the same question over and over. "My pencil broke. How can I do my math?" "I'm finished with my workbook. What should I do now?" "Steven hit me!"

At the secondary school level, teachers must deal daily with over 100 students who use dozens of kinds of materials and often change rooms for each class. Secondary students are also more likely to challenge teachers' authority. The effective managers studied by Emmer, Evertson, and their colleagues had planned rules and procedures for coping with these situ

The teacher has established four rules and posted them: be considerate; speak softly; complete your daily assignments; and walk indoors. Rules like this can help create a positive, friendly atmosphere—everyone's energy is freed to concentrate on learning, and activities flow smoothly. *(Tom McCarthy/The Image Bank)*

ations. We all know what rules and procedures mean, but let's look at what these words imply for classroom management specifically.

procedures: prescribed steps for an activity

Procedures describe how to accomplish activities in the classroom. How will materials and assignments be distributed and collected? Under what conditions can students leave the room? How do students respond to the bell at the beginning and end of a period? How will grades be determined? In addition, science, physical education, home economics, vocational subjects, and art classes need special procedures related to equipment, safety, and supplies. Procedures are seldom written down. They are simply the ways of getting things done in class. The Guidelines on the following pages should help you plan your procedures.

rules: statements specifying expected and forbidden behaviors; dos and don'ts

Rules specify expected and forbidden actions in the class. They are the dos and don'ts of classroom life. Unlike procedures, rules are often written down and posted. In establishing rules, you should consider what kind of atmosphere you want to create. What student behaviors do you need in order to teach effectively? What limits do the students need to guide their behavior (Canter & Canter, 1976)? It is better to have a few general rules that cover many specifics rather than to list all the dos and don'ts. But if specific actions are forbidden, such as chewing gum in class or smoking in the restrooms, then a rule should make this clear.

Rules for Elementary School. Evertson and her colleagues (1984) give five examples of general rules for elementary school classes.

1. *Be polite and helpful.* This applies to behavior toward adults and other students.
2. *Take care of your school.* This might include picking up litter, caring for school property, returning library books, and not marking on walls, desks, or buses.
3. *Behave in the cafeteria.* Here students need guidance and clear examples, including how to act in line, what kind of talking is permitted, what to do with trays and trash, and whether sharing of food is permitted.
4. *Do not hit, shove, or hurt others.* Again, students need clear explanations of what the teacher means by *hurting*.
5. *Keep the bathroom clean.*

Guidelines

Establishing Class Procedures

Determine your procedures for student upkeep of desks, storage areas, classroom equipment, and other facilities.

Examples
1. *Some teachers set aside a cleanup time each day or once a week in self-contained classes.*
2. *You might demonstrate and have students practice how to push chairs under the desk, take and return materials stored on shelves, sharpen pencils, use the sink or water fountain, assemble lab equipment, set up the sewing machine, and so on.*
3. *In some classes a rotating monitor is in charge of equipment or materials.*
4. *Be clear about which materials can be used anytime and which require permission from the teacher.*

Decide how students will be expected to enter and leave the room.

Examples
1. *How will students know what they should do as soon as they enter the room? Some teachers have a standard assignment ("Have your homework out and be checking it over."). Other teachers have a different warm-up exercise on the board each day.*
2. *Under what conditions can students leave the room? When do they need permission? How do they get it? How must they line up if the whole group is leaving?*
3. *If students are tardy or late, how do they gain admission to the room?*
4. *Many teachers require students to be in their seats and quiet before they can leave at the end of class. The teacher, not the bell, dismisses class.*

Establish a signal and teach it to your students.

Examples
1. *In the classroom, some teachers flick the lights, sound a chord on a piano or recorder, move to the podium and stare silently at the class, use a phrase like "Eyes, please," take out their grade books, or move from the classroom door to the front of the class.*

Whatever the rule, students need to be taught the behaviors that it includes and excludes. Examples, practice, and discussion will be required before learning is complete.

Avoiding Confusion

As you've seen, different activities often require different rules. This can be confusing for elementary students until they have thoroughly learned all the rules. To prevent confusion, you might consider making signs that list the rules for each activity. Then you can post the appropriate sign before the activity as a reminder. Of course, these rules must be explained and discussed before the signs can have their full effect (Canter & Canter, 1976). Figure 10–1 on page 360 shows one teacher's effective signs.

Rules for Secondary School.   Emmer and colleagues suggest five examples of rules for secondary students:

2. *In the halls, a raised hand, one clap, or some other signal may mean "stop."*
3. *On the playground, a raised hand or whistle may mean "line up."*

Set procedures for student participation in class.

Examples
1. *Will you have students raise their hands for permission to speak or simply require that they wait until the speaker has finished?*
2. *How will you signal that you want everyone to respond at once? Some teachers raise a cupped hand to their ear. Others preface the question with "Everyone. . . ."*
3. *How will students get help? Must they raise their hands, or can they come to your desk?*
4. *Make sure you are clear about differences in procedures for different activities: reading group, learning center, discussion, teacher presentation, seatwork, film, peer learning group, library, public-address announcement, and so forth.*
5. *How many students at a time can be at the pencil sharpener, teacher's desk, learning center, sink, bookshelves, reading corner, or bathroom? More than two or three students in one place at one time can lead to trouble.*

Determine how you will communicate, collect, and return assignments.

Examples
1. *Some teachers reserve a particular corner of the board for listing assignments. Others write assignments in colored chalk. Some teachers dictate assignments and require students to write them in a special notebook. For younger students it may be better to prepare assignment sheets or folders, color-coding them for math workbook, reading packet, and science kit.*
2. *Some teachers collect assignments in a box or bin; others have a student collect work so they can introduce the next activity. Some teachers have students pass assignments to the front in a particular way. The same procedures are often used for returning assignments.*

Secondary Rules

1. *Bring all needed materials to class.* The teacher must specify type of pen, pencil, paper, notebook, texts, and so on.
2. *Be in your seat and ready to work when the bell rings.* Many teachers combine this rule with a standard beginning procedure for the class, such as a warm-up exercise on the board or a requirement that students have paper with a proper heading ready when the bell rings.
3. *Obtain permission before speaking or leaving your seat.* There may be exceptions to this rule, such as allowing students to sharpen pencils or come to the teacher's desk when the teacher is not presenting a lesson.
4. *Respect and be polite to everyone.* This covers fighting, verbal abuse, and general troublemaking.
5. *Respect other people's property.* This means property belonging to the school, the teacher, or other students.

Again, these rules must be explained and taught.

Figure 10–1   **Rules for Different Work Areas in an Elementary Class**

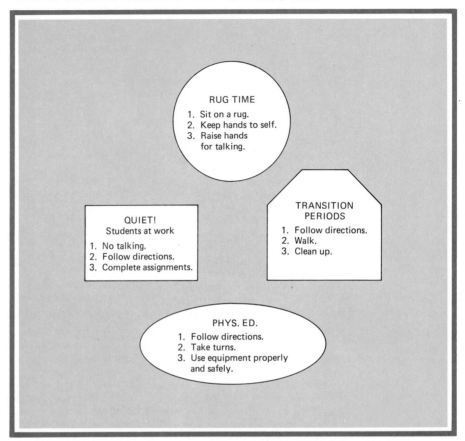

Adapted from Canter and Canter (1976), Rules for different work areas in an elementary class. In Assertive discipline: A take-charge approach for today's educator. *Los Angeles: Canter & Associates.*

Consequences.   As soon as you decide on your rules and procedures, you must consider what you will do when a student breaks a rule or does not follow a procedure. It is too late to make this decision after the rule has been broken. For many infractions, the logical consequence is having to go back and "do it right." Students who run in the hall may have to return to where they started and walk properly. Incomplete papers can be redone. Materials left out should be put back. Sometimes consequences are more complicated. For example, one interruption during a meeting means a warning; two interruptions mean extra work or no more participation in the discussion.

You will have to determine positive and negative consequences for student actions. In Chapter 6 we discussed the role of consequences in class management. The main point here is that these decisions must be made early on, so students know before they break a rule or use the wrong procedure what this will mean for them. Which brings us to a very important topic in managing a class—

Getting Started: The First Weeks of Class

What do effective teachers really do during those first critical days and weeks? You may recall that Emmer, Evertson, and their colleagues observed elementary and secondary classrooms on the very first day of school, throughout the first weeks, and less frequently for the rest of the year. One study from their classroom management projects carefully analyzed the first weeks' activities and found striking differences between effective and ineffective elementary teachers (Emmer, Evertson, & Anderson, 1980).

Effective Managers for Elementary Students.   In the effective teachers' classrooms the very first day was well organized. Name tags were ready. There was something interesting for each child to do right away. Materials were set up. The teachers had planned carefully to avoid any last-minute tasks that might take them away from their students. These teachers dealt with the children's pressing concerns first. "Where do I put my things? How do I pronounce my teacher's name? How do I get the teacher's attention? Can I whisper to my neighbor? Where is the bathroom?" The effective teachers had a workable, easily understood set of rules and taught the students the most important rules right away. They taught the rules like any other subject, with lots of explanation, examples, and practice.

Throughout the first weeks, the effective managers continued to spend quite a bit of time teaching rules and procedures. Some used guided practice to teach procedures; others used rewards to shape behavior. Most taught

Teachers should deal with young students' most pressing concerns on the first day of class: Where do I keep my materials? How do I get to the bathroom? What do we do for lunch? How should I address my teacher? *(Ken Karp)*

students to respond to a bell or some other signal. These teachers worked with the group as a whole on enjoyable academic activities. They did not rush to get students into groups or to get them started in readers. This whole-class work gave the teachers a better opportunity to continue monitoring all students' learning of the rule and procedures. Misbehavior was stopped quickly, firmly, but not harshly.

An Ineffective Start

In the classrooms that later had many management problems, the first weeks were quite different. Rules were not workable. They were either vague or too complicated. Neither positive nor negative behaviors had clear, consistent consequences. Procedures for accomplishing routine activities varied from day to day. The procedures were not taught or practiced. Students wandered aimlessly, not knowing exactly how to deal with essentials such as sharpening pencils or getting permission to go to the restroom. They had to ask each other what they should be doing. Often they talked to one another because they had nothing productive to do. The teachers frequently left the room. Many became absorbed in paperwork or in helping just one student.

The first few weeks are clearly an important investment in positive management for the whole year. In the study we have just seen, effective managers may have lost some instructional time during the first few weeks of the year by focusing on rules and procedures, but they definitely gained time over the entire year. Their classes were seldom interrupted by student misbehavior or thrown off course by general confusion and disorganization.

Suggestions for a Good Start

Dreikurs and colleagues have some other recommendations for getting started effectively in an elementary school classroom (Dreikurs, Grunwald, & Pepper, 1971). The teacher should have a variety of activities planned so that each student will form a good impression of the new class and will not be bored by one or two long lessons the first day. The teacher should be familiar with the students' names, be able to pronounce them correctly, and have some positive information about each student that can be mentioned in a private greeting. The first morning, the teacher should make sure students can recognize and pronounce his or her name. The teacher should direct praise and positive expectations toward the group as a whole, to begin to build group spirit. Statements such as "I think this is going to be a good class" or "We are going to learn a lot together," said with genuine conviction, are better than statements that emphasize differences among individual students, such as "Jason has already learned how to put his materials away quickly before lunch."

Effective Managers for Secondary Students. What about getting started in a secondary school class? It appears that many of the differences between effective and ineffective elementary school teachers hold at the secondary level as well. Again, effective managers focus on establishing rules, procedures, and expectations on the first day of class. These standards for academic work and class behavior are clearly communicated to students and consistently enforced during the first weeks of class. Student behavior is closely monitored, and infractions of the rules are dealt with quickly. In classes with lower-ability students, work cycles are shorter; students are not required to spend long, unbroken periods on one type of activity. Instead, they are moved smoothly through several different tasks each period. In general, effective teachers carefully follow each student's progress, so students cannot avoid work without facing consequences (Emmer & Evertson, 1982).

With all this close monitoring and consistent enforcement of the rules, you may wonder if effective secondary teachers must be grim and humorless. Not necessarily. The effective managers in one study also smiled and joked more with their students (Moskowitz & Hayman, 1976). As any experienced teacher can tell you, there is much more to smile about when the class is cooperative and well behaved.

MAINTAINING EFFECTIVE MANAGEMENT: MOTIVATION AND PREVENTION

But a good start is only that—just a beginning. Effective teachers build on this beginning. They maintain their management system by keeping students engaged in productive work and preventing problems.

Encouraging Engagement

Motivation Plus

We have already discussed several ways to keep students engaged. In the chapter on motivation, for example, we noted such approaches as building positive attitudes toward learning, stimulating curiosity, relating lessons to student interests, encouraging cooperative learning, building reinforcement into activities, and fostering feelings of competence. What else can teachers do?

Lesson Format. The format of a lesson affects student involvement. In general, as teacher supervision increases, student engaged time also increases (Emmer & Evertson, 1981). Rosenshine (1979) reported, for example, that supervised students are off task only about 5 percent of the time. But unsupervised students working alone and pacing themselves are off task about 15 percent of the time and in transition from one activity to another about 10 percent of the time. This does not mean that teachers should eliminate independent work for students. It simply means that this type of activ-

If students are to stay productively engaged when the teacher is not watching, they must have a task with reasonable goals, readily available materials, and clear-cut steps. *(Hugh Rogers/Monkmeyer Press)*

ity usually requires careful monitoring. *Independent* does not necessarily mean "left completely alone without guidance."

When the task provides continuous cues for the student about what to do next, involvement will be greater (Kounin & Gump, 1974). This may be one reason why we persist in arts or crafts projects. As long as the project is unfinished, it is fairly clear what we should do next. The lack of closure pulls us on. Similarly, activities with clear steps are likely to be more absorbing, since one step leads naturally to the next. When students have all the materials they need to complete a task, they tend to stay involved (Kounin & Doyle, 1975). And as you now know, if their curiosity is piqued or they are personally interested in the question, students will be motivated to continue seeking an answer. They will stay involved and resist distractions.

Involvement without Supervision. Of course, teachers can't supervise every student all the time or rely on curiosity. Something else must keep students working and completing assignments on their own. In their study of elementary and secondary teachers, Evertson, Emmer, and their colleagues found that effective class managers at both levels had well-planned systems for encouraging students to manage their own work (Evertson et al., 1984; Emmer et al., 1984). The Guidelines are based on their findings.

These strategies should help keep students engaged, with and without your supervision. What else can you do to maintain your management system? The ideal way to manage problems, of course, is to prevent them in the first place.

Prevention Is the Best Medicine

Jacob Kounin (1970) also studied classroom management by comparing effective teachers, whose classes were relatively free of problems, with ineffective teachers, whose classes were continually plagued by chaos and disruption. Observing both groups in action, Kounin found that they were not very different in the way they handled discipline once problems arose. The difference was that the successful managers were much better at preventing problems.

Kounin noted that effective teachers were skilled at leading groups and keeping activities moving. They made sure students had something productive to do at all times and were not waiting for work or watching others work. Activities were well organized and moved at a good pace. Besides being experts at group management, these effective teachers were also aware of individual students, so no one could "hide" in the group.

Kounin concluded that effective classroom managers were especially skilled in four areas: "withitness," overlapping activities, group focusing, and movement management (Doyle, 1977). More recent research confirms the importance of these factors (Emmer & Evertson, 1981).

withitness:
according to Kounin, awareness of everything happening in a classroom

Withitness. **Withitness** means communicating to students that you are aware of everything that is happening in the classroom, that you aren't missing anything. "With-it" teachers seem to have eyes in the back of their heads. They avoid becoming absorbed or interacting with only a few students, since this encourages the rest of the class to wander.

Guidelines

Encouraging Student Responsibility

Make basic work requirements clear.

Examples
1. *Specify and post the routine work requirements for headings, paper size, pen or pencil use, and neatness.*
2. *Establish and explain rules about late or incomplete work and absences. If a pattern of incomplete work begins to develop, deal with it early; speak with parents if necessary.*
3. *Make due dates reasonable, and stick to them unless the student has a very good excuse for lateness.*

Communicate the specifics of assignments.

Examples
1. *With younger students, have a routine procedure for giving assignments, such as writing them on the board in the same place each day. With older students, assignments may be dictated, posted, or given in a syllabus.*
2. *Remind students of upcoming assignments. Even college students forget requirements that are listed on the syllabus but never mentioned again.*
3. *If an assignment is complicated or has several parts, give students a sheet describing what to do, what resources are available, when work is due, and so on. Older students should also be told your grading criteria.*
4. *Demonstrate how to do the assignment, do the first question together, or provide a sample work sheet to make sure students know what to do.*

Monitor work in progress.

Examples
1. *When you make an assignment in class, make sure each student gets started correctly. If you check only those who raise their hands for help, you will miss students who think they know what to do but don't really understand, students who are too shy to ask for help, and students who don't plan to do the work at all.*
2. *Check progress periodically. In discussions and recitations, make sure everyone has a chance to respond. That way you can check each student, not just the volunteers.*

Give frequent academic feedback.

Examples
1. *Elementary students should get papers back the day after they are handed in.*
2. *A teacher described by Evertson and colleagues (1984) had students come to her desk one at a time each day to discuss their work. Completed work was quickly graded and the grade recorded as the student watched. This way the students saw immediate results of their efforts.*
3. *Of course, good work can be displayed in class and graded papers sent home to parents each week.*
4. *Students of all ages can keep records of grades, projects completed, and extra credits earned.*
5. *For older students you might break up long-term assignments into several phases, giving feedback at each point. For example, students may be required to turn in a topic, then a list of books, then an outline, then a rough draft, and finally a finished paper.*

These teachers prevent minor disruptions from becoming major. They also know who instigated the problem, and they make sure the right people are dealt with. In other words, they do not make what Kounin called *timing errors* (waiting too long before intervening) or *target errors* (blaming the wrong student and letting the real perpetrators escape responsibility for their behavior).

If two problems occur at the same time, effective managers deal with the more serious one first. For example, a teacher who tells two students to stop whispering but ignores even a brief shoving match at the pencil sharpener communicates to students a lack of awareness. Students begin to believe they can get away with almost anything if they are clever (Charles, 1981).

Being with it does not mean publicly correcting every minor infraction of the rules. This kind of public attention may actually reinforce the misbehavior, as we saw in Chapter 5. Teachers who frequently correct students do not necessarily have the most well behaved classes (Irving & Martin, 1982). The key is to know what is happening and what is important so you can prevent problems. Emmer and colleagues (1984) suggest four simple ways to stop misbehavior quickly:

1. Make eye contact with or move closer to the offender. Other nonverbal signals, such as pointing to the work students are supposed to be doing, might be helpful. Make sure the student actually stops the inappropriate behavior and gets back to work. If you do not, students will learn to ignore your signals.

2. If students are not performing a class procedure correctly, remind the students of the procedure and have them follow it correctly.

3. In a calm, unhostile way, ask the student to state the correct rule or procedure and then to follow it.

4. Tell the student in a clear, assertive, and unhostile way to stop the misbehavior. (We will discuss more about assertive messages to students later in the chapter.)

overlapping:
supervising several activities at once

Overlapping and Group Focus. **Overlapping** means keeping track of and supervising several activities at the same time. Success in this area also requires constant monitoring of the class. In many ways, a teacher must continually manage what Dunkin and Biddle (1974) have called a three-ring circus. For example, a teacher might have to check the work of an individual and at the same time keep a small group working by saying, "Right, go on" (Charles, 1981).

group focus:
keeping as many students as possible involved in activities

Maintaining a **group focus** means keeping as many students as possible involved in appropriate class activities and avoiding narrowing in on just one or two students. All students should have something to do during a lesson. If someone is working a problem at the board, the other students should be working the same problem at their desks. The teacher might ask everyone to write the answer to a question, then call on individuals to respond while the other students compare their answers. Choral responses might be required while the teacher moves around the room to make sure everyone is participating (Charles, 1981). Some teachers have their students use small blackboards or colored cards for responding in groups. This lets the teacher check for understanding as well. For example, during a grammar lesson the teacher might say, "Everyone who thinks the answer is *have run*, hold up the red side of your card. If you think the answer is *has run*, hold up the green side" (Hunter, 1980). This is a way teachers can ensure that all students are involved and check that they all understand the material.

movement management: ability to keep lessons and groups moving smoothly

Movement Management. **Movement management** involves keeping lessons and the group moving with smooth transitions, an appropriate (and flexible) pace, and variety. The effective teacher avoids abrupt transitions, such as announcing a new activity before gaining the students' attention or starting a new activity in the middle of something else (Charles, 1981). In these situations, one-third of the class will be doing the new activity, many will be on the old lesson, several will be asking other students what to do, some will be taking the opportunity to have a little fun, and most will be confused.

Losing Time and Attention

Another transition problem Kounin noted is the slowdown, or taking too much time to start a new activity. Sometimes teachers give too many directions. "Everyone take out a piece of paper. . . . Now get a pencil. . . . Print your name in the upper left-hand corner. . . . Let's see the names. . . . Now put the date in the upper left corner. . . . Today is. . . ." By the time the teacher finishes, the students have lost interest in the project and gone on to entertain themselves.

Problems also arise when teachers have students work one at a time while the rest of the class waits and watches. Charles (1981, pp. 52–54) gives this example:

> During a science lesson the teacher began, "Row one may get up and get their beakers. Row two may get theirs. Now row three. Now, row one may line up to put salt in their beakers. Row two may follow them," and so forth. When each row had gotten the salt, the teacher had them go row by row to get some water. This left the rest of the class sitting at their desks with no direction. At best they were doing nothing. Probably they were dreaming up something with which to entertain themselves.
>
> . . . After every child had the necessary elements . . . the teacher proceeded. "Okay, Roy, now pour the vinegar into the water while we watch. Now Susie, it's your turn. Patti, you're next." The teacher had the students do the activity singly when it would have made sense to have the class do it together.

A teacher who successfully demonstrates withitness, overlapping activities, group focus, and movement management tends to have a class filled with actively engaged students who do not escape his or her all-seeing eye. This need not be a grim classroom. It is more likely a busy place where students are actively learning and gaining competence and a sense of self-worth rather than misbehaving in order to get attention and achieve status.

Of course, no classroom is problem-free. This is especially true in the upper grades. Let's look at some particular problems for secondary teachers and the responses of the effective teachers studied by Emmer and his colleagues (1984).

Special Problems with Secondary Students

Incomplete Work

Many secondary students never complete their work. Besides encouraging student responsibility, what else can teachers do to deal with this frustrating problem? Since students at this age have many assignments and teachers have many students, both teacher and students may lose track of what has and hasn't been completed. The teacher must keep accurate records so everyone will be sure what the students are actually doing. But the most important thing is to enforce the established consequences for incomplete work. Do not pass a student because you know he or she is "bright enough" to pass. Make it clear to these students that the choice is theirs: they can do the work and pass or refuse to do the work and face the consequences.

The Same Rule Broken

There is also the problem of students who continually break the same rules, always forgetting materials, for example, or speaking without raising their hands. What should you do? Seat these students away from others who might be influenced by them. Try to catch them before they break the rules, but if rules are broken, be consistent in applying established consequences. Do not accept promises to do better next time. Teach the students how to monitor their own behavior; some of the self-management techniques described in Chapter 6 should be helpful. Finally, remain friendly with the students. Try to catch them in a good moment so you can talk to them about something other than their rule breaking.

The Defiant Student

The defiant, hostile student can pose serious problems. If there is an outbreak, try to get out of the situation as soon as possible; everyone loses in a public power struggle. One possibility is to give the student a chance to save face and cool down by saying, "It's your choice to cooperate or not. You can take a minute to think about it." If the student complies, the two of you can talk later about controlling the outbursts. If the student refuses to cooperate, you can tell him or her to wait in the hall until you get the class started on work; then step outside for a private talk. If the student refuses to leave, send another class member for the assistant principal. Again, follow through. If the student complies before help arrives, do not let him or her off the hook. If outbursts occur frequently, you might have a conference with the counselor, parents, or other teachers. If the problem is an unreconcilable clash of personalities, the student should be transferred to another teacher.

Violence

Violence or destruction of property is a difficult and potentially dangerous problem. The first step is to send for help and get the names of participants and witnesses. Then get rid of any crowd that may have gathered; an audience will only make things worse. Do not try to break up a fight without help. Make sure the school office is aware of the incident. Usually the school has a policy for dealing with these situations.

THE NEED FOR COMMUNICATION

Communication between teacher and students is essential when problems arise. Communication is more than "teacher talks—student listens." It is more than simply the words exchanged between individuals. We communicate in many ways.

Communication and Metacommunication

TEACHER: Carl, where is your homework?

CARL: I left it in my Dad's car this morning.

TEACHER:	Again? You will have to bring me a note tomorrow from your father saying that you actually did the homework. I won't grade it without the note.
MESSAGE RECEIVED BY CARL:	You are lying. I can't trust you. I need proof you did the work.
TEACHER:	Sit at every other desk. Put all your things under your desk. Jane and Laurel, you are sitting too close together. One of you move up here!
MESSAGE RECEIVED BY JANE AND LAUREL:	I expect you two to cheat on this test.

A new student comes to Ms. Lincoln's kindergarten. The child is messy and unwashed. Ms. Lincoln puts her hand lightly on the girl's shoulder and says, "I know you will like it here." Her muscles tense, and she leans away from the child.

MESSAGE RECEIVED BY THE STUDENT:	I don't like you. I think you are bad.

In all interactions, a message is sent and a message is received. Sometimes teachers believe they are sending one message, but their voices, body positions, choices of words, and gestures may communicate a different message. The underlying or hidden message is the **metacommunication.**

meta-communication: hidden message

Students may hear the metacommunication and respond to it without ever stopping to think, "The teacher said . . . but I know she means. . . ." For example, a student may respond with hostility if she or he feels insulted by the teacher (or by another student) but may not be able to say exactly where the feeling of being insulted came from. Perhaps it was in the teacher's tone of voice, not the words actually spoken. In such cases, the teacher may feel attacked for no reason. "What did I say? All I said was. . . ." The first principle of communication is that people respond to what *they* think was said or meant, not necessarily to the speaker's intended message.

The first step in communicating with students is really hearing what they are saying. True listening requires attention, openness, and sensitivity to the feelings behind the students' words. *(Richard Hutchings/ Photo Researchers)*

There are many exercises you can try in your college courses or in your classroom to practice sending and receiving messages accurately. Students in my classes told me about one instructor who encourages accurate communication by using the paraphrase rule. Before any participant, including the teacher, is allowed to respond to any other participant in a class discussion, he or she must summarize what the previous speaker said. If the summary is wrong, indicating the speaker was misunderstood, the speaker must explain again. The respondent then tries again to paraphrase. The process continues until the speaker agrees that the listener has heard the correct message.

There are several advantages to using the paraphrase rule. People must listen more carefully to each other, since they must paraphrase correctly before speaking themselves. They also learn to be clearer in their communications by hearing how others interpret their messages. And sometimes two people find they only *think* they disagree (or agree) on a subject: often one person disagrees with something the other person never meant to say.

Paraphrasing is more than a classroom exercise. It can be the first step in communicating with students. Before teachers can deal appropriately with any student problem, they must know what the real problem is. A student who says, "That was the dumbest book. Why did we have to read it?" may really be saying, "The book was too difficult for me. I couldn't read it, and I feel dumb." A teacher who responds to the *why* question with a justification for the choice of reading material has missed the point. The student may feel even worse as a result: "Now I'm not just dumb, I've also missed out on this thing the teacher thinks is so important. I'll never catch up. I might as well just give up instead!"

Diagnosis: Whose Problem Is It?

As a teacher, you may find many student behaviors unacceptable, unpleasant, or troubling. It is often difficult to stand back from these problems, take an objective look, and decide on an appropriate response. According to Thomas Gordon (1974), the key to good teacher-student relationships is determining why you are troubled by a particular behavior and whose problem it is. Gordon has developed a systematic procedure for helping teachers diagnose problem situations. The teacher must begin by asking who "owns" the problem. The answer to this question is critical. If it is really the student's problem, the teacher must become a counselor and supporter, helping the student find his or her own solution. The teacher must not assume responsibility for the problem. But if the teacher does "own" the problem, it *is* the teacher's responsibility to find a solution through problem solving with the student.

Diagnosing who owns the problem is not always straightforward. Let's look at three troubling situations to get some practice in this skill:

1. A student writes obscene words and draws sexually explicit illustrations in an encyclopedia.
2. A student tells you that his mother and father had a bad fight and he hates his father.
3. A student quietly reads a newspaper in the back of the room.

Why are these behaviors troubling? If you cannot accept the student's behavior because it has a real effect on you as a teacher—if you are blocked from reaching your goals by the student's action—then *you* own the problem. It is your responsibility to confront the student and seek a solution. A teacher-owned problem appears to be present in the first situation described above—the young pornographer.

If you feel annoyed by the behavior because it is getting in the student's own way or because you are embarrassed for the child, but the behavior does not directly interfere with your teaching, then it is probably the student's problem. The test question is this: Does this student's action tangibly affect you or prevent you from fulfilling your role as a teacher? The student who hates his father would not prevent you from teaching, even though you might wish the student felt differently. The problem is really the student's, and he must find his own solution. (In both the first and second situations, teachers may want to help students confront moral or emotional problems. Nevertheless, teachers must still clarify *whose* emotions and values are involved, how they are involved, and why.)

Situation 3 is more difficult to diagnose. I have had lengthy debates in my class about whose problem it is when a student reads a newspaper in class. One argument is that the teacher is not interfered with in any way, so it is the student's problem. Another argument is that teachers might find the paper reading distracting during a lecture, so it is *their* problem, and they must find a solution. In a gray area such as this, the answer probably depends on how the teacher actually experiences the student's behavior. Having decided who owns the problem, it is time to act.

Counseling: The Student's Problem

Let's pick up the situation in which the student found the reading "dumb." How might a teacher handle this positively?

STUDENT: This book is really dumb! Why did we have to read it?

TEACHER: You are upset that you had to read the book. It seemed like a worthless assignment to you. [Teacher paraphrases the student's statement, trying to hear the emotions as well as the words.]

STUDENT: Yeah! Well, it wasn't really worthless. I mean, I don't know if it was. I couldn't read it.

TEACHER: You had difficulty with the book. It was too hard to read it, and that bothers you.

STUDENT: Sure, I felt really dumb. I know I can write a good report, but I need a different book for reading.

TEACHER: Would you like to choose one?

STUDENT: Great! I have two ideas. . . .

**empathetic
listening:** hearing
the intent and
emotions behind
what another says
and reflecting them
back by
paraphrasing
Here the teacher used what Charles Kelley (1974) calls **empathetic listening** to allow the student to find a solution. (As you can see, this approach relies heavily on paraphrasing.) By trying to hear the student and by avoiding the tendency to jump in too quickly with advice, solutions, criticisms, reprimands, or interrogations, the teacher keeps the communication lines open. Here are a few *unhelpful* responses the teacher might have made:

I chose the book because it is the best example of __ in our library. You will need to have read it before your English II class next year. [The teacher justifies his choice; as has been noted, this prevents the student from admitting that this "important" assignment is too difficult.]

Did you really read it? I bet you didn't do the work, and now you want out of the assignment. [The teacher accuses, and the student hears, "He doesn't trust me!" and must defend herself or accept the teacher's view.]

Your job is to read the book, not ask me why. I know what's best. [The teacher pulls rank, and the student hears, "You are too dumb or immature to decide what is good for you!" The student can rebel or passively accept the teacher's judgment.]

Empathetic, or active, listening can be a helpful response when students bring problems to you. You must reflect back to the student what you hear him or her saying. This reflection is more than a parroting of the student's words; it should capture the emotions, intent, and meaning behind them. Sokolove, Garrett, Sadker, and Sadker (1986, p. 241) have summarized the components of active listening:

1. Blocking out external stimuli
2. Attending carefully to both the verbal and nonverbal messages
3. Differentiating between the intellectual and emotional content of the message
4. Making inferences regarding the speaker's feelings.

When students realize they really have been heard and not evaluated negatively for what they have said or felt, they feel freer to trust the teacher and to talk more openly. Sometimes the true problem surfaces later in the conversation.

Confrontation and Assertive Discipline

Now let's assume a student is doing something that actively interferes with teaching. The teacher decides the student must stop. The problem is the teacher's. Confrontation, not counseling, is required.

"I" message:
clear,
nonaccusatory
statement of how
something is
affecting you

"I" Messages.   Gordon (1974) recommends sending an **"I" message** in order to intervene and change a student's behavior. Basically, this means telling a student in a straightforward, assertive, and nonjudgmental way what she or he is doing, how it affects you as a teacher, and how you feel about it. The student is then free to change voluntarily, and often does so. Here are two "I" messages:

When you leave your locker open, I sometimes bump into it and hurt myself.

When you all call out answers, I cannot concentrate on each answer, and I feel frustrated.

assertive discipline:
clear, firm,
unhostile response
style

Assertive Discipline.   Lee and Marlene Canter (1976) suggest other approaches for dealing with a teacher-owned problem. They call their method **assertive discipline.** Teachers are assertive when they make their expectations clear and follow through with established consequences. Students then have a straightforward choice: they can follow the rules or accept the con-

A private conversation can often soothe wounds, calm nerves, and help to get at the root of a problem or conflict. A willingness to talk and to listen is a prized quality in a teacher. *(Richard Hutchings/Photo Researchers)*

sequences. Many teachers are ineffective with students because they are either wishy-washy and passive or hostile and aggressive.

Passive Style

The passive style can take several forms. Instead of telling the student directly what to do, the teacher tells, or often asks, the student to *try* or to *think* about the appropriate action. The passive teacher might comment on the problem behavior without actually telling the child what to do differently. This kind of comment is often a rhetorical question—"Why are you doing that? Don't you know the rules?" or "Sam, are you disturbing the class?" Or teachers may clearly state what should happen but never follow through with the established consequences, giving the students "one more chance" every time. Finally, teachers may ignore behavior that should receive a response or wait too long before responding.

Hostile Style

A hostile response style involves different mistakes. Teachers may make "you" statements that condemn the student without stating clearly what the student should be doing—"You should be ashamed of the way you're behaving!" or "You never listen!" or "You are acting like a baby!" Teachers may also threaten the students angrily but follow through too seldom, perhaps because the threats are too vague—"You'll be very sorry you did that when I get through with you!"—or too severe. For example, one teacher observed by Canter and Canter (1976) told a student in a physical education class that he would have to sit on the bench for three weeks. A few days later the team was short one member and the teacher let the student play, never returning him to the bench to complete the three-week sentence. At times teachers get so fed up with students that they respond with physical force. Often a teacher who has been passive becomes hostile and explodes when students persist in misbehaving.

True Assertiveness

In contrast with both the passive and hostile styles, an assertive response communicates to the students that you care too much about them and the process of learning to allow inappropriate behavior to persist. (Recall the difference between assertive and aggressive? See Chapter 3.) Assertive teachers clearly state what they expect. To be most effective, the teachers often look into a student's eyes when speaking, address the student by name, and perhaps touch the student's shoulder. The teacher's voice is calm, firm, and confident. They are not sidetracked by accusations such as "You just don't understand!" or "You don't like me!" Assertive teachers do not get into a debate about the fairness of the rules. They expect changes, not promises or apologies. Table 10–1 gives examples of passive, hostile, and assertive responses to two common situations.

Conflict and Negotiations. If "I" messages or assertive responses fail and a student persists in misbehaving, teacher and student are in a conflict. Both believe one cannot win unless the other loses.

Several pitfalls now loom. The two individuals become less able to perceive each other's behavior accurately. Research has shown that the angrier you get with another person, the more you see the other as the villain and yourself as an innocent victim. The other's mistakes are vividly clear to you, but your own actions seem perfectly justified. Since you feel the other person is in the wrong, and since he or she feels just as strongly that the conflict is all your fault, very little mutual trust is possible. A cooperative solution to the problem is almost impossible. In fact, by the time the discussion has gone on a few minutes, the original problem is lost in a sea of charges, countercharges, and self-defense (Johnson, 1972).

Methods of Conflict Resolution

There are three methods of resolving a conflict between teacher and student. One is for the teacher to impose a solution. This may be necessary during an emergency, as when a defiant student refuses to go to the hall to discuss a public outbreak. The second method is for the teacher to give in to the student's demands. You might be convinced by a particularly compelling student argument. But generally it is a bad idea to be talked out of a position.

Problems arise when either the teacher or the student gives in completely. In each case, someone is the loser and has no impact on the final decision. Gordon recommends a third approach, which he calls the *no-lose method*. Here the needs of both the teacher and the students are taken into account in the solution. No one person is expected to give in completely, and all participants retain respect for themselves and each other. The no-lose method is a six-step problem-solving strategy:

1. *Define the problem.* What exactly are the behaviors involved? What does each person want? (Use active listening to help students pinpoint the real problem.)
2. *Generate many possible solutions.* Brainstorm, but remember, don't allow any evaluations of ideas yet.
3. *Evaluate each solution.* Any participant may veto any idea. If no solutions are found to be acceptable, brainstorm again.
4. *Make a decision.* Choose one solution through consensus, with no voting allowed. In the end everyone must be satisfied with the solution.
5. *Determine how to implement the solution.* What will be needed? Who will be responsible for each task? What is the timetable?
6. *Evaluate the success of the solution.* After trying the solution for a while, ask, Are we satisfied with our decision? How well is it working? Should we make some changes?

I have described the suggestions of Charles Kelley, Lee and Marlene Canter, and Thomas Gordon for counseling and confronting students because these approaches give teachers specific strategies to try in difficult situ-

Table 10–1 Passive, Hostile, and Assertive Teacher Responses

Problem Situation:	A third-grade teacher has a number of children who frequently push and shove in order to be first in line. This results in constant fighting and yelling before the class goes outside. Before lunch the problem occurs again.
Passive Response:	The teacher walks up to the children and says, "I don't know what's wrong with you children. You're pushing and shoving again. You children need to learn how to line up like good boys and girls. Now I want you all to try to do that."
Hostile Response:	The teacher walks up to the children who are pushing and roughly yanks them to the back of the line. Then the teacher says angrily, "You push and shove others, I'll push and shove you!"
Assertive Response:	The teacher firmly tells the children, "Stop pushing and shoving." To back up these words, the teacher makes all the children who are pushing and shoving go to the back of the line.
Problem Situation:	Students in an eighth-grade science class frequently cheat on tests. During an exam the teacher observes several students openly looking at their neighbors' papers.
Passive Response:	The teacher says, "Don't forget, I have told you if I catch anyone cheating they will be sorry. So I hope any of you who may be thinking of cheating won't do it."
Hostile Response:	The teacher storms up to the students caught cheating and rips up their papers, shouting, "I hate cheaters. You should be ashamed of yourselves!"
Assertive Response:	The teacher calls the cheating students up to the desk and firmly but quietly tells them, "There is no cheating in this class! I saw you looking at each other's papers, so you all get an F on the test."

Adapted from Canter and Canter (1976), Passive, hostile, and assertive teacher responses. In Assertive discipline: A take-charge approach for today's educator. *Los Angeles: Canter & Associates.*

ations. I have used these methods and found them helpful. By focusing on listening and problem solving, I find it easier to see the student's side of an issue and to remain positive toward students as individuals, even when their behavior leads to problems.

SUMMARY

1. Classroom management is a major challenge and an essential task for teachers. Classrooms are by nature multidimensional, full of simultaneous activities, fast-paced and immediate, unpredictable, public, and affected by the history of students' and teachers' actions. A manager must juggle all these elements every day.

2. Productive classroom activity requires cooperation. Maintaining cooperation is a different task for different age groups.

3. Managers must allow ample time for learning, improve the quality of time use by keeping students actively engaged, and make sure participation structures for every activity are clear, straightforward, and consistent.

4. The most effective teachers set rules and establish procedures for handling predictable problems. Consequences should be established for following and breaking the rules, so the teacher and the students know what will happen in either case.

5. It seems to be essential for effective classroom management to spend the first days of class teaching basic rules and procedures. During these first days, all students should be occupied with organized, enjoyable activities so that they spend little time with nothing to do and learn to function cooperatively in the group.

6. Quick, firm, clear, and consistent responses to infractions of the rules characterize effective teachers.

7. To create a positive environment and prevent problems, teachers must take individual differences into account, maintain student motivation, and reinforce positive behavior.

8. Successful problem preventers are skilled in four areas described by Kounin: withitness, overlapping, group focusing, and movement management.

9. Communication between teacher and student is essential when problems arise. All interactions between people, even silence or neglect, communicate some meaning.

10. Techniques such as paraphrasing, empathetic listening, determining whether the teacher or the student is responsible for the problem, assertive discipline, avoidance of passive and hostile responses, and active problem solving with students help teachers open the lines of positive communication.

KEY TERMS

allocated time	group focus
engaged time	movement management
participation structures	metacommunication
procedures	empathetic listening
rules	"I" message
withitness	assertive discipline
overlapping	

SUGGESTIONS FOR FURTHER READING AND STUDY

CHARLES, C. M. (1981). *Building classroom discipline: From models to practice.* New York: Longman. Describes 7 models of discipline, including those of Kounin and Canter, then presents 20 strategies based on insights from these models.

DOYLE, W. (1986). Classroom organization and management. In M. Wittrock (Ed.), *Handbook of research on teaching* (3rd ed.) (pp. 392–431). New York: Macmillan. This is a wide-ranging discussion of the research on classroom management. Doyle builds a complex model of the classroom and the managerial demands of teaching.

DREIKURS, R., GRUNWALD, B. B., & PEPPER, F. C. (1971). *Maintaining sanity in the classroom: Illustrated teaching techniques.* New York: Harper & Row. This very useful book for teachers gives both a theoretical framework and many techniques for dealing with the whole range of classroom problems.

EMMER, E. T., & EVERTSON, C. M. (1981). Synthesis of research on classroom management. *Educational Leadership, 38,* 342–345. In just a few pages these two experts on classroom management summarize the results of the best research in the area.

EMMER, E., EVERTSON, C., SANFORD, J., CLEMENTS, B., & WORSHAM, M. (1984). *Classroom management for secondary teachers.* Englewood Cliffs, NJ: Prentice-Hall. This is an indispensable guide for secondary teachers. All of the ideas are based on the practices of effective class managers. The same team—Evertson, C., Emmer, E., Sanford, J., Clements, B., & Worsham, M. (1984)—wrote *Classroom management for elementary teachers.* Englewood Cliffs, NJ: Prentice-Hall.

GARRETT, S. S., SADKER, M., & SADKER, D. (1986). Interpersonal communication skills. In J. Cooper (Ed.), *Classroom teaching skills* (3rd ed.). Lexington, MA: Heath. Here you will learn about communication skills step by step and get the chance to practice in several activities.

GORDON, T. (1974). *T.E.T.: Teacher effectiveness training.* New York: Peter H. Wyden. Gordon's very popular book gives many examples of his now-famous active listening and "I" messages, along with other problem-solving techniques for dealing with classroom problems.

JONES, V., & JONES, L. (1986). *Comprehensive classroom management: Creating positive learning environments* (2nd ed). Boston: Allyn & Bacon. A very complete guide to class management, this book deals with motivation, instruction, group dynamics, problem prevention, and courses of action when prevention fails.

Teachers' Forum

The Sum of Experience: Management Tips

Suppose a group of beginning teachers comes to you beset by worries about managing their classes—frustrated by wasted time, disruptions, and uncooperativeness and eager to know if there really are any practical principles they can follow. If you had to sum up your experience and your ideas on classroom management, what would be the essential points you'd want to get across to these new teachers?

Caring and Consistency

Establish an open, loving, caring environment so that your charges can receive lots of positive strokes. Know your students and their backgrounds. Be alert to the signs they send—I'm tired, I'm hurt, I'm hungry—and be ready to act, before they "act out." Be sure your expectations and rules are clearly understood, and be consistent with their applications. Be aware that our tolerance levels vary from day to day; but if we permit inappropriate behavior today, we will see it again tomorrow. Busy, involved students have little time or interest in misbehavior. Be ready to change your pace, plans, or activities if necessary. Keep your voice well modulated. Learn to give silent messages to offenders. Be ready to relieve tensions with a smile or a laugh.

Joan H. Lowe, Fifth-Grade Teacher
Russell Elementary School, Hazelwood, Missouri

Setting the Tone

Good organization is essential for good classroom management. Plan your day so that there are easy transitions from one activity to another. Have work available for students to begin as soon as they arrive—this will set the tone for the day. It often helps to involve the students in the decisions about what is acceptable behavior and what is not and what the consequences of unacceptable behavior should be.

Carol Gibbs, Sixth-Grade Teacher
Happy Valley School, Rossville, Georgia

The Basic Assumptions

There's no substitute for well-organized, enthusiastic teaching. If your students are interested and you are well prepared, behavior is easier to manage. Start with these assumptions: you like to teach; your students want to learn; you have something important to give them. Establish, from the beginning, the division of roles: you are the teacher, fully in charge; they are the students, there to learn. A folksy, chummy, pal-like demeanor diminishes your authority. Whatever your game plan for discipline, whether it be names posted, seating changed, extra assignments, removal from class, or after-school detainment, administer it consistently—this means consistency in your expectations and in what you will not tolerate. Carry out your plan with firmness, but with no shouting. Do it fairly, without sarcasm or shaming. And from the beginning, try hard to create a climate of optimism and cheerfulness, expecting the very best effort from everyone. Your classroom is a good place to be. Learning something is the most satisfying thing in the world. Hindsight has taught me that the best teachers do these things. I wish I had taught this way more often.

Harriet Chipley, Elementary Art Teacher
Lookout Mountain Elementary School, Lookout Mountain, Tennessee

Smooth Transitions

A teacher in your school comes to you for help: his students are having consistent trouble whenever they have to change activities or locations. All the transitions take too long; students keep talking and won't settle down to work. If they are supposed to bring materials with them from one place to another, they invariably forget. What advice would you offer your colleague?

Analyze the Situation and Be Clear

An attempt should be made to pinpoint the reason(s) for the students' unsatisfactory response. On the one hand, the students may be immature and may need guidance in the logistics of changing from one activity to another—perhaps a short lesson on arranging and organizing materials. On the other hand, students may be testing your limits and theirs. In this case, the teacher should state his expectations about conduct clearly, letting the students know very definitely that they are responsible to be in their places with materials ready at a certain designated time.

In either case, it would be helpful for the teacher to post for all to see a list of rules for class procedures; to give a warning signal to students a few minutes before the bell rings, so that they can close out one activity and get ready for the next; and to be certain that all classroom management procedures are clearly spelled out and remain consistent.

Katherine P. Stillerman, Seventh-Grade Language Arts and Social Studies Teacher
Pine Forest Junior High School, Fayetteville, North Carolina

Discipline: The Delicate Balance

Many beginning teachers want so much to be accepted by their students that any distinction between being friendly and being friends becomes blurred. Others go to the opposite extreme and interpret advice to be assertive as a warning that they must be grim disciplinarians. Is there a viable middle ground? What advice would you give new teachers about establishing appropriate relationships with students? What does being assertive mean to you as a teacher? Does the adage "Don't smile until Christmas" have any value?

Friendly but in Charge

Everyone wants to be received favorably and to be well liked. But students expect an authority figure to be in charge of the class. They need someone they can turn to if they have a problem, someone who can guide them through difficult times. Someone who acts and talks to them as a peer will have trouble being believed and respected as the person in charge. The students will feel they have as much authority and independence as the teacher. A teacher can certainly joke and have fun with students, but he or she needs to know where and when to draw the line—without any arguments—*before* the situation gets out of hand. Be firm, fair, caring, supportive, and understanding, and your students will not only like you, they will respect you.

Ida Pofahl, Second-Grade Teacher
Denison Elementary School, Denison, Iowa

Earning Respect

My observations lead me to believe that discipline problems occur when students do not respect their teacher. My strongest suggestion is to *earn* your students' respect, and not to assume that students will automatically respect you simply because of your position. You can earn their respect with your competence, preparation, flexibility, and understanding. *Show* them (don't tell them) that you respect each of them as individuals. There are few discipline problems between people who respect and care for each other. And if you have nothing to smile about until Christmas, you shouldn't be a teacher.

R. Chris Rohde, High School Chemistry Teacher
Chippewa Falls Senior High School, Chippewa Falls, Wisconsin

11

Setting Objectives and Planning

Overview
Teacher Planning   383
Objectives for Learning   383
The Value of Objectives   383
Kinds of Objectives   385
Criticisms   388
In Summary: What Are the Advantages?   389
Task Analysis   390
The Basic Method   390
An Example of Task Analysis   391
Taxonomies   392
The Cognitive Domain   393
The Affective Domain   394
The Psychomotor Domain   395
The Big Picture: Course Objectives   396
Basic Formats For Teaching   398
Recitation and Questioning   398
Lecturing and Explaining   401
Group Discussion   402
Seatwork and Homework   403
Individualized Instruction   405
Settings for Achieving Objectives   408
Interest-Area Arrangements   408
Personal Territories   410
Summary/Key Terms
Suggestions for Further Reading and Study
Teachers' Forum

OVERVIEW   Each Sunday night, thousands of teachers across the country sit planning the upcoming week. Often they begin by outlining the main activities: lecture on Monday, film on Tuesday, and so on. Although this seems like a reasonable way to proceed, an important step may be missing. The teacher may not have asked, What is the purpose of these activities? The teacher may not have really decided what the students are supposed to learn. If the teacher is unclear about the purpose of the activities, the students will probably be even more confused. They are likely to greet any new material with the common refrain, "Will this be on the test?"

Because teachers so frequently begin in the middle by selecting activities rather than at the beginning by determining purposes, I have devoted a large part of this chapter to objectives. We look first at some basic definitions of instructional objectives, their function in the classroom, several different kinds of objectives, and a number of criticisms. Next, we consider how to select objectives, for a lesson or a whole course, based on task analysis and taxonomies of learning outcomes.

Once a teacher has a clear set of purposes in mind, the next step is to decide how to structure the lesson. We discuss several teaching strategies based on the size of the group and the role of the teacher. These strategies include recitation, lecturing, group discussion, seatwork, and individualized instruction. In the final section we consider how to match the physical environment of the classroom to the objectives and activities of the lesson.

By the time you have finished this chapter, you should be able to do the following:

- Describe the functions and levels of teacher planning.
- Give several reasons for using instructional objectives.
- Write objectives, applying Mager's or Gronlund's approach.
- Use task analysis to develop a sequence of objectives.
- Create objectives for cognitive, affective, and psychomotor learning.
- Plan objectives for an entire course.
- Describe situations in which each of the possible formats would be most appropriate—recitation, lecture, group discussion, seatwork, or individualized instruction.
- Draw floor plans that fit your learning goals and teaching methods.

TEACHER PLANNING

In the past few years educational researchers have become very interested in teachers' planning. They have interviewed teachers about how they plan, asked teachers to "think out loud" while planning or keep journals describing their plans, and even studied teachers intensively for months at a time. What have they found? First, planning is a very important step in teaching. In many ways, the plan determines what students will learn because planning transforms the available curriculum into activities, assignments, and tasks for students. Whatever students encounter in class activities will determine to a large extent what they learn. When a teacher decides to devote 5 hours to language arts and 15 minutes to science in a given week, the students in that class will learn more language than science. And once a plan is set, most teachers really try to "get through" all the material (Clark & Peterson, 1986; Denham & Liberman, 1980; Doyle, 1983).

Second, teachers engage in several levels of planning—by the year, term, unit, week, and day. All the levels must of course be coordinated. Accomplishing the year's plan requires breaking the work into terms, the terms into units, and the units into weeks and days. Planning done at the beginning of the year is particularly important because many routines and patterns are established early. For experienced teachers, unit planning seems to be the most important level, followed by weekly and then daily planning (Clark, 1983; Clark & Peterson, 1986).

Third, plans reduce but do not eliminate uncertainty in teaching. Even the best plans cannot (and should not) control everything that happens in class. Clark (1983) has suggested that beginning teachers think of their plans as "flexible frameworks for action, as devices for getting started in the right direction, as something to depart from or elaborate on, rather than as rigid scripts" (p. 13).

Finally, there is no one model for effective planning. Experienced teachers don't necessarily continue to follow the lesson-planning models they learned during their teacher-preparation programs, but many think it was helpful to learn this detailed system as a foundation (Clark & Peterson, 1986). Once you gain experience and many aspects of teaching become more automatic, you should be able to develop your own style of planning.

In the next pages we will examine an approach to planning that can provide an initial foundation. The main steps in this planning model are setting learning objectives, specifying evaluation procedures, and selecting learning activities. Objectives, evaluation procedures, learning activities, settings, and materials must be coordinated throughout the process.

OBJECTIVES FOR LEARNING

The eight items listed in the overview at the beginning of this chapter are examples of instructional objectives. Although there are many different approaches to writing objectives, each assumes that the first step in teaching is to decide what changes should take place in the learner—what is meant to be the outcome of teaching. This leads us to a general definition of an **instructional objective:** it is a clear and unambiguous description of your educational intentions for your students.

instructional objective: clear statement of what students are intended to learn through instruction

The Value of Objectives

Some advocates of instructional objectives have been extremely enthusiastic. At times their zeal has done a disservice to their cause, but many of the advantages they claim for objectives are worth examining.

Student Achievement.　The effects of providing students with instructional objectives are not clear-cut. Having objectives seems to improve achievement, but only under certain conditions. First, objectives can promote learning with activities like lectures, films, and research projects that are loosely organized and less structured. With very structured materials like programmed instruction, objectives seem less important (Tobias & Duchastel, 1974). Second, if the importance of some information is not clear from the learning materials and activities themselves, instructional objectives will probably help focus student attention and thus increase achievement (Duchastel, 1979). Finally, having objectives at the beginning of a reading passage seems to help students remember very specific verbal information from the passage. But when the task involves simply getting the gist of the passage or transferring the information to a new situation, objectives are not as effective. In these situations, it is better to use questions that focus on meaning, inserting the questions right before the passage to be read (Hamilton, 1985).

Improved Communication. In day-to-day classroom interaction, a good number of a teacher's verbal and nonverbal messages may be ambiguous. For example, a teacher may know that one goal of teaching is to foster good citizenship. Everyone would agree that good citizenship is important. This kind of vague purpose is a good example of what Dyer (1967) has called "word magic." Goals stated in word magic sound great. But no one really knows what they mean. What will the students be doing when they are good citizens? One day the teacher may consider that questioning authority is a sign of good citizenship. Another day the same action may be considered bad citizenship (especially if it is the teacher's authority being ques-

When Objectives Help

Word Magic

What kinds of objectives might the teacher have set for this class's study of *Romeo and Juliet?* Acting out a scene may very well help these students to analyze themes, characters, and language and to understand the play's relevance and power. *(Will/Deni McIntyre/Photo Researchers)*

tioned). Specifying learning objectives can help teachers clarify for themselves the changes they believe are important for their students. This will not only make the changes more easily attainable but will also improve communication between teacher and student.

Planning and Testing.   Each day teachers must plan to do something; they must select or create activities and put those activities into some meaningful order. But an infinite number of possible activities exist. Which ones are best? Some criteria must be used to make these decisions. A reasonable approach is to select activities that will help students learn something worth knowing—or, in other words, help them master important objectives. If intended changes in student behavior are not made the central concern in planning, other concerns can take their place. Planning may become haphazard. It may begin to revolve around whatever happens to be available that week in the audiovisual center.

Evaluation Implies
Objectives

In almost every class, teachers must evaluate performance. Distinctions are made between good and poor work. All evaluation, in fact, implies learning objectives. Even if a teacher never specifies objectives, students will become aware of them when the tests or assignments are graded. If, for example, the top grades go to students who are best at memorizing facts, the students will realize that the objective was to memorize facts. If, on the other hand, the objectives are supplied in advance, both students and teacher will know what the criteria are. Students' understanding of the objectives will make studying easier and more efficient. For the teacher, an early statement of objectives will make preparing tests a simpler task.

Kinds of Objectives

One of the factors that distinguishes the various approaches to writing objectives is the level of specificity required.

From the General to the Specific.   In our discussion thus far, you have seen the words *goal, purpose, outcome,* and *objective.* As you may have guessed, there are several levels of goals for education. At a very general, abstract level are the grand goals society might have for graduates of public schools—like increased intellectual development and effective citizenship. At the other end of the continuum are specific subobjectives describing single behaviors. Wayne Johnson, for example, should hold a pencil properly, and Mary Delgado should spell the word *vote* correctly.

Balancing General
and Specific

At the most general level, goals are so vague that they become meaningless as potential guidelines for instruction—this is word magic at work again. One teacher's definition of how to promote intellectual development might be very different from another teacher's. On the other hand, listing every new behavior for every student in the class would require a computer and many bottles of aspirin. In addition, objectives that are too specific may teach poor study habits by focusing the student's attention on specific facts and encouraging the students to skip anything that is not mentioned in the objective (TenBrink, 1986).

Most psychologists and educators agree that we need something between grand generalities and specific item-by-item instructions for each student.

But here the agreement ends. The individual's view of learning will of course influence her or his objectives. Objectives written by people with behavioral views focus on observable and measurable changes in the learner and use terms like *list*, *define*, *add*, or *calculate*. Objectives written by cognitivists emphasize internal changes. Their objectives are more likely to include words like *understand*, *recognize*, *create*, or *apply*. Not surprisingly, cognitive objectives tend to be more general and less clearly measurable than behavioral objectives. They also tend to be less restricting.

operationalize:
make measurable by making specific

There is a way to consider both the cognitive and behavioral perspectives in writing objectives. Look at the examples in Table 11–1. The more general cognitive objectives in the left-hand column have been **operationalized** to form the more specific behavioral objectives in the right-hand column; that is, the more general objectives have been made measurable. Suppose your goals are for students to reason, understand, and appreciate. How can you tell if they have accomplished these goals? One way is to give the students a specific, measurable task that will provide evidence for the change. Let's look at one well-developed method of writing more specific objectives.

Mager: Start with the Specific. Robert Mager has developed a very influential system for writing instructional objectives. Mager's idea is that objectives ought to describe "what the student will be doing when demonstrating his achievement and how you will know he is doing it" (Mager, 1962, p. 53). Mager's objectives are generally regarded as behavioral.

According to Mager, a good objective has three parts. First, it describes the intended student behavior—what must the student *do*? Second, it lists the conditions under which the behavior will occur—how will this behavior be recognized or tested? Third, it gives the criteria for acceptable performance on the test. Table 11–2 shows how the system works.

Using Mager's format, we can develop an objective for this chapter:

In class, without the aid of any course material, write three instructional objectives appropriate for students in your subject area. Each objective must contain all three components described by Mager.

Table 11–1 **Objectives: General and Specific**

General Objectives	More Specific Objectives
The student reasons in solving simple arithmetic problems.	The student solves simple arithmetic problems written in a new form: $3 + 4 = ?$ and $3 + 4 = x$.
The student understands the concept of meter in poetry.	The student scans poems in various meters and correctly identifies the meters.
The student appreciates teamwork.	The student passes the ball when appropriate.

Table 11–2
Mager's Three-Part System

Part	Central Question	Example
Student behavior	Do what?	Mark statements with an F for fact or an O for opinion
Conditions of performance	Under what conditions?	Given an article from a newspaper
Performance criteria	How well?	75% of the statements correctly marked

From R. F. Mager, Preparing instructional objectives. © *1962 by Fearon, Palo Alto, CA. Reprinted by permission.*

Mager's system, with its emphasis on final behavior, requires a very explicit statement. Mager contends that such an effort is worthwhile. He believes that often students can teach themselves if they are given well-stated objectives. Norman Gronlund offers a different approach.

Gronlund: Start with the General. Gronlund (1978) believes that an objective should be stated first in general terms (understand, appreciate, and so on). Then the teacher should clarify by listing a few sample behaviors that would provide evidence that the student has attained the objective. Gronlund's system is often used for writing cognitive objectives.

Look at the example in Table 11–3. Gronlund's point is that the goal here really is *to understand.* The teacher does not want the student to stop with defining, identifying, or distinguishing. Instead, the teacher looks at performance on these sample tasks to decide if the student really does understand. The teacher could just as well have chosen three different tasks to indicate understanding.

Gronlund's emphasis on specific objectives as samples of more general student ability is important. A teacher could never list all the behaviors that might be involved in truly understanding some subject area. But stating an initial general objective makes it clear that understanding is the purpose.

Table 11–3
Gronlund's Combined System of Writing Objectives

Part	Example
General objective	Understands the terms used in plane geometry
Subobjective A	Defines the terms in his or her own words
Subobjective B	Identifies the meaning of the terms when used in context
Subobjective C	Distinguishes between those terms that are similar in meaning

Adapted from N. E. Gronlund (1978), Stating behavioral objectives for classroom instruction (2nd ed.). *Toronto: Macmillan, pp. 4–5.*

The most recent research on instructional objectives tends to favor approaches similar to Gronlund's. It seems reasonable to state a few central objectives in general terms and clarify them with samples of specific behaviors (Dressel, 1977; Hamilton, 1985).

Criticisms

As noted at the beginning of the section, not all educators believe writing objectives is valuable. Many of the criticisms are worth considering. We will look at three common criticisms of objectives and then offer a set of Guidelines to help teachers avoid problems.

The Time Factor. A number of critics have argued that specifying an objective for every learning outcome requires more time than most teachers have. Those in favor of objectives have called this an admission of laziness. But MacDonald-Ross's (1974) finding that 10,000 objectives would be necessary to define all the outcomes of a typical educational psychology text lends support to the notion that time is a factor worth considering. Two possible solutions are to acknowledge that not all outcomes can be specified and to get help from outside sources. Many publications provide lists of potential objectives. One source is the Instructional Objectives Exchange, which has collected and rated objectives in many areas. Originally a nonprofit organization, this is now a private company.

10,000 Objectives?

The Trivialization Factor. According to some critics, since trivial, short-term goals are easier to specify than higher-level, more relevant goals, instructional objectives are likely to be basically irrelevant. The curriculum can stagnate if objectives are too precise and teachers try to stick to the objectives year after year. Teachers bound to such objectives may ignore any new developments that don't fit in with the objectives. Of course, using objectives will not force a teacher to teach low-level abilities or to resist changes in the curriculum, but it might strengthen these possibilities.

Spoon-feeding?

Many critics feel that the use of instructional objectives has a potential effect of spoon-feeding students. If only low-level abilities are specified as outcomes, and tests are merely a collection of instructional objectives turned into questions, spoon-feeding is indeed likely. The students' opportunities to question and explore might well be limited. But this does not have to be the case. Consider this objective, prepared for a relatively high-level secondary course in history:

> In class, without access to notes, given three presidential elections between 1900 and 1944, write a 200-word essay describing how domestic policy might have changed if the defeated presidential candidate had been elected.

For the test, the teacher selects the elections of 1900, 1912, and 1940. Since these particular years were not specified in the objective, students must know a number of facts. What president was chosen in each election year between 1900 and 1944? Who ran against each? What was the domestic policy advocated by each candidate? What were key events during each president's term in office? Besides understanding these facts and concepts, the students would have to be able to make inferences, give evidence to

How subjective should objectives be? Writing objectives for the arts can prove difficult: personal judgments are often implied and perhaps are unavoidable. Can "good" artwork be broken down into specifics? What role does the teacher's intuition play? *(Rogers/ Monkmeyer Press)*

support hypotheses, and think divergently (come up with many possible right answers). This is hardly spoon-feeding!

The Difficulty of Writing Objectives for Some Subjects.   It may be relatively easy to write objectives for math classes, but what about objectives in art classes? Advocates of objectives insist that teachers in all fields, even in the humanities and arts, make judgments about student work. Therefore, the criteria for making judgments can be applied to determine learning objectives (Popham, 1969). The argument is that if you can judge a good painting when you see one, you can write objectives that specify the criteria you use to decide if the painting is good. This seems to make some sense but is not necessarily true in all cases. As MacDonald-Ross (1974) has pointed out, just because you can recognize a good painting, perhaps intuitively, it does not mean you can write objectives describing how all good painting would be evaluated. And judgment of what is "good" is subjective, after all.

So the problem of writing objectives in some subjects is real. Again, it might be worthwhile to supplement the objectives you write with those available from such sources as the Instructional Objectives Exchange.

In Summary: What Are the Advantages?

Because instructional objectives were developed primarily in industry and the military, the techniques often sound somewhat mechanistic. But this need not be the case. In fact, there is nothing less humane than playing the guess-what-you-should-be-learning game with students. Using instructional objectives properly can be a way of humanizing the educational process. Certainly a hard look at what students should be able to do when they have completed a unit can help a teacher distinguish important and enduring outcomes from irrelevant ones. A teacher who considers which objectives are most attainable must take into account the strengths and weaknesses of each student and is thus more likely to tailor teaching to the individuals in

Subjective/Objective

Guidelines

Instructional Objectives

Avoid word magic—phrases that sound noble and important but say very little.

Examples
1. *Keep the focus on specific changes that will take place in the students in your class.*
2. *Ask students to explain the meaning of the objectives. If they can't give specific examples of what you mean, the objectives are not communicating your intentions to your students.*

Suit the activities to the objectives.

Examples
1. *If the goal is the memorization of vocabulary, give the students memory aids and practice exercises.*
2. *If the goal is the ability to develop well-thought-out positions, consider position papers, debates, team projects, or mock trials.*
3. *If you want students to become better writers, give many opportunities for writing and rewriting.*

Make sure your tests are related to your objectives.

Examples
1. *Write objectives and rough drafts for tests at the same time.*
2. *Weight the tests according to the importance of the various objectives and the time spent on each.*

---

the class. And offering objectives to students gives each a chance to take more responsibility for her or his own learning. The Guidelines should help you whether you decide to make thorough use of objectives or just to prepare them for certain assignments.

TASK ANALYSIS

When teachers try to decide what students should learn, they confront an overwhelming number of possibilities. Several solutions have been proposed to this dilemma. Here we will look at one of the most influential methods of determining learning objectives, task analysis.

The Basic Method

task analysis: system for breaking down a task hierarchically into basic skills and subskills

The procedure involved in **task analysis** was originally developed by R. B. Miller (1962) to help the armed services train personnel. Miller's system begins with a definition of the final performance requirement, what the trainee (or student) must be able to do at the end of the program or unit. Then the objectives that will lead to the final goal are specified. The procedure simply breaks skills and processes down into subskills and subprocesses.

In the classroom, the teacher begins by asking: "What will the students have to do before they can reach the final goal I have in mind?" The answer to this question may help identify several underlying skills. Let's say five skills are identified. The teacher then asks: "What must the students be able to do to succeed at each of these five skills?" The answer this time should produce a number of subskills for each of the basic skills. This working backward should give a full picture of all the abilities a student must have to accomplish the objective successfully. (You may remember from Chapter 8 that working backward is a problem-solving heuristic.)

An Example of Task Analysis

Consider an example. Assume students must write a position paper based on library research. What skills and subskills are required for this assignment? Figure 11–1 offers the beginning of a task analysis for this assignment.

If the teacher assigned the position paper without analyzing the task in this way, what could happen? Some of the students might not know how to use the card catalog. They might search through one or two encyclopedias, then write a summary of the issues based only on the encyclopedia articles. The teacher wanted a synthesis of several sources, but these students used only one type of source. They would receive low grades on the assignment. Another group of students might know how to use the card catalog, tables of contents, and indexes but have difficulty reaching conclusions. They might hand in lengthy papers listing a number of summaries about different ideas. These students would also get low grades, but for different reasons. A final group of students might be able to draw conclusions, but their written presentations might be so confusing and grammatically incorrect that the teacher could not understand what they were trying to say. Each of the groups failed, but for different reasons.

Figure 11–1   **Task Analysis for a Library Assignment**

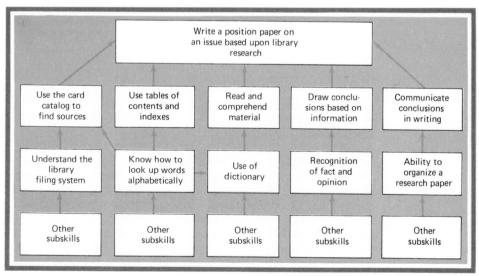

A teacher who assigns a research report and assumes that all students already know how to use a card catalog may be in for a shock. A task analysis of the skills needed for researching and writing papers may help prevent such surprises. *(Mimi Forsyth/Monkmeyer Press)*

A task analysis gives a picture of the logical sequence of steps leading toward the final goal. An awareness of this sequence can help teachers make sure that students have the necessary skills *before* they are given an assignment. In addition, when students have difficulty, the teacher can pinpoint problem areas. If a task analysis had been done on the assignment we just discussed, the teacher could have written several different objectives for the students. Some students would have had to work on mastering the supporting objectives before they could tackle the final assignment. Other students could have gone right to the library and begun work.

The process can also work in reverse. Student errors can highlight the subskills required to complete a task successfully. If you have not done a task analysis before giving an assignment, you can use the information from student errors to analyze the task before presenting it to next year's class. Each year of experience can lead to better teaching.

TAXONOMIES

taxonomy: classification system

cognitive domain: in Bloom's taxonomy, memory and reasoning objectives

affective domain: emotional objectives

psychomotor domain: physical ability objectives

Several decades ago, as interest in defining educational objectives was increasing, a group of experts in educational evaluation led by Benjamin Bloom studied the idea of defining objectives very systematically. They developed a **taxonomy,** or classification system, of educational objectives. Objectives were divided into three **domains: cognitive, affective,** and **psychomotor.** A handbook describing the objectives in each area was eventually published. In real life, of course, behaviors from these three different domains occur simultaneously. While students are writing (psychomotor), they are also remembering or reasoning (cognitive), and they are likely to have some emotional response to the task as well (affective). One reason for considering these areas separately is to accentuate the affective and psychomotor areas, since schools often focus on cognitive changes alone.

The Cognitive Domain

Six basic objectives are listed in Bloom's taxonomy of the cognitive domain (Bloom, Engelhart, Frost, Hill, & Krathwohl, 1956):

Cognitive
Objectives

1. *Knowledge:* Remembering or recognizing something previously encountered without necessarily understanding, using, or changing it.
2. *Comprehension:* Understanding the material being communicated without necessarily relating it to anything else.
3. *Application:* Using a general concept to solve a particular problem.
4. *Analysis:* Breaking something down into its parts.
5. *Synthesis:* Creating something new by combining different ideas.
6. *Evaluation:* Judging the value of materials or methods as they might be applied in a particular situation.

It may be helpful to consider these objectives as a hierarchy, each skill building on those below, but this may not be an accurate picture. It is very difficult to divide intellectual abilities into separate skills that build on each other. For example, Pring (1971) suggests that you cannot separate comprehension of terms or symbols from a working knowledge of how to apply them. In certain fields, such as mathematics, the levels in the hierarchy do not seem to fit the structure of knowledge in the subject very well. But Bloom's taxonomy does encourage educators to think systematically about objectives and broadens our view about possible outcomes (Furst, 1981).

Consider how the taxonomy might suggest objectives for a course. Table 11–2 gave one example of a specific objective at the analysis level in a social studies class—distinguishing between fact and opinion in news stories. At the synthesis level, an objective for the class could be written this way:

Higher-Level
Cognitive Examples

Given a list of three facts, write a two-paragraph news story taking a position on an issue and documenting the position with the facts.

At the level of evaluation, the objective might be written like this:

Given two articles that present contradictory views of a recent event, decide which article gives the fairer presentation and justify your choice.

Using Cognitive Objectives for Evaluation. The progression from one level to another in the taxonomy of objectives can also be helpful in planning evaluation, since different types of test items are appropriate for objectives at the various levels. Gronlund (1982) has suggested that knowledge objectives can best be measured by true-false, short-answer, matching, or multiple-choice tests. Such tests will also work with the comprehension, application, and analysis levels of the taxonomy.

But these types of tests will not be adequate for measuring synthesis and evaluation objectives. Here the *essay test* is more appropriate. Essay tests will also work at the middle levels of the taxonomy but are not as efficient for measuring the more straightforward knowledge objectives. So for measuring middle-level objectives you have a choice of methods. When it comes to the lowest and highest levels, however, you must take care to see that the evaluation methods fit the objectives.

The Affective Domain

The objectives in the taxonomy of the affective domain run from least committed to most committed (Krathwohl, Bloom, & Masia, 1956). At the lowest level, a student would simply pay attention to a certain idea. At the highest level, the student would adopt an idea or a value and act consistently with that idea. There are five basic objectives in the affective domain.

Affective Objectives

1. *Receiving:* Being aware of or attending to something in the environment; this is the I'll-listen-to-the-concert-but-I-won't-promise-to-like-it level.

2. *Responding:* Showing some new behavior as a result of experience; at this level a person might applaud after the concert or hum some of the music the next day.

3. *Valuing:* Showing some definite involvement or commitment; at this point a person might choose to go to a concert instead of a film.

4. *Organization:* Integrating a new value into one's general set of values, giving it some ranking among one's general priorities; this is the level at which a person would begin to make long-range commitments to concert attendance.

5. *Characterization by value:* Acting consistently with the new value; at this highest level, a person would be firmly committed to a love of music and show it openly and consistently.

Like the basic objectives in the cognitive domain, these five objectives are very general. To write specific learning objectives, you must state what students will actually be doing when they are receiving, responding, valuing, and so on. For example, an objective for a nutrition class at the valuing level might be stated:

An Example

After completing the unit on consumer action, at least 50 percent of the class will support the junk-food boycott project by giving up candy for a month.

Evaluating Affective Objectives. There are at least two ways in which assessing affective objectives may be helpful. Evaluation of these objectives can serve diagnostic purposes, to see what values students bring to class. Final evaluation may also help teachers gauge their success in bringing about a desired change in attitudes or values.

Suppose, for example, that an important goal in a science class is commitment to ethics in conducting and reporting research. If the teacher learns at the beginning of the course that students approve of falsifying scientific results to further one's position, the teacher will have a ready-made affective goal to pursue throughout the course. If the teacher learns that students still feel this way at the end of a course, the teacher may wish to approach that topic a little differently the next time.

Measurement Difficulties

But it is difficult to measure the attainment of affective objectives. How can the teacher in the nutrition example be sure that students have given up candy in support of a junk-food boycott? The best method may be to ask them to report anonymously on their candy consumption; if students have to sign their names to their responses, the process may counteract the desire to reach another affective goal, honesty. Also, if students are graded on their success in boycotting candy, this process might really encourage the students to give false reports. In most cases, it is best not to grade affective measures.

The Psychomotor Domain

Until recently, this area has been overlooked for the most part by teachers not directly involved in physical education. A taxonomy of the objectives in the psychomotor domain was not developed until the early 1970s (Harrow, 1972). It is arranged from the lowest level of observable movements to the highest. There are six basic objectives.

Psychomotor
Objectives

1. *Reflex movements:* Actions that occur involuntarily in response to some stimulus (stretching, blinking, posture adjustments).
2. *Basic fundamental movements:* Innate movement patterns formed from a combination of reflex movements (walking, running, jumping, pushing, pulling).
3. *Perceptual abilities:* Translation of stimuli received through the senses into appropriate movements (following verbal instructions, dodging a moving ball, maintaining balance, jumping rope).
4. *Physical abilities:* Basic movements and abilities that are essential to the development of more highly skilled movements (distance running, weight lifting, toe touching, basic ballet exercises).
5. *Skilled movements:* More complex movements requiring a certain degree of efficiency (movement patterns involved in sports, dance, and the fine arts).
6. *Nondiscursive communication:* Ability to communicate through body movement (gestures, facial expressions, choreographed dance movements).

Objectives in the psychomotor domain should be of interest to a wide range of educators, including those in fine arts, vocational-technical education, and special education. Many other subjects, such as chemistry, physics, and biology, also require specialized movements and well-developed

Psychomotor and affective objectives often overlap. Led by an enthusiastic teacher, these children are using physical and perceptual abilities and at the same time learning to value health and exercise. *(Ellis Herwig/Stock, Boston)*

hand and eye coordination. Using lab equipment or art materials means learning new physical skills. Here are two psychomotor objectives:

Examples

Four minutes after completing a one-mile run in eight minutes or under, your heart rate will be below 120.

Without referring to notes or diagrams, assemble the appropriate laboratory apparatus to distill _____.

Methods of Evaluating Psychomotor Objectives. Learning in the psychomotor area really means developing a particular performance ability. How do you assess a student's performance? The obvious answer is to ask the student to demonstrate the skill and observe the student's proficiency. In some cases, the performance of the skill results in a product, so assessment of the product can be substituted for observation of the actual performance. An art student learning to use the potter's wheel, for example, should be able to produce a pot that is symmetrical, stands by itself, and meets a number of other criteria.

When students are actually performing, you need a checklist or rating scale to help you focus on the important aspects of the skill being evaluated. A checklist usually gives the measurable dimensions of performance, along with a series of blank spaces for judgments. An example is found in Table 11–4. A rating scale generally follows the same plan but has a numerical scale (often from 1 to 5) to rate each aspect of performance, rather than blanks for yes or no judgments.

Once you have learned to write and evaluate objectives in all three domains, your job is not over. You will be teaching more than single skills and lessons. You must plan an integrated program of study and then evaluate progress in that program.

behavior-content matrix: a planning method that integrates expected student behaviors with course topics to arrive at specific objectives

The Big Picture: Course Objectives

In planning objectives for an entire unit, many teachers develop a **behavior-content matrix**. The first step is to decide the general objectives for the

Table 11–4 | **Checklist for Evaluating the Use of an Oral Thermometer**

_____	1.	Removes thermometer from container by grasping nonbulb end.
_____	2.	Wipes thermometer downward from nonbulb end with fresh wiper.
_____	3.	Shakes down thermometer to less than 96° while holding nonbulb end.
_____	4.	Places bulb end of thermometer under patient's tongue.
_____	5.	Tells patient to close lips but to avoid biting down on thermometer.
_____	6.	Leaves thermometer in patient's mouth for 3 minutes.
_____	7.	Removes thermometer from patient's mouth by grasping nonbulb end.
_____	8.	Reads temperature to the nearest two-tenths of a degree.
_____	9.	Records temperature reading on patient's chart.
_____	10.	Cleans thermometer and replaces in container.

Adapted from N. E. Gronlund (1977), Constructing achievement tests (2nd ed.). Englewood Cliffs, NJ: Prentice-Hall, p. 98. Adapted with permission of publisher.

Table 11–5 A Behavior-Content Matrix for a Unit on Decimals

Content	Behaviors				Total Objectives
	Knowledge	Comprehension	Application	Analysis	
Multiplication		1	1	1	3
Addition and Subtraction			1	1	2
Division		1	1	1	3
Renaming	2	2		1	5
Definitions	2			1	3
Total Objectives	4	4	3	5	16

From J. R. Hills (1976), Measurement and evaluation in the classroom. *Columbus, OH: Merrill, p. 8.*

course, stated in broad terms. Each general objective is then broken down into two components. The first is student behavior—that is, knowledge of facts, knowledge of concepts, ability to generalize, and so on. The second component is course content—that is, the subjects to be covered in the course. If one of the general objectives in an English class was to enhance appreciation of American literature, student behaviors might include knowledge (of authors, historical periods, book titles, themes, and styles), ability to compare (different styles, different themes), and ability to criticize. The course content component would include the different novels, poems, short stories, and so on that you wished to cover.

Drawing It Up   In drawing up the matrix or chart, the teacher lists student behaviors across the top, usually from simplest to most complex, and content areas down the side. At each square where a particular behavior intersects with a particular content area, the teacher can write instructional objectives. In this way, the teacher makes sure all important behaviors and topics are *considered* as possible objectives. Priorities can be set, with several objectives for some squares and none for others, depending on the outcomes the teacher is seeking. At test time, the teacher can emphasize key areas by asking more questions from the most important squares. If you look at Table 11–5, you will see that this teacher has decided to emphasize knowledge and comprehension of renaming and knowledge of definitions in this unit on decimals. The numbers indicate how many objectives are to be written for each behavior and content intersection.

If you develop a behavior-content matrix for a course, you may avoid many of the potential problems with instructional objectives. You are less likely to present trivial objectives or spoon-feed students. A behavior-content matrix also makes it possible to see all the objectives of a course at once and to organize them in the most logical sequence. Examples of plans for many different subject areas at both the elementary and secondary levels can be found in a handbook by Bloom, Hastings, and Madaus (1971).

Let us assume you have developed the objectives for your class and have a general idea of the goals for the entire year. What next? You still need to decide what to do on Monday. The following section describes a variety of methods for turning objectives into action in the classroom.

BASIC FORMATS FOR TEACHING

We begin with the strategy many people associate most directly with teaching: reciting and answering questions.

Recitation and Questioning

recitation: format of teacher questioning, student response, and teacher feedback

The **recitation** approach to teaching has been with us for many years. A teacher poses questions, and students answer them. The teacher's questions generally follow some sort of plan to develop a framework for the subject matter involved. The students' answers are often followed by reactions from the teacher, such as statements of praise, correction, or requests for further information. The pattern from the teacher's point of view consists of structure (setting a framework), solicitation (asking questions), and reaction (praising, correcting, and expanding) (Clark, Gage, Marx, Peterson, Staybrook, & Winne, 1979). These steps are repeated over and over again.

Let us consider the heart of recitation, the soliciting or questioning phase, by looking first at the different kinds of questions that might be asked and then at ways of responding to student answers.

Kinds of Questions. Much has been written to describe the kinds of questions teachers could ask. Some educators have estimated that high school teachers ask an average of 395 questions per day (Gall, 1970). What are these questions like? Bloom's taxonomy of objectives in the cognitive domain is often used to categorize questions. Table 11–6 offers examples of different questions at the different levels.

We discussed convergent and divergent thinking when we looked at theories of intelligence and creativity and returned to the subject when we dealt with problem solving. Questions may also be **convergent** (asking for only one right answer) or **divergent** (asking for many possible answers). Questions about concrete facts are convergent: Who ruled England in 1540? Who wrote *Peter Pan?* Questions dealing with opinions or hypotheses are divergent: Why did the United States go to war in 1898? What do you think of nuclear power plants?

convergent questions: questions having a single correct answer

divergent questions: questions for which there are no single correct answers

Quite a bit of space in education textbooks has been devoted to urging teachers to ask both high-level (analysis, synthesis, and evaluation) and divergent questions. Is this really an effective approach? Recent research has provided several surprises.

Fitting the Questions to the Students. Stallings and Kaskowitz (1975) and Soar (1973) have found that the frequency of knowledge questions, comprehension-level questions, convergent questions, and single-answer questions is positively related to student learning. In these studies, high-level questions were negatively related to student learning. But three facts should be

Table 11–6 Classroom Questions for Objectives in the Cognitive Domain

Category	Type of Thinking Expected	Examples
Knowledge (recognition)	Recalling or recognizing information as learned	Define. . . . What is the capital of . . . ? What did the text say about . . . ?
Comprehension	Demonstrating understanding of the material; transforming, reorganizing, or interpreting	Explain in your own words. . . . Compare. . . . What is the main idea of . . . ? Describe what you saw. . . .
Application	Using information to solve a problem with a single correct answer	Which principle is demonstrated in . . . ? Calculate the area of . . . Apply the rules of . . . to solve . . .
Analysis	Critical thinking; identifying reasons and motives; making inferences based on specific data; analyzing conclusions to see if supported by evidence	What influenced the writings of . . . ? Why was Washington, D.C. chosen . . . ? Which of the following are facts and which are opinions? Based upon your experiment, what is the chemical . . . ?
Synthesis	Divergent, original thinking; original plan, proposal, design, or story	What's a good name for this . . . ? How could we raise money for . . . ? What would the United States be like if the South had won . . . ?
Evaluation	Judging the merits of ideas, offering opinions, applying standards	Which U.S. senator is the most effective? Which painting do you believe to be better? Why? Why would you favor . . . ?

Adapted from M. Sadker and D. Sadker (1986), Questioning skills. In J. Cooper (Ed.), Classroom teaching skills: A handbook (3rd ed.). Lexington, MA: D.C. Heath, pp. 143–160.

kept in mind in interpreting these results. The students were in primary grades; they were from low socioeconomic backgrounds; and their achievement was measured with test questions at the knowledge and comprehension levels.

Other investigators have reached different conclusions. For example, Redfield and Rousseau (1981) examined 14 studies and concluded that higher-order questions can lead to achievement gains when teachers are trained to use this approach appropriately.

It appears that both types of questions can be effective (Gall, 1984). However, different patterns seem to be better for different students. The best pattern for younger students and for lower-ability students of all ages is simple questions allowing a high percentage of correct answers, ample encouragement, help when the student does not have the correct answer, and praise. For high-ability students, the successful pattern includes harder questions at both higher and lower levels and more critical feedback (Medley, 1977; Ward & Tikunoff, 1976).

No matter what their age or ability, all students should have some experience with thought-provoking questions and, if necessary, help in learning how to answer them. As we saw in Chapter 8, in order to master critical thinking and problem-solving skills, we must have a chance to practice them. Students also need time to think about their answers. But research shows that teachers wait an average of only *one second* for students to answer (Rowe, 1974). Consider the following slice of classroom life (Sadker & Sadker, 1986, p. 170):

<table>
<tr><td>Enough Time to Think?</td><td>TEACHER:</td><td>Who wrote the poem "Stopping by Woods on a Snowy Evening"? Tom?</td></tr>
<tr><td></td><td>TOM:</td><td>Robert Frost.</td></tr>
<tr><td></td><td>TEACHER:</td><td>Good. What action takes place in the poem? Sally?</td></tr>
<tr><td></td><td>SALLY:</td><td>A man stops his sleigh to watch the woods get filled with snow.</td></tr>
<tr><td></td><td>TEACHER:</td><td>Yes. Emma, what thoughts go through the man's mind?</td></tr>
<tr><td></td><td>EMMA:</td><td>He thinks how beautiful the woods are . . . . (She pauses for a second)</td></tr>
<tr><td></td><td>TEACHER:</td><td>What else does he think about? Joe?</td></tr>
<tr><td></td><td>JOE:</td><td>He thinks how he would like to stay and watch. (Pauses for a second)</td></tr>
<tr><td></td><td>TEACHER:</td><td>Yes—and what else? Rita? (Waits half a second) Come on, Rita, you can get the answer to this. (Waits half a second) Well, why does he feel he can't stay there indefinitely and watch the woods and the snow? . . .</td></tr>
<tr><td></td><td>SARAH:</td><td>Well, I think it might be—(Pauses a second)</td></tr>
<tr><td></td><td>TEACHER:</td><td>Think, Sarah. (Teacher waits for half a second) All right then—Mike? (She waits again for half a second) John? (Waits half a second) What's the matter with everyone today? Didn't you do the reading?</td></tr>
</table>

The types of questions asked and the amount of time allowed for answering can make the difference between a classroom full of eager students and a sea of blank faces. *(Paul Conklin/ Monkmeyer Press)*

Very little thoughtful responding can take place in this situation. When teachers learn to wait at least five seconds before calling on a student to answer, students tend to give longer answers; more students are likely to participate, ask questions, and volunteer appropriate answers; student comments involving analysis, synthesis, inference, and speculation tend to increase; the students generally appear more confident in their answers (Rowe, 1974; Sadker & Sadker, 1986; Swift & Gooding, 1983). This seems like a simple improvement in teaching, but five seconds of silence is not that easy to handle. It takes practice. You might try asking students to jot down ideas or even discuss the question with another student. This makes the wait more comfortable and gives students a chance to think. Of course, if it is clear that students are lost or don't understand the question, waiting longer will not help. When your question is met with blank stares, rephrase the question or ask if anyone can explain the confusion.

Responding to Student Answers.   What do you do after the student answers? The most common response, occurring about 50 percent of the time in most classrooms, is simple acceptance—"OK" or "Uh-huh" (Sadker & Sadker, 1986). But there are better reactions, depending on whether the student's answer is correct, partially correct, or wrong. Rosenshine and Stevens (1986) provide these guidelines. If the answer is quick, firm, and correct, simply accept the answer or ask another question. If the answer is correct but hesitant, give the student feedback on *why* the answer is correct— "That's right, Chris, because the Senate does not have the power to . . . ." This allows you to explain the material again. If this student is unsure, others may be confused as well. If the answer is partially or completely wrong but the student has made an honest attempt, you should probe for more information, give clues, simplify the question, review the previous steps, or reteach the material. If the student's wrong answer is silly or careless, however, it is probably better to simply correct the answer and go on. Whatever you do, don't let misunderstandings go uncorrected.

Lecturing and Explaining

Some studies have found that lecturing takes up one-sixth to one-fourth of all classroom time. Teachers in the high grades, of course, lecture more than teachers in the low grades (Dunkin & Biddle, 1974). You will probably learn about how to lecture in your methods classes. Many different approaches are available; the system you choose depends on your objectives and the subject you are teaching. You will certainly want to keep in mind the age of your students. The younger your students, the briefer and simpler your explanations should be. You may also want to follow a basic four-part format suggested by Shostak (1986).

1. Introduce the presentation so as to put your students in an interested, receptive frame of mind. This is often called *set induction* or creating an **anticipatory set** (Hunter, 1982). Techniques for set induction include brief reviews, advance organizers, curiosity-provoking questions, and demonstrations.
2. Make your presentation. Ausubel's expository teaching has much to offer here, even though Ausubel's approach depends more on interaction than on lecturing. Organization, clarity, comparisons, and examples are critical for effective explanations.

anticipatory set:
an interested,
receptive frame of
mind in students

3. Keep students engaged and attentive throughout the presentation. Here the ideas we have already discussed in the chapters on cognitive perspectives and motivation should be helpful.

4. End with a summary and reinforcement so students have a sense of closure and satisfaction.

When to Lecture?

In considering the lecture method, you will have to make decisions about when to use it. Lecturing is appropriate for communicating a large amount of material to many students in a short period of time. The teacher can integrate information from many sources and give students a more complete understanding of a subject in less time than it would take for the students to integrate all the information themselves. Lecturing is a good method for introducing a new topic, giving background information, and motivating students to learn more on their own. Lecturing also helps students learn to listen accurately and critically. Finally, lecturing gives a teacher a chance to see which students appear confused and to make on-the-spot changes to help them understand (Gilstrap & Martin, 1975). Lectures are therefore most appropriate for cognitive and affective objectives at the lower levels of the taxonomies described earlier—for knowledge, comprehension, application, receiving, responding, and valuing.

Disadvantages

With all these advantages, lecturing may sound like the ideal method. But consider these four disadvantages. First, you may find that some students have trouble listening for more than a few minutes at a time and simply tune you out. Second, lecturing puts the students in a passive position and may prevent them from asking or thinking of questions. Third, students learn and comprehend at different paces, whereas a lecture proceeds at the lecturer's own pace. Finally, the material covered in a lecture may often be communicated just as well in a text assignment or a handout (Gilstrap & Martin, 1975). If your objectives include having students analyze a problem, create solutions, arguments, essays, poems, short stories, paintings, and so on, or evaluate work, then you must go beyond lecturing to methods that require more direct student involvement.

Group Discussion

Group discussion is in some ways similar to the recitation strategy described earlier. A teacher may pose questions, listen to student answers, react, and probe for more information. But in a true group discussion the teacher tries to assume a less dominant role. Students ask and answer each other's questions and respond to each other's answers. The teacher becomes the moderator, trying to involve as many of the students as possible in the discussion, keeping the discussion on the topic (one of the hardest tasks), and helping students summarize and draw conclusions.

Usefulness

Again, choices about when to use group discussion can best be made with an understanding of the advantages and disadvantages of the method in relation to your objectives. On the positive side, the students are directly involved and have the chance to participate. Group discussion helps students learn to express themselves clearly, to justify opinions, and to tolerate different views. Group discussion also gives students a chance to ask for clarification and get more information. Finally, students can assume responsibility by sharing the leadership of the group with the teacher (Gilstrap & Martin, 1975). Thus, group discussions are appropriate for objectives like evaluation of ideas, development of tolerant attitudes, and synthesis of personal viewpoints. Discussions are also useful when students are trying to understand difficult concepts that go against common sense. As we saw in Chapter 8, many scientific concepts, like the role of light in vision or Newton's laws of motion, are difficult to grasp because they contradict common-sense notions. By thinking together, challenging each other, and suggesting and evaluating possible explanations, students are more likely to reach a genuine understanding.

Limitations   Of course, there are disadvantages. First, class discussions are quite unpredictable and may easily digress into exchanges of ignorance. Second, some members of the group may have great difficulty in participating and may become anxious if forced to speak. Third, a good deal of preparation may be necessary to ensure that participants have a common background of knowledge on which to base the discussion. Finally, large groups are often unwieldy. In many cases, a few students will dominate the discussion while the others daydream. The Guidelines on the next page may help you keep your group discussions on track.

Seatwork and Homework

seatwork:
independent
classroom work

Although students spend many hours every week on **seatwork** and homework, little is known about how to use these techniques effectively. There is some evidence that well-designed homework increases student achievement (Walberg, Pascal, & Weinstein, 1985). There is little research on the effects of seatwork, but it is clear that this technique is often overused. Seatwork should follow up a lesson and give students supervised practice. It should *not* be the main mode of instruction.

If properly designed and supervised, both seatwork and homework can help students master a range of objectives, from simple drill and practice of knowledge to thoughtful evaluations of complex ideas. Several conditions must be met to make the work worthwhile. Of course, the assignments or seatwork must be meaningful extensions of the class lessons, not just busywork. To benefit from these assignments, students must stay involved and do the work. The first step toward involvement is getting everyone started right. Students should understand the assignment. It may help to do the first few questions as a class, to clear up any misconceptions. Finally, students must be held accountable for completing the work correctly, not just for filling in the page. This means the work should be checked, errors should be corrected, and the results should count toward the class grade (Brophy & Good, 1986).

Monitoring   Seatwork particularly requires careful monitoring. As you saw in the previous chapter, effective teachers supervise students, keeping them actively involved in the materials so that the time spent on seatwork is not wasted. Being available to students doing seatwork is more effective than offering help to students before they ask for it. To be available, you should move around the class and avoid spending too much time with one or two students. Short, frequent contacts are best (Brophy & Good, 1986; Rosenshine, 1977).

Guidelines

Leading Class Discussions

Invite the participation of shy children.

Examples
1. "What's your opinion, Joel?"
2. "We need to hear from some other students. What do you think, Kevin?"
3. Don't wait until there is a deadly silence to ask shy students to reply. Most people, even those who are verbal and confident, hate to break a silence.
4. Be sure that questions directed to shy students can be answered easily.

Direct student comments and questions back to another student.

Examples
1. "That's an unusual idea, Steve. Kim, what do you think of Steve's idea?"
2. "That's an important question, John. Maura, do you have any thoughts about how you'd answer that?"
3. Encourage students to look at and talk to one another rather than wait for your opinion.

Make sure you understand what a student has said. If you are unsure, other students may be unsure as well.

Examples
1. Ask a second student to summarize what the first student said; then the first student can try again to explain if the summary is incorrect.
2. "Karen, I think you're saying . . . . Is that right, or have I misunderstood?"

Probe for more information.

Examples
1. "That's a strong statement. Do you have any evidence to back it up?"
2. "Tell us how you reached that conclusion. What steps did you go through?"

Bring the discussion back to the subject.

Examples
1. "Let's see, we were discussing . . . and Sarah made one suggestion. Does anyone have a different idea?"
2. "Before we continue, let me try to summarize what has happened thus far."

Give time for thought before asking for responses. Some students find it easier to speak if they write down a few ideas first.

Example
1. "How would your life be different if television had never been invented? Jot down your ideas on paper, and we will share reactions in a minute." After a few minutes: "Jean, will you tell us what you wrote?"

When a student finishes speaking, look around the room to judge reactions.

Examples
1. If other students look puzzled, ask them to describe why they are confused.
2. If students are nodding assent, ask them to give an example of what was just said or further evidence to back up the argument.

Adapted from R. Dreikurs, B. B. Grunwald, & F. C. Pepper (1971), Maintaining sanity in the classroom: Illustrated teaching techniques. New York: Harper and Row, pp. 100–120.

Seatwork does not have to mean confinement to one's desk or the drudgery of filling in a dull workbook; it can cover a range of objectives. With all the materials she needs at hand and an unambiguous assignment, this student is unlikely to be distracted. *(Four by Five)*

What kinds of tasks and materials keep students involved? One clue is found in a study by Kounin and Doyle (1975). When the teachers in this study arranged materials beforehand for their preschool students, the students were more attentive to the task. When the students had to stop to find needed materials, they often became distracted. So structure is especially important when students work on their own. Students should see the connection between the seatwork and the lesson. The objectives should be clear, all the materials that might be needed should be provided, and the work should be easy enough that students can succeed on their own. Success rates should be high—near 100 percent. When seatwork is too difficult, students often resort to guessing or copying just to finish (Anderson, 1985).

Individualized Instruction

individualized instruction: approach designed to meet individual students' needs, interests, abilities, and work pace

Individualized instruction does not necessarily mean independent work. **Individualized instruction** involves each student working with learning plans designed to meet his or her own needs, interests, and abilities.

Modifying Lessons to Fit Individual Needs. To tailor a learning activity to individual students, a teacher might vary one or more of the following: (1) the pace of learning; (2) the instructional objectives; (3) the activity or the materials; (4) the reading level; and (5) the methods by which students are to demonstrate what they have learned.

Perhaps the simplest form of individualized instruction is to let students work at their own pace on the same assignment. The material must be broken down into a sequence of objectives and learning activities or assignments. After mastering one objective, a student can move on to the next.

The second variable in individualized instruction is the choice of learning objectives. If you establish a set of objectives, then pretest the class on the objectives, you may find that many students are already able to do much of the work. Instead of insisting that each student move through the same sequence of objectives, you can tailor the objectives to the needs, interests, and abilities of different students or different groups of students. A low-ability student might need to work on objectives related to concrete skills. The steps in the task and the objectives would have to be small and specific. A gifted student might work toward objectives that call for high-level thinking and abstraction. For this student, the steps need not be small. Clearly, you need a variety of objectives across many ability levels to accommodate a heterogeneous group of students.

Another variable in individualized instruction is the learning activity itself. Even if students are moving toward the same objectives, they might use different means to achieve those objectives. One student might rely on the textbook, while another might read library books or newspaper stories. A third student could use audiovisual resources. Students with reading problems, students who have impaired vision, or students who have difficulty remembering what they read might listen to tapes or play simulation games together. Gifted students might do independent library or field research. Individual contracts, which we discussed in Chapter 6, are possibilities. In your methods courses you may learn about other approaches, such as learning centers and individualized learning packages.

A fourth variable has just been touched on—reading level. All your students may be capable of working toward the same objective, but some may require material at a lower reading level than the rest. Most of the students in a high school class may be able to write a two-page paper comparing the Great Depression and the present economic situation, but some of them may need background reading material at the junior high level or even lower. It is not always possible to find such a wide range of reading materials. Information sources other than the printed word—tapes, films, photographs, cartoons, and so on—may have to be included.

A last variable that can be tailored to fit the needs of individual students is the way in which students are required to demonstrate their new learning. Students who have difficulty with written expression might first be given oral tests or asked to tape their answers to written tests on cassettes. Gifted students might demonstrate learning by completing major papers or projects. For other students, frequent tests might be better. Some learning can also be expressed nonverbally, by drawing pictures, graphing relationships, making a model, or assembling a collage.

Whatever method is chosen to individualize instruction, a teacher must know the subject well in order to analyze the task—to break it down into small units and to arrange the units into a meaningful sequence. Most of the methods also rely heavily on clear objectives. Since students are often working on their own, without the teacher's direct control, they must know what they are expected to learn before they can make good choices about how to learn. Objectives define these expectations.

Field research might be just the right way to individualize instruction for a gifted student. Perhaps this student working at an archaeological site will log her findings, write a scholarly paper or a fictionalized account about the historical period she's investigating, or even decide to pursue archaeology as a career—all are possible. This kind of project can spark imaginations. *(Mimi Forsyth/Monkmeyer Press)*

Research on Individualized Instruction.   In practice, the results of individualized instruction have not always matched the expectations. When used as the *only* form of instruction, these approaches are not superior to traditional methods for elementary and secondary students. But individualized methods do seem quite effective for college students (Bangert, Kulik, & Kulik, 1983). It is possible that completely individualized systems leave elementary and secondary students on their own too much. Time is wasted. Only the most motivated and self-directed students can stay involved. Most students don't get the direct teaching and explanation that they need. The teacher's time is absorbed with preparing and correcting individual assignments—leaving less time for demonstrating, presenting, explaining, and reteaching.

This doesn't mean that teachers should make every student work at the same pace, on the same objectives and activities, at the same reading level. Many elements of individualized instruction can be incorporated into regular class lessons. For example, students can work at their own pace on assignments matched to their ability but study and practice together in cooperative, mixed-ability learning groups like those described in Chapter 9. This variation of cooperative learning, called *Team Assisted Individualization,* has proved very effective in elementary school mathematics classes (Slavin & Karweit, 1985). Good teachers have been individualizing for years when they make sure that the books chosen for library assignments match the reading levels of the students. Individualized assignments can provide remediation and enrichment, if carefully designed and monitored. At times it makes sense to send some children into a different grade for instruction in one subject. Two second-grade students, for example, joined my daughter's sixth-grade class for science. No extra lesson planning was required for this, just some coordinating of schedules.

Today, no discussion of teaching methods would be complete without an examination of computer-assisted instruction. This is such an important area that I have devoted an Epilogue to it. In addition, on the disk that accompanies this text, you will find several examples of computer programs for teaching a variety of subjects.

SETTINGS FOR ACHIEVING OBJECTIVES

In recent years, psychologists have become interested in the role of the physical environment in classroom learning. Instead of taking the room arrangement for granted, many teachers have discovered how to match the setting to objectives and activities. To understand the impact of the physical environment on learning in classrooms, you should be familiar with two basic ways of organizing space.

Territoriality

Indignant cries of "This is my desk!" are familiar to many elementary school teachers. In most traditional classrooms, a student's desk is inviolable territory. Territoriality rules in this type of classroom arrangement. The space is divided into individual territories that belong to their owners, at least until the teacher changes everyone's seat. This type of organization is particularly suitable for lessons addressed to the whole class.

Function

A second way of arranging space is by function. In this arrangement, space is divided into interest areas or work centers that contain curriculum materials for specific topics, directions for activities, and work surfaces. Everyone has access to all areas. This type of arrangement is best for situations where small groups work simultaneously on a variety of activities.

These two ways of organizing space are not mutually exclusive; many teachers use a design that combines the two. Individual students' desks are placed in the center, with interest areas in the back or around the periphery of the room. This allows the flexibility needed for both large- and small-group activities.

Interest-Area Arrangements

Recent research on this topic has shown that the design of interest areas can influence the way the areas are used by students. For example, working with a classroom teacher, Carol Weinstein (1977) was able to make changes in interest areas that helped the teacher meet her objectives of having more girls involved in the science center and having all students experiment more with a variety of manipulative materials. In a second study, changes in a library corner led to more involvement in literature activities throughout the class (Morrow & Weinstein, 1983).

Teachers are often puzzled by how to design interest areas that match their objectives for the students. Here are several suggestions.

Decide What Activities You Want the Classroom to Accommodate. For example, if you are in a self-contained elementary classroom, you might wish to set up interest areas for reading, arts and crafts, science, and math. If you are teaching one particular subject on the junior or senior high level, you may wish to divide your room into several areas, perhaps for audiovisual activities, small-group instruction, quiet study, and projects. List these activities in a column, and next to each note whether any pose special spatial requirements. For example, art and science should be near the sink; science should also be near windows if you wish to grow plants; a quiet study area should not be in front of the door; small-group instruction should be near the board.

Draw Several Floor Plans, Then Choose the Best.   Use graph paper if possible, and draw to scale. As you work, keep in mind these principles:

Design Principles

1. *What are the fixed features?* What are the "givens" of the room that you must deal with—where are the doors, windows, sockets? You don't want an audiovisual center in a corner without an electrical socket!

2. *Have easy access to materials.* Materials should have a clearly labeled place of their own, and these places must be easy to reach if you want students to use the materials. Shelves toward the center of the room seem to be more likely to attract attention than those placed in the corners. There should be enough shelves so that materials do not have to be placed in piles on top of each other.

3. *Students need clean, convenient surfaces on which to use equipment.* The closer this surface is to the materials, the better.

4. *Work areas should be private and quiet.* Tables or work areas should not be placed in the middle of traffic lanes, and a person should not have to pass through one area to get to another. Noisy activities should be placed as far as possible from quiet ones, and you can increase the feeling of quiet and privacy by placing partitions such as bookcases or pegboards between areas or within large areas.

5. *There should be ease of supervision in each area.* If you plan to put up partitions, make sure they are low enough for you to see over them comfortably. If your classroom is too much like a maze, you will have difficulty supervising activities in a quiet, efficient way.

6. *Avoid dead spaces and "racetracks."* Check to see that you have not placed all the interest areas around the outside of the room, leaving a large dead space in the middle. You also want to avoid placing a few items of furniture right in the middle of this large space, creating a "racetrack" around the furniture. Both encourage rowdiness, perhaps because they resemble playgrounds and so communicate to the pupils that it is permissible to run here.

7. *Provide choices.* Different people have different spatial needs. Some people prefer closed, small spaces in which to work; others may find such places too confining.

8. *Provide flexibility.* At times you may wish to have students work alone, in small groups, or with many others. If you cannot arrange to have spaces for all these possibilities at one time, try to ensure that your design is flexible enough so that it can be changed to meet the requirements of new activities.

Try the New Arrangement; Evaluate and Make Changes.   Only by monitoring the use of the environment can difficulties be identified and solved. Even then, the suggestions presented here cannot guarantee that students will select materials and work purposefully with them. Rather, the common goal of these suggestions is to remove as much physical friction from the classroom system as possible, so that students can easily select and use materials. Incidentally, do not neglect to enlist the aid of your students. They have to live in the room, too, and designing a classroom can be a very educational, challenging experience!

Personal Territories

environment-behavior research: research on effects of physical settings on behavior and attitudes

Can the physical setting influence teaching and learning in classrooms organized by territories? Almost all the **environment-behavior research** in these classrooms has examined the relationship between seating position and variables such as students' attitudes toward school, grades, and class participation. Let's look briefly at a few of the most intriguing studies.

Firsthand experience in traditional classrooms tells us that the most interested students sit at the front, and those who yearn for an early escape station themselves as close to the door as possible. Does research support this observation? In an extensive research project examining elementary and secondary classes, Adams and Biddle (1970) found that verbal interaction was concentrated in the center front of the classroom and in a line directly up the center of the room. The data were so dramatic that Adams and Biddle coined the term **action zone** to refer to this area of the room.

action zone: area of a classroom where the greatest amount of interaction takes place

Do students who are interested in a course and who wish to participate select seats in the front, or do teachers assign front seats to students who tend to participate? Does a front-seat position somehow cause students to become more interested and involved in class? These questions remain unresolved, but front-seat location does seem to increase participation from those students who are predisposed to speak in class, whereas a seat in the back will make it more difficult to participate and easier to sit back and daydream (Woolfolk & Brooks, 1983). In addition, even though most rooms have an action zone where participation is greatest, this area is not always front and center. In some classes it may be on one side or near a particular learning center (Good, 1983).

Varying Seating Plans

Many teachers vary the seating in their classrooms so the same students are not always consigned to the back of the room. Another reason to change seating is to make the arrangement more appropriate for particular objectives and activities, as we've discussed. Since too much rearranging can be a waste of time and an invitation to chaos, Musgrave (1975) distinguishes between home-base formations, semipermanent arrangements that are suitable for a wide number of teaching and learning situations, and special formations, which give needed variety and are suited to a particular lesson.

Figure 11–2 shows several home-base formations other than rows and columns. Horizontal rows share many of the advantages of row and column arrangements. Both are useful for independent seatwork, presentations, and recitations; they encourage students to focus on the teacher; and they simplify housekeeping. Horizontal rows permit students to work more easily in pairs. This formation is also best for demonstrations, since students are closer to the teacher. However, it is a poor arrangement if a teacher wishes to encourage large-group interaction.

Clusters of four or circle arrangements are best for student interaction. Circles are especially useful for discussions but still allow for independent seatwork. Clusters permit students to talk, help one another, share materi-

Figure 11–2 Some Home-Base Formations

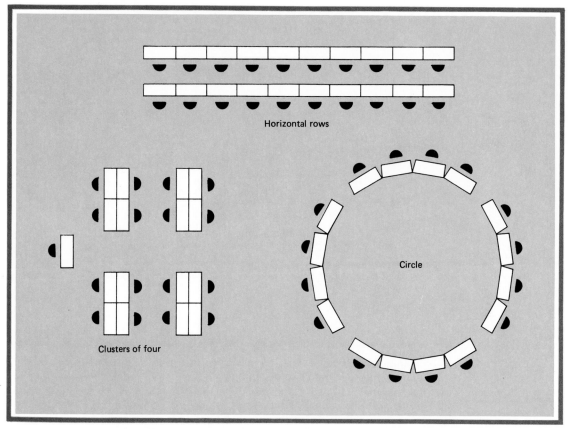

Horizontal rows

Clusters of four

Circle

Adapted from G. R. Musgrave (1975), Individualized instruction: Teaching strategies focusing on the learner. *Boston: Allyn and Bacon, pp. 49, 52, 54.*

als, and work on group tasks. Both arrangements, however, are poor for whole-group presentations and may make class control more difficult.

Figure 11–3 shows several special formations. The debate arrangement and interest stations are probably familiar. The stack formation, where students sit close together near the focus of attention (the back row may even be standing), should only be used for short periods of time, since it is not comfortable for a long period and can lead to discipline problems. On the other hand, it can create a feeling of group cohesion and is helpful when the teacher wants students to watch a demonstration, brainstorm on a class problem, or see a small visual aid.

Although the physical environment can hinder or aid the realization of a teacher's goals in ways that are real and important, it is not all-powerful. Arranging desks in a circle will not guarantee increased participation in a discussion. A cozy reading area will not solve reading problems. Nevertheless, it is essential that teachers consider the classroom space at the same time that they focus on the objectives and teaching methods. All play an important role in the establishment of an optimal learning environment.

Figure 11–3 **Some Special Formations**

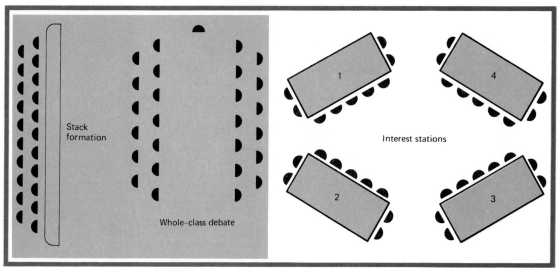

Adapted from G. R. Musgrave (1975), Individualized instruction: Teaching strategies focusing on the learner. *Boston: Allyn and Bacon, pp. 48, 63, 65.*

SUMMARY

1. Planning on several different levels is an important step in teaching, though there is no single model to depend on.

2. Instructional objectives state a teacher's intentions for what students will learn. Objectives help provide structure, let students know what they are studying for or working toward, improve teacher-student communication, and provide guidance in writing fair and balanced tests.

3. Critics of instructional objectives have argued persuasively that objectives are time-consuming, tend to be irrelevant because trivial objectives are easier to create, tend to be too difficult to create for some subjects, and place too many restrictions on students' inclination to explore on their own.

4. Two approaches to writing objectives are Mager's specific behavior objectives and Gronlund's combination of general and specific objectives.

5. Using task analysis, a teacher identifies all the skills and subskills necessary to master a goal or objective. Specific objectives are written for each subskill, forming a logical sequence of steps.

6. Bloom and others have developed taxonomies categorizing basic objectives in the cognitive, affective, and psychomotor domains. A taxonomy encourages systematic thinking about relevant objectives and ways to evaluate them.

7. One straightforward method for planning an entire unit is a behavior-content matrix, which can help teachers integrate desired student behaviors with specific items of course content.

8. The teaching format for putting objectives into action should be suited to the objectives. Recitation can involve various types of questions, which should fit students' abilities and motivation levels; teacher responses to answers should not be too hasty in most cases and should provide appropriate feedback. Lecturing is efficient for communicating a large amount of new material to a large group but may keep students too passive and ignore individual learning rates.

Group discussion encourages involvement, clarity of expression, tolerance, and responsibility but can digress unpredictably and leave out the anxious or unmotivated. Homework and seatwork are useful if they involve real work, are specific, engage students, and are well supervised.

9. In individualized instruction the teacher can vary the pace, objectives, activities, reading level, or method by which students demonstrate learning.

10. There are two basic kinds of spatial organization, territorial (the traditional classroom arrangement) and functional (dividing space into interest or work areas). Flexibility is often the key. Access to materials, convenience, privacy when needed, ease of supervision, and a willingness to reevaluate plans are important features in choosing physical arrangements.

KEY TERMS

instructional objective	psychomotor domain	anticipatory set
operationalize	behavior-content matrix	seatwork
task analysis	recitation	individualized instruction
taxonomy	convergent questions	environment-behavior research
cognitive domain	divergent questions	action zone
affective domain		

SUGGESTIONS FOR FURTHER READING AND STUDY

BANGERT, R. L., KULIK, J. A., & KULIK, C. (1983). Individualized systems of instruction in secondary schools. *Review of Educational Research, 53*, 143–158. This review of the effects of individualized instruction reaches some surprising conclusions.

COOPER, J. (Ed.). (1986). *Classroom teaching skills* (3rd ed.). Lexington, MA: D. C. Heath. Three chapters in this book are designed to develop your teaching skills. Each chapter has objectives, activities, and a mastery test. The chapters are: Sadker, M., & Sadker, D. (1986), "Questioning Skills"; Shostak, R. (1986), "Lesson Presentation Skills"; TenBrink, T. D. (1986), "Writing Instructional Objectives."

FURST, E. J. (1981). Bloom's taxonomy of educational objectives for the cognitive domain: Philosophical and educational issues. *Review of Educational Research, 51*, 441–454. A thoughtful critique of Bloom's taxonomy.

GALL, M. (1984). Synthesis of research on teachers' questioning. *Educational Leadership, 41*, 40–47. A brief but thorough look at the kinds of questions teachers ask and their effects on student learning.

GRONLUND, N. E. (1978). *Stating behavioral objectives for classroom instruction* (2nd ed.). Toronto: Macmillan. This is a very practical book about using instructional objectives.

KAPFER, M. B. (Ed.). (1978). *Behavioral objectives: The position of the pendulum.* Englewood Cliffs, NJ: Prentice-Hall. This book has chapters by many experts on the use of behavioral objectives in instruction.

MAGER, R. (1962). *Preparing instructional objectives.* Palo Alto, CA: Fearon. Perhaps the most influential work on how to write behavioral objectives. Mager's book is written with style and humor in branching-program format.

REDFIELD, D. L., & ROUSSEAU, E. W. (1981). A meta-analysis of experimental research on teacher-questioning behavior. *Review of Educational Research, 51*, 181–193. These researchers compare the results of many studies on teacher questions and student learning.

WALBERG, H. J., PASCAL, R. A., & WEINSTEIN, T. (1985). Homework's powerful effects on learning. *Educational Leadership, 42*, 76–79. A very prohomework statement. For a criticism of this article and a rebuttal from the authors, see the May 1986 issue of *Educational Leadership.*

WEINSTEIN, C. (1979). The physical environment of the school and student behavior. *Review of Educational Research, 49*, 577–610. This article offers a thorough review of research on the physical aspects of schools and classrooms and their effects on student behavior.

Teachers' Forum

What Are Lesson Plans Worth?

Some very experienced teachers believe that writing out lesson plans is a complete waste of time. How would you respond?

Lesson Plans Work

Throughout my teaching experience, I have found that my students' most successful learning experiences come from those lessons I have planned the most carefully. Lesson plans give structure to activities, relating them to past and future learning. Plans allow me to narrow my instructional focus to specific objectives without losing sight of the general goals of education. They also provide a useful reference tool: I can go back to previous plans to determine which methodology and which materials were most successful in what circumstances. And with carefully written plans, I can be more accurate in my evaluations of a child's performance.

Arleen Wyatt, Third-Grade Teacher
Happy Valley School, Rossville, Georgia

Objectives: Sources and Standards

How do you establish instructional goals for your students and your subject(s)? Have you found teachers' manuals or curriculum guides helpful? What makes for the most effective objectives?

Gifted Objectives

Compared to regular instructional programs, there are few materials available for teaching gifted and talented students, so teachers of these students write much of the curriculum themselves, sharing developed units with other gifted teachers. We might choose unit topics that could be presented at an introductory level in a regular classroom and expanded and presented at a more advanced level for the gifted classes. Or we might choose topics that would not fit into a regular classroom program at all. A curriculum for the gifted and talented should provide a varied, differentiated program that helps move students into areas of skill development not possible in the regular classroom setting. The curriculum should establish objectives at the highest levels of affective and cognitive skills—analysis, synthesis, evaluation. It should be open-ended and allow each student to choose what to investigate, to develop goals and methods, to determine what will constitute a finished product, to evaluate that product, and to demonstrate the product to others.

Richard D. Courtright, Gifted and Talented Elementary Teacher
Ephesus Road Elementary School, Chapel Hill, North Carolina

Letting Students Know

Do you tell your students what your objectives are? Do you tell them what your performance standards are as well? Why or why not?

Purposes and Standards Make the Difference

We all—adults and children—need to know that what we're learning serves some purpose. Without this, learning becomes trivial. If reasons are stated in terms children can understand, they are much more willing to tackle the work. They also need to know what's expected of them: is this particular lesson simply to introduce them to a new concept, or will they be expected to master the concept, and if so, in what kind of time framework? They must know, too, when their efforts are acceptable, and why.

Ida Pofahl, Second-Grade Teacher
Denison Elementary School, Denison, Iowa

The Choice Is Yours: Help!

Sometimes student teachers get "stuck" on a particular teaching method. Students can get stuck in their roles, too—some students always participate, and some never do. How would you help student teachers expand their repertoire of teaching strategies and decide on appropriate ones? How would you help them ensure the participation of all students?

Experimenting and Monitoring

When working with a student teacher to develop a curriculum, I use a planning web to identify the content and list the many ways each section can be taught. The student teacher selects a different strategy for each section. This way, he or she can experiment with several methods, gain practice with each, and choose those with which he or she is most comfortable. To monitor the number of students who participate, I tape or video several lessons; the student teacher listens to or watches the tapes and notes the proportion of teacher versus student participation. I also observe lessons and mark on a seating chart the number of responses each student makes during a class period. Then the student teacher and I discuss various strategies for achieving greater participation.

Ruth Roberts, Seventh-Grade Earth Science and Biology Teacher
Greece Athena Junior High School, Rochester, New York

Seatwork: Always Boring?

A common criticism of seatwork is that it is busywork: students get bored, their attention wanders, and the time ends up wasted. How can seatwork assignments be structured so that they are valid, positive learning experiences?

A Difficult but Worthwhile Endeavor

Seatwork can be a valid teaching tool if properly planned. The success of a seatwork assignment hinges on several variables that teachers must take into account—the who, what, where, when, how, and why of the students and the assignment: the personalities of the students and the Gestalt of the whole class; the background knowledge students bring to the subject and to the task; the physical environment and its conduciveness to the task; how fatigued, distracted, or stimulated students are at the particular time of day; the procedure and the essential materials and their accessibility; and the existing motivation for the task as well as the extra reinforcement necessary to encourage self-directed work.

In addition, teachers need a thorough knowledge of the subject matter, legitimate long-range goals, and specific, behaviorally stated short-range objectives. Seatwork then becomes one of the comprehensive, productive, daily assignments that are the culmination of this kind of extensive planning. As for the students, they must see a legitimate correlation between an assignment's purpose and its actual completion. There must be a predetermined criterion for success, and actual completion of the task must be also be reinforced. Seatwork can and should be exciting and motivating!

Laura Atkinson, Special Education Teacher
Chapel Hill, North Carolina

12

Effective Teaching

Overview
The Search for the Keys to Success 418
Do Teachers Make a Difference? 419
Methods for Studying Effective Teaching 420
An Example of a Research Program 420
Characteristics of Effective Teachers 421
Meanwhile, What's Happening with the Students? 426
Academic Tasks 426
Effective Teaching for Different Subjects 429
Basic Skills: Direct Instruction 430
Beyond the Basics 434
Effective Teaching with Different Students 434
Different Strategies for Younger and Older Students 435
Students with Different Aptitudes 435
Integrating Ideas about Effective Teaching 440
A Second-Grade Class That Works 440
A Fifth-Grade Class That Works 442
A Secondary Class That Works 443
Teacher Effectiveness: Conclusions 444
Summary/Key Terms
Suggestions for Further Reading and Study
Teachers' Forum

Teachers make many decisions affecting the lives of students. These decisions range from how to position desks to how long to spend teaching reading or reviewing homework each day. Even when students are working independently or in small unsupervised groups, they are influenced by decisions the teacher has made about such things as materials, grouping, and timing.

In this chapter, we examine in depth what is known about the role of the teacher in student learning. Are there particular characteristics that distinguish effective from ineffective teachers? Then we'll shift to the student. Students learn by participating in the tasks set for them by teachers. But students are not passive containers, waiting to be filled with knowledge. They are powerful players in a dynamic situation. We will look at how they exert their power to influence teaching and learning.

Next we turn to the teaching of basic skills. Research in recent years has identified a cluster of principles that can guide the teaching of basic, explicit information and procedures. Finally, we will explore effective teaching beyond the basics and discuss how to match teaching strategies to the demands of the subject matter and the aptitudes of the students.

By the time you finish this chapter, you are likely to have many new ideas about methods and approaches to try in the classroom. More specifically, you should be able to do the following:

- Describe a number of characteristics that effective teachers seem to share.
- List steps that can ensure clarity in presentation.
- Discuss the role of academic tasks in learning.
- Give examples of lessons based on the principles of direct instruction, on the Hunter model, and on the Missouri Mathematics Program.
- Plan a unit in your subject for a low-ability class.
- Choose one lesson in your own area and explain how you would go about presenting it to the students you will be teaching.

THE SEARCH FOR THE KEYS TO SUCCESS

The search for the secret of successful teaching is not a new one. But until recently it hasn't been very successful. In the 1950s the Committee on Criteria of Teaching Effectiveness of the American Educational Research Association stated, "After 40 years of research on teacher effectiveness, during which a vast number of studies have been carried out, one can point to few outcomes . . . that a teacher-education faculty can employ in planning or improving teacher-education programs" (AERA, 1953, p. 657). In the 1960s and 1970s, several widely publicized studies concluded that teachers have very little impact on student learning (Coleman, Campbell, Wood, Weinfeld, & York, 1966; Jencks et al., 1972). Based on these reports, it seemed that factors such as social class and student ability were the main influences on learning. Many people wondered . . .

Do Teachers Make a Difference?

Response to Coleman and Jencks

A closer look at the Coleman and Jencks reports reveals many problems in the design of this research (Good, 1982; Program on Teaching Effectiveness, 1976). These studies looked mainly for correlations between such things as the verbal ability or social class of the teachers and the general intellectual skills of the students. Schoolwide averages were generally used. The studies did not try to relate what actually happened in individual classrooms to the achievement of students, nor did they examine the effects of individual teachers within each school. Since the research was purely correlational, we have no basis for inferring any causal relationships. There appears to be no relationship between the average social class of the teachers in a school and the general intellectual skills of the students, but this does not really answer the basic question: Do individual teachers make a difference in the day-to-day learning of their students?

Partly in response to the Coleman and Jencks reports, many researchers set out to answer this question. Their efforts have had profound implications for teaching. Based on their research, many states have changed regulations for teacher certification. The findings of these studies are required reading in many teacher-preparation programs and are included on most national tests for teachers. In this chapter you will see what we have learned from this explosion of research on teaching.

This teacher obviously takes her job seriously. Do her efforts make a substantial difference for her students? What could she do to be more effective with her class? Recent research has a number of answers. *(Richard Hutchings/ Photo Researchers)*

Methods for Studying Effective Teaching

How would you go about identifying the keys to successful teaching? You might ask students, principals, college professors of education, or experienced teachers to list the characteristics of good teachers. Or you could do intensive case studies of a few classrooms over a long period. You might observe classrooms, rate different teachers on certain traits, and then see which traits were associated with teachers whose students achieved the most or were the most motivated to learn. (To do this, of course, you would have to decide how to measure achievement and motivation.) You could identify teachers whose students, year after year, learned more than students working with other teachers; then you could watch the more successful teachers and note what they do. You might also train teachers to apply several different strategies to teach the same lesson and then determine which strategy led to the greatest student learning. All these approaches and more have been applied to the study of teaching. Let's take a closer look at an important series of projects, described by Evertson and Green (1986).

An Example of a Research Program

A Series of Studies

You have just seen that in the early 1970s many researchers decided to challenge the conclusions of the Coleman and Jencks reports by examining the actual relationships between teachers' classroom behaviors and student learning. One investigation, the Texas Teacher Effectiveness Project (1970–1973), studied about 30 second- and third-grade teachers (Brophy, 1973; Good, Biddle, & Brophy, 1975). The teachers were chosen because the students in their classes had consistently done better or worse than expected on standardized achievement tests each year for three or four years. In other words, the teachers seemed to have stable effects—good or bad—on student learning. A great deal of information was collected. Interactions between teachers and students were observed and analyzed. The teachers were interviewed and given questionnaires to complete. Researchers noted each teacher's materials and methods. Student achievement in mathematics and language was assessed, and several target students in each class were observed intensively. Based on this information, the researchers calculated the correlations between various teaching behaviors and student learning.

The next step was the Texas Junior High Study (1974–1975). Many of the procedures developed for the elementary sample just described were used to study 29 mathematics and 31 English teachers in several junior high schools. This time observation instruments were expanded and additional information was gathered. For example, student ratings of teachers were added, and observers kept track of how much time was spent in each class activity. Again, the investigators identified correlations between different aspects of teaching and student learning (Evertson, Anderson, & Brophy, 1978).

Also during 1974 and 1975 the researchers tested 22 teaching procedures derived from the correlational findings of previous work. This project was called the First-Grade Reading Group Study (Anderson, Evertson, & Brophy, 1979). You were introduced to this project briefly in Chapter 1 when we discussed how results of correlational research can suggest treatments to be tested in experiments. The example of calling on students in order around a reading circle was taken from the First-Grade Reading Group Study.

Much of this early work suggested that management is a very important factor in effective teaching. So the next phase (1977–1984) in this series of projects focused on classroom management. We discussed this work by Emmer, Evertson, and their colleagues in Chapter 10. As you may remember, this time the researchers stationed themselves in the classrooms on the first day of school. They made videotapes and detailed narrative records in every class. After identifying what effective teachers seemed to do to establish and maintain good management, the investigators developed a training manual and tested it with other teachers (Emmer, Evertson, Clements, Sanford, & Worsham, 1984; Evertson et al., 1984). Other projects, based on these findings, continue today.

What the Research Teaches Us

What can we see in this series of studies? First, we see how one study builds on those before, the results of one suggesting new variables or new approaches for another. More specifically, we see examples of what has been called the *descriptive-correlational-experimental loop*. Careful observation and the identification of relationships between teaching and learning can form the basis for developing teaching approaches that are then tested in experimental studies. Finally, we have gained some specific knowledge about effective teaching from these projects and studies. The rest of the chapter is based on the knowledge from these and other investigations.

Characteristics of Effective Teachers

Some of the earliest research on effective teaching focused on the teachers themselves. Researchers thought that the key to success in teaching must lie in the characteristics of teachers (Medley, 1979). Although this assumption proved incorrect, or at least incomplete, it did teach us some lessons about effective teaching. Let's examine three teacher characteristics: knowledge, clarity, and warmth.

Knowledge and Education.   Do teachers who know more about their subject areas have a more positive impact on their students? The relationship

Knowledge of Subject

between a teacher's knowledge of the subject and her or his students' learning is not clearly defined and appears to be indirect. Teachers who know more about their subject do not necessarily have students who learn more. But teachers who know more may tend to make clearer presentations or to use more effective teaching strategies (McDonald, 1976c). Knowledge is probably necessary but not sufficient for effective teaching.

Knowledge of Methods

There is evidence that a teacher's knowledge of teaching methods is related to student learning (McDonald, 1976b). A study by Cantrell, Stenner, and Katzenmeyer (1977) found that teachers who scored high on a test of the behavioral principles of classroom management (the information found in Chapters 5 and 6) and who had positive attitudes toward students were more successful than teachers with less knowledge of these methods. And another study of 31 Head Start teachers found that the ones with more formal education, teaching experience, and hours of training were more successful in helping students achieve educational and social objectives (Seefeldt, 1973).

Today researchers are again interested in studying teachers' knowledge. But instead of using college grades, scores on achievement tests, or number of courses taken as measures of knowledge, they are looking to cognitive psychology for new approaches. Some educational psychologists are investigating the cognitive skills required in teaching by contrasting expert and novice teachers' understanding of their subject matter and of the process of teaching itself (Leinhardt & Greeno, 1986; Leinhardt & Smith, 1985). They are finding that expert teachers differ from novice teachers in much the same ways that expert physicians, physicists, or chess players (as you saw in Chapter 8) differ from novices in these fields. For example, expert teachers have richer and more elaborate categories for understanding problems in teaching. They work from integrated, underlying principles instead of dealing with surface features or specifics of each new situation. Many of their teaching routines have become automatic, so they have more working memory for being creative or dealing with new problems as they arise. They also waste less class time. For example, one study found that expert math teachers could go over the previous day's work with the class in 2 or 3 minutes, compared with 15 minutes for novices (Leinhardt, 1986). Even though these experts may have different ways of understanding their subject matter or different classroom routines, their knowledge is solid and thoroughly developed and enables them to handle most questions or situations easily.

Organization and Clarity.   Students discussing a teacher are likely to say things like, "Oh, he's very clear," "She's too confusing," or "Those two! They're too hard to follow!" In fact, when Barak Rosenshine and Norma Furst (1973) reviewed about 50 studies of teaching, they concluded that clarity was the most promising teacher behavior for future research on effective teaching. Let's look at some of the evidence.

Teachers at both the elementary and secondary levels who are systematic and consistent in their teaching tend to maintain better morale in their classrooms than disorganized teachers (Ryans, 1960). At the college level, teachers rated as clear and organized by students also tend to receive more positive overall student evaluations (Murray, 1983). Teacher clarity seems to affect student learning as well. For example, the students of ninth-grade algebra teachers who were rated as clear by students and classroom observers improved more in their comprehension of algebraic concepts than the students of teachers rated as unclear (McConnell, 1977). Similar results have been found with other subjects (Kennedy, Cruickshank, Bush, & Meyers, 1978) and at other grade levels, including college (Good & Grouws, 1977; Hines, Cruickshank, & Kennedy, 1982, 1985; Land & Smith, 1979).

Clarity and
Knowledge Linked There may be important connections among clarity, knowledge of the subject, and student learning. Hiller (1971) studied over 30 twelfth-grade social studies teachers during two minilessons. Teachers with more knowledge of the subject tended to be less vague in their explanations to the class. The less vague the teacher, the more the students learned. Vagueness was assessed on the basis of the number of occurrences of 233 words and phrases, such as *somewhere, not many, not sure, anyway*, and *sometimes*.

Lack of knowledge may cause teachers to be vague—or to be anxious and nervous, which also causes them to be vague. Either way, students get lost (Dunkin & Biddle, 1974). Perhaps the effect of a teacher's lack of knowledge depends on how the teacher copes with the situation. An advanced understanding of chemistry will probably be less important in fourth-grade science than in eleventh-grade chemistry. But if lack of knowledge causes the teacher to feel anxious or to choose a poor teaching method to hide the ignorance, the teacher's lack of knowledge can interfere with student learning at any grade level.

Most studies of teacher clarity involve students at the later elementary, secondary, and college levels. In the very early grades there is less extended verbal teaching and more small-group, drill-and-practice, and individual work. Being clear probably is less important in these situations but becomes increasingly significant as teaching includes more explanation and lecture (Rosenshine, 1979).

Guidelines for
Clarity

Recent research offers guidelines for greater clarity in teaching (Evertson et al., 1984; Hines, Cruickshank, & Kennedy, 1982, 1985). When planning a lesson, try to anticipate the problems your students will have with the material. Turn to teachers' manuals and experienced teachers for help with this. You might also do the written parts of the lesson yourself to identify potential problems. Have definitions ready for new terms, and prepare several relevant examples for concepts. Think of analogies that will make ideas easier to understand. Organize the lesson in a logical sequence; include checkpoints incorporating oral or written questions or problems to make sure the students are following the explanations.

During the lesson, emphasize the important aspects of the material. You can do this at the outset by stating clearly the purpose of the activity. Give step-by-step directions if possible. Make sure students have mastered one step before going on to the next. Use models, examples, and illustrations. Summarize parts of the lesson as you go along. Watch your pace. After more difficult sections, stop and give students a chance to think. Probe to make sure they understand. Don't overlook anyone; some students are experts at hiding in a group or following the lead of the better pupils and guessing right answers. Ask students to summarize your main points (you may be surprised at their responses). Reteach if students have not understood. Answer students' questions with an explanation, example, or analogy.

In general, stick with your plan and do not digress. Signal transitions from one major topic to another with phrases such as *the next area . . ., now we will leave . . . and turn to . . .,* or *the second step is. . . .* You might help students follow the lesson by outlining topics or listing key points on the board or on an overhead projector. Continually monitor the group to see if everyone is following the lesson. Look for confident nods or puzzled stares. You should be able to tell if most students are keeping up.

Avoiding Vague
Language

Throughout the lesson, choose words that are familiar to the students. Define new terms and relate them to what the students already know. Be precise. Avoid vague words and ambiguous phrases: steer clear of the *somes—something, someone, sometime, somehow;* the *not verys—not very much, not very well, not very hard, not very often;* and other unspecific fillers, such as *most, not all, sort of,* and *more or less.* Use specific (and, if possible, colorful) names instead of *it, them,* and *thing.* Also, refrain from using pet phrases such as *you know* and *OK?*

After the lesson, make sure once again that students have understood the material. You might have the students do a few problems at their desks while you walk around the room and spot-check. This way, you can correct misunderstandings immediately. If homework is assigned, check it quickly for any problems that require immediate additional explanation. A final idea is to record a lesson on tape to check yourself for clarity. This might prove an ear-opening experience.

Warmth and Enthusiasm. As you know well, some teachers are much more enthusiastic than others. According to Rosenshine and Furst (1973), ratings of teachers' enthusiasm for their subject have been found by several studies to be related to student achievement gains. Warmth, friendliness, and understanding seem to be the teacher traits most strongly related to student attitudes (Murray, 1983; Ryans, 1960; Soar & Soar, 1979). In other words, teachers who are warm and friendly tend to have students who like them and the class in general.

Again, these are correlational studies. The results do not tell us that teacher enthusiasm *causes* student learning or that warmth *causes* positive attitudes, only that the two variables tend to occur together. Teachers trained to be more enthusiastic have students who are more attentive and involved but not necessarily better on tests of content (Gillett & Gall, 1982).

Knowing that warmth and enthusiasm are good qualities for teachers will not tell you how to act in the classroom. Warmth and enthusiasm are **high-inference characteristics:** they are difficult to define objectively. Just how do warm, enthusiastic teachers communicate? Do they use particular behaviors or skills that can be defined more specifically? Mary Collins (1978) has operationalized (see Chapter 11) enthusiasm to include rapid, varied, and excited vocal delivery, lively eyes, demonstrative gestures, use of descriptive

high-inference characteristics: characteristics that are difficult to define objectively

Two important elements of instruction are communicating information and providing encouragement for students as they learn. Effective teachers are skilled at both. They seem to say to their students, I know you can learn this if we work together. The results can be very satisfying. *(William Strode/ Woodfin, Camp & Associates)*

Guidelines

Effective Teaching

Organize your lessons carefully.

Examples
1. *Provide objectives that help students focus on the purpose of the lesson.*
2. *Begin lessons by writing a brief outline on the board, or work on an outline with the class as part of the lesson.*
3. *If possible, break the presentation into clear steps or stages.*
4. *Review periodically.*

Strive for clear explanations.

Examples
1. *Use concrete examples or analogies that relate to the students' own lives. Explain supply and demand by noting the falling prices of certain record albums when supply exceeds demand because a new singer or group has become more popular. Have several examples for particularly difficult points.*
2. *Give explanations at several levels so all students, not just the brightest, will understand.*
3. *Focus on one idea at a time and avoid digressions.*

Communicate an enthusiasm for your subject and the day's lesson.

Examples
1. *Tell students why the lesson is important. Have a better reason than "This will be on the test" or "You will need to know it next year." Emphasize the value of the learning itself.*
2. *Be sure to make eye contact with the students.*
3. *Vary your pace and volume in speaking. Use silence for emphasis.*

Keep all students involved.

Examples
1. *Make sure students who finish early have something productive to do. Possibilities include work for extra credit, content-related games or puzzles, homework assignments, the chance to help slower students, and a pass to the library or computer lab.*
2. *Reinforce students for independent work and for sticking with a task.*

Adapt your teaching to student needs and interests.

Examples
1. *Use student questionnaires to make adjustments in your teaching.*
2. *Combine a focus on academic skills with special student interests whenever possible.*
3. *Use games, simulations, films, and demonstrations.*

Constantly broaden your knowledge in your area.

Examples
1. *Read journals that report new research and suggest new ideas.*
2. *Go to workshops and conventions; take a course at a nearby college.*

words, an easygoing acceptance of students' ideas and questions, and a high energy level. What else might you add from your own observations?

The research we have looked at has identified teacher knowledge, clarity, organization, and enthusiasm as important characteristics of effective teachers. The Guidelines summarize the practical implications of this work for the classroom.

Limitations of Research on Teacher Characteristics. Helpful as they have been, the studies of specific teacher characteristics or actions have certainly not provided all the answers about effective teaching. Most of these studies simply reported correlations between teacher and student behaviors; no causal relationships were established. Findings have also been inconsistent. Teacher behavior is not always stable from class to class or from day to day. In fact, some studies have found little or no relationship between teachers' behavior on one occasion and their behavior on another (see, for example, Shavelson & Dempsey, 1975).

What does this mean? Is the inconsistency a problem? Probably not. As researchers began to look beyond the teacher's characteristics and behavior to the larger situation (the subject matter, objectives, students, settings, and materials), they made some important discoveries. No one way of teaching is right for every class or lesson. As Brophy and Good (1986, p. 360) have stated, "Effective instruction involves selecting (from a larger repertoire) and orchestrating those teaching behaviors that are appropriate to the context and the teacher's goals, rather than mastering and consistently applying a few 'generic' teaching skills." The expert teacher knows not only what to do but when, where, with whom, and how long to do it. So the focus of research on effective teaching has shifted from teacher behaviors to a wide range of variables involved in effective instruction (Rosenshine, 1977; Waxman & Walberg, 1982). For one thing, researchers realized that a very important factor had often been overlooked—the students.

MEANWHILE, WHAT'S HAPPENING WITH THE STUDENTS?

A Complex Relationship

The relationships between teaching strategies and student learning are complicated. The actions of a teacher cannot magically result in student learning; only the student can do the learning. One of the themes of this book is that the way students process information determines to a large extent what they learn and remember. At the most basic level, students must first pay attention to information. As you saw in Chapter 10, a main task of teaching is to keep students involved in productive learning activities. Teachers make more time for learning by improving classroom management and keeping students motivated and involved.

But time and engagement will not guarantee accurate or lasting learning. The time must be used well. Filling the time with the latest teaching methods will not guarantee success, either. The real issues are, What are the students doing? What are they thinking? How are they processing the information? What the teacher plans, says, and does influences what the students will do and therefore, to a large extent, what the students will learn. The task the teacher sets for the students is an important link between teaching and learning.

Academic Tasks

There are many ways to characterize the tasks that teachers set for students. Tasks have a certain content: they involve facts, concepts, opinions, and principles, whether assigned in history or geometry or home economics.

Tasks also involve certain operations: they require students to memorize, infer, classify, or apply. As students work on a task, they are both learning information and practicing operations (Doyle, 1983). This description may remind you of the behavior-content matrix for setting learning objectives, discussed in the previous chapter.

Let's take a moment to look at the second element of an academic task—the operation required. Doyle (1983) has suggested that there are four general categories of academic tasks, defined by the operations required.

1. *Memory tasks* simply require students to recognize or reproduce information they have encountered before, as in matching states and capitals or reciting lines from a play.

2. *Routine or procedural tasks* involve using an algorithm (prescribed set of steps) to solve a problem. If students apply the procedure correctly, they will get the right answer: if they use the formula πr^2, they will find the area of a circle.

3. *Comprehension tasks* require students to go a step beyond—to transform information, choose the best among many approaches, combine several ideas to solve a new problem, or write a passage in a particular style.

4. *Opinion tasks* ask students to state a preference, such as which character in a story is their favorite.

You may see similarities between these tasks and Bloom's taxonomy in the cognitive domain, described in Chapter 11. Both Doyle and Bloom would probably agree that students will learn the operations they practice. For example, to learn to write poetry, you must obviously do some writing. Simply memorizing definitions or steps won't make you a poet.

A second way to characterize tasks is by the *risk* involved. Some tasks are riskier than others because failure is more likely. For example, opinion tasks are very low-risk tasks: there are no right or wrong answers. Simple mem-

Lab work may involve straightforward procedural tasks—the student simply follows a list of steps. Designing and carrying out an experiment, however, require a different sort of task and a different kind of thinking. *(Nancy J. Pierce/Photo Researchers)*

ory or procedural tasks also involve few risks, because getting the right answer is easy: you just follow the steps. But the stakes can be very high with longer and more complex memory or procedural tasks. Reciting 100 lines from a Shakespeare play is risky, especially if you are graded on how well you do, because there is a great deal to memorize. Involved procedural tasks, such as solving quadratic equations, can also be risky, since there are many possibilities for mistakes.

Finally, tasks can either have clear-cut answers or be ambiguous. Opinion and understanding tasks are ambiguous: it is hard to predict the right answer (if there is one) or how to find it. If you were asked, as I was in my freshman government class, to write a paper on the central problem of the democratic form of government, you wouldn't know for sure what the right answer was or even if there *was* a right answer. (This may involve the teacher's opinion, in which case you'd be on treacherous ground.) Memory and procedural tasks, on the other hand, are unambiguous. If you are reciting a soliloquy from *Hamlet*, the "right" answer is clear, even though the task is difficult. Figure 12–1 summarizes how tasks can be categorized by risk and ambiguity.

What does this have to do with effective teaching? Most students want to lower the risk and decrease the ambiguity involved in schoolwork, since

Clear-cut or Ambiguous?

Figure 12–1   Ambiguity and Risk Associated with Academic Tasks in Classrooms

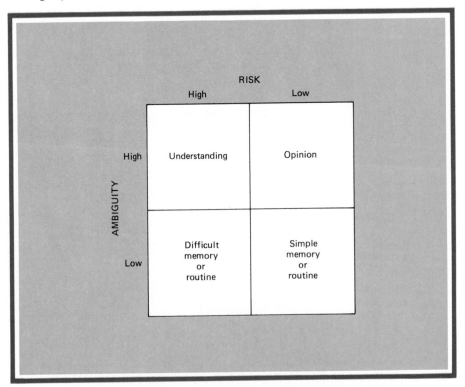

Adapted from Doyle, W. (1983), Academic work. Review of Educational Research, 53, *p. 183.*

their grades are at stake. Many times teachers plan a complex comprehension task that is both ambiguous and risky. They want their students to learn to think and solve problems. But the students may want more guidance: management problems may arise if they are very confused. They may ask for models, rules, minimums, or formulas: "How many references do you want?" "How many pages?" "Will we have to know dates and names?" "Give us a model to follow." In other words, the students negotiate the task. So the teacher changes the task by stating the three points that should be addressed, giving a minimum number of references or a page limit, and providing books that would be helpful. The comprehension task becomes a procedural one. Since students learn what they do, they learn how to do the procedure—and how to negotiate with teachers (Doyle, 1983). But these students probably won't learn the more complicated problem-solving skills that the teacher had intended to develop. Certainly creativity will not be encouraged.

Obviously, some balance is needed. Instructions should be clear, but not too restricting. Tasks that help students learn to remember facts will not necessarily help them learn to comprehend or understand. Teachers must make wise choices, then stick with them, even when students try to negotiate changes.

As we examine different systems for effective teaching, remember that the academic task set for the students is a major influence on what they will learn. Very different systems of teaching may actually have the same effects; similar-looking systems may have very different effects. The key lies in the thoughts and actions of the students. What are they trying to accomplish? What do *they* think is the point of the task? Are they practicing thinking or just applying a procedure?

EFFECTIVE TEACHING FOR DIFFERENT SUBJECTS

A great deal of progress has been made lately in understanding how to teach basics like reading and mathematics. We will look at some of the research, but a warning is in order. In describing effective instruction in this section we will be speaking about one very specific kind of effectiveness: improvement on academic tests. Most of the studies define effectiveness in those terms.

There are several related limitations to bear in mind. First, the research applies best to the teaching of clearly structured knowledge and skills, such as science facts, mathematics computations, reading vocabulary, and grammar rules (Rosenshine & Stevens, 1986). These involve tasks that are relatively unambiguous; they can be taught step by step. So the research does not really pertain to objectives such as helping students to write creatively or mature emotionally. Second, the studies generally focus on the American classroom as it is at present. Other forms of education may be equally or more effective. Finally, the results generally hold for a group of students. We cannot say if methods that are successful on the average will be successful with particular individuals. The research presented here should give you some guidelines for experimenting in your own class. But your own judgment of the impact of each strategy on your students should be your criterion for using or abandoning any of the approaches.

(margin note: Negotiating the Task)

(margin note: Limitations of Research)

Basic Skills: Direct Instruction

**direct instruction/
explicit teaching:**
instruction for
mastery of basic
skills

active teaching:
another term for
direct instruction

Several psychologists have identified one teaching approach that is related to improved student learning. Barak Rosenshine calls this approach **direct instruction** (1979), or more recently, **explicit teaching** (1986). Tom Good uses the term **active teaching** for a similar approach. The goal of direct instruction is mastery of basic skills as measured by the tests commonly given in schools. In Rosenshine's words:

> Direct instruction refers to academically focused, teacher-directed classrooms using sequenced and structured materials. It refers to teaching activities where goals are clear to students, time allocated for instruction is sufficient and continuous, coverage of content is extensive, the performance of students is monitored, . . . and feedback to students is immediate and academically oriented. In direct instruction the teacher controls instructional goals, chooses materials appropriate for the student's ability, and paces the instructional episode. Interaction is . . . structured, but not authoritarian. Learning takes place in a convivial academic atmosphere. (Rosenshine, 1979, p. 38)

Let's look at a typical situation.

Lee Cohen teaches third grade in a moderate-sized suburban school. She allocates 60 minutes a day, in two 30-minute sessions, to reading instruc-

Is this an effective teaching approach? It all depends. Is the material fairly basic, straightforward, and sequential? Is the workbook at the students' level, neither too easy nor too hard? Do the exercises reinforce the teacher's explanations? Do the students know how to do the work and why it is necessary? If so, then the students in this circle will probably benefit from their lesson. *(Cary Wolinsky/Stock, Boston)*

tion. Most of the time her students stay focused on the reading task because she constantly monitors the room, even when she is working with small groups or individuals. Students who are not working are brought back to the task by some communication from the teacher. Often the message is a glance or a private reminder. The tone is firm but gentle. Both teacher and students are aware of the objectives for most of the activities. Lee has chosen the materials carefully and arranged the activities logically. Her presentations are clear and well organized with lots of examples. She often stops to review and to check the students' understanding. Before students attempt any assignments on their own, Lee makes sure they know what to do and how to do it. If necessary, she goes back and reteaches parts of the lesson. Transitions from one activity to the next are smooth and orderly. The central figure in the classroom is definitely the teacher, but a pleasant atmosphere prevails. There is a sense of seriousness about the academic work and mutual respect between students and teacher.

A number of variations and elaborations on the basic model of direct instruction have been proposed. We will look at three in the next few pages.

Six Teaching Functions.   Rosenshine and Stevens (1986) have identified six teaching functions based on the research on effective instruction. These could serve as a checklist or a framework for teaching basic skills.

1. *Review and check the previous day's work.* Reteach if students misunderstood or made errors.
2. *Present new material.* Make the purpose clear, teach in small steps, provide many examples and nonexamples, and be sure students understand.
3. *Provide guided practice.* Question students, give practice problems, and listen for misconceptions and misunderstandings. Reteach if necessary. Continue guided practice until students answer about 80 percent of the questions correctly.
4. *Give feedback and correctives* based on student answers. Reteach if necessary.
5. *Provide independent practice.* Let students apply the new learning on their own, either in seatwork or homework. The success rate during independent practice should be about 95 percent. This means that students must be well prepared for the work by the presentation and guided practice and that assignments must not be too difficult. The point is for the students to practice until the skills become overlearned and automatic. Hold students accountable for the work they do—check it.
6. *Review weekly and monthly* to consolidate learning. Include some review items as homework. Test often, and reteach material missed on the tests.

These are not steps to be followed in a particular order, but elements of effective instruction. For example, feedback, review, or reteaching should occur whenever necessary and should match the aptitudes of the students.

Hunter's Mastery Teaching Program.   Even before the research on basic skills became influential, Madeline Hunter had developed a system for designing lessons that had much in common with direct instruction. The most recent version of this system is the Hunter Mastery Teaching Program (Hunter, 1982). Like Rosenshine, Hunter emphasizes review, guided practice, checking for understanding, and independent practice, but she also

Table 12–1   The Hunter Mastery Teaching Program: Selected Principles

Get students set to learn: Make the best use of the prime time at the beginning of the lesson.

> Give students a review question or two to consider while you call the roll, pass out papers, or do other "housekeeping" chores. Follow up—listen to their answers, and correct if necessary.

> Create an *anticipatory set* to capture the students' attention. This might be an advance organizer, an intriguing question, or a brief exercise. For example, at the beginning of a lesson on categories of plants you could ask, "How is pumpkin pie similar to cherry pie but different from sweet potato pie?" Answer: Pumpkins and cherries are both fruits, unlike sweet potatoes.

> Communicate the lesson objectives (unless withholding this information for a while is part of your overall plan).

Provide information effectively.

> Determine the basic information and organize it. Use this basic structure as scaffolding for the lesson.

> Present information clearly and simply. Use familiar terms, examples, illustrations.

> Model what you mean. If appropriate, demonstrate or use analogies—"If the basketball Ann is holding were the sun, how far away do you think I would have to hold this pea to represent Pluto . . .?"

Check for understanding, and give guided practice.

> Ask a question and have every student signal an answer—"Thumbs up if this statement is true, down if it's false."

> Ask for a choral response: "Everyone, is this a dependent or an independent clause?"

> Sample individual responses: "Everyone, think of an example of a closed system. Jon, what's your example?"

Allow for independent practice.

> Get students started right by doing the first few questions together.

> Make independent practice brief. Monitor responses, giving feedback quickly.

adds ideas about how to get students ready to learn and how to present material effectively. Table 12–1 is a summary of Hunter's approach.

Good and Grouws's Missouri Mathematics Program.   Tom Good and Doug Grouws have spent years studying mathematics teachers who consistently improve the achievement of their students. Based on their research, they have developed a model for teaching mathematics that appears to be successful with elementary and middle school students. Again, the program emphasizes review, guided practice, checking for understanding, and independent practice.

Good and Grouws believe that the presentation or development portion of the lesson is critical. The most successful teachers emphasize understanding and meaning in their presentations. They do not simply teach procedures and rules but strive to make students comprehend the material. Demonstrations, illustrations, concrete examples, diagrams, models, and clear explanations are important aspects of their presentations (Good & Grouws, 1979; Good, Grouws, & Ebmeier, 1983). A model for a math lesson is given in Table 12–2.

Table 12–2 **Missouri Mathematics Program: Key Instructional Elements**

Opening (first 8 minutes except Mondays)

1. Briefly review the concepts and skills associated with the homework.
2. Collect and deal with homework assignments.
3. Ask students to do several mental computation exercises. ("Think: what's 4 × 4? Now, what's 40 × 4?")

Development (about 20 minutes)

1. Briefly focus on prerequisites—the skills and concepts that will be needed in the lesson.
2. Focus on meaning and on promoting student understanding by using lively explanations, demonstrations, and illustrations. Keep the pace lively.
3. Assess student comprehension frequently. Use both rapid short-answer questions (but give students enough time to respond) and single practice problems.
4. Repeat and elaborate on meaning as necessary. Use examples and analogies.

Seatwork (about 15 minutes)

1. Provide uninterrupted successful practice. Most students should get at least 80 percent of their items correct.
2. Momentum—keep the ball rolling; get everyone involved, then sustain involvement.
3. Alerting—let students know their work will be checked at the end of the period.
4. Accountability—check the students' work.

Homework Assignment

1. Assign homework at the end of each math class except Fridays. The work should take about 15 minutes.
2. Include one or two review problems in homework assignments.

Special Reviews

1. Weekly review/maintenance: during the first 20 minutes each Monday. Focus on skills and concepts covered the previous week.
2. Monthly review/maintenance on every fourth Monday. Focus on skills and concepts covered since the last monthly review.

Adapted from T. Good, D. Grouws, & H. Ebmeier (1983), Active mathematics teaching. *New York: Longman.*

Direct instruction appears to be one successful system for teaching basic skills. Are the principles of direct instruction appropriate for other types of skills? There is disagreement on this question.

Beyond the Basics

Penelope Peterson (1979) has compared the more traditional teacher-centered instruction with more open, informal methods. She concluded that teacher-centered instruction leads to better performance on achievement tests, while the open, informal methods like discovery learning or inquiry approaches are associated with better performance on tests of creativity, abstract thinking, and problem solving. In addition, the open methods are better for improving attitudes toward school and stimulating curiosity, cooperation among students, and lower absence rates (Stallings & Kaskowitz, 1975). According to these conclusions, when the goals of teaching involve problem solving, creativity, and mastering processes and when the students are average or above in their knowledge of a subject, many approaches besides direct instruction should be effective. Is this true?

Results of research on effective teaching in different subjects do support these conclusions. For example, McDonald (1976a) found that effective methods for teaching both math and English with younger students and for teaching math with fifth graders fit the principles of direct instruction. These topics tend to be explicit, inherently structured, and straightforward. Approaches that proved effective included teacher-led instruction with small groups, use of a large amount of material that covered a wide range of content and skills, and rapid correction of errors. Less effective were methods that relied on questioning and discussion. But successful approaches for teaching English with the older students involved discussion, questioning, independent work, in-depth analysis, and complex material—very different from the drill-and-practice, teacher-led learning of direct instruction.

Different Goals,
Different Methods

The learning goals for English in the upper grades are more likely to involve abstract thinking, creativity, and problem solving. These goals probably require methods other than direct instruction. This is in keeping with Tom Good's conclusion that teaching should become less direct (1) as students mature and (2) when the goals involve affective development and problem solving or critical thinking (Good, 1982). Of course, every subject, even college English or chemistry, can require some direct instruction. If you are teaching when to use *who* and *whom* or how to set up laboratory apparatus, direct instruction may be the best approach. The message for teachers is to match instructional methods to learning goals.

EFFECTIVE TEACHING WITH DIFFERENT STUDENTS

In Chapter 4 we explored several ways that students differ: socioeconomic status, culture, intelligence, creativity, and cognitive style. In Chapter 9 we discussed the need for achievement, locus of control, and anxiety. In analyzing effective teaching, we must ask whether one method of teaching can be equally effective with everyone. Even without turning to research for an answer, you might say no—and you would be right. Let's examine what research on teaching effectiveness tells us about dealing with differences.

Different Strategies for Younger and Older Students

Age may be an important element in choosing instructional strategies. Some educators believe that teaching students in the preschool years through third grade is so different from teaching older students that the teachers of these groups should complete separate and vastly different training programs (Brophy, 1976). In the early grades, effective instruction seems to involve (1) little discussion, (2) highly structured teacher presentation of new material, (3) immediate chances to practice new skills, (4) drill and more drill, (5) speedy individual feedback, (6) many carefully chosen and well-supervised individual learning exercises, and (7) a warm, nurturing teaching style (Brophy, 1976; Brophy & Evertson, 1976).

Rationale for Separate Approaches

Students in the early grades are mastering basic skills. They must learn these skills thoroughly so that performance becomes almost automatic. Students in the higher grades are using the basic skills to learn facts and concepts in various subjects. Only in the grades above third and fourth are class discussion, independent learning, and lectures likely to be helpful. One rationale for these two separate approaches, with third and fourth grade as the dividing line, is that many students below fourth grade are still thinking preoperationally (Brophy, 1976). In order to benefit from ideas presented in a purely verbal format, a student must be able to think and process information at a concrete operational level or beyond. Of course, using the third and fourth grade as a dividing line is not a perfect solution. Some third-grade students and even whole third-grade classes can handle more verbal teaching and discussion than others. (A more complete discussion of the teaching implications of differences in developmental levels appears in Chapter 2.)

Students with Different Aptitudes

Solutions Suggested and Debated

Although most teachers do not teach a wide range of ages in one class, they are usually expected to work with students of varying aptitudes. The question of how to adapt teaching to the needs of the individual student has been studied and debated for years. Countless answers have been suggested, and many solutions attempted. Honors courses, vocational courses, experiences in the performing arts, cooperative work-study programs, independent study, and many other options available to older students are all attempts to adapt to individual interests and aptitudes. As we saw in Chapter 4, another approach has been compensatory, remedial, or lower-track classes for students whose achievement is below average.

But whatever the merits or limitations of these approaches, no one method can be equally successful with all the individuals in a class, even if they are all fairly similar in ability (a rare occurrence). This has been demonstrated repeatedly by psychologists doing research on aptitude-treatment interactions.

aptitude-treatment interaction (ATI): interaction of individual differences in learning with particular teaching methods

Aptitude-Treatment Interactions. The term **aptitude-treatment interaction,** or **ATI,** refers to the ways individual differences that affect learning—verbal ability, anxiety, cognitive style, or need to achieve—interact with particular teaching methods. The result is as we've seen: no single method is effective for everyone (Cronbach & Snow, 1977). In other words, what works well with one person may not work well with another. You encountered a few examples of ATIs in Chapter 9 when we discussed how approaches like programmed instruction and competitive grading can have very different effects on nonanxious and highly anxious students.

Recent studies by Penelope Peterson and colleagues at the University of Wisconsin provide examples of ATI research (Peterson, Janicki, & Swing, 1980). In one of these studies, two experienced social studies teachers taught each of their three ninth-grade classes with an inquiry, lecture-recitation, or public issues approach. The students in each class varied in verbal ability, anxiety level, attitude toward social studies, and personality factors; some, for example, expressed their need to achieve by conforming and others were motivated to work independently. Results indicated that student differences *did* interact with the teaching method. As you can see in Figure 12–2, students with high verbal ability performed best on a test when they had had the lecture-recitation lesson, and students with lower verbal ability performed best when they had participated in the public issues approach.

higher-order interaction: interaction involving more than two variables

The interaction shown in Figure 12–2 is only one of the results of Peterson's study. Several other high-order interactions were identified. **Higher-order interactions** involve more than two variables. These interactions become increasingly complex and difficult to interpret. For example, Peterson found a three-way interaction involving student anxiety, student ability, and type of instruction. Anxiety did not affect how well high-ability students responded to any of the teaching methods, but it *was* a factor for low-ability students. High-anxiety, low-ability students did poorly with the public issues approach but responded well to the inquiry method. Low-anxiety, low-ability students had the opposite reaction, performing better with public issues than with inquiry.

Even with such promising results, it has been difficult to draw clear implications for teaching from the ATI studies. With the possible exception of student ability, most aptitudes interact differently with treatments, depending on the situation or study. Many of the interactions identified are higher-order. Using these relationships as guidelines for teaching would be quite difficult (Good & Stipek, 1983).

However, although guidance about specific aptitude-treatment matches is hard to find at this point, there is one important general implication of the ATI research: when students are having difficulty learning with one teaching approach, it makes sense to try something else. If you can form some hypotheses about your students' particular needs and the reasons your current approach does not fit these needs, you should be able to find a better alternative. Once more, flexibility is the key. Be prepared to adapt your methods to different students, subjects, and objectives.

Ability Differences and Prior Knowledge. There is one area of ATI research where findings have fairly clear and consistent implications for teaching. This is the research that has focused on academic ability and prior knowledge. In ATI research the term *ability* refers not to a theoretical notion of potential but instead to readiness for instruction (Cronbach & Snow, 1977; Good & Stipek, 1983). In the classroom, readiness to learn usually means having the necessary background knowledge to understand new material. Of course, other factors, including motivation, academic self-concept, and

Figure 12–2   **An Aptitude-Treatment Interaction in the Teaching of Social Studies**

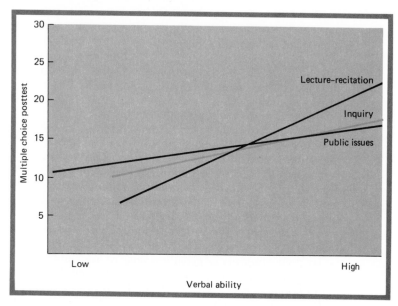

Adapted from P. Peterson, T. C. Janicki, and S. R. Swing (1980), Aptitude-treatment interaction effects of three social studies teaching approaches. Review of Educational Research, 17, p. 354. Copyright © 1980, AERA, Washington, DC.

level of cognitive development, influence how easily an individual will comprehend new material.

If we look at ATI studies involving prior knowledge, we can identify some consistent findings. When students are quite knowledgeable about a particular subject, different teaching methods do not seem to affect achievement. But when students have little prior knowledge, the method does make a difference. The less students know, the more they need instructional support, probably in the form of improved materials, help in focusing and sustaining attention, systematic feedback, and explicit teaching or direct instruction (Rosenshine & Stevens, 1986; Tobias, 1981, 1982).

Dealing with Limited Knowledge

For example, effective materials might be organized around clear instructional objectives and include visual support such as graphs, diagrams, models, and photographs. Help in focusing attention could mean any of the special techniques already described for increasing academic engaged time. One goal of this extra instructional support is to reduce the information processing demands on the students (Corno, 1980; Snow, 1977). Appropriate materials and methods help the students organize the information, direct their attention to its critical features, and relieve some of the burden on their memories.

These principles should serve as general guidelines for you in teaching students who have limited knowledge of your subject. But these students often have other problems as well. They may lack interest or motivation. Often they have failed repeatedly in school, and their attitudes are not positive. Some, unable to work independently for more than a short time, may disrupt class. Frequently teachers are given a whole class of these "low achievers." Even though such a class may be smaller than average, its discipline problems are usually greater than average (Evertson, 1982).

Lesson Formats for Low-Ability Classes.   In most secondary school subjects, teachers follow a lesson format that involves an opening, a presentation that develops the content of the lesson, student work on problems or questions based on the presentation, and a closing. In a low-ability class, this standard format can invite problems because the students are expected to pay attention to one activity for long blocks of time.

Tasks in Small Doses

Teachers who are successful with low-ability classes tend to have more than one cycle of presentation and student seatwork in each period (Ebmeier & Ziomek, 1982). The teacher may make a short presentation, have the students work briefly, continue the lesson with more content development and then more student practice on the skill being developed, and perhaps give another presentation followed by student seatwork (Evertson, 1982). This pattern keeps the students attentive by giving small doses of both information and individual work. The teacher can make sure every student understands each step. The different activities are short enough to be within the students' attention spans.

To give students a greater sense of responsibility for their own work, Emmer and colleagues (1984) have suggested short daily assignments. Students should keep a record of grades on every assignment and of average grades for each week so they can see the results of their work (or lack of work). Class participation should be a part of the grading system, with daily or weekly grades awarded for appropriate contributions. In addition, students can be taught some of the learning and metacognitive strategies that more successful students tend to apply automatically (see Chapters 7 and 8). It is especially important to give low-achieving students techniques for monitoring their own learning and problem-solving processes so they can tell when they are using these strategies correctly (Brown, Campione, & Day, 1981).

A Supportive
Friendly Place

With all this emphasis on structure, the atmosphere of the class should remain as friendly and supportive as possible. Students who have failed repeatedly are more likely to need the kind of genuine, constant encouragement and nurturing that is effective with younger students (Stallings, 1981). Approaches that have proved successful with low-achieving students in the basic-skills area are contrasted with less successful approaches in Table 12–3. You might be surprised—the less effective approaches in the second

Table 12–3   Teaching Basic Skills: Are You Helping or Hindering Low Achievers?

Helpful Approaches	Less Successful Approaches
Instruction broken down into steps Short activities sequenced by the teacher	Long, unbroken periods of seatwork or independent work Student choice of activities
Plenty of practice Clear, immediate feedback and praise	Little practice or independent practice No prompt feedback
A lot of supervision and help Whole-class and/or group settings	Individualized, self-paced, independent work Pupil self-control or self-direction
Interruptions avoided	Interruptions from teacher or other students
A level of difficulty that guarantees a high rate of success	Overly challenging materials or questions—students unlikely to know most answers
Many opportunities and much encouragement to answer teacher's questions	Few opportunities and little encouragement to answer questions frequently
Convergent questions—one correct answer	Open-ended questions
	Nonacademic conversation
Calling on nonvolunteers or calling on students according to set patterns	Calling only on volunteers
Staying with student until question is answered	Letting others answer when response is not immediate
Short and frequent paper-and-pencil activities	Games, arts, crafts, interest centers
Specific praise for good performance	Vague or general praise; random praise when not especially deserved
Material covered thoroughly	A great deal of material covered quickly

Adapted from E. T. Emmer, C. M. Evertson, B. S. Clements, J. P. Sanford, & M. E. Worsham (1984), Organizing and managing the junior high school classroom. Englewood Cliffs, NJ: Prentice-Hall; and H. H. Ebmeier & R. L. Ziomek (1982), Increasing engagement rates of low and high achievers. Paper presented at the annual meeting of the American Educational Research Association, New York.

column may *sound* good. But remember, it is the coordination of the approach with the type of material (basic skills) and the achievement level of students (low achievers) that matters.

Teaching High Achievers.   The research on aptitude-treatment interactions indicates that a wider range of methods and approaches can be effective with high achievers. During lecture-discussion sessions, these students tend to learn more if the teacher keeps the pace of the class rapid and the tasks challenging, asks both factual questions and questions requiring higher-level thinking, sets high standards, and points out errors clearly (Brophy & Evertson, 1976). The more nurturing style of teaching seems less important in encouraging learning in high achievers, although this would not hold for every individual. Presentations can be longer, and more material can be covered in one session. Guided practice sessions can be shorter. Less review and independent practice is necessary (Rosenshine, 1986). In the next chapter we will look more closely at how to teach very able students.

INTEGRATING IDEAS ABOUT EFFECTIVE TEACHING

Complications

Teaching is complicated. Some of the methods that are supposed to work for every situation simply do not. As a teacher, you will have to make judgments based on your students and the subjects you teach. You will probably have to teach one way for one group of students and another way for others. Young students, students with lower abilities, and highly anxious students may need more structure, support, and direction. Older and higher-ability students may need more freedom as well as stricter performance standards. The Guidelines on pages 442–443 should help you make some of these decisions.

Synthesizing
Research Findings

How are the many different ideas about effective teaching to be integrated? The findings of several recent studies of effective teaching can be combined only to a certain extent. We have already seen that different techniques are more or less successful with different kinds of students. We must remember that even if several studies agree that one particular approach is associated with learning gains, the measure of gain is usually based on a class average. In each class, some individuals may do very poorly when taught by the method that has seemed most effective for the majority of the students. With these cautions in mind, let's turn to several imaginary practical examples. First we'll look at two elementary teachers who practice many of the strategies discussed in this chapter. We'll also look at a secondary classroom that seems to work.

A Second-Grade Class That Works

In this class, students generally work on individually tailored assignments at their seats while the teacher works with small groups. For reading, a variety of materials keep the students interested. In mathematics, a single workbook is used to move students step by step through the basic mathe-

Effective teaching means constant monitoring, especially in the early grades. A teacher must make sure the students understand the assignment and have all the information and materials they need. Monitoring also means the teacher is immediately available to those who need a bit of extra help or a second explanation. *(Barbara Burnes/Photo Researchers)*

matics skills. This work is supplemented by lots of concrete experiences with counting, weighing, mixing, cutting, and other activities designed to build number concepts.

The teacher seldom instructs the class as a whole, although small groups are used more for reading than for mathematics. Work is assigned according to the achievement level of each student, and all students spend quite a bit of time on drill and repetition. The teacher is careful to prepare students for seatwork so that they will get lots of successful practice. Students also receive rapid feedback about right and wrong answers. Whenever necessary, the teacher stops and reteaches material.

The teacher monitors student progress by constantly moving around the room, watching for students who need help. The class is managed positively whenever possible, through praise, support, and encouragement. Although the lessons are carefully planned, the teacher takes advantage of the unusual and unpredictable. When students rush to the window to watch the first snowfall of the season, the teacher uses this opportunity to teach new "snow vocabulary." In order to make smooth transitions from one activity to another, the teacher avoids stopping any activity abruptly. New activities are introduced with a few sentences about why the task is important, what the objective of the lesson is, or what the class will be doing for the next few minutes. The teacher likes the students and strongly believes all of them can learn.

A Fifth-Grade Class That Works

If you spent much time in this class, you would hear the teacher asking questions, listening carefully to answers, explaining, probing, correcting, and asking more questions. Many of the discussions focus on short stories or articles the whole class has read. Even though the teacher does not use individualized instruction, each student's work is monitored, and most of the students are involved most of the time. In math lessons, the teacher works with the whole class or sometimes with small groups but does not send any students off to work on their own. The students usually complete the math workbook by the end of the year.

Although the atmosphere of the class is businesslike, here too the teacher is willing to capitalize on the unexpected. The discovery of some graffiti on

Guidelines

Organizing Instruction

Vary the amount of structure to fit the needs of the students.

Examples
1. *Give clear directions and very specific objectives (written or oral) when working with younger, more anxious, or more dependent students.*
2. *Encourage independence in older and higher-achieving students by providing less structure for some assignments. Give them a topic and suggest they propose a reading list and tentative outline.*

Allow students in junior and senior high school ample opportunity to explore a limited amount of material in depth. Focus on one novel for several weeks or on one essay or one historical figure for several days.

Examples
1. *Hold debates after students finish reading an essay. The next day, have students change sides and defend the opposite position.*
2. *Have thought-provoking questions ready for discussion. Was Robert E. Lee right to take on leadership of the Confederate army, even though he was opposed to the dissolution of the country? How might the world be different today if Lincoln, the Kennedys, or King had not been assassinated?*
3. *Ask students to write proposals for turning a novel into a film and present their proposals to the class as if to prospective producers.*
4. *Have different groups of students take the positions of a novel's protagonist(s) and antagonist(s) and defend their actions, debate their differences, or draw up a profile of their most important traits.*

Use unexpected events as vehicles for teaching.

Examples
1. *Teach new words and concepts related to electricity and sound transmission when students are excited by an electrical storm.*
2. *Discuss seeing events from several different perspectives after a disappointing loss in sports or after the announcement of schoolwide election results.*

the back wall leads to a class project—the creation of a mural in an appropriate place—as well as to some interesting discussions about self-expression and the limits of individual freedom. The students understand the reason for most of the assignments. When the teacher gives a minilecture or explains a concept, the presentation is generally very clear. The teacher likes and accepts the students and believes they all can learn.

A Secondary Class That Works

Less is known about effective teaching patterns in the secondary grades. We do know that more lecturing, explaining, and discussing occur in the secondary classroom. Based on the research on college classrooms and some

---

Match teaching strategies to objectives.

Examples
1. *Use explicit teaching for well-defined, sequential content and skills and more open methods for more abstract, higher-level objectives.*
2. *Be aware of students' attempts to negotiate tasks and reduce ambiguity and risk. If you want students to tackle difficult, ambiguous tasks, lower the risk involved by making the work ungraded, giving students the chance to revise and redo, or dividing the tasks into small steps.*

Make sure the objectives for various materials are clear.

Examples
1. *In the elementary grades, provide certain basic materials, such as workbooks, that present information in a meaningful sequence.*
2. *When teaching with supplemental materials in any grade, make sure the purpose of the materials and the instructions are clear.*

Balance cognitive and affective objectives.

Examples
1. *In the early grades, include a pleasant, ungraded activity each day, preferably in the afternoon.*
2. *In the later grades, allow students free time when work is completed to participate in a variety of self-selected projects.*
3. *Have a surprise Friday celebration for work well done.*

Be flexible: if one approach does not work with some students, try a different strategy.

Examples
1. *If teacher praise does not seem motivating to a student, try a self-management approach or provide more challenging work.*
2. *If a student does not understand a concept, use more concrete examples or let a peer explain it.*

studies using student ratings as criteria for effective teaching, we can create a hypothetical class. But you should remember that there are probably many patterns of effectiveness for the different ages and subjects at the secondary level.

An effective secondary class might have a teacher who is both well organized and enthusiastic. Lectures would be clear but not too long. While speaking, the teacher might move around the room, making eye contact with as many students as possible. Materials would be at the appropriate level of difficulty for each student. This might require quite a range of materials, since the range of abilities is often very great in secondary classes. The teacher would tailor the lessons as much as possible to the needs of individual students. Some students might be given one assignment; others might be given a number of choices. Still others might be told to design their own projects.

Teacher Effectiveness: Conclusions

If you teach your fourth-grade students mathematics in a large group, will they automatically learn? Not if your explanations are confused and vague. Not if you lose control of the class. Not if you hate talking to the whole class, become very anxious, and make no sense as a result. Could a dynamic, knowledgeable, well-organized, enthusiastic teacher have positive results using a less effective grouping strategy to teach mathematics? It is very possible. Could a biology teacher produce students who did well on achievement tests at the end of the year but hated the subject so much that they vowed never to dissect another animal as long as they lived? Again, it is possible.

Making Choices

As a teacher, you must make a number of decisions about the organization of classroom instruction. There are no guarantees that the methods you choose will work. In making choices, you must consider the effects the methods are likely to have when used with your subject and your students. You should also consider your own strengths. Finally, you must consider the overall goals you wish to achieve.

We have seen that factors such as teacher control of the class, drill, factual questions, clarity, and task orientation are all associated with student learning, at least in certain classes and with certain students. Keep in mind that by *student learning* we mean the kind of cognitive learning measured by most classroom and standardized tests. As Rosenshine (1979) has said, this may seem like a grim picture of teaching. Actually, effective classrooms are pleasant and convivial places. Really expert teachers know how to give students some needed drill and practice in the form of games, puzzles, jokes, and riddles (Leinhardt, 1986).

Some studies have found that more open and flexible, and less structured, less teacher-controlled methods may lead to lower absence rates, more cooperation among students, and higher scores on nonverbal problem-solving tests of reasoning (Stallings & Kaskowitz, 1975). The best teachers probably make use of the research findings on teacher effectiveness but also include activities that foster emotional and social growth and some lessons that are just fun. After all, we want students to learn to read, but we also want them to enjoy reading and stay in school.

Rosenshine (1977, pp. 23–24) describes some small "free" schools that combine both the more structured and the more open approaches:

Combining Approaches

> Mornings in these schools are spent in structured programs in reading, writing, and mathematics. The teachers make the assignments, but the children complete them anywhere in the room in a relaxed and informal manner. These assignments are from the same sequential, structured workbooks and readers that are used in traditional schools. Although each child works at his own task and at his own pace, no more than two activities, such as reading and writing, occur at the same time. Although the atmosphere is relaxed, informal, and respectful, the setting is large-group, teacher-centered, and structured. Afternoons are given to projects, exploration, messing around, trips, and discussion. Fridays are for hobbies and crafts. Thus, the school teaches didactic goals, such as reading and math, in a didactic way, and spends the remaining time on more open activities.

SUMMARY

1. For years, researchers have tried to unravel the mystery of effective teaching. Studies reported in the 1960s and early 1970s focused on general ability levels and social class of teachers and average measures of student ability. Later research has tried to determine if individual teachers make a difference in the daily lives and learning of their students.

2. Results of research on teacher behaviors indicate that thorough and expert knowledge of a subject, organization and clarity in presentation, and enthusiasm all play important parts in effective teaching. But no one way of teaching has been found to be right for each class, lesson, or day.

3. The student's role is also important. What students work on—the actual task—strongly influences what they learn. A task can be characterized by what sort of operation (memory, procedure, comprehension, or opinion), what level of risk, and how much ambiguity it involves.

4. A balance must be struck between breaking down a task in negotiation with students and sticking with a difficult assigned task to encourage thinking.

5. Direct instruction seems most appropriate for teaching basic skills. A framework for direct instruction might involve reviewing yesterday's work, presenting new material, giving guided practice, giving feedback and corrections, providing independent practice, and reviewing weekly and monthly. Hunter's mastery teaching and the Missouri Mathematics Program are also elaborations on direct instruction in the basics.

6. Beyond the basics—for abstract problem solving, affective development, and creativity, for older students and complex subjects like high school English—more open, inquiry-type approaches seem to be effective.

7. Teachers must deal with a wide range of student aptitudes for learning. Aptitude-treatment interaction research has attempted to determine how particular methods affect students of different abilities. One clear implication is that teachers must be flexible and be willing to try a new approach if one is not working well.

8. Degree of prior knowledge can influence the effect of teaching methods. Students with little prior knowledge need much more of a direct-instruction approach.

9. Low-ability students need a supportive atmosphere, a great deal of structure, and lessons broken up into small doses of presentation and seatwork—not too

much of any one task at once. A wider range of methods and a faster pace are more appropriate for high achievers.

10. Though there are no guarantees about which methods to use, it is clear that effective classrooms are pleasant, convivial, and fun. Teachers must consider all the essential factors of the task and the students as well as their own personal strengths and goals.

KEY TERMS

high-inference characteristics

direct instruction/explicit teaching

active teaching

aptitude-treatment interaction (ATI)

higher-order interaction

SUGGESTIONS FOR FURTHER READING AND STUDY

BERLINER, D.C. (1983). Developing conceptions of classroooom environments: Some light on the T in studies of ATI. *Educational Psychologist, 18,* 1–13. Describes 11 basic activity structures that occur in classrooms.

BROPHY, J. (1982). Successful teaching strategies for the inner-city child. *Phi Delta Kappan, 63,* 527–530. Research-based suggestions for helping these students to be successful in school.

EPSTEIN, J. (Ed.). (1981). *Masters: Portraits of great teachers.* New York: Basic Books. A series of essays about gifted teachers written by their equally able students.

GOOD, T. (1979). Teacher effectiveness in the elementary school: What we know about it now. *Journal of Teacher Education, 30,* 52–64. A thoughtful integration of the research on effective elementary school teaching.

GOOD, T., GROUWS, D., & EBMEIER, H. (1983). *Active mathematics teaching.* New York: Longman. Summarizes the development of the Missouri Mathematics Program.

HUNTER, M. (1982). *Mastery teaching.* El Segundo, CA: TIP Publications. Teachers all over the country are reading this book about how to conduct effective lessons, motivate students, and help students get the most from the material.

LEINHARDT, G. (1986). Expertise in mathematics teaching. *Educational Leadership, 43,* 28–33. A close-up look at a very gifted teacher. Contains ideas for improving your own teaching and helping others do the same.

LORTIE, D. (1975). *Schoolteacher: A sociological study.* Chicago: University of Chicago Press. A classic study of teaching as an occupation. Emphasizes teachers' views, beliefs, and feelings about their lives in the classroom.

PETERSON, P. L., JANICKI, T. C., & SWING, S. R. (1980). Aptitude-treatment interaction effects of three social studies teaching approaches. *American Educational Research Journal, 17,* 339–360. Examines relationships between teaching approaches and student attributes.

Research on teaching. *The Elementary School Journal.* (1983), *83* (4). A special issue including articles by Jere Brophy on classroom organization, Barak Rosenshine on teaching functions, Rhona Weinstein on how children perceive teachers and instructional methods, and Steward Purkey on effective schools.

ROSENSHINE, B. (1986). Synthesis of research on explicit teaching. *Educational Leadership, 43,* 60–69. A concise and readable summary of what we know about how to teach explicit information. Rosenshine has been one of the best and most sensible synthesizers of research on teaching.

TIMPSON, W. M., & TOBIN, D. N. (1982). *Teaching as performing: A guide to energizing your public presentation*. Englewood Cliffs, NJ: Prentice-Hall. Being a better teacher by taking your "cues" from performers.

WITTROCK, M. (Ed.). (1986). *Handbook of research on teaching* (3rd ed.). New York: Macmillan. Not so much a book as a library of outstanding articles on teaching. Contains sections on methods, research, the context of teaching, and the adaptation of teaching to differences in learners, as well as chapters on teaching mathematics, science, writing, social studies, and many other subjects.

Teachers' Forum

Engaged Time

We know that effective teaching relies in part on students' active involvement in lessons. What strategies do you use to keep students involved? How do you keep the rest of the class engaged when only a few are answering questions?

A Constant Challenge

Keeping all students involved is always a challenge. One way to meet the challenge is to make sure that all students believe they may be called on at any time. In my experience, secondary students should be selected to answer questions randomly. The question should be asked first, before anyone is called on. After the first student has responded, that answer can be used to generate a new question for others.

Another technique to help keep students focused on the task is to walk around the classroom while asking questions. Students tend to daydream less if the teacher is standing nearby. A third technique is to have students write individual responses to questions. After they've all had enough time to write their responses, an individual student can be called on. This way, all students think through the question and answer it, even if they don't respond orally.

Jane C. Dusell, High School English Teacher
Medford Senior High School, Medford, Wisconsin

Challenge or Prescribe?

You have just finished grading the first library research papers of the year, and the results are disastrous. The idea seemed simple enough. You gave each student a different current topic, then told them to look up their topics in different periodicals and write a two-page summary of the information they found, listing sources. From the results, you can see that some students used nothing but encyclopedias, others just stated their own opinions, and some copied their entire papers from the sources. Originally, you'd decided that to break the assignment down further would be to spoon-feed students. What has gone wrong? What can you do?

In-Class References

Usually in such cases I do a research paper with my fourth-grade students. I bring in periodicals so that the students *see* the references. I have students tell what they have read, and I encourage them to record these words and not the words of the author. At all levels I would make every effort to give individual topics that were of interest to them. For the students who used only one reference, I would consider requiring them to hand in notes from various sources on different days.

Louise Harrold Melucci, Fourth-Grade Teacher
Greenwood School, Warwick, Rhode Island

Each Reason and Every Step Are Important

Perhaps the students were bored by their topics—or perhaps the teacher did not point out clearly enough why each topic had value or what the essential, interesting features were for students to look for. Many of the students might not have been ready to take on this kind of comprehension and summarizing task. Some might need remedial work with reading comprehension—how to skim for main points, take notes, and so on. Others may simply not have understood what summarizing involved. It is also possible that some students wanted to make the task easy for themselves and see what they could get away with.

It might be best to (1) have a lesson on what research is and why it is relevant; (2) ask students for a list of topics of immediate interest to them that they'd like to research; (3) pick one topic to work on as a class; (4) read several references on that topic together in class and work up a class summary—ask for oral contributions in students' own words, or have each student write down what they think are the essential points, then pool these responses and vote on the points to include; (5) be sure to distinguish between opinion and research summaries—have several examples of both; (6) list all the references for the class topic on the board, pointing out why citing sources is important—it's just credit where credit is due; (7) make a bulletin-board display (for younger students) or start a news-magazine type article (for older students) based on the class topic, using the summary as a starting point; (8) assign papers on topics each student picks from the original list.

Simone Wharton, High School English Teacher
New York, New York

Different Ability Levels

Should high- and low-ability students be taught differently? This is a controversial topic among educators. What is your position on this issue? What characteristics of your teaching are consistent for students of all ability levels? How do you modify your teaching for the different ability levels?

Each Student's Contribution Matters

I try to make learning fun and to capture the students' full attention. I reduce the possibility of failure as much as possible, at the same time stressing that in my classroom I expect students' full energy to be applied to learning. I also emphasize that they should strive for correctness but that mistakes are just a part of learning something new.

I try to give every student a chance to succeed, both privately and publicly. I find that although my low-ability students still have trouble with things like grammar and composition, they can succeed in other areas at the same level as their high-ability classmates.

Once, in a Shakespeare class, one of my high-ability students was giving her opinion of a play we were reading; she was discussing a bit of literary criticism she'd read on her own, outside of class. She was repeating a lot of what the critic had said, using his vocuabulary. One of the low-ability students couldn't stand it anymore and asked her what she was trying to say. She couldn't put it into her own words, and it led to a long and interesting discussion involving all levels of students, about literary criticism, critics, and the value of the students' own ideas. There were no hard feelings, just discussion. They realized that they, too, were critics, that they could form their own reactions to a work, and that these reactions were important.

Karen L. Eitreim, High School German and English Teacher
Richland High School, Richland, Washington

Avoiding Assumptions

I believe it is wrong to make assumptions about the abilities of students (or anyone else). In most situations, students seem to live up to your expectations. I completely ignore previous academic records, IQ scores, or guidance counselor recommendations. My experience indicates that many who have been pigeonholed as low-ability students can show remarkable insight and problem-solving skills. Without actually saying so, I communicate to them that I believe in them and that *they* are the ones who establish their limits. I show my respect for and understanding of their answers and contributions, so that I can establish a nonthreatening learning environment. As the course progresses, I pose increasingly abstract, complex problems, which do not have right or wrong answers. This gives all students a chance to think, respond, and participate, regardless of their ability level.

R. Chris Rohde, High School Chemistry Teacher
Chippewa Falls Senior High School, Chippewa Falls, Wisconsin

13

Teaching Exceptional Students

Overview
What Does It Mean to Be Exceptional?   452
What's in a Name?: Cautions in the Use of Labels   453
Beyond the Labels: Teaching Students   454
Students with Learning Problems   455
Physical and Health Problems: Orthopedic Handicaps, Epilepsy,
   Cerebral Palsy   456
Impaired Vision or Hearing   457
Communication Disorders   460
Behavior Disorders   462
Specific Learning Disabilities: What's Wrong When Nothing Is
   Wrong?   465
Mental Retardation   466
Mainstreaming   469
Public Law 94-142   470
Making the Programs Work   472
Resources for Mainstreaming   472
Students with Special Abilities: The Gifted   474
Who Are the Gifted?   474
Recognizing Gifted Students   476
Teaching the Gifted   477
Multicultural and Bilingual Education   479
Making Multicultural Education Work   479
Bilingual Education   481
Summary/Key Terms
Suggestions for Further Reading and Study
Teachers' Forum

Teachers today must be able to work with a wide range of students. In the past, students with identifiable learning problems—students we now call exceptional—were often segregated in special education classes. Today, many spend at least part of the day with regular teachers. Also, in the classrooms of the 1980s and 1990s there is great cultural diversity among students.

Exceptional students include both the handicapped and the gifted. Handicapped students may be mentally retarded, physically handicapped, emotionally disturbed, or learning disabled or have communication or behavior problems. Recent changes in federal legislation require that many handicapped students formerly taught in special classes must now be taught in the regular classroom. One consequence of these legal rulings is that you probably will have at least one exceptional student in your class, whatever grade you teach. We will discuss the new laws, their effects on classrooms, and how to cope with these effects.

This chapter is organized around the kinds of problems and abilities students might have. As we discuss each problem area, we will consider how a teacher might recognize problems, seek help from school and community resources, and plan instruction based on the individuals' strengths and weaknesses.

By the time you complete this chapter, you should be able to do the following:

- Discuss the potential problems in categorizing and labeling students.
- List indicators of hearing, vision, language, and behavior problems, as well as indicators of specific learning disabilities and mental retardation.
- Adapt teaching methods to meet the needs of exceptional students.
- Discuss the implications of Public Law 94-142 for your teaching.
- Describe how you might recognize and teach a gifted student in your class.
- Explain the options for multicultural and bilingual teaching.

WHAT DOES IT MEAN TO BE EXCEPTIONAL?

One problem facing exceptional students until recently was a lack of options. If a child could not be taught in the regular classroom with standard methods, the school had the right to refuse to educate that child at all. A student who was mildly cerebral palsied or partially sighted might need only extra materials, equipment, or tutoring to succeed in a normal classroom. Yet the school could deny its facilities to the student, forcing him or her to attend a separate program designed for individuals with much more serious handicaps. This situation has changed dramatically in the past decade.

The practice of separating students with learning problems and physical handicaps from "normal" students relied on the process of labeling. Today labeling is a very controversial issue.

What's in a Name? Cautions in the Use of Labels

No child is born "mildly retarded" or "learning disabled" in the same way that a child is born female or with the blood type O. The decision that an individual is retarded is a judgment based on the way the individual performs certain tasks. As Jane Mercer has stated, "Persons have no names and belong to no class until we put them in one. Whom we call mentally retarded, and where we draw the line between the mentally retarded and the normal, depend upon our interest and the purpose of our classification" (1973, p. 1).

Labels and Decisions.   For many years, the purpose of labels was diagnostic. Assigning labels was a way of determining eligibility for special services in the school or community. The focus of special education was diagnosis and classification, deciding what was "wrong" with students so they could receive the appropriate "treatment." The model for this procedure is basically the disease model used by physicians: the assumption is that each disease has a particular treatment, which usually is effective.

The Disease Model

Unfortunately, few specific "treatments" automatically follow from a diagnosis such as mental retardation. Many different teaching strategies and materials are appropriate for students labeled retarded. Similarly, a student categorized as partially sighted may benefit from the same techniques used to teach students whose sight is perfect but who have great difficulty remembering what they see. Critics of labeling claim the categories have no educational relevance, since a label does not tell the teacher which methods or materials to use with individual students.

Labels as Stigmas.   Many educators believe children labeled as different from peers are permanently stigmatized. Teachers, friends, and the students themselves set expectations for achievement that are based on the labels and

Many different approaches can be helpful with exceptional students. Play therapy, for example, encourages language and social skills through interaction with the teacher; it also provides an outlet for pent-up feelings and creative impulses. *(Alan Carey/The Image Works)*

not on the individuals' real abilities. When everyone assumes a student will fail, he or she often responds with failure. Several research studies have demonstrated the powerful effects of labels (for example, Foster, Ysseldyke, & Reese, 1975; Gottlieb, 1974). In these studies, the same information (test scores, videotape interview, and so on) about a student was presented to two different groups of teachers. One group was told that the student was normal. The other group was told the student had a particular problem (for example, that he or she was retarded, emotionally disturbed, "dull," or learning disabled). The teachers who believed the student had some kind of problem usually saw the student's behavior as disturbed. In other words, the expectation of a problem led to the perception of a problem—whether it was there or not. (See Chapter 9 for more on teacher expectations.)

Labels are not the sole source of stigma for exceptional students. There is evidence that the behavior of "special" students is one cause of difficulties in their interpersonal relationships; that is, students who are very slow learners, who disrupt class, or who repeatedly fail are liked less by their classmates regardless of the presence or absence of a formal label (Gottlieb, 1974). However, the presence of a label may add to these difficulties, especially for older students.

On the other hand, some educators argue that for younger students at least, being labeled as special helps protect the child. For example, if classmates know a student is retarded, they will adjust their standards and be more willing to accept his or her limitations. Being classified also means that parents and teachers have some guidelines in seeking information on particular problems. And of course, labels still sometimes serve the purpose of opening doors to special programs or financial assistance.

Labels probably both stigmatize and help students (Burbach, 1981; MacMillan, 1982). But until we are able to make diagnoses with great accuracy, we should be very cautious about describing a complex human being with one word.

Beyond the Labels: Teaching Students

When teachers or parents confront a student who clearly cannot cope with the world as easily as others the same age, they must do something. Avoiding special attention and help in order to avoid placing a label on such students is not a satisfactory response. The best way to prevent the students, their peers, and their teachers from forming negative attitudes about the situation is to help these students learn and help them change their behavior. Let's look at three examples of successful intervention.

Sandy, Bill, and Jean: Different People—Different Approaches. Sandy is an 8-year-old girl in a suburban school. Although her teachers have given her hours of extra attention, Sandy is falling farther and farther behind in all subjects. She requires much longer to learn and must move very slowly, practicing new skills more than other children. Sandy also has difficulty in her relationships with peers. She sometimes explodes angrily.

An individual intelligence test is given, and Sandy receives a score of 60. She is low in all abilities measured on an achievement test. Because she needs special help in all subject areas, Sandy is assigned to a self-contained

Labels and Expectations

Benefits of Labels

A Special Class Placement

class for children who need more individual attention than the regular teachers can give. Sandy still joins her old class for art (one of Sandy's strengths) and recess. The regular teacher works with the special teacher to plan a behavior management program focused on Sandy's relationships with classmates and on her tantrums.

Using a Resource Room

Bill is a handsome 13-year-old. He is quite bright but avoids writing whenever possible. His grades are beginning to suffer because his schoolwork requires more and more writing. Testing reveals that Bill has great difficulty translating the information he hears into its written equivalent. He becomes confused and cannot seem to write what he has in mind. His sentences become disorganized and are left unfinished. Bill is assigned to the resource room for one hour each day to work on written expression. The resource teacher's aide also gives Bill some tests from his regular classes orally so he can begin to salvage his sinking grades. In addition, the resource teacher helps Bill's regular teachers adapt his assignments to avoid his writing problem until he can make some progress in overcoming it.

Tutors and Building Alterations

Jean is a 17-year-old who has a congenital orthopedic problem. She has had major surgery on three occasions and countless minor operations and physical therapy treatments. Although very bright, Jean has had to miss quite a bit of school, and her grades have suffered. Testing has revealed no learning problems other than a mild hearing impairment. A hearing aid has practically eliminated this source of difficulty. It has been decided that tutors and home teachers will be provided when Jean is out of school. The only extra help Jean needs during the time she attends school is assistance with her wheelchair, books, and materials. A few changes have been made in Jean's high school—ramps have been installed, and Jean's classes have all been moved to the first floor. Students have been assigned to help Jean get from one class to another and to carry her books. Two of these helpers have become her close friends. The three girls plan to go to the same college and be roommates.

Teaching to Strengths or Weaknesses. You can see that some of the approaches for Sandy, Bill, and Jean involve building on their strong areas to compensate for weaknesses. Other approaches involve trying to correct the weaknesses directly. Which is better?

Flexibility Is the Key

There is disagreement among professionals on this question. Suppose a student has great difficulty reading. Because all subjects require some reading—even subjects he understands well, such as mathematics and science—he has fallen far behind in all his classes. If you were the student's teacher, would you concentrate on teaching him to read or on using methods that did not rely on reading? Since the answer to this question varies for each student, it is probably best to try both approaches. Do not let students fall behind in all other subjects by insisting that they learn only from the printed word. But don't give up on teaching them to read! Flexibility is crucial for regular teachers working with handicapped students.

STUDENTS WITH LEARNING PROBLEMS

In this section we take an in-depth look at the major problems. Remember that many students have more than one handicapping condition.

Physical Problems: Orthopedic Handicaps, Epilepsy, and Cerebral Palsy

orthopedic devices: devices like braces and wheelchairs that aid the physically handicapped

Many students have health problems that do not interfere with their progress in school. Some students must have special **orthopedic devices**, such as braces, shoes, crutches, or wheelchairs, to participate in a normal school program. Accidents, disease, or birth defects can lead to conditions that require these devices. If the school has the necessary architectural features, such as ramps, elevators, and accessible restrooms, and if teachers allow for the physical limitations of students, very little needs to be done to alter the usual educational program. We will look at two physical problems, epilepsy and cerebral palsy, in more detail, since these conditions are so often misunderstood.

epilepsy: disorder marked by seizures and caused by abnormal electrical discharges in the brain

Epilepsy. Many of us tend to have more misinformation than information about **epilepsy.** Its exact causes are unknown, but the seizures that accompany some forms of it result from uncontrolled, spontaneous firings of neurons in the brain. Not all seizures are the result of epilepsy; temporary conditions such as high fevers or infections can also trigger seizures.

There are two types of epilepsy you might encounter in the classroom. *Petit mal epilepsy* is characterized by a brief loss of contact with the outside world. The student may stare, fail to respond to questions, drop objects, and miss what has been happening for 1 to 30 seconds. *Grand mal epilepsy* is characterized by uncontrolled jerking movements that ordinarily last 2 to 5 minutes, followed by a deep sleep or coma. Upon regaining consciousness, the student may be very weary, confused, and in need of extra sleep (Hallahan & Kauffman, 1986).

Petit Mal

The major problem for students with petit mal seizures is that they miss the continuity of the class interaction. If their seizures are frequent, they will find the lessons confusing. As a teacher, you should simply question these students to be sure they are understanding and following the lesson. Be prepared to repeat yourself periodically. Since petit mal seizures are not dramatic, the condition can easily go undetected. If a child in your class appears to daydream frequently, does not seem to know what is going on at times, or cannot remember what has just happened when you ask, you should consult the school psychologist or nurse.

Grand Mal

A grand mal seizure requires a reaction from the teacher. The old idea of putting a stick or pencil in a student's mouth to protect the tongue during a seizure should be *forgotten.* Anything hard might injure the child. The major danger to students having a grand mal seizure is hurting themselves by striking a hard surface during the violent jerking. But do not try to restrain the child's movements. Simply lower the child gently to the floor, away from furniture or walls. Move hard objects away. Turn the child's head gently to the side and loosen any tight clothing. Some experts advise gently placing a soft material like a handkerchief between the back teeth. Find out from the student's parents how the seizure is usually dealt with. If one seizure follows another and the student does not regain consciousness in between, get medical help right away (Hallahan & Kauffman, 1986).

During a seizure the student may perspire heavily, foam at the mouth, and lose bladder or bowel control. As a teacher, your reaction is very important. The other students in the class will be upset if you are upset. If you seem fearful or disgusted, they will learn to respond in similar ways. The class should be prepared for the possibility of seizures occurring during school. Some students may believe that epilepsy is contagious; this and any other mistaken notions should be corrected. A student who has been through a seizure should not be greeted by a classroom of staring children when consciousness returns.

Cerebral Palsy.

cerebral palsy:
condition involving a range of motor or coordination difficulties due to brain damage

spasticity:
involuntary muscular contractions, characteristic of some forms of cerebral palsy

Cerebral Palsy.   Damage to the brain before, during, or in the early years after birth can cause a child to have difficulty moving and coordinating his or her body. The problem may be very mild, so the child simply appears a bit clumsy, or so severe that voluntary movement is practically impossible. The most common form of **cerebral palsy** is characterized by **spasticity** (involuntary contraction of muscles).

The damage to the brain may be such that only movement is affected. Children with this form of cerebral palsy may simply wear a brace or use a wheelchair and need no special educational program. But many children with cerebral palsy have secondary handicaps (Bigge & Sirvis, 1982). In the classroom, these secondary handicaps are the greatest concern—and these are generally what the regular teacher can help with most. For example, many children with cerebral palsy also have hearing impairments, speech problems, or mild mental retardation. The strategies described in the upcoming pages for dealing with these problems should prove helpful in such situations.

Adjustment and Self-Concept.   Although many students with health problems seem to need only medication or special equipment in order to learn in the regular classroom, they may also need extra emotional support and counseling. A student wearing a brace may be no different from others when it comes to translating French or solving long-division problems, but that student's life outside the classroom may be quite different.

Need for Praise

It is especially important for students with serious health problems to receive genuine praise and recognition for their successes. Because physical handicaps often interfere with normal play and physical activity, the development of peer relationships may be affected. Teachers should be sensitive to the social successes of all their students, but handicapped students sometimes need extra support in their attempts to become a part of the classroom group.

Impaired Vision or Hearing

Students with severe hearing or vision losses, especially younger students who have not yet learned how to function in regular classrooms, spend most of their school time in special classes. Students with mild impairments and students with more severe problems who have had special training are frequently placed in regular classrooms for most or all of their instruction.

Hearing Impairment.   Hearing losses may be caused by genetic factors, maternal infections such as rubella during pregnancy, complications during birth, or early-childhood diseases such as mumps or measles. Many children today are protected from hearing loss by vaccinations against such infections.

Clearly, many experiences in regular classrooms can be both educational and enjoyable for hearing-impaired children. With some careful planning, these students can be full participants in their class. And activities that involve *all* the senses—not just sight and hearing—benefit every student. *(Cary Wolinsky/Stock, Boston)*

Signs of hearing problems are turning one ear toward the speaker, favoring one ear in conversation, or misunderstanding conversation when the speaker's face cannot be seen. Other indications include not following directions, seeming distracted or confused at times, frequently asking people to repeat what they have said, mispronouncing new words or names, and being reluctant to participate in class discussions (Charles & Malian, 1980). Take note particularly of students who have frequent earaches, sinus infections, or allergies (Hallahan & Kauffman, 1986).

In the past, educators have debated whether oral or manual approaches are better for children with hearing impairments. Oral approaches involve **speech reading** (also called lip reading) as well as training students to use whatever limited hearing they might have. Manual approaches include **sign language** and **finger spelling.** Research indicates that children who learn some manual method of communicating perform better in academic subjects and are more socially mature than students who are exposed only to oral methods. Today the trend is to combine both approaches (Hallahan & Kauffman, 1986).The Guidelines should help if you have hearing-impaired students in a regular class.

speech reading:
using visual cues to understand language

sign language:
communication system of hand movements that symbolize words and concepts

finger spelling:
communication system that "spells out" each letter with a hand position

Visual Impairment.   Mild vision problems can be overcome with corrective lenses. Difficulties sometimes arise when a student forgets or refuses to wear glasses. One solution in these situations is a token reinforcement program. For example, the teacher makes the following contract with the student: "At ten random times during the day I will stop by your desk. If you are wearing your glasses at that moment, you get a check on this card taped to the top of your desk. As soon as you have five checks (or whatever number is appropriate), you may choose a reward from this list."

Guidelines

Teaching the Hearing-Impaired Student

Make sure the student is seated where he or she can see your lip and facial movements clearly.

Examples
1. Lighting should be sufficient for clear vision, but students should not be facing windows or bright light.
2. Do not stand with your back to the windows or a bright light; this casts your face in shadow and makes lip reading difficult.
3. Don't seat the child too close to you, either. A distance of about six feet is best.

Speak naturally, in complete grammatical sentences.

Examples
1. Do not overemphasize lip movements or speak more slowly than usual.
2. Do not speak too loudly, especially if the student is wearing a hearing aid.

Avoid visual distractions that would draw attention away from the lips.

Examples
1. Excessive makeup or jewelry can be distracting.
2. Overuse of hand gestures can be confusing.

Make it easy for the student to see your face.

Examples
1. Use an overhead projector so you can speak and write while maintaining eye contact with students. Don't talk to the chalkboard.
2. Try not to move around the room while speaking.

Encourage the student to face the speaker during class discussions.

Examples
1. Allow the student to move around the room to get the best possible view of the speaker.
2. Use small-group discussions.

Make sure directions, assignments, and class materials are understood.

Examples
1. Write assignments or directions on the board, or use handouts. Use visual aids as much as possible.
2. If necessary, ask a hearing student to take notes for the hearing-impaired student.
3. Ask hearing-impaired students to repeat or explain class material. Do not simply ask, "Do you understand?" These children often become good imitators, following the lead of other students and appearing to understand.

Learn how a hearing aid operates.

Examples
1. Ask the child or special teacher to demonstrate it to the class.
2. Encourage the child to assume responsibility for the care of the hearing aid.

If applicable, give the whole class some exposure to sign language.

Examples
1. Ask a hearing-impaired student if she or he is willing to give a minilesson in signing. Offer your assistance.
2. Arrange to see a play performance that is simultaneously interpreted in sign language.

Keep in close contact with other professionals involved in the child's education.

Examples
1. Exchange visits with the special-class teacher.
2. Check with the child's therapist regularly, noting changes and different needs.

Only about .1 percent of the students in this country have visual impairments so serious that special educational services are needed. Most of this group needing special services is classified as having **low vision.** This means they can see objects close to them but have difficulty seeing at a distance. These children may need only large-print readers to remain in the regular classroom. A small group of students, about 1 in every 2,500, are **educationally blind.** These students must have Braille materials (Kirk & Gallagher, 1983).

low vision: vision limited to close objects

educationally blind: needing Braille materials in order to learn

Special materials and equipment that help visually handicapped students to function in regular classrooms include large-print typewriters; variable-speed tape recorders (allowing teachers to make time-compressed tape recordings, which speed up the rate of speech without changing the voice pitch and allow students to review material quickly); special calculators; the abacus; three-dimensional maps, charts, and models; and special measuring devices. For students with visual problems, the quality of the print is often more important than the size, so watch out for hard-to-read handouts and ditto sheets. You can buy ditto masters that print in black, red, or green. These may be easier to read than the standard purple we all know and love. The Instructional Materials Reference Center of the American Printing House for the Blind (1839 Frankfort Avenue, Louisville, KY 40206) has catalogs of instructional materials for visually impaired students.

Signs of Vision Problems

Students who have difficulty seeing often hold books very close to or very far from their eyes. They may squint, rub their eyes frequently, or complain that their eyes burn or itch. The eyes may actually be swollen, red, or encrusted. Students with vision problems may misread material on the chalkboard, describe their vision as being blurred, be very sensitive to light, or hold their heads at an odd angle (Charles & Malian, 1980; DeMott, 1982). Any of these signs of impairment should be reported to a qualified school professional.

Communication Disorders

Causes

Language is a complex, learned behavior. Language disorders may arise from many sources, since so many different aspects of the individual are involved in learning language. A child with a hearing impairment will not learn to speak normally. A child who hears inadequate language at home will learn inadequate language. Children who are not listened to or whose perception of the world is distorted by emotional problems will reflect these problems in their language development. Since speaking involves movements, any impairment of the motor functions involved with speech can cause language disorders. And because language development and thinking are so interwoven, any problems in cognitive functioning can affect ability to use language.

speech impairment: inability to produce sounds effectively for speaking

Speech Impairments. Students who cannot produce sounds effectively for speaking are considered to have a **speech impairment.** About 5 percent of school-age children have some form of speech impairment. Articulation problems and stuttering are the two most common problems.

articulation disorder: any pronunciation difficulty, such as the substitution, distortion, or omission of sounds

Articulation disorders include substituting one sound for another ("I *t*ought I *t*aw a pu*dd*y *t*at"), distorting a sound (*shoup* for *soup*), adding a sound (*ideer* for *idea*), or omitting sounds (*po-y* for *pony*) (Cartwright, Cartwright, & Ward, 1981). But keep in mind that most children are 6 to 8 years

Early intensive work with a speech therapist is often very important for children with speech impairments or language disorders. Many problems are correctable if students receive the right help. *(Alan Carey/The Image Works)*

old before they can successfully pronounce all English sounds in normal conversation. The sounds of the consonants *l, r, y, s,* and *z* and the consonant blends *sh, ch, zh,* and *th* are the last to be mastered.

stuttering: repetitions, prolongations, and hesitations that block flow of speech

Stuttering generally appears between the ages of 3 and 4. It is not yet clear what causes stuttering; stuttering, though, can cause embarrassment and anxiety for the sufferer. In about 50 percent of cases, stuttering disappears during early adolescence (Wiig, 1982). The Guidelines on the next page give some ideas for dealing with this problem in the classroom.

voicing problem: inappropriate pitch, quality, loudness, or intonation

Voicing problems, a third type of speech impairment, include speaking with an inappropriate pitch, quality, or loudness or in a monotone (Wiig, 1982). A student with any of these problems should be referred to a speech therapist. Recognizing the problem is the first step. Be alert for students whose pronunciation, loudness, voice quality, speech fluency, expressive range, or rate is very different from that of their peers. Pay attention also to students who seldom speak. Are they simply shy, or do they have difficulties with language?

Four Types

Oral Language Disorders.   There are four types of language disorders: (1) the absence of verbal language, due possibly to deafness at birth, brain damage, or severe emotional problems; (2) usage of qualitatively different language—merely echoing what is said, failing to adapt language to the context, or using nonsense language—caused by hearing loss, learning disabilities, mental retardation, or emotional problems; (3) delayed language development, possibly caused by hearing loss, brain damage, emotional problems, poor teaching or parenting, or inadequate language models; and (4) interrupted language development, often due to hearing loss or injury later in childhood (Hallahan & Kauffman, 1986). As we noted in Chapter 2, language *differences* are not necessarily language *disorders.* Students with language disorders are those who are markedly deficient compared with other students of their own age and cultural group. Students who seldom speak, who use few words or very short sentences, or who rely only on gestures to communicate should be referred to a qualified school professional for observation or testing.

Guidelines

Helping the Student Who Stutters

Concentrate on what is said, not on the trouble the student has in saying it.

Examples
1. *Don't correct or finish the sentence for the student. Allow the student time to speak.*
2. *Monitor your nonverbal communication. Does your expression show impatience?*

Give the student some classroom responsibility.

Examples
1. *Appoint the student to a position that will gain him or her respect from classmates.*
2. *Let the student demonstrate skills that require little speaking.*

Try to establish a regular routine.

Examples
1. *The student should follow the same rules as any other student, but pressure should not be put on speaking.*
2. *Develop a schedule so the student knows what's coming next most of the time.*
3. *Do not call on the student suddenly, with no warning.*
4. *Signal the student a little before his or her turn is coming up. You might use patterned turns, such as going around the circle.*

Do not allow the student to use stuttering to avoid a class assignment.

Examples
1. *If a task is oral and the student feels unable to do it, assign the work in written form.*
2. *Some days will be easier than others. Encourage interaction and recitation on good days.*

Do not allow peers to make fun of the stutterer.

Examples
1. *Model patience and interest when the child talks.*
2. *Read a story written from an exceptional student's viewpoint and discuss it with the class.*
3. *Talk privately with any students who ridicule and explain the effects of their behavior on the stutterer.*

Behavior Disorders

Definition

Students with behavior disorders can be among the most difficult to teach in a regular class. Luckily there are strategies, based on behavior modification, that are very effective in helping these students. Behavior becomes a problem when it deviates so much from appropriate behaviors for the child's age group that it significantly interferes with (1) the child's own growth and development and/or (2) the lives of others. Clearly, deviation implies a difference from some standard, and standards of behavior differ from one situation, age group, culture, and historical period to another. What passes for team spirit in the football bleachers might be seen as disturbed behavior in a religious service in our culture.

Until recently, *emotional disturbance* was often considered synonymous with *behavior disorder*, but this has led to definition and classification difficulties. Quay (1979) has provided a helpful way of classifying behavior disorders into four categories based on clusters of related traits. Children who have *conduct disorders* are aggressive, destructive, disobedient, uncooperative, distractible, disruptive, and persistent. They have been corrected and punished for the same misbehaviors countless times. Many of these children are disliked by the adults and even the other children in their lives. The most successful strategies for helping these children are the behavior management approaches described in Chapters 5 and 6. These students need very clear rules and consequences, consistently enforced. The future is not promising for students who do not learn to control their behavior and who also fail academically (Hallahan & Kauffman, 1986).

Children who are extremely anxious, withdrawn, shy, depressed, and hypersensitive, who cry easily and have little confidence, are said to have an *anxiety-withdrawal disorder*. These children have few social skills and consequently very few friends. The most successful approaches with them appear to involve the direct teaching of social skills (Gresham, 1981).

The third category is *immaturity*. Characteristics include a short attention span, frequent daydreaming, little initiative, messiness, and poor coordination. If an immature student is not too far behind others in the class, she or he may respond to the behavior management strategies described in Chapters 5 and 6. But if this approach fails or the problem is severe, you should

This teacher is making sure both students receive the contact, attention, and support they need—they don't have to misbehave to make their needs clear. As they develop a greater sense of safety and security, they are also learning to cooperate in group activities. *(Alan Carey/The Image Works)*

consult the school psychologist, guidance counselor, or another mental health professional.

The final category of behavior disorders is *socialized aggression.* Students in this group are often members of gangs. They may steal or vandalize because their peer culture expects it.

These four categories are very general. Let's look at some more specific problems.

hyperactivity: behavior disorder marked by atypical, excessive restlessness and inattentiveness

Hyperactivity. You have probably heard and may even have used the term **hyperactivity.** The notion is a modern one; there were no children considered hyperactive 30 or 40 years ago. Today, if anything, the term is applied too often and too widely. Hyperactivity is not one particular condition; it is "a set of behaviors—such as excessive restlessness and short attention span—that are quantitatively and qualitatively different from those of children of the same sex, mental age, and SES" (O'Leary, 1980, p. 195).

Hyperactive children are not only more physically active and inattentive than other children; they also have difficulty responding appropriately and working steadily toward goals (even their own goals), and they may not be able to control their behavior on command, even for a brief period. The problem behaviors are generally evident in all situations and with every teacher. It is hard to know how many children could be classified as hyperactive. The most common estimate is 5 percent of the elementary school population (O'Leary, 1980). More boys than girls are identified as hyperactive. Adolescents are rarely classified in this category (Haring & McCormick, 1986).

Causes

There is great disagreement about the cause or causes of hyperactivity. The list includes subtle damage to the brain, often called minimal brain damage (MBD), slower than normal neurological development, chemical imbalances in the body, genetic factors, food allergies, lead poisoning, maternal drinking or smoking during pregnancy, and simply inappropriate learning (Reid & Hresko, 1981). There is evidence for each of these possibilities. Certain treatments work better with some individuals than with others, so the underlying problem may not be the same for each child.

Drug Therapy

As a teacher or parent, you are more concerned with cures than causes. Unfortunately, there are no completely effective approaches. Many children, about 700,000, receive stimulant medication, usually Dexedrine or Ritalin. These stimulants in particular dosages tend to have paradoxical effects on these children: short-term effects include possible improvements in social behaviors such as cooperation, attention, and compliance. Research suggests that about 70 percent of hyperactive children are more manageable when on medication. But for many there are negative side effects (increased heart rate and blood pressure, interference with growth rate, insomnia, weight loss, nausea) (O'Leary, 1980; Walden & Thompson, 1981). In addition, there is little known about the long-term effects of drug therapy. There is also no evidence of improvement in academic learning or peer relationships—two areas where hyperactive children have great problems. Since students may appear to improve dramatically in their behavior, parents and teachers, relieved to see change, may assume the problem has been cured. It hasn't. The students still need special help in learning.

The methods that have proved most successful in helping hyperactive students learn new skills are based on the behavioral principles described in

Chapters 5 and 6—for example, token reinforcement programs, contingency contracts, and self-management procedures. These methods should be thoroughly tested with the student before drugs are used. Even if students in your class are on medication, it is critical that they also learn the academic and social skills they will need to survive. Again, this will not happen by itself, even if behavior improves with medication (Kneedler, 1984).

Suicide. Lately many people have become concerned about the seeming increase in suicide among adolescents. Suicide is one of the most common causes of death among young people. Attempted suicides must be taken seriously. As James Toolan (1981) has written:

> [An] attitude concerning suicide that we must always question is the one expressed by the comment, "Oh well, it was just a gesture—an attempt to gain attention." The "Friday night special" in the emergency room presents the typical young female who is upset because her boyfriend or husband has gone off with another woman. Band-Aids are put on her wrists or her stomach [is] washed out, and she is sent home and told not to come back. But why would anyone make a suicidal gesture unless he or she were desperate? Her boyfriend did run out on her—she has a right to be depressed—but does she have to use this method of calling attention to her plight? People who resort to this extreme are in my opinion really desperate. They urgently need help and should be seen as soon as possible after the attempt. (pp. 311–312)

Specific Learning Disabilities: What's Wrong When Nothing Is Wrong?

How do you explain what is wrong with a student who is not mentally retarded, emotionally disturbed, educationally deprived, or culturally different, who has normal vision, hearing, and language capabilities, and who still cannot learn to read, write, or compute? One explanation is that the student has a **specific learning disability.** This is a relatively new category of exceptional students. The category is controversial, partly because professionals cannot agree on who belongs in it. The federal government gives this definition:

> "Specific learning disability" means a disorder in one or more of the basic psychological processes involved in understanding or using language, spoken or written, which may manifest itself in an imperfect ability to listen, think, speak, read, write, spell, or to do mathematical calculations. The term includes such conditions as perceptual handicaps, brain injury, minimal brain dysfunction, dyslexia, and developmental aphasia. (*Federal Register,* August 23, 1977)

The definition goes on to say that these disorders of listening, thinking, and so on are *not* due primarily to other conditions, such as mental retardation, emotional disturbance, or educational disadvantages.

Students with Learning Disabilities. As with any of the groups of handicapped students described thus far, students with learning disabilities are not all alike. Many different characteristics have been attributed to learning disabled students; the most common are specific difficulties in one or more academic areas, poor coordination, problems paying attention, hyperactivity and impulsivity, problems organizing and interpreting visual and auditory information, disorders of thinking, memory, speech, and hearing, and sharp emotional ups and downs (Hallahan & Kauffman, 1986). As you can see, many students with other handicaps, such as hyperactivity, and many normal students might have some of the same characteristics. To complicate the situation even more, not all students with learning disabilities will have these problems, and few will have *all* of the problems.

Causes Unclear

There is no agreement about the causes of learning disabilities. Explanations include lack of dominance of one side of the brain, mild or slight physical damage to the brain, chemical imbalances in the body due to allergies to foods and additives, poor early nutrition, genetic factors, immaturity of the central nervous system, underdeveloped perceptual motor skills, poor teaching, lack of motivation, and inadequate structure in the educational program (Mercer, 1982). You can see that some explanations refer to factors within the child and others refer to environmental factors.

Early diagnosis is important so that learning disabled students do not become terribly frustrated and discouraged. The students themselves do not understand why they have such trouble learning. They may try to compensate and develop bad learning habits in the process, or they may begin avoiding certain subjects out of fear of not being able to handle the work. To prevent these things from happening, the teacher should refer these students to the appropriate professionals in the school.

There is also controversy over how best to help these students. Many programs have been developed to "train" the underlying learning processes; Marianne Frostig's techniques for improving visual perception provide an example (Frostig & Horne, 1964). In general, attempts to train perceptual processes directly have not been very successful in improving academic performance (Reid & Hresko, 1981). A more promising approach seems to be to emphasize study skills and methods for processing information in a given subject like reading or math. Many of the principles of cognitive learning can be applied to help all students improve their attention, memory, and problem-solving abilities. No set of teaching techniques will be effective for every learning disabled child. You should work with the special education teachers in your school to design appropriate instruction for individual students. The Guidelines may also help.

Mental Retardation

mental retardation:
significantly below-average intellectual and adaptive social behavior, evident before age 18

Before the 1970s, **mental retardation** was often defined simply as a score below a particular cutoff point on an intelligence test. Since one school district might use a cutoff of, say, 75 and another a cutoff of 67, a student could be labeled mentally retarded in one district but not in another. Using an IQ score alone is *never* an appropriate way to classify a student as retarded. Almost every definition of mental retardation includes the idea that mentally retarded individuals cannot adapt adequately to their environment.

Definition and Prevalence. According to the American Association on Mental Deficiency (AAMD), there are three key factors in mental retardation.

Guidelines

Learning Disabled Students

Allow students to use their learning strengths to master course content.

Examples
1. If a student cannot read, find other ways to present the facts and ideas.
2. A student who cannot write but who speaks well can use a tape recorder for some assignments.

Work on the learning problem directly.

Examples
1. If the student cannot read, teach reading—don't make the student do a social studies assignment from a textbook.
2. If the student has difficulty remembering, teach memory strategies and systems for making written records.

Break assignments into very small steps.

Examples
1. Identify the steps that give the student the most trouble and concentrate on them.
2. Use task analysis to put material into a meaningful sequence (see Chapter 11).

Make sure students are being reinforced for their successes.

Examples
1. Experiment with token reinforcement systems.
2. Allow students to serve as tutors for subjects they know well.

Students should be exposed to special teaching approaches effective with learning disabled students.

Examples
1. Learn some of these teaching methods and incorporate them into your classroom. They may be useful with slow learners as well.
2. Encourage the student to obtain special tutoring if possible.
3. Consider using computer-based instruction to individualize teaching.

Do not use the LD label, or let the student use it, as an excuse.

Examples
1. Keep appropriate expectations for performance; learning disabled students are usually of average or above-average intelligence.
2. Remember that learning disabled is the most general of the exceptional-student categories. It does not describe a specific condition.

Identifying Mental Retardation: Three Factors

1. Intellectual function must be significantly below average. (This is usually defined as a score lower than two standard deviations below the mean on an individual intelligence test—for example, a score below 70 on the WISC–R.)

2. Adaptive behavior must also be so deficient that the individuals do not meet the standards of personal independence and social responsibility expected of people their age in their own cultural group.

3. Finally, these deficiencies of intellectual functioning and adaptive behavior must have appeared before age 18. Problems occurring after that are assumed to be due to other factors, such as brain damage or emotional disturbance.

Of the three factors, "the test of social adequacy is the most basic indicator of retarded mental development. If a person is socially and economically self-sufficient, low test scores are relatively meaningless" (Smith & Neisworth, 1975, p. 307). This caution is especially important when interpreting the scores of students from different cultures. Students who have limited verbal ability but are perfectly capable in social situations and have adequate adaptive behavior are *not* retarded.

Prevalence

Only about 1 to 2 percent of the population fits this definition of retarded in both intellectual functioning and adaptive behavior (Hallahan & Kauffman, 1986). Of this group, most—about 75 percent—are mildly retarded. Only 20 percent of all retarded individuals are moderately retarded, and only 5 percent are severely or profoundly affected. Table 13–1 describes typical behaviors for mildly, moderately, severely, and profoundly retarded people at preschool and school-age levels.

Causes. We know of organic (physical) causes of retardation for only about 10 to 25 percent of the individuals involved. One is **Down syndrome,** a condition caused by having an extra chromosome (though the extra chromosome does not appear to be inherited). Children with Down syndrome range in intelligence from very severely retarded to almost normal.

Down syndrome: retardation caused by presence of extra chromosome

Other known cases of mental retardation include maternal infections such as rubella during pregnancy, blood-type incompatibility between the mother and the unborn baby, premature birth, and an inherited disease called phenylketonuria, or PKU (Kirk & Gallagher, 1983).

Teaching Retarded Students. As a regular teacher, you will have very little contact with severely or moderately retarded children, but you may encounter mildly retarded children. In the early grades these students may simply learn more slowly than their peers. By the third or fourth grade, they will probably have fallen far behind.

Learning Goals for the Mildly Retarded

Learning goals for mildly retarded students between the ages of 9 and 13 include basic reading, writing, arithmetic, learning about the local environment, social behavior, and personal interests. In junior and senior high school, the emphasis is on vocational and domestic skills; literacy for living (using the telephone book, reading signs, labels, and newspaper ads, completing a job application); job-related behaviors like courteousness and punctuality; health self-care; and citizenship skills (Robinson & Robinson, 1976).

Effects of Regular Class Placement

The impact of regular-class placement on retarded students is not clear. Simply placing a retarded student in a regular class does not guarantee that he or she will be accepted (Gottlieb, Alter, & Gottlieb, 1983). In fact, there is evidence that retarded students are *more* accepted when they spend *less* time in the regular class. Without extra support from teachers, retarded students can be as isolated from nonretarded peers in a regular class as they are in a special class. Many children must be taught how to make and keep friends, and retarded children often need this kind of guidance most of all.

The Guidelines on page 470 list suggestions for teaching students with below-average general intelligence.

Table 13–1 **Developmental Characteristics of Mentally Retarded Individuals**

Degree of Retardation	IQ Range	Preschool Years (0–5)	School Years (6–20)
Mild	50–55 to approx. 70	Capable of developing social and communication skills Minimal sensorimotor retardation Retardation may not be obvious at this age	By late teens, can attain about 6th-grade academic level Social conformity and acceptance with guidance "Educable"
Moderate	35–40 to 50–55	Can talk or communicate Poor social awareness Fair motor development Moderate supervision necessary Training in self-help useful	Progress beyond 2nd-grade academic level unlikely Training in social and occupational skills beneficial Can learn to get around alone in familiar places
Severe	20–25 to 35–40	Minimal speech; few or no communication skills Poor motor development Self-help training generally unprofitable	Can talk or learn to communicate Systematic training in basic hygiene and other self-care habits beneficial
Profound	Below 20–25	Minimal sensorimotor functioning capacities Nursing care required	Some motor development Limited self-help training may be useful

Adapted from S. A. Kirk & J. J. Gallagher (1979), Educating exceptional children (3rd ed.). Boston: Houghton Mifflin, p. 142, reprinted by permission of Houghton Mifflin Co.; and from H. G. Grossman (Ed.) (1983), Classification in mental retardation. Washington, DC: American Association on Mental Deficiency, p. 13.

MAINSTREAMING

We have been discussing the many special problems of exceptional students in detail because you may well encounter such students in your classroom, no matter what grade or subject you teach. Recent legislation has played an important role in bringing these students into the mainstream.

Guidelines

Teaching Retarded Students

1. Determine readiness: however little a child may know, he or she is ready to learn a next step.
2. Objectives should be simply stated and presented.
3. Specific learning objectives should be based on an analysis of the child's learning strengths and weaknesses.
4. Present material in small, logical steps. Practice extensively before going on to the next step.
5. Skills and concepts should be practical, based on the demands of adult life.
6. Do not skip steps. Students with average intelligence can form conceptual bridges from one step to the next. Retarded children need every step and bridge made explicit. Make connections for the students. Do not expect them to "see" the connections.
7. You may have to present the same idea in many different ways.
8. Go back to a simpler level if you see the student is not following.
9. Be especially careful to motivate the student and maintain attention.
10. Find materials that do not insult the student. A junior high boy may need the low vocabulary of "See Spot run" but will be insulted by the age of the characters and the content of the story.
11. Focus on a few target behaviors or skills so you and the student have a chance to experience success. Everyone needs positive reinforcement.
12. Retarded students must overlearn, repeat, and practice more than children of average intelligence. They must be taught how to study, and they must frequently review and practice their newly acquired skills in different settings.

Public Law 94-142

On November 29, 1975, the Education for All Handicapped Children Act was signed by President Gerald R. Ford. The major purpose of the law is to ensure that all handicapped children have available to them a free public education appropriate to their needs. PL 94-142 has three major points of interest to teachers: the concept of least restrictive placement; the individualized education program (IEP); and the protection of the rights of handicapped students and their parents.

least restrictive placement: placement of each child in as normal an educational setting as possible

Least Restrictive Placement.   The law requires states to develop procedures for educating each child in the **least restrictive placement.** This means a setting that is as normal and as much in the mainstream of education as possible. Some handicapped students might spend most of the day in a special class but attend one or two regular classes in physical education and art. Mainstreaming does *not* mean that students with severe physical, emotional, or cognitive problems must be placed in regular schools that cannot meet their needs. But students who can benefit from involvement with their nonhandicapped peers should be educated with them, even if doing so calls for special aids and services and training or consultation for the regular teaching staff.

It is probably clear to you now that each student is unique and may need a different program to make progress. The drafters of PL 94-142 recognized this.

individualized education program (IEP): annually revised program for an exceptional student, detailing present achievement level, goals, and strategies, drawn up by teachers, parents, specialists, and student (if possible)

Individualized Education Program. The **individualized education program,** or **IEP** is written by a team that includes the student's teacher or teachers, a qualified school psychologist or special education supervisor, the parent(s) or guardian(s), and the student (when possible). The program must be updated each year and must state in writing:

1. The student's present level of achievement.
2. Goals for the year and short-term measurable instructional objectives leading to those goals.
3. A list of specific services to be provided to the student and when those services will be initiated.
4. A description of how fully the student will participate in the regular school program.
5. A schedule telling how the student's progress toward the objectives will be evaluated and approximately how long the services described in the plan will be needed.

The Rights of Students and Parents. Several stipulations in PL 94-142 protect the rights of parents and students. Schools must have procedures for

Individual attention from a specially trained teacher or counselor, oral instead of written tests, detailed feedback, guidance in practical career and life skills, and encouragement can all help to prevent a mainstreamed student's difficulties from interfering with potential progress. The IEP has been an attempt to ensure this kind of support for exceptional students. *(Jerry Howard/Stock, Boston)*

maintaining the confidentiality of school records. Testing practices must not discriminate against students from different cultural backgrounds. Parents have the right to see all records relating to the testing, placement, and teaching of their child. If they wish, parents may obtain an independent evaluation of their child. Parents may bring an advocate or representative to the meeting at which the IEP is developed. Students whose parents are unknown or unavailable must be assigned a surrogate parent to participate in the planning. Parents must receive written notice (in their native language) before any evaluation or change in placement is made. Finally, parents have the right to challenge the program developed for their child and are protected by due process of law. Clearly, all these safeguards can complicate the process of planning for exceptional students. But the rights of handicapped students and their parents were not protected well enough by earlier procedures.

The Future of PL 94-142

The future of PL 94-142 is not certain; the legislation may be changed or even repealed. Still, the economic realities of the educational system probably will require regular teachers to handle more instead of fewer handicapped students, since the money for expensive specialists and programs will not be available in most schools.

Making the Programs Work

Lloyd Dunn (1973a) has suggested 11 designs for teaching exceptional students. These designs are presented in Table 13–2. At the top of the list are the plans that integrate (mainstream) the student most completely into the regular school program. As you move down the list, the plans remove the student more and more from the regular program.

Ideally, each student is assigned to the most integrated program he or she can handle. Then students are moved up to a more integrated program as soon as possible. For example, students with severe reading problems might first be assigned to Plan 4 or 5. They would spend a large portion of the day in a resource room or special education classroom learning to read and would also attend regular classes where reading was not as important. As they progressed in reading, they would spend less time in the special class and more time in regular classes. At some point they might stop going to the special class but meet with a reading tutor a few times a week (Plan 3). Finally, they would attend only regular classes, but their teachers might be given special materials to use in teaching them as well as consultation in how to help them continue to improve while in the regular classes (Plans 1 or 2).

Resources for Mainstreaming

How is the regular classroom teacher to deal with mainstreaming? Many regular teachers have not had any special training in teaching exceptional students, partly because the focus on mainstreaming is a relatively new one. (Whether the new focus and the new law—if it remains in effect—will make a difference is not yet known.) Some educators have criticized the move toward mainstreaming for precisely this reason: teachers in regular classes

Table 13–2   Plans for Teaching Exceptional Students: From Most to Least Integrated

Plan 1 Student enrolled in regular day class; special education instructional materials and equipment available in regular class

Plan 2 Student enrolled in regular day class; special education instructional materials and equipment available, plus special education consulting service for regular teacher

Plan 3 Student enrolled in regular day class; itinerant or school-based special education tutors used

Plan 4 Student enrolled in regular day class; special education resource room and teacher used as necessary

Plan 5 Student spends part of day in special day class where enrolled; receives some academic instruction in regular class

Plan 6 Student in self-contained special day class where enrolled; receives no academic instruction in regular class

Plan 7 Student divides time between regular school (special class) and special day school; receives no instruction in regular class

Plan 8 Student attends special day school full time

Plan 9 Student attends special boarding school or residential facility

Plan 10 Student receives instruction at hospital

Plan 11 Student receives instruction at home

Adapted from L. M. Dunn (1973), An overview. In L. M. Dunn (Ed.), Exceptional children in the schools: Special education in transition (2nd ed.). New York: Holt, Rinehart, & Winston. Copyright © 1973 by Holt, Rinehart, & Winston, Inc. Reprinted by permission of Holt, Rinehart, & Winston, CBS College Publishing.

have not been prepared for students with special learning problems. Critics have also noted that just placing an exceptional student in a class with non-handicapped peers will not automatically mean that the student will learn more. This is a point addressed throughout this book: it is the specific instructional strategies that count, not just the grouping or placement or general ideas.

Certainly, despite financial crunches, administrators must *not* use mainstreaming as a way to cut costs, simply by moving handicapped students into the less expensive regular classrooms. In order for teachers to be able to create a learning environment appropriate for exceptional students, the school must provide a certain amount of materials, methods, knowledge, skills, and support in some form. What kind of help is available?

resource room: classroom with special materials and a specially trained teacher

Resource Rooms and Helping Teachers.   A **resource room** is a classroom with special materials and equipment and a specially trained teacher. It can be used in many ways. Students may come to the resource room each day for 30 minutes to several hours. During this time, they receive instruction individually or in small groups. Students are helped to overcome learning problems by developing skills they lack or by learning how to compensate for weaknesses. The rest of the day the students are in regular classes. The resource teacher works every day with several groups of students from all grades in the school.

The resource room can also be used as a crisis center. Individual students may spend an hour, a day, or a week during a crisis, when their regular teacher is unable to give them the necessary attention and guidance. Many resource teachers are trained in crisis intervention and counseling. They can help both the regular teacher and the student get through a difficult situation.

Besides working with students directly, a resource teacher may also work with them indirectly by giving the regular teacher ideas, materials, or actual demonstrations of teaching techniques. Ideally, all the teaching techniques found effective with a particular student in the resource room will be taught to the regular teachers so that they can take over most of the responsibility for the student's instruction.

Special Materials and Equipment. It is sometimes possible to provide special materials and equipment so that a handicapped student will not have to leave the regular class for instruction. Having large-print books and special recordings will allow many partially sighted or blind students to remain in class. Some students have excellent vision but cannot read or interpret information they receive visually. These students may need tutors who will read to them and record class material for listening at home. Students who can read but are far behind their classmates in reading level are often helped by high-interest, low-vocabulary books. The stories in these books are written to interest older students, but the vocabulary is very simple.

For some students with coordination problems, special writing equipment is available. Large-print typewriters may be helpful to students with vision problems. Learning to type has been demonstrated in one study to help high school students who were at least two years behind in reading improve their achievement (Fuhr, 1972).

STUDENTS WITH SPECIAL ABILITIES: THE GIFTED

There is another group of students with special educational needs who are often overlooked by the schools: the gifted and talented. In the past, providing an enriched education for extremely bright or talented students was seen as undemocratic, elitist, and un-American. Why use extra resources for students who already have so much ability when handicapped students need the resources so desperately? But there is a growing recognition that gifted students are being poorly served by most public schools. It is a tragedy whenever students are prevented from fulfilling their potential, whether they are retarded or gifted.

Who Are the Gifted?

gifted students: very bright, creative, and talented students

There is no agreement about what constitutes a **gifted student.** Individuals can have many different gifts. Renzulli (1982) suggests that we distinguish between academic giftedness and "creative/productive" giftedness. The academically gifted learn lessons very easily and quickly and generally score well on tests of intelligence. However, these indicators do not predict success in later life. Those in the second group tend to excel in situations that require the application of information to solve problems in new and effective ways. These characteristics are more likely to be associated with success in later life.

Using these ideas, Renzulli has defined giftedness as a combination of three basic characteristics: above-average general ability; a high level of task commitment or motivation to achieve in certain areas; and a high level of creativity. With these three characteristics, the gifted individual can make valuable contributions to society.

In this text we include very bright, creative, and talented students in the gifted category. Truly gifted children are not the students who simply learn quickly with little effort. The work of gifted students is original, extremely advanced for their age, and potentially of lasting importance.

What do we know about these remarkable individuals—those whom the former U.S. Commissioner of Education Sidney P. Marland, Jr., has called "our most neglected students"? A classic study of the characteristics of the gifted was started decades ago by Terman and associates (1925, 1947, 1959). This huge project is following the lives of 1,528 gifted males and females and will continue until the year 2010. The subjects all have IQ scores in the top 1 percent of the population (140 or above on the Standard-Binet individual test of intelligence). They were identified on the basis of teacher recommendations and IQ tests, so they probably fall into Renzulli's academically gifted category.

Terman and colleagues found that these gifted children were larger, stronger, and healthier than the norm. They often walked sooner and were more athletic. However, nongifted siblings of gifted children are also larger and healthier than the general population. It appears that physical health

Keeping up with gifted students can be difficult—and exciting. Sometimes the right program for gifted students already exists, but in another location, perhaps at a local college or university. High school students, for instance, can leave school early to work with college majors in a given field like chemistry or advanced mathematics. Flexibility and imagination are the keys to providing the gifted with appropriate academic challenges. *(John Ficara/Woodfin, Camp & Associates)*

and achievement may go along with being gifted, but being gifted does not always go along with being physically able (Laycock & Caylor, 1964).

Emotional Adjustment

Another surprising finding was that Terman's subjects were more emotionally stable than their peers and became better-adjusted adults than the average. They had lower rates of delinquency, emotional problems, divorces, drug problems, and so on. Of course, the teachers in Terman's study who made the nominations may have selected students who were better adjusted initially. It would be incorrect to say that every gifted person is superior in adjustment and emotional health. Many problems confront a gifted child. After all, "to have the intelligence of an adult and the emotions of a child combined in a childish body is to encounter certain difficulties" (Hollingworth, 1942, p. 282). These difficulties can include boredom and frustration in school as well as isolation (sometimes even ridicule) from peers because of seemingly unbridgeable differences in interests and concerns. For example, schoolmates may be consumed with a passion for baseball or anxious only about passing math class, whereas the gifted child is fascinated with Beethoven or Rembrandt or focused on an abstract moral issue. Gifted children may also find it difficult to accept their own emotions, since the mismatch between mind and emotion can be great.

Recognizing Gifted Students

It may seem to you that identifying a gifted child would be simple. This is not always the case. Many parents provide early educational experiences for their children. A preschool or primary student coming to your class may read above grade level, play an instrument quite well, or whiz through every assignment. How do you separate the gifted from hard-working or parentally pressured students? Since many talents and abilities are involved, there are many ways to recognize gifted students.

Individual Intelligence Tests. The best single predictor of academic giftedness is still the individual IQ test. Many schools identify the academically gifted as those who score in the top 3 percent for their ethnic or cultural group (an IQ of about 130 for white, native-born Americans). An individual intelligence test is costly, time-consuming, and far from perfect. Many eminent individuals, including Copernicus, Rembrandt, Bach, Lavoisier, and Locke, might not have made this cutoff (Cox, 1926).

Teacher Observation. Teachers are successful about 10 to 50 percent of the time in picking out the gifted children in their classes (Fox, 1981). Seven questions emerged from a study by Walton (1961) as the best to ask teachers in identifying gifted children:

Checklist for the Gifted

1. Who learns easily and rapidly?
2. Who uses a lot of common sense and practical knowledge?
3. Who retains easily what he has heard?
4. Who knows about many things that other children are unaware of?
5. Who uses a large number of words easily and accurately?
6. Who recognizes relations and comprehends meanings?
7. Who is alert and keenly observant and responds quickly?

Other Sources of Information.   Group achievement and intelligence tests tend to underestimate the IQs of very bright children. Still, these tests are often administered routinely and may give some useful information, if the results are interpreted with caution. When schools rely on a cutoff of 130 on a group test such as the Otis Quick-Scoring Mental Ability Test, they are likely to miss 50 to 75 percent of the students who would score 130 or above on the individual tests of IQ. A cutoff score of 115 will identify around 90 percent of these students (Fox, 1981).

Tests

Group tests might be appropriate for screening but are not appropriate for making placement decisions. Several studies at the University of Connecticut have found that students scoring in the top 20 percent but below the top 5 percent on traditional measures of academic ability performed just as well in a special program for the gifted as students in the same program who scored in the top 5 percent (Reis, 1981).

Relying on Experts

Especially for recognizing artistic talent, experts in the field can be called in to judge the merits of a child's creation. Science projects, exhibitions, performances, auditions, and interviews are all possibilities. Creativity tests may provide additional information. Not all children with very high IQs score high on creativity tests, and vice versa. However, scores on creativity and IQ tests are positively related, and tests of creativity may identify some children not picked up by other measures, particularly minority students who may be at a disadvantage on the other types of tests.

Teaching the Gifted

There are at least two issues in making educational plans for gifted students. One is how students should be grouped and paced. The other is what teaching methods are most effective.

Enrichment and Acceleration.   Some educators believe that gifted students should be *accelerated*—moved quickly through the grades. Other educators prefer *enrichment*—giving the students additional, more sophisticated, and more thought-provoking work but keeping them with their age-mates in school. Fox (1979) has suggested that both acceleration and an enriched curriculum are appropriate for especially able students.

Effects of Acceleration

There continues to be popular resistance to plans that allow gifted students to begin school early or to accelerate. Most careful studies indicate that truly gifted students who begin primary, elementary, junior high, high school, college, or even graduate school early do as well as and usually better than nongifted students who are progressing at the normal pace. Social and emotional adjustment does not appear to be impaired. Gifted students tend to prefer the company of older playmates and may be miserably bored if kept with children of their own age. Skipping grades may not be the best solution for a particular gifted student, but it does not deserve the bad name it has received (Daurio, 1979; Kulik & Kulik, 1984).

Creative Options

Increasingly, more flexible programs are being instituted for gifted students. Before- or after-school programs, summer institutes, courses at nearby colleges, classes with local artists, musicians, or dancers, independent research projects, selected classes in high school for younger students, honor classes, and special-interest clubs are all options for giving gifted students appropriate learning experiences. There is evidence that grouping gifted students together, at least for part of the school day, is beneficial to them (Martinson, 1961). But simply grouping students together will not, of course, automatically lead to excellence. The teaching methods, materials, and curricula must be appropriate.

Teaching Strategies.   Teaching methods for gifted students should encourage abstract thinking (formal operational thought), creativity, and independence, not simply the learning of greater quantities of facts. A number of these ideas are included in the Guidelines. In working with gifted and talented students, teachers must be imaginative, flexible, and unthreatened by the capabilities of these students. They must ask themselves, What does this child need most? What is she or he ready to learn? Who can help us to help? Answers might come from faculty members at nearby colleges, retired

Guidelines

Teaching Gifted Students

Allow time, quiet, and privacy for independent work.

Examples
1. *Allow students to pursue independent projects in the library, community, or art room.*
2. *Some class time can be devoted to independent work.*
3. *Help students find the resources they need. If you can't help, try to find a community expert or mentor who can.*

Use advanced learning materials and computers to allow students to master material independently.

Examples
1. *Have a variety of advanced texts available to take home.*
2. *Keep an advanced reading list to which students can add titles and comments.*
3. *If computers are available, encourage students to design teaching programs for computer-based instruction.*

Use delayed, intrinsic, and social reinforcement rather than immediate and concrete rewards.

Examples
1. *Avoid emphasizing grades.*
2. *Have students share their creations with the class.*
3. *Have students analyze and criticize their own work.*
4. *Use gifted students as peer tutors.*

Involve students in planning their own curriculum.

Examples
1. *Help students set their own learning goals.*
2. *Have problem-solving sessions to identify assignments.*

Focus on problem solving, divergent thinking, and long-term projects rather than on frequent tests of factual information.

Examples
1. *Avoid frequent testing and grading.*
2. *Focus on a few large projects instead of many small assignments.*

professionals, books, museums, or older students. Strategies might be as simple as letting the child do math with the next grade or as complicated as helping parents find an appropriate residential school or an interesting, challenging after-school or summer program.

MULTICULTURAL AND BILINGUAL EDUCATION

Since the beginning of the twentieth century, American institutions have tended to promote a blending of the diverse subcultures of the nation into a single unit. As new immigrants arrived, they were expected to be assimilated—that is, to enter the melting pot and become like those who had arrived earlier. The concept of **multicultural education** rejects both assimilation and the existence of separate cultures. According to this concept, American society should undergo a gradual transformation to a society that values diversity, or **cultural pluralism.**

multicultural education: education that teaches the value of cultural diversity

cultural pluralism: cultural diversity; position that stresses different cultures' distinctive identities within larger society

Making Multicultural Education Work

How can an educational program be designed to meet the needs of members of various ethnic minority groups? Students must feel secure in order to learn. A comfortable and nonthreatening learning environment can be created by accepting each student's individuality and beginning with routines that do not conflict with any student's culture. Where English is not a student's first language, some specific issues arise. In schools where there are

Spelling may not be perfect yet, but in this bilingual elementary classroom, there's a lot of learning going on. The caption the children have illustrated for an Acadian history lesson reads, "The Acadians who come to the United States have no money. They have no houses. They speak no English. But they are courageous. They are going to succeed." The children are not only gaining fluency in both French and English; they are also building pride in their Acadian heritage. *(Cary Wolinsky/Stock, Boston)*

large minority-language (say, Spanish-speaking) populations, the classroom can be made more like home by using the child's home language for instruction in the early years.

Ethnic Pride,
Broadened Horizons Self-esteem and pride are important accomplishments of the school years. Sometimes the self-image and occupational aspirations of minority children have actually declined in their early years in public school, probably because of the emphasis on majority-culture values, accomplishments, and history (Diggs, 1974). By presenting the accomplishments of particular members of an ethnic group or by bringing that culture into the classroom (in the form of, say, foods, dress, or music), teachers can help students maintain a sense of pride in their cultural group. Students from other cultures will also benefit from learning more about the diversity of American society.

Tiedt and Tiedt (1979) have provided a great many useful suggestions for multicultural teaching. Here are just a few:

Multicultural
Teaching Ideas Ask students to draw pictures or bring in photographs of themselves. Have each student list all her or his group memberships on a page with this picture. Display the pages around the room or bind them into a book (see Figure 13–1).

Study one cultural group in depth, such as Native Americans, Puerto Ricans, Chicanos, Afro-Americans, or Vietnamese-Americans.

Create a learning center based on a particular culture. Use maps, postcards, books, encyclopedias, recordings of the native language, posters, flags. Have students draw maps, calculate distances, convert money, act out historical events or important holiday traditions, write their own "encyclopedia" articles or travelogues, or write for more information to the appropriate public or private agencies within that country.

Introduce lessons based on a multicultural calendar. Tiedt and Tiedt provide a calendar for each school month showing the important holidays of various cultures and the contributions of these groups to American society.

Figure 13–1   **A Student's "Self-Portrait": We All Belong to Many Groups**

Sue Wong is . . .

a girl
a daughter
a member of the Wong family
a Californian
a San Franciscan
a member of this class
a twelve-year-old
a Chinese-American
a U.S. citizen

From P. L. Tiedt & I. M. Tiedt (1979), Multicultural education: A handbook of activities, information, and resources. Boston: Allyn & Bacon, p. 144. © 1979 by Allyn & Bacon. Reprinted by permission.

Bilingual Education

All citizens should learn the official language of their country. But when and how should instruction in that language begin? Is it better to teach minority students in the United States to read first in their native language or to begin reading instruction in English? Do these children need some oral lessons in English before reading instruction can be effective? Should other subjects, such as mathematics and social studies, be taught in the primary (home) language until the children are fluent in English?

There are two basic positions on these questions, which have given rise to two contrasting teaching approaches (Engle, 1975). In the **native-language approach,** it is considered to be essential that the child learn the majority language, but it is also assumed that students have the right to keep their own native language. Teachers work with the language the children have learned at home and gradually build knowledge of the majority language, as appropriate. The **direct method,** on the other hand, emphasizes development of the majority language and does not use the child's native language as a medium of instruction.

native-language approach: instruction in native language, with gradual teaching of majority language

direct method: instruction in majority language

Research evidence can be shown to support either approach, but final answers are not yet possible. Engle (1975) has made some generalizations about the research findings on bilingual education. Students should be taught to speak the second language before they learn to read in it. Often programs in bilingual education will not show student gains for several years. No matter what program of instruction is used, bilingual students will initially make slower progress than their single-language counterparts. They pay a price for the later potential gain of fluency in two languages. Bilingual progress over the years, however, need not retard development of the primary language.

SUMMARY

1. In the past, education for children with learning problems or physical handicaps followed a medical disease model—diagnosis and treatment. Treatment often meant segregation into separate programs regardless of the degree of the problem. Labels based on diagnoses can easily become stigmas; they can also open doors to financial help and programs where needed.

2. The key to helping handicapped students is to focus not on labels but on each individual's behavior, especially learning strengths and weaknesses. Whether the primary thrust of teaching should be to correct weaknesses or to build on strengths has been debated; probably both approaches must be used in tandem.

3. Physical and health problems include orthopedic handicaps, epilepsy, and cerebral palsy. Often several health problems occur together.

4. A combination of oral and manual approaches is favored today in teaching the hearing impaired. Visually impaired students can be helped with special materials and equipment.

5. Communication disorders include speech impairments (articulation disorders, stuttering, and voicing problems) and language disorders (absence of speech, abnormal use of language, delayed development, and interrupted development).

6. Behavior disorders have sometimes been linked with emotional disturbance; they interfere with a child's own development and/or with others' lives. Major types of these disorders, according to one useful classification system, are conduct disorders, anxiety-withdrawal disorders, immaturity, and socialized aggression. Hyperactivity is often considered a behavior disorder. The extent of emotional disturbance among adolescents has become a cause of concern—there are some indications that teenage suicides are on the rise.

7. A specific learning disability can involve many different characteristics. Emphasis on study, memory, and problem-solving skills seems to be beneficial.

8. The mentally retarded have significantly below-average intellectual skills and cannot adapt adequately to social norms.

9. Public Law 94-192, enacted in 1975, requires education in the least restrictive placement and the development of an individualized education program for each handicapped student. The law also protects the rights of the student and his or her parents.

10. Many regular classroom teachers lack training in instructing handicapped students. Sources of assistance include resource rooms, resource teachers, and special materials and equipment.

11. Gifted students—those who are exceptionally bright, creative, and talented—have often been unable to fulfill their potential in public school.

12. Acceleration and enrichment may both be appropriate for these exceptionally able students.

13. The assimilation approach to the education of children of cultural and linguistic minority groups is being challenged by the concept of multicultural education, which favors cultural diversity. Incorporating aspects of minority cultures into classroom work can enhance minority students' self-esteem.

14. The native-language approach and the direct method have both been used in educating minority-language children. Which approach is "better" remains controversial.

KEY TERMS

orthopedic devices

epilepsy

cerebral palsy

spasticity

speech reading

sign language

finger spelling

low vision

educationally blind

speech impairment

articulation disorder

voicing problems

stuttering

hyperactivity

specific learning disability

mental retardation

Down syndrome

least restrictive placement

individualized educational program (IEP)

resource room

gifted student

muticultural education

cultural pluralism

native-language approach

direct method

SUGGESTIONS FOR FURTHER READING AND STUDY

CHARLES, C. M., & MALIAN, I. M. (1980). *The special student: Practical help for the classroom teacher*. St. Louis: C.V. Mosby. An excellent overview of the legal requirements and teaching methods for working with exceptional students in the regular classroom.

THE COUNCIL FOR EXCEPTIONAL CHILDREN (1920 Association Drive, Reston, VA 22091) publishes several journals for teachers, including *Journal for the Education of the Gifted, Teaching Exceptional Children,* and *Exceptional Children* (this journal reports results of research).

GRESHAM, F. (1981). Social skills training with handicapped children. *Review of Educational Research, 51,* 139–176. A good look at the research on a promising approach.

HALLAHAN, D. P., & KAUFFMAN, J. M. (1986). *Exceptional children: Introduction to special education* (3rd ed.). Englewood Cliffs, NJ: Prentice-Hall. One of the best introductions to the field, this book has chapters about mental retardation, learning disabilities, speech and language disorders, hearing and visual impairment, physical handicaps, giftedness,and current trends in special education.

KIRK, S. A., & GALLAGHER, J. J. (1983). *Educating exceptional children* (4th ed.). Boston: Houghton Mifflin. A classic in the field of special education, organized like the Hallahan and Kauffman text, by categories of exceptionality.

KULIK, J. A., & KULIK, C. L. (1984). Effects of accelerated instruction on students. *Review of Educational Research, 54,* 409–425. Demonstrates that acceleration is a very reasonable alternative for many students.

LARRIVEE, B. (1985). *Effective teaching for successful mainstreaming.* New York: Longman. Recommendations for teaching mainstreamed students that are based on a study of effective practices.

O'LEARY, K. D. (1980). Pills or skills for hyperactive children? *Journal of Applied Behavior Analysis, 13,* 191–204. A very thorough review of the research on different methods for helping hyperactive children.

REID, D. K., & HRESKO, W. P. (1981). *A cognitive approach to learning disabilities.* New York: McGraw-Hill. The new cognitive orientation to learning disabled students.

Teaching Gifted Children and *Learning Disabilities Guide,* each published nine times a year by Croft-NEI, 24 Rope Ferry Road, Waterford, CT 06386.

WITTROCK, M. (1986). *Handbook of research on teaching* (3rd ed.). New York: Macmillan. A very thorough, up-to-date volume with several chapters on teaching exceptional children. Topics include the gifted and talented, bilingual students, the mildly retarded, and adaptation of instruction to individual differences.

WOODWARD, D. M. (1981). *Mainstreaming the learning disabled adolescent: A manual of strategies and materials.* Rockville, MD: Aspen Systems Corp. It is difficult to find a book on this topic. Woodward's text is a very practical resource for teachers.

WOOLFOLK, A. E. (1982). The schools and individual excellence. *Journal for the Education of the Gifted, 7,* (1), 39–49. Describes several factors in schooling that contribute to the psychological development of highly productive and talented individuals.

Teachers' Forum

Exceptional Approaches

What teaching approaches have you found to be particularly useful with students who have special learning needs?

Art for Their Sake The art curriculum is an excellent vehicle for handling the exceptional child. The clear intention is to stimulate individual and personal responses to a given task. In an environment that stresses different and creative solutions, all children are encouraged to find their own answers, regardless of their developmental level. Indeed, many exceptional students whose academic disabilities are severe sometimes have great creative ability.

I think now of one particular student whose ability in every area is very limited. He cannot understand much about the aesthetic concepts taught, but the art room has been a happy experience for him. He seems to take pleasure in whatever he does there. In an atmosphere of praise and encouragement, his peers give him helpful hints, and we all salute his efforts.

Harriet Chipley, Elementary Art Teacher
Lookout Mountain Elementary School, Lookout Mountain, Tennessee

Helping Students Accept the Handicapped

In your class you have two mainstreamed students: a girl with cerebral palsy and a boy with a severe speech impairment. Although both are above average intellectually, their handicaps cause them to seem "dumb." The other students avoid these two and are beginning to call them names like "weirdo" and "retard." How can you help these mainstreamed students to become accepted members of the class?

Offer a Chance Accepting handicapped children is considerably easier if the teacher accepts them
to Identify and is not uncomfortable about the impairments. The class has to be prepared to receive and accept children who are different. There are many books containing stories of handicapped children, which if read and discussed can help these children who are more fortunate gain an understanding of others. Another useful technique is role playing. A teacher I know had her class spend an entire day using just one hand. After this experience, most were able to understand and even identify with a handicapped child with only one good hand.

Charlotte Ross, Second-Grade Teacher
Covert Avenue School, Elmont, New York

Preventing Further Slippage

You have a student who is mainstreamed part of the time and who works the rest of the time in a resource room on material related to what you're doing in class. The student is continuing to get farther and farther behind. What do you do?

Knowing One's I would confer with the resource-room teacher and examine the diagnostic evalua-
Responsibilities tion to determine if the child has the mental capability to do the work. If he does not, an individualized education program (IEP) needs to be written commensurate with his needs. If he does, I would discuss the situation with the student to figure

out what the problem is. If it is a matter of not understanding the material in the resource room, I have a responsibility to get additional help for that student or provide material that explains the concepts involved. Often students have problems structuring time effectively. If the student is behind because he doesn't know where to begin, setting up a concrete schedule will help to make the task more manageable. If the student simply isn't motivated to do the work, I have the responsibility of making certain he understands the consequences of his decision.

Linda Stahl, High School Psychology Teacher
Ponca City Senior High School, Ponca City, Oklahoma

Skipping a Grade

Imagine that you have an exceptionally bright student in your class, who is way beyond the others in her ability to deal with abstract concepts. She also seems much more mature than her classmates, and she doesn't have many friends among them. Her parents would like to have her advanced to the next grade. The guidance counselor thinks that she should remain where she is and be given more challenging work. The administration has asked your opinion. What would you advise, and how would you justify your advice to administrators, counselor, and parents?

Social Needs Count Because she is much more mature than the other students, I would support skipping a grade. The schools and their staffs should minister to the *whole* youngster. Since this student is having social problems in her current placement, I would explain to the administration and the counselor that skipping a grade would be ministering to the girl's social needs. Since she is bright, her academic needs can be satisfied *either* by giving her more challenging work or by allowing her to skip a grade.

Louise Harrold Melucci, Fourth-Grade Teacher
Greenwood School, Warwick, Rhode Island

Considering the Individual Case I think it's important to know how old the child is—the difference between fifth and sixth grades, say, can be much greater than that between eleventh and twelfth. In the end, however, it depends on the individual case. Some questions to ask: If the student has few friends in her current grade, does she already have friends in the next grade? Is she isolated now because of some underlying problem, and how can the school or teachers help with this? What do you know about the class she might be placed in? Is she shy or outgoing? In the later prepuberty years and in adolescence, sexual maturity can make a big difference. Will she be in "over her head"? Or is she ready for a change like that? Will greater academic satisfaction offset any other potential difficulties? What other academic options are available—high-ability reading or math classes? taking some subjects with another grade but remaining with her current homeroom? Are there resources for tutoring or supervised courses somewhere else? Sometimes a shortage of teachers willing to take on extra supervision can in itself make grade skipping worthwhile. What about independent projects—or will this isolate her further?

There are always trade-offs when these sorts of decisions are made. Sometimes the decision will really not make that much difference one way or the other. It is difficult, since a school-age child is usually in some sort of transition, to reach a perfect scholastic/cognitive/emotional matchup. After all, many of us as adults are still struggling with reaching a balance.

Simone Wharton, High School English Teacher
New York, New York

14

Using Standardized Tests in Teaching

Overview
Measurement and Evaluation   488
Norm-Referenced Tests   489
Criterion-Referenced Tests   490
What Do Test Scores Mean?   492
Basic Concepts   492
Types of Scores   493
Interpreting Test Scores   498
Types of Standardized Tests   502
Achievement Tests: What Has the Student Learned?   503
Diagnostic Tests: What Are the Student's Strengths and
   Weaknesses?   507
Aptitude Tests: How Well Will the Student Do in the Future?   508
Current Issues in Standardized Testing   510
The Role of Testing   511
Advantages in Taking Tests: Fair and Unfair   512
Summary/Key Terms
Suggestions for Further Reading and Study
Teachers' Forum

Would it surprise you to learn that published tests such as the college entrance exams and IQ tests are creations of the twentieth century? In the nineteenth and early twentieth centuries, college entrance was generally based on grades, essays, and interviews. From your own experience, you know that testing has come a long way since then.

What would you like to know about testing? How should you prepare yourself or your students for tests? How should you make up tests? How should you interpret standardized test scores? This chapter will focus on the last question, leaving the others for Chapter 15. Dealing with standardized tests involves some very specific considerations. An understanding of how standardized test scores are determined, what they really mean, and how they can be used (or misused) will give you a framework for ensuring that the tests you give, whether standardized or not, are appropriate.

First we consider testing in general, including the various methods of interpreting test scores. Then we look at the different kinds of standardized tests used in schools. By the time you have completed this chapter, you should be able to do the following:

- Calculate mean, median, mode, and standard deviation.
- Define percentile ranks, standard deviations, z scores, T scores, and stanine scores.
- Explain how to improve reliability and validity in testing.
- Interpret the results of achievement, aptitude, and diagnostic tests in a realistic manner.
- Take a position on the truth-in-testing issue and defend your position.
- Describe how to prepare students (and yourself) for taking standardized tests.

MEASUREMENT AND EVALUATION

evaluation:
decision making about student performance and appropriate teaching strategies

All teaching involves **evaluation.** At the heart of evaluation is judgment—making decisions based on values. In the process of evaluation, we compare information to criteria and then make judgments. Teachers must make all kinds of judgments. "Should we use a different text this year?" "Is the film appropriate for my students?" "Will Sarah do better if she repeats the first grade?" "Should Terry get a B− or a C+ on the project?"

measurement:
evaluation expressed in quantitative (number) terms

Measurement is evaluation put in quantitative terms—the description of an event or characteristic in numbers. Measurement tells how much, how often, or how well by providing scores, ranks, or ratings. Instead of saying "Sarah doesn't seem to understand addition," a teacher might say "Sarah answered only 2 of the 15 problems correctly on her addition work sheet." Measurement also allows a teacher to compare one student's performance on one particular task with a standard or with the performances of the other students.

Not all the evaluative decisions made by teachers involve measurement. Some decisions are based on information that is difficult to express numerically: student preferences, information from parents, previous experiences, even intuition. But measurement does play a large role in many classroom decisions, and properly done, it can provide unbiased data for evaluations.

The answers given on any type of test have no meaning by themselves; we must make some kind of comparison to interpret test results. Two basic types of comparison are possible. A test score can be compared to the scores obtained by other people who have taken the same test. If you took a college entrance exam, the score you received told you (and the admissions offices of colleges) how your performance compared to performances of many other people who had previously taken the same test or one like it. The second type of comparison is to a fixed standard or minimum passing score. Most tests required for a driver's license are based on this kind of comparison.

Norm-Referenced Tests

In **norm-referenced** testing, the other people who have taken the test provide the *norms* for determining the meaning of a given individual's score. You can think of a norm as being the typical level of performance for a particular group. By comparing the individual's raw score (the actual number correct) to the norm, we can determine if the score is above, below, or around the average for that group.

There are at least three types of norm groups (comparison groups) in education. One frequently used norm group is the class or school itself. When a teacher compares the score of one student in a tenth-grade American history class with the scores of all the other students in the class, the class itself is the norm group. If the teacher happens to have three American history classes, all of about the same ability, then the norm group for evaluating individual performance might be all three classes.

Norm groups may also be drawn from wider areas. Sometimes, for example, school districts develop achievement tests. When students take this kind of test, their scores are compared to the scores of all the other students at their grade level throughout the district. A student whose score on the achievement test was in the top 25 percent at a particularly good school might be in the top 15 percent for the entire district. Finally, some tests have national norm groups. When students take the college entrance exam, their scores are compared with the scores of students all over the country.

Advantages

Norm-referenced tests are constructed with certain objectives in mind, but the test items themselves tend to cover many different abilities rather than assess a limited number of specific objectives. Norm-referenced tests are especially useful in measuring overall achievement when students have come to understand complex material by different routes. Norm-referenced tests are also appropriate when only the top few candidates can be admitted to a program.

Limitations

Hopkins and Antes (1979) have listed several limitations of norm-referenced measurements. Results of a norm-referenced test do not tell you whether students are ready to move on to more advanced material. Knowing that a student is in the top 3 percent of the class on a test of algebraic

Have you ever wondered why you've had to take so many standardized tests? Results of these tests may have proved very useful in a number of ways: to counsel you about courses or colleges, to see how well your school as a whole was doing in fostering achievement, and even to determine who in your class or school would graduate. *(Mimi Forsyth/Monkmeyer Press)*

concepts will not tell you if he or she is ready to move on to trigonometry. *Everyone* in the class might have failed to achieve sufficient mastery of algebraic concepts.

Norm-referenced tests are also not particularly appropriate for measuring affective and psychomotor objectives. To measure psychomotor learning, a clear description of standards is necessary to judge individuals. Even the best gymnast in any school performs certain exercises better than others and needs specific guidance about how to improve. In the affective area, attitudes and values are personal; comparisons among individuals are not really appropriate. For example, what is an "average" performance on a measure of political values or opinions? Finally, norm-referenced tests tend to encourage competition and comparison of scores. Some students compete to be the best. Others, realizing that being the best is impossible, may compete to be the worst! Either goal has its casualties.

Criterion-Referenced Tests

criterion-referenced testing: testing in which scores are compared to a set performance standard

When test scores are compared not to those of others but to a given criterion or standard of performance, the test is called **criterion-referenced.** In deciding who should be allowed to drive a car, it is important to determine just what standard of performance is appropriate for selecting safe drivers. It does not matter how your test results compare to the results of others. If your performance on the test was in the top 10 percent but you consistently ran through red lights, you would not be a good candidate for receiving a license, even though your score was high.

Mastery of
Objectives

Criterion-referenced tests measure the mastery of very specific objectives. The results of a criterion-referenced test should tell the teacher exactly what the students can do and what they cannot do, at least under certain conditions. For example, a criterion-referenced test would be useful in measuring the ability to add three-digit numbers. A test could be designed with 20 different problems. The standard for mastery could be set at 17 out of 20 correct. (The standard is often somewhat arbitrary but may be based on such things as the teacher's experience with other classes or the difficulty of the problems.) If two students receive scores of 7 and 11, it does not matter that one student did better than the other, since neither met the standard of 17. Both need more help with addition.

There are many such instances in the teaching of basic skills when comparison to a preset standard is more important than comparison to the performance of others. It is not very comforting to know, as a parent, that your child is better than most of the students in class in reading if all the students are unable to read material suited for their grade level. Sometimes standards for meeting the criterion must be set at 100 percent correct. You would not like to have your appendix removed by a surgeon who left surgical instruments inside the body only 10 percent of the time.

Appropriateness

But criterion-referenced tests are not appropriate for every situation. Not every subject can be broken down into a set of specific objectives that exhausts all possible learning outcomes. And as we noted in Chapter 11, often the true objective is understanding, appreciating, or analyzing. Moreover, although standards are important in criterion-referenced testing, they often tend to be arbitrary, as you have already seen. When deciding whether a student has mastered the addition of three-digit numbers comes down to the difference between 16 or 17 correct answers, it seems hard to justify one particular standard over another. Finally, at times it is valuable to know how the students in your class compare to other students at their grade level both locally and nationally. Remember, too, that admission to college is based in part on a test given to students all over the country. You will want your students who plan to go to college to have a good chance to do well on such a test. Table 14–1 offers a comparison of norm-referenced and criterion-referenced tests.

Table 14–1   **Deciding on the Type of Test to Use**

Norm-referenced tests may work best when you are
- Measuring general ability in certain areas, such as English, algebra, general science, or American history.
- Assessing the range of abilities in a large group.
- Selecting top candidates when only a few openings are available.

Criterion-referenced tests may work best when you are
- Measuring mastery of basic skills.
- Determining if students have prerequisites to start a new unit.
- Assessing affective and psychomotor objectives.
- Grouping students for instruction.

WHAT DO TEST SCORES MEAN?

On the average, more than 1 million standardized tests are given each school day in classes throughout this country (Lyman, 1978). Most of these are norm-referenced standardized tests.

Basic Concepts

standardized tests: tests given, usually nationwide, under uniform conditions and scored according to uniform procedures

Standardized tests are the official-looking pamphlets and piles of forms purchased by school systems and administered to students. More specifically, a standardized test is "a task or set of tasks given under standard conditions and designed to assess some aspect of a person's knowledge, skill, or personality. . . . A test yields one or more objectively obtained quantitative scores, so that, as nearly as possible, each person is assessed in the same way" (Green, 1981, p. 1001). The tests are meant to be given under carefully controlled conditions, so that students all over the country undergo the same experience when they take the tests. Standard methods of developing items, administering the test, scoring it, and reporting the scores are all implied by the term *standardized test.*

norming sample: large sample of students serving as a comparison group for scoring standardized tests

The test items and instructions have also been tried out to make sure they work and then rewritten and retested as necessary. The final version of the test is administered to a **norming sample,** a large sample of subjects as similar as possible to the students who will be taking the test in school systems throughout the country. This norming sample serves as a comparison group for all students who later take the test.

The test publishers provide one or more ways of comparing each student's raw score (number of correct answers) with the norming sample. Let's look at some of the measurements on which comparisons and interpretations are based.

frequency distribution: record showing how many scores fall into set groups

Frequency Distributions. A **frequency distribution** is simply a listing of the number of people who obtain each score or fall into each range of scores on a test or other measuring device. For example, on a spelling test 19 students made these scores: 100, 95, 90, 85, 85, 85, 80, 75, 75, 75, 70, 65, 60, 60, 55, 50, 50, 45, 40. As you can see, 1 student made a score of 100, 3 made 85, and so on. This kind of information is often expressed as a simple graph where one axis (the x or horizontal axis) indicates the possible scores and the other axis (the y or vertical axis) indicates the number of subjects who attained each score. A graph, in this case a **histogram,** or bar graph, of the spelling test scores is shown in Figure 14–1.

histogram: bar graph of a frequency distribution

mean: arithmetical average

Measurements of Central Tendency and Standard Deviation. You have probably had a great deal of experience with means. A **mean** is simply the arithmetical average of a group of scores. To calculate the mean, you add the scores and divide the total by the number of scores in the distribution. For example, the total of the 19 spelling scores is 1,340, so the mean is 1,340/19, or 70.53. The mean offers one way of measuring **central tendency,** the score that is typical or representative of the whole distribution.

central tendency: typical score for a group of scores

median: middle score in a group of scores

Two other measures of central tendency are the median and the mode. The **median** is the middle score in the distribution, the point at which half the scores are larger and half are smaller. The median of the 19 scores is

Figure 14–1   Histogram of a Frequency Distribution

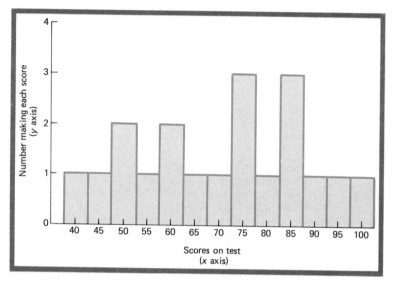

75. Nine scores in the distribution are greater than or equal to 75, and nine are less. The **mode** is the score that occurs most often. The distribution in Figure 14–1 actually has two modes, 75 and 85. This makes it a **bimodal distribution.**

The measure of central tendency gives a score that is representative of the group of scores, but it does not tell you anything about how the scores are distributed. Two groups of scores may both have a mean of 50 but be alike in no other way. One group might contain the scores 50, 45, 55, 55, 45, 50, 50; the other group might contain the scores 100, 0, 50, 90, 10, 50, 50. In both cases the mean, median, and mode are all 50, but the distributions are quite different.

The **standard deviation** is a measure of how the scores spread out around the mean. The larger the standard deviation, the more spread out the scores in the distribution. The smaller the standard deviation, the more the scores are clustered around the mean. For example, in the distribution 50, 45, 55, 55, 45, 50, 50, the standard deviation is much smaller than in the distribution 100, 0, 50, 90, 10, 50, 50. Another way of saying this is that distributions with very small standard deviations have less **variability** in the scores.

The standard deviation is relatively easy to calculate if you remember your high school math. It does take time, however. The process is similar to taking an average, but square roots are used. To calculate the standard deviation, you follow these steps:

1. Calculate the mean (written as $\overline{X}$) of the scores.
2. Subtract the mean from each of the scores. This is written as $(X - \overline{X})$.
3. Square each difference (multiply each difference by itself). This is written $(X - \overline{X})^2$.
4. Add all the squared differences. This is written $\Sigma (X - \overline{X})^2$.

mode: most frequently occurring score

bimodal distribution: distribution with two modes

standard deviation: measure of how scores are spread around the mean

variability: degree of difference or deviation from mean

Calculating the Standard Deviation

5. Divide this total by the number of scores. This is written $\frac{\Sigma(X - \overline{X})^2}{N}$.

6. Find the square root. This is written $\sqrt{\frac{\Sigma(X - \overline{X})^2}{N}}$,

which is the formula for calculating the standard deviation.

The *Student Guide* that accompanies this text provides a more complete explanation of the standard deviation and a shortcut method for estimating it with classroom test data.

Using the SD

Knowing the mean and the standard deviation of a group of scores gives you a better picture of the meaning of an individual score. For example, suppose you received a score of 78 on a test. You would be very pleased with the score if the mean of the test were 70 and the standard deviation were 4. In this case, your score would be 2 standard deviations above the mean, a score well above average.

Consider the difference if the mean of the test had remained at 70 but the standard deviation had been 20. In the second case, your score of 78 would be less than 1 standard deviation from the mean. You would be much closer to the middle of the group, with an above-average but not a high score. Knowing the standard deviation tells you much more than simply knowing the range of scores. One or two students may do very well or very poorly no matter how the majority scored on the tests.

The Normal Distribution. Standard deviations are very useful in understanding test results. They are especially helpful if the results of the tests form a **normal distribution,** like those in the two example tests in Figure 14–2. You may have met the normal distribution before. It is the bell-shaped curve, the most famous frequency distribution because it describes many naturally occurring physical and social phenomena. Many scores fall in the middle, giving the curve its puffed appearance. You find fewer and fewer scores as you look out toward the end points, or *tails,* of the distribution.

normal distribution: the most commonly occurring distribution, in which scores are distributed evenly around mean

Figure 14–2 **Two Tests with the Same Mean and Different Standard Deviations**

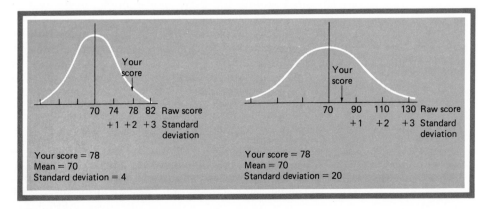

Your score = 78
Mean = 70
Standard deviation = 4

Your score = 78
Mean = 70
Standard deviation = 20

Figure 14–3 **The Normal Distribution**

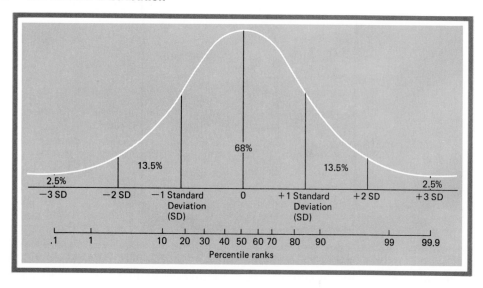

Properties of the Normal Distribution

The normal distribution has been thoroughly analyzed by statisticians. The mean of a normal distribution is also its midpoint. Half the scores are above the mean, and half are below it. In a normal distribution, the mean, median, and mode are all the same point.

Another convenient property of the normal distribution is that the percentage of scores falling within each area of the curve is known, as you can see in Figure 14–3. A person scoring within 1 standard deviation of the mean obviously has a lot of company. Many scores pile up here. In fact, 68 percent of all scores are located in the area plus and minus 1 standard deviation from the mean. About 16 percent of the scores are higher than 1 standard deviation above the mean. Of this higher group, only 2.5 percent are better than 2 standard deviations above the mean. Similarly, only about 16 percent of the scores are less than 1 standard deviation below the mean, and of that group only about 2.5 percent are worse than 2 standard deviations below. At 2 standard deviations from the mean in either direction, the scorer has left the pack behind.

The SAT college entrance exam offers one example of a normal distribution. The mean of the SAT is 500 and the standard deviation is 100. If you know people who made scores of 700, you know they did very well. Only about 2.5 percent of the people who take the test do that well because only 2.5 percent of the scores are better than 2 standard deviations above the mean in a normal distribution.

Types of Scores

Now you have enough background for a discussion of the different kinds of scores you may encounter in reports of results from standardized tests.

Percentile Rank Scores. The concept of ranking is the basis for one very useful kind of score reported on standardized tests: a **percentile rank** score. In percentile ranking, each student's raw score is compared with the raw scores obtained by the students in the norming sample. The percentile rank shows the percentage of students in the norming sample who scored at or below a particular raw score. If a student's score is the same or better than three-quarters of the students in the norming sample, the student would score in the 75th percentile, or have a percentile rank of 75. You can see that this does *not* mean that the student had a raw score of 75 correct answers or even that the student answered 75 percent of the questions correctly. Rather, the 75 refers to the percentage of people in the norming sample whose scores on the test were equal to or below this student's score. A percentile rank of 50 means that a student has scored as well or better than 50 percent of the norming sample and achieved an average score.

Figure 14–4 illustrates one problem in interpreting percentile scores. Differences in percentile ranks do not mean the same thing in terms of raw score points in the middle of the scale as they do at the fringes. The graph shows Joan's and Alice's percentile scores on the fictitious Test of Excellence in Language and Arithmetic. Both students are about average in arithmetic skills. One equaled or surpassed 50 percent of the norming sample; the other, 60 percent. But in the middle of the distribution, this difference in percentile ranks means a raw score difference of only a few points. Their raw scores actually were 75 and 77. In the language test, the difference in percentile ranks seems to be about the same as the difference in arithmetic, since one ranked at the 90th percentile and the other at the 99th. But the difference in their raw scores on the language test is much greater. It takes a greater difference in raw score points to make a difference in percentile rank at the extreme ends of the scale. On the language test the difference in raw scores is about 10 points.

Grade-Equivalent Scores. **Grade-equivalent scores** are generally obtained from separate norming samples for each grade level. The average of the scores of all the tenth graders in the norming sample defines the tenth-grade

percentile rank: percentage of those in the norming sample who scored at or below individual's score

grade-equivalent score: measure of grade level based on comparison with norming samples from each grade

Figure 14–4 Percentile Ranking on a Normal Distribution Curve

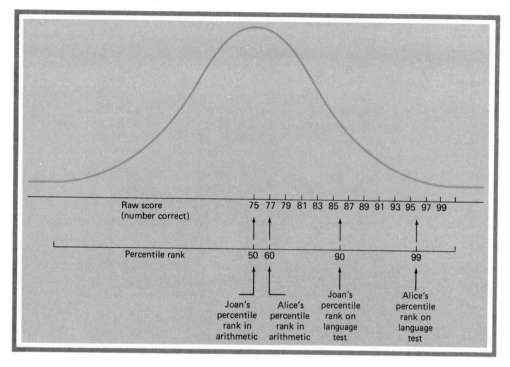

equivalent score. Suppose the raw-score average of the tenth-grade norming sample was 38. Any student who attains a raw score of 38 on that test will be assigned a grade-equivalent score of tenth grade. Grade-equivalent scores are generally listed in numbers, such as 8.3, 4.5, 7.6, 11.5, and so on. The whole number gives the grade and the decimals stand for tenths of a year, but they are usually interpreted as months.

Problems with Grade-Equivalent Scores

Suppose a student with the grade-equivalent score of 10 is a seventh grader. Should this student be promoted immediately? No! Different forms of the test are used at different grade levels, so the seventh grader may not have had to answer items that would be given to tenth graders. The high score may represent superior mastery of material at the seventh-grade level, rather than a capacity for doing advanced work. Even if an average tenth grader did as well as our seventh grader on this particular test, the tenth grader would certainly know much more than this test covered.

Because grade-equivalent scores are misleading and so often misinterpreted, especially by parents, most educators and psychologists strongly believe they should not be used at all. There are several other forms of reporting available that are more appropriate.

Standard Scores.   As you may remember, one problem with percentile ranks is the difficulty in making comparisons among ranks. A discrepancy of a certain number of raw-score points has a different meaning at different places on the scale. With standard scores, on the other hand, a difference of 10 points is the same everywhere on the scale.

standard scores:
scores based on the
standard deviation

z score: standard
score indicating
number of standard
deviations above or
below mean

Standard scores are based on the standard deviation. A very common standard score is called the **z score**. A z score tells how many standard deviations above or below the average a raw score is. In the example described earlier, in which you were fortunate to get a 78 on a test where the mean was 70 and the standard deviation was 4, your z score would be +2, or 2 standard deviations above the mean. If a person were to score 64 on this test, the score would be 1.5 standard deviation units *below* the mean, and the z score would be −1.5. A z score of 0 would be no standard deviations above the mean—in other words, right on the mean.

To calculate the z score for a given raw score, just subtract the mean from the raw score and divide the difference by the standard deviation. The formula is:

$$z = \frac{X - \overline{X}}{SD}$$

T score: standard
score with a mean
of 50 and a
standard deviation
of 10

Since it is often inconvenient to use negative numbers, other standard scores have been devised to eliminate these difficulties. The **T score** has a mean of 50 and uses a standard deviation of 10. If you multiply the z score by 10 (which eliminates the decimal) and add 50 (which gets rid of the negative number), you get the equivalent T score as the answer. The person whose z score was −1.5 would have a T score of 35:

$$-1.5 \times 10 = -15$$
$$-15 + 50 = 35$$

The scoring of the College Entrance Examination Board test is based on a similar procedure. The mean of the scores is set at 500, and a standard deviation of 100 is used.

Before we leave this section on types of scores, we should mention one other widely used method. **Stanine scores** (the name comes from "standard nine") are standard scores. There are only nine possible scores on the stanine scale, the whole numbers 1 through 9. The mean is 5, and the standard deviation is 2. Each unit from 2 to 8 is equal to half a standard deviation. Stanine scores also provide a method of considering a student's rank, because each of the nine scores includes a specific range of percentile scores in the normal distribution. For example, a stanine score of 1 is assigned to the bottom 4 percent of scores in a distribution. A stanine of 2 is assigned to the next 7 percent. Of course, some raw scores in this 7 percent range are better than others, but they all get a stanine score of 2.

stanine scores:
whole-number
scores from 1 to 9,
each representing a
wide range of raw
scores

Each stanine score represents a wide range of raw scores. This has the advantage of encouraging teachers and parents to view a student's score in more general terms instead of making fine distinctions based on a few points. Figure 14–5 compares the four types of standard scores we have considered, showing how each would fall on a normal distribution curve.

Interpreting Test Scores

One of the most common problems with the use of tests is misinterpretation of scores. Often this takes the form of believing that the numbers are precise measurements of a student's ability. No test provides a perfect picture of a person's abilities; a test is only one small sample of behavior. You probably have had the experience of feeling that you really understood a subject only to have the test ask several questions you were not expecting or felt were simply unfair. Was the test an accurate measure of your ability? Two factors are important in developing good tests: reliability and validity. Both must be considered in interpreting test scores.

Reliability. If you took a standardized test on Monday, then took the same test again one week later and received about the same score each time, you would have reason to believe the test was reliable. If 100 people took the test one day and then repeated it again the following week and the ranking of the individual scores was about the same for both tests, you would be even more certain the test was reliable. (Of course, this assumes that no one looks up answers or studies before the second test.) A reliable test gives a consistent and stable "reading" of a person's ability from one occasion to the next, assuming the person's ability remains the same. A reliable thermometer works in a similar manner, giving you a reading of 100°C each time you measure the temperature of boiling water. Measuring a test's **reliability** in this way gives an indication of *test-retest reliability*. If a group of people takes two equivalent versions of a test and the scores on both tests are comparable, this indicates *alternate-form reliability*.

reliability: consistency of test results

Figure 14–5 **Four Types of Standard Scores on a Normal Distribution Curve**

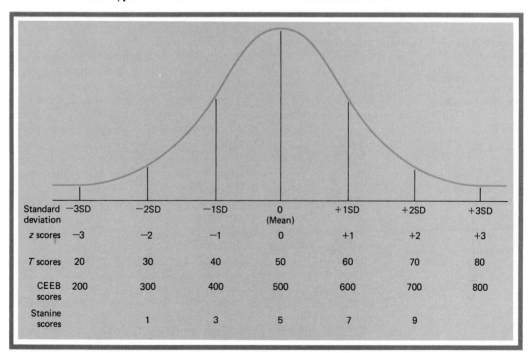

	−3SD	−2SD	−1SD	0 (Mean)	+1SD	+2SD	+3SD
Standard deviation	−3SD	−2SD	−1SD	0 (Mean)	+1SD	+2SD	+3SD
z scores	−3	−2	−1	0	+1	+2	+3
T scores	20	30	40	50	60	70	80
CEEB scores	200	300	400	500	600	700	800
Stanine scores		1	3	5	7	9	

Reliability can also refer to the internal consistency or the precision of a test. This type of reliability, known as *split-half reliability,* is calculated by comparing performance on half of the test questions with performance on the other half. If someone, for example, did quite well on all the odd-numbered items and not at all well on the even-numbered items, we could assume that the items were not very consistent or precise in measuring what they were intended to measure (Cronbach, 1970).

True Score. All tests are imperfect estimators of the qualities or skills they are trying to measure. There is error involved in every testing situation. Sometimes the errors are in your favor, and you may score higher than your ability might warrant. This occurs when you happen to review a key section just before the test or are unusually well rested and alert the day of an unscheduled "pop" quiz. Sometimes the errors go against you. You don't feel well the day of the examination, have just gotten bad news from home, or focused on the wrong material in your review. But if you could be tested over and over again without becoming tired and without memorizing the answers, the average of the test scores would bring you close to a **true score.** In other words, a student's true score can be thought of as the mean of all the scores the student would receive if the test were repeated many times.

true score: hypothetical average of all scores if repeated testing under ideal conditions were possible

But in reality students take a test only once. That means that the score each student receives is made up of the hypothetical true score plus some amount of error. How can error be reduced so that the actual score can be brought closer to a true score? As you might guess, this returns us to the question of reliability. The more reliable the test, the less error in the score actually obtained. On standardized tests, test developers take this into consideration and make estimations of how much the students' scores would probably vary if they were tested repeatedly. This estimation is called the **standard error of measurement.** It represents the standard deviation of the distribution of scores from our hypothetical repeated testings. Thus, a reliable test can also be defined as a test with a small standard error of measurement.

standard error of measurement: hypothetical estimate of variation in scores if testing were repeated

The most effective way to improve reliability is to add more items to the test. Generally speaking, longer tests are more reliable than shorter tests. In their interpretation of tests, teachers must also take the margin for error into consideration.

Confidence Interval. Teachers should never base an opinion of a student's ability or achievement on the exact score the student obtains. Many test companies now report scores using a **confidence interval** or "standard error band" that encloses the student's actual score. This makes use of the standard error of measurement and allows a teacher to consider the range of scores within which a student's true score might be.

confidence interval: range of scores within which a particular score is likely to fall

Let us assume, for example, that two students in your class take a standardized achievement test in Spanish. The standard error of measurement for this test is 5. One student receives a score of 79; the other, a score of 85. At first glance, these scores seem quite different. But when you consider the standard error bands around the scores instead of the scores alone, you see that the bands overlap. The first student's true score might be anywhere between 74 and 84 (that is, the actual score of 79 plus and minus the standard error of 5). The second student's true score might be anywhere between 80 and 90. If these two students took the test again, they might even switch rankings. It is crucial to keep in mind the idea of standard error bands when selecting students for special programs. No child should be rejected simply because his or her obtained score misses the cutoff by one or two points. The student's true score might well be above the cutoff point.

Validity.   If a test is sufficiently reliable, the next question is whether it is *valid*. A test has **validity** if it measures what it is supposed to measure or predicts what it is supposed to predict. To be a valid test of Spanish grammar and vocabulary, the questions must measure just those things and not reading speed or lucky guessing. Tests of mathematics achievement ought to measure what students have learned in mathematics and not level of anxiety about math. A test is judged to be valid in relation to a specific purpose.

validity: degree to which a test measures what it is intended to measure

There are several ways to determine whether or not a test is valid for a specific purpose (Gronlund, 1985). If the purpose of a test is to measure the skills covered in a particular course or unit, the inclusion of questions on all the important topics and on no extraneous topics would provide *content-related evidence* of validity. Have you ever taken a test that dealt only with a few ideas from one lecture or a few pages of the textbook? That test would certainly show no evidence of content-related validity.

Validity of SATs

Some tests are designed to predict outcomes. The SATs, for example, are intended to predict performance in college. If SAT scores correlate with academic performance in college as measured by, say, grade-point average in the first year, then we have *criterion-related evidence* of validity for the SAT. In other words, the test scores are fairly accurate predictors of how well the student would do in college.

Most standardized tests are designed to measure some psychological characteristic or "construct" such as reasoning ability, reading comprehension, achievement motivation, intelligence, creativity, and so on. It is a bit more difficult to gather *construct-related evidence* of validity, yet this is a very important requirement. A test might be a good predictor of an outcome but still be an unsatisfactory measure of the construct under consideration. For example, both family income and intelligence test scores predict school

How do the results of the well-known SAT affect a student's life? That depends on where the scores are sent. Some colleges rely more heavily on the predictive powers of this test than do others. *(Hugh Rogers/ Monkmeyer Press)*

achievement. Assuming that intelligence test scores and school achievement ought to be related, what makes the intelligence test a better measure of intelligence than family income? This has to do with our understanding of the construct of intelligence—our conceptual framework. Construct-related evidence of validity is gathered over many years. It is seen in a pattern of scores. For example, older children can answer more questions on intelligence tests than younger children. This fits with our construct of intelligence. If the average 5-year-old answered as many questions correctly on a test as the average 13-year-old, we would doubt that the test really measured intelligence. Construct-related evidence for validity can also be demonstrated when the results of a test correlate with the results of other well-established and valid measures of the same construct.

Threats to Validity

A number of factors may interfere with the validity of tests given in classroom situations. One problem has already been mentioned—a poorly planned test with little or no relation to the important topics. Standardized tests must also be chosen so that the items on the test actually measure content covered in the classes. This match is absent more often than we might assume. And students must have the necessary skills to take the test. If students score low on a science test not because they lack knowledge about science but because they have difficulty reading the questions, do not understand the directions, or do not have enough time to finish, the test is not a valid measure of science achievement.

A test must be reliable in order to be valid. For example, if an intelligence test yields different results each time it is given to the same child over a few months, then by definition it is not reliable. And it couldn't be a valid measure of intelligence because intelligence is assumed to be fairly stable, at least over a short period of time. However, reliability will not guarantee validity. If that intelligence test gave the same score every time for a particular child but didn't predict school achievement, speed of learning, or other characteristics associated with intelligence, then performance on the test would not be a true indicator of intelligence. The test would be reliable but invalid.

The Guidelines should help you increase the reliability and validity of the standardized tests you give.

TYPES OF STANDARDIZED TESTS

Several kinds of standardized tests are used in schools today. If you have seen cumulative folders, with testing records for individual students over several years, you know how many ways students are tested in schools in this country. There are three broad categories of standardized tests: achievement, diagnostic, and aptitude (including interest). As a teacher, you will probably encounter achievement and aptitude tests most frequently. An excellent source of information on all types of published tests is a series called the *Mental Measurements Yearbooks*. These yearbooks, once edited by Oscar K. Buros and now done by psychologists at the University of Nebraska, contain reviews of every major test, with information on the strengths and weaknesses of each, appropriate age levels, and how to order.

Categories

Guidelines

Increasing Reliability and Validity

Make sure the test actually covers the content of the unit of study.

Examples
1. *Compare test questions to course objectives. A behavior-content matrix might be useful here.*
2. *Use local achievement tests and local norms when possible.*
3. *Check to see if the test is long enough to cover all important topics.*
4. *Are there any difficulties your students experience with the test, such as not enough time, level of reading, and so on? If so, discuss these problems with appropriate school personnel.*

Make sure students know how to use all the test materials.

Examples
1. *Several days before the testing, do a few practice questions with a similar format.*
2. *Demonstrate the use of the answer sheets, especially computer-scored answer sheets.*
3. *Ask all students questions to make sure they understand.*
4. *Check with new students, shy students, slower students, and students who have difficulty reading to make sure they understand the questions.*
5. *Make sure students know if and when guessing is appropriate.*

Follow instructions for administering the test exactly.

Examples
1. *Practice giving the test before you actually use it.*
2. *Follow the time limits exactly.*

Make students as comfortable as possible during testing.

Examples
1. *Do not create anxiety by making the test seem like the most important event of the year.*
2. *Help the class relax before beginning the test, perhaps by telling a joke or having everyone take a few deep breaths. Don't be tense yourself!*
3. *Make sure the room is quiet.*
4. *Discourage cheating by monitoring the room. Don't become absorbed in your own paperwork.*

Remember that no test scores are perfect.

Examples
1. *Interpret scores using bands instead of a single score.*
2. *Ignore small differences between scores.*

Achievement Tests: What Has the Student Learned?

achievement tests: standardized tests measuring how much students have learned in a given content area

The most common standardized tests given to students are **achievement tests.** These are meant to measure how much a student has learned in specific content areas such as reading comprehension, language usage, grammar, spelling, number operations, computation, science, social studies, mathematics, and logical reasoning.

As a teacher, you will undoubtedly give standardized tests. The results will be meaningless unless you administer them properly, following the procedures exactly as given in the instructions. If you are well prepared, organized, and relaxed, it will help your students relax and perform better on the test.

Frequently Used Achievement Tests.   Achievement tests can be designed to be administered to a group or individually. Group tests are generally used for screening, to identify children who might need further testing. Results *Group or Individual* of group tests can also be used as a basis for grouping students according to achievement levels. Individual achievement tests are generally given to determine a child's academic level more precisely or to help diagnose learning problems.

Norm-referenced achievement tests that are commonly given to groups include the California Achievement Test, the Metropolitan Achievement Test, the Stanford Achievement Test, the Comprehensive Test of Basic Skills, the SRA Achievement Series, and the Iowa Test of Basic Skills. Individually administered norm-referenced tests include Part II of the Woodcock-Johnson Psycho-Educational Battery: Tests of Achievement; the Wide-Range Achievement Test; the Peabody Individual Achievement Test; and the Kaufman Assessment Battery for Children. These tests vary in their reliability and validity.

Using Information from a Norm-Referenced Achievement Test.   What kind of specific information do achievement test results offer teachers? Test publishers usually provide individual profiles for each student, showing scores on each subtest. Figure 14–6 is an example of an individual profile

"WHAT WITH THE PRIMARY MENTAL ABILITY TEST AND THE DIFFERENTIAL APTITUDE TEST AND THE READING READINESS TEST AND THE BASIC SKILLS TEST AND THE I.Q. TEST AND THE SEQUENTIAL TEST OF EDUCATIONAL PROGRESS AND THE MENTAL MATURITY TEST, WE HAVEN'T BEEN LEARNING ANYTHING AT SCHOOL."

© 1978 American Scientist Magazine. Sidney Harris.

Figure 14–6   **An Individual Test Record**

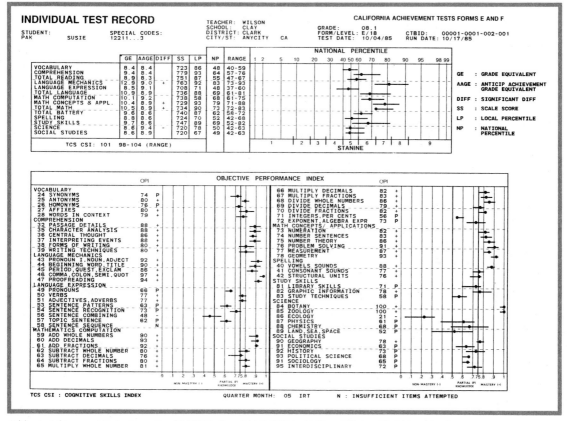

California Achievement Tests, *Forms E and F (1985). Copyright © 1985 by McGraw-Hill, Inc. All rights reserved.*

for an eighth grader, Susie Pak, on the California Achievement Test. Note that the Individual Test Record reports the scores in many different ways. On the top of the form, after the identifying information about Susie's teacher, school, district, grade, and so on, is a list of the various tests— Vocabulary, Comprehension, Total Reading (Vocabulary and Comprehension combined), Language Mechanics, and so on. Beside each test are several different ways of reporting her score on that test:

Different Types of Scores

GE: Susie's grade-equivalent score.

AAGE: Anticipated achievement grade-equivalent score, which is the *average* grade-equivalent score on this test for students around the country who are at Susie's grade level.

DIFF: An indication of whether or not the difference between Susie's actual and anticipated grade-equivalent scores is statistically significant (+ means her actual grade-equivalent score is significantly higher than the average, − means her score is significantly lower than the average).

SS: Susie's standard score.

LP: Susie's local percentile score; this tells us where Susie stands in relation to other students at her grade level in her district.

NP: Susie's national percentile score, telling us where Susie stands in relation to students at her grade level across the country.

RANGE: The range of national percentile scores in which Susie's true score is likely to fall. You may remember from our discussion of *true scores* that this range, or *confidence interval band*, is determined by adding and subtracting the standard error of the test from Susie's actual score. There is a 95 percent chance that Susie's true score is within this range.

Beside the scores is a graph showing Susie's national percentile and stanine scores, with the standard error bands indicated around the scores. Bands that show any overlap are probably not significantly different. But when there is no overlap between bands for two test scores, we can be reasonably certain that Susie's achievement in these areas is actually different.

Analyzing a Profile

Let's look at Susie's scores more carefully. In language mechanics she has a grade-equivalent score of 12.9, which is equal to a standard score of 763. This is at the 92nd percentile for Susie's district and at the 83rd percentile nationally. Her true national percentile score is probably in the range from 73 to 93 (that is, plus and minus 1 standard error of measurement from the actual score of 83). By looking at the graph, we can see that Susie's language mechanics score is equal to a stanine of 7. We can also see that her score bands on vocabulary and comprehension overlap a bit, so her achievement in these areas is probably similar, even though there seems to be a difference when you look at the NP scores alone. When we compare language mechanics and language expression, on the other hand, we see that the bands do not overlap. Susie probably is stronger in mechanics than in expression.

You may also have noticed that the difference between Susie's actual and anticipated grade-equivalent scores in language mechanics is significant. She scored significantly higher than the average student in her grade on this part of the test. But as discussed earlier, it is best not to interpret grade-equivalent scores literally. Susie is much better than the average eighth grader in language mechanics (in fact, she is as good or better than 92 percent of students at her grade level locally), but it's very unlikely that she could handle twelfth-grade English classes.

Conclusions Drawn

The profile in Figure 14–6 tells us a number of things. First, we can see that Susie is apparently strongest in language mechanics and math concepts and applications and weakest in language expression and science. But she is significantly below the average for her grade level only in science. By comparing the two columns under LP (local percentiles) and NP (national percentiles), we can see that the eighth graders in Susie's district are achieving below the national level on every test except math computations. This is evident because Susie's performance places her generally in the 70th to 90th percentile range for her district but only in the 50th to 70th percentile range nationally. For example, Susie's performance in vocabulary is well above average for her district (86th percentile) but only average (48th percentile) for eighth graders nationally.

The scores we have just described are all norm-referenced. But results from standardized tests like the one Susie took can also be interpreted in a criterion-referenced way. The bottom portion of Susie's Individual Test Record in Figure 14–6 breaks down the larger categories of the top section and shows criterion-referenced scores that indicate mastery, partial knowledge, or nonmastery for specific skills like use of synonyms and antonyms, character analysis in reading comprehension, and abilities in geometry and physics. Teachers could use these results to get a relatively good idea of Susie's strengths and weaknesses with these specific skills and thus to determine her progress toward objectives in a given subject.

Diagnostic Tests: What Are the Student's Strengths and Weaknesses?

diagnostic tests: individually administered tests to identify special learning problems

If teachers want to identify more general learning problems, they may need to refer to results from the various diagnostic tests that have been developed. Most **diagnostic tests** are given to students individually by a highly trained professional. The goal is usually to identify the specific problems a student is having. Achievement tests, both standardized and teacher-made, identify weaknesses in academic content areas like mathematics, computation, or reading; individually administered diagnostic tests identify weaknesses in learning processes. There are diagnostic tests to assess the ability to hear differences between sounds, remember spoken words or sentences, recall a sequence of symbols, separate figures from their background, express relationships, coordinate eye and hand movements, describe objects orally, blend sounds together to form words, recognize details in a picture, coordinate movements, and many other abilities needed to receive, process, and express information.

Frequently Used Diagnostic Tests. Some diagnostic tests measure a student's ability in a variety of areas. These tests include the Detroit Test of Learning Aptitude and Part I of the Woodcock-Johnson Psycho-Educational Battery: Tests of Cognitive Ability. Others, however, assess a student's ability in a more specific area. Tests of motor skills include the Bender Gestalt Test and the Purdue Perceptual Motor Survey.

For assessing specific areas of perception, commonly used tests include

This child is taking an individual achievement test, perhaps as part of a battery of tests. The psychologist can use the test results, as well as her observations of how the child approaches each task, to diagnose learning strengths and problems. *(Jim Cartier/Photo Researchers)*

the Wepman Auditory Discrimination Test, the Goldman-Fristoe-Woodcock Test of Auditory Discrimination, the Frostig Developmental Test of Visual Perception, and the Motor-Free Visual Perception Test.

Elementary school teachers are more likely than secondary teachers to receive information from diagnostic tests. There are few such tests for older students. If you become a high school teacher, your students are more likely to be given aptitude tests.

Aptitude Tests: How Well Will the Student Do in the Future?

aptitude tests:
tests for predicting future performance

Both achievement and aptitude tests measure developed abilities. Achievement tests may measure abilities developed over a short period of time, such as during a week-long unit on map reading, or over a longer period of time, such as a semester. **Aptitude tests** are meant to measure abilities developed over many years and to predict how well a student will do in learning unfamiliar material in the future. The greatest difference between the two types of tests is that they are used for different purposes—achievement tests to measure final performance (and perhaps give grades), and aptitude tests to predict how well people will do in particular programs like college or professional school (Anastasi, 1981).

Scholastic Aptitude.   The purpose of a scholastic aptitude test, like the SAT or ACT, is to predict how well you would do in college. Colleges use such scores to help decide on acceptances and rejections. The SAT may have seemed like an achievement test to you, measuring what you had already learned in high school. Although the test is designed to avoid drawing too heavily on specific high school curricula, the questions are very similar to achievement test questions.

SATs as Predictors

Standardized aptitude tests such as the SAT (and the SCAT for younger students) seem to be fairly reliable in predicting future achievement. Since standardized tests are less open to teacher bias, they may be even fairer predictors of future achievement than high school grades are. Indeed, some psychologists believe grade inflation in high schools has made tests like the SAT even more important.

IQ and Scholastic Aptitude.   In Chapter 4 we discussed one of the most influential aptitude tests of all, the IQ test. The IQ test as we know it could well be called a test of scholastic aptitude. Figure 14–7 shows how IQ scores are distributed based on the results of the major individual tests. Now that you understand the concept of standard deviation, you will be able to appreciate several statistical characteristics of the tests.

For example, the IQ score is really a standard score with a mean of 100 and a standard deviation of 15 (for the Wechsler Scales, the Cognitive Abilities section of the Woodcock-Johnson Psycho-Educational Battery, and the Global Scale of the Kaufman Assessment Battery for Children) or 16 (for the Stanford-Binet and the McCarthy Scales for Children). Thus, about 68 percent of the general population would score between +1 and −1 standard deviations from the mean, or between about 85 and 115. Only about 2.5 percent of the general population would have a score higher than 2 standard deviations above the mean—that is, above 130 on the Wechsler Scales.

Figure 14–7   **The Distribution of IQ Scores**

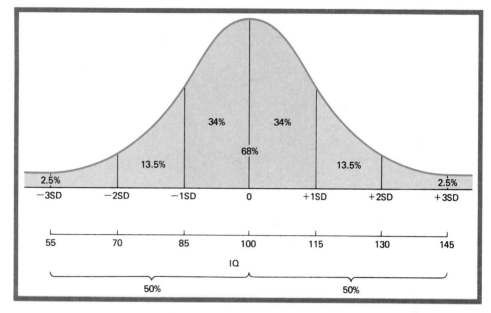

A difference of a few points between two students' IQ scores should not be viewed as important. Scores between 90 and 109 are within the average range. In fact, scores between 80 and 119 are considered to range from low average to high average. To see the problems that may arise, consider the following conversation:

A Few Points May Not Matter

PARENT: We came to speak with you today because we are shocked at our son's IQ score. We can't believe he has only a 99 IQ when his sister scored much higher on the same test. We know they are about the same. In fact, Sammy has better marks than Lauren did in the fifth grade.

TEACHER: What was Lauren's score?

PARENT: Well, she did much better. She scored a 103!

Clearly, brother and sister have both scored within the average range. The standard error of measurement on the WISC-R varies slightly from one age to the next, but the average standard error is 3.19. So the bands around Sammy's and Lauren's IQ scores—about 96 to 102 and 100 to 106—are overlapping. Either child could have scored 100, 101, or 102. The scores are so close that, on a second testing, Sammy might score slightly higher than Lauren.

Vocational Aptitude and Interest.   In schools, the guidance counselor is generally the person most concerned with students' career decisions. It is the responsibility of people in the guidance office to know what aptitude test scores really mean and how to help each student make an appropriate decision. Two kinds of tests, vocational aptitude and vocational interest, may provide useful information for educational planning. But as with any tests, interpretation must be cautious.

If you teach in a junior high or high school, your school may administer vocational aptitude tests to the students. One test designed to measure aptitudes relevant to career decisions is the Differential Aptitude Test (DAT). Students in grades 8 through 12 may take the test. Questions cover seven areas: (1) verbal reasoning; (2) numerical ability; (3) abstract reasoning; (4) clerical speed and accuracy; (5) mechanical reasoning; (6) space relations; and (7) spelling and language.

The test results on the DAT are converted into percentiles, and a percentile band is reported for each subtest. After the tests have been scored, the guidance counselors in a school should be able to help students relate their DAT profile scores to career-planning decisions. In general, people in different occupational groups do tend to have different patterns of scores on the DAT, which gives the test some validity.

vocational interest tests: tests indicating possible areas of career interest

In many high schools, **vocational interest tests** are also given. Three examples are the Kuder Preference Record, the Strong-Campbell Interest Blank, and Part III of the Woodcock-Johnson Psycho-Educational Battery: Tests of Interest Level. In these tests students may be asked to indicate which of several activities (such as collecting books, collecting shells, or collecting postcards) they would like most and which they would like least. The pattern of the students' answers is then compared to the answer patterns of adults working in different occupations. It must be remembered, however, that the results on such a test indicate interests, *not* aptitude or talent.

Occupational interest tests cannot tell you exactly what students will be or should be when they grow up. Results of such tests should be interpreted in the light of all the other information available about a student, as well as with some healthy skepticism. As a teacher, information you gain about a student's interests from test results can be used most appropriately to help motivate the student. No career option should be permanently closed to an adolescent on the basis of an occupational interest test.

CURRENT ISSUES IN STANDARDIZED TESTING

As mentioned at the beginning of this chapter, before the early twentieth century standardized tests were practically nonexistent. Two factors changed the picture. In 1916 Lewis Terman revised the procedure developed by Binet in France and gave us the Stanford-Binet Intelligence Scale. But the greatest change came when the United States entered World War I in 1917. The army needed a method for evaluating recruits. To solve this problem, psychologists created the Army Alpha and Beta group intelligence tests. By 1919 these had been given to 1.7 million people and had provided valuable information for placing recruits in appropriate training programs.

An Ongoing Controversy

This success encouraged great interest. Psychologists began to expand testing to civilian populations in high schools, colleges, and industry. Controversy and concern about the widespread use of tests began at that point and has continued ever since (Haney, 1981). In this section we will consider two basic questions: What role should testing play in making decisions about people? Do some students have an unfair advantage in taking tests?

The Role of Testing

Thus far, our discussion of standardized testing has focused on the characteristics of the instruments themselves. But tests are not simply procedures used in research. Many decisions about individuals are made every day based on the results of tests. Should Trevor move on to the next math unit, or does he need more drill on long division? Should Kay be issued a driver's license? How many and which students from the eighth grade would benefit from an accelerated program in science? Who belongs in a special class for the mentally retarded? Who will be admitted to college or professional school? In answering these questions, it is important to distinguish between the quality of the test itself and how the test is used. Even the best instruments can be and have been misused. For example, in earlier years a large number of minority students were inappropriately classified as mentally retarded on the basis of generally valid and reliable individual intelligence scales.

Behind all the statistics and terminology are issues related to values and ethics. Who will be tested? What are the consequences of choosing one test over another for a particular purpose with a given group? What is the effect on students of being tested? How will the test scores of minority students be interpreted? What do we really mean by intelligence, competence, and scholastic aptitude, and do our views agree with those implied by the tests we use to measure these constructs (Messick, 1981)? How will test results be integrated with other information about the individual to make judgments? Answering these questions requires choices based on values, as well as accurate information about what tests can and cannot tell us.

Minimum Competency Tests. I have mentioned in previous chapters that many Americans believe schools should do a better job of teaching the basics. The 1984 Gallup Poll found that 65 percent of the respondents favored a standard, nationwide examination for a high school diploma. This is a surprisingly large number, considering the distrust of tests and dislike for government intervention shared by a large portion of the population (Lerner, 1981). Is the level of competence in reading, writing, and arithmetic too low among today's high school graduates, and will competency testing help?

In answer to the first question, *A Nation at Risk* (National Commission on Excellence in Education, 1983) reported that about 23 million American adults were functionally illiterate. About 13 percent of the teenagers in the United States (and up to 40 percent of minority youth) were also functionally illiterate. And in many studies comparing U.S. students with students from other industrialized nations, the American students have placed last in academic achievement.

Will requiring minimum competency tests for promotion and finally for graduation improve the situation? As usual, experts disagree. Lerner believes the close monitoring and clear standards required by minimum competency testing would encourage teachers and students to spend more time teaching and learning the basics. Since academic engaged time is one of the few factors that seems clearly associated with learning, this increased attention should improve achievement. Besides, "no other approach is demonstrably superior to it" (Lerner, 1981, p. 1062).

Decisions Based on Test Results

Values and Ethics

The Problem of Illiteracy

But many psychologists and teachers believe such tests would be undesirable. Their argument is teachers would have less and less freedom in deciding what and how to teach. The tests would control the curriculum. In working to get everyone to the minimum level, teachers would have to ignore the faster students. A few slower students might monopolize the teacher's attention. New ways of organizing classes would be necessary to prevent holding everyone back. Finally, tests might discriminate against minority students.

Minimum
Competency: Legal
Issues

This last factor had a great impact when Florida instituted a functional literacy test for high school graduation. Although the citizens of the state were in favor of the testing, a federal judge ordered the process stopped on the grounds that the tests perpetuated the effects of past discrimination against minority students. Evidence presented during the trial *Debra P.* v. *Turlington* indicated that 20 percent of black seniors and only 2 percent of white seniors were denied diplomas on the basis of the tests. Many of these black students had spent some of their early school careers in segregated schools. The judge felt that denying them diplomas punished these students for having gone to inferior schools and thus violated their right to equal protection under the law (Haney, 1981).

Truth in Testing.   Recently, many critics of standardized tests have joined together to call for "consumer action" in testing, and the truth-in-testing movement was born. Supporting this movement are various organizations around the country that have lobbied for the admissions testing process to be more open to public scrutiny. These groups want the public to have complete information about the reliability, validity, costs, and development procedures related to nationwide tests. In addition, they want an individual test-taker to be able to receive the correct answers to questions after completing any test.

On January 1, 1980, a truth-in-testing law went into effect in New York State, covering all major college and professional school admissions tests. Other states are considering legislation similar to New York's. Since litigation and legislation in this area are constantly changing, it is impossible to give an up-to-the-minute picture, but the trend is toward greater openness in testing.

Effects of Truth in
Testing

An advantage of making testing more open is that the sort of mistakes in scoring that have occurred can be caught. The public may become more sophisticated about testing in general, and publishers may have to be more careful to ensure reliability and validity in their tests. Better assessment procedures, particularly for minority students, may be a consequence (Bersoff, 1981). The disadvantage is that new tests will have to be created continually, adding greatly to the cost of testing for individual students. In addition, it is difficult for researchers to accumulate information and compare results across studies when the tests keep changing.

Advantages in Taking Tests: Fair and Unfair

In this section we will consider three basic issues: Are standardized tests biased against minority students? Can people gain an advantage on admissions tests through coaching? Can they be taught test-taking skills?

As you saw in Chapter 4, the average performance of students from lower SES and from minority groups is below that of middle-class students on most standardized measures of mental abilities, although the discrepancies are decreasing for some minority groups (Burton & Jones, 1982). Are tests such as the individual measures of intelligence or college admissions tests biased against minorities? This is a complex question.

IQ: Middle-Class Abilities?

A standard IQ test can be seen as a sample of the student's current abilities to function in a middle-class school culture, a culture that emphasizes verbal skills. In this sense, some students do have less ability than others because they lack familiarity and training in these culturally influenced skills.

Some people argue that the society, not the intelligence test, is unfair, since many students are denied advantages available to others. As Sattler (1974, p. 34) states: "In a sense, *no test can be culture-fair in a culture that is not fair.*" IQ tests measure quite well some of the abilities needed to make it in school. A student who does poorly on an IQ test probably will have more trouble succeeding in school than a student who scores high on the same test. In fact, IQ tests are the most reliable single predictors of school achievement (Sattler, 1982). But this should not be surprising. Remember, Binet and Simon threw out all the test questions that did not predict school achievement when they developed the first IQ test.

Research on test bias shows that most standardized tests predict school *achievement* equally well for all groups of students. Items that might appear on the surface to be biased against minorities are not necessarily harder for minorities to answer correctly (Jensen, 1980). But even though standardized aptitude and achievement tests are not biased against minorities in predicting school performance, many people believe there are factors related to the specific content and procedures of such tests that put minority students at a disadvantage. Here are a few factors they suggest:

Potential Difficulties for Minorities

1. The language of the test and the tester are often different from those of the students.
2. The questions asked tend to center on experiences and facts more familiar to the dominant culture.
3. Answers that support middle-class values often are rewarded with more points.
4. Being very verbal and talking a lot is rewarded as well. Of course, this is easier if a student feels comfortable in the situation.
5. Minority children may not be oriented toward achievement and may not appreciate the value of doing well on tests.

culture-fair/culture-free tests: tests without cultural bias

Concern about cultural bias in testing has led some psychologists to try to develop **culture-fair** or **culture-free tests.** These efforts have not been very successful. On many of the so-called culture-fair tests, the performance of students from deprived socioeconomic backgrounds and minority groups has been the same or worse than their performance on the standard Wechsler and Binet scales (Costello & Dickie, 1970; Jensen, 1974; Sattler, 1982).

Testing on Trial. The question of bias in IQ testing found its way into the courts. In the early 1970s, the issue in *Diana* v. *State Board of Education* was the overrepresentation of Mexican-American children in California's public school classes for the mildly mentally retarded. The plaintiff charged that the percentage of Mexican-American children in these classes was higher than the percentage in the school population because IQ tests, given in English, were biased against these children. The court ordered the schools to correct the disproportions and to administer placement tests in a student's native language. The native language requirement for testing later became a part of federal law, PL 94–142, the Education for All Handicapped Children Act.

Court Ruling

In 1971, also in California, *Larry P.* v. *Riles.* was initiated on behalf of minority children placed in classes for the mildly retarded. The issue again was overrepresentation of certain groups of students in these classes and bias in the IQ tests. In 1979, the court ruled that no intelligence tests could be used to place minority students in special classes for the retarded unless the tests met these standards (Bersoff, 1981):

1. The scores from the tests had to predict academic achievement and classroom performance fairly well.
2. All groups of students (blacks, Mexican-Americans, whites) had to have the same pattern of scores on the tests *and the same mean scores.*

The second requirement meant that standard individual IQ tests could not be a part of the evaluation and placement process for minority students.

In making the decision, the judge assumed that any test yielding different mean scores for different groups of students was automatically biased. This rejects the possibility that some groups of students, for whatever reason, might be less able in the particular school-related skills measured by the tests. In 1984, the Ninth Circuit Court of Appeals upheld the 1979 ruling. As of this writing, no further appeals were pending, but the case could still go to the Supreme Court (Presse & Reschly, 1986).

In the years since the schools in California stopped including IQ tests with the placement procedures, the actual number of students enrolled in classes for the mildly retarded has decreased substantially, but the percentage of minority students remains almost the same, around 50 percent. The IQ testing was only one of many elements in the decision to place a student in a special class. First, the child had to fail in the regular class. Then other test results and teacher recommendations were examined. Simply eliminating IQ testing cannot be expected to help the children who are failing in school. The real question is how to give these students an appropriate education.

What We've Learned

In summarizing her review of test bias, Nancy Cole (1981) has said: "First, we have learned there is not large-scale, consistent bias against minority groups in the technical validity sense in the major, widely used and widely studied tests. Second, we have learned that the lack of such bias means neither that the use made of the tests is necessarily socially good nor that improvements in the test cannot be made" (p. 1075).

Coaching and Test-Taking Skills. Courses to prepare students for college entrance exams are becoming more popular. In a survey of seven northeastern states, Alderman and Powers (1980) found that almost one-third of the high schools offered special programs for students taking the SAT. As you

© 1986 Joel Pett in the Kappan.

Effects of Coaching

probably know from experience, commercial courses are available as well. It is hard to evaluate the effects of these courses. In general, research has indicated that short high school training programs yield average gains of 10 points in SAT verbal scores and 15 points in SAT math scores, whereas longer commercial programs show gains of about 20 verbal and 30 math points. A gain of 20 to 30 points would mean that you got about three additional items correct (Messick, 1980; Messick & Jungeblut, 1981). Kulik, Kulik, and Bangert (1984) analyzed the results of 40 different studies on aptitude and achievement test training and found that there were more substantial gains when students practiced on a parallel form of a test for brief periods. The design of the coaching program may be the critical factor.

Practice Helps

Two other types of training can make a difference in test scores. One is simple familiarity with the procedures of standardized tests. Students who have a lot of experience with standardized tests do better than those who do not. Some of this advantage may be due to greater self-confidence, less tendency to panic, familiarity with different types of questions (for example, analogies like house : garage :: _____ : car), and practice with the various answer sheets (Anastasi, 1981). Even brief orientations about how to take tests can help students who lack familiarity and confidence.

Metacognitive Training

A second type of training that appears to be very promising is instruction in general cognitive skills such as problem solving, careful analysis of questions, consideration of *all* the alternatives, noticing details and deciding which are relevant for the solution, avoiding impulsive answers, and checking work. These are the kinds of metacognitive and study skills we have discussed before. This type of training is likely to generalize to many tasks (Anastasi, 1981). The Guidelines on the following pages give some ideas about how to be a more effective test-taker.

New Directions in Testing. In response to dissatisfaction with traditional forms of assessment, new approaches have emerged to deal with some of the most common testing problems. But each of these approaches has its own problems.

Guidelines

Taking a Test

Use the night before the test effectively.

Examples
1. *Study the night before the exam, ending with a final look at a summary of the key points, concepts, and relationships.*
2. *Get a good night's sleep. If you know you generally have trouble sleeping the night before an exam, try getting extra sleep on several previous nights.*

Set the situation so you can concentrate on the test.

Examples
1. *Give yourself plenty of time to eat and get to the exam room.*
2. *Don't sit near a friend. It may make concentration difficult. If your friend leaves early, you may be tempted to do so too so you can compare notes.*

Make sure you know what the test is asking.

Examples
1. *Read the directions carefully. If you are unsure, ask the instructor or proctor for clarification.*
2. *Read each question carefully to spot any tricky words, such as not, except, all of the following but one.*
3. *On an essay test, read every question first, so you know the size of the job ahead of you and can make informed decisions about how much time to spend on each question.*
4. *On a multiple-choice test, read every alternative, even if you find an early one that seems right.*

Use time effectively.

Examples
1. *Begin working right away and move as rapidly as possible while your energy is high.*
2. *Do the easy questions first.*
3. *Don't get stuck on one question. If you are stumped, mark the question so you can return to it easily later, and go on to questions you can answer more quickly.*
4. *If you are unsure about a question, answer it but mark it so you can go back if there is time to reconsider it more carefully.*
5. *On a multiple-choice test, if you know you will not have time to finish, give yourself a few minutes to fill in all the remaining questions with the same letter if there is no penalty for guessing.*
6. *If you are running out of time on an essay test, do not leave any questions blank. Briefly outline a few key points to show the instructor you "knew the answer and just needed more time."*

One criticism that has been voiced against traditional forms of intelligence testing has been that such tests are merely samples of performance at one particular point in time. These tests, critics say, fail to capture the child's potential for future learning. Reuven Feuerstein's Learning Potential Assessment Device attempts to look at the *process* of learning rather than its product (Feuerstein, 1979). The child is presented with various reasoning and memory tasks. When necessary, the examiner teaches the child how to solve the problems and then assesses how well the child has benefited from in-

Know when to guess on multiple-choice or true-false tests.

Examples
1. *Always guess when only right answers are scored.*
2. *Always guess when you can eliminate some of the alternatives.*
3. *Don't guess if there is a penalty for guessing, unless you can confidently eliminate at least one alternative.*

Notice patterns in the right response on multiple-choice and true-false tests.

Examples
1. *Are correct answers always longer? shorter? in the middle? more likely one letter, or more often true than false?*
2. *Does the grammar give the right answer away or eliminate any alternatives?*

Check your work.

Examples
1. *Even if you can't stand to look at the test another minute, reread each question to make sure you answered the way you intended.*
2. *If you are using a machine-scored answer sheet, check occasionally to be sure the number of the question you are answering corresponds to the number of the answer on the sheet.*

On essay tests, answer as directly as possible.

Examples
1. *Avoid flowery introductions. Answer the question in the first sentence and then elaborate.*
2. *Don't save your best ideas till last. Give them early in the answer.*
3. *Unless the instructor requires complete sentences, consider listing points, arguments, and so on by number in your answer. It will help you organize your thoughts and concentrate on the important aspects of the answer.*

Learn from the testing experience.

Examples
1. *Pay attention when the teacher reviews the answers to the test. You can learn from your mistakes, and the same question may reappear in a later test.*
2. *Notice if you are having trouble with a particular kind of item; try to adjust your study approach next time to handle this type of item better.*

Adapted from W. Pauk (1974), How to study in college (2nd ed.). Boston: Houghton Mifflin, pp. 176–185; and R. E. Sarnacki (1979), An examination of test-wiseness in the cognitive test domain. Review of Research in Education, 49, pp. 252–279.

struction. This approach reflects Vygotsky's ideas about the zone of proximal development. Results of the test have been difficult to interpret. Nevertheless, it offers a thought-provoking and radically different approach to intelligence testing.

Another criticism leveled at intelligence and achievement tests is that they yield little information that is really relevant or helpful to teachers. If a seventh-grade student is found to have an IQ of 112 on a Wechsler intelligence test and a grade equivalent of 6.7 in reading comprehension on the Stanford

**curriculum-based
assessment:** system
for testing based on
mastery of
curriculum
objectives

Achievement Test, what does this tell the classroom teacher about what and how to teach? Proponents of **curriculum-based assessment** argue that testing should be based on the curriculum the child is expected to learn (Deno, 1985). Test items must refer to a specific set of curriculum objectives; a student's performance indicates which objectives the student has not yet mastered, and instruction can then be directed to precisely those objectives. This approach, which has become quite popular in special education, is thought to maximize instructional time by giving teachers clear directions. One problem with using curriculum-based assessment, however, is that mastery levels for each objective must be defined by each teacher. There are also practical concerns: a teacher must juggle the individual instructional needs of all students in the classroom.

With a move to curriculum-based assessment, local schools and teachers become responsible for constructing tests. This brings us to classroom testing and grading—the topic of the next chapter.

SUMMARY

1. Evaluation of students can be based on measurements from either norm-referenced tests, in which a student's performance is compared to the average performance of others, or criterion-referenced tests, in which scores are compared to a preestablished standard.

2. Standardized tests are most often norm-referenced and have been tried out, revised, and in final form administered to a norming sample, which becomes the comparison group for scoring.

3. Important aspects of measurement in standardized testing are the frequency distribution, the central tendency, and the standard deviation. The mean (arithmetical average), median (middle score), and mode (most common score) are all measures of central tendency. The standard deviation reveals how scores spread out around the mean.

4. A normal distribution is a frequency distribution represented as a bell-shaped curve. Many scores cluster in the middle; the farther from the midpoint, the fewer the scores. Half the scores are above the mean; half are below.

5. There are several basic types of standardized test scores: percentile rankings, indicating the percentage of others who scored at or below an individual's score; grade-equivalent scores, which indicate how closely a student's performance matches average scores for a given grade; and standard scores, which are based on the standard deviation. T and z scores are both common standard scores. A stanine score is a standard score that incorporates elements of percentile rankings.

6. Care must be taken in interpreting test results. Each test is only a sample of a student's performance on a given day. The score is only an estimate of a student's hypothetical true score.

7. Some tests are more reliable than others—that is, they yield more stable and consistent estimates. The standard error of measurement takes the possibility for error into account and is one index of test reliability.

8. Some tests are more valid than others, in the sense that they measure what they are supposed to measure and the meaning of the scores is clear. Evidence of validity can be content-related, criterion-related, or construct-related. Reliability does not guarantee validity.

9. Three kinds of standardized tests are used frequently in schools: achievement, diagnostic, and aptitude. Profiles from norm-referenced achievement tests can also be used in a criterion-referenced way to help a teacher assess a student's strengths and weaknesses in a particular subject.

10. Controversy over standardized testing has focused on the role and interpretation of tests, the fairness and usefulness of minimum competency testing, the availability of information about tests to the public (truth in testing), and the degree of bias against minorities.

11. It is *how* test results are used that is the major issue for teachers. Teachers should use results to improve instruction, not to stereotype students or justify lowered expectations.

12. Performance on standardized tests can be improved if students are given experience with this type of testing and training in study skills and problem solving.

KEY TERMS

evaluation	mode	reliability
measurement	bimodal distribution	true score
norm-referenced testing	standard deviation	standard error of measurement
criterion-referenced testing	variability	confidence interval
standardized tests	normal distribution	validity
norming sample	percentile rank	achievement tests
frequency distribution	grade-equivalent score	diagnostic tests
histogram	standard scores	aptitude tests
mean	z score	vocational interest tests
central tendency	T score	culture-fair/culture-free tests
median	stanine scores	curriculum-based assessment

SUGGESTIONS FOR FURTHER READING AND STUDY

American Psychologist. (1981, October). In this special issue on testing, there are many short articles on test bias, coaching, the uses of tests, admissions, and minimum competency. There is also a "primer" on testing concepts.

Exceptional Children. (1985, November). A special issue on curriculum-based assessment.

LAMBERT, N. M. (1981). Psychological evidence in *Larry P.* v. *Wilson* files: An evaluation by a witness for the defense. *American Psychologist, 36,* 937–952. Reading this article, you will see how tests have come under attack in the courts and what some of the counterarguments are.

LYMAN, H. B. (1986). *Test scores and what they mean* (4th ed.). Englewood Cliffs, NJ: Prentice-Hall. A very readable text.

MILLMAN, J., & PAUK, W. (1969). *How to take tests.* New York: McGraw-Hill, 1969. This book has helped many improve their test-taking skills.

The search for solutions to the testing problem. *Educational Leadership.* (1985, October). There are 16 articles in this special section on testing, from general considerations of the role of testing in a democratic society to specific considerations like computerized testing.

SHAVER, J. P. (1985). Chance and nonsense: A conversation about interpreting tests of statistical significance. *Phi Delta Kappan,* Part 1, September, pp. 57–60; Part 2, October, pp. 138–141. In this two-part series, a special education teacher has an enlightening conversation in the teachers' lounge with a very knowledgeable colleague who can explain statistics clearly and sensibly.

What is the proper role of testing? *Phi Delta Kappan.* (1985, May). Articles in this special section cover the decline in SAT scores, reform movements in testing, how to test writing skills, and several other current issues.

WILEY, D. E. (1982). The vicious and the virtuous: ETS and college admissions. *Contemporary Education Review, 1,* 85–101. A very thoughtful consideration of admissions tests, their content, strengths, weaknesses, and the role they play in educational decisions.

Teachers' Forum

Achievement Tests

Achievement tests have become a way of life in schools. But the tests are an expense to the schools and a source of anxiety to the students (and teachers). What are the advantages and disadvantages of these tests? How can the results be used?

A Balanced View　The advantages: Achievement tests (1) provide a basis of comparison for evaluating strengths and correcting weaknesses of students, classes, schools, and districts. (2) They provide support for teacher judgment. (3) They serve as tools for evaluating the worth of texts, instructional materials, and curriculum.

The disadvantages: (1) Tests do not always test what is taught. (2) Some administrators use tests to evaluate teachers and principals, pitting school against school and teacher against teacher. (3) Some teachers are pressured into teaching the tests, thereby invalidating the results. (4) Some students are not "test takers" and some are "superguessers," making results unreliable. (5) Test results are too often just filed and forgotten. . . . I use these test results to measure each individual's growth and plan for any significant deviation from the norm.

Joan H. Lowe, Fifth-Grade Teacher
Russell Elementary School, Hazelwood, Missouri

ESL Students and Test Results

Your district is giving standardized achievement tests. Two of your students have recently moved to the United States and are still having some problems with reading quickly, even though they have passed ESL (English as a Second Language) tests. You notice that they have not completed nearly as much of the achievement test as your other students, although you know that they are both bright children. They will not get high scores on the test because they simply cannot get much of the test completed. What would you do?

Making　I would give each student an *additional* answer sheet on which I would direct them
Adjustments　to continue the test beyond the time limit. For example, had they completed 28 questions, I would tell them to begin on line 29 of the *second* answer sheet. The students would be given a *specific* amount of time, but under no condition would the additional time exceed the original allotted time. The teacher should copy the answers from the first answer sheet to the second. Both sheets should be submitted and corrected, and the ESL students will each have two scores.

Louise Harrold Melucci, Fourth-Grade Teacher
Greenwood School, Warwick, Rhode Island

Analyze the　Since the students are not discouraged enough to give up working on the test, they
Available　should be encouraged to finish what is possible. Achievement tests are used to mea-
Information　sure general ability rather than just reading skills. Children should not be penalized for being slow readers. The results of most standardized tests have item analyses that the teacher can and should study for correct and incorrect answers. By analyzing the questions answered, the teacher can see the children's strengths and weaknesses. Though the composite scores may be lowered, there will still be enough information to be useful.

Ida Pofahl, Second-Grade Teacher
Denison Elementary School, Denison, Iowa

Coaching?

You have just been told that all teachers in your school must give standardized achievement tests to their students. The administration has said that the test results will be used to measure only the students, not the teachers. Nevertheless, a general hope has been expressed that the students will do well on the tests. Should you coach your students in any way in preparation for the tests? Note that the tests are generally designed based on the assumption that students receive no special training for the specific material the tests cover.

No to Coaching

In view of everything that has come to light recently we, as teachers, know that some blame and doubt have been directed toward our performance in the classroom. We also realize that many feel results of standardized tests can be attributed directly to the teacher. I would take *no* steps in preparing my students for a test of this nature. I should hope that the tests would indicate how well students have achieved in certain areas, not how well a teacher has prepared them to take such tests. Preparation for achievement tests would, by its very nature, be counterproductive.

James C. Fulgham, High School Latin and English Teacher
Brainerd High School, Chattanooga, Tennessee

Reducing Anxiety

I firmly believe that the greatest help I can give to my students in this situation is to instruct them in general test-taking techniques and to reduce the anxiety that invariably accompanies any standardized testing program. I would reassure them that these types of tests provide very useful information for future course selection and career choices but are not something to worry about or study for. I think that anxiety can be reduced by covering examples of the types of questions they will encounter, discussing when it is in their best interest to "guess," and demonstrating the way to pace themselves to get through the material.

Linda Stahl, High School Psychology Teacher
Ponca City Senior High School, Ponca City, Oklahoma

Be a Good Coach!

Coaching is an excellent analogy—the coach prepares and psyches up the players, telling them how to perform and what to expect, but the players go on the field and *they* execute what they've learned. Teachers need to coach in order to maximize the results of the *accurate* assessment of student performance. To prepare for the achievement test, the teacher should tell the students the number, topics, and duration of the subtests, then explain that there are questions they will be unable to answer because of the nature of achievement tests. The teacher should give practice in filling in circles or boxes in booklets or on answer sheets similar to the test (most publishers provide these) and advise students whether it would be beneficial to guess at an answer they don't know (this information is in the testing manual).

The teacher can also change the room to the testing arrangement four or five days ahead of time so students, especially those in open classrooms, will be accustomed to it. Next, the teacher should send home a letter suggesting that parents enforce a recommended bedtime during the days of testing. Yes, coach the students. You can't play the game for them, but you can do everything possible to ensure their *best* performance.

Richard D. Courtright, Gifted and Talented Elementary Teacher
Ephesus Road Elementary School, Chapel Hill, North Carolina

15

Classroom
Evaluation
and Grading

Overview
Classroom Evaluation and Testing   524
Two Uses of Tests
Objective Testing   526
Essay Testing   527
Planning a Measurement Program   531
Planning Evaluation   531
Cautions: Being Fair   533
Effects of Grades and Grading on Students   535
The Effect of High Grades   535
The Effect of Low Grades   535
Effects of Feedback   537
Working for a Grade versus Working to Learn   539
Grading and Reporting: Nuts and Bolts   542
Criterion-Referenced versus Norm-Referenced Grading   542
Preparing Report Cards   544
The Point System   546
Percentage Grading   546
The Contract System   548
The Mastery Approach   549
Grading on Effort and Improvement   550
Beyond Grading: Communication   551
Summary/Key Terms
Suggestions for Further Reading and Study
Teachers' Forum

When they think about elementary or secondary school, many people vividly remember being tested and graded. In this chapter, we will look at both tests and grades, focusing not only on the effects these are likely to have on students but also on practical means for developing more efficient methods of testing and grading.

We begin with a consideration of the many types of tests teachers prepare each year. Then we turn to grades, looking first at ways teachers can overcome any biases they may bring to the grading process and then at the effects grades are likely to have on students. Because there are so many grading systems, we also spend some time examining the advantages and disadvantages of one system over another. Finally, we turn to the very important topic of communication with students and parents. How will you justify the grades you give?

By the time you have finished this chapter, you should be able to do the following:

- Create multiple-choice and essay test items for your subject area.
- Identify possible sources of bias in your own grading policies.
- Make a plan for testing students on a unit of work.
- Discuss the potential positive and negative effects of grades on students.
- Give examples of criterion-referenced and norm-referenced grading systems.
- Assign grades to a hypothetical group of students and defend your decisions in a class debate.
- Role-play a conference with parents who do not understand your grading system or their child's grades.

CLASSROOM EVALUATION AND TESTING

As a teacher, you may or may not be involved in the decision about which grading system will be adopted for your school or your class. Many school districts have a standard approach to grading. Still, you will have some choice about how you will use your district's grading system. Will you give tests? How many? What kinds? Will students do projects? How will homework influence grades? Will you grade on students' current academic performance or on their degree of improvement?

We discussed standardized tests in the previous chapter. But many tests given in classrooms are not provided by outside sources; they are created by the teacher.

Two Uses of Tests

Planning instruction necessarily entails determining how to measure achievement. To be sure students have learned anything, you must observe or test

formative measurement: ungraded testing used before or during instruction to aid in planning and diagnosis

pretest: formative test for assessing students' knowledge, readiness, and abilities

diagnostic test: formative test to determine students' areas of weakness

summative measurement: testing that follows instruction and assesses achievement

their performance in some way. Bloom, Hastings, and Madaus (1971) divide measurement of achievement into two categories: formative and summative.

Formative measurement occurs before or during instruction. It has two basic purposes: to guide the teacher in planning and to help students identify areas that need work. In other words, it helps *form* educational plans. Often students are given a formative type of test prior to instruction, a **pretest.** This helps teachers determine what students already know. Sometimes a test is also given to see what areas of weakness remain when instruction has been partially completed. This is generally called a **diagnostic test** but should not be confused with the standardized diagnostic tests of more general learning abilities. A classroom diagnostic test identifies a student's areas of achievement and weakness. Pretests and diagnostic tests are not graded.

Summative measurement occurs at the end of a sequence of instruction. Its purpose is to let the teacher and the students know the level of accomplishment attained. Summative measurement provides a *summary* of accomplishment. The final exam is a classic example.

The distinction between formative and summative measurement is based on how the measurement is used. The same test can be used for either purpose. If the goal is to obtain information about student learning for planning purposes, the testing is formative. If the purpose is to assess final achievement (and help determine a course grade), the measurement is summative.

Although summative testing is the best-known form of classroom assessment, formative tests also have an important role to play. You yourself have probably had the experience of thinking you really understood something until you took the final exam. Then you realized how and why your interpretation was incorrect. If this information had been available before the test, you could have used it to improve your mastery of the topic. Since teachers cannot possibly interview every student on every topic to determine who understands what, formative tests can be very effective. Older students are often able to apply the information from formative tests to "re-teach" themselves. Since formative tests do not count toward the final grade, students who tend to be very anxious on "real" tests may find this low-pressure practice in test taking especially helpful.

Tests are a way of life in today's classrooms. Test results may be used to see how well students are learning and whether teaching should be modified—a formative use of the information. Or the testing may be used to determine grades—a summative application. *(Mimi Forsyth/Monkmeyer Press)*

A variation of formative measurement is ongoing measurement, often called **data-based instruction** (Lovitt, 1977). This approach uses daily "probes," or brief tests of specific skills, to give a very precise picture of the student's current performance. This method has been used primarily with students who have learning problems, since it provides systematic evaluation of both student performance and the teaching methods used. If a student shows inadequate progress on the daily probes, the teacher should consider modifying or switching instructional strategies. Once the student has demonstrated mastery of a specific skill, a new skill can be introduced.

Let us look now at some common formats for testing—objective and essay questions.

data-based instruction: method using daily probes of specific-skill mastery

Objective Testing

Multiple-choice questions, matching exercises, true or false statements, and short-answer or fill-in items are all types of **objective testing.** The word *objective* in relation to testing does not refer to a goal, as in "instructional objectives." Here, *objective* means "not open to many interpretations," or "not subjective." The scoring of these types of items is relatively straightforward compared to the scoring of essay questions.

Gronlund (1982) suggests that teachers should begin by trying to construct multiple-choice items and switch to other formats only if the subject matter or learning outcome involved makes this desirable. If a number of similar concepts need to be interrelated, a matching item might serve best. If it is difficult to come up with several wrong answers for a multiple-choice item, a true-false question may well solve the problem. Alternatively, the student might be asked to supply a short answer that completes a statement ('fill in the blank"). In addition, variety can lower anxiety, since the entire grade does not depend on one type of question that may be difficult for a particular student. Here we will look closely at the multiple-choice format, since it is the most versatile.

objective testing: multiple-choice, matching, true-false, short-answer, and fill-in items; scoring answers does not require interpretation

Using Multiple-Choice Tests. People often assume that multiple-choice items are appropriate only for asking factual questions. But these items can test higher-level objectives as well, even though writing such "higher-level" items tends to be more difficult (Carter, 1984). A multiple-choice item can assess more than recall and recognition if it requires the student to deal with new material by applying the concept or principle being tested. How might this be done?

In Chapter 11 we discussed Bloom's taxonomy of objectives in the cognitive domain. At the fourth level of the taxonomy is *analysis*. One aspect of analysis is the ability to recognize unstated assumptions. The following multiple-choice item is designed to evaluate this kind of higher-level objective:

Higher-Level Items

An educational psychology professor states, "A z score of +1 on a test is equivalent to a percentile rank of approximately 84." Which of the following assumptions is the professor making?

1. The scores on the test range from 0 to 100.
2. The standard deviation of the test scores is equal to 3.4.
3. The distribution of scores on the test is normal. (CORRECT ANSWER)
4. The test is valid and reliable.

All test items require skillful construction, but good multiple-choice items are a real challenge. Let's examine some suggestions offered by Gronlund (1982) for constructing and grading multiple-choice tests.

Multiple Choice: Construction and Grading. Some students jokingly refer to multiple-choice tests as "multiple-guess" tests. Your goal in writing test items is to design them so that they measure student achievement rather than test-taking and guessing skills.

The **stem** of a multiple-choice item is the part that asks the question or poses the problem. The choices that follow are called alternatives. The wrong answers are called **distractors** because their purpose is to distract students who have only a partial understanding of the material. If there were no plausible distractors, students with only a vague understanding would have no difficulty in finding the right answer.

Stating the correct answer so that it is the *only* right answer or clearly the *best* answer is tricky. You probably have been on the student side of discussions about whether the correct answer was really correct or whether several of the answers might be correct. The teacher is likely to feel just as bad as the students when half the class selects the same wrong answer and only three people choose the so-called right answer. Often this means the item was poorly constructed. The Guidelines on the following pages should make writing multiple-choice questions easier.

Essay Testing

Some learning objectives are best measured by requiring students to create answers on their own. An essay question is in order in these cases. The most difficult part of essay testing is judging the quality of the answers, but writing good, clear questions is not particularly easy, either. We will look at a number of the factors involved in writing, administering, and grading essay tests, with most of the specific suggestions taken from Gronlund (1982). We will also consider factors that can bias the scoring of essay questions and ways you can overcome these problems.

Constructing Essay Tests. True essay tests (as opposed to tests with questions that can be answered in a few sentences) can cover less material than objective tests can. This is because answering essay questions takes more time. Thus, for the sake of efficiency, essay tests should generally be limited to the evaluation of the more complex learning outcomes.

Clarity and Precision

An essay question should give students a clear and precise task. It should indicate the elements to be covered in the answer. Gronlund suggests the following as an example of an essay question that might appear in an educational psychology course to measure an objective at the *synthesis* level (fifth level) of Bloom's taxonomy in the cognitive domain:

> For a course that you are teaching or expect to teach, prepare a complete plan for evaluating student achievement. Be sure to include the procedures you would follow, the instruments you would use, and the reasons for your choices.

This question requires students to apply information and values derived from course material to produce a complex new product.

Guidelines

Writing Objective Test Items

The stem should be clear, simple, and present only a single problem. Unessential details should be left out.

Poor   *There are several different kinds of standard or derived scores. An IQ score is especially useful because . . .*

Better   *An advantage of an IQ score is . . .*

The problem in the stem should be stated in positive terms. Negative language is confusing. If you must use words such as *not, no,* or *except,* underline them or type them in all capitals.

Poor   *Which of the following is not a standard score?*

Better   *Which of the following is NOT a standard score?*

Do not expect students to make extremely fine discriminations.

Poor   *The percentage of area in a normal curve falling between $+1$ and -1 standard deviations is about:*
a. 66%.   *c. 68%.*
b. 67%.   *d. 69%.*

Better   *The percentage of area in a normal curve falling between $+1$ and -1 standard deviations is about:*
a. 14%.   *c. 68%.*
b. 34%.   *d. 95%.*

As much wording as possible should be included in the stem so phrases will not have to be repeated in each alternative.

Poor   *A percentile score*
a. indicates the percentage of items answered correctly.
b. indicates the percent of correct answers divided by the percent of wrong answers.
c. indicates the percent of people who scored at or above.
d. indicates the percent of people who scored at or below.

Better   *A percentile score indicates the percent of*
a items answered correctly.
b. correct answers divided by the percent of wrong answers.
c. people who scored at or above.
d. people who scored at or below.

Each alternative answer should fit the grammatical form of the stem, so that no answers are obviously wrong.

Poor   *The Stanford-Binet test yields an*
a. IQ score.   *c. vocational preference.*
b. reading level.   *d. mechanical aptitude.*

Better   *The Stanford-Binet is a test of*
a. intelligence.   *c. vocational preference.*
b. reading level.   *d. mechanical aptitude.*

Categorical words such as *always, all, only,* or *never* should be avoided unless they can appear consistently in all the alternatives. Most smart test takers know they ought to avoid the categorical answers.

Poor A student's true score on a standardized test is
a. never equal to the obtained score.
b. always very close to the obtained score.
c. always determined by the standard error of measurement.
d. usually within a band that extends from + 1 to − 1 standard errors of measurement on each side of the obtained score.

Better Which one of the statements below would most often be correct about a student's true score on a standardized test?
a. It equals the obtained score.
b. It will be very close to the obtained score.
c. It is determined by the standard error of measurement.
d. It could be above or below the obtained score.

The *poor* alternative given in the item above has a second problem. The correct answer is much longer and more detailed than the three distractors. This is a clue that *d* is the correct choice.

You should also avoid including two wrong answers that have the same meaning. If only one answer can be right and if two answers are the same, then these two must both be wrong. This narrows down the choices considerably.

Poor The most frequently occurring score in a distribution is called the
a. mode.   c. arithmetic average.
b. median.   d. mean.

Better The most frequently occurring score in a distribution is called the
a. mode.   c. standard deviation.
b. median.   d. mean.

Using the exact wording found in the textbook is another technique to avoid. Poor students may recognize the answers without knowing what they mean.

Overuse of *all of the above* and *none of the above* should be avoided. Such choices may be helpful to students who are simply guessing. In addition, using *all of the above* may trick a quick student who sees that the first alternative is correct and does not read on to discover that the others are correct, too.

Obvious patterns on a test also aid students who are guessing. The position of the correct answer should be varied, as should its length.

Gronlund (1982) has offered a number of specific suggestions for constructing and administering essay tests. First, students should be given ample time for answering. If more than one essay is being completed in the same class period, you may want to suggest time limits for each. Remember, however, that time pressure increases anxiety and may prevent accurate evaluation of some students.

Coverage
Limitations

Whatever your approach, do not include a large number of essay questions in an attempt to make up for the limited amount of material an essay test can cover. It would be better to plan on more frequent testing than to include more than two or three essay questions in a single class period. Combining an essay question with a number of objective items is one way to avoid the problem of limited sampling.

Evaluating Essays: Dangers. In 1912 Starch and Elliot began a series of experiments that shocked educators into critical consideration of subjectivity in testing. These researchers wanted to find out the extent to which teachers were influenced in scoring essay tests by personal values, standards, and expectations. For their initial study, they sent copies of English examination papers written by two high school students to the first-year English teachers in 200 high schools. Each teacher was asked to score the papers according to his or her school's standards. A percentage scale was to be used with 75 percent as a passing grade.

Same Essays,
Different Scores

The results? Neatness, spelling, punctuation, and communicative effectiveness were all valued to different degrees by different teachers. The scores on one of the papers ranged from 64 to 98 percent, with a mean of 88.2. The average score for the other paper was 80.2, with a range between 50 and 97. The following year Starch and Elliot (1913a, 1913b) published similar findings in a study involving history and geometry papers. The most important result of these studies was the discovery that the problem of subjectivity in grading was not confined to any particular subject area. The main difficulties were the individual standards of the grader and the unreliability of scoring procedures.

Certain qualities of an essay itself may influence grades. For example, in a study of grading practices at 16 law schools, Linn, Klein, and Hart (1972) found that neatly written, verbose, jargon-filled essays with few grammatical and construction errors were given the best grades. Recent evidence indicates that teachers may tend to reward quantity rather than quality in essays. In a series of studies, many high school and college English teachers

Rewarding Verbosity

rated pairs of student essays that were identical in every way but linguistic style. One essay was quite verbose, with flowery language, complex sentences, and passive verbs. The other essay was written in the simple, straightforward language most teachers claim is the goal for students of writing. The teachers consistently rated the verbose essay higher and even perceived different errors in this type of paper. When interviewed by a reporter, one of the experimenters, Rosemary Hake, said:

> The teachers tended to find errors of logic and meaning in the verbose papers and mechanical errors in the others—even though the papers were identical in the errors they contained. The operating principle seemed to be that the higher the level of the language, the greater the importance of the errors. (Fiske, 1981, p. C1)

Evaluating Essays: Methods. Gronlund (1982) has offered a number of strategies for grading essays to avoid these undesirable influences. When possible, a good first step is to construct a model answer; then you can assign points to its various parts. Points might also be given for the organization of the answer, as well as the internal consistency. Grades such as 1 to 5 or A, B, C, D, and F can then be assigned, and the papers sorted into piles by grade. As a final step, the papers in each pile should be skimmed to see if they are relatively comparable in quality. These techniques will help ensure fairness and accuracy in grading.

Ensuring Fairness

When grading essay tests with several questions, it makes sense to grade all responses to one question before moving on to the next. This helps prevent the quality of a student's answer to one question from influencing your evaluation of the student's other answers. After you finish reading and scoring the first question, shuffle the papers so that no students end up having all their questions graded first, last, or in the middle (Hills, 1976).

You may achieve greater objectivity if you ask students to put their names on the back of the paper, so that grading is anonymous. A final check on your fairness as a grader is to have another teacher who is equally familiar with your goals and subject matter grade your tests. This can give you valuable insights into areas of bias in your grading practices. But if you decide to do this, be sure that each of you makes comments on separate sheets of paper so you do not influence each other.

holistic scoring: evaluation of a piece of written work as a whole, without separate grades for individual elements

In recent years, educators concerned with the writing process have developed an approach to evaluating written work known as **holistic scoring.** The philosophy underlying the holistic approach is that a written passage is greater than the sum of its parts. When teachers focus on the specific parts of an essay, such as vocabulary, grammar, spelling, or inclusion of particular details, they may miss important qualities like the essential message and persuasiveness. Rather than assigning separate grades for style, grammar, and content, for example, the holistic approach would evaluate the essay as a whole and give just one grade. To make sure holistic scores are reliable, White (1984) has recommended that teachers read essays in one session and at the outset choose sample essays for different levels to serve as models—choose one essay as a model for an A, one for a B, and so on.

Now that we have examined both objective and essay testing, we can compare the two approaches. Table 15–1 on the next page presents a summary of the important characteristics of each.

PLANNING A MEASUREMENT PROGRAM

Teaching involves instruction and evaluation. Both are most effective when they are well organized and planned. The behavior-content matrix presented in Chapter 11 offers one way of making sure instruction follows a logical and rational plan. Evaluation should also follow a logical plan: each part of an evaluation program should be designed to suit a specific purpose.

Planning Evaluation

Every test requires planning. If you use a behavior-content matrix to plan instruction, it can also act as your guide in developing a plan for the unit

Table 15–1 **Comparing Objective and Essay Tests**

	Objective Tests	Essay Tests
Useful for measuring . . .	Outcomes at the knowledge, comprehension, application, and analysis levels of Bloom's taxonomy	Synthesis and evaluation outcomes; also comprehension, application, and analysis outcomes
Number of items/range of material covered	Large number of items/broad coverage of course content	Relatively small number of items/limited but often in-depth coverage
Preparation problems	Difficult and time-consuming	Difficult for good items, but easier than objective items
Scoring	Objective, simple, and highly reliable	Subjective, difficult, and less reliable
Sources of score distortions	Students' level of reading ability; guessing	Students' writing ability; bluffing
Probable effect on learning	Encourage students to remember, interpret, and analyze the ideas of others	Encourage students to organize, integrate, and express their own ideas

Adapted from N. E. Gronlund (1982), Constructing achievement tests *(3rd ed.). Englewood Cliffs, NJ: Prentice-Hall, p. 73.*

test. Whatever method you select, you will need to decide how many items students can complete during the testing period and then make sure that the items you write cover all the objectives you have set for the unit. More important objectives should have more items.

Priorities and Objectives

An example of a plan that might be appropriate for a 40-question unit test in government is given in Table 15–2. From the test plan, you can see that this teacher has decided the most important topic is major political issues and has accordingly allotted a total of 15 questions to it. The least important topic is methods of inquiry. Also, the teacher wants to emphasize students' ability to make generalizations (14 questions) while giving considerable attention to understanding concepts and locating information. Interpreting graphs is the least important skill, but it is not to be overlooked.

By preparing such a plan, a teacher can avoid a situation where she or he has written 15 great questions (out of 40), only to discover that all 15 ask students to deal with concepts about the same topic. Making a test plan will also improve the validity of tests. You will be able to ask a reasonable number of questions about each key topic, measuring the skills you hoped to develop. Using a test plan is not time-consuming, especially if you work from the outside totals in toward the specific types of questions.

In making a general test plan, you will also have to consider the issues of frequency and variety. Frequent testing encourages the retention of information and appears to be more effective than a comparable amount of time spent reviewing and studying the material (Nungester & Duchastel, 1982). In addition to formal tests, you may want to use corrected homework as part of formative or summative evaluation. Participation in certain activities may be credited toward the grade. For example, students may be required to participate in debates, role playing, demonstrations, group projects, or games. The quality of their participation may or may not be graded; participation itself is the primary goal. In some subjects teachers keep samples, tape recordings, or portfolios of students' work. When the time comes to assign grades, these work samples give evidence of progress. In Chapter 11 we examined methods for assessing affective and psychomotor objectives. These methods might be included in an overall measurement program.

Other Things Count, Too

Cautions: Being Fair

You saw earlier that factors such as flowery language can influence teachers when they grade essay tests. But the influences do not stop with writing style. Oral expression can also affect a student's course grades. It appears that using standard American English with appropriate intonation and speaking with a soft, moderately pitched, good-quality voice are associated with receiving better grades from teachers (Frender, Brown, & Lambert, 1970; Naremore, 1970; Seligman, Tucker, & Lambert, 1972). (See, your mother was right. Be neat and speak softly. You may get a better grade for the same work!)

Voice Quality and Grades

Table 15–2 **Test Plan for a Unit on Government**

Topics	Skills Tested				
	Understanding Concepts	Making Generalizations	Locating Information	Interpreting Graphs	Total Questions
Social trends	4	4	1	1	**10**
National political events	2	3	3	2	**10**
Methods of inquiry	1	1	2	1	**5**
Major political issues	3	6	4	2	**15**
Total questions	**10**	**14**	**10**	**6**	**40**

How well is this student communicating? Will an evaluation of his oral report be a part of his final grade? Has the teacher communicated to him beforehand what's expected and how much his work will count? And will the teacher be influenced by the way the student talks—his voice quality or his accent? *(Richard Hutchings/Photo Researchers)*

Teachers' Expectations

As we saw in Chapter 9, a teacher's expectations can be a strong influence in the classroom. In general, it appears that teachers' expectations about the ability of students can greatly influence grading practices. In several studies, college students have been given tests to score, along with fictitious information about the general ability of the students who supposedly did the work. Higher scores went to "students" who the graders believed had a high level of ability (Cahen, 1966; Simon, 1969).

Even a student's name can influence grading. In one study, elementary school teachers gave higher grades to papers supposedly written by Michael or David than to the same papers written by Elmer and Hubert. For girls, the name Adelle on the paper resulted in more points than the names Karen or Bertha (Hills, 1976).

Much of Chapter 9 focused on student attributions about their own failures and successes. Again, the attributions a teacher makes about the causes of student successes or failures can also affect the grades that students receive. Teachers are more likely to give higher grades for effort (a controllable factor) than for ability (an uncontrollable factor). Lower grades are more likely when teachers attribute a student's failure to lack of effort instead of lack of ability (Weiner, 1979). It is also possible that grades can be influenced by a **halo effect**—that is, by the tendency to view particular aspects of a student based on a general impression, either positive or negative. As a teacher, you may find it difficult to avoid being affected by positive and negative halos. A very pleasant student who seems to work hard and causes little trouble may be given the benefit of the doubt (B− instead of C+), whereas a very difficult student who seems to refuse to try might be a loser at grading time (D instead of C−).

But what about the recipients of these grades? Is it enough that the teacher's evaluation practices are fair? Student attributions and expectations are also part of the complex equation of classroom evaluation.

halo effect: tendency for a general impression of a person to influence our perception of any aspect of that person

EFFECTS OF GRADES AND GRADING ON STUDENTS

It might be worthwhile at this point for you to consider how the many grades you have received over the years have affected you. Since you are a college student, you have probably received your share of high grades. Without them, you might not have reached this educational level. Did you ever receive an F? If you did, how did you feel? What did you do as a result?

Grades have many different effects on students. But based on what we know about attributions, expectations, and motivation, we can say that at least three factors play a part in determining the effect of any grade: (1) the student's attribution of the cause for the grade; (2) the grade the student expected to receive; and (3) the grade the student is accustomed to receiving.

Three Factors

The Effect of High Grades

For the student who generally achieves high marks, grades tend to be a positive reinforcer. The student is likely to study in the same way and to try to continue the kind of learning that has been rewarded in the past. Some research indicates that if teachers reward conforming answers—answers that agree with or duplicate material from lectures or the textbook—students will try to conform to teacher views in future assignments, even if they did not previously share those views (Bostrum, Vlandis, & Rosenbaum, 1961). In addition, there is some evidence that high grades are generally more often achieved by conforming students than by "creative" students (Holland, 1960; Kelley, 1958) and that students who share the teacher's values tend to receive higher grades (Cronbach & Snow, 1977).

Conformity, Consistency, and Unexpected Successes

These findings refer to continually successful students. Such students probably develop a positive view of themselves as academic achievers over time. But suppose a student is not consistently successful. What would be the effect of unexpected high grades? They might lead to rising levels of aspiration and perhaps to increased effort. For a student who has neither worked hard nor received high grades in the past, a reward for honest initial efforts at a new learning task can be influential, depending again on the student's attributions about the causes of the new success.

The Effect of Low Grades

Some students have received so many C's and D's by the time they finish high school that they may begin to feel they have earned a C or D in life as well. As we have seen, repeated failure can lead to a destructive cycle: failure, lower level of aspiration, reduced efforts to succeed, failure, lower level of aspiration, and so on. Grades assigned to these students are often perceived as punishment—but punishment for what? A student who has been studying a bit, coming to school regularly, and putting in some effort on tests can easily begin to believe it is *these* behaviors that are being punished. If there are no other rewards forthcoming in school for these behaviors, they are likely to diminish or disappear.

"IT MAY BE A REPORT CARD TO YOU, BUT IN MY HOUSE, IT'S AN ENVIRONMENTAL IMPACT STATEMENT."

Adverse Effects

There is some evidence that high standards, a competitive class atmosphere, and a large percentage of lower grades are associated with increased absenteeism and increased dropout rates (Moos & Moos, 1978; Trickett & Moos, 1974). This seems especially likely with disadvantaged students (Wessman, 1972). Highly competitive classes may be particularly hard on anxious students or students who lack self-confidence. So while high standards and competition do tend generally to be related to increased academic learning, it is clear that a balance must be struck between high standards and a reasonable chance to succeed.

Constructive Failure

It may sound as though low grades and failure should be avoided in schools. But the situation is not that simple. (It never is in teaching!) After reviewing many years of research on the effects of failure from several perspectives, Margaret Clifford (1979, 1984) concluded that failure can have both positive and negative effects on subsequent performance, depending on the situation and the personality of the students involved.

For example, one study required subjects to complete three sets of problems. On the first set, the experimenters arranged for subjects to experience either 0, 50, or 100 percent success. On the second set, it was arranged for all subjects to fail completely. On the third set of problems, the experimenters merely recorded how well the subjects performed. Those who had succeeded only 50 percent of the time before the failure experience performed the best. It appears that a history of complete failure or 100 percent success may be bad preparation for learning to cope with failure, something we must all learn. Some level of failure may be helpful for most students, especially if teachers help the students see connections between hard work and improvement. Efforts to protect students from failure and guarantee success may be counterproductive. Clifford (1979) summarizes the dangers of easy success:

> Success which comes too easily is not likely to be as highly valued as success which is difficult to achieve. With our educational practices designed to ensure success we may be conditioning students to be intolerant of performance which is less than perfect, to be conservative risk takers in learning situations, to retreat when they encounter failure, and to covet the known rather than venture into the unknown. (p. 50)

The more able your students, the more challenging and important it will be to help them learn to "fail successfully" (Foster, 1981).

Being Held Back

So far, we have been talking about the effects of failing a test or perhaps a course. But what about the effect of failing an entire grade—that is, of being "held back"? According to Holmes and Matthews (1984), being held back injures students' self-esteem. In their view, students generally do better academically when promoted, since the "potential for negative effects" of being held back "consistently outweighs positive outcomes" (Holmes & Matthews, 1984, p. 232).

Effects of Feedback

The results of several studies of feedback fit well with the notion of "successful" or constructive failure. These studies have concluded that it is more helpful to tell students when they are wrong than when they are right, but the most productive approach is to tell them *why* they are wrong so they can learn more appropriate strategies (Bloom & Bourdon, 1980). Students often need help in figuring out why their answers are incorrect. Without such feedback, they are likely to make the same mistakes again. Yet this type of feedback is rarely given. In one study, only about 8 percent of the teachers noticed a consistent type of error in a student's arithmetic compu-

Feedback to students should be immediate and specific. This student needs to know what she did right, what her mistakes were, why they are mistakes, and how she can correct them next time. *(David S. Strickler/Monkmeyer Press)*

tation and informed the student (Bloom & Bourdon, 1980). However, with some instruction, teachers can easily learn to give effective feedback (Elawar & Corno, 1985).

Logical Mistakes

Results of research on cognitive learning demonstrate that students are very logical and "intelligent" in making errors—few mistakes are random. (This may remind you of the phase of overregularization that children go through when they learn language.) The student usually applies some rule or procedure to answer a question or solve a problem in class. The rule may be wrong and may need to be corrected before the student will understand the material. Table 15–3 shows several examples of mistaken rules (or "buggy" algorithms) that have appeared in the arithmetic computations of students.

Written Comments

Early research indicated that written comments by teachers on completed assignments can lead to improved performance in the future (Page, 1958).

Table 15–3   **Correcting Mistaken Rules**

143 − 28 ___ 125	The smaller digit in each column has been subtracted from the larger digit, regardless of which is on top; or in order to borrow, 10 has been added to the top digit of a column without subtracting 1 from the next column to the left.
1300 − 522 ____ 878	When borrowing from a column whose top digit is 0, the student writes 9 but does not continue borrowing from the column to the left of the 0.
140 − 21 ___ 121	Whenever the top digit in a column is 0, the student writes the bottom digit in the answer; i.e., $0 - N = N$.
140 − 21 ___ 120	Whenever the top digit in a column is 0, the student writes 0 in the answer; i.e., $0 - N = 0$.
1300 − 522 ____ 788	When borrowing from a column where the top digit is 0, the student borrows from the next column to the left correctly but writes 10 instead of 9 in this column.
321 − 89 ___ 231	When borrowing into a column whose top digit is 1, the student does not add in the 1 and uses 10 instead of 11.
662 − 357 ____ 205	Having borrowed once, the student continues to borrow from every column whether necessary or not.
662 − 357 ____ 115	The student always subtracts all borrows from leftmost digit in the top number.

Adapted from J. S. Brown & R. R. Burton (1978), *Diagnostic Models for Procedural Bugs in Basic Mathematical Skills. Cognitive Science, 2, 155–192.* Copyright 1978 by Ablex Publishing Corp. Reprinted by permission.

In more recent work, the emphasis has been on identifying characteristics of effective written feedback. With older students (late elementary through high school), written comments are most helpful when they are personalized rather than stereotyped and when they provide constructive criticism. This means the teacher should make specific comments on errors or faulty strategies but balance this criticism with suggestions about how to improve as well as with comments on the positive aspects of the work (Elawar & Corno, 1985; Stewart & White, 1976). Working with sixth-grade teachers, Elawar and Corno (1985) found that feedback was dramatically improved when the teachers used these four questions as a guide: "What is the key error? What is the probable reason the student made this error? How can I guide the student to avoid the error in the future? What did the student do well that could be noted?" (p. 166). Here are some examples of teachers' written comments that proved helpful (Elawar & Corno, 1985, p. 164):

Effective Feedback: Older Students

> Juan, you know how to get a percent, but the computation is wrong in this instance. . . . Can you see where? (Teacher has underlined the location of errors.)
>
> You know how to solve the problem—the formula is correct—but you have not demonstrated that you understand how one fraction multiplied by another can give an answer that is smaller than either ($1/2 \times 1/2 = 1/4$).

Effective Feedback: Younger Students

For younger students, oral feedback may be much more important than written comments. Marble, Winne, and Martin (1978) reached a similar conclusion in a study of written comments in eighth-grade science classes. They have suggested that the teacher's time might be better spent giving students immediate oral feedback. As has been noted, oral feedback that helps students pinpoint and correct key misconceptions is especially helpful.

While extensive written comments may be inappropriate for younger students, brief written comments are a different matter. Short, cogent comments can be fun for teacher and students alike. With younger students, the comments may be as simple as "Wow," "Bravo," "Super," "A winner." One elementary teacher I know just writes down the first printable word that pops into her head; students never know what will come next. My daughter understood that her paper was particularly good whenever her second-grade teacher drew a "popcorn man" saying "terrific" in the corner of her test or essay. Having a cartoonlike popcorn man on her paper was more reinforcing than simply receiving a good grade. Such comments also take some of the emphasis off the grade itself.

Working for a Grade versus Working to Learn

Is there really a difference between working for a grade and working to learn? The answer to this question depends in part on how a grade is determined. If grades are based on tests that require detailed memorization of facts, dates, and definitions, the students' study time will probably be spent learning these details. There will be little opportunity to explore the thought questions that may be found at the end of the chapter. But would students actually explore these questions if their work were not graded?

Cullen and Cullen (1975) gave three groups of high school students a one-page library assignment and varied grading conditions in an attempt to find

Teachers must be careful that their systems for grading encourage eagerness to learn and to continue learning. If the grading system emphasizes external rewards alone, students' genuine interest in the subject may diminish. *(John Coletti/Stock, Boston)*

out whether the presence or absence of a grade made a difference. One group was told that completing the paper would mean "extra credit"—that is, it would add points to their grade, but they would not lose points if they did not do the paper. Another group was told that if they did not complete the extra assignment, their course grades would go down. The last group was invited to complete the paper simply for their own interest and enjoyment.

Papers were completed by 41 percent of the group who could improve their grades, 64 percent of the group who could lose points, and only 14 percent of those who had no grade incentive. This study demonstrated that if some assignments count toward the grade and others do not, students are likely to put their efforts where the grades are and let opportunities to complete projects "just for fun" slip through their fingers.

Motivation: Continuing or Diminishing?

Some research indicates that if students receive external rewards for doing something they enjoy anyway, their motivation may actually diminish. They may be less likely to do the task for its own sake. Salili, Maehr, Sorenson, and Fyans (1976) found that actual performance on a task was not affected by the evaluation conditions but that future performances often were. The three types of evaluation in their study were (1) external evaluation—scores reported to the teacher and figured into the final grade; (2) self-evaluation—only the student knew his or her own score; and (3) peer evaluation—scores were indicated publicly but not included in the final grade. While performance on the task at hand was not affected, students in the external evaluation group were less motivated to work on similar tasks in the future.

Other researchers (Lepper & Greene, 1975; Lepper, Greene, & Nisbett, 1973) have found that external rewards can decrease both current performance and motivation to continue. (We discussed this issue in Chapter 9.) One recommendation based on these findings would be to give a few *required* but *ungraded* assignments. Even when the work is ungraded, students should receive feedback on good and improvable aspects.

As a teacher, you can use grades to motivate the kind of learning you intend students to achieve in your course. If you test only at a very simple but detailed level of knowledge, you may force students to choose between higher aspects of learning and a good grade in your course. If you set objectives more appropriately, including all applicable levels of cognitive, affective, and psychomotor functioning, you will allow students to equate studying for learning with studying for a grade. When a grade reflects meaningful learning, working for a grade and working to learn become the same thing.

The Guidelines summarize the many different effects grades can have on students.

Guidelines

Minimizing the Detrimental Effects of Grading

Avoid reserving high grades and high praise for answers that conform to your ideas or to those in the textbook.

Examples
1. *Give extra points for correct and creative answers.*
2. *Withhold your opinions until all sides of an issue have been explored.*
3. *Reinforce students for disagreeing in a rational, productive manner.*
4. *Give partial credit for partially correct answers.*

Make sure each student has a reasonable chance to be successful, especially at the beginning of a new task.

Examples
1. *Pretest students to make sure they have prerequisite abilities.*
2. *Individualize instruction based on pretest results.*
3. *Base grades to some degree on improvement rather than absolute performance.*
4. *When appropriate, provide opportunities for students to retest to raise their grades, but make sure the retest is as difficult as the original.*

Balance written and oral feedback.

Examples
1. *Consider giving short, lively written comments with younger students and more extensive written comments with older students.*
2. *When the grade on a paper is lower than the student might have expected, be sure the reason for the lower grade is clear.*
3. *Tailor comments to the individual student's performance; avoid writing the same phrases over and over.*
4. *Note specific errors, possible reasons for errors, ideas for improvement, and work done well.*

Make grades as meaningful as possible.

Examples
1. *Tie grades to the mastery of important objectives.*
2. *Give ungraded assignments to encourage exploration.*

Base grades on more than just one criterion.

Examples
1. *Use essay questions as well as multiple-choice items on a test.*
2. *Grade oral reports and class participation.*

GRADING AND REPORTING: NUTS AND BOLTS

Now that we have seen a few of the factors that might bias grading and some of the effects of grades on students, let us examine grading practices themselves. You should be in a good position to evaluate each approach by considering its potential effect on students, how well it fits with the subject matter you will be teaching, and how vulnerable it would be to bias.

In determining a final grade, the teacher must make a major decision. Should a student's grade reflect the amount of material learned and how well it has been learned, or should the grade reflect the student's status in comparison with the rest of the class? In other words, should grading be criterion-referenced or norm-referenced?

Criterion-Referenced versus Norm-Referenced Grading

criterion-referenced grading: assessment of each student's mastery of course objectives

In **criterion-referenced grading,** the grade represents a list of accomplishments. If clear objectives have been set for the course, the grade may represent a certain number of objectives met satisfactorily. When a criterion-referenced system is used, criteria for each grade generally are spelled out in advance. It is then up to the student to strive for and reach a level that matches the grade she or he wants to receive. Theoretically, in this system all students can achieve an A if they master the necessary number of specified objectives.

norm-referenced grading: assessment of students' achievement in relation to one another

If grading is **norm-referenced,** the major influence on a grade is the student's standing in comparison with others who also took the course. If a student studies very hard but almost everyone else does too, the student may receive a disappointing grade, perhaps a C.

Different kinds of information are conveyed by criterion-referenced and norm-referenced grading. Since any number of students can achieve any grade in a criterion-referenced system, there is no need to discriminate among the students. There are enough high grades to go around for those who will work for them. The grade does not imply that the student did better or worse than anyone else. It reflects achievement, not a student's status relative to other members of the class. Motivation to succeed tends to be higher among students when they know they are not obliged to compete for the small number of high grades available (Kurtz & Swenson, 1951).

In practice, many school systems would look askance at a teacher who turned in a roster filled with A's and explained that all the students had attained the course objectives. Administrators might say that if all the objectives could be so easily attained by all the students, then more or tougher objectives were needed. Nevertheless, a criterion-referenced system may be acceptable in some schools. Let's consider an example.

A Criterion-Referenced System. Criterion-referenced grading has the advantage of relating judgments about a student to the achievement of clearly defined instructional objectives. Some school districts have developed reporting systems where report cards list objectives along with judgments about the student's attainment of each. Reporting is done at the end of each unit of instruction. The junior high report card shown in Table 15–4 demonstrates the relationship between evaluation and the goals of the unit.

Table 15–4   Criterion-Referenced Grades at the Secondary Level

JERICHO JUNIOR HIGH SCHOOL
JERICHO, NEW YORK

EVALUATION

Teacher _____   Student _____

Counselor _____   Dates (from) _____ (to) _____

Unit: Analogy as a Thought Process   Grade _____   Subject: English

Code: 1 The student has met the objective.
        2 The student has demonstrated progress toward meeting the objective.
        3 The student has not at this time met the objective.
        4 The student has not demonstrated whether or not the objective has
           been met.
        5 The objective does not apply at this time.

BASIC INFORMATION:

_____ a. The student can identify comparisons that use *like, as, than,* and *is.*
_____ b. The student can identify comparisons that do not use *like, as, than,* or
           is. (The teacher threw the student out of class. Student = ball.)
_____ c. The student can recognize the similarity in two unlike items.

UNDERSTANDING:

_____ a. The student can distinguish between the *is* of identity and the *is* of
           comparison. *(I am John. I am a block of wood.)*
_____ b. The student can distinguish between the literal sense of a poem and the
           meaning suggested by its imagery.

APPLICATION:

_____ a. The student can compose original sentences that make a comparison
           without using words such as *like, as,* or *than.*
_____ b. Given a comparison, the student can extend it into a paragraph.

grading on the curve: norm-referenced grading that compares students' performance to an average level

A Norm-Referenced System.   One very popular type of norm-referenced grading is **grading on the curve.** As noted in the previous chapter, the characteristics of the normal curve, or normal distribution, are well known. For example, we know that two-thirds of the distribution (68 percent) are clustered within 1 standard deviation of the mean. In grading on the curve, the middle of the normal distribution or "average" performance becomes the anchor on which grading is based. In other words, teachers look at the average level of performance, assign what they consider an "average grade" for this performance, and then grade superior performances higher and inferior performances lower.

If grading were done strictly on the normal curve, there would be an equal number of A's and F's, a larger number of B's and D's, and an even larger number of C's. The grades would have to form a bell-shaped curve. For example, a teacher might decide to give 10 percent A's and F's, 20 percent B's and D's, and 40 percent C's. This is a very strict interpretation of grading on the curve, and it makes sense only if achievement in the class follows the normal curve.

Curve Approaches   Grading on the curve can be done with varying levels of precision. The simplest approach is to rank-order the students' raw scores on a test and use this ranked list of scores as the basis for assigning grades. Such a distribution might look like this: 92 91 91 90 83 80 78 76 72 68 65 61 57 54 53 49 48 47 46 43 38 36 29 29. Knowing that two-thirds of the scores in a normal distribution should be in the middle, you might bracket off the middle two-thirds of the scores and plan to give those students C's (or B's, if you believed B was an average grade for the class in question). Some people prefer to use the middle one-third of the students rather than two-thirds as the basis for the average grade. Based on these two approaches, grades might be assigned as follows:

Middle Two-Thirds Assigned C's

A | B | C | D | F
92 | 91 91 90 | 83 80 78 76 72 68 65 61 57 54 53 49 48 47 46 43 | 38 36 | 29 29

Middle One-Third Assigned C's

A | B | C | D | F
92 | 91 91 90 83 80 78 76 | 72 68 65 61 57 54 53 49 | 48 47 46 43 38 36 | 29 29

Fairness and Common Sense   This approximation to grading on the curve is very rough indeed. In these examples the distance between one letter grade and another is sometimes one point! Given the amount of error in testing, this assignment of grades is probably not fair. You can correct some of these problems by introducing common sense into the process. For example, you may believe the following grade assignment is fairer:

Adjusted Grades

A | B | C | D | F
92 91 91 90 | 83 80 78 76 72 | 68 65 61 57 54 53 | 49 48 47 46 43 38 36 | 29 29

In this case the instructor has used the natural gaps in the range of scores to locate boundaries between grades. Between the A and B categories are 7 points, between the B and C, 4 points, and so on.

Preparing Report Cards

No matter what kind of grading system you use, you will undoubtedly give several tests. And you will probably assign homework or projects. Let's assume your unit evaluation plan includes two short tests (mostly multiple-choice questions with one essay), homework, a project, and a unit test. If you use a criterion-referenced system for testing and grading, how will you convert scores on these individual performances to the overall indications of mastery on a report card such as that in Table 15–4? What about using a norm-referenced system? How do you combine results from individual tests and assignments to yield a final distribution of scores for the unit grade?

Criterion-Referenced Grades

Let us consider criterion-referenced grading first. If you adopt this system, you cannot average or combine test scores or homework grades in a mathematical way. Since each test and assignment measures the mastery of a particular objective (or set of objectives), it would be meaningless to average, say, the students' mastery of addition of two-digit numbers with their mastery of measurement with a ruler, although both might be objectives in arithmetic. On the report card, the various objectives are listed, and the student's level of proficiency in each is indicated.

Norm-Referenced Grades

Norm-referenced grading is a different story. In order to assign grades, the teacher must merge all the scores from tests and projects into one final score. Final grades are assigned based on how each student's final score compares with that of the rest of the students. But the usual procedure of simply adding up all the scores and averaging the total is often not appropriate, and it can be misleading. For example, assume two students took two tests. The tests are equally important in the overall unit. The students' scores are shown below (from Chase, 1978, p. 328).

	Test 1 Class Mean = 30 Standard Deviation = 8	Test 2 Class Mean = 50 Standard Deviation = 16	Total Raw Score
Leslie	38	50	88
Jason	30	66	96

Total Scores Can Be Misleading

If we compute an average or if we rank the students based on their totals, Jason would be ahead of Leslie. But if we look at the class mean and standard deviation for each test, we see a different picture. On one test, Leslie's score was 1 standard deviation above the mean, and on the other her score was at the mean; Jason's record is exactly the same.

	Test 1	Test 2
Leslie	+1 SD	Mean
Jason	Mean	+1 SD

If these two tests are really equally important, Jason and Leslie have identical records in relation to the rest of the class on these tests. To compare students' performances on several tests, the scores for each must be converted to a standard scale like a T score. As you may recall from Chapter 14, a T score is a standard score into which a raw score is transformed. The mean is automatically 50 and the standard deviation is 10. More detailed instructions about how to convert raw scores into T scores are available in

Terwilliger (1971). Most teachers do not calculate T scores for all their students, but the example illustrates the importance of using common sense in grading. Gross totals do not always reflect how well one student is doing in relation to others in the class.

The Point System

One popular system for combining grades from many assignments is a point system. Each test or assignment is given a certain number of total points, depending on its importance. A test worth 40 percent of the grade could be worth 40 points. A paper worth 20 percent could be worth 20 points. Points are then awarded on the test or paper based upon specific criteria. An A+ paper, one that meets all the criteria, could be given the full 20 points; an average paper might be given 10 points. If tests of comparable importance are worth the same number of points, are equally difficult, and cover a similar amount of material, we can expect to avoid some of the problems encountered with Jason and Leslie, when the means and standard deviations of two supposedly comparable tests varied so greatly.

Let us assume a grade book indicates the scores shown in Table 15–5. How would you assign grades to students for this unit of work? Here are several possibilities:

1. Find the total number of points for each student and rank the students. Assign grades by looking for natural gaps of several points or imposing a curve (a certain percentage of A's, B's, and so on).
2. Convert each score to a percentage and average the percentages. Rank the students on percentages and proceed as above to look for gaps or impose a curve. Compare the results of this approach with the results of the one above.
3. Rank the students on each assignment. Then calculate each student's average rank for all five assignments. (If two students tie for one rank, they split the difference between that rank and the one below. For example, if two students tie for third place, they each get 3.5 and there is no fourth place.) Use the average rankings to determine overall ranks, then look for gaps or impose a curve on the overall ranks.

You might enjoy having your educational psychology class divide into groups and assign grades to the students in Table 15–5, based on the three different methods. Then compare each group's grades. Even better, have several groups try each method. You can see if your group's grades correspond to those of the other groups using the same method.

Percentage Grading

There is another approach to assigning grades to a group of students like those in Table 15–5. The teacher can assign grades based on how much knowledge each student has mastered—what percent of the total knowledge he or she understands. To do this, the teacher might score tests and other classwork with percentage scores (based on how much is correct—50 percent, 85 percent, etc.), then average these scores to reach a course score. These scores are then converted into letter grades, according to predetermined cutoff points. Then any number of students can earn any grade. This

Table 15–5 **Points Earned on Five Assignments**

Student	Test 1 20% 20 points	Test 2 20% 20 points	Unit Test 30% 30 points	Homework 15% 15 points	Project 15% 15 points	Total
Amy	10	12	16	6	7	_____
Bert	12	10	14	7	6	_____
Cathy	20	19	30	15	13	_____
Doug	18	20	25	15	15	_____
Étienne	6	5	12	4	10	_____
Frieda	10	12	18	10	9	_____
Grace	13	11	22	11	10	_____
Herbert	7	9	12	5	6	_____
Isaac	14	16	26	12	12	_____
Joy	20	18	28	10	15	_____
Keith	19	20	25	11	12	_____
Linda	14	12	20	13	9	_____
Melody	15	13	24	8	10	_____
Ned	8	7	12	8	6	_____
Olivia	11	12	16	9	10	_____
Peter	7	8	11	4	8	_____
	—	—	—	—	—	_____

procedure is very common; you may have experienced it yourself from the student's end. Let us look at it more closely, because it has some frequently overlooked problems.

Percentages and Letter Grades

The grading symbols of A, B, C, D, and F are probably the most popular means of reporting at the present time. School systems often establish equivalent percentage categories for each of these symbols. The percentages vary from school district to school district, but two typical ones are as follows:

90–100% = A; 80–89% = B; 70–79% = C; 60–69% = D; below 60% = F
94–100% = A; 85–93% = B; 76–83% = C; 70–75% = D; below 70% = F

As you can see, although both districts have an A to F five-point grading system, the average achievement required for each grade is different.

But can we really say what the total amount of knowledge available in, for example, eighth-grade science is? Are we sure we can accurately measure what percentage of this body of knowledge each student has attained? To use **percentage grading** appropriately, we would have to know exactly what there was to learn and exactly how much of that each student *had* learned. These conditions are seldom met, even though teachers use the cutoff points to assign grades as if measurement were so accurate that a one-point difference was meaningful: "In spite of decades of research in educational and psychological measurement, which has produced more defensible methods, the concept [of percentage grading], once established, has proved remarkably resistant to change" (Zimmerman, 1981, p. 178).

percentage grading: converting class performances to percentage scores and assigning grades based on predetermined cutoff points

Suppose teachers are required to adhere to such a grading system, using the percentage average from grade books to assign the appropriate letter grade automatically. By giving very easy tests, they can ensure that a large number of students will do well and receive high grades in the course. By administering more difficult tests, the teacher can produce a greater number of lower and failing grades.

No Absolutes

Any grading system prescribed or suggested by the school can be influenced by particular concerns of the teacher. Do not be fooled by the seeming security of absolute percentages. Your own grading philosophy will continue to operate, even in this system. Because there is more concern today with specifying objectives and criterion-referenced evaluation, especially at the elementary-grade levels, several new methods for evaluating student progress against predetermined criteria have evolved. We will look at two: the contract system and mastery learning.

The Contract System

contract system: system in which each student agrees to work for a particular grade according to agreed-upon standards

When applied to the whole class, the **contract system** indicates the type, quantity, and quality of work required for each number or letter grade in the system. Students agree or "contract" to work for particular grades by meeting the specified requirements. For example, the following standards may be established:

F: Not coming to class regularly or not turning in the required work.

D: Coming to class regularly and turning in the required work on time.

C: Coming to class regularly, turning in the required work on time, and receiving a check mark on all assignments to indicate they are satisfactory.

B: Coming to class regularly, turning in the required work on time, and receiving a check mark on all assignments except three that achieve a check-plus, indicating superior achievement.

A: As above, plus a successful oral or written report on one of the books listed for supplementary reading.

This example contains more subjective judgment than would be ideal. However, contract systems reduce student anxiety about grades and can eliminate subjective judgment to whatever extent the teacher wants by specifying the quantity and quality required for various grades. The contract system can be applied to individual students and functions much like an independent study plan.

Unfortunately, the system can also lead to overemphasis on quantity of work. Teachers may be too vague about the standards that differentiate acceptable from unacceptable work. It is sometimes difficult to tell a student that a particular assignment is completely unsatisfactory ("Is it that bad?"), so many teachers end up accepting almost every piece of work. In addition, if a school system requires a five-point grading system and all students contract for and achieve the highest grade, the teacher will wish administrative approval for the system had been obtained in advance.

revise option: chance to revise and improve work in a contract system

The contract system can be modified by including a **revise option.** Then students whose work has not been satisfactory or who earned a check but hoped for a check-plus could be allowed to revise their work. A check might be worth 75 points and a check-plus 90 points; a check-plus earned after revision could be worth 85 points—more than a check but less than a check-plus earned the first time around. This system allows students to improve their work but also rewards getting it right the first time. Some quality control is possible, since students earn points not just for quantity but also for quality. In addition, the teacher might be less reluctant to judge a project unsatisfactory, since students can improve their work (King, 1979).

The Mastery Approach

mastery learning: approach in which achievement of specific objectives is the main focus

As mentioned earlier, many psychologists are not satisfied with the normal curve model of grading. They believe effective instruction ought to ensure that most students master a majority of the learning objectives. **Mastery learning** is an approach to teaching and grading based on the assumption that given enough time and the proper instruction, most students can master a majority of the learning objectives (Bloom, 1968; Guskey & Gates, 1986).

To use the mastery approach, teachers must break a course down into small units of study. Each unit might involve mastering several specific objectives. Students are informed of the objectives and the criteria for meeting each. Students who do not reach the minimum level of mastery or who reach this minimum but want to improve their performance (thus raising their grade) can recycle through the unit and take another form of the unit test.

Under a mastery system, grades can be determined by the actual number of objectives mastered, the number of units completed, the proficiency level reached on each unit, or some combination of these methods. Students can work at their own pace, finishing the entire course quickly if they are able or taking a long time to reach a few objectives. Of course, if only a few objectives are met by the end of the marking period, the student's grade will reflect this. The Keller Plan discussed in Chapter 5 is a version of a mastery approach.

Limitations and Requirements

There are problems with this approach. Since all students do not cover the same material, the course must be self-contained. Using a mastery approach to teach Algebra I would not ensure that all students had the prerequisites for Algebra II, since some might never get past solving an equation with one unknown. In addition, teachers must have a variety of materials to allow students to recycle through objectives they failed to meet the first time. Usually, just dealing with the same materials all over again will not help. If the entire school uses a mastery system, however, some of these problems are solved.

It is also important to have several tests for each unit. Students quickly figure out that taking the test and failing is better preparation for passing the unit than studying all the material, since an attempt at the test tells them exactly what to study before taking the next test (Cox & Dunn, 1979). This approach can lead to memorizing and learning a few specifics but not really to an understanding of the material.

Thus far we have been talking about mastery learning as an individualized approach, with students moving at their own pace through the material. This seems to be the best use of mastery learning. When a whole group moves through units at the same pace, many of the advantages of mastery learning are lost. The faster students have to wait until everyone in the class reaches the required level of mastery. This holds back the more able students and limits the level of achievement possible in the class (Arlin, 1984).

Persistence of
Achievement
Differences

In practice, mastery learning has not helped to erase achievement differences among students, as some proponents have hoped. Individual differences in achievement persist, unless the teacher holds back the faster students while the slower ones catch up (Arlin, 1984). Left to work at their own pace, some students will learn much more and leave a unit with much better understanding than others. Some will work much harder to take advantage of the learning opportunities (Grabe & Latta, 1981). Some will be frustrated instead of encouraged by the chance to recycle ("You mean I have to do it *again?!*"). And finally, the word *mastery* may be misleading. Completing a mastery unit successfully usually means that the students are ready to move to the next unit, not that they are "masters" of the information (Cox & Dunn, 1979).

Grading on Effort and Improvement

Grading on effort and improvement is not really a complete grading system but rather a theme that can run through most grading methods.

Should teachers grade students based on how much they learn or on the final level of learning? One problem with using improvement as a standard for grading is that the best students improve the least, since they are already the most competent. Do you want to penalize these students because they knew quite a bit initially and the teaching and testing have limited how much learning they can demonstrate? After all, unless you assign extra work, students will run out of things to do.

individual learning expectation: personal average score

One solution is to use the **individual learning expectation** system described in Chapter 9. With this system students earn improvement points on tests or assignments for scoring above their personal base (average) score in that subject or for making a perfect score. These improvement points can be counted when figuring a final grade or simply used as a basis for earning other classroom rewards. (See Chapter 9 for a complete discussion of how to use this approach.)

dual marking system: assigning two grades, one reflecting achievement, the other effort, attitude, and actual ability

Many teachers try to include some judgment of effort in final grades. But effort is difficult to assess. Are you certain your perception of each student's effort is correct? Clement (1978) suggests a system for including a judgment about effort in the final grade called the **dual marking system.** Students are assigned two grades. One (usually a letter) indicates the actual level of achievement. The other, a number, indicates the relationship of the achievement to the student's actual ability and effort. For example, a grade of B could be qualified as follows (Clement, 1978, p. 51):

B_1: Outstanding effort, better achievement than expected, good attitude

B_2: Average effort, satisfactory in terms of ability

B_3: Lower achievement than ability would indicate, poor attitude

Of course, this system assumes that the teacher can adequately judge true ability and effort. A grade of D_1, D_2, or F_2 could be quite insulting! A grade of A_3 or F_1 should not be possible. But the system does have the advantage of recognizing hard work and giving feedback about a seeming lack of effort. An A_2 might tell very bright students: "You're doing well, but I know you could do better." This could help the students to expect more of themselves and not slip by on high ability. The overall grade—A, B, C—still reflects achievement and is not changed (or biased) by teachers' subjective judgment of effort.

Few teachers are able to create a grading system completely to their own liking; the school system generally has ideas of its own. The Guidelines on the following pages should help you work within whatever system you use.

BEYOND GRADING: COMMUNICATION

No number or letter grade conveys the totality of a student's experience in a class or course. Both students and teachers sometimes become too focused on the end point—the grade. Children and adolescents spend the majority of their waking hours for many months of the year in school, where teachers are the relevant adults. This gives teachers the opportunity and the responsibility to know their students as people.

Clear and open communication with both students and parents is an important element of teaching and a valuable adjunct to the grading system. What shows up only in black and white on the report card may have many shades of gray—or many vivid colors. Students for their part need to know that teachers and parents understand them as people and are working as a team. *(Catherine Ursillo/Photo Researchers)*

Guidelines

Using Any Grading System

Explain your grading policies to students early in the course and remind them of the policies regularly.

Examples
1. Give older students a grading handout describing the assignments, tests, grading criteria, and schedule of testing.
2. Explain to younger students in a low-pressure manner how their work will be evaluated.

Set reasonable standards.

Examples
1. Discuss workload and grading standards with more experienced teachers.
2. Give a few formative tests to get a sense of your students' range of abilities before you give a graded test.
3. Take tests yourself first to gauge the difficulty of the test and to estimate the time your students will need.

Base your grades on as much objective evidence as possible.

Examples
1. Plan in advance how and when you will test.
2. Keep a portfolio of student work. This may be useful in student or parent conferences.

Be sure students understand test directions.

Examples
1. Outline the directions on the board.
2. Ask several students to explain the directions.
3. Go over a sample question first.

Ask clear questions that focus on the important material covered in class.

Examples
1. Check your questions to see if they have too many and's, or's, or in addition's.
2. Stay close to your test plan in which the key course objectives are outlined.

Student Conferences   Every subject area can allow time for teachers to observe students at work and interacting with one another. With a little reorganization, it should also be possible to use some class time as "conference time" when the teacher sees students individually. It is common in elementary schools for teachers to assign marks or make comments concerning each student's nonacademic achievement. Enthusiasm, ability to work with others, conformity to classroom rules, self-confidence, and other aspects of social and motivational behavior may be included in the report. Some secondary schools also report this type of information to parents.

Conferences and careful observation of students in a somewhat structured way can make such judgments more accurate and valuable, subjective though they will continue to be. Observing particular students in a planned

Watch for cheating during tests.

Examples
1. *Walk around the room.*
2. *Be firm but reasonable when you encounter cheating.*

Correct, return, and discuss test questions as soon as possible.

Examples
1. *Have students who wrote good answers read their responses for the class; make sure they are not the same students each time.*
2. *Discuss why wrong answers, especially popular wrong choices, are incorrect.*
3. *As soon as they finish a test, give students the answers to questions and the page numbers where answers are discussed in the text.*

As a rule, do not change a grade.

Examples
1. *Make sure you can defend the grade in the first place.*
2. *DO change any clerical or calculation errors.*

Guard against bias in grading.

Examples
1. *Ask students to put their names on the backs of their papers.*
2. *Use an objective point system or model papers when grading essays.*

Keep pupils informed of their standing in the class.

Examples
1. *Write the distribution of scores on the board after tests.*
2. *Schedule periodic conferences to go over work from previous weeks.*

Give students the benefit of the doubt. All measurement techniques involve error.

Examples
1. *Unless there is very good reason not to, give the higher grade in borderline cases.*
2. *If a large number of students miss the same question in the same way, revise the question for the future and consider throwing it out for that test.*

Adapted from A. M. Drayer (1979), Problems in middle and high school teaching: A handbook for student teachers and beginning teachers. *Boston: Allyn and Bacon, pp. 182–187.*

way, on some regular schedule, will keep you from being attentive only to the troublemakers and failing to notice the little boy in the back who missed the eye screening and is squinting at the blackboard.

Parent Conferences   Conferences with parents are often expected of teachers in elementary school and can be equally important in junior high and high school. At every level, the success of the conference depends on a number of factors. At the simplest level, both parties must be present. Schedule conferences at a time convenient for parents and confirm appointments in writing or by phone.

Clearly, the more skilled teachers are at communicating, the more effective they will be at conducting these conferences. Listening and problem-solving skills such as those discussed in Chapter 10 can be particularly important. Especially when dealing with parents or students who are angry or upset, make sure you really hear the *concerns* of the participants, and not just their words.

The conference should not be a time for lecturing parents or students. As the professional, the teacher needs to take a leadership role while remaining sensitive to the needs of the other participants. The atmosphere should be friendly and unrushed. Any observations about the student should be as factual as possible, based on observation or information from assignments. Information gained from a student or a parent alone should be kept confidential. Table 15–6 offers some helpful guidelines on planning and conducting conferences.

Privacy Act

An important ruling, the Buckley Amendment, is likely to have an effect on you as a teacher. Also called the Family Educational Rights and Privacy

Table 15–6 **Guidelines for a Successful Parent-Teacher Conference**

> **Plan ahead.**
> What are your goals?
> Problem solving?
> Sharing test results?
> Asking questions that you want answered?
> Providing information you want to share? Emphasize the positive. Be specific and describe behavior.
> Describing your "next steps" in the classroom?
> Making suggestions for use at home?
>
> **Begin with a positive statement.**
> "Howard has a great sense of humor."
> "Giselle really enjoys materials that deal with animals."
> "Sandy is sympathetic when somebody has a problem."
>
> **Listen actively.**
> Empathize with the parents.
> Accept their feelings: "You seem to feel frustrated when Lee doesn't listen."
>
> **Establish a partnership.**
> Ask parents to follow through on class goals at home: "If you ask to see the homework checklist and go over it at home with Iris, I'll review it and chart her progress at school."
>
> **Plan follow-up contacts.**
> Write notes or make phone calls to share successes.
> Keep parents informed *before* problems develop.
>
> **End with a positive statement.**
> "José has made several friends this year."
> "Courtney should be a big help in the social studies play that a group is developing."

Adapted from D. P. Fromberg & M. Driscoll (1985), The successsful classroom: Management strategies for regular and special education teachers. New York: Teachers College Press, p. 181.

Act of 1974 and the Educational Amendments Act of 1974, this law states that all educational agencies must make test results and any other information in students' records available to the students and/or their parents. If the records contain information students or parents believe is incorrect, they can challenge such entries and have the information removed if they win the challenge. This means that the information in a student's records must be based on firm, defensible evidence. Tests must be valid and reliable. Your grades must be justified by thorough testing and observation.

SUMMARY

1. Two very important and difficult tasks for teachers are testing students and assigning grades. Many schools have established policies about testing and grading practices, but individual teachers decide how these practices will be carried out.

2. In the classroom, tests may be formative (ungraded, diagnostic) or summative (graded, summarizing the student's learning).

3. Two common formats are the objective test and the essay test.

4. Objective tests, which can include multiple-choice, true-false, fill-in and/or matching items, should be written with specific guidelines in mind.

5. Writing and scoring essay questions require careful planning plus criteria to discourage bias in scoring.

6. Many factors besides quality of work can influence grades: the teacher's beliefs about the student's ability or effort, the student's handwriting or voice quality, the student's general classroom behavior, perhaps even the student's name.

7. The effects of grades on students depend in part on the students' attributions of their successes and failures, as well as on their grading history.

8. High grades tend to encourage continued effort and higher levels of aspiration; low grades tend to discourage effort and lead to lower levels of aspiration.

9. Students need experience in coping with failure, so standards must be high enough to encourage effort. Occasional failure, if appropriate feedback is provided, can be positive.

10. Grading can be either criterion- or norm-referenced.

11. Criterion-referenced report cards usually indicate how well each of several objectives has been met by the individual student.

12. One popular norm-referenced system is grading on the curve, based on a ranking of students in relation to the average performance level.

13. Tests and papers are often scored on a point system. Many schools use percentage grading systems, but the difficulty of the tests and the scoring criteria often influence the results. The difference between a B and a C may only be a matter of one or two points on paper, but the effect of the difference can be large for a student.

14. Two alternatives to traditional grading are the contract and mastery approaches.

15. No matter what system you use, you will have to decide whether you want to grade on effort, improvement, or some combination and whether you want to limit the number of good grades available.

16. Not every communication from the teacher needs to be tied to a grade. Communication with students and parents can be an important step in understanding students and creating effective instruction. Students and parents now have a legal right to see all the information in the students' records.

KEY TERMS formative measurement   criterion-referenced grading

pretest   norm-referenced grading

diagnostic test   grading on the curve

summative measurement   percentage grading

data-based instruction   contract system

objective testing   revise option

stem   mastery learning

distractors   individual learning expectation

holistic scoring   dual marking system

halo effect

SUGGESTIONS FOR FURTHER READING AND STUDY

BLOCK, J. J., & ANDERSON, L. W. (1975). *Mastery learning in classroom instruction.* New York: Macmillan. This is a volume in the Current Topics in the Classroom Series. Although very short (about 90 pages), it covers such topics as a philosophy of mastery learning, planning and constructing mastery units, preparing students to use the mastery approach, and assigning and reporting grades.

BLOOM, B. S., HASTINGS, J. T., & MADAUS, G. F. (Eds.). (1971). *Handbook on formative and summative evaluation of student learning.* New York: McGraw-Hill. An encyclopedia on the subject of creating classroom tests. There are chapters describing formative and summative classroom evaluation in almost every subject area.

CATTERMOLE, J., & ROBINSON, N. (1985). Effective home/school communication—From the parents' perspective. *Phi Delta Kappan, 67,* 48–50. This short article reports the results of a survey that asked parents how they usually learn about their children's schoolwork and how they would prefer to learn.

CLIFFORD, M. M. (1984). Thoughts on a theory of constructive failure. *Educational Psychologist, 19,* 108–120. This article discusses the potential value of failure for future learning and describes circumstances under which failure can be helpful or harmful.

CONNER, K., et al. (1985). Using formative testing at the classroom, school, and district levels. *Educational Leadership, 43,* 63–67. The seven authors explain how formative testing can improve learning for a classroom, a school, or a whole district and what has to be done to implement it.

GLASER, R. (1981). The future of testing: A research agenda for cognitive psychology and psychometrics. *American Psychologist, 36,* 923–936. Glaser shows the role of cognitive science in designing and interpreting tests.

GRONLUND, N. E. (1982). *Constructing achievement tests* (3rd ed.). Englewood Cliffs, NJ: Prentice-Hall. A complete guide to creating and scoring multiple-choice, essay, matching, true-false, and short-answer tests. An essential work for teachers who test, and that's everyone!

GRONLUND, N. E. (1973). *Preparing criterion-referenced tests for classroom instruction.* New York: Macmillan. The book is a very brief and understandable introduction to the principles and uses of criterion-referenced testing. There are chapters on mastery learning, developmental learning, test planning, writing test questions, and applications of criterion-referenced testing in many situations.

Teachers' Forum

Explaining Scores

You have used a norm-referenced system to grade a recent 50-item test. One of your students received a 35, considerably below the class average; on your scale his grade was a D. But both the student and his parents are upset and want to know why he got a D instead of a C—35 out of 50 is 70 percent, after all. What do you say to them?

Up to the Teacher

Explaining grades to a student is difficult; explaining grades to a parent can be nearly impossible. I would show the student and his parents the grade distribution for the test and the student's placement. . . . Unless the school has a clearly defined grading policy, grading is largely a matter of professional discretion. Both the parents and the student need to understand that it is the teacher who defines the parameters for the class, determines the scope and sequence of the content and activities, and selects the appropriate grading structure.

Jane C. Dusell, High School English Teacher
Medford Senior High School, Medford, Wisconsin

Showing the Evidence

I would show all the scores in the class—numbers only, without any names—to the parents and student. I would explain which scores are A's, B's, C's, and so on and point out that 35 right answers out of a possible 50 was just not an average grade or C on this particular test. I think the parents and student need to *see* the scores of the entire class. In this case, a picture is worth a thousand words.

Louise Harrold Melucci, Fourth-Grade Teacher
Greenwood School, Warwick, Rhode Island

Ideal Grading

If you could pick any way to grade your students or give feedback, what would you do?

Involving Students and Parents

I would use frequent individual student conferences as well as in-depth written progress reports. In both cases, students are made aware of the areas in which they are doing well and those in which they are having difficulty. A plan is developed between student and teacher to specify ways to improve. Parents receive a copy of the progress report and the improvement plan. Advantages include student involvement, especially in the designing of improvement plans, and parental notification in a more detailed form than just a letter grade.

Carol Gibbs, Sixth-Grade Teacher
Happy Valley School, Rossville, Georgia

Honesty and Fairness

I'm not sure there is an ideal grading system. Children are very sharp. They know how they are doing before we ever try to evaluate them. The best way to evaluate children is to be honest and fair with them.

In the primary grades, I evaluate children on their performance at their levels of ability and maturity. I let parents know that at this level (above, below, or at grade level), your child is doing this. This way, even the child who is performing below grade level can be acknowledged for effort and progress.

In the upper grades, you need a more sophisticated and formal grading system that the students understand. It must be one that does not defeat them before they start. Since we all have good days and bad days, perhaps we could give students an option of selecting five of their best pieces of work in a unit or eliminating the lowest grade on one or two out of five papers.

Carolyn R. Cook, Kindergarten Teacher
Ramona Elementary School, Ramona, California

Value of Written
Statements

Ideally, I would not use a formal grading system but would write comments about each student's progress. "Roger is doing a terrific job" seems to me to carry much more weight than an A, and written statements allow credit for poor students who are trying. These statements also let the teacher point out specific strengths and weaknesses.

Osborn Howes, Eighth-Grade English, Economics, and History Teacher
Hall School, Larkspur, California

We Learned That Already!

You are teaching basic skills to elementary students and using a criterion-referenced grading system. At the beginning of the year, you administer a test of skills that were part of last year's curriculum. Much to your distress, many of the students fail to meet the mastery criterion. You decide to go back and help them master the skills before starting on new material. After a few weeks, some of the parents begin complaining that their children have already learned the material and got A's and B's in it from their last teacher. What would your reaction be?

Listening,
Explaining, and
Encouraging
Involvement

First, I would listen sympathetically to their complaints and concerns, to ascertain that the stated complaint is indeed the problem. Then I would explain the concept of criterion referencing. I would emphasize that review is a confirmation of background: it gives the child a chance to be successful immediately, thus enhancing self-concept, and to approach new material with confidence. I would also emphasize that a child progresses at different rates; periods of rapid growth often alternate with periods of slower growth. Then I would point out that the review period is temporary. I would encourage active, ongoing parental participation in developing a supplemental enrichment program for use at home and in the community. Parents need to know that their input and participation are crucial in educating their children.

Laura Atkinson, Special Education Teacher
Chapel Hill, North Carolina

Evaluating Ourselves

Describe what you would regard as the most accurate, acceptable, and useful way to have your own teaching evaluated.

Working with
Administrators

Philosophically, I feel that good teaching is too subjective to measure. Pragmatically, when my teaching is evaluated, I prefer to use self-evaluation along with the input of an administrator. After assessing my students' needs and comparing them to my methods and materials, I develop personal goals for the year. These are shared with my principal. During periodic conferences, we review my progress toward these goals. At the end of the year, an evaluation of my teaching is easily rendered. This personalizes the evaluation process in a way that benefits both me and my children.

Arleen Wyatt, Third-Grade Teacher
Happy Valley School, Rossville, Georgia

EPILOGUE
Teaching and Learning in the Computer Age

Overview
Computer Literacy: What Is It?   560
The Origins and Basics of Computer-Based Education   561
Approaches and Availability   562
Components and Functions: Hardware   563
Putting Computers to Work in Today's Classrooms   564
Computers as Tutors: CBI and Its Software   565
Advantages of CBI   567
Limitations of CBI   569
What the Research Shows   570
Computers as Instructional Tools   571
Word Processing   571
Data Processing   571
Computer-Managed Instruction   572
Computers as Tutees: Programming   572
What the Future Holds   574
Summary/Key Terms
Suggestions for Further Reading and Study

"We stand at the beginning of a major revolution in the way people learn, a revolution that Eric Ashby called 'the fourth revolution.' . . . We are moving rapidly toward a future when computers will comprise the dominant delivery system in education for almost all age levels in most subject areas" (Bork, 1985).

Could this be an accurate prediction? Talmis, a research company, reported a total of 1,035,000 computers in schools as of June 1985. This was a 64 percent increase over 1984 and more than a 3000 percent increase over 1981. Over 91 percent of the schools in the United States are reported to be using computers (*Electronic Learning*, May/June 1986, p. 6).

That computer usage is rapidly increasing in schools is probably not surprising news. But you may be asking what implications computers will have for you as a future educator. Although computers have been put to many uses over the past three decades, it is only recently that they have had a significant impact on schools. This epilogue is intended to acquaint you with past and current developments, including the origin of computers, their features and operation, and their specific applications to education. We will pay special attention to microcomputers, the major force behind today's computer revolution. These small, relatively inexpensive systems make it possible for homes and schools to enter the computer age.

When you complete this epilogue you should be able to:

- Describe major events in the history of computer-based education.
- Distinguish the types of computer applications and systems used in education.
- List the types of software available for classroom use.
- Select appropriate hardware and software for computer-based education.
- Evaluate the strengths and limitations of computer-based lessons.
- Discuss issues concerning the teaching of programming.

COMPUTER LITERACY: WHAT IS IT?

computer literacy: knowledge of the computer's basic operations and its potential and limitations

Computer literacy, much like charity or generosity, is a concept that is easy to endorse but whose meaning is difficult for people to agree on. To some educators it means fluency in computer programming; to others it may mean an understanding of how computers operate, knowledge of applications, expertise at software selection and evaluation, or all of these skills combined. Why does computer literacy have so many different meanings? James Poirot (1986) has suggested that people define computer literacy on the basis of their own needs and experience. Thus, a third-grade art teacher may (and probably should) have a different conception of computer literacy than a tenth-grade math teacher, a district superintendent, or a school librarian. We will briefly examine some of the most popular views.

There are certainly points of agreement about computer literacy. A person does *not* need to know everything about the inner workings of computers to use them. How much do you know, for instance, about how a hand calculator works? What about a telephone? Gaining a general understanding about computer memory and basic operations should serve most educators' needs quite well. Teachers *should* know the potential advantages and limitations of different types of instructional and management software (Barger, 1984). And they should realize that computers are not intrinsically better teachers than humans or other media. Functions such as drill or record keeping are well suited to a computer's capabilities, but explaining a concept, motivating a class, or demonstrating a physical skill (ever see a computer do a handstand?) are not (Clark, 1983, 1985). Finally, computers are not effective by themselves. The quality of the software determines effectiveness.

Does Literacy Include Programming?

Do you have to learn to program a computer to be computer-literate? This is a very controversial issue. A growing number of experts appear to support the compromise position that some knowledge of programming is helpful (Barger, 1984; Bork, 1985; Anderson, Klassen, & Johnson, 1986). From this perspective, programming should be combined with other types of computer experiences to create a broader computer literacy.

THE ORIGINS AND BASICS OF COMPUTER–BASED EDUCATION

The history of educational computing parallels the rapid advancements in computer technology. A very early prototype was the Mark I computer, developed at Harvard in 1939. It was mostly a mechanical device, operated by extremely noisy relay switches. Then came the *first-generation computers,* which operated with vacuum tubes. Most prominent among this group was ENIAC (Electronic Numerical Integrator and Calculator), built at the University of Pennsylvania in 1947. Its cost was a ''mere'' $500,000 (1946 dollars!), and it occupied about 1,400 square feet.

microchip: a tiny piece of silicon on which electronic circuits are implanted

Technology improved steadily over the years. Vacuum tubes were replaced by transistors that reduced the bulk of computers by a factor of ten (Thompson, 1979) in the *second generation* of computers. In the 1960s, however, the development of the **microchip,** a one-quarter-square-inch piece of silicon on which thousands of electronic circuits could be implanted, sent these transistor-laden creatures the way of the dinosaur almost overnight. *Third-generation* computers were born. Microchips enabled transmissions of impulses (switchings) to take place in several nanoseconds (a nanosecond is one-thousand-millionth of a second) (Shane, 1982). Awe-inspiring figures, no doubt, but what does it all mean? The answer is cost efficiency, high power, and seemingly limitless possibilities for miniaturization. The *fourth-generation* descendant of ENIAC is a device that sells for a very small fraction of ENIAC's cost and has the bulk and weight of a typewriter.

The pioneers of the computer age were engineers, mathematicians, and physicists. Neither their inventions nor their interests were geared toward education. But the rapidly expanding computer industry needed to train new personnel quickly and efficiently. What better way to do this than by using the computers themselves? Thus, in the late 1950s members of the computer industry became some of the first users of computer-based education, or **CBE** (Suppes & Macken, 1978).

CBE: computer-based education

Interest in programmed instruction provided impetus for the involvement of educators soon thereafter (Burns & Bozeman, 1982). If you have read the section on programmed instruction in Chapter 5 and have had any previous exposure to CBE, you can appreciate how natural computers are for presenting programmed lessons. Throughout the 1960s many projects were initiated by corporations and universities to develop and evaluate such applications. By the late 1960s, numerous CBE systems were emerging all over the country.

microcomputers: small computer systems that use microchips

Still, only a very small proportion of children were receiving any exposure to computers. Was CBE available at your elementary school or high school? Probably not. The emergence of **microcomputers** changed all that.

Approaches and Availability

How is CBE made available in classrooms? Although various possibilities have been proposed (Bork, 1978), for simplicity we will restrict our analysis to two basic approaches—time sharing and stand-alone.

time-sharing system: system in which separate terminals are connected to one central computer

Time Sharing.   In a **time-sharing system,** students sit at separate terminals connected to a main computer through direct wiring, phone lines, or microwaves. The main computer may be in the same room as the terminals, in another room in the school, or many miles away. The terminal will typically contain a keyboard that receives student responses and a television-type screen (cathode ray tube, or CRT) that displays information from the computer. The terminal does not function as a computer, but only as a device for transmitting information.

The PLATO system provides an excellent example of time sharing. Operated by the Computer-Based Education Research Laboratory at the University of Illinois and Control Data Corporation, it has over 1,000 terminals connected to its main computer in Urbana, Illinois. Communication between the computer and the user terminal takes place by microwaves for nearby locations and over telephone lines for remote locations. Lessons appear on a special plasma panel that can produce animation as well as complex graphics. Teachers can write their own lessons in a special language called TUTOR. Users have access to any PLATO lesson stored in a central library and can communicate directly with any other user of the system.

stand-alone unit: computer that functions independently; microcomputers fit in this category

Stand-Alone.   The second major type of computer system is the **stand-alone unit.** Here each "terminal" is actually a computer, capable of storing and processing information. The most obvious example of a stand-alone unit is the conventional microcomputer. A student working with a microcomputer receives a lesson independently of all other students and of any other computer. But an individual microcomputer can also be made part of a time-sharing system by connecting it to a central computer. PLATO terminals have recently been developed that function in both stand-alone and time-sharing capacities.

Which is more effective? Each can be advantageous, depending on the circumstances. Time sharing offers the advantage of a coordinated system that centralizes storage of records and permits access to a library of programs. A disadvantage, however, is that when the main computer is not

downtime: period when central computer is not functioning

operating for some reason (this is called **downtime**), computer lessons are unavailable. Another consideration is that a time-sharing operation may be expensive; it requires special terminals and hookups to a large computer. Stand-alone units eliminate the downtime problem and may reduce expenses, but they sacrifice centralization.

Components and Functions: Hardware

Microcomputers, like people, come in many different shapes and sizes but share certain features. All microcomputers can receive, process, and transmit information. A typical microcomputer (Figure A) looks something like a typewriter that grew a television set where its "typing" head should be. The typewriter part, or keyboard, is the primary means through which the user transmits information to the computer. The part that looks like a television, the **monitor,** displays information from the computer. The heart of the computer, not visible in the diagram, is its central processing unit (CPU), made up of the microchips mentioned earlier. Using the computer's memory, the CPU coordinates the logical decisions and calculations requested by the user.

monitor: screen displaying information

hardware: computer's physical equipment

peripherals: accessories not performing basic computing functions

What we have been describing is **hardware**—the physical equipment that goes into a computer system. The items of hardware that do not perform the main computing functions are called **peripherals.** Two peripherals already introduced are the keyboard and monitor. Let's look at some others.

disk drive: device for storing information on and reading it from disks

disk: a storage medium; in operation, something like a combination of cassette and phonograph record

Disk Drive. If your only peripherals were a keyboard and monitor, you could send and receive information but would have no way of storing it. Whenever you wanted to use a program, you would have to enter it manually into the computer's memory. A **disk drive** is a device for storing information on, and reading it from, a plastic **disk** similar to a cassette tape. The disk drive can read, or *access*, any location on the disk instantaneously. It is a reliable, efficient, and almost essential peripheral for CBE functions.

Figure A **Microcomputers and Peripherals**

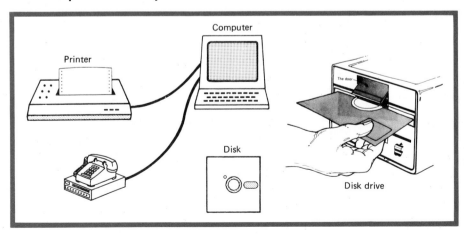

Printer. Displays on a monitor are only temporary; once a new one appears, what was previously on the screen can no longer be seen. Printers, like typewriters, print information on paper, providing a **hard copy.** Teachers can have a variety of materials printed as hard copies: student records, take-home exercises, letters and memos, and program lists.

Game Paddles and Joy Sticks.   Many computer games and some CAI lessons call for rapid, coordinated responses that cannot be achieved through the pressing of keys. A game paddle, a relatively inexpensive peripheral, makes such responding possible through manipulation of push buttons and circular dials. Joy sticks serve a similar function with a single lever.

Mouse. The mouse is a hand-held device that enables you to control the computer without having to type commands. By moving the mouse on a table, you can move the *cursor* (a special prompt indicating position) across the monitor screen to select different symbols that represent commands. This rapid and fluent type of control makes the mouse extremely effective for creating graphics.

modem: device permitting transfer of information from one computer to another over phone lines

Modem. The **modem,** which is essentially a telephone coupler, allows a microcomputer to be connected to a main computer or other microcomputers over regular phone lines. As a result, you can share information with someone thousands of miles away or access data sources such as the stock market, news wire services, and the Library of Congress.

For the most part, the essential peripherals are the keyboard, monitor, and disk drive. The cost of this basic setup is about $500 to $3,000, depending on size, capabilities, and manufacturer. By adding peripherals, you can build a more powerful and flexible system. Another factor in price (though it has become less important) is the size of the computer's memory, expressed in number of **kilobytes** or *K* (roughly, the capacity to store 1,000 characters). For simple home or educational applications, as little as 16K may suffice. Many commercial programs, however, require between 48K and 64K, and some more elaborate programs as much as 128K or more.

kilobytes: units able to store about 1,000 characters of text each

PUTTING COMPUTERS TO WORK IN TODAY'S CLASSROOMS

What part can computers play in education? Robert Taylor (1980) has envisioned three roles. The first is as a *tutor* that presents material, evaluates responses, and decides what to present next. The second role is as a *tool* that helps students and teachers perform calculations, analyze data, keep records, or write papers. The third role is as a *tutee* that is instructed what to do by the student or teacher through programming. The tutor role is the most traditional and is embodied in what is known as computer-based instruction. The other two roles represent newer ideas. In this section we will focus on the tutor role.

Computers as Tutors: CBI and Its Software

CBI: computer-based instruction

software: computer programs

Computer-based instruction, or **CBI,** is the direct application of the computer to teaching. The PLATO system, mentioned earlier, is an example. The computer, not a person or textbook, presents the lesson using **software** (programs that give it instructions). CBI is also known as computer-assisted learning (CAL), instructional application of computers (IAC), and computer-assisted instruction (CAI). Although CAI was once the most popular term, it is used less frequently now, probably because it has been associated with early teaching orientations that are less sophisticated than those available today (Siegal & Davis, 1986). At one time, only two categories of CBI—drill programs and tutorial programs—were recognized (Suppes & Morningstar, 1972). Now, new categories are being discussed in the literature. The following scheme—a mixture of the old and the new—should give you a solid background in the various forms of CBI. The instructional disk that accompanies this text has several examples of CBI.

Drill and Practice. This is the classic form of CBI. Drill-and-practice models do exactly what their name indicates—provide drill and practice in a selected subject. They are generally the easiest programs to write and are readily available. Examples include programs that ask students to solve multiplication problems, convert Fahrenheit temperatures to Celsius, spell words correctly, identify state capitals, and diagram sentences. In a typical drill-and-practice program, the initial difficulty level may be chosen by the teacher. When subsequent lessons begin, the computer checks its records (stored on a disk) of the student's final performance level during the previous session and begins at that point. An appropriate item is presented, and the student enters a response and is immediately informed whether that answer is correct. If so, the program continues with the next item; if not, an additional chance may be given. If the student fails to answer correctly after several tries, the correct answer will then be shown.

Examples of drill and practice are numerous; we can look at only a few. Typing Tutor (Microsoft) drills letter combinations and phrases for beginning typists. Milliken Math Series (Milliken Software) gives elementary students practice in basic mathematics skills. The Notable Names Matching Quizzes on the disk for this text are also examples.

Tutorial. In drill-and-practice programs, you receive both immediate and summary feedback on the accuracy of your responses but no information about *why* particular answers are correct or incorrect. In contrast, tutorial programs *are* instructional. They present information as a lecturer or tutor might do. Tutorials are also *interactive:* they solicit responses from a student and then decide what to do next. Depending upon the student's response, a tutorial might route the student to a remedial segment of the program, branch to the next lesson, or ask another question. A good tutorial should give students the feeling that they are actually involved in a dialogue with the author. Sometimes it is helpful to have intermittent testing to evaluate the student's understanding and reinforce a feeling of success.

The Interactive Element

Tutorials are more expensive and more difficult to write than drill-and-practice programs, but there is a definite payoff. Alfred Bork (1985), for example, translated a section of his introductory physics course into a tutorial for students. This meant he no longer had to function primarily as a lecturer; he was free for more one-on-one interaction with students having difficulty. Commercial software companies, such as PLATO, Conduit, MECC, and Broderbund, offer extensive tutorial material in virtually all school subjects.

Simulations. Simulations allow us to represent real or imaginary events that could not be brought into a classroom. As such, they constitute one of the most powerful and potentially valuable applications of educational computing. They are also relatively difficult to write, as you might imagine. There are several types (Alessi & Trollip, 1985). *Physical* and *procedural* simulations teach sequences of skills required for operating equipment or conducting scientific experiments. A classic illustration is Flight Simulator II (subLOGIC Corporation), in which the student becomes the pilot of a small airplane flying from New York to Los Angeles. Students can practice take-offs, landings, and other exercises without running the risk of hurting themselves or expensive equipment. In a *situational* simulation, the student may play different roles within a historical or fictitious context. For example, in Oregon Trail (Minnesota Educational Computing Consortium), the student is cast as a pioneer attempting to survive the trip from Missouri to Oregon in the 1800s. The "pioneer" must carefully plan the trip, determining what resources to purchase (food versus warm clothing, for example) and when and how to respond to accidents and dangers that might be encountered along the trail. In *process* simulations certain parameters (conditions) are defined by the student to simulate events or situations in the real world. In the ecology program Balance (Diversified Educational Enterprises), the student chooses the initial number of wolves and deer in the forest, the number of wolves shot annually by hunters, and so on. By running the program several times with different parameters, the student can readily see the effects of these variables on the population of the two species.

Two simulation programs are contained in the "applications" section of the supplementary disk for this text. Both allow you to "experience" a Piagetian interview (Chapter 2) and to classify the child's level of cognitive development without the need for real materials or an actual subject.

Instructional Games. Computer games are expressly designed to create a learning environment that is stimulating and enjoyable. One popular type is the Adventure Game, in which the player becomes the main character in a quest of some type, such as rescuing a princess who has been kidnapped, defeating an evil magician who is terrorizing a kingdom, finding a treasure hidden in a haunted house, or freeing oneself from captivity on a mysterious island. The value of these games is their emphasis on problem-solving skills and divergent thinking.

A second popular category is the *arcade-type* game of hand-eye coordination and perceptual judgment. A third is the *logic game*, such as Rocky's Boots (The Learning Company). Here young children must build "logic machines" based on the conjunctions *and, or,* and *nor*. The children construct "gates" that will accept some things (an *and* operation), such as red circles and orange squares, and exclude others (an *or* operation), such as blue or red squares.

Physical and Procedural Types

Situational Types

Process Types

Arcades and Logic

Advantages of CBI

What are the advantages of CBI over conventional teaching methods? There are several.

Self-Pacing.   It is an established fact in education that students learn at different rates. CBI is particularly well suited to accommodate these differences. The fast worker or high achiever can move through a CBI lesson rapidly and progress to the next lesson without having to wait for classmates to catch up. Students experiencing difficulty can move at a slower pace, reviewing troublesome sections and requesting additional practice until they have mastered the lesson. Lecture and recitation teaching methods, on the other hand, are group-paced:all students receive the instruction at the same time and at the same rate.

Drill and Practice.   Although most teachers would agree that "practice makes perfect," providing the right amount of practice for each individual is almost impossible. In this regard, the computer, with its nearly limitless patience and endurance, has an important advantage. It can drill a student as long as the student holds up. A spelling program, for example, can store hundreds of words on a disk and present different sets of words in different orders to all the individuals in a class. Using a *random-number function*, a math program may actually create new problems, as many as the student requests.

Personalization.   Like programmed instruction, CBI is designed to foster active student responding. Immediate feedback lets students know whether

Computers make learning fun for many youngsters in many different ways. The fun can be shared—the interactions involved in solving problems together can be educational as well. An additional consideration: in today's society, and probably even more in tomorrow's, a working knowledge of computers is a definite plus.
(Lawrence Migdale/ Photo Researchers)

their responses are correct or incorrect. Unlike programmed instruction, many CBI programs can also give other information about responses, along with such pertinent data as students' names and pretest scores. All this information can be stored and used to generate personalized messages and prescriptions. Based on prior learning history and current performances, one student may be branched to a remedial section of a program, another to a tutorial section, and a third to a drill-and-practice section. Further, within the drill section, the difficulty level and/or number of problems may be increased or decreased according to the learner's needs (Park & Tennyson, 1980; Ross, 1984; Tennyson & Rothen, 1977).

A Personalized Program

The potential of CBI to personalize instruction was recently demonstrated by Ross and associates in teaching elementary school mathematics (Anand & Ross, in press; Ross, McCormick, Krisak, & Anand, 1985). Lessons on dividing fractions were personalized for students by incorporating information about their friends, hobbies, and birthdays. A student could work a problem in which her best friends, Sally and Bob, divided her favorite food, pizza, among guests at her July 12th birthday party. These personalized lessons resulted in higher achievement and more favorable attitudes toward this math task than did work on conventional word problems.

Computer Learning Is Fun.   Computers seem to have an intrinsic appeal for children. Teachers often comment about students' increased enthusiasm for learning once they have a computer in their classroom. Several school districts, such as Hueneme School District in California, have reported increases in attendance among computer-using students (*Electronic Education,* April 1986). It's clear that if students want to go to school, they will learn more. Computers, in fact, are so appealing to many students that teachers have found them effective as incentives for completing other tasks. (Remember the Premack principle from Chapter 6?)

Interaction.   Thinkers from Socrates to Piaget have strongly emphasized the importance of active participation in the learning process. As Jerome Bruner has said, "Knowing is a process, not a product" (1966, p. 72). One of the computer's main advantages is its capacity to keep the learner constantly active, gathering information, determining solutions, making responses, and checking results.

Multisensory Presentations.   Picture the following scene. Billy, a second grader, is receiving a CBI lesson on sentence construction. A list of words is displayed on the monitor, from which he is to choose appropriate articles, nouns, and verbs and construct an English sentence. He types his entry: *The boy chases the ball.* Suddenly the screen flashes in all different colors, a buzzer sounds, and his sentence appears in large letters in the middle of the screen accompanied by the message "Good work, Billy, that is a proper sentence." The screen goes blank, and a few seconds later a little ball starts rolling across the screen with a boy chasing it; clicking sounds represent the boy's steps. The sentence has come alive! Computers can engage several senses and skills at once, using text, illustrations, movement, and sound. This kind of diversity not only reduces boredom but also provides alternative learning methods—another way into the material—for a particular skill such as reading text or interpreting pictures.

Simulating Real-Life Events. Certain skills are extremely difficult or prohibitively expensive to teach under realistic conditions. The vocational education instructor, for instance, might find his principal somewhat reluctant to approve a request to purchase a gasoline engine for each of his 20 students. Similarly, the physics teacher may detect an uneasiness among parents when she asks their permission to teach the principles of flight by giving the students rides in a glider she built. Actual experience may be the best teacher, but if that is not feasible, an excellent alternative can be working with a simulation or model. The computer's capabilities for graphics, animation, and user interaction make simulation a natural and highly valuable educational component (Dellow & Ross, 1982–1983).

Limitations of CBI

Given all these potentially positive benefits, we must balance the picture with a look at some of CBI's limitations.

Lack of Human Qualities. Feedback and encouragement from a computer hardly have the same meaning as they do when they come from a human being. All of us have been in situations in which desire for approval from meaningful others inspired our best performances and the greatest pride when we finished. Recognition from a teacher, a parent, or classmates can be an extremely powerful motivating force in children's lives. A positive message from a computer ("Nice going, Fred"), though appreciated, is delivered without the all-important ingredients of feeling and conviction.

Limited Sensitivity. Sensitivity is another human quality computers lack. Even with the most elaborate programming, CBI lacks the flexibility that teachers can provide in their interactions with students. A perceptive teacher can evaluate how a student is performing and feeling at a particular time and then decide on an appropriate course of action—discontinuing the lesson, varying the teaching method, providing reinforcement, or switching to another subject. The computer's repertoire, in contrast, is limited to the small domain of response options programmed into the lesson.

Restricted Text Display. Although computers can do wonderful things with graphics and sounds, many students find them awkward for reading text. A textbook contains a complete set of material in a relatively small, manageable package. Each page can contain a considerable amount of text, and you can hold the book at whatever distance is easiest for reading. In contrast, the computer's monitor presents a relatively small display. Going through different sections and reading the text is much more difficult than in a book. In short, computers make very costly and inefficient "page turners." Lessons that require extensive textual explanation are probably best presented exclusively or in part through printed manuals (Bork, 1985).

Simulations Are Not Reality. There are many skills that require practice in a realistic setting. CBI can do an excellent job teaching a child the rules of baseball, but it's a poor substitute for a coach and playing field for developing throwing, fielding, and batting skills. The same applies to playing the piano, giving a speech, using a dictionary, and driving a car. Computer simulations would hardly provide sufficient preparation for these activities. Would you trust the operation of a real nuclear reactor to the local champ on a nuclear reactor, simulator or fly with someone who has logged 2,000 hours on a flight simulator but only 3 hours in the air?

Software Limitations. CBI refers only to a *system* of teaching. As such, its effectiveness depends upon the quality of the software available. Software, no matter how it is acquired, often does not teach the subject in the manner desired. Low-quality or inappropriate software leads to ineffective CBI. And CBI is not valuable unless it supports specific curriculum objectives. Many teachers end up using CBI for much the same reason that George Leigh Mallory gave for climbing Mt. Everest—"Because it is there!" But using CBI just because it is available is a poor decision.

Hardware Limitations. Although unavailability of software is a serious problem, the real crisis today for many schools is a shortage of hardware to support CBI. With decreases in computer costs and higher budget priorities assigned to computer resources, the hardware issue is gradually becoming less of a problem. But for schools in poorer communities, computer-based education may still be only a promise for the distant future.

Logistical Problems. In addition to finances, there are other logistical problems in making CBI available to students. Where should the computers be located? Who gets to use them at what times? How should equipment be safeguarded? Similar decisions must be made with software.

What the Research Shows

As the use of CBI expands, its effectiveness relative to other methods is becoming an increasingly important consideration in educational policies. Numerous studies of CBI effectiveness have been performed. Let us briefly examine the main findings.

CBI at College

Kulik, Kulik, and Cohen (1980) analyzed findings from 59 independent studies of computer-based college teaching. They concluded that in comparison with conventional instruction, CBI (1) made small but significant contributions to course achievement; (2) produced slightly more favorable attitudes toward instruction and the subject matter; and (3) substantially reduced the amount of time needed for instruction. Comparable support for CBI has been obtained in many different teaching contexts, including military education (Orlansky & String, 1981), elementary schools (Kulik, Kulik, & Bangert-Drowns, 1981), and secondary schools (Kulik, Bangert, & Williams, 1983). The question of how instructors feel about CBI has received less attention, but where evaluations have been made, favorable attitudes generally seem to be the rule (Alderman, Appel, & Murphy, 1978; Hansen, Ross, & Bowman, 1978; Ragosta, Holland, & Jameson, 1982).

In interpreting these findings, remember that many variables that cannot be experimentally controlled influence learning in real life. For this reason, making valid comparisons of teaching methods is very difficult. Richard Clark (1983, 1984, 1985) has suggested that computers themselves do not influence learning. He has argued that the reported advantages of a medium like CBI over a medium like traditional instruction are really a function of the differences between the instructional methods or of the content taught, not a function of intrinsic properties of each medium per se. In much of the research done in this area, the establishment of CBI as a feasible method was the main concern. The CBI programs studied have thus tended to be programs that were carefully thought out and appropriately applied. Another factor to consider is the Hawthorne effect, discussed in the appendix to Chapter 1. CBI is new and exciting and traditional instruction is old and routine, and this may work to CBI's advantage.

CBI as Teacher's Complement

In light of all these considerations, CBI is most sensibly regarded as a resource for helping teachers, not as a replacement for them. The strengths and limitations of computers in educational roles *complement* those of human teachers. Teachers who are concerned about being replaced by computers are often the teachers with the least amount of computer exposure and experience. Teachers who have just worked with computers for the first time have generally characterized their experiences with computers very favorably.

COMPUTERS AS INSTRUCTIONAL TOOLS

In addition to their tutoring role, computers can also be valuable tools. This section will examine some of the common applications.

Word Processing

word processing: electronically creating and editing text on monitor

When is the last time you used a conventional typewriter that prints characters on paper as you press its keys? Maybe as recently as today. But before long you may need to visit a museum to see one. Word-processing software is the reason why. **Word processing** allows you to create and edit text electronically on the monitor screen. Text can be automatically realigned, margins set, and sentences moved around as you desire. The draft can then be run through an *on-line* dictionary program (on-line means individual items of data are directly accessible through the computer terminal) that will check the spelling of words and flag those that are incorrect. Research on word processing in schools suggests that children enjoy working with word processors and are more likely to edit and revise their writing when using them (Daiute, 1985). More research is needed, but few question the potential of word processors to revolutionize the teaching and practice of writing.

Data Processing

data processing: using computers to store, manipulate, and retrieve large amounts of information

data bases: data files

Data processing involves using computers to store, manipulate, and retrieve large quantities of information. The information is stored in and retrieved from data files called **data bases.** Library data bases, for example, allow users to search for a book by author, title, and subject, just as with conventional card catalogs, but more quickly and easily. Another example is Dialog, an information-retrieval source that stores more than 75 million records of information, including indexes for newspapers and periodicals, and about

200 data bases for subjects such as science, engineering, law, social science, and business (Friedlander, 1985; Solomon, 1986). Three others, The Source, CompuServe, and Knowledge Index are general information services that offer access to encyclopedias, news, and electronic mail.

Computer-Managed Instruction

CMI: computer-managed instruction

Computers can also be used as a management tool (this is called **CMI, computer-managed instruction**). Computerized grade books have become very popular in recent years. These programs help track student grades using the traditional grade-book format (names in rows, scores in columns) and have features for weighting grades, calculating averages and other statistics, and constructing graphs and charts. The supplementary disk for this text includes such a program, called The Gradebook, which you may use to enter, display, statistically summarize, and graph actual test scores and grades, as well as to compare the effects of different grading systems (see Chapter 15).

Another CMI tool can help with testing. Testing programs allow teachers to enter, edit, select, and print test items. This makes it easier to prepare new tests and to revise existing ones. After the test is given, student answers can be stored to provide summary information such as item difficulty and effectiveness and thus help teachers improve the quality of test items.

The success of CBE clearly depends on the quality of the materials selected. The Guidelines sum up our overview of computer resources with a checklist for selecting hardware and software that meet your needs.

COMPUTERS AS TUTEES: PROGRAMMING

Several rationales have been proposed for teaching computer programming in schools. First, students must be prepared to live in a computer-oriented society. Second, students who hope to pursue programming careers should be equipped with a good foundation. Finally, programming can help develop students' intellectual functioning (Coburn et al., 1985). Not all CBE experts would agree with these rationales, however. Let's look more closely at the role of programming.

Computer languages, like human languages, come in many different forms. Since the advent of microcomputers in the 1970s, the most popular language taught in schools has been **BASIC** (Beginner's All-Purpose Symbolic Instruction Code), developed in the late 1960s. BASIC is the language that is *resident* in most microcomputers, meaning that it is built-in to the computer's permanent memory and thus may be used without being loaded from a disk. Computer manufacturers selected BASIC over other languages for two reasons: (1) it has a reputation for being an easy language to learn (compared with earlier languages such as FORTRAN and COBOL), and (2) storing its instructions requires relatively little space in memory.

BASIC: programming language; acronym for Basic All-Purpose Symbolic Instruction Code

A newer language rapidly growing in popularity is **Pascal,** developed in the 1970s. Pascal was specifically designed to facilitate the construction of highly structured and readable programs. Accordingly, some experts believe that learning Pascal helps beginning students to develop good programming habits (Bork, 1985). Pascal, in fact, is the language used by the Educational

Pascal: programming language

Guidelines

A Checklist for Selecting Microcomputer Hardware and Software

Evaluate how well the available types and brands of hardware fit your needs.

Examples
1. Make sure that memory capacity is neither too small nor excessive.
2. Compare prices of different brands and of the same models sold by different vendors.
3. Be certain that appropriate software is easily accessible for the model purchased.
4. Check that appropriate peripherals, such as a disk drive, can be acquired if they are not standard features of the model.
5. Make sure servicing is readily available.
6. Ask different vendors to demonstrate their products at your school.
7. Observe CBE systems at other schools and talk to teachers about advantages and disadvantages of their brands and models.

Keep apprised of the latest quality software available in your teaching area.

Examples
1. Check catalogs sold in bookstores.
2. Check advertisements and reviews in computer magazines.
3. Talk with other teachers using CBE.
4. Keep a file of evaluations for software that you have used or that has been recommended.

Take advantage of any free software that is available.

Examples
1. Check computer magazines.
2. Join a local computer club.
3. Arrange trades with others who collect software.

Select software that supports your classroom needs.

Examples
1. CBI software should teach content that supports your instructional objectives.
2. Content should be taught in the same manner (for example, using the same terminology or formulas) as the textbook and other materials that you use.
3. Avoid software that performs meaningless tasks or tasks that are done more easily by conventional means (for example, balancing a checkbook).
4. Explore all types of software—word processors, data bases, testing programs, and grade books.

Bear in mind the attributes and potential of effective software, and evaluate programs accordingly.

Examples
1. Are screens neat and uncluttered?
2. Are long text explanations avoided?
3. Is the pacing controlled by the user?
4. How interactive is the program?
5. Is feedback appropriate—rewards for correct responses but no rewards or special emphasis (like humorous comments or novel displays) for errors?
6. Are the computer's capabilities for multisensory presentations fully exploited?
7. Is the program user-friendly—is it easy to use, with clear instructions?
8. Is it user-proof, so students cannot terminate a program by mistake or cause it to run incorrectly?

Testing Service in testing high school students on the Advanced Placement Exam in computer science.

A third popular language is **LOGO,** developed by Seymour Papert in the 1960s. LOGO is designed for young children and emphasizes discovery learning, imagery, and the meaningful use of mathematical concepts in solving problems. According to Papert, who studied with Piaget in Geneva, LOGO puts the child into "Mathland," where mathematics becomes a natural language for instructing the computer to draw and rotate geometric figures and other designs (1980). LOGO's distinguishing characteristic is its "turtle graphics" capability: figures of various shapes can be created by giving the "turtle" (a triangular prompt) special commands about how to move and turn on the screen.

Which language is most desirable for teaching children programming? Critics of BASIC, such as Papert (1980) and Bork (1985), argue that BASIC is too abstract and unstructured for children and leads to poor programming habits. Luehrmann (1986) has defended BASIC by emphasizing its popularity over the years and has argued that there is no one "right" computer language, just as there is no "right" human language. Indeed, at present there is no convincing evidence that one language is intrinsically superior to another or better for children to learn. It seems safe to predict that all three languages, BASIC, Pascal, and LOGO, will continue to be widely used over the next decade.

Programming and Intellectual Skills

Another controversial issue is whether learning to program improves cognitive abilities. Since logical thinking and systematic problem solving are such important skills in the writing of programs, the notion that better thinking skills might result from learning to write programs is quite appealing. Papert (1980) has claimed, for example, that as children learn to write LOGO programs, they expand their intellectual skills. Olson (1985) has suggested that since programming requires children to be very explicit, it may teach them to become more effective communicators. Unfortunately, research studies have failed to provide clear confirmation of these effects. In some instances learning a language such as BASIC or LOGO has proved beneficial on measures of thinking skills (Clements & Gullo, 1984; Soloway, Lockhhead, & Clement, 1982), but in other instances no benefits have been found (Gregg, 1978; Mayer, Dyck, & Vilberg, 1986; Pea & Kurland, 1983). Perhaps it is asking too much to expect a few weeks' training or even an entire course in programming to have noticeable effects on thinking habits that have developed over many years. But the present generation of elementary school students is receiving far more exposure to computer programming than any comparable group in the past. With such long-term and concentrated experience, any positive consequences of programming should eventually be clear.

WHAT THE FUTURE HOLDS

The only certainty about the future of educational computing is that computers and software will continue to change and improve rapidly. Faster and more powerful machines will certainly be developed, but cost and size are likely to remain fairly constant. Software will become more "intelligent" by imitating the way students think as they learn (Self, 1974; Suppes, 1984).

These systems, which are presently in their infancy, are referred to as Intelligent Computer-Assisted Instruction (ICAI). New and exciting computer-assisted devices will become available to meet the educational needs of physically, mentally, and emotionally handicapped students. We will see a great deal more of interactive video systems that combine CBI with audiovisual presentations (stored on disk or tape). And it is certain that educational computing will continue to expand in schools and training programs.

It no longer makes any sense to speculate about computers' fading away like other educational innovations of the past; CBE is definitely here to stay. Teachers will recognize that CBE can relieve them of the drudgery of routine tasks such as drill exercises, record keeping, and test preparation and scoring. As a result, they will have more time for tutoring, explaining, motivating, prescribing, and the many other activities that they, as human beings, do best.

SUMMARY

1. Computer literacy involves knowledge of basic principles of computer operations and of the potential, the advantages, and the limitations of different types of software. Some knowledge of programming may also play a part.

2. Starting with the development of ENIAC, the first general-purpose electronic computer, in 1946, advancements in computer technology took place rapidly. The microcomputer is a fourth-generation computer.

3. Interest in computer-based education (CBE) was spurred in part by the programmed-instruction movement in the late 1950s and early 1960s.

4. CBE can be made available through time-sharing systems, in which separate computer terminals transmit information to and from a central computer with a large library of programs, and through less costly stand-alone systems, in which the computers operate as self-sufficient units.

5. Microcomputers are inexpensive, portable, easily accessible, and extremely well equipped for CBE applications.

6. Essential microcomputer hardware (physical equipment) consists of the computing unit (CPU) itself and peripherals such as a keyboard and monitor for transmitting information. Other common peripherals are disk drives, printers, game paddles, modems, and "mice."

7. Computers in education have three potential roles: as tutors that present material and give feedback; as tools that assist teachers and students in tasks; and as tutees that are instructed (programmed) by students and teachers. The tutor role has been implemented in computer-based instruction, or CBI.

8. CBI software takes the common forms of drill-and-practice, tutorial, simulation, and game programs.

9. Computers can facilitate learning and teaching through self-pacing, infinite capacity to drill, personalization, motivation, interaction, multisensory presentations, and simulation of reality.

10. Limitations of computers include their lack of human qualities and their inability to provide meaningful support and encouragement; their lack of flexibility and creativity in making instructional decisions; their inappropriateness for presenting extensive amounts of text; the dependence on the quality of software available; the high cost of hardware; and logistical problems in maintaining computer resources within a school.

11. The research evidence, overall, generally supports CBI, indicating small to moderate achievement gains, considerable savings in course completion time, and more favorable student attitudes toward instruction.

12. The computer as a tool has been put to work in word-processing programs and data bases, and in computer-managed instruction (CMI) with grade-book and testing programs.

13. Using the computer as a tutee or student involves teaching programming. Currently popular programming languages include BASIC, LOGO, and Pascal. It is not clear whether one language is better than another or whether learning how to program actually improves thinking skills.

14. The future will bring more powerful and efficient machines, more "intelligent" software, more computer assistance for handicapped individuals, more interactive video, and a continued expansion of computer uses in schools. An educational resource with great potential, the computer is best viewed as a complement to the teacher.

KEY TERMS			
	computer literacy	hardware	word processing
	microchip	peripherals	data processing
	CBE	disk drive	data bases
	microcomputers	hard copy	CMI
	time-sharing system	modem	BASIC
	stand-alone unit	kilobytes	Pascal
	downtime	CBI	LOGO
	monitor	software	

SUGGESTIONS FOR FURTHER READING AND STUDY

ALESSI, S. M., & TROLLIP, S. R. (1985). *Computer-based instruction: Methods and development.* Englewood Cliffs, NJ: Prentice-Hall. A thorough explanation of the history and current status of CBI.

BORK, A. (1983). *Personal computers for education.* New York: Harper & Row. A very readable, brief introduction to CBI.

COBURN, P., KELMAN, P., ROBERTS, N., SNYDER, T. F. F., WATT, D. H., & WEINER, C. (1985). *Practical guide to computers in education.* Reading, MA: Addison-Wesley. A good introduction for beginners.

Electronic Education. A monthly computer magazine with software reviews.

Electronic Learning. Another useful computer magazine that reviews software.

LATHROP, A., & GOODSON, B. (1983). *Courseware in the classroom.* Reading, MA: Addison-Wesley. The emphasis here is on the selection and use of software.

PAPERT, S. (1980). *Mindstorms: Children, computers, and powerful ideas.* New York: Basic Books. A classic in the field by one of the real innovators.

WALKER, D. F., & HESS, R. D. (1984). *Instructional software: Principles and perspectives for design and use.* Belmont, CA: Wadsworth. Contains excellent criteria for evaluating hardware and software.

Glossary

Abstract A brief summary of the key procedures and results of a research study.

Accommodation In Piaget's theory, the alteration of existing cognitive structures (schemes) in response to new information. Accommodation is one of the processes of adaptation.

Accountability The notion that teachers should be held responsible (accountable) for what and how much students learn in school; also, the responsibility itself.

Achievement motivation Motivation for achievement in a field for its own sake rather than for extrinsic reward; the desire to excel.

Achievement tests Tests that measure how much a student has learned in a subject area.

Action zone The area in classrooms, arranged in rows and columns that includes the front row and the center columns. Students seated in this area tend to interact more with the teacher and to be higher achievers.

Activate To bring from long-term memory into working memory.

Active teaching Principles of instruction similar to direct instruction in which the teacher actively directs learning and carefully monitors students to make sure they are doing the work, much of which involves mastering basic skills.

Adaptation According to Piaget the tendency of all species to adjust to the environment. Two complementary processes are involved: accommodation and assimilation.

Adolescent egocentrism Assumption during adolescence that everyone else shares one's thoughts, feelings, and concerns.

Advance organizer In Ausubel's approach to teaching, an initial statement about subject matter that provides a structure for the information that follows, thereby making it easier to learn and remember. An organizer both introduces and sums up the material to be learned.

Affective domain In Bloom's taxonomy, emotional objectives.

Affective education Education that focuses on emotional growth.

Aggression Hostile behavior.

Algorithm Step-by-step procedure for solving a problem; a prescription for a solution.

Allocated time Time set aside for learning.

Antecedents Events that precede a behavior.

Anticipatory set An interested, receptive frame of mind in students.

Anxiety A feeling of general uneasiness and tension; a sense of foreboding.

Aptitude tests Tests that predict future performance. The SAT, for example, is designed to predict how well one would do in college.

Aptitude-treatment interaction The interaction between an individual student's capabilities and different teaching methods. As a result of this interaction, a particular teaching method may not be equally effective with all students.

Articulation disorder Any pronunciation difficulty, such as the substitution, distortion, or omission of sounds.

Assertive discipline An approach to classroom management developed by Canter and Canter that stresses the rights of teachers to teach and the rights of students to learn. Teachers respond to students in a clear, firm, unhostile way.

Assimilation In Piaget's theory, the fitting of new information into previously established cognitive structures (schemes). This is one of the processes of adaptation.

577

Attribution theories Cognitive views of motivation that emphasize the role of the individual's explanations for his or her own successes and failures.

Autonomy Independence. The conflict of autonomy v. shame and doubt marks Erikson's second stage of development, during which young children begin to explore their environment actively.

Aversive stimulus An unpleasant stimulus, one that a subject will work to avoid.

BASIC An acronym for Beginners All-purpose Symbolic Instruction Code, the most popular programming language for microcomputers.

Behavioral learning theories Theories that focus on observable behaviors instead of on internal events such as thinking and emotions.

Behavior-content matrix A teacher planning method for integrating objectives with course content. A matrix or chart is designed with desired student behaviors listed across the top and course content down the side. At each point of intersection of these two components the teacher can design specific instructional objectives.

Being needs Maslow's term for the three higher level needs in his hierarchy: intellectual achievement, aesthetic appreciation, and self-actualization.

Bimodal distribution A group of scores that has two modes—two different scores that tie for being the most frequently occurring score (mode).

Bottom-up processing Making sense of information by analyzing the basic elements and combining them to form larger units. For example, reading would involve analyzing and recognizing letters and words and then building meaning from these basics.

Brainstorming A strategy for developing creative thought. Ideas are generated but not evaluated until all possible suggestions have been made.

Branching program Programmed instruction materials that use a multiple-choice and multiple-sequence format. Each incorrect response directs students to various remediation frames that clarify the material and send students back to try again.

CBE Acronym for computer-based education—general applications of computers to classroom teaching and management.

CBI Acronym for computer-based instruction.

Central tendency A score that is typical or representative of a group of scores. The three measures of central tendency are mean, median, and mode.

Cerebral palsy Difficulty in movement and coordination resulting from brain damage prior to, during, or soon after birth.

Chunking Grouping individual bits of data into meaningful larger units. This allows us to "extend" the limited capacity of the short-term memory.

Classical conditioning A type of learning, first identified by Pavlov, in which a neutral stimulus is paired with a stimulus that elicits an emotional or physiological response. After repeated pairings, the previously neutral stimulus alone will elicit a similar response.

Classification Grouping objects into multiple categories. This is an important cognitive ability mastered in Piaget's concrete operational stage. It is linked to the ability to focus on one or more characteristics of objects at once.

Classroom management Maintaining a healthy learning environment, relatively free of behavior problems.

CMI An acronym for computer-managed instruction—the use of computers for testing, record keeping, scheduling, and so on.

Coding system An organizational framework that enhances understanding; a hierarchy of ideas. The more specific examples are placed under the broader concepts.

Cognitive development Gradual, orderly changes by which mental processes become more complex and sophisticated; the development of thinking and problem-solving abilities.

Cognitive domain In Bloom's taxonomy, memory and reasoning objectives.

Cognitive learning theories Theories that focus on internal mental processes like memory, abstract thinking, and problem solving. Cognitive theorists contend that learning is the result of each individual's attempts to make sense of the world.

Cognitive strategies In Gagné's hierarchy, strategies for retrieving, processing, and monitoring information. These are the most complex skills in the hierarchy.

Cognitive styles Different ways of perceiving and organizing information.

Collective monologue Form of speech in which children in a group talk but do not really interact or communicate.

Compensation A Piagetian term for the principle that changes in one dimension can be offset by the changes in another dimension. In order to solve conservation problems, one must understand this principle; this occurs during the concrete operational stage.

Components In an information processing view, basic problem-solving processes that underlie intelligence.

Computer literacy Knowledge of the computer's basic operation, potential, and limitations.

Concepts General categories of ideas, objects, people, or experiences, whose members share certain properties.

Concrete operations The third stage of Piaget's theory of cognitive development, during which children become able to think logically, but only about problems that can be visualized or considered in concrete terms.

Conditioned response (CR) In classical conditioning, a learned response made to a previously neutral stimulus. This response is acquired through repeated pairings of the neutral stimulus with an unconditioned stimulus.

Conditioned stimulus (CS) A previously neutral stimulus that is paired with an unconditioned stimulus and eventually produces a response when presented alone.

Confederate An assistant in an experiment who pretends to be a subject as part of the experimental manipulation.

Confidence interval The student's score plus and minus the standard error of measurement of the test.

Consequences Events that follow a behavior.

Conservation The concept that certain properties of an object (weight, length, etc.) remain the same regardless of changes in its other properties (shape, position, etc.). Conservation is mastered during Piaget's stage of concrete operations.

Contiguity A principle of learning stating that whenever two events occur together repeatedly they will become associated. Later, when only one of these events occurs (a stimulus), the other will be remembered too (a response). Also, the pairing itself.

Contingency contract A behavioral program in which teachers draw up individual contracts with students. The contracts outline specifically what the student must do to be rewarded and what the reward will be.

Continuous reinforcement A schedule in which every correct response is reinforced.

Contract system A grading system in which students agree to work for a particular grade by meeting agreed-upon standards.

Control group In an experiment, a group of subjects that receives no special treatment and serves as a basis for comparison.

Convergent questions Questions that have only one correct answer.

Convergent thinking A more common type of thinking that results in one conventional solution or the single correct answer to a problem.

Correlation A statistical description of how closely two variables are related.

Creativity An individual's capacity to produce imaginative, original products or solutions to problems.

Criterion-referenced grading In this grading system the criteria for each grade are spelled out in advance and everyone has a chance to earn the highest possible grade.

Criterion-referenced testing Testing in which scores are compared to a set performance standard.

Crystallized intelligence The many abilities that are highly valued and taught by the culture (reading, making change, or balancing a checkbook). These abilities are not affected by aging.

Cueing Providing a stimulus that "sets up" a desired response.

Cultural pluralism Cultural diversity; the existence of many different cultures within a group; encouraging different cultures to maintain their distinctive qualities within the larger society.

Culture The values, beliefs, attitudes, and rules that define regional, ethnic, religious, or other groups.

Culture-fair/culture-free tests Tests designed to eliminate bias in favor of or against any cultural group.

Curriculum-based assessment Testing in which test items refer to a specific set of curriculum objectives; scoring is based on mastery of these objectives.

Data-based instruction Ongoing formative measurement that relies on daily probes to test mastery of specific skills.

Data bases Data files in a computer system.

Data processing Using computers to store, manipulate, and retrieve large amounts of information.

Decentration The ability to focus on more than one aspect of an object or situation at a time; mastered during Piaget's concrete operational stage.

Declarative knowledge Verbal information; knowledge of facts, concepts, and principles.

Decoding Translating the printed word into speech. Younger and poorer readers spend most of their mental energy on decoding.

Deficiency needs Maslow's term for the four lowest needs in his hierarchy: survival, safety, belonging, and self-esteem. When these needs are not met, motivation to satisfy them increases. Once met, however, motivation to satisfy them decreases.

Defining attributes   Features that are shared by the members of a category and that combine to characterize or define the category. These features are also referred to as distinctive features. For example, one defining attribute of the category *square* is four equal sides.

Dependent variable   In experiments, the variable that may change as a result of changes in the independent variable.

Development   The orderly changes that occur in an individual over time from conception to death.

Developmental crisis   In Erikson's theory, a specific conflict faced at each of eight developmental stages. The way each crisis is resolved affects the resolution of the next crisis.

Deviation IQ   A score determined by comparing the individual's performance on an intelligence test with the average performance for that age group. The average is usually set at 100.

Diagnostic tests   (1) Individually administered standardized tests used to identify specific learning problems. (2) Ungraded, nonstandardized formative tests given at a midpoint in instruction to determine students' areas of achievement and weakness.

Dialect   A rule-governed variation of a language spoken by a particular ethnic, social, or regional group.

Direct instruction   An instructional method that emphasizes the mastery of basic skills. This method is characterized by several basic themes: clear organization of content, student involvement, engaged time, a strong sense of direction, mastery of materials, and a pleasant, busy atmosphere.

Direct method   An approach to bilingual education in which the main goal is the development of the majority language; the student's primary language is not used as a medium of instruction.

Direct observation   A method for collecting information in which a researcher watches the individual or situation and records behavior without any intervention.

Discovery learning   Bruner's approach to teaching, in which students are exposed to specific examples and use these to discover general principles and relationships. Contrast with *expository teaching*.

Discrimination   In classical and operant conditioning, distinguishing between and responding differently to two similar stimuli.

Disk   A medium used for storing information apart from the computer's memory; in operation, something like a cross between a cassette and a phonograph record.

Disk drive   A device for storing information on and retrieving it from disks.

Distractors   The wrong answers among the alternatives in a multiple-choice question. They should be plausible in order to be chosen by students who have only a partial understanding of the subject.

Distributed practice   Practicing material to be remembered for brief periods of time. There are rest times in between practice times.

Divergent questions   Questions for which there are no single correct answers.

Divergent thinking   Imaginative problem solving; coming up with several different and unusual solutions to any single problem. This type of thought is often equated with creativity. Contrast with *convergent thinking*.

Down syndrome   Retardation caused by the presence of an extra chromosome.

Downtime   The time when a central computer is out of service for any reason.

Dual marking system   Assigning two grades—a letter reflecting achievement and a number (usually a subscript) indicating effort, attitude, and ability. The number qualifies the letter grade.

Education   A formal process through which society transmits its values, beliefs, knowledge, and symbolic systems to new members.

Educationally blind   Vision so limited that special teaching materials are necessary.

Educational psychology   A discipline concerned with understanding and improving the teaching and learning processes; it uses the theories and methods of psychology as well as its own unique theories and methods.

Egocentrism   Assumption that others experience the world the same way you do.

Eg-rule method   A teaching method that moves from specific examples to general rules or definitions.

Elaboration   Adding and extending meaning by connecting new information with knowledge already in long-term memory.

Empathetic listening   Hearing the intent and emotions behind what another says and then paraphrasing what you've heard. This can be a very useful approach in communicating with students.

Empathy   The ability to feel an emotion as it is experienced by another.

Engaged time   The time students spend actively learning.

Environment-behavior research Studies the effect of the physical classroom setting on the behavior and attitudes of students and teachers.

Epilepsy A general name given to a group of nervous diseases marked by spontaneous neuron firings in the brain that result in seizures (of varying degrees).

Episodic memory The part of long-term memory that holds information associated with particular times and places. Compare *semantic memory*.

Equilibration In Piaget's theory, searching for a balance between one's cognitive schemes and one's experiences or perceptions of the environment. This is the process by which actual changes in thinking take place.

Evaluation The inspection of all information available concerning the students, teacher, and educational program to ascertain the degree of change in the students and to make valid judgments concerning the educational program being used.

Experimentation A method of research in which investigators manipulate one or more variables (independent variables) and measure the effects of this manipulation on another set of variables (dependent variables).

Expository teaching Ausubel's approach to instruction, based on reception rather than discovery. Teachers present material in complete, organized form, moving from the broadest ideas to more specific concepts and examples. Use of advance organizers is an important feature.

Extinction The gradual disappearance of a learned response. In operant conditioning, this occurs when reinforcement is withheld. In classical conditioning, extinction will result when the conditioned stimulus is presented repeatedly without any longer being paired with the unconditioned stimulus.

Extrinsic motivation. Motivation created by external events or rewards outside the learning situation itself.

Faces of intellect In Guilford's theory, the three basic categories of thinking—operations (evaluation, convergent production, divergent production, memory, cognition), contents (figural, symbolic, semantic, behavioral), and products (units, classes, relations, systems, transformations, implications). We operate on a particular content to achieve a product. There are 120 separate intellectual abilities.

Feature analysis Recognizing examples of concepts by checking for distinctive features or characteristics that define the concept; recognizing new stimuli by identifying elements. For example, we recognize the letter *A* by checking for two lines meeting at approximately a 45 degree angle with a horizontal line going across about halfway down. This is the basic process involved in bottom-up processing.

Field-dependent A cognitive style in which patterns are perceived as wholes. Field-dependent people have trouble breaking down a pattern into component parts or focusing on only a single aspect of a situation.

Field-independent Cognitive style marked by the ability to focus on separate parts of a pattern. Field-independent people are good at analysis and organization.

Figure-ground A principle of Gestalt psychology that refers to the way individuals organize stimuli to create reality. According to this principle, people tend to focus on a basic figure so that it clearly stands out and the stimuli surrounding it become the background.

Finger spelling Communication system that "spells out" each letter of the alphabet with a hand position.

Fixed-interval schedule A reinforcement schedule in which a predetermined interval must occur between each reinforced response, regardless of the number of responses the subject makes.

Fixed-ratio schedule A schedule of reinforcement in which a predetermined, fixed number of responses must occur in between each reinforced response.

Fluid intelligence Basic thinking and problem-solving abilities that develop without formal education. These abilities decline with age. Contrast with *crystallized intelligence.*

Foreclosure According to Marcia, one of the alternatives, or identity statuses, available to adolescents going through Erikson's stage of identity v. role confusion. In identity foreclosure, the adolescent has accepted parental choices for life-style and career without really considering other options.

Formal operations Mental tasks involving abstract thinking and coordination of a number of variables. These tasks are mastered in Piaget's final stage of cognitive development. "Formal operations" sometimes refers to the stage itself.

Formative measurement Occurs before or during instruction for the purpose of guiding or forming educational plans.

Frames The small steps or units used in programmed instruction. Most of these steps contain some text and at least one question requiring a response from the students.

Frequency distribution   Record showing how many test scores fall into set groupings.

Functional fixedness   The inability to use things in a new way. This is one possible barrier to problem solving.

Generalization   In classical and operant conditioning, the process by which a response conditioned to one stimulus "spreads" to similar stimuli. The more similar the stimulus, the greater the chance for generalization.

Generativity   In Erikson's theory, a sense of concern for future generations, expressed by having children, by creativity, and/or by productively working toward a better world. Generativity is the positive outcome of Erikson's seventh developmental stage, generativity v. stagnation.

Gestalt   German word for pattern or whole.

Gestalt theory   Holds that people tend to organize their perceptions into patterns in order to make sense of the world around them.

Gifted students   Very bright, creative, and talented students.

Goal-directed actions   Deliberate actions toward a goal; one of the major cognitive accomplishments of Piaget's sensorimotor period.

Goal structure   Johnson and Johnson's term for the way in which students strive toward a goal in relation to others. There are three such structures: cooperative, competitive, and individualistic.

Grade-equivalent score   The measure of grade level based on a comparison with average scores from each grade. If your score on a test equals the average score for students who are halfway through the 11th grade, then your grade equivalent score would be 11.5 on that test. This score is so often misinterpreted that it should never be used.

Grading on the curve   Assigning grades so that they follow a normal curve, with an equal number of A's and F's, B's and D's, and the largest number of C's.

Group focus   A teacher's ability to keep as many students as possible involved in class activities.

Guided discovery   An adaptation of discovery learning in which the teacher provides some direction by asking leading questions and giving appropriate feedback.

Halo effect   The tendency to view particular aspects of a student's performance based on one's general impression of that student.

Hard copy   Computer data printed on paper.

Hardware   The physical equipment that goes into

a computer, consisting of mechanical, magnetic, electrical, and electronic devices.

Hawthorne effect   An influence that can occur in experiments when subjects know they are being studied and change their behavior as a result.

Heritability ratio   That proportion of a particular characteristic's variability that is due to genetic factors, assuming the individuals have experienced the same environmental conditions.

Heuristic   General strategy used in attempting to solve problems.

Higher-order interactions   Complex relationships between three or more variables in an experiment. These interactions make findings increasingly hard to interpret.

High-inference characteristics   Characteristics that are difficult to define objectively.

Histogram   A bar graph showing how many people achieved each score or set of scores on a test; more generally, the frequency of occurrence of each observation.

Holistic scoring   Evaluation of a piece of written work as a whole, without separate grades for individual elements.

Holophrases   Single words used during an early stage of language development to communicate a whole thought or complex idea, for example saying "Juice!" to communicate "My juice is gone and I want more!"

Humanistic psychology   The branch of psychology concerned with the total person and the fulfillment of the individual's positive potential.

Hyperactivity   Behavior disorder marked by atypical amounts of movement, restlessness, and inattentiveness.

Hypothesis   Prediction or assumption that forms the basis for an investigation or research study.

Identity   (1) In Piaget's theory, the principle that a person or object remains the same over time; children master this principle during the concrete operational stage. Conservation depends in part on an understanding of identity. (2) In broader psychological terms, a sense of self; the complex answer to the question, Who am I?

Identity achievement   According to Marcia, one of the alternatives during Erikson's identity v. role confusion stage. The adolescent has a strong sense of commitment to life choices, made after free and serious consideration of options.

Identity diffusion   According to Marcia, one of the four alternatives during Erikson's identity v. role confusion stage. The adolescent feels no clear sense of self, is uncertain what he or she wants, and remains uncommitted to any career or moral choices.

"I" message A clear, nonaccusatory statement describing how something affects you practically and emotionally. Gordon recommends that teachers send "I" messages to students in order to change problem behaviors. The approach frees students to change their behavior voluntarily.

Impulsive Cognitive style of responding quickly but often inaccurately.

Independent variable In experiments, this is the variable changed or treated to determine the effects of these changes on other variables being studied. See also *dependent variable*.

Individualized education program (IEP) An annually revised program written for the student by the teacher, parents, a qualified school official, and the student (whenever possible). This program should set forth goals, services, and teaching strategies for that student. The IEP was mandated by the Education for All Handicapped Children Act.

Individualized instruction Instruction that has been designed to meet the needs, interests, and abilities of the individual student.

Individual learning expectation A recomputable personal average score in a subject.

Inductive reasoning The formulation of general principles based on knowledge of specific examples and details.

Industry Eagerness to engage in productive work. Industry is the positive outcome of Erikson's fourth stage of development, industry v. inferiority.

Information processing The human mind's activity of taking in, storing, and using information; also, the cognitive model that relies on an analogy of the human mind to the computer to explain learning and memory.

Initiative Willingness to begin new activities and explore new directions. Initiative is the positive outcome of Erikson's third stage of development, initiative v. guilt.

Insight Sudden recognition of a solution to a problem.

Instructional objectives Clear and unambiguous descriptions of the goals or changes in the students the teacher wishes to observe as a result of instruction.

Integrity Sense of self-acceptance and fulfillment. This is the positive outcome of Erikson's final stage of development, integrity v. despair, reached in old age.

Intelligence The individual's current level of mental functioning (a product of inherited abilities and experiences); the ability or abilities to acquire, remember, retrieve, and use knowledge to solve problems and adapt to the world.

Intelligence quotient (IQ) A score determined by dividing the individual's mental age by chronological age and multiplying by 100. The formula is $IQ = MA/CA \times 100$.

Intermittent reinforcement A schedule in which correct responses are reinforced frequently, but not every time. This schedule is most effective in maintaining already acquired responses.

Intrinsic motivation An internal source of motivation such as curiosity or the desire to learn; motivation associated with activities that are their own reward.

Intuitive thinking According to Bruner, the ability to go beyond the information given and develop hypotheses based on sudden, dramatic perceptions; making imaginative leaps to workable solutions of a problem or complete understanding of a concept.

Keller Plan/PSI A system of individualized instruction that does not require any special materials or computers. This system uses many of the principles of programmed instruction (specific goals, small steps, immediate feedback, and self-pacing) and incorporates lectures, proctored testing, and tutoring. This plan is also referred to as the Personalized System of Instruction (PSI).

Keyword method A mnemonic device that links new words or concepts with similar-sounding cue words; often used in learning foreign-language vocabulary.

Kilobyte (K) A measure of the computer's memory capacity. Roughly speaking, a kilobyte is the capacity to store 1,000 characters.

Latchkey children Children without adult supervision for some part of the day; in most cases, these are children who return from school in the afternoon to an empty house.

Law of effect Thorndike's law of learning: any action that produces a satisfying state will be repeated in a similar situation.

Laws Principles that have stood the test of time and repeated investigation.

Learned helplessness A sense that one is doomed to fail, based on past experiences, This sense can stifle motivation and prevent people from attempting new tasks.

Learning A relatively permanent change in an individual's capabilities as a result of experience or practice. These internal changes cannot be directly observed, so they must be inferred from changes in the individual's directly observable behaviors.

Least restrictive placement Placement of each child in the most normal educational situation that is possible, given the child's special problems and needs. Mandated by the Education for All Handicapped Children Act.

Level of aspiration The individual's goals for achievement, often a compromise between ideal desires and the fear of failure.

Levels of processing theory A theory of memory stating that the *depth* of processing of information determines how well we will remember that information. Information processed superficially will not be remembered as well as information that is thoroughly processed and connected with existing knowledge. This theory was first proposed as an alternative to the multistore (short-term/long-term) model of memory.

Linear programs A type of programmed instruction materials advocated by Skinner. Linear programs have two important features: (1) students must actively create an answer as opposed to choosing one from a multiple-choice format; and (2) frames are designed to keep the amount of errors at a minimum.

Linguistic comprehension Understanding the meaning of individual sentences in a text.

Loci method A peg-type mnemonic in which items to be memorized are associated with specific places. For recall, the places serve as cues for the items.

Locus of control Perception of "where" the responsibility for one's successes and failures lies—either within oneself or outside of oneself. Usually discussed with attribution theories of motivation.

LOGO Computer programming language designed for young children and emphasizing imagery, discovery learning, and manipulation of mathematical concepts in problem solving.

Longitudinal study A research study of the same subjects over several years to observe changes that take place across time.

Long-term memory An apparently permanent and for practical purposes unlimited memory store.

Low vision Some useful vision within a few feet but limited distance vision.

Mainstreaming The movement of students with special learning needs out of special education classes and into regular classes.

Massed practice Studying material for a single extended period of time.

Mastery learning An approach to teaching and grading that focuses on achieving specific objectives. It is based on the assumption that every student is capable of achieving most of the course objectives if given enough time and the proper instruction.

Maturation Genetically programmed changes that occur naturally and spontaneously. These changes proceed regardless of outside influences.

Mean The arithmetical average of a group of scores. This is the most commonly used measure of central tendency.

Meaningful verbal learning Verbal information, ideas, and relationships among ideas.

Means-ends analysis Problem-solving strategy (heuristic) in which the final goal is subdivided into intermediate goals.

Measurement Numerical description of an object, event, characteristic, or performance; evaluation expressed in quantitative terms.

Median The central score of a distribution; the score that divides the distribution into two equal subgroups. This is the second most common measure of central tendency. Compare *mean* and *mode*.

Mental age A concept used in intelligence testing. Mental age is a derived score based on the assigned age level of the items completed correctly by the test taker.

Mental retardation Significantly below average intellectual functioning accompanied by poor behavioral adaptation, both of which are evident before age 18.

Metacognition Knowledge about and monitoring of our own cognitive processes such as thinking, learning, and remembering. You use metacognitive abilities, for example, to recognize when one strategy is not working and a new approach is called for.

Metacommunication An underlying or hidden message of a communication. Although this may not be the message the speaker intended to send, it may be the message that is received.

Metalinguistic awareness Knowledge about language; understanding of the rules and exceptions of language usage.

Microchip A tiny piece of silicon on which electronic computer circuits are implanted.

Microcomputers Small, self-contained computers (about the size of a television or even smaller) that have large capacities, made possible by the invention of the microchip.

Minimum competency testing A system that requires students to pass a test of basic information or skills before they can graduate or continue to the next level.

Mnemonics The art of memory; also techniques for remembering. The purpose of mnemonics is to connect new information with previously existing knowledge. Mnemonics strategies are most useful when the information to be learned has very little inherent meaning.

Mode The score that occurs most often in a distribution. This is one of three measures of central tendency. See also *mean* and *median.*

Modem A device permitting the transfer of information from one computer to another over telephone lines.

Monitor A video display unit, which uses a cathode ray tube (CRT) to generate characters. It resembles a regular TV set but has a higher degree of resolution (greater clarity).

Moral dilemmas Hypothetical situations in which the "correct" or "moral" course of action is unclear. Used by Kohlberg to determine stages of moral reasoning.

Moratorium Identity crisis. According to Marcia, a moratorium involves an active struggle during adolescence to shape an identity. According to Erikson, a moratorium is a probably healthy delay in an adolescent's commitment to career and life choices. A moratorium occurs during Erikson's stage of identity v. role confusion.

Motivation The general process by which behavior is initiated and directed toward a goal; also, the factors involved in so energizing and directing behavior.

Movement management According to Kounin, a teacher's ability to keep lessons and groups moving smoothly.

Multicultural education Educational goals and methods that teach students the value of cultural diversity.

Native-language approach An approach to bilingual education in which teachers work with the student's native language and gradually teach the majority language.

Need Deficiency or requirement; what an individual requires for his overall well-being.

Negative reinforcement The strengthening of a behavior by the removal of an aversive stimulus. For example, a child is allowed to come out of the corner when he or she is quiet.

Neobehavorists A group of behavioral psychologists who have expanded their view of learning to incorporate changes in certain internal, unobservable states such as expectations, beliefs, thoughts, etc.

Normal distribution A bell-shaped distribution. In a normal curve, scores are distributed symmetrically about the mean, and the mean, median, and mode are all the same.

Norming sample A large sample of people as similar as possible to the students who will be taking a particular standardized test. The norming sample serves as a comparison group for scoring the tests.

Norm-referenced grading This system reflects a student's standing in comparison with others in the class; few students can earn the highest possible grade in this system.

Norm-referenced testing Tests in which scores are determined by a comparison to the performances of other people who have taken the test.

Objective testing Testing that uses multiple choice, fill-in, true-false, matching, or short-answer items. Knowledge, comprehension, application, and analysis objectives are best measured through the use of objective tests. Scoring does not require interpretation.

Object permanence Piaget's term for the understanding that an object exists in the environment apart from one's perception of it and action on it. Children make this important cognitive step during the sensorimotor stage of development.

Observation A research method in which investigators watch and record behaviors without any intervention.

Observational learning Learning by observing and imitating others. The consequences of others' actions are also influential.

One-way logic The ability of preoperational children to think through an operation logically in only one direction. Children at this stage are unable to reverse the direction of the operation.

Operant conditioning A type of learning in which voluntary behaviors are strengthened or weakened depending upon their consequences or antecedents.

Operants A Skinnerian term for behaviors that are not simple responses to stimuli but rather are deliberate actions made on the environment. According to Skinner, these operants are affected by their consequences (or antecedents).

Operationalize To make measurable, by making specific; to define objectives in specific terms so that they can be more easily observed and measured.

Operations Actions carried out through logical mental processes rather than through physical manipulations.

Organization Piaget's term for the ongoing process of arranging information and experience into meaningful patterns and structures (schemes).

Origins De Charms's term for individuals who

take responsibility for setting and reaching their own goals.

Orthopedic devices Devices such as braces, crutches, wheelchairs, and so on used by the physically handicapped.

Overgeneralization In learning language, children may use one word for many similar objects, for example, calling all four-legged animals "dogs." In concept learning, overgeneralization means inclusion of nonmembers of a category.

Overlapping A teacher's ability to supervise and keep track of several activities simultaneously.

Overlearning Practicing a task until it is learned perfectly. At this point practice no longer leads to improvement. The skill is resistant to forgetting and is easily retrieved when needed.

Overregularization In learning language, children may learn a rule and apply it to all situations, even when the result is incorrect, for example, adding *ed* to all words to express past tense (*breaked, comed, gived*).

Participation structures Rules defining how to participate in different activities.

Part learning Breaking down a list of items to be learned into smaller segments. This concentration on a limited number of items is useful because only a few items can enter long-term storage at one time.

Pascal A popular computer programming language.

Pawns De Charms's term for individuals who feel powerless and think they have no control over their fate.

Peer rating A method for collecting information about students by asking their classmates to make judgments, rankings, ratings, or other evaluations.

Pegword method A peg-type mnemonic in which the items of a list to be learned are associated with cue words (pegwords) and images.

Percentage grading Converting performance on class work to a percentage and then assigning grades based on a predetermined cutoff point. For example, 93 to 100 percent is an A, 84 to 92 percent is a B, and so on.

Percentile rank A comparison of an individual's raw score with the raw scores of the norming sample. This comparison tells the test taker the percentage of students in the norming sample whose scores fall at or below his or her own score.

Perception Interpretation of sensory information.

Peripherals Accessory devices for computers, such as printers and modems, that do not perform the primary computing functions.

Personal development Changes in an individual's personality over time.

Physical development Orderly changes in bodily functions and structure that occur over time.

Polygenetic Influenced by more than one set of genes. Many human traits, from height to intelligence, are polygenetic.

Positive practice A method of correcting students by having them practice the correct response several times immediately after making an error.

Positive reinforcement The strengthening of a behavior by the presentation of a desired stimulus or reward after the behavior. Some examples are food, physical contact, and social praise.

Prägnanz A basic principle of the Gestalt theory of perception, stating that we make sense of what we perceive by reorganizing it to be simpler, more complete, and more regular. In other words, we try to make what we experience fit a category we already know.

Premack principle A principle developed by David Premack, stating that a high-frequency behavior (or preferred activity) may act as reinforcement for a low-frequency behavior (or less-preferred activity). In the application of this principle the low-frequency behavior should come first.

Preoperational Before the development and mastery of logical operations. The preoperational stage is the second stage in Piaget's theory of cognitive development.

Presentation punishment The presentation of an aversive stimulus that decreases or suppresses the behavior that produced it. Examples: spanking, reprimands, running laps.

Pretest A formative test given before instruction to determine what the students already know and what they are ready to learn.

Principle A relationship between two or more factors that has been established through repeated study and experimentation.

Proactive interference An explanation of forgetting in long-term memory: old information interferes with new information. Compare *retroactive interference.*

Problem solving Creating new solutions to novel problems rather than simply applying previously learned rules.

Procedural knowledge Knowing how to do something; knowledge of strategies; application and manipulation of declarative knowledge.

Procedures Systems for dealing with routine and predictable tasks in the classroom, such as handing out papers or correcting homework.

Programmed instruction A set of instructional materials that students can use to teach themselves about a particular topic. This instructional approach features self-pacing, immediate feedback, and division of materials into small units (frames).

Propositional network Set of interconnected units of knowledge called propositions; one of the structures in which long-term knowledge is held. A proposition is the smallest unit of information that can be judged true or false.

Prototype The best representative of a particular category.

Psychology The study of human behavior, mental processes, development, and learning.

Psychomotor domains In Bloom's taxonomy, physical ability objectives.

Psychosocial Describes the relationship between the individual's needs and the social environment. Erikson's theory of development is a psychosocial one.

Punishment Anything that weakens or suppresses behavior.

Random Without a definite pattern or plan; following no rule.

Receptors The parts of the body that receive sensory information.

Reciprocal teaching A method based on modeling for teaching reading comprehension strategies.

Recitation A specific teaching format in which the teacher asks questions, students respond, and the teacher gives feedback by praising, correcting, or expanding student responses.

Reflective Cognitive style of responding slowly, carefully, and accurately.

Rehearse Repeated practice. Information can be retained in short-term memory by rehearsal.

Reinforcement Using consequences to strengthen behavior; also, any consequence that strengthens a behavior.

Reliability Consistency of test results in repeated administrations.

Removal punishment The removal of a pleasant or desired stimulus so that a behavior is decreased or suppressed. Examples: fines, loss of privileges.

Replication The process of repeating research to ensure that different experimenters will get the same results.

Reprimands Criticisms for misbehavior. When used as a method for stopping a problem behavior, soft private reprimands are much more effective than loud public reprimands.

Resource room A separate classroom in which a student can receive extra help in a problem area. A resource room is generally equipped with special materials and a specially trained teacher.

Response Any physiological or psychological change or process that results from stimulation; an observable reaction to a stimulus.

Response cost A behavioral method for decreasing undesirable behavior that involves the loss of a reinforcer as a result of the infraction of rules.

Response set Rigidity; tendency to continue responding in a familiar way, even when the situation requires a new response.

Resultant motivation The overall tendency of one's motivation; whichever is the overriding need—the need to achieve or the need to avoid failure.

Retroactive interference An explanation of forgetting in long-term memory: new information interferes with old. Compare *proactive interference*.

Reversible thinking In Piaget's theory, the mental ability to think back through an operation from the end to the beginning. This ability is necessary for solving conservation tasks.

Revise option The option to improve on work already completed in a contract grading system.

Ripple effect The "contagious" spreading of behaviors through imitation.

Rule-eg method A teaching method in which a general definition or rule is stated first and then particular examples of that rule are considered.

Rules Statements that specify essential expected and forbidden behaviors; classroom dos and don'ts. Setting clear, straightforward rules is an important aspect of classroom management.

Satiation One method used to stop a problem behavior: students are required to continue the behavior until they are tired of it. In using this approach teachers must take care not to give in before the students do.

Schemata (sing., schema) In cognitive learning, large, basic units for organizing information. Schemata serve as guides describing what to expect in a given situation, how elements should fit together, the usual relationships among elements, and so on. A schema is like a model or stereotype.

Schemes A Piagetian term for the cognitive frameworks or systems individuals use to organize experiences and perceptions of their environment. These basic cognitive units become increasingly complex with development. This term refers both to ideas and to motor patterns of behavior.

Seatwork That portion of students' schoolwork that is done independently. Seatwork often includes reading, drills, answering questions, completing work sheets, etc.

Self-actualization Maslow's term for the realization of personal potential; self-fulfillment.

Self-concept How people view themselves physically, emotionally, socially, and academically; all self-perceptions, taken together.

Self-efficacy An individual's belief about or perception of personal competence in a given situation.

Self-fulfilling prophecy A phenomenon in which believing or predicting that something will occur causes it to happen; also, the expectation itself.

Self-instruction A method for controlling your own behavior by reminding yourself of the sequence of steps to follow in completing a particular task. This approach has been especially helpful in training impulsive children to be more deliberate.

Self-management Setting one's own goals, monitoring one's progress, and reinforcing oneself. A teacher may help students develop self-management skills through programs that allow them to set their own goals, observe and keep records of their own work and progress, and evaluate their own performance.

Self-report A method for collecting information about a person in which the individual being studied responds to questions and provides data directly to the experimenter.

Semantic memory The part of long-term memory that holds general knowledge unconnected to time or place. Compare *episodic memory*.

Semantics Meanings; the ways meaning is organized in language.

Sensorimotor Involving the senses and motor activity. The sensorimotor stage is the earliest stage of development in Piaget's theory. It occurs during infancy (0-2 yrs.) and is marked by exploration of the environment through motor action and sense perception.

Sensory register A brief holding point for sensory information. During this brief period we select information for further processing.

Serial-position effect A phenomenon in which items at the beginning and end of a list are most easily remembered.

Seriation Arranging objects or events in sequential order along some dimension. This cognitive ability is mastered during Piaget's concrete operational stage.

Shaping A behavior management method for developing an appropriate behavior in which the teacher rewards responses that are suc-

cessively more similar to the ultimate desired response (successive approximations). In order to use this method, teachers must break down the desired complex behavior into a number of smaller steps.

Short-term memory Working memory; a memory store holding a limited amount of information for a relatively short period (approximately 20 seconds). After that, information will disappear unless rehearsed.

Sign language A system of hand signals and symbols that communicate words and concepts.

Skinner box A small experimental chamber designed by Skinner and equipped with a food tray and a bar (for rats) or a disc (for pigeons) connected to a food hopper.

Social cognition The process of understanding the thoughts, viewpoints, emotions, and intentions of other people; our conceptions of others.

Social cognitive theory A theoretical orientation in psychology that draws on both cognitive and behavioral perspectives; according to this theory we learn a great deal by observing others.

Social development Changes over time in the way an individual relates to other people and to society.

Social isolation The removal of a disruptive student from the classroom and from contact with others for about 5 to 10 minutes. Also called timeout from reinforcement.

Socioeconomic status (SES) A sociological term used to describe variations in wealth, power, background, and prestige of individuals in society; relative standing in society based on these factors.

Software The programs and accompanying documentation for use with computers.

Spasticity Involuntary contraction of muscles, characteristic of many forms of cerebral palsy.

Specific learning disability A problem with acquisition and use of language, which may show up as a difficulty with reading, writing, reasoning, or mathematical calculating. Learning disabilities are not related to level of intelligence.

Speech impairment An inability to produce effective speech sounds due to stuttering or difficulties in articulation, or voicing.

Speech reading Using visual cues to understand language. Lip reading is really a form of speech reading.

Stand-alone unit A computer unit that functions independently of other units. Microcomputers belong to this category.

Standard deviation A measure of how scores are spread around the mean.

Standard error of measurement A hypothetical estimate of how much an individual's score would vary if a test were given repeatedly. A reliable test should have a small standard error of measurement.

Standardized tests Tests that have been tried out with many students and revised based upon these trials. Standardized tests have standard administration and scoring procedures.

Standard scores Scores based on the standard deviation.

Stanine scores Whole-number scores from 1 to 9, each representing a wide range of raw scores. Stanine scores combine some of the properties of percentile ranks with some of the properties of standard scores.

Stem The question or problem part of a multiple-choice item.

Stimulus Any event in the environment that activates behavior.

Story grammars Typical structures or organizations for stories; basic plot schemata or models that allow one to predict what will happen and thus enhance understanding and memory of reading material.

Structure Bruner's term for the fundamental ideas, relationships, and patterns that make up a subject matter; basic framework of ideas.

Student Teams-Achievement Divisions (STAD) A cooperative learning system developed by Slavin that uses heterogeneous groups, elements of competition, and rewards to increase student motivation.

Stuttering A problem in speaking that involves repeating or prolonging sounds, thus interrupting the normal flow of speech.

Subjects The people or animals studied in a research project.

Subsumer Ausubel's term for the general concept that heads the coding system of a subject area. It is given this name because all other more specific concepts are subsumed under it.

Summative measurement Testing that occurs at the end of an instructional unit for the purpose of assessing students' final levels of achievement.

Sustaining expectation effect A phenomenon in which student performance is maintained at a certain level because the teacher does not recognize improvements.

Task analysis A system for breaking down a task into fundamental skills and subskills. The first step is to define the final performance goal and then list the skills necessary to attain that goal.

These skills are then broken down into subskills until a full picture is attained of all abilities (in proper sequence) necessary to achieve the ultimate goal.

Taxonomy A classification system. Bloom developed a taxonomy for educational objectives that consists of three domains: cognitive, affective, and psychomotor.

Teacher ratings A method for collecting information about students by asking teachers to make judgments, rankings, ratings, or other evaluations.

Telegraphic speech A stage in learning language when children use only essential words, as in a telegram—"Eric want cookie!"

Test A series of questions, exercises, or other tasks for measuring ability, skill, knowledge, performance, etc.

Theory An integration of all known principles, laws, and information pertaining to a specific area of study. This structure allows the investigator to offer explanations for related phenomena and create solutions to unique problems.

Time-sharing system A system in which separate computer terminals are connected to and dependent on a central computer for operation.

Tip-of-the-tongue phenomenon Sense of being about to recall something—as if the information you want were on the tip of your tongue.

Token reinforcement A behavioral program in which students can earn tokens both for good academic work and for classroom behavior. When a number of tokens have been accumulated, students may exchange them for toys, food, free time, privileges, or other desired rewards.

Top-down processing Making sense of information by inference; using context or general knowledge to recognize and understand individual elements. In reading, you use the sense of the story to recognize unfamiliar words and fill in meaning. The alternative is bottom-up processing.

Transfer A phenomenon in which something that was previously learned facilitates (*positive transfer*) or hinders (*negative transfer*) current learning; the influence of previously learned information on new situations or tasks.

True score The mean of all scores an individual would receive if the same test were taken an infinite number of times under ideal conditions. This is a theoretical concept never obtained in practice.

T score A standard score that converts the average raw score to 50 and uses a standard deviation of 10, so that the inconvenience of negative scores, as in z scores, is eliminated.

Unconditioned response (UR) In classical conditioning, an emotional or physiological response that occurs to a particular stimulus without the benefit of any previous learning; an innate response. For example, a loud buzzer will cause a startle response without any previous conditioning.

Unconditioned stimulus (US) In classical conditioning, any stimulus that automatically produces an emotional or physiological response without the benefit of any previous learning (an unconditioned response). For example, in Pavlov's experiments, meat produced the physiological response of salivation in the dogs.

Undergeneralization The exclusion of some true members from a category; limiting a concept; for example, excluding penguins and ostriches from the category of birds.

Validity The degree to which a test measures what it is intended to measure.

Variability The degree of difference or deviation from the mean.

Variable Any characteristic that can change or vary from one person or situation to the next. Age, sex, test scores, attitudes, and number of books read are examples of variables.

Variable-interval schedule A reinforcement schedule in which a predetermined time interval, which varies from trial to trial, must pass between each reinforced response.

Variable-ratio schedule A schedule of reinforcement in which a predetermined number of responses, which varies from trial to trial, must occur between each reinforced response.

Vocational interest tests Tests that are used to indicate the careers a student might be interested in. To determine interests, a student's responses are compared to the responses of adults in various vocations.

Voicing problem Inappropriate pitch, quality, loudness, or intonation.

Withitness According to Kounin, a teacher's awareness of everything that happens in the classroom and the ability to communicate this awareness.

Word processing The electronic creation and editing of text on a computer monitor.

Zone of proximal In Vygotsky's theory of cognitive development, the phase at which a child can master a task if given appropriate guidance and support.

z score A standard score that indicates how many standard deviations above or below the mean a raw score is.

References

ADAMS, A., CARNINE, D., & GERSTEN, R. (1982). Instructional strategies for studying content area texts in the intermediate grades. *Reading Research Quarterly, 18,* 27–53.

ADAMS, R. S., & BIDDLE, B. J. (1970). *Realities of teaching: Explorations with video tape.* New York: Holt, Rinehart & Winston.

AIKEN, W. M. (1942). *Story of the eight-year study.* New York: Harper.

AKIN, J. N. (1985). *Teacher Supply/Demand 1985.* Madison, WI: Association for School, College, and University Staffing.

ALDERMAN, D. L., APPEL, L. R., & MURPHY, R. T. (1978). PLATO and TICCIT: An evaluation of CAI in the community college. *Educational Technology, 18,* 40–45.

ALDERMAN, M. K. (1985). Achievement motivation and the preservice teacher. In M. Alderman & M. Cohen (Eds.), *Motivation theory and practice for preservice teachers* (pp. 37–49). Washington, DC: Eric Clearinghouse on Teacher Education.

ALDERMAN, D. L., & POWERS, D. E. (1980). The effects of special preparation on SAT-verbal scores. *American Educational Research Journal, 17,* 239–253.

ALESSI, S. M., & TROLLIP, S. R. (1985). *Computer-based instruction: Methods and development.* Englewood Cliffs, NJ: Prentice-Hall.

ALLINGTON, R. (1980). Teacher interruption behaviors during primary-grade oral reading. *Journal of Educational Psychology, 71,* 371–377.

ALWIN, D., & THORNTON, A. (1984). Family origins and schooling processes: Early versus late influence of parental characteristics. *American Sociological Review, 49,* 784–802.

AMERICAN ASSOCIATION OF COLLEGES FOR TEACHER EDUCATION. (1985). 1985 Report to the profession. *Briefs, 6*(6), 1–13.

AMERICAN EDUCATIONAL RESEARCH ASSOCIATION, Committee on the Criteria of Teaching Effectiveness. (1953). *Journal of Educational Research* (2nd Rep.), 46, 641–658.

AMERICAN PSYCHOLOGICAL ASSOCIATION. (1976). *Preliminary report of the commission on behavior modification: Case study issues raised by behavior modification in the schools.* Washington, DC: Author.

AMES, C. (1985). Attributions and cognition in motivation theory. In M. Alderman & M. Cohen (Eds.), *Motivation theory and practice for preservice teachers* (pp. 16–21). Wash-ington, DC: Eric Clearinghouse on Teacher Education.

AMES, R., & LAU, S. (1982). An attributional analy-sis of student help-seeking in academic set-tings. *Journal of Educational Psychology, 74,* 414–423.

ANAND, P., & ROSS, S. M. (in press). Using com-puter-assisted instruction to personalize math learning materials for elementary school chil-dren. *Journal of Educational Psychology.*

ANDERSON, J. R. (1980). *Cognitive psychology and its implications.* San Francisco: W. H. Freeman.

ANDERSON, J. R. (1985). *Cognitive psychology and its implications* (2nd ed.). San Francisco: W. H. Freeman.

ANDERSON, L. (1985). What are students doing when they do all that seatwork? In C. Fisher & D. Berliner (Eds.), *Perspectives on instructional time.* New York: Longman.

ANDERSON, L., EVERTSON, C. M., & BROPHY, J. E. (1979). An experimental study of effective teaching in first-grade reading groups. *Elemen-tary School Journal, 79,* 193–222.

ANDERSON, R. E., KLASSEN, D. L., & JOHNSON, D. C. (1986). In defense of a comprehensive view of computer literacy—A reply to Luehrmann. In T. R. Cannings & S. W. Brown (Eds.), *The information-age classroom: Using the computer as a tool.* Irvine, CA: Franklin, Beedle & Associates.

ARLIN, M. (1984). Time, equality, and mastery learning. *Review of Educational Research, 54,* 65–86.

ARMBRUSTER, B. B., & ANDERSON, T. H. (1981). Research synthesis on study skills. *Edu-cational Leadership, 39,* 154–156.

ARMBRUSTER, F. E. (1977, August 28). The more we spend, the less children learn. *The New York Times Magazine.*

ARMENTO, B. A. (1977). *Teacher verbal cognitive behaviors related to student achievement on a social science concept test.* Unpublished doc-toral dissertation, Indiana University.

ASHTON, P. T. (1978). Cross-cultural Piagetian research: An experimental perspective. *Har-vard Educational Review* (Reprint Series No. 13).

ASHTON-WARNER, S. (1963). *Teacher.* New York: Simon & Schuster.

ATKINSON, R. C. (1975). Mnemotechnics in sec-ond-language learning. *American Psycholog-ist, 30,* 821–828.

ATKINSON, R. C., & RAUGH, M. R. (1975). An application of the mnemonic keyword method to the acquisition of Russian vocabulary. *Jour-nal of Experimental Psychology: Human Learn-ing and Memory, 104,* 126–133.

AU, K. H. (1980). Participation structures in a read-ing lesson with Hawaiian children: Analysis of a culturally appropriate instructional event. *Anthropology and Education Quarterly, 11,* 91–115.

AU, K. H., & MASON, J. M. (1981). Social organi-zation factors in learning to read: The balance of rights hypothesis. *Reading Research Quar-terly, 17,* 115–152.

AUSUBEL, D. P. (1963). *The psychology of mean-ingful verbal learning.* New York: Grune and Stratton.

AUSUBEL, D. P. (1977). The facilitation of mean-ingful verbal meaning in the classroom. *Educa-tional Psychologist, 12,* 162–178.

AYLLON, T., & ROBERTS, M. D. (1974). Eliminat-ing discipline problems by strengthening aca-demic performance. *Journal of Applied Behavior Analysis, 7,* 71–76.

BABAD, E. Y., INBAR, J., & ROSENTHAL, R. (1982). Pygmalion, Galatea, and the Golem: Investigations of biased and unbiased teachers. *Journal of Educational Psychology, 74,* 459–474.

BACKMAN, M. (1972, Winter). Patterns of mental abilities: Ethnic, socioeconomic, and sex dif-ferences. *American Educational Research Jour-nal, 9*(1), 1–11.

BAKER, L., & BROWN, A. L. (1984). Metacognitive skills and reading. In P. D. Pearson, M. Kamil, R. Barr, & P. Mosenthal (Eds.), *Handbook of reading research* (pp. 353–394). New York: Longman. (a)

BAKER, L., & BROWN, A. (1984). Cognitive monitoring in reading. In J. Flood (Ed.), *Under-standing reading comprehension* (pp. 21–44). Newark, DE: International Reading Associa-tion. (b)

BALDWIN, J. D., & BALDWIN, J. I. (1986). *Behavioral principles in everyday life* (2nd ed.). Englewood Cliffs, NJ: Prentice-Hall.

BALL, S. (1977). A postscript: Thoughts toward an integrated approach to motivation. In S. Ball (Ed.), *Motivation in education.* New York: Academic Press.

BALLARD, K. D., & GLYNN, T. (1975). Behavioral self-management in story writing with elemen-

591

tary school children. *Journal of Applied Behavior Analysis, 8,* 387–398.

BANDURA, A. (1963). The role of imitation in personality development. *Journal of Nursery Education, 18,* 207–215.

BANDURA, A. (1971). *Social learning theory.* New York: General Learning Press.

BANDURA, A. (1973). *Aggression: A social learning analysis.* Englewood Cliffs, NJ: Prentice-Hall.

BANDURA, A. (1977). *Social learning theory.* Englewood Cliffs, NJ: Prentice-Hall.

BANDURA, A. (1978). The self-system in reciprocal determinism. *American Psychologist, 33,* 344–358.

BANDURA, A. (1986). *Social foundations of thought and action.* Englewood Cliffs, NJ: Prentice-Hall.

BANDURA, A., ROSS, D., & ROSS, S. A. (1963). Vicarious reinforcement and imitative learning. *Journal of Abnormal and Social Psychology, 67,* 601–607.

BANGERT, R., KULIK, J., & KULIK, C. (1983). Individualized systems of instruction in secondary schools. *Review of Educational Research, 53,* 143–158.

BARGER, R. (1984). Computer literacy: Toward a clearer definition. In J. H. Tashner (Ed.), *Computer literacy for teachers: Issues, questions and concerns.* Phoenix, AZ: The Oryx Press.

BARRON, F., & HARRINGTON, D. M. (1981). Creativity, intelligence, and personality. In M. Rosenzweig & L. W. Porter (Eds.), *Annual Review of Psychology.* Palo Alto, CA: Annual Reviews, Inc.

BARTLETT, F. C. (1932). Remembering: A study in experimental and social psychology. New York: Macmillan.

BARTON, E. J. (1981). Developing sharing: An analysis of modeling and other behavioral techniques. *Behavior Modification, 5,* 386–398.

BATTING NINE HUNDRED. (1986, May/June). *Electronic Learning,* p. 6.

BAUMRIND, D. (1973). The development of instrumental competence through socialization. In A. Pick (Ed.), *Minnesota symposium on child psychology* (Vol. 7). Minneapolis: University of Minnesota Press.

BECKER, W. C., ENGELMANN, S., & THOMAS, D. R. (1975). *Teaching 1: Classroom management.* Chicago: Science Research Associates.

BEE, H. (1981). *The developing child* (3rd ed.). New York: Harper and Row.

BEEZER, B. (1985). Reporting child abuse and neglect: Your responsibilities and your protections. *Phi Delta Kappan, 66,* 434–436.

BELL, R. Q. (1979). Parent, child, and reciprocal influences. *American Psychologist, 34,* 821–826.

BENBOW, C., & STANLEY, J. (1983). Differential course-taking hypothesis revisited. *American Educational Research Journal, 20,* 469–473.

BENBOW, C. P., & STANLEY, J. C. (1980). Sex differences in mathematical ability: Fact or artifact? *Science, 210,* 1262–1264.

BERGER, K. S. (1980). *The developing person.* New York: Worth.

BERGER, K. S. (1983). *The developing person through the life span.* New York: Worth.

BERLINER, D. (1983). Developing concepts of classroom environments: Some light on the *T* in studies of ATI. *Educational Psychologist, 18,* 1–13.

BERRUETA-CLEMENT, J. R., SCHWEINHART, L. J., BARNETT, W. S., EPSTEIN, A. S., & WEIKART, D. P. (1984). *Changed lives: The effects of the Perry Preschool Program on youths through age nineteen.* Ypsilanti, MI: High Scope Press.

BERSOFF, D. N. (1981). Testing and the law. *American Psychologist, 36,* 1046–1056.

BEYER, B. K. (1984). Improving thinking skills: Practical approaches. *Phi Delta Kappan, 65,* 556–560.

BEYER, B. K. (1985). Practical strategies for the direct teaching of thinking skills. In A. Costa (Ed.), *Developing minds: A resource book for teaching thinking* (pp. 145–150). Alexandria, VA: Association for Supervision and Curriculum Development.

BIGGE, J., & SIRVIS, B. (1982). Physical and multiple handicaps. In N. Haring (Ed.), *Exceptional children and youth.* Columbus, OH: Charles E. Merrill.

BIRNS, B. (1976). The emergence and socialization of sex differences in the earliest years. *Merrill-Palmer Quarterly, 22,* 229–254.

BLACKHAM, G., & SILBERMAN, A. (1979). *Modification of child and adolescent behavior* (3rd ed.). Belmont, CA: Wadsworth.

BLOCK, J. (1983). Differential premises arising from differential socialization of the sexes: Some conjectures. *Child Development, 54,* 1335–1354.

BLOOM, B. (1968). Learning for mastery. *Evaluation Comment,* 1(2). Los Angeles: University of California, Center for the Study of Evaluation of Instructional Programs.

BLOOM, B. (1973). Individual differences in achievement. In L. J. Rubin (Ed.), *Facts and feelings in the classroom.* New York: Viking.

BLOOM, B. S. (1976). *Human characteristics and school learning.* New York: McGraw-Hill.

BLOOM, B. S., ENGELHART, M. D., FROST, E. J., HILL, W. H., & KRATHWOHL, D. R. (1956). *Taxonomy of educational objectives. Handbook I: Cognitive domain.* New York: David McKay.

BLOOM, B. S., HASTINGS, J. T., & MADAUS, G. F. (1971). *Handbook on formative and summarized evaluation of student learning.* New York: McGraw-Hill.

BLOOM, R., & BOURDON, L. (1980). Types and frequencies of teachers' written instructional feedback. *Journal of Educational Research, 74,* 13–15.

BORK, A. (1978). Machines for computer-assisted learning. *Educational Technology, 18,* 17–20.

BORK, A. (1984). Computers in education today—and some possible futures. *Phi Delta Kappan, 66,* 239–243.

BORK, A., & FRANKLIN, S. (1979). Personal computers in learning. *Educational Technology, 19,* 7–12.

BORKOWSKI, J. G., JOHNSTON, M. B., & REID, M. K. (in press). Metacognition, motivation, and the transfer of control processes. In S. J. Ceci (Ed.), *Handbook of cognition: Social and neurological aspects of learning disabilities.* Hillsdale, NJ: Erlbaum.

BORNSTEIN, P. H. (1985). Self-instructional training: A commentary and state-of-the-art. *Journal of Applied Behavior Analysis, 18,* 69–72.

BOSTROM, R. N., VLANDIS, J. W., & ROSENBAUM, M. E. (1961). Grades as reinforcing contingencies and attitude change. *Journal of Education Psychology, 52,* 112–115.

BOURNE, L. E., DOMINOWSKI, R. L., LOFTUS, E. F., & HEALY, A. (1986). *Cognitive processes* (2nd ed.). Englewood Cliffs, NJ: Prentice-Hall.

BRANSFORD, J. D., STEIN, B. S., VYE, N. J., FRANKS, J. J., AUBLE, P. M., MEZYNSKI, K. J., & PERFETTO, G. A. (1982). Differences in approaches to learning: An overview. *Journal of Experimental Psychology: General, 111,* 390–398.

BRAUN, C. (1976). Teacher expectation: Sociopsychological dynamics. *Review of Educational Research, 46* (2), 185–212.

BRENNER, L. P., & AGEE, C. C. (1979). The symbiosis of PLATO and microcomputers. *Educational Technology, 19,* 45–52.

BRETHERTON, I. (1985). Attachment theory: Retrospect and prospect. In I. Bretherton & E. Walters (Eds.), Growing points of attachment theory and research. *Monographs of the Society for Research in Child Development, 50*(1–2, Serial No. 209).

BREWER, W. F. (1974). There is no convincing evidence for operant and classical conditioning in humans. In W. B. Weimer & D. S. Palermo (Eds.), *Cognition and symbolic processes.* Hillsdale, NJ: Erlbaum.

BRIDGEMAN, D. (1977, August). *Cooperative, interdependent learning and its enhancement of role-taking in fifth-grade students.* Paper presented at a meeting of the American Psychological Association, San Francisco.

BRODZINSKY, D. M. (1982). The relationship between cognitive style and cognitive development: A two-year longitudinal study. *Developmental Psychology, 18,* 617–626.

BROLYER, C. R., THORNDIKE, E. L., & WOODYARD, E. R. (1927). A second study of mental discipline in high school students. *Journal of Educational Psychology, 18,* 377–404.

BROMLEY, D. B. (1978). Natural language and the development of the self. In C. B. Keasey (Ed.), *Nebraska Symposium on Motivation, 1977.* Lincoln, NE: University of Nebraska Press.

BROPHY, J. (1973). Stability of teacher effectiveness. *American Educational Research Journal, 10,* 245–252.

BROPHY, J. E. (1976). Reflections on research in elementary schools. *Journal of Teacher Education, 27,* 31–34.

BROPHY, J. E. (1981). Teacher praise: A functional analysis. *Review of Educational Research, 51,* 5–21.

BROPHY, J. E. (1982, March). *Research on the self-fulfilling prophecy and teacher expectations.* Paper presented at the annual meeting of the American Educational Research Association, New York.

BROPHY, J. E., & EVERTSON, C. (1976). *Learning from teaching: A developmental perspective.* Boston: Allyn & Bacon.

BROPHY, J., & EVERTSON, C. (1978). Context variables in teaching. *Educational Psychologist, 12,* 310–316.

BROPHY, J., & GOOD, T. (1986). Teacher behavior and student achievement. In M. Wittrock (Ed.), *Handbook of research on teaching* (3rd ed., pp. 328–375). New York: Macmillan.

BROWN, A. L., BRANSFORD, J. D., FERRARA, R. A., & CAMPIONE, J. C. (1983). Learning, remembering, and understanding. In P. Mussen (Ed.), *Carmichael's manual of child psychology. Vol. 3: Cognitive development* (E. Markman & J. Flavell, Volume Eds.). New York: Wiley.

BROWN, A. L., CAMPIONE, J. C., & DAY, J. D. (1981). Learning to learn: On training students to learn from tests. *Educational Researcher, 9,* 14–21.

BROWN, A. L., & SMILEY, S. S. (1977). Rating the importance of structural units of prose passages: A problem of metacognitive development. *Child Development, 48,* 1–8.

BROWN, J. S., & BURTON, R. R. (1978). Diagnostic models for procedural bugs in basic mathematical skills. *Cognitive Science, 2,* 155–192.

BROWN, R. (1973). *A first language: The early stages.* Cambridge, MA: Harvard University Press.

BROWN, R., & HANLON, C. (1970). Derivational complexity and order of acquisition in child speech. In J. M. Hays (Ed.), *Cognition and the development of language*. New York: Wiley.

BROWN, R., & McNEILL, D. (1966). The "tip-of-the-tongue" phenomenon. *Journal of Verbal Learning and Verbal Behavior, 5,* 325–337.

BRUNER, J. S. (1960). *The process of education*. New York: Vintage Books.

BRUNER, J. S. (1966). *Toward a theory of instruction*. New York: Norton.

BRUNER, J. S. (1973). *Beyond the information given: Studies in the psychology of knowing*. New York: Norton.

BURBACH, H. J. (1981). The labeling process: A sociological analysis. In J. Kauffman & D. Hallahan (Eds.), *Handbook of special education*. Englewood Cliffs, NJ: Prentice-Hall.

BURTON, N. W., & JONES, L. V. (1982). Recent trends in achievement levels of black and white youth. *Educational Researcher, 11,* 10–14.

BURTON, R. V. (1963). The generality of honesty reconsidered. *Psychological Review, 70,* 481–499.

CAHEN, L. (1966). *An experimental manipulation of the halo effect*. Unpublished doctoral dissertation, Stanford University.

CALLAHAN, R. E. (1962). *Education and the cult of efficiency: A study of the social forces that have shaped the administration of the public schools*. Chicago: University of Chicago Press.

CAMPOS, J. J., BARRETT, K. C., LAMB, M. E., GOLDSMITH, H. H., & STERNBERG, C. (1983). Socioemotional development. In P. Mussen (Ed.), *Handbook of child development* (Vol. 2). New York: Wiley.

CANTER, L., & CANTER, M. (1976). *Assertive discipline: A take-charge approach for today's educator*. Los Angeles: Lee Canter and Associates.

CANTRELL, R. P., STENNER, A. J., & KATZENMEYER, W. G. (1977). Teacher knowledge, attitudes, and classroom teaching correlates of student achievement. *Journal of Educational Psychology, 69,* 180–190.

CARTER, K. (1984). Do teachers understand principles of writing tests? *Journal of Teacher Education, 35,* 57–60.

CARTWRIGHT, G. P., CARTWRIGHT, C. A., & WARD, M. E. (1981). *Educating special learners*. Belmont, CA: Wadsworth.

CASE, R. (1978). Piaget and beyond: Toward a developmentally-based theory and technology of instruction. In R. Glaser (Ed.), *Advances in instructional psychology* (Vol. 1). Hillsdale, NJ: Erlbaum. (a)

CASE, R. (1978). Developmentally-based theory and technology of instruction. *Review of Educational Research, 48,* 439–463. (b)

CASE, R. (1980). Intellectual development: A systematic reinterpretation. In F. Farley & N. J. Gordon (Eds.), *Psychology and education: The state of the union*. Berkeley, CA: McCutchan.

CASE, R. (1985). A developmentally-based approach to the problem of instructional design. In R. Glaser, S. Chipman, & J. Segal (Eds.), *Teaching thinking skills* (Vol. 2, pp. 545–562). Hillsdale, NJ: Erlbaum.

CATTELL, R. B. (1963). The fluid and crystallized intelligence: A critical experiment. *Journal of Educational Psychology, 54,* 1–22.

CAZDEN, C. B. (1968). Some implications of research on language development for preschool education. In R. Hess & R. Bear (Eds.), *Early education: Current theory, research and action*. Chicago: Aldine.

CHAPMAN, D. W., & HUTCHESON, S. M. (1982). Attrition from teaching careers: A discriminant analysis. *American Educational Research Journal, 19,* 93–106.

CHARLES, C. M. (1981). *Building classroom discipline: From models to practice*. New York: Longman.

CHARLES, C. M., & MALLIAN, I. M. (1980). *The special student: Practical help for the classroom teacher*. St. Louis: C. V. Mosby.

CHASE, C. I. (1978). *Measurement for educational evaluation* (2nd ed.). Reading, MA: Addison-Wesley.

CHOMSKY, N. (1965). *Aspects of a theory of syntax*. Cambridge, MA: M.I.T. Press.

CHRISTY, P. R. (1975). Does use of tangible rewards with individual children affect peer observers? *Journal of Applied Behavior Analysis, 8,* 187–196.

CLAIBORN, W. L. (1969). Expectancy effects in the classroom: A failure to replicate. *Journal of Education Psychology, 60,* 377–383.

CLAIRIZIO, H. F. (1971). *Toward positive classroom discipline*. New York: Wiley.

CLARK, C. M., GAGE, N. L., MARX, R. W., PETERSON, P. L., STAYBROOK, N. G., & WINNIE, P. H. (1979). A factorial experiment on teacher structuring, soliciting, and reacting. *Journal of Educational Psychology, 71,* 534–550.

CLARK, R. E. (1983). Reconsidering research on learning from media. *Review of Educational Research, 53,* 445–459.

CLARK, R. E. (1984). Research on student thought processes during computer-based instruction. *Journal of Instructional Development, 7,* 2–5.

CLARK, R. E. (1985). Evidence for confounding in computer-based instruction studies: Analyzing the meta-analyses. *Educational Communication and Technology Journal, 33,* 249–262.

CLARK-STEWART, K. A., & FEIN, G. G. (1983). Early childhood programs. In P. Mussen (Ed.), *Handbook of child development* (Vol. 2). New York: Wiley.

CLEMENT, S. L. (1978). Dual marking system: Simple and effective. *American Secondary Education, 8,* 49–52.

CLEMENTS, D. H., & GULLO, D. F. (1984). Effects of computer programming on young children's cognition. *Journal of Educational Psychology, 76,* 1051–1058.

CLIFFORD, M. M. (1979). Effects of failure: Alternative explanations and possible implications. *Educational Psychologist, 14,* 44–52.

CLIFFORD, M. M. (1984). Educational psychology. In *Encyclopedia of Education* (pp. 413–416). New York: Macmillan.

CLIFFORD, M. M. (1984). Thoughts on a theory of constructive failure. *Educational Psychologist, 19,* 108–120.

COATES, J. F. (1978). Population and education: How demographic trends will shape the U.S. *The Futurist, 12,* 35–42.

COATES, T. J., & THORESEN, C. E. (1979). Behavioral self-control and educational practice or do we really need self-control? In D. C. Berliner (Ed.), *Review of research in education*, (Vol. 7). Itasca, IL: F. E. Peacock.

COBBETT, W. (1824, November 20). *Political Register*, L11.

COBURN, P., KELMAN, P., ROBERTS, N., SNYDER, T. F. F., WATT, D. H., & WEINER, C. (1985). *Practical guide to computers in education*. Reading, MA: Addison-Wesley.

COHEN, M. (1985). Extrinsic and intrinsic motivation. In M. Alderman & M. Cohen (Eds.), *Motivation theory and practice for preservice teachers* (pp. 6–15). Washington, DC: Eric Clearinghouse on Teacher Education.

COLE, N. S. (1981). Bias in testing. *American Psychologist, 36,* 1067–1077.

COLEMAN, J. S., CAMPBELL, J., WOOD, A. M., WEINFELD, F. D., & YORK, R. L. (1966). *Equality of educational opportunity*. Washington, DC: United States Department of Health, Education and Welfare, Office of Education.

COLLINS, A., & SMITH, E. (1980). *Teaching the process of reading comprehension* (Tech. Rep. No. 182). Urbana-Champaign: University of Illinois, Center for the Study of Reading.

COLLINS, M. L. (1978). Effects of enthusiasm training on preservice elementary teachers. *Journal of Teacher Education, 24,* 53–57.

COOPER, H. (1979). Pygmalion grows up: A model for teacher expectation communication and performance influence. *Review of Educational Research, 49,* 389–410.

COOPER, H. M., & GOOD, T. (1983). *Pygmalion grows up: Studies in the expectation communication process*. New York: Longman.

COOPER, H. M., & TOM, D. H. (1984). Teacher expectation research: A review with implications for classroom instruction. *Elementary School Journal, 85,* 77–90.

COPI, I. M. (1961). *Introduction to logic*. New York: Macmillan.

CORNBLETH, C., DAVIS, O.L., JR., & BUTTON, C. (1974). Expectations for pupil achievement and teacher-pupil interaction. *Social Education, 38,* 54–58.

CORNO, L. (1980). Individual and class level effects of parent-assisted instruction in classroom memory support systems. *Journal of Educational Psychology, 72,* 278–292.

CORNO, L., & SNOW, R. E. (1986). Adapting teaching to individual differences in learners. In M. Wittrock (Ed.), *Handbook of research on teaching* (3rd ed.). New York: Macmillan.

COSTA, A. L. (Ed.). (1985). *Developing minds: A resource book for teaching thinking*. Alexandria, VA: Association for Supervision and Curriculum Development.

COSTELLO, J., & DICKIE, J. (1970). Leiter and Stanford-Binet IQ's of preschool disadvantaged children. *Psychological Reports, 28,* 755–760.

COVINGTON, M. (1984). Strategic thinking and the fear of failure. In J. Segal, S. Chipman, & R. Glaser (Eds.), *Thinking and learning skills: Relating instruction to basic research*. Hillsdale, NJ: Erlbaum.

COVINGTON, M. (1984). The self-worth theory of achievement motivation. *The Elementary School Journal, 85,* 5–20.

COVINGTON, M., & BEERY, R. (1976). *Self-worth and schooling*. New York: Holt, Rinehart & Winston.

COVINGTON, M., & OMELICH, C. (1979). It's best to be able and virtuous, too: Student and teacher evaluative responses to successful effort. *Journal of Educational Psychology, 71,* 688–700.

COX, C. C. (1926). The early mental traits of three hundred geniuses. In L. M. Terman (Ed.), *Genetic studies of genius* (Vol 2). Stanford, CA: Stanford University Press.

COX, W. F., & DUNN, T. G. (1979). Mastery learning: A psychological trap? *Educational Psychologist, 14,* 24–29.

CRAIG, G. (1986). *Human development* (4th ed.). Englewood Cliffs, NJ: Prentice-Hall.

CRAIK, F. I. M. (1979). Human memory. *Annual Review of Psychology, 30,* 63–102.

CRAIK, F. I. M., & LOCKHART, R. S. (1972). Levels of processing: A framework for memory research. *Journal of Verbal Learning and Verbal Behavior, 11,* 671–684.

CRONBACH, L. J. (1970). *Essentials of psychological testing* (3rd ed.). New York: Harper and Row.

CRONBACH, L. J., & SNOW, R. L. (1977). *Aptitudes and instructional methods*. New York: Irvington.

CROUSE, J. M. (1971). Ketroactive interference in reading prose materials. *Journal of Educational Psychology, 62,* 39–44.

DAIUTE, C. (1985). Writing and computers. *The Harvard Education Letter, 1(4).*

DAMON, W. (1977). *The social world of the child.* San Francisco: Jossey-Bass.

DANNER, F. W. (1976). Children's understanding of intersentence organization in the recall of short descriptive passages. *Journal of Educational Psychology, 68,* 174–183.

DANSEREAU, D. F. (1985). Learning strategy research. In J. Segal, S. Chipman, & R. Glaser (Eds.), *Thinking and learning skills. Vol. 1: Relating instruction to research.* Hillsdale, NJ: Erlbaum.

DARLEY, J., & FAZIO, R. (1980). Expectancy confirmation processes arising in the social interaction sequence. *American Psychologist, 35.* 867–881.

DARLING-HAMMOND, L. (1984). *Beyond the commission reports: The coming crisis in teaching.* Santa Monica, CA: Rand.

DAURIO, S. P. (1979). Educational enrichment versus acceleration: A review of the literature. In W. George, S. Cohn, & J. Stanley (Eds.), *Educating the gifted: Acceleration and enrichment.* Baltimore: Johns Hopkins Press.

DAVIDSON, J. (1982). The group mapping activity for instruction in reading and thinking. *Journal of Reading, 26,* 52–56.

DAVIS, G. A. (1976). Research and development in training creative thinking. In J. Levin & V. Allen (Eds.), *Cognitive learning in children: Theories and strategies.* New York: Academic Press.

DAVIS, J., LAUGHLIN, P., & KOMORITA, S. (1976). The social psychology of small groups: Cooperative and mixed-motive interaction. In M. Rosenzweig & L. Porter (Eds.), *Annual Review of Psychology, 27,* 501–542.

DE CHARMS, R. (1968). *Personal causation.* New York: Academic Press.

DE CHARMS, R. (1976). *Enhancing motivation: Change in the classroom.* New York: Irvington.

DE CHARMS, R. (1983). Intrinsic motivation, peer tutoring, and cooperative learning: Practical maxims. In J. Levine & M. Wang (Eds.), *Teacher and student perceptions: Implications for learning* (pp. 391–398). Hillsdale, NJ: Erlbaum.

DECI, E. (1975). *Intrinsic motivation.* New York: Plenum.

DEIDERICH, P. B. (1973). *Short-cut statistics for teacher-made tests.* Princeton, NJ: Educational Testing Service.

DE LISI, R., & STAUDT, J. (1980). Individual differences in college students' performance on formal operations tasks. *Journal of Applied Developmental Psychology, 1,* 201–208.

DELLOW, D. A., & ROSS, S. M. (1982–1983). Implications of personal computers for social science faculty. *Community College Social Science Journal, 4,* 72–75.

DE MOTT, R. M. (1982). Visual impairments. In N. Haring (Ed.), *Exceptional children and youth.* Columbus, OH: Charles E. Merrill.

DEMPSTER, F. N. (1981). Memory span: Sources of individual and developmental differences. *Psychological Bulletin, 89,* 63–100.

DENHAM, C., & LIEBERMAN, A. (1980). *Time to learn.* Washington, DC: National Institute of Education.

DENO, S. L. (1985). Curriculum-based measurement: The emerging alternative. *Exceptional Children, 52,* 219–232.

DINNEL, D., & GLOVER, J. A. (1985). Advance organizers: Encoding manipulations. *Journal of Educational Psychology, 77,* 514–522.

DOCTOROW, M., WITTROCK, M. C., & MARKS, C. (1978). Generative processes in reading comprehension. *Journal of Educational Psychology, 70,* 109–118.

DONALDSON, M. (1985). The mismatch between school and children's minds. In N. Entwistle (Ed.), *New directions in educational psychology. Vol. 1: Learning and teaching.* Philadelphia: Falmer Press.

DOYLE, W. (1977). The uses of nonverbal behaviors: Toward an ecological model of classrooms. *Merrill-Palmer Quarterly, 23,* 179–192.

DOYLE, W. (1979). Making managerial decisions in classrooms. In D. Duke (Ed.), *Classroom management: 78th Yearbook of the National Society for the Study of Education* (Part 2). Chicago: University of Chicago Press.

DOYLE, W. (1980). *Classroom management.* West Lafayette, IN: Kappa Delta Pi.

DOYLE, W. (1983). Academic work. *Review of Educational Research, 53,* 287–312.

DOYLE, W. (1985, May/June). Recent research on classroom management: Implications for teacher preparation. *Journal of Teacher Education,* pp. 31–35.

DOYLE, W. (1986). Classroom organization and management. In M. Wittrock (Ed.), *Handbook of research on teaching* (3rd ed., pp. 392–431). New York: Macmillan.

DOYLE, W., HANCOCK, G., & KIFER, E. (1971, March). Teacher's perceptions: Do they make a difference? Paper presented at a meeting of the American Educational Research Association, New York.

DRABMAN, R. A., & SPITALNIK, R. (1973). Social isolation as a punishment procedure: A controlled study. *Journal of Experimental Child Psychology, 16,* 236–249.

DRAYER, A. M. (1979). *Problems in middle and high school training: A handbook for student teachers and beginning teachers.* Boston: Allyn & Bacon.

DREIKURS, R., GRUNWALD, B. B., & PEPPER, F. C. (1971). *Maintaining sanity in the classroom: Illustrated teaching techniques.* New York: Harper and Row.

DRESSEL, P. L. (1977). The nature and role of objectives in instruction. *Educational Technology, 17,* 7–15.

DUCHASTEL, P. (1979). Learning objectives and the organization of prose. *Journal of Educational Psychology, 71,* 100–106.

DUNCKER, K. (1945). On solving problems. *Psychological Monographs, 58* (5, Whole No. 270).

DUNKIN, M. J., & BIDDLE, B. J. (1974). *The study of teaching.* New York: Holt, Rinehart & Winston.

DUNN, L. M. (1973). An overview. In L. M. Dunn (Ed.), *Exceptional children in the schools: Special education in transition.* New York: Holt, Rinehart & Winston.

DURKIN, D. (1979). What classroom observations reveal about reading comprehension instructions. *Reading Research Quarterly, 14,* 481–533.

DWECK, C. (1983). Theories of intelligence and achievement motivation. In S. Paris, G. Olson, & H. Stevenson (Eds.), *Learning and motivation in the classroom.* Hillsdale, NJ: Erlbaum.

DYER, H. S. (1967). The discovery and development of educational goals. *Proceedings of the 1966 Invitational Conference on Testing Problems.* Princeton, NJ: Educational Testing Service.

EATON, J. F., ANDERSON, C. W., & SMITH, E. L. (1984). Students' misconceptions interfere with science learning: Case studies of fifth-graders. *Elementary School Journal, 84,* 365–379.

EMBEIER, H. H., & ZIOMEK, R. L. (1982, March). Increasing engagement rates of low and high achievers. Paper presented at the annual meeting of the American Educational Research Association, New York.

EDWARDS, K. J., & DE VRIES, D. L. (1974). *The effects of teams-games-tournament and two instructional variations on classroom student attitudes, and student achievement* (Rep. No. 172). Baltimore: The Johns Hopkins University, Center for Social Organization of Schools.

EGGEN, P. D., KAUCHAK, D. P., & HARDER, R. J. (1979). *Strategies for teachers: Information processing in the classroom.* Englewood Cliffs, NJ: Prentice-Hall.

EISEMAN, J. W. (1981). What criteria should public school moral education programs meet? *The Review of Education, 7,* 213–230.

EISNER, E. (1983, January). The art and craft of teaching. *Educational Leadership,* pp. 4–13.

ELASHOFF, J. D. & SNOW, R. E. (1971). *Pygmalion reconsidered.* Worthington, OH: Charles A. Jones.

ELAWAR, M. C., & CORNO, L. (1985). A factorial experiment in teachers' written feedback on student homework: Changing teacher behavior a little rather than a lot. *Journal of Educational Psychology, 77,* 162–173.

ELKIND, D. (1970). *Children and adolescents.* New York: Oxford University Press.

ELKIND, D. (1981). Obituary—Jean Piaget (1896–1980). *American Psychologist, 36,* 911–913.

EMMER, E. T., & EVERTSON, C. M. (1981). Synthesis of research on classroom management. *Educational Leadership, 38,* 342–345.

EMMER, E. T., & EVERTSON, C. M. (1982). Effective classroom management at the beginning of the school year in junior high school classes. *Journal of Educational Psychology, 74,* 485–498.

EMMER, E. T., EVERTSON, C., SANFORD, J. P., CLEMENTS, B., & WORSHAM, M. (1984). *Classroom management for secondary teachers.* Englewood Cliffs, NJ: Prentice-Hall.

EMMER, E. T., & MILLETT, G. (1970). *Improving teaching through experimentation: A laboratory approach.* Englewood Cliffs, NJ: Prentice-Hall.

ENGLE, P. L. (1975). Language medium in early school years for minority language groups. *Review of Educational Research, 45,* 283–326.

ERICKSON, F., & SCHULTZ, J. (1977). When is context? Some issues and methods in the analysis of social competence. *Quarterly Newsletter for the Institute for Comparative Human Development, 1(2),* 5–10.

ERIKSON, E. (1963). *Childhood and society* (2nd ed.). New York: Norton.

ERIKSON, E. (1974). *Dimensions of a new identity.* New York: Norton.

ESTES, W. K. (1975). The state of the field: General problems and issues of theory and metatheory. In W. K. Estes (Ed.), *Handbook of learning and cognitive processes. Vol. 1: Concepts and issues.* Hillsdale, NJ: Erlbaum.

EVANS, E. D. (1976). *Transition to teaching.* New York: Holt, Rinehart & Winston.

EVERTSON, C. M. (1982). Differences in instructional activities in high and low achieving junior high classes. *Elementary School Journal, 82,* 329–350.

EVERTSON, C. M., ANDERSON, L., & BROPHY, J. (1978). *The Texas junior high school study: Final report of process–product relationships* (ERIC No. ED 173 744). Austin: University of Texas Research and Development Center for Teacher Education.

EVERTSON, C. M., EMMER, E. T., CLEMENTS, B. S., SANFORD, J. P., & WORSHAM, M. E. (1984). *Classroom management for elementary teachers.* Englewood Cliffs, NJ: Prentice-Hall.

EVERTSON, C. M., & GREEN, J. (1986). Observation as inquiry and method. In M. Wittrock (Ed.), *Handbook of research on teaching* (3rd ed., pp. 162–213). New York: Macmillan.

FARNHAM-DIGGORY, S. (1972). *Cognitive processes in education: A psychological preparation for teaching and curriculum development.* New York: Harper and Row.

FAW, H. W., & WALLER, T. G. (1976). Mathemagenic behaviors and efficiency in learning from prose. *Review of Educational Research, 46,* 691–720.

FEIN, G. (1978). *Child development.* Englewood Cliffs, NJ: Prentice-Hall.

FEITLER, F., & TOKAR, E. (1982). Getting a handle on teacher stress: How bad is the problem? *Educational Leadership, 39,* 456–458.

FELDMAN, R., & PROHASKA, T. (1979). The student as Pygmalion: Effects of student expectancy of the teacher. *Journal of Educational Psychology, 71,* 485–493.

FELIXBROD, J. J. (1974). *Effects of prior locus of control over reinforcement on current performance and resistance to extinction.* Unpublished doctoral dissertation, State University of New York at Stony Brook.

FENEMA, E., & SHERMAN, J. (1977). Sex-related differences in mathematics achievement, spatial visualization and affective factors. *American Educational Research Journal, 14*(1), 51–71.

FERSTER, C. B., & SKINNER, B. F. (1957). *Schedules of reinforcement.* New York: Appleton-Century-Crofts.

FETTERMAN, N., & ROHRKEMPER, M. (1986, April). *The utilization of failure: A look at one social/instructional environment.* Paper presented at the annual meeting of the American Educational Research Association, San Francisco.

FEUERSTEIN, R. (1979). *The dynamic assessment of retarded performers: The Learning Potential Assessment Device, theory, instruments, and techniques.* Baltimore: University Park Press.

FINN, J. (1972). Expectations and the educational environment. *Review of Educational Research, 42,* 387–410.

FISHBEIN, J., & WASIK, B. (1981). Effect of the Good Behavior game on disruptive library behavior. *Journal of Applied Behavior Analysis, 14,* 89–93.

FISKE, E. B. (1981, October 27). Teachers reward muddy prose, study finds. *The New York Times,* p. C1.

FLAVELL, J. H. (1976). Metacognitive aspects of problem solving. In L. Resnick (Ed.), *The nature of intelligence.* Hillsdale, NJ: Erlbaum.

FLAVELL, J. H. (1977). *Cognitive development.* Englewood Cliffs, NJ: Prentice-Hall.

FLAVELL, J. H. (1984). Cognitive development during the post-infancy years. In H. W. Stevenson & J. Qicheng (Eds.), *Issues in cognition: Proceedings of a joint conference in psychology* (pp. 1–17). Washington, DC: National Academy of Science, American Psychological Association.

FLAVELL, J. H. (in press). Cognitive monitoring. In W. P. Dickson (Ed.), *Children's oral communication skills.* Orlando, FL: Academic Press.

FLAVELL, J. H., FRIEDRICHS, A. G., & HOYT, J. D. (1970). Developmental changes in memorization processes. *Cognitive Psychology, 1,* 324–340.

FLAVELL, J. H., & WELLMAN, H. M. (1977). Metamemory. In R. V. Kail & J. W. Hagen (Eds.), *Perspectives on the development of memory and cognition.* Hillsdale, NJ: Erlbaum.

FORREST, D. L., & WALLER, T. G. (1980, April). *What do children know about their reading and study skills?* Paper presented at the annual meeting of the American Educational Research Association, Boston.

FOSTER, G. G., YSSELDYKE, J. E., & REESE, J. H. (1975). I wouldn't have seen it if I hadn't believed it. *Exceptional Children, 41,* 469–473.

FOSTER, W. (1981, August). *Social and emotional development in gifted individuals.* Paper presented at the Fourth World Conference on Gifted and Talented, Montreal.

FOX, L. H. (1979). Programs for the gifted and talented: An overview. In A. Passow (Ed.), *The gifted and talented: Their education and development.* Chicago: University of Chicago Press.

FOX, L. H. (1981). Identification of the academically gifted. *American Psychologist, 36,* 1103–1111.

FOXX, R. M., & JONES, J. R. (1978). A remediation program for increasing the spelling achievement of elementary and junior high school students. *Behavior Modification, 2,* 211–230.

FRECHLING, J. A., EDWARDS, S., & RICHARDSON, W. M. (1981, April). *The declining enrollment problem: A study of why parents withdraw their children from public schools.* Paper presented at the annual meeting of the American Educational Research Association, Los Angeles.

FREDERIKSEN, N. (1984). Implications of cognitive theory for instruction in problem solving. *Review of Educational Research, 54,* 363–407.

FRENDER, R., BROWN, B., & LAMBERT, W. (1970). The role of speech characteristics in scholastic success. *Canadian Journal of Behavioral Science, 2,* 299–306.

FRIEDLANDER, B. (1985, November/December). Get your class in-line and on-line with a modem. *Electronic Education,* pp. 14–15.

FROMBERG, D. P., & DRISCOLL, M. (1985). *The successful classroom: Management strategies for regular and special education teachers.* New York: Teachers College Press.

FROSTIG, M., & HORNE, D. (1964). *The Frostig program for the development of visual perception: Teacher's guide.* Chicago: Follett.

FUHR, M. L. (1972). The typewriter and retarded readers. *Journal of Reading, 16,* 30–32.

FULLER, F. G. (1969). Concerns of teachers: A developmental conceptualization. *American Educational Research Journal, 6,* 207–226.

FURMAN, W., & BIERMAN, K. L. (1984). Children's conceptions of friendship: A multimethod study of developmental changes. *Developmental Psychology, 20,* 925–931.

FURST, E. J. (1981). Bloom's taxonomy of educational objectives for the cognitive domain: Philosophical and educational issues. *Review of Educational Research, 51,* 441–454.

FURTH, H., & WACHS, H. *Thinking goes to school: Piaget's theory in practice.* New York: Oxford University Press, 1974.

GAGNÉ, E. D. (1985). *The psychology of school learning.* Boston: Little, Brown.

GAGNÉ, R. (1985). *The conditions of learning and theory of instruction* (4th ed.). New York: Holt, Rinehart & Winston.

CAGNÉ, R. (1977). *The conditions of learning* (3rd ed.). New York: Holt, Rinehart & Winston.

GAGNÉ, R. M. (1974). *Essentials of learning for instruction.* Hinsdale, IL: Dryden Press.

GAGNÉ, R. M. (1982, March). *Some issues in the psychology of mathematics instruction.* Paper presented at the annual meeting of the American Educational Research Association, New York.

GAGNÉ, R. M., & SMITH, E. (1962). A study of the effects of verbalization on problem solving. *Journal of Experimental Psychology, 63,* 12–18.

GALL, M. (1984). Synthesis of research on teachers' questioning. *Educational Leadership, 41,* 40–47.

GALL, M. D. (1970). The use of questions in teaching. *Review of Educational Research, 40,* 707–721.

GALLUP, A. M. (1984). Gallup Poll of teachers' attitudes toward the public schools. *Phi Delta Kappan, 66,* 97–107.

GALLUP, A. M. (1985). The 17th annual Gallup Poll of the public's attitudes toward the public schools. *Phi Delta Kappan, 67,* 35–47.

GALLUP, G. (1982, September). Fifteenth annual Gallup poll of public attitudes toward the public schools. *Phi Delta Kappan, 64,* 34–46.

GARDNER, H. (1983). *Frames of mind: The theory of multiple intelligences.* New York: Basic Books.

GARNER, R., & KRAUS, C. (1982). Monitoring of understanding among 7th graders: An investigation of good comprehender–poor comprehender differences on knowing and regulating reading behaviors. *Educational Research Quarterly, 6,* 5–12.

GARRETT, S. S., SADKER, M., & SADKER, D. (1986). Interpersonal communication skills. In J. Cooper (Ed.), *Classroom teaching skills* (3rd ed.). Lexington, MA: D. C. Heath.

GELMAN, R. (1979). Preschool thought. *American Psychologist, 34,* 900–905.

GELMAN, R., & BAILLARGEON, R. (1983). A review of some Piagetian concepts. In P. Mussen (Ed.), *Carmichael's manual of child psychology. Vol. 3: Cognitive development* (E. Markman & J. Flavell, Volume Eds.). New York: Wiley.

GENTNER, D. (1975). Evidence for the psychological reality of semantic components: The verbs of possession. In D. Norman & D. Rumelhart (Eds.), *Explorations in cognition.* San Francisco: W. H. Freeman.

GARBER, G., & GROSS, L. (1974). Violence profile No. 6: Trends in network television drama and viewer conceptions of social reality, 1967–73. *Monographs of the Annenberg School of Communications.* Philadelphia: University of Pennsylvania.

GILLETT, M., & GALL, M. (1982, March). *The effects of teacher enthusiasm on the at-task behavior of students in the elementary grades.* Paper presented at the annual meeting of the American Educational Research Association, New York.

GILLIGAN, C. (1977). In a different voice: Women's conceptions of self and of morality. *Harvard Educational Review, 47,* 481–517.

GILSTRAP, R. L., & MARTIN, W. R. (1975). *Current strategies for teachers: A resource for personalizing education.* Pacific Palisades, CA: Goodyear.

GINSBURG, H. (1985). Piaget and education. In N. Entwistle (Ed.), *New directions in educational psychology. Vol. 1: Learning and teaching.* Philadelphia: Falmer Press.

GINSBURG, H., & OPPER, S. (1979). *Piaget's theory of intellectual development* (2nd ed.). Englewood Cliffs, NJ: Prentice-Hall.

GOIN, M. T., PETTERS, E. E., & LEVIN, J. R. (1986, April). Effects of pictorial mnemonic strategies on the reading performance of students classified as learning disabled. Paper presented at the annual meeting of the Council for Exceptional Children, New Orleans.

GOLDBERG, D. (1985, January 5). Letting in "latchkey children." *New York Times Winter Survey of Education,* pp. 47–48.

GOOD, T. (1983). Research on classroom teaching. In L. Shulman & G. Sykes (Eds.), *Handbook of teaching and policy* (pp. 42–80). New York: Longman.

GOOD, T. L. (1970). Which students do teachers call on? *Elementary School Journal, 70,* 190–198.

GOOD, T. L. (1979). Teacher effectiveness in the

elementary school: What we know about it now. *Journal of Teacher Education, 30,* 52–64.

GOOD, T. L. (1983). Classroom research: A decade of progress. *Educational Psychologist, 18,* 127–144.

GOOD, T. L., & BECKERMAN, T. M. (1978). Time on task: A naturalistic study in sixth-grade classrooms. *Elementary School Journal, 73,* 193–201.

GOOD, T., BIDDLE, B., & BROPHY, J. (1975). *Teachers make a difference.* New York: Holt, Rinehart & Winston.

GOOD, T. L., & BROPHY, J. E. (1984). *Looking in classrooms* (3rd ed.). New York: Harper and Row.

GOOD, T. L., & GROUWS, D. (1977). Teaching effects: A process-product study in fourth-grade mathematics classrooms. *Journal of Teacher Education, 28,* 49–54.

GOOD, T. L., & GROUWS, D. (1979). The Missouri mathematics effectiveness project: An experimental study in fourth grade classrooms. *Journal of Educational Psychology, 71,* 355–362.

GOOD, T., GROUWS, D., & EBMEIER, H. (1983). *Active mathematics teaching.* New York: Longman.

GOOD, T. L., & MARSHALL, S. (1984). Do students learn more in heterogeneous or homogeneous groups? In P. Peterson, L. C. Wilkinson, & M. Hallinan (Eds.), *The social context of instruction: Group organization and group processes* (pp. 15–38). Orlando, FL: Academic Press.

GOOD, T. L., & STIPEK, D. J. (1983). Individual differences in the classroom: A psychological perspective. In G. Fenstermacher & J. Goodlad (Eds.), *1983 National Society for the Study of Education Yearbook.* Chicago: University of Chicago Press.

GORDON, A. (1982). From theory to practice: Some implications. In L. Feagans & D. C. Farran (Eds.), *The language of children reared in poverty: Implications for evaluation and intervention* (pp. 241–244). New York: Academic Press.

GORDON, N. J. (1981). Social cognition. In F. Farley & N. Gordon (Eds.), *Psychology and education: The state of the union.* Berkeley, CA: McCutchan.

GORDON, T. (1974). *Teacher effectiveness training.* New York: Peter H. Wyden.

GOTTLIEB, J. (1974). Attitudes toward retarded children: Effects of labeling and academic performance. *American Journal of Mental Deficiency, 79,* 268–273.

GOTTLIEB, J., ALTER, M., & GOTTLIEB, B. (1983). Mainstreaming mentally retarded children. In J. Matson & J. Mulich (Eds.), *Handbook of mental retardation* (pp. 67–77). Elmsford, NY: Pergamon Press.

GRABE, M., & LATTA, R. M. (1981). Cumulative achievement in a mastery instructional system: The impact of differences in resultant achievement motivation and persistence. *American Educational Research Journal, 18,* 7–14.

GREEN, B. F. (1981). A primer of testing. *American Psychologist, 36,* 1001–1012.

GREEN, J., & WEADE, R. (1985). Reading between the lines: Social cues to lesson participation. *Theory into Practice, 24,* 14–21.

GREGG, L. W. (1978). Spatial concepts, spatial names, and the development of exocentric representations. In R. Siegler (Ed.), *Children's thinking: What develops?* Hillsdale, NJ: Erlbaum.

GRESHAM, F. (1981). Social skills training with handicapped children. *Review of Educational Research, 51,* 139–176.

GRINDER, R. E. (1981). The "new" science of edu-

cation: Educational psychology in search of a mission. In F. H. Farley & N. J. Gordon (Eds.), *Psychology and education: The state of the union.* Berkeley, CA: McCutchan.

GRONLUND, N. E. (1977). *Constructing achievement tests* (2nd ed.). Englewood Cliffs, NJ: Prentice-Hall.

GRONLUND, N. E. (1978). *Stating behavioral objectives for classroom instruction* (2nd ed.). Toronto: Macmillan.

GRONLUND, N. E. (1985). *Measurement and evaluation in teaching* (5th ed.). New York: Macmillan.

GROSSMAN, H. J. (Ed.). (1983). *Classification in mental retardation.* Washington, DC: American Association on Mental Deficiency.

GUERNEY, L. F. (1981, April). *Psychoeducational programming for children coping with parental separation and divorce.* Paper presented at the annual meeting of the American Educational Association, Los Angeles.

GUILFORD, J. P. (1967). *The nature of human intelligence.* New York: McGraw-Hill.

GUSKEY, T. R., & GATES, S. L. (1986). Synthesis of research on mastery learning. *Education Leadership, 43,* 73–81.

HALLAHAN, D., & KAUFFMAN, J. (1986). *Exceptional children: Introduction to special education* (3rd ed.). Englewood Cliffs, NJ: Prentice-Hall.

HAMILTON, R. J. (1985). A framework for the evaluation of the effectiveness of adjunct questions and objectives. *Review of Educational Research, 55,* 47–86.

HANEY, W. (1981). Validity, vaudeville, and values: A short history of social concerns over standardized testing. *American Psychologist, 36,* 1021–1034.

HANSEN, D. N., ROSS, S. M., & BOWMAN, H. L. (1978, December). Cost effectiveness of navy computer-managed instruction. In T. A. Ryan (Ed.), *Systems research in education.* Columbia, SC: University of South Carolina.

HANSEN, R. A. (1977). Anxiety. In S. Ball (Ed.), *Motivation in education.* New York: Academic Press.

HANSFORD, B. C., & HATTIE, J. A. (1982). The relationship between self and achievement/performance measures. *Review of Educational Research, 52,* 123–142.

HARING, N. G., & McCORMICK, L. (Eds.). (1986). *Exceptional children and youth* (4th ed.). Columbus, OH: Charles E. Merrill.

HARROW, A. J. (1972). *A taxonomy of the psychomotor domain: A guide for developing behavioral objectives.* New York: David McKay.

HARVARD UNIVERSITY. (1985, June). Preschool: It does make a difference. *Harvard Education Letter,* pp.–3.

HARVARD UNIVERSITY. (1986, March). When the student becomes the teacher. *Harvard Education Letter,* pp. 5–6.

HAVIGHURST, R. J. (1981). Life-span development and educational psychology. In F. H. Farley & N. J. Gordon (Eds.), *Psychology and education: The state of the union.* Berkeley, CA: McCutchan.

HAYES, J. R., WATERMAN, D. A., & ROBINSON, C. S. (1977). Identifying relevant aspects of a problem text. *Cognitive Science, 1,* 297–313.

HAYES, S. C., ROSENFARB, I., WULFERT, E., MUNT, E. D., KORN, Z., & ZETTLE, R. D. (1985). Self-reinforcement effects: An artifact of social standard setting? *Journal of Applied Behavior Analysis, 18,* 201–214.

HESS, R., & McDEVITT, T. (1984). Some cognitive consequences of maternal intervention techniques: A longitudinal study. *Child Development, 55,* 1902–1912.

HETHERINGTON, E. M. (1979). Divorce: A child's perspective. *American Psychologist, 34,* 851–858.

HETHERINGTON, E. M., & PARKE, R. D. (1979). *Child psychology: A contemporary viewpoint.* New York: McGraw-Hill.

HILGARD, E. R., ATKINSON, R. L., & ATKINSON, R. C. (1979). *Introduction to psychology* (7th ed.). New York: Harcourt Brace Jovanovich.

HILL, K. T., & EATON, W. O. (1977). The interaction of test anxiety and success-failure experiences in determining children's arithmetic performance. *Developmental Psychology, 13,* 205–211.

HILL, K. T., & WIGFIELD, A. (1984). Test anxiety: A major educational problem and what can be done about it. *Elementary School Journal, 85,* 105–126.

HILL, W. F. (1985). *Learning: A survey of psychological interpretations* (4th ed.). New York: Harper and Row.

HILLER, J. H. (1971). Verbal response indicators of conceptual vagueness. *American Educational Research Journal, 8,* 151–161.

HILLS, J. R. (1976). *Measurement and evaluation in the classroom.* Columbus, OH: Charles E. Merrill.

HINES, C. V., CRUICKSHANK, D. R., & KENNEDY, J. L. (1982, March). *Measures of teacher clarity and their relationships to student achievement and satisfaction.* Paper presented at the annual meeting of the American Educational Research Association, New York.

HINES, C., CRUICKSHANK, D. R., & KENNEDY, J. (1985). Teacher clarity and its relation to student achievement and satisfaction. *American Educational Research Journal, 22,* 87–99.

HINSLEY, D., HAYES, J. R., & SIMON, H. A. (1977). From words to equations. In P. Carpenter & M. Just (Eds.), *Cognitive processes in comprehension.* Hillsdale, NJ: Erlbaum.

HOFFMAN, L. W. (1977). Changes in family roles, socialization, and sex differences. *American Psychologist, 32*(8), 644–657.

HOFFMAN, M. L. (1978). Empathy: Its development and prosocial implications. In C. B. Keasey, (Ed.), *Nebraska Symposium on Motivation, 1977.* Lincoln, NE: University of Nebraska Press.

HOFFMAN, M. L. (1979). Development of moral thought, feeling, and behavior. *American Psychologist, 34,* 958–966.

HOLLAND, J. L. (1960). Prediction of college grades from personality and aptitude variables. *Journal of Educational Psychology, 51,* 245–254.

HOLLINGWORTH, L. S. (1942). *Children above 180 IQ.* New York: Harcourt Brace Jovanovich.

HOLMES, C. T., & MATTHEWS, K. M. (1984). The effects of nonpromotion on elementary and junior high school pupils: A meta-analysis. *Review of Educational Research, 54,* 225–236.

HOPKINS, C. O., & ANTES, R. L. (1979). *Classroom testing: Administration, scoring, and score interpretation.* Itasca, IL: F. E. Peacock.

HORN, J. L., & DONALDSON, G. (1980). Cognitive development in adulthood. In O. Brim & J. Kagan (Eds.), *Constancy and change in human development.* Cambridge, MA: Harvard University Press.

HOWE, H. (1983, November). Education moves center stage: An overview of recent studies. *Phi Delta Kappan, 65,* 167–172.

HUDGINS, B. B. (1977). *Learning and thinking: A primer for teachers.* Itasca, IL: F. E. Peacock.

HUESMAN, L. R., LAGARSPETZ, K., & ERON, L. (1984). Intervening variables in the TV violence-aggression relation: Evidence from two countries. *Developmental Psychology, 20,* 746–775.

HUNDERT, J., & BUCHER, B. (1978). Pupil's self-scored arithmetic performance: A practical procedure for maintaining accuracy. *Journal of Applied Behavior Analysis, 11*, 304.

HUNT, J. (1981). Comments on "The modification of intelligence through early experience" by Ramey and Haskins. *Intelligence, 5*, 21–27.

HUNT, J. McV. (1961). *Intelligence and experience*. New York: Ronald.

HUNT, M. (1982, January 24). How the mind works. *The New York Times Magazine*, pp. 30–35.

HUNTER, M. (1982). *Mastery teaching*. El Segundo, CA: TIP Publications.

HYDE, J. (1981). How large are cognitive gender differences? *American Psychologist, 36*, 292–301.

IRVING, O., & MARTIN, J. (1982). Withitness: The confusing variable. *American Educational Research Journal, 19*, 313–319.

IRWIN, J. W. (1986). *Teaching reading comprehension*. Englewood Cliffs, NJ: Prentice-Hall.

JACKSON, P., & LAHADERNE, H. (1971). Inequalities of teacher-pupil contacts. In M. Silberman (Ed.), *The experience of schooling*. New York: Holt, Rinehart & Winston.

JENCKS, C., SMITH, M., ACLAND, H., BANE, M., COHEN, D., GINTIS, H., HEYNS, B., & MICHELSON, S. (1972). *Inequality: A reassessment of the effect of family and schooling in America*. New York: Basic Books.

JENSEN, A. R. (1980). *Bias in testing*. New York: Free Press.

JENSEN, A. R. (1974). How biased are culture-loaded tests? *Genetic Psychology Monographs, 90*, 185–244.

JENSEN, A. R. (1981). Raising the IQ: The Ramey and Haskins study. *Intelligence, 5*, 29–40.

JOHNSON, D., & JOHNSON, R. (1975). *Learning together and alone: Cooperation, competition, and individualization*. Englewood Cliffs, NJ: Prentice-Hall.

JOHNSON, D., & JOHNSON, R. (1978). Many teachers wonder . . . will the special-needs child ever really belong? *Instructor, 87*, 152–154.

JOHNSON, D. W. (1972). *Reaching out: Interpersonal effectiveness and self-actualization*. Englewood Cliffs, NJ: Prentice-Hall.

JONES, V. F., & JONES, L. S. (1986). *Comprehensive classroom management: Creating positive learning environments* (2nd ed.). Boston: Allyn & Bacon.

JOYCE, B., & WEIL, M. (1986). *Models of teaching*. Englewood Cliffs, NJ: Prentice-Hall.

KAGAN, J. (1979). Family experience and the child's development. *American Psychologist, 34*, 886–891.

KAGAN, J., ROSMAN, B. L., DAY, D., ALBERT, J., & PHILLIPS, W. (1964). Information processing in the child: Significance of analytic and reflective attitudes. *Psychological Monographs, 78* (1, Whole No. 570).

KAGAN, S. (1983). Social orientation among Mexican-American children: A challenge to traditional classroom structures. In E. Garcia (Ed.), *The Mexican-American child: Language, cognition, and social development*. Tempe, AZ: Center for Bilingual Education.

KARWEIT, N. (1981). Time in school. *Research in Sociology of Education and Socialization, 2*, 77–110.

KARWEIT, N., & SLAVIN, R. (1981). Measurement and modeling choices in studies of time and learning. *American Educational Research Journal, 18*, 157–171.

KASH, M. M., & BORICH, G. (1978). *Teacher behavior and pupil self-concept*. Reading, MA: Addison-Wesley.

KATZ, L. G. (1972). *Developmental stages for pre-school teachers*. Urbana, IL: ERIC Clearinghouse on Early Childhood Education.

KEARSLEY, G. (1984). Instructional design and authoring software. *Journal of Instructional Development, 7*, 11–16.

KELLER, F. S. (1966). A personal course in psychology. In R. Ulrich, T. Stachnik, & J. Mabry (Eds.), *Control of human behavior* (Vol. 1). Glenview, IL: Scott, Foresman.

KELLEY, E. G. (1958). A study of consistent discrepancies between instructor grades and test results. *Journal of Educational Psychology, 49*, 328–335.

KENDALL, P. C. (1981). Cognitive-behavioral interventions with children. In B. B. Lahey & A. E. Kazdin (Eds.), *Advances in clinical psychology* (Vol. 4). New York: Plenum.

KENNEDY, J. L., CRUICKSHANK, D. C., BUSH, A. J., & MYERS, R. (1978). Additional investigations into the nature of teacher clarity. *Journal of Educational Research, 72*, 3–10.

KEOGH, B. K., & MARGOLIS, J. (1976). Learn to labor and to wait: Attentional problems of children with learning disorders. *Journal of Learning Disabilities, 9*, 276–286.

KING, G. (1979, June). Personal communication. University of Texas at Austin.

KIRBY, F. D., & SHIELDS, F. (1972). Modification of arithmetic response rate and attending behavior in a seventh-grade student. *Journal of Applied Behavior Analysis, 5*, 79–84.

KIRK, S., & GALLAGHER, J. J. (1979). *Educating exceptional children* (3rd ed.). Boston: Houghton Mifflin.

KIRK, S., & GALLAGHER, J. (1983). *Educating exceptional children* (4th ed.). Boston: Houghton Mifflin.

KLAHR, D. (1978, March). *Information processing models of cognitive development: Potential relevance to science instruction*. Paper presented at the meeting of American Educational Research Association.

KLAUSMEIER, H. J. (1976). Instructional design and the teaching of concepts. In J. Levin & V. Allen (Eds.), *Cognitive learning in children: Theories and strategies*. New York: Academic Press.

KLAUSMEIER, H., & SIPPLE, T. S. (1982). Factor structure of the Piagetian stage of concrete operations. *Contemporary Educational Psychology, 7*, 161–180.

KNAPCZYK, D. R., & LIVINGSTON, G. (1974). The effects of prompting question-asking upon on-task behavior and reading comprehension. *Journal of Applied Behavior Analysis, 7*, 115–121.

KNEEDLER, P. (1985). California assesses critical thinking. In A. Costa (Ed.), *Developing minds: A resource book for teaching thinking*. Alexandria, VA: Association for Supervision and Curriculum Development.

KNEEDLER, R. (1984). *Special education for today*. Englewood Cliffs, NJ: Prentice-Hall.

KOHLBERG, L. (1963). The development of children's orientations toward moral order: Sequence in the development of moral thought. *Vita Humana, 6*, 11–33.

KOHLBERG, L. (1975). The cognitive-developmental approach to moral education. *Phi Delta Kappan, 56*, 670–677.

KOHLBERG, L. (1981). *The philosophy of moral development*. New York: Harper and Row.

KOLATA, G. B. (1980). Math and sex: Are girls born with less ability? *Science, 210*, 1234–1235.

KOLESNIK, W. B. (1978). *Motivation: Understanding and influencing human behavior*. Boston: Allyn & Bacon.

KOUNIN, J. (1970). *Discipline and group management in classrooms*. New York: Holt, Rinehart & Winston.

KOUNIN, J. S., & DOYLE, P. H. (1975). Degree of continuity of a lesson's signal system and task involvement of children. *Journal of Educational Psychology, 67*, 159–164.

KRATHWOHL, D. R., BLOOM, B. S., & MASIA, B. B. (1956). *Taxonomy of educational objectives. Handbook II: Affective domain*. New York: David McKay.

KULIK, C., & KULIK, J. (1982). Effects of ability grouping on secondary school students: A meta-analysis of evaluation findings. *American Educational Research Journal, 19*, 415–428.

KULIK, J., BANGERT, R., & WILLIAMS, G. (1983). Effects of computer-based teaching on secondary school students. *Journal of Educational Psychology, 75* (1), 19–26.

KULIK, J. A., & KULIK, C. L. (1984). Effects of accelerated instruction on students. *Review of Educational Research, 54*, 409–425.

KULIK, J. A., KULIK, C. C., & BANGERT, R. L. (1984, April). Effects of practice on aptitude and achievement test scores. *American Educational Research Journal, 21*, 435–447.

KULIK, J., KULIK, C., & BANGERT-DROWNS, R. (1984). *Effects of computer-based education on secondary school pupils*. Paper presented at the annual meeting of the American Educational Research Association, New Orleans, LA.

KULIK, J. A., KULIK, C. C., & COHEN, P. A. (1979). A meta-analysis of outcome studies of Keller's Personalized System of Instruction. *American Psychologist, 34*, 307–318.

KULIK, J. A., KULIK, C. C., & COHEN, P. A. (1980). Effectiveness of computer-based college teaching: A meta-analysis of findings. *Review of Educational Research, 50*, 525–544.

KURDEK, L. A., & KRILE, D. (1982). A developmental analysis of the relation between peer acceptance and both interpersonal understanding and perceived self-competence. *Child Development, 53*, 1485–1491.

KURTZ, J. J., & SWENSON, E. J. (1951). Factors related to over-achievement and under-achievement in school. *School Review, 59*, 472–480.

LAMB, M. (1978). The father's role in the infant's social world. In J. H. Stevens & M. Mathews (Eds.), *Mother/child/father/child relationships*. Washington, DC: National Association for the Education of Young Children.

LAMB, M. E. (1979). Parental influences and the father's role: A personal perspective. *American Psychologist, 34*, 938–943.

LAMB, M. E. (1982). Parent-infant interaction, attachment, and socioemotional development in infancy. In R. Emde & R. Harmon (Eds.), *The development of attachment and affiliative systems*. New York: Plenum.

LAND, M. L., & SMITH, L. R. (1979). Effect of low inference teacher clarity inhibitors on student achievement. *Journal of Teacher Education, 31*, 55–57.

LANGER, P. C. (1972). What's the score on programmed instruction? *Today's Education, 61*, 59.

LAOSA, L. (1982). School, occupation, culture, and family: The impact of parental schooling on the parent-child relationship. *Journal of Educational Psychology, 74*, 791–827.

LAOSA, L. (1984). Ethnic, socioeconomic, and home language influences on early performance on measures of ability. *Journal of Educational Psychology, 76*, 1178–1198.

LARSEN, G. Y. (1977). Methodology in developmental psychology: An examination of research on Piagetian theory. *Child Development, 48*, 1160–1166.

LATHROP, A., & GOODSON, B. (1983). *Courseware in the classroom: Selecting,* organizing, and using educational software. Reading, MA: Addison-Wesley.

LAYCOCK, F., & CAYLOR, J. S. (1964). Physiques of gifted children and their less gifted siblings. *Child Development, 35*, 63–74.

LAZAR, I., & DARLINGTON, R. (1982). Lasting effects of early education: A report from the Consortium for Longitudinal Studies. *Monographs of the Society for Research in Child Development, 47* (2–3, No. 195).

LEFCOURT, H. (1966). Internal versus external control of reinforcement: A review. *Psychological Bulletin, 65*, 206–220.

LEINHARDT, G. (1986). Expertise in mathematics teaching. *Educational Leadership, 43*, 28–33.

LEINHARDT, G., & GREENO, J. D. (1986). The cognitive skill of teaching. *Journal of Educational Psychology, 78*, 75–95.

LEINHARDT, G., & SMITH, D. (1985). Expertise in mathematics instruction: Subject matter knowledge. *Journal of Educational Psychology, 77*, 247–271.

LEPPER, M. R., & GREENE, D. (1975). Turning play into work: Effects of adult surveillance and extrinsic reward on children's motivation. *Journal of Personality and Social Psychology, 31*, 479–486.

LEPPER, M. R., & GREENE, D. (1978). *The hidden costs of rewards: New perspectives on the psychology of human motivation*. Hillsdale, NJ: Erlbaum.

LEPPER, M. R., GREENE, D., & NISBETT, R. (1973). Undermining children's intrinsic interest with extrinsic reward: A test of the "overjustification" hypothesis. *Journal of Personality and Social Psychology, 28*, 129–137.

LERNER, B. (1981). The minimum competency testing movement: Social, scientific, and legal implications. *American Psychologist, 36*, 1057–1066.

LEVER, J. (1978). Sex differences in the complexity of children's play and games. *American Sociologist Review, 43*, 471–483.

LEVIN, J. R. (1985). Educational applications of mnemonic pictures: Possibilities beyond your wildest imagination. In A. A. Sheikh (Ed.), *Imagery in the educational process*. Farmingdale, NY: Baywood.

LEVIN, J. R., DRETZKE, B. J., McCORMICK, C. B., SCRUGGS, T. E., McGIVERN, S., & MASTROPIERI, M. (1983). Learning via mnemonic pictures: Analysis of the presidential process. *Educational Communication and Technology Journal, 31*, 161–173.

LEVITAN, T. E., & CHANANIE, L. C. (1972). Responses of female primary school teachers to sex-typed behaviors in male and female children. *Child Development, 43*, 1309–1316.

LEWIS, J., JR. (1981). Do you encourage teacher absenteeism? *The American School Board Journal, 168*, 29–30.

LICKONA, T. (1977, March). How to encourage moral development. *Learning*, pp. 38–42.

LIEBERT, R. M., & SCHWARTZBERG, N. S. (1977). Effects of mass media. In M. Rosenzweig & L. Porter (Eds.), *Annual review of psychology*. Palo Alto, CA: Annual Reviews.

LIEBERT, R. M., SPRAFKIN, J. N., DAVIDSON, E. S. (1982). *The early window: Effects of television on children and youth*. Elmsford, NY: Pergamon.

LIEBERT, R. M., WICKS-NELSON, R., & KAIL, R. V. (1986). *Developmental psychology* (4th ed.). Englewood Cliffs, NJ: Prentice-Hall.

LINDSAY, P. H., & NORMAN, D. A. (1977). *Human information processing: An introduction to psychology* (2nd ed.). New York: Academic Press.

LINDVALL, C. M., TAMBURINO, J. L., & ROBINSON, L. (1982, March). *An exploratory investigation of the effect of teaching primary grade children to use specific problem-solving strategies in solving simple arithmetic story problems*. Paper presented at the annual meeting of the American Educational Research Association, New York.

LINN, R., KLEIN, S., & HART, F. (1972). The nature and correlates of law school essay grades. *Educational and Psychological Measurement, 32*, 267–279.

LOCKWOOD, A. (1978). The effects of value clarification and moral development curricula on school-age subjects: A critical review of recent research. *Review of Educational Research, 48*, 325–364.

LOEHLIN, J. C., LINDZEY, G., & SPUHLER, J. N. (1979). Cross-group comparisons of intellectual abilities. In L. Willerman & R. Turner (Eds.), *Readings about individuals and group differences*. San Francisco: W. H. Freeman.

LOVITT, T. C. (1977). *In spite of my resistance, I've learned from children*. Columbus, OH: Charles E. Merrill.

LUEHRMANN, A. L. (1981). Computer literacy— what should it be? *The Mathematics Teacher, 74* (9).

LUEHRMANN, A. (1984). Computer literacy: The what, why, and how. In D. Peterson (Ed.), *Intelligent schoolhouse: Readings on computers and learning* (pp. 53–58). Reston, VA: Reston Publishing Company.

LUEHRMANN, A. L. (1986). Don't feel bad teaching BASIC. In T. R. Cannings & S. W. Brown (Eds.), *The information-age classroom: Using the computer as a tool*. Irvine, CA: Franklin, Beedle & Associates.

LUFLER, H. S. (1978). Discipline: A new look at an old problem. *Phi Delta Kappan, 59*, 424–426.

LUITEN, J., AMES, W., & ACKERSON, G. (1980). A meta-analysis of the effects of advance organizers on learning and retention. *American Educational Research Journal, 17*, 211–218.

LYMAN, H. B. (1986). *Test scores and what they mean* (4th ed.). Englewood Cliffs, NJ: Prentice-Hall.

MACCOBY, E. E., & JACKLIN, C. N. (1974). *The psychology of sex differences*. Stanford, CA: Stanford University Press.

McCALL, R. B. (1981). Nature-nurture and the two realms of development: A proposed integration with respect to mental development. *Child Development, 52*, 1–12.

McCLELLAND, D. (1985). *Human motivation*. Glenview, IL: Scott, Foresman.

McCLELLAND, D. C. (1973). Testing for competence rather than for intelligence. *American Psychologist, 28*, 1–14.

McCLELLAND, D., ATKINSON, J. W., CLARK, R. W., & LOWELL, E. L. (1953). *The achievement motive*. New York: Appleton-Century-Crofts.

McCLELLAND, D., & PILON, D. (1983). Sources of adult motives in patterns of parent behavior in early childhood. *Journal of Personality and Social Psychology, 44*, 564–574.

McCONNELL, J. W. (1977, April). *Relationships between selected teacher behaviors and attitudes/achievement of algebra classes*. Paper presented at the annual meeting of the American Educational Research Association, New York.

McCORMICK, C. B., & LEVIN, J. R. (in press). Mnemonic prose-learning strategies. In M. Pressley & M. McDaniel (Eds.), *Imaginery and related mnemonic processes* New York: Springer/Verlag.

McDONALD, F. (1976, April). *Designing research for policy-making*. Paper presented at the annual meeting of the American Educational Research Association, San Francisco. (a)

McDONALD, F. (1976). *Teachers do make a difference*. Princeton, NJ: Educational Testing Service. (b)

MacDONALD-ROSS, M. (1974). Behavioral objectives: A critical review. *Instructional Science, 2*, 1–51.

McGINLEY, P., & McGINLEY, H. (1970). Reading groups as psychological groups. *Journal of Experimental Education, 39*, 36–42.

McLAUGHLIN, T. F. (1981). The effects of a classroom token economy on math performance in an intermediate grade school. *Education and Treatment of Children, 4*, 139–147.

McLAUGHLIN, T. F., & GNAGEY, W. J. (1981, April). *Self-management and pupil self-control*. Paper presented at the annual meeting of the American Educational Research Association, Los Angeles.

MacMILLAN, D. (1982). *Mental retardation in school and society*. Boston: Little, Brown.

McNEILL, D. (1966). Developmental psycholinguistics. In F. Smith & G. Miller (Eds.), *The genesis of language: A psycholinguistic approach*. Cambridge, MA: MIT Press.

McNEMAR, Q. (1964). Lost: Our intelligence? Why? *American Psychologist, 19*, 871–882.

McWILLIAMS, E. D. (1974). Report of progress for the field test of the MITRE/BYU TICCIT System of CAI. Sponsored by the National Science Foundation.

MADSEN, C. H., BECKER, W. C., & THOMAS, D. R. (1968). Rules, praise, and ignoring: Elements of elementary classroom control. *Journal of Applied Behavior Analysis, 1*, 139–150.

MADSEN, C. H., BECKER, W. C., THOMAS, D. R., KOSER, L. & PLAGER, E. (1968). An analysis of the reinforcing function of "sit down" commands. In R. K. Parker (Ed.), *Readings in educational psychology*. Boston: Allyn & Bacon.

MAEHR, M. L. (1974). *Sociocultural origins of achievement*. Monterey, CA: Brooks/Cole.

MAGER, R. (1962). *Preparing instructional objectives*. Palo Alto, CA: Fearon.

MAHONEY, K. B., & HOPKINS B. L. (1973). The modification of sentence structure and its relationship to subjective judgments of creativity in writing. *Journal of Applied Behavior Analysis, 6*, 425–434.

MAHONEY, M. J., & THORESEN, C. E. (1974). *Self-control: Power to the person*. Monterey, CA: Brooks/Cole.

MAIER, N. R. F. (1933). An aspect of human reasoning. *British Journal of Psychology, 24*, 144–155.

MAIER, S. F., SELIGMAN, M. E. P., & SOLOMON, R. L. (1969). Pavlovian fear conditioning and learned helplessness. In B. Campbell & R. Church (Eds.), *Punishment and aversive control*. New York: Appleton-Century-Crofts.

MARBLE, W. O., WINNE, P. H., & MARTIN, J. F. (1978). Science achievement as a function of method and schedule of grading. *Journal of Research in Science Teaching, 15*, 433–440.

MARKMAN, E. M. (1977). Realizing that you don't understand: A preliminary investigation. *Child Development, 48*, 986–992.

MARKMAN, E. M. (1979). Realizing that you don't understand: Elementary school children's awareness of inconsistencies. *Child Development, 50*, 643–655.

MARSH, H. W., & SHAVELSON, R. (1985). Self-concept: Its multifaceted, hierarchical structure. *Educational Psychologist, 20*, 107–123.

MARSHALL, S. (1984). Sex differences in children's mathematics achievement: Solving computations and story problems. *Journal of Educational Psychology, 76*, 194–204.

MARTINSON, R. A. (1961). *Educational programs*

for gifted pupils. Sacramento: California Department of Education.

MASLOW, A. H. (1968). Toward a psychology of being (2nd ed.). Princeton, NJ: Van Nostrand.

MASLOW, A. H. (1970). Motivation and personality (2nd ed.). New York: Harper and Row.

MATARAZZO, J. D. (1972). Wechsler's measurement and appraisal of adult intelligence (5th ed.). Fair Lawn, NJ: Oxford University Press.

MAYER, R. E. (1979). Can advance organizers influence meaningful learning? Review of Educational Research, 49, 371–383.

MAYER, R. E. (1982). Memory for algebra story problems. Journal of Educational Psychology, 74, 199–216.

MAYER, R. E. (1983). Thinking, problem solving, cognition. San Francisco, CA: W. H. Freeman.

MAYER, R. E., & BROMAGE, B. (1980). Different recall protocols for technical texts due to advance organizers. Journal of Educational Psychology, 72, 209–225.

MAYER, R. E., DYCK, J. L., & VILBERG, W. (1986, April). Cognitive consequences of learning BASIC computer programming. Paper presented at the annual meeting of the American Educational Research Association, San Francisco.

MEDLEY, D. M. (1977). Teacher competence and teacher effectiveness: A review of process-product research. Washington, DC: American Association of Colleges for Teacher Education.

MEDLEY, D. M. (1979). The effectiveness of teachers. In P. Peterson & H. Walberg (Eds.), Research on teaching: Concepts, findings, and implications. Berkeley, CA: McCutchan.

MEICHENBAUM, D. (1977). Cognitive behavior modification: An integrative approach. New York: Plenum.

MEICHENBAUM, D., BURLAND, S., GRUSON, L., & CAMERON, R. (1985). Metacognitive assessment. In S. Yussen (Ed.), The growth of reflection in children. Orlando, FL: Academic Press.

MENDELS, G. E., & FLANDERS, J. P. (1973). Teacher's expectations and pupil performance. American Educational Research Journal, 10, 203–212.

MERCER, C. (1982). Learning disabilities. In H. Haring (Ed.), Exceptional children and youth. Columbus, OH: Charles E. Merrill.

MERCER, J. (1973). Labeling the mentally retarded. Berkeley, CA: University of California Press.

MERRILL, M. C., SCHNEIDER, E. W., & FLETCHER, K. A. (1980). TICCIT. Englewood Cliffs, NJ: Educational Technology Publications.

MESSER, S. (1970). Reflection-impulsivity: Stability and school failure. Journal of Educational Psychology, 61, 487–490.

MESSER, S. (1976). Reflection-impulsivity: A review. Psychological Review, 83, 1026–1052.

MESSICK, S. (1980). The effectiveness of coaching for the SAT: Review and reanalysis of research from the fifties to the FTC. Princeton, NJ: Educational Testing Service.

MESSICK, S., & JUNGEBLUT, A. (1981). Time and method in coaching for the SAT. Psychological Bulletin, 89, 191–216.

METCALFE, B. (1981). Self-concept and attitude toward school. British Journal of Educational Psychology, 51, 66–76.

MEYER, B. J. F., BRANDT, D. M., & BLUTH, G. J. (1980). Use of top-level structure in text: Key for reading comprehension of ninth-graders. Reading Research Quarterly, 15, 72–103.

MILLER, G. A. (1956). The magical number seven, plus or minus two: Some limits on our capacity for processing information. Psychological Review, 63, 81–97.

MILLER, G. A., GALANTER, E., & PRIBRAM, K. H. (1960). Plans and the structure of behavior. New York: Holt.

MILLER, P. H. (1983). Theories of developmental psychology. San Francisco: W. H. Freeman.

MILLER, R. B. (1962). Analysis and specification of behavior for training. In R. Glaser (Ed.), Training research and education: Science edition. New York: Wiley.

MOOS, R. H., & MOOS, B. S. (1978). Classroom social climate and student absences and grades. Journal of Educational Psychology, 70, 263–269.

MORGAN, M. (1984). Reward-induced decrements and increments in intrinsic motivation. Review of Educational Research, 54, 5–30.

MORGAN, M. (1985). Self-monitoring of attained subgoals in private study. Journal of Educational Psychology, 77, 623–630.

MORRIS, C. G. (1982). Psychology: An introduction (4th ed.). Englewood Cliffs, NJ: Prentice-Hall.

MORRIS, C. G. (1985). Psychology (5th ed.). Englewood Cliffs, NJ: Prentice-Hall.

MORROW, L., & WEINSTEIN, C. (1986). Encouraging voluntary reading: The impact of a literature. Reading Research Quarterly, 21, 330–346.

MORROW, L. M., & WEINSTEIN, C. S. (in press). Increasing children's use of literature through program and physical design changes. Elementary School Journal.

MOSKOWITZ, B. A. (1978). The acquisition of language. Scientific American, 239, 92–108.

MOSKOWITZ, G., & HAYMAN, M. L. (1976). Successful strategies of inner-city teachers: A year-long study. Journal of Educational Research, 69, 283–289.

MURRAY, H. G. (1983). Low inference classroom teaching behavior and student ratings of college teaching effectiveness. Journal of Educational Psychology, 75, 138–149.

MUSGRAVE, G. R. (1975). Individualized instruction: Teaching strategies focusing on the learner. Boston, MA: Allyn & Bacon.

MUSSEN, P., CONGER, J. J., & KAGAN, J. (1979). Child development and personality (5th ed.). New York: Harper and Row.

NAREMORE, R. (1970, March). Teacher differences in attitudes toward children's speech characteristics. Paper presented at the meeting of the American Educational Research Association.

NATIONAL ASSESSMENT OF EDUCATIONAL PROGRESS. (1976). Functional literacy: Basic reading performance. Denver, CO: Author.

NATIONAL COMMISSION ON EXCELLENCE IN EDUCATION. (1983). A nation at risk: The imperative for educational reform. Washington, DC: U.S. Government Printing Office.

NATIONAL EDUCATION ASSOCIATION. (1984). Nationwide teacher opinion poll. Washington, DC: Author.

NATIONAL EDUCATION ASSOCIATION. (1985). Estimates of School Statistics, 1984–85. Washington, DC: Author.

NEIMARK, E. (1975). Intellectual development during adolescence. In F. D. Horowitz (Ed.), Review of child development research (Vol. 4). Chicago: University of Chicago Press.

NEISSER, U. (1979). The concept of intelligence. In R. Sternberg & D. Detterman (Eds.), Human intelligence: Perspectives on its theory and measurement. Norwood, NJ: Ablex.

NELSON, K. (1981). Individual differences in language development: Implications for development and language. Developmental Psychology, 17, 170–187.

NORMAN, D. P. (1982). Learning and memory. San Francisco: W. H. Freeman.

NUNGESTER, R. J., & DUCHASTEL, P. C. (1982). Testing versus review: Effects on retention. Journal of Educational Psychology, 74, 18–22.

O'CONNOR, R. D. (1969). Modification of social withdrawal through symbolic modeling. Journal of Applied Behavior Analysis, 2, 15–22.

O'DAY, E. F., KULHAVY, R. W., ANDERSON, W., & MALCZYNSKI, R. J. (1971). Programmed instruction: Techniques and trends. New York: Appleton-Century-Crofts.

OGDEN, J. E., BROPHY, J. E., & EVERTSON, C. M. (1977, April). An experimental investigation of organization and management techniques in first-grade reading groups. Paper presented at the annual meeting of the American Educational Research Association, New York.

O'LEARY, K. D. (1980). Pills or skills for hyperactive children? Journal of Applied Behavior Analysis, 13, 191–204.

O'LEARY, K. D., KAUFMAN, K. F., KASS, R. E., & DRABMAN, R. S. (1970). The effects of loud and soft reprimands on the behavior of disruptive students. Exceptional Children, 37, 145–155.

O'LEARY, K. D., & O'LEARY, S. (Eds.). (1977). Classroom management: The successful use of behavior modification (2nd ed.). Elmsford, NY: Pergamon.

O'LEARY, S. G., & O'LEARY, K. D. (1976). Behavior modification in the schools. In H. Leitenberg (Ed.), Handbook of behavior modification and behavior therapy. Englewood Cliffs, NJ: Prentice-Hall.(a)

O'LEARY, S. G., & O'LEARY, K. D. (1976). Behavior modification in schools: Concepts, procedures, and ethical issues. Report prepared for the Protection of Human Subjects of Biomedical and Behavior Research. Washington, DC: Department of Health, Education and Welfare.(b)

OLLENDICK, T. H., DAILEY, D., & SHAPIRO, E. S. (1983). Vicarious reinforcement: Expected and unexpected effects. Journal of Applied Behavior Analysis, 16, 485–491.

OLLENDICK, T. H., MATSON, J. L., ESVELDT-DAWSON, K., & SHAPIRO, E. S. (1980). Increasing spelling achievement: An analysis of treatment procedures utilizing an alternating treatments design. Journal of Applied Behavior Analysis, 13, 645–654.

OLSON, D. R. (1985). Computers as tools of the intellect. Educational Researcher, 14, 5–7.

OOSTHOEK, H., & ACKERS, G. (1973). The evaluation of an audio-taped course (II). British Journal of Educational Technology, 4, 55–73.

ORLANSKY, J., & STRING, J. (1981). Computer-based instruction for military training. Defense Management Journal, 2nd Quarter, 46–54.

ORNSTEIN, A. C. (1980). Teacher salaries: Past, present, and future. Phi Delta Kappan, 61, 677–679.

ORNSTEIN, A. C., & MILLER, H. L. (1980). Looking into education: An introduction to American education. Chicago: Rand McNally.

OSBORN, A. F. (1963). Applied imagination (3rd ed.). New York: Scribner's.

O'SULLIVAN, J. T., & PRESSLEY, M. (1984). Completeness of instruction and strategy transfer. Journal of Experimental Child Psychology, 38, 275–288.

PAGE, E. B. (1958). Teacher comments and student performances: A 74-classroom experiment in school motivation. Journal of Educational Psychology, 49, 173–181.

PALINSCAR, A. S., & BROWN, A. L. (1984). Reciprocal teaching of comprehension-fostering and comprehension-monitoring activities. Cognition and Instruction, 1, 117–175.

PALLAS, A. M., & ALEXANDER, K. (1983). Sex differences in quantitative SAT performance:

New evidence on the differential coursework hypothesis. *American Educational Research Journal, 20,* 165–182.

PAPALIA, D. E., & OLDS, S. W. (1981). *Human development.* New York: McGraw-Hill.

PAPERT, S. (1980). *Mindstorms.* New York: Basic Books.

PARK, O., & TENNYSON, R. D. (1980). Adaptive design strategies for selecting number and presentation order of examples in coordinate concept acquisition. *Journal of Educational Psychology, 72,* 362–370.

PATTISON, P., & GRIEVE, N. (1984). Do spatial skills contribute to sex differences in different types of mathematical problems? *Journal of Educational Psychology, 76,* 678–689.

PAUK, W. (1974). *How to study in college* (2nd ed.). Boston: Houghton Mifflin.

PAULMAN, R. G., & KENNELLY, K. J. (1984). Test anxiety and ineffective test taking: Different names, same construct? *Journal of Educational Psychology, 76,* 279–288.

PAVIO, A. (1971). *Imagery and verbal processes.* New York: Holt, Rinehart & Winston.

PEA, R. D., & KURLAND, M. K. (1985). On the cognitive effects of learning computer programming. *New Ideas in Psychology,* 137–167.

PEECK, J., van den BOSCH, A. B., & KREUPELING, W. J. (1982). Effect of mobilizing prior knowledge on learning from text. *Journal of Educational Psychology, 74,* 771–777.

PELHAM, W. E. (1981). Attention deficits in hyperactive and learning-disabled children. *Exceptional Education Quarterly, 2,* 13–23.

PEPER, R. J., & MAYER, R. E. (1986). Generative effects of note taking during science lectures. *Journal of Educational Psychology, 78,* 34–38.

PERKINS, D. N. (1986). Thinking frames. *Educational Leadership, 43,* 4–11.

PETERS, E. E., & LEVIN, J. R. (1986). Effects of a mnemonic imagery strategy on good and poor readers' prose recall. *Reading Research Quarterly, 21,* 179–192.

PETERSON, P. (1979). Direct instruction reconsidered. In P. Peterson & H. Walberg (Eds.), *Research on teaching: Concepts, findings, and implications.* Berkeley, CA: McCutchan.

PETERSON, P., & FENNEMA, E. (1985). Effective teaching, student engagement in classroom activities, and sex-related differences in learning mathematics. *American Educational Research Journal, 22,* 309–337.

PETERSON, P., JANICKI, T. C., & SWING, S. R. (1980). Aptitude-treatment interaction effects of three social studies teaching approaches. *American Educational Research Journal, 17,* 339–360.

PETKOVICH, M. D., & TENNYSON, R. D. (1984). Clark's "learning from media": A critique. *Educational Communication Technology Journal, 32,* 233–241.

PETTEGREW, L. S., & WOLF, G. E. (1982). Validating measures of teacher stress. *American Educational Research Journal, 19,* 373–396.

PFEFFER, C. R. (1981). Developmental issues among children of separation and divorce. In I. Stuart & L. Abt (Eds.), *Children of separation and divorce.* New York: Van Nostrand Reinhold.

PFIFFNER, L. J., ROSEN, L. A., & O'LEARY, S. G. (1985). The efficacy of an all-positive approach to classroom management. *Journal of Applied Behavior Analysis, 18,* 257–261.

PIAGET, J. (1954). *The construction of reality in the child* (M. Cook, Trans.). New York: Basic Books.

PIAGET, J. (1963). *Origins of intelligence in children.* New York: Norton.

PIAGET, J. (1967). *Six psychological studies.* New York: Random House.

PIAGET, J. (1970). *The science of education and the psychology of the child.* New York: Orion Press.

PIAGET, J. (1974). *Understanding causality* (D. Miles and M. Miles, Trans.). New York: Norton.

PIDGEON, D. A. (1970). *Expectation and pupil performance.* London: National Foundation for Educational Research.

PIPPERT, R. A. (1969). *A study of creativity and faith.* Manitoba Department of Youth and Education, Monograph No. 4.

PLATT, W., & BAKER, B. A. (1931). The relation of the scientific "hunch" to research. *Journal of Chemical Evaluation, 8,* 1969–2000.

POIROT, J. (1986, January). Computer literacy: What is it? *Electronic Learning,* pp. 33–36.

POLIT, D. E., NUTTALL, R. L., & NUTTALL, E. V. (1980). The only child grows up: A look at some characteristics of adult only children. *Family Relations, 29,* 99–106.

POPHAM, W. J. (1969). Objectives and instruction. In W. J. Popham, E. W. Eisner, H. J. Sullivan, & L. I. Tyler (Eds.), *Instructional objectives* (Monograph Series on Curriculum Evaluation, No. 3). Chicago: Rand McNally.

POSNER, M. I. (1973). *Cognition: An introduction.* Glenview, IL: Scott, Foresman.

PRAWAT, R. S., ANDERSON, A., DIAMOND, B., McKEAGUE, D., & WHITMER, S. (1981, April). *Teacher thinking about the affective domain: An interview study.* Paper presented at the annual meeting of the American Educational Research Association, Los Angeles.

PREMACK, D. (1965). Reinforcement theory. In D. Levine (Ed.), *Nebraska symposium on motivation* (Vol. 13). Lincoln, NE: University of Nebraska Press.

PRESSE, D. P., & RESCHLY, D. J. (1986). Larry P.: A case of segregation, testing, or program efficacy? *Exceptional Children, 52,* 333–346.

PRESSLEY, M. (1982). Elaboration and memory development. *Child Development, 53,* 296–309.

PRESSLEY, M., BORKOWSKI, J. G., & O'SULLIVAN, J. T. (1984). Memory strategy instruction is made of this: Metamemory and durable strategy use. *Educational Psychologist, 19,* 94–107.

PRESSLEY, M., LEVIN, J., & DELANEY, H. D. (1982). The mnemonic keyword method. *Review of Research in Education, 52,* 61–91.

PRICE, G., & O'LEARY, K. D. (1974). Teaching children to develop high performance standards. Unpublished manuscript, State University of New York at Stony Brook.

PRING, R. (1971). Bloom's taxonomy: A philosophical critique. *Cambridge Journal of Education, 1,* 83–91.

PROGRAM ON TEACHING EFFECTIVENESS. (1976). *A factorially designed experiment on teacher structuring, soliciting, and reacting* (Research and Development Memorandum No. 147). Stanford, CA: Stanford Center for Research and Development in Teaching.

PULLING IT TOGETHER IN PORT HUENEME. (1986, April). *Electronic Education,* p. 14.

PURKEY, W. W. (1970). *Self-concept and school achievement.* Englewood Cliffs, NJ: Prentice-Hall.

QUAY, H. C. (1979). Classification. In H. Quay & J. Werry (Eds.), *Psychopathological disorders of childhood* (2nd ed.). New York: Wiley.

RAGOSTA, M., HOLLAND, P. W., & JAMESON, D. T. (1982, June). *Computer-assisted instruction and compensatory education: The ETS/LAUSD study* (Executive Summary to U.S.

National Institute of Education, Contract No. 0400-78-0065). Princeton, NJ: Educational Testing Service.

RAMEY, C. T., & HASKINS, R. (1981). The modification of intelligence through early experience. *Intelligence, 5,* 5–19. (a)

RAMEY, C. T., & HASKINS, R. (1981). Early education, intellectual development, and school performance: A reply to Authur Jensen and J. McVicker Hunt. *Intelligence, 5,* 41–48. (b)

RASCHE, D. B., DEDRICK, C. V., STRATHE, M. I., & HAWKES, R. R. (1985). Teacher stress: The elementary teacher's perspective. *Elementary School Journal, 85,* 559–564.

RAUDSEPP, E., & HAUGH, G. P. (1977). *Creative growth games.* New York: Harcourt Brace Jovanovich.

RAVITCH, D. (1985). Scapegoating the teachers. In F. Schultz (Ed.), *Annual editions: Education, 1985/1986* (pp. 212–221). Guilford, CT: Duskin.

REDFIELD, D. L., & ROUSSEAU, E. W. (1981). A meta-analysis of experimental research on teacher questioning behavior. *Review of Educational Research, 51,* 181–193.

REED, S. K. (1982). *Cognition: Theory and applications.* Monterey, CA: Brooks/Cole.

REID, D. K., & HRESKO, W. P. (1981). *A cognitive approach to learning disabilities.* New York: McGraw-Hill.

REIS, S. M. (1981). *An analysis of the productivity of gifted students participating in programs using the revolving door identification model.* Storrs, CT: University of Connecticut, Bureau of Educational Research.

RESNICK, L. B. (1981). Instructional psychology. *Annual Review of Psychology, 32,* 659–704.

REYNOLDS, W. M. (1980). Self-esteem and classroom behavior in elementary school children. *Psychology in the Schools, 17,* 273–277.

RICKARDS, J., & AUGUST, G. J. (1975). Generative underlining strategies in prose recall. *Journal of Educational Psychology, 67,* 860–865.

RIST, R. (1970). Student social class and teacher expectations: The self-fulfilling prophecy in ghetto education. *Harvard Educational Review, 40,* 411–451.

ROBERSON, S. D., KEITH, T. Z., & PAGE, E. B. (1983). Now who aspires to teach? *Educational Researcher, 12,* 13–21.

ROBIN, A. L. (1976). Behavioral instruction in college classrooms. *Review of Educational Research, 46,* 313–355.

ROBINSON, C. S., & HAYES, J. R. (1978). Making inferences about relevance in understanding problems. In R. Revlin & R. E. Mayer (Eds.), *Human reasoning.* Washington, DC: Winston.

ROBINSON, D. W. (1978). Beauty, monster, or something in between? 22 views of public schooling. *The Review of Education, 4,* 263–274.

ROBINSON, F. P. (1961). *Effective study.* New York: Harper and Row.

ROBINSON, N. M., & ROBINSON, H. B. (1976). *The mentally retarded child* (2nd ed.). New York: McGraw-Hill.

ROEDELL, W. C., SLABY, R. G., & ROBINSON, H. B. (1976). *Social development in young children: A report for teachers.* Washington, DC: National Institute of Education.

ROEMER, R. E. (1978). The social conditions for schoolings. In A. B. Calvin (Ed.), *Perspectives on education.* Reading, MA: Addison-Wesley.

ROETHLISBERGER, F. J., & DICKSON, W. J. (1939). *Management and the worker.* Cambridge, MA: Harvard University Press.

ROGERS, D. (1985). *Adolescents and youth* (5th ed.). Englewood Cliffs, NJ: Prentice-Hall.

ROGOFF, B., & WERTSCH, J. V. (Eds.). (1984). *Children's learning in the "zone of proximal development."* San Francisco: Jossey-Bass.

ROLLINS, H. A., McCANDLESS, B. R., THOMPSON, M., & BRASSELL, W. R. (1974). Project Success Environment: An extended application of contingency management in inner-city schools. *Journal of Educational Psychology, 66,* 167–178.

ROSCH, E. (1973). On the internal structure of perceptual and semantic categories. In T. Moore (Ed.), *Cognitive development and the acquisition of language.* New York: Academic Press.

ROSCH, E. H. (1975). Cognitive representations of semantic categories. *Journal of Experimental Psychology: General, 104,* 192–233.

ROSEN, L. A., O'LEARY, S. G., JOUCE, S. A., CONWAY, G., & PFIFFNER, L. J. (1984). The importance of prudent negative consequences for maintaining the appropriate behavior of hyperactive students. *Journal of Abnormal Child Psychology, 12,* 581–604.

ROSEN, R., & HALL, E. (1983). *Sexuality and modern life.* New York: Random House.

ROSENBERGER, G. (1985, August 18). Letting in "latchkey children." *New York Times Fall Survey of Education,* pp. 17–18.

ROSENSHINE, B. (1977, April). *Primary grades instruction and student achievement.* Paper presented at the annual meeting of the American Educational Research Association, New York.

ROSENSHINE, B. (1979). Content, time, and direct instruction. In P. Peterson & H. Walberg (Eds.), *Research on teaching: Concepts, findings, and implications,* Berkeley, CA: McCutchan.

ROSENSHINE, B. (1986). Synthesis of research on explicit teaching. *Educational Leadership, 43*(7), 60–69.

ROSENSHINE, B., & FURST, N. (1973). The use of direct observation to study teaching. In R. Travers (Ed.), *Second handbook of research on teaching.* Chicago: Rand McNally.

ROSENSHINE, B., & STEVENS, R. (1986). Teaching functions. In M. Wittrock (Ed.), *Handbook of research on teaching* (3rd ed., pp. 376–391). New York: Macmillan.

ROSENTHAL, R. (1973). The Pygmalion effect lives. *Psychology Today,* pp. 56–63.

ROSENTHAL, R. (1976). *Experimenter effects in behavioral research* (enlarged ed.). New York: Halsted Press.

ROSS, S. M. (1984). Matching the lesson to the student: Alternative adaptive designs for individualized learning systems. *Journal of Computer-Based Instruction, 11,* 42–47.

ROSS, S. M. (1986). *BASIC programming for educators.* Englewood Cliffs, NJ: Prentice-Hall.

ROSS, S. M., McCORMICK, D., KRISAK, N., & ANAND, P. (1985). Personalizing context in teaching mathematical concepts: Teacher-managed and computer-managed models. *Educational Communication Technology Journal, 33,* 169–178.

ROTTER, J. (1954). *Social learning and clinical psychology.* Englewood Cliffs, NJ: Prentice-Hall.

ROWE, M. B. (1974). Wait-time and rewards as instructional variables: Their influence on language, logic, and fate control. Part 1: Wait-time. *Journal of Research in Science Teaching, 11,* 81–94.

RUMELHART, D. (1977). Understanding and summarizing brief stories. In D. Laberge & S. J. Samuels (Eds.), *Basic processes in reading.* Hillsdale, NJ: Erlbaum.

RUMELHART, D. E., & ORTONY, A. (1977). The representation of knowledge in memory. In R. Anderson, R. Spiro, & W. Montague (Eds.), *Schooling and the acquisition of knowledge.* Hillsdale, NJ: Erlbaum.

RUST, L. W. (1977). Interests. In S. Ball (Ed.), *Motivation in education.* New York: Academic Press.

RYANS, D. G. (1960). *Characteristics of effective teachers, their descriptions, comparisons and appraisal: A research study.* Washington, DC: American Council on Education.

SADKER, M. & SADKER, D. (1985, March). Sexism in the schoolroom of the '80s. *Psychology Today,* pp. 54–57.

SADKER, M., & SADKER, D. (1986). Questioning skills. In J. Cooper (Ed.), *Classroom teaching skills* (3rd ed., pp. 143–180). Lexington, MA: D. C. Heath.

SALILI, F., MAEHR, M. L., SORENSEN, R. L., & FYANS, L. J. (1976). A further consideration of the effect of evaluation on motivation. *American Educational Research Journal, 13*(2), 85–102.

SANDEFUR, J. T. (1985). Competency assessment of teachers. *Action in Teacher Education, 7,* (1–2), 1–6.

SANTOGROSSI, D. A., O'LEARY, K. D., ROMANCZYK, R. G., & KAUFMAN, K. F. (1973). Self-evaluation by adolescents in a psychiatric hospital school token program. *Journal of Applied Behavior Analysis, 6,* 277–288.

SARASON, S. B., DAVIDSON, K. S., LIGHTALL, F. F., WAITE, R. R., & RUEBUSH, B. H. (1960). *Anxiety in elementary school children.* New York: Wiley.

SARNACKI, R. E. (1979). An examination of test-wiseness in the cognitive test domain. *Review of Research in Education, 49,* 252–279.

SATTLER, J. (1974). *Assessment of children's intelligence.* Philadelphia: Saunders.

SAVAGE, T. V. (1983). The academic qualifications of women choosing education as a major. *Journal of Teacher Education, 34,* 14–19.

SCARR, S., & CARTER-SALTZMAN, L. (1982). Genetics and intelligence. In R. Sternberg (Ed.), *Handbook of human intelligence.* New York: Cambridge University Press.

SCHAB, F. (1980). Cheating in high school: Differences between the sexes (revisited). *Adolescence, 15,* 959–965.

SCHIEDEL, D., & MARCIA, J. (1985). Ego integrity, intimacy, sex role orientation, and gender. *Developmental Psychology, 21,* 149–160.

SCHLECHTY, P. C., & VANCE, V. (1981). Do academically able teachers leave education? The North Carolina case. *Phi Delta Kappan, 63,* 106–112.

SCHLECHTY, P. C., & VANCE, V. (1983). Recruitment, selection, and retention: The shape of the teaching force. *Elementary School Journal, 83,* 469–487.

SCHOOL SALES SURGE (1985, November/December). *Electronic Learning,* p. 12.

SCHUG, M. (1985). Teacher burnout and professionalism. In F. Schultz (Ed.), *Annual Editions: Education, 1985/1986* (pp. 212–221). Guilford, CT: Duskin.

SCHUNK, D. H. (1982). Effects of effort attributional feedback on children's perceived self-efficacy and achievement. *Journal of Educational Psychology, 74,* 548–558.

SCHUNK, D. (1985). Social comparison, self-efficacy, and motivation. In M. Alderman & M. Cohen (Eds.), *Motivation theory and practice for preservice teachers* (pp. 22–36). Washington, DC: Eric Clearinghouse on Teacher Education.

SCRUGGS, T. E., MASTROPIERI, M. A., McLOONE, B., LEVIN, J. R., & MORRISON, C. R. (1985). *Mnemonic facilitation of learning-disabled students' memory for expository prose.* Unpublished manuscript, Utah State University, Logan.

SEEFELDT, C. (1973). Who should teach young children? *Journal of Teacher Education, 24,* 308–311.

SEIBER, J. E., O'NEIL, H. F., & TOBIAS, S. (1977). *Anxiety, learning, and instruction.* Hillsdale, NJ: Erlbaum.

SELF, J. A. (1974). Student models in computer-aided instruction. *International Journal of Man-Machine Studies, 6,* 261–276.

SELIGMAN, C., TUCKER, G., & LAMBERT, W. (1972). The effects of speech style and other attributes on teachers' attitudes toward pupils. *Language in Society, 1,* 131–142.

SERRALDE de SCHOLZ, H. C., & McDOUGALL, R. (1978). Comparison of potential reinforcer ratings between slow learners and regular students. *Behavior Therapy, 9,* 60–64.

SHANE, H. G. (1982). The silicon age and education. *Phi Delta Kappan, 63,* 303–308.

SHANTZ, C. (1975). The development of social cognition. In E. M. Hetherington (Ed.), *Review of CHild development research* (Vol. 5). Chicago: University of Chicago Press.

SHANTZ, D. W., & VOYDANOFF, D. A. (1973). Situational effect on retaliatory aggression at three age levels. *Child Development, 44,* 149–153.

SHAVELSON, R. J., & BOLUS, R. (1982). Self-concept: The interplay of theory and methods. *Psychology, 74,* 3–17.

SHAVELSON, R. J., HUBNER, J. J., & STANTON, G. C. (1976). Self-concept: Validation of construct interpretations. *Review of Educational Research, 46,* 407–442.

SHAVELSON, R. S., & DEMPSEY, N. *Generalizability of measures of teacher effectiveness and teaching process* (Beginning Teacher Evaluation Study, Tech. Rep. No. 3). San Francisco: Far West Laboratory for Educational Research and Development.

SHOSTAK, R. (1986). Lesson presentation skills. In J. Cooper (Ed.), *Classroom teaching skills* (3rd ed., pp. 114–138). Lexington, MA: D. C. Heath.

SHUELL, T. J. (1981). Dimensions of individual differences. In F. H. Farley & N. J. Gordon (Eds.), *Psychology and education: The state of the union.* Berkeley, CA: McCutchan. (a)

SCHUELL, T. J. (1981, April). *Toward a model of learning from instruction.* Paper presented at a meeting of the American Educational Research Association, Los Angeles. (b)

SIEGAL, M. A., & DAVIS, D. M. (1986). *Understanding computer-based education.* New York: Random House.

SIGEL, I. E., & BRODZINSKY, D. M. (1977). Individual differences: A perspective for understanding intellectual development. In H. Hom & P. Robinson (Eds.), *Psychological processes in early education.* New York: Academic Press.

SILBERMAN, C. (1966). Technology is knocking at the schoolhouse door. *Fortune, 74,* 120–125.

SILBERMAN, H. R., MELARAGNO, R. J., COULSON, J. E., & ESTEVAN, D. (1961). Fixed sequence versus branching auto-instructional methods. *Journal of Educational Psychology, 52,* 166–172.

SIMON, D. P., & CHASE, W. G. (1973). Skill in chess. *American Scientist, 61,* 394–403.

SIMON, W. (1969). Expectancy effects in the scoring of vocabulary items: A study of scorer bias. *Journal of Educational Measurement, 6,* 159–164.

SINCLAIR, H. (1973). From pre-operational to concrete thinking and parallel development of symbolization. In M. Schwebel & J. Raph (Eds.), *Piaget in the classroom.* New York: Basic Books.

SKINNER, B. F. (1953). *Science and human behavior*. New York: Macmillan.

SKINNER, B. F. (1954). The science of learning and the art of teaching. *Harvard Educational Review, 24*, 86–97.

SKINNER, B. F. (1984). The shame of American education. *American Psychologist, 39*, 947–954.

SLAVIN, R. (1977). Classroom reward structure: An analytic and practical review. *Review of Educational Research, 47*, 633–650.

SLAVIN, R. (1978). Student teams and achievement divisions. *Journal of Research and Development in Education, 12*, 38–48.

SLAVIN, R. (1980). Effects of individual learning expectations on student achievement. *Journal of Educational Psychology, 72*, 520–524.(a)

SLAVIN, R. (1980). *Using student team learning* (rev. ed.). Baltimore: The Johns Hopkins University, Center for Social Organization of Schools.(b)

SLAVIN, R. E. (1983). *Cooperative learning*. New York: Longman.

SLAVIN, R. (1986). *Educational psychology: Theory into practice*. Englewood Cliffs, NJ: Prentice-Hall.

SLAVIN, R., & KARWEIT, N. J. (1984). *Mathemtics achievement effects of three levels of individualization: Whole class, ability grouped, and individualized* (Report No. 349). Baltimore: The Johns Hopkins University, Center for Social Organization in Schools.

SLAVIN, R., & KARWEIT, N. (1985). Effects of whole class, ability grouped, and individualized instruction on mathematics achievement. *American Educational Research Journal, 22*, 351–368.

SMITH, F. (1975). *Comprehension and learning: A conceptual framework for teachers*. New York: Holt, Rinehart & Winston.

SMITH, S. M., GLENBERG, A., & BJORK, R. A. (1978). Environmental context and human memory. *Memory and Cognition, 6*, 342–353.

SNOW, R. E. (1977). Research on aptitude for learning: A progress report. In L. Shulman (Ed.), *Review of research in education*. Itasca, IL: F. E. Peacock.

SNOW, R. E. (1969). Unfinished Pygmalion. *Contemporary Psychology, 14*, 197–199.

SNOWMAN, J. (1984). Learning tactics and strategies. In G. Phye & T. Andre (Eds.), *Cognitive instructional psychology*. Orlando, FL: Academic Press.

SOAR, R. S. (1973). *Follow-through classroom process measurement and pupil growth 1970–1971: Final report*. Gainesville, FL: University of Florida.

SOAR, R., & SOAR, R. (1979). Emotional climate and management. In P. Peterson & H. Walberg (Eds.), *Research on teaching: Concepts, findings, and implications*. Berkeley, CA: McCutchan.

SOLOMON, G. (1986, March). Electronic research. *Electronic Learning*, pp. 37–40.

SOLOWAY, E., LOCKHEAD, J., & CLEMENT, J. (1982). Does computer programming enhance problem solving ability? Some positive evidence on algebra word problems. In R. J. Seidel, R. E. Anderson, & S. B. Hunter (Eds.), *Computer literacy*. New York: Academic Press.

SPEARMAN, C. (1927). *The abilities of man: Their nature and measurement*. New York: Macmillan.

SPIELBERGER, C. D. (Ed.). (1966). *Anxiety and behavior*. New York: Academic Press.

SROUFE, L. A., FOX, N. E., & PANCAKE, V. (1983). Attachment and dependency in developmental perspective. *Child Development, 54*, 1615–1627.

STALLINGS, J. (1980). Allocated academic learning time revisited, or beyond time on task. *Educational Researcher, 9*, 11–16.

STALLINGS, J. A., & KASKOWITZ, D. H. (1975, April). *A study of follow-through implementation*. Paper presented at the annual meeting of the American Educational Research Association, Washington, DC.

STANLEY, J. (1980). On educating the gifted. *Educational Researcher, 9*, 8–12.

STARCH, D., & ELLIOT, E. C. (1912). Reliability of grading high school work in English. *Scholastic Review, 20*, 442–457.

STARCH, D., & ELLIOT, E. C. (1913). Reliability of grading work in history. *Scholastic Review, 21*, 676–681.(a)

STARCH, D., & ELLIOT, E. C. (1913). Reliability of grading work in mathematics. *Scholastic Review, 21*, 254–259.(b)

STARR, R. H., JR (1979). Child abuse. *American Psychologist, 34*, 872–878.

STEIN, B. S., LITTLEFIELD, J., BRANSFORD, J. D., & PERSAMPIERI, M. (1984). Elaboration and knowledge acquisition. *Memory and Cognition, 12*, 522–529.

STERNBERG, R. (1985). *Beyond IQ: A triarchic theory of human intelligence*. New York: Cambridge University Press.

STERNBERG, R. J. (1986). *Intelligence applied: Understanding and increasing your own intellectual skills*. New York: Harcourt Brace Jovanovich.

STERNBERG, R., & DAVIDSON, J. (1982, June). The mind of the puzzler. *Psychology Today*, pp. 37–44.

STEWART, J. R. (1980). Teachers who stimulate curiosity. *Education, 101*, 158–165.

STEWART, L. G., & WHITE, M. A. (1976). Teacher comments, letter grades and student performance: What do we really know? *Journal of Educational Psychology, 68*(4), 488–500.

STRAUS, M. A., GELLES, R. J., & STEINMETZ, S. K. (1980). *Behind closed doors: Violence in the American family*. New York: Doubleday.

STROTHER, D. B. (1984). Latchkey children: The fastest-growing special interest group in the schools. *Phi Delta Kappan, 66*, 290–293.

SULZER-AZAROFF, B., & MAYER, G. R. (1986). *Achieving educational excellence using behavioral strategies*. New York: Holt, Rinehart & Winston.

SUPPES, P. (1984). Observations about the application of artificial intelligence research to education. In D. F. Walker & R. D. Hess (Eds.), *Instructional software: Principles and perspectives for design and use* (pp. 298–306). Belmont, CA: Wadsworth.

SUPPES, P., JERMAN, M. & BRIAN, D. (1968). *Computer-assisted instruction: The 1965–66 Stanford arithmetic program*. New York: Academic Press.

SUPPES, P., & MACKEN, E. (1978). The historical path from research and development to operational use of CAI. *Educational Technology, 18*, 9–12.

SUPPES, P., & MORNINGSTAR, M. (1972). *Computer-assisted instruction at Stanford, 1966–1968: Data, models, and evaluation of the arithmetic programs*. New York: Academic Press.

SWANSON, R. A., & HENDERSON, R. W. (1977). Effects of televised modeling and active participation on rule-governed question production among native American pre-school children. *Contemporary Educational Psychology, 2*, 345–352.

SWIFT, J., & GOODING, C. (1983). Interaction of wait-time, feedback, and questioning instruction in middle school science teaching. *Journal of Research in Science Teaching, 20*, 721–730.

SWITZER, E. B., DEAL, T. E., & BAILEY, J. S. (1977). The reduction of stealing in second graders using a group contingency program. *Journal of Applied Behavior Analysis, 10*, 267–272.

TANNER, J. (1970). Physical growth. In P. Mussen (Ed.), *Carmichael's manual of child psychology* (3rd ed., Vol. 1). New York: Wiley.

TAYLOR, J. B. (1983). Influence of speech variety on teachers' evaluation of reading comprehension. *Journal of Educational Psychology, 75*, 662–667.

TAYLOR, R. P. (Ed.). (1980). *The computer in the school: Tutor, tool, tutee*. New York: Teachers College Press.

TENBRINK, T. D. (1986). Writing instructional objectives. In J. Cooper (Ed.), *Classroom teaching skills* (3rd ed., pp. 71–110). Lexington, MA: D. C. Heath.

TENNYSON, R. D. (1981, April). *Concept learning effectiveness using prototype and skill development presentation forms*. Paper presented at the annual meeting of the American Educational Research Association, Los Angeles.

TENNYSON, R. D., & ROTHEN, W. (1977). Pretask and on-task adaptive design strategies for selecting number of instances in concept acquisition. *Journal of Educational Psychology, 69*, 586–592.

TERMAN, L. M., BALDWIN, B. T., & BRONSON, E. (1925). Mental and physical traits of a thousand gifted children. In L. M. Terman (Ed.), *Genetic studies of genius* (Vol. 1). Stanford, CA: Stanford University Press.

TERMAN, L. M., & ODEN, M. H. (1947). The gifted child grows up. In L. M. Terman (Ed.), *Genetic studies of genius* (Vol. 4). Stanford, CA: Stanford University Press.

TERMAN, L. M., & ODEN, M. H. (1959). The gifted group in mid-life. In L. M. Terman (Ed.), *Genetic studies of genius* (Vol. 5). Stanford, CA: Stanford University Press.

TERWILLIGER, J. S. (1971). *Assigning grades to students*. Glenview, IL: Scott, Foresman.

THOMPSON, T. J. (1979). An overview of microprocessor central processing units (CPUs). *Educational Technology, 10*, 41–44.

THORNDIKE, E. L. (1913). Educational psychology. In *The psychology of learning* (Vol. 2). New York: Teachers College, Columbia University.

THORNDIKE, R., HAGEN, E., & SATTLER, J. (1986). *The Stanford-Binet Intelligence Scale* (4th ed.). Chicago: Riverside.

THURSTONE, L. L. (1938). Primary mental abilities. *Psychometric Monographs*, No. 1.

TOBIAS, S. (1979). Anxiety research in educational psychology. *Journal of Educational Psychology, 71*, 573–582.

TOBIAS, S. (1981). Adaptation to individual differences. In F. Farley & N. Gordon (Eds.), *Psychology and education: The state of the union*. Berkeley, CA: McCutchan.

TOBIAS, S. (1982, January). Sexist equations. *Psychology Today*, pp., 14–17.(a)

TOBIAS, S. (1982). When do instructional methods make a difference? *Educational Researcher, 11*(4), 4–10.(b)

TOBIAS, S., & DUCHASTEL, P. (1974). Behavioral objectives, sequence, and anxiety in CAI. *Instructional Science, 3*, 232–242.

TORRANCE, E. P. (1972). Predictive validity of the Torrance tests of creative thinking. *Journal of Creative Behavior, 6*, 236–262.

TORRANCE, E. P., & HALL, L. K. (1980). Assessing the future reaches of creative potential. *Journal of Creative Behavior, 14*, 1–19.

TRAVERS, R. M. W. (1977). *Essentials of learning* (4th ed.). New York: Macmillan.

TRAVERS, R. M. W. (1982). *Essentials of learning: The new cognitive learning for students of education* (5th ed.). New York: Macmillan.

TRICKETT, E., & MOOS, R. (1974). Personal correlates of contrasting environments: Student satisfaction with high school classrooms. *American Journal of Community Psychology, 2*, 1–12.

TULVING, E. (1972). Episodic and semantic memory. In E. Tulving & W. Donaldson (Eds.), *Organization of memory.* New York: Academic Press.

TYLER, L. E. (1974). *Individual differences: Abilities and motivational directions.* New York: Appleton-Century-Crofts.

URE, A. (1861). *The philosophy of manufactures: Or an exposition of the scientific, moral, and commercial economy of the factory system of Great Britain* (3rd ed.). London: H. G. Bohn.

VAILLANT, G. E., & VAILLANT, C. O. (1981). Natural history of male psychological health, X: Work as a predictor of positive mental health. *The American Journal of Psychiatry, 138*, 1433–1440.

VAN MONDRANS, A. P., BLACK, H. G., KEYSOR, R. E., OLSEN, J. B., SHELLEY, M. F., & WILLIAMS, D. D. (1977). Methods of inquiry in educational psychology. In D. Treffinger, J. Davis, & R. R. Ripple (Eds.), *Handbook on teaching educational psychology.* New York: Academic Press.

VEENMAN, S. (1984). Perceived problems of beginning teachers. *Review of Educational Research, 54*, 143–178.

VIDLER, D. C. (1977). Curiosity. In S. Ball (Ed.), *Motivation in education.* New York: Academic Press.

VITELLO, S. J., & SOSKIN, R. (1984). *Mental retardation: Its social and legal context.* Englewood Cliffs, NJ: Prentice-Hall.

VYGOTSKY, L. S. (1978). *Mind in society: The development of higher mental processes.* Cambridge, MA: Harvard University Press.

WADSWORTH, B. J. (1978). *Piaget for the classroom teacher.* New York: Longman.(a)

WADSWORTH, B. J. (1978). *Piaget's theory of cognitive development: An introduction for students of psychology and education* (2nd ed.). New York: Longman.(b)

WALBERG, H. J., PASCAL, R. A., & WEINSTEIN, T. (1985). Homework's powerful effects on learning. *Educational Leadership, 42*(7), 76–79.

WALBERG, H. J., & UGUROGLU, M. E. (1980). Motivation and educational productivity: Theories, results, and implications. In L. J. Fyans, Jr. (Ed.), *Achievement motivation: Recent trends in theory and research.* New York: Plenum.

WALDEN, E. L., & THOMPSON, S. A. (1981). A review of some alternative approaches to drug management of hyperactive children. *Journal of Learning Disabilities, 14*, 213–217.

WALKER, D. F., & HESS, R. D. (1984). *Instructional software: Principles and perspectives for design and use.* Belmont, CA: Wadsworth.

WARD, B., & TIKUNOFF, W. (1976). The effective teacher application problem: Application of selected research results and methodology to teaching. *Journal of Teacher Education, 27*, 48–52.

WAXMAN, H. C., & WALBERG, H. J. (1982). The relation of teaching and learning: A review of reviews of process-product research. *Contemporary Educational Review, 1*, 103–120.

WEAVER, W. T. (1979). The need for new talent in teaching. *Phi Delta Kappan, 61*, 29–46.

WEBB, N. (1985). Verbal interaction and learning in peer-directed groups. *Theory into Practice, 24*, 32–39.

WEBB, N. M. (1980). A process-outcome analysis of learners in group and individual settings. *Educational Psychology, 15*, 69–83.

WECHSLER, D. (1958). *The measurement and appraisal of adult intelligence* (4th ed.). Baltimore: Williams & Wilkins.

WECHSLER, D. (1974). *Manual for the Wechsler Intelligence Scale for Children—Revised.* New York: The Psychological Corporation.

WEINER, B. (1979). A theory of motivation for some classroom experiences. *Journal of Educational Psychology, 71*, 3–25.

WEINER, B. (1980). The role of affect in rational (attributional) approaches to human motivation. *Educational Researcher, 9*, 4–11.

WEINER, B. (1984). Principles for a theory of student motivation and their application within an attributional framework. In R. Ames & C. Ames (Eds.), *Research on motivation in education* (Vol. 1). Orlando, FL: Academic Press.

WEINER, B., RUSSELL, D., & LERMAN, D. (1978). Affective consequences of causal ascriptions. In J. H. Harvey, W. J. Ickes, & R. F. Kidd (Eds.), *New directions in attribution research* (Vol. 2). Hillsdale, NJ: Erlbaum.

WEINSTEIN, C. S. (1977). Modifying student behavior in an open classroom through changes in the physical design. *American Educational Research Journal, 14*, 249–262.

WEINSTEIN, C. E., & MAYER, R. E. (1985). The teaching of learning strategies. In M. C. Wittrock (Ed.), *Handbook of research on teaching* (3rd ed.). New York: Macmillan.

WERTSCH, J. V. (1985). Adult-child interaction as a source of self-regulation in children. In S. Yussen (Ed.), *The growth of reflection in children.* Orlando, FL: Academic Press.

WESSELLS, M. G. (1982). *Cognitive psychology.* New York: Harper and Row.

WESSMAN, A. (1972). Scholastic and psychological effects of a compensatory education program for disadvantaged high school students: Project A B C. *American Educational Research Journal, 9*, 361–372.

WEST, C. K., FISH, J. A., & STEVENS, R. J. (1980). General self-concept, self-concept of academic ability and school achievement: Implication for causes of self-concept. *Australian Journal of Education, 24.*

WHITE, B. L., KABAN, B. T., ATTANUCCI, J., & SHAPIRO, B. B. (1978). *Experience and environment: Major influences on the development of the young child.* Englewood Cliffs, NJ: Prentice-Hall.

WHITE, E. M. (1984). Holisticism. *College Composition and Communication, 35*, 400–409.

WHITE, K. R. (1982). The relation between socioeconomic status and academic achievement. *Psychological Bulletin, 91*(3), 461–481.

WHITE, R. W. (1959). Motivation reconsidered: The concept of competence. *Psychological Review, 66*, 297–333.

WHY TEACHERS FAIL. (1984, September 24). *Newsweek*, pp. 64–70.

WIIG, E. H. (1982). Communication disorders. In H. Haring (Ed.), *Exceptional children and youth.* Columbus, OH: Charles E. Merrill.

WILKINS, W. E., & GLOCK, M. D. (1973). *Teacher expectations and student achievement: A rep-

lication and extension.* Ithaca, NY: Cornell University Press.

WILLIAMS, J. P. (1976). *Individual differences in achievement test presentation and evaluation anxiety.* Unpublished doctoral dissertation, University of Illinois, Urbana-Champaign.

WINETT, R. A., KRASNER, L., & KRASNER, M. (1971). Child-monitored token reading program. *Psychology in the Schools, 8*, 259–262.

WINETT, R. A., & WINKLER, R. C. (1972). Current behavior modification in the classroom: Be still, be quiet, be docile. *Journal of Applied Behavior Analysis, 15*, 499–504.

WINOGRAD, P., & JOHNSTON, P. (1982). Comprehension monitoring and the error-detection paradigm. *Journal of Reading Behavior, 14*, 61–76.

WISCONSIN RESEARCH AND DEVELOPMENT CENTER. (1979, Spring). Images are a key to learning. *Wisconsin Research and Development Center News*, pp. 1–2.

WITKIN, H. A., MOORE, C. A., GOODENOUGH, D. R., & COX, R. W. (1977). Field-dependent and field-independent cognitive styles and their educational implications. *Review of Educational Research, 47*, 1–64.

WITTROCK, M. C. (1978). The cognitive movement in instruction. *Educational Psychologist, 13*, 15–30.

WITTROCK, M. C. (1982, March). *Educational implications of recent research on learning and memory.* Paper presented at the annual meeting of the American Educational Research Association, New York.

WLODKOWSKI, R. J. (1981). Making sense out of motivation: A systematic model to consolidate motivational constructs across theories. *Educational Psychologist, 16*, 101–110.

WOMEN ON WORDS AND IMAGES. (1975). *Dick and Jane as victims: Sex stereotyping in children's readers* (expanded ed.). Available from author, P. O. Box 2163, Princeton, NJ.

WOOLFOLK, A. E., & BROOKS, D. (1982). Nonverbal communication in teaching. In E. Gordon (Ed.), *Review of research in education* (Vol. 10). Washington, DC: American Educational Research Association.

WOOLFOLK, A. E., & BROOKS, D. (1985). The influence of teachers' nonverbal behaviors on students' perceptions and performance. *Elementary School Journal, 85*, 514–528.

WOOLFOLK, A. E., & WOOLFOLK, R. L. (1974). A contingency management technique for increasing student attention in a small group. *Journal of School Psychology, 12*, 204–212.

WOOLFOLK, A. E., & WOOLFOLK, R. L. (in press). Time-management: An experimental investigation with preservice teachers. *Journal of School Psychology.*

YOUNG, T. (1980). Teacher stress: One school district's approach. *Action in Teacher Education, 2*, 37–40.

YOUNISS, J. (1980). *Parents and peers in social development.* Chicago: University of Chicago Press.

YUSSEN, S. R. (Ed.). (1985). *The growth of reflection in children.* Orlando, FL: Academic Press.

ZIMMERMAN, B. J., & PIKE, E. O. (1972). Effects of modeling and reinforcement on the acquisition and generalization of question-asking behavior. *Child Development, 43*, 892–907.

ZIMMERMAN, D. W. (1981). On the perennial argument about grading "on the curve" in college courses. *Educational Psychologist, 16*, 175–178.

Name Index

A

Ackers, G., 342
Ackerson, G., 279, *307*
Acland, H., 142, 419
Adams, A., 293
Adams, R.S., 410
Aiken, W.M., 114
Ainsworth, M.D.S., 89
Akin, J.N., 20
Albert, J., 156
Alderman, D.L., 514, 570
Alderman, M.K., 323, 324, *345*
Alessi, S.M., 566, *576*
Alexander, K., 146
Allers, R.D., *158*
Allington, R., 336
Alter, M., 468
Alwin, D., 126
Ames, C., 317, *345*
Ames, R., 317, *345*
Ames, W., 279, *307*
Anand, P., 568
Anastasi, A., 508, 515
Anderson, A., 115
Anderson, C.W., 291
Anderson, J.H., 165
Anderson, J.R., 240, 246, 247, 262, *266*, 405
Anderson, L.M., 200, 356, 361, 420
Anderson, L.W., *556*
Anderson, R.E., 561
Anderson, T.H., 293, 295, 299
Anderson, W., 188, 190
Antes, R.L., 489
Appel, L.R., 570
Applegate, J., *29*
Archer, S., 94
Arlin, M., 550

Armbruster, B.B., 295, 299
Armbruster, F.E., 115
Armento, B.A., 353
Ashton, P.T., 55, 69, 70
Ashton-Warner, S., 324
Atkinson, J.W., 321
Atkinson, R.C., 104, 129, 236, 257
Atkinson, R.L., 104, 129
Attanucci, J., 128
Au, K.H., 354
Auble, P.M., 252
Ausubel, D.P., 165
Ayllon, T., 225

B

Babad, E.Y., 339
Backman, M., 126
Bailey, J.S., 215
Baillargeon, R., 65
Baker, L., 259, 261
Baldwin, J.D., 178, 185, *193*
Baldwin, J.J., 178, 185, *193*
Ball, S., 339
Ballard, K.D., 223
Bandura, A., 113, 114, 166, 184, 185, 187, *193*, 223, 314
Bane, M., 142, 419
Bangert, R.L., 190, 407, *413*, 515
Bangert-Drowns, R., 570
Barger, R., 561
Barnett, W.S., 99, 144
Barrett, K.C., 90
Barron, F., 150
Barton, E.J., 185
Baumrind, D., 128–29, 134
Becker, W.C., 22, 199, 205, 213
Beckerman, T.M., 353

Bee, H., 113
Beery, R., 323
Beezer, B., 133, *158*
Bell, R.Q., 133, 134, *158*
Bell, T.H., 14
Benbow, C.P., 146
Berger, K.S., 77, 133
Berliner, D.C., 354, *446*
Berrueta-Clement, J.R., 99, 144
Bershon, B.L., *81*
Bersoff, D.N., 512, 514
Beyer, B.K., 304
Biddle, B.J., 366, 401, 410, 420, 422
Bierman, K.L., 101
Bigge, J., 457
Bigge, M.L., *266*
Binet, A., 138–39, 510
Birns, B., 97
Bjork, R.A., 253
Black, H.B., 39
Blackham, G., 203
Block, J.J., 97, *556*
Bloom, B.S., 106, 354, 392–94, 397, 525, 549, *556*
Bloom, R., 537, 538
Bluth, G.J., 294
Bolus, R., 106
Borich, G., 6–7, *119*
Bork, A., 18, 19, 560–62, 565, 569, 572, 574, *576*
Borkowski, J.G., 258, 260
Bornstein, P.H., 224
Bourdon, L., 537, 538
Bourne, L.E., 280
Bower, G.H., 183, *193*, 302, 314
Bowman, H.L., 570
Bozeman, W.C., 562
Brandt, D.M., 294
Bransford, J.D., 74, 252, *266*, *307*

Brassell, W.R., 216
Braun, C., 331, 334
Bretherton, I., 89
Brewer, W.F., 171
Bridgeman, D., 326
Brodzinsky, D.M., 152, 153, 156
Brolyer, C. R., 297
Bromley, D.B., 105
Brooks, D., 134, 336, 410
Brophy, J.E., 22, 24, 149, 200, 331,
        333, 336, 338, 339, 352, 403,
        420, 426, 435, 440, *446*
Brown, A.L., 74, 259, 261, 262, *266*,
        307, 439
Brown, B., 533
Brown, J.S., 289, 538
Brown, R., 74, 75, 251
Bruner, J.S., 114, 165, 274–76, 281,
        568
Bucher, B., 222
Buckley, N.K., *229*
Burbach, H.J., 454
Burland, S., 73
Burns, P.K., 562
Burton, N.W., 289, 513
Burton, R.R., 538
Burton, R.V., 112
Bush, A.J., 422
Buss, A.R., 125
Button, C., 332, 336
Bybee, R.W., *81*

C

Cahen, L., 534
Callahan, R.E., 114
Cameron, R., 73
Campbell, J.R., 418–19
Campione, J.C., 74, 259, *307*, 439
Campos, J.J., 90
Canter, L., 357, 358, 361, 372, 374,
        375
Canter, M. 357, 358, 361, 372, 374,
        375
Cantrell, R.P., 421
Carnine, D., 293
Carter, K., 526
Carter-Saltzman, L., 143
Cartwright, C.A., 460
Cartwright, G.P., 460
Case, R., 56, 67, 72
Casey, R., *29*
Casserly, P., 146
Cattell, R.B., 147
Cattermole, J., *556*
Caylor, J.S., 476
Cazden, C., 79
Chananie, L.C., 98
Chapman, D.W., 11

Charles, C.M., 366, *377*, 458, 460,
        483
Chase, C.I., 545
Chase, W.G., 290
Chomsky, N., 75
Christy, P.R., 227
Claiborn, W.L., 332
Clarizio, H.F., 173
Clark, C.M., 383, 398
Clark, R., 321, 383, 561, 570
Clark-Stewart, K.A., 98–99
Clement, S.L., 550
Clements, B.S., 356, 357, 364, 366,
        367, *377*, 421, 423, 438, 439
Clements, D.H., 574
Clifford, M.M., *345*, 536, 537, *556*
Coates, J.F., 20
Coates, T.J., 221
Cobbett, W., 304
Coburn, P., 572, *576*
Cocchiarella, M.J., 350
Cohen, D., 142, 419
Cohen, M.W., 324, 331, *345*
Cohen, P.A., 191, 570
Cole, N., 514
Coleman, J.S., 418–19
Collins, M., 262, 424
Conford, E., 114
Conger, J.J., 49
Conner, K., *556*
Conway, G., 200
Cooper, H.M., 33, 339
Cooper, J., *413*
Copi, I.M., 289
Cornbleth, C., 332, 336
Corno, L., 149, *159*, 438, 538, 539
Costa, A.L., 304, *307*
Costello, J., 513
Coulson, J.E., 190
Covington, M., 323
Cox, C.C., 476
Cox, R.W., 155
Cox, W.F., 549, 550
Craig, G., 102, 130
Craik, F.I., 248, *266*
Cronbach, L., 191, 436, 437, 500, 535
Crouse, J.M., 250
Crowder, N.A., 189
Cruickshank, D.C., 422
Cruickshank, D.R., 422, 423
Cullen, F.T., 539
Cullen, J.B., 539

D

Dailey, D., 185
Daiute, C., 571
Damon, W., 100
Danner, F.W., 261
Dansereau, D., 260

Darley, J., 339
Darling-Hammond, L., 4, 9, 10
Darlington, R., 99, 144
Daurio, S.P., 477
Davidson, E.S., 113
Davidson, J., 283, 290, 295, *307*
Davidson, K.S., 339
Davis, D.M., 565
Davis, G.A., 149
Davis, J.A., 326
Davis, O.L., Jr., 332, 336
Day, D., 156
Day, J.D., 259, *307*, 439
Deal, T.E., 215
de Charms, R., 329, 330
Deci, E., 220, 226, 331
Dedrick, C.V., 8, 11, *29*
Delaney, H.D., 257, *267*
De Lisi, R., 65
Dellow, D.A., 569
De Mott, R., 460
Dempsey, N., 426
Dempster, F.N., 244
Denham, C., 383
Deno, S.L., 518
Derry, S.J., *266*
De Vries, D.L., 326
Diamond, B., 115
Dickie, J., 513
Dickson, W.J., 40
Diggs, R.W., 480
Dinnel, D., 280
Doctorow, M., 294
Dominowski, R.L., 280
Donaldson, G., 148
Donaldson, M., 77
Doyle, P.H., 364, 405
Doyle, W., 5, 336, 351, 352, 354,
        364, *377*, 383, 427, 429
Drabman, R.A., 212
Drabman, R.S., 211
Drayer, A.M., 553
Dreikurs, R., 362, *377*
Dressel, P.L., 388
Dretzke, B.J., 257
Driscoll, M., 222
Duchastel, P., 384, 533
Duncker, K., 287
Dunkin, M.J., 366, 401, 422
Dunn, L., 472, 473
Dunn, T.G., 549, 550
Durkin, D., 291
Dweck, C., 316
Dyck, J.L., 574
Dyer, H.S., 384

E

Eaton, J.F., 291
Eaton, W.O., 340

Ebmeier, H.H., 433, 438, *446*
Edwards, K.J., 326
Edwards, S., 13
Eggen, P.D., 282, *307*
Eiseman, J.W., 117
Eisner, E.W., 3
Elashoff, J.D., 331
Elawar, M.C., 538, 539
Elkind, D., 50, 64
Elliott, E.C., 530
Elliot-Faust, D., *267*
Emmer, E.T, 242, 356–58, 361, 363, 364, 366, 367, *377*, 421, 423, 428, 439
Engelhart, M.D., 393
Engelmann, S., 205, 213
Engle, P., 481
Epstein, A.S., 99, 144
Epstein, J., *446*
Erickson, F., 354
Erikson, E., 86–96, 107, *119*
Eron, L., 113
Estes, W.K., 166
Estevan, D., 190
Esveldt-Dawson, K., 202
Evans, E.D., 12
Evertson, C.M., 22, 24, 200, 352, 356, 357, 361, 363, 364, 366, 367, *377*, 420, 421, 423, 435, 438–40

F

Farley, F.H., *28*
Farnham-Diggory, S., 68
Faw, H.W., 278, 279
Fazio, R., 339
Fein, G.G., 98–99, 102
Feitler, F., 350
Feldman, R., 41–43
Felixbrod, J., 221
Fenker, R., *307*
Fennema, E., 146
Ferrara, R.A., 74
Ferster, C.B., 179
Feshbach, F., 350
Fetterman, N., 321
Feuerstein, R., 516
Finn, J., 338
Fish, J.A., 106
Fishbein, J., 214
Fiske, E.B., 530
Flanders, J.P., 331
Flavell, J.H., 71, 73, *81*, 258, 259
Flora, R., *29*
Forrest-Pressley, D.L., *267*
Foster, G.G., 454
Foster, W., 537
Fox, L.H., 476, 477
Fox, N.E., 90

Foxx, R.M., 202
Franks, J.J., 252
Frechling, J.A., 13
Frederiksen, N., 152, *307*
Freeman, W.H., 246
Frender, R., 533
Freud, S., 86, 88
Friedlander, B., 572
Friedrichs, A.G., 73
Fromberg, D.P., 3, 222
Frost, E.J., 393
Frostig, M., 466
Fuhr, M.L., 474
Fuller, F.F., 12
Furman, W., 101
Furst, E.J., 393, *413*
Furst, N., 37, 422, 424
Furth, H., 68
Fyans, L.J., 540

G

Gage, N.L., 398
Gagné, R.M., 236, 237, 272–74, 283, 289
Galanter, E., 235
Gall, M.D., 398, 399, *413*, 424
Gallagher, J.J., 23, 460, 468, 469, *483*
Gallup, A.M., 14, 15, *28–29*, 350
Gardner, H., 136, 137, *159*
Garner, R., 261
Garrett, S.S., 372, *377*
Gelles, R.J., 133
Gelman, R., 59, 65
Gentner, D., 246, 247
Gersten, R., 293
Gillett, M., 424
Gilligan, C., 112
Gilstrap, R.L., 402, 403
Ginsburg, H., 53, 58, 68
Gintis, H., 142, 419
Glaser, R., 165, 291, *556*
Gleitman, H., 137, 142
Glenberg, A., 253
Glock, M.D., 331, 332
Glover, J.A., 280
Glynn, T.L., 223
Gnagey, W.J., 221
Goin, M.T., 257
Goldberg, D., 15
Goldsmith, H.H., 90
Good, T.L., 33, 148, 149, 332, 333, 336, 338, 350, 353, 403, 410, 419, 420, 422, 426, 430, 433, 434, 437, *446*
Goodenough, D.R., 155
Gooding, C., 401
Goodson, B., *576*
Gordon, N.J., *28*, 116

Gordon, T., 370, 372, *377*
Gottlieb, B., 468
Gottlieb, J., 454, 468
Grabe, M., 550
Green, B.F., 492
Green, J., 355, 420
Greene, D., 220, 226, 540
Greeno, J.D., 422
Gregg, L.W., 574
Gresham, F., 463, *483*
Grieve, N., 146
Grinder, R.E., 21
Gronlund, N.E., 387–88, 393, 396, *413*, 501, 526, 527, 530–32, *556*
Grouws, D., 422, 433, *446*
Grunwald, B.B., 362, *377*
Gruson, L., 73
Guerney, L.F., 130
Guilford, J.P., 136–37
Gullo, D.F., 574
Gump, P.V., 364

H

Hagan, E., 139
Hall, E., 103
Hall, J.F., *266*
Hall, L.K., 150
Hallahan, D.P., 456, 458, 461, 463, 466, 468, *483*
Hamilton, R.J., 294, 384, 388
Hancock, G., 336
Haney, W., 510, 512
Hanlon, C., 74
Hansen, D.N., 570
Hansen, R.A., 339
Hansford, B.C., 106
Harder, R.J., 282, *307*
Haring, N.G., 464
Harrington, D.M., 150
Harris, V.W., 214
Harrow, A.J., 395
Hart, F., 530
Hart, L.A., *266*
Haskins, R., 143
Hastings, J.T., 397, 525, *556*
Hattie, J.A., 106
Haugh, G.P., 287
Havighurst, R.J., 148
Hawkes, R.R., 8, 11, *29*
Hayes, J.R., 285
Hayes, S.C., 221, 223
Hayman, M.L., 363
Healy, A., 280
Henderson, R.W., 207
Hersh, R.H., 112, 116, *119*
Hess, R.D., 128, *576*
Hetherington, E.M., 129, 130, 132
Heyns, B., 142, 419

Higbee, K.L., *266*
Hilgard, E.R., 104, 129, 183, *193*, 302, 314
Hill, K.T., 340–42
Hill, W.F., 164, 168, 183, *193*
Hill, W.H., 393
Hiller, J.H., 422
Hills, J.R., 531, 534
Hines, C.V., 422, 423
Hinsley, D., 285
Hoffman, L., 97, 132
Hoffman, M., 107, 108
Holland, J.L., 535
Holland, P.W., 570
Hollingworth, L.S., 476
Holmes, C.T., 537
Holt, J., 14
Hopkins, B.L., 215
Hopkins, C.O., 489
Horn, J.L., 148
Horne, B., 466
Howe, H., 14
Hoyt, J.D., 73
Hresko, W.P., 464, 466, *483*
Hubner, J.J., 106, 114
Huesmann, L.R., 113
Hundert, J., 222
Hunt, J.McV., 67, 144
Hunter, I.M., 367
Hunter, M., 401, 431, *446*
Hutcheson, S.M., 11
Hyde, J., 146

I

Illich, I., 14
Inbar, J., 339
Irving, O., 366
Irwin, J.W., *266*, 295

J

Jacklin, C.N., 146
Jackson, P., 98
Jacobson, L., 331
Jameson, D.T., 570
Janicki, T.C., 436, *446*
Jencks, C., 142, 419
Jensen, A.R., 144, 145, 513
Johnson, D., 326, 374, 561
Johnson, J., *29*
Johnson, R. 326
Johnston, M.B., 260, 261
Jones, J.R., 202
Jones, L., 337, *377*, 513
Jones, V.F., 337, *377*
Jungeblut, A., 515

K

Kaban, B.T., 128
Kagan, J., 49, 134, 156
Kagan, S., 127
Kail, R.V., 101
Kapfer, M.B., *413*
Karweit, N.L., 149, 353, 407
Kash, M.M., 6–7, *119*
Kaskowitz, D.H., 398, 434, 444
Kass, R.E., 211
Katz, L.G., 12
Katzenmeyer, W.G., 421
Kauchak, D.P., 282
Kauffman, J., 456, 458, 461, 463, 466, 468, *483*
Kaufman, K.F., 211, 222
Kaufman, P., 242
Kavchak, D.P., *307*
Keith, T.Z., 11, 15, *29*
Keller, F.S., 191
Kelley, C., 371
Kelley, E.G., 535
Kelman, P., 572, *576*
Kendall, P.C., 224
Kennedy, J.J., 422
Kennedy, J.L., 422, 423
Kennelly, K.J., 341, 342
Keogh, B.K., 241
Keysor, R.E., 39
Kifer, E., 336
King, G., 549
Kirk, S.A., 23, 460, 468, 469, *483*
Klahr, D., 71
Klassen, D.L., 561
Klatzky, R.L., *266*
Klausmeier, H.J., 66, 282
Klein, S., 530
Knapczyk, D.R., 181
Kneedler, P., 303
Kneedler, R., 465
Kohlberg, L., 109–12, 117
Kolata, G.B., 146
Kolesnik, W.B., 318, 321
Komorita, S., 326
Korn, Z., 221, 223
Koser, L., 22
Kounin, J.S., 186, 364, 367, 405
Kozol, J., 14
Krasner, L., 217
Krasner, M., 217
Krathwohl, D.R., 393, 394
Kraus, C., 261
Kreupeling, W.J., 236
Krisak, N., 568
Krumboltz, H.D., 208, 210, *229*
Krumboltz, J.D., 208, 210, *229*
Kulhavy, R.W., 188, 190
Kulik, C., 149, 190, 191, 407, *413*, 477, *483*, 515, 570

Kulik, J.A., 149, 190, 191, 407, *413*, 477, *483*, 515, 570
Kurland, M.K., 574
Kurtz, J.J., 542

L

Lagarspetz, K., 113
Lahaderne, H., 98
Lamb, M.E., 88, 90, 97
Lambert, N.M., *519*
Lambert, W., 533
Land, M.L., 422
Langer, P.C., 190
Laosa, L., 126
Larkin, J., *307*
Larrivee, B., *483*
Larsen, G.Y., 50
Lashley, T., *29*
Lathrop, A., *576*
Latta, R.M., *550*
Lau, S., 317
Laughlin, P., 326
Laycock, F., 476
Lazar, I., 99, 144
Lefcourt, H., 316
Leinhardt, G., 422, 444, *446*
Lepper, M.R., 220, 226, 540
Lerman, D., 317
Lerner, B., 511
Lever, J., 101
Levin, J.R., 255, 257, *267*, *307*
Levitan, T.E., 98
Lickona, T., 116
Liebert, R.M., 101, 113
Lightall, F.F., 339
Lindsay, P.H., 237, 238, 250, 251, 256
Lindvall, C.M., 285, 286
Lindzey, G., 126, 143
Linn, R., 530
Lipman, M., 304
Littlefield, J., 252
Livingston, G., 181
Lockhart, R.S., 248, *266*
Lockhead, J., 574
Lockwood, A., 116
Loehlin, J.C., 126, 143
Loftus, E.F., 280
Long, L., 132
Long, T.J., 132
Lortie, D., *446*
Lovitt, T.C., 526
Lowell, E.L., 321
Luehrmann, A.L., 574
Lufler, H.S., 313
Luiten, J., 279, *307*
Lyman, H.B., 492, *519*

M

McCall, R.B., 144
McCandless, B.R., 216
McClelland, D.C., 142, 321, 323
McConnell, J.W., 422
McCormick, C.B., 255, 257
McCormick, D., 568
McCormick, L., 464
McDermott, J., *307*
McDevitt, T., 128
McDonald, F., 421, 434
MacDonald-Ross, M., 388, 389
McDougall, R., 203
McGinley, H., 335
McGinley, P., 335
McGivern, S., 257
McKeague, D., 115
McKenzie, T.L., 223
McLaughlin, T.F., 221
McLoone, B., 257
MacMillan, D.L., 454
McNeill, D., 78, 251
McNemar, Q., 136
Maccoby, E.E., 146
Macken, E., 561
Madaus, G.F., 397, 525, *556*
Madsen, C.H., 22, 199
Maehr, M.L., 127, 540
Mager, G., *29*
Mager, R., 386–87, *413*
Mahoney, M.J., 176
Maier, S.F., 287, 317
Malczynski, R.J., 188, 190
Malian, J.M., 458, 460, *483*
Marble, W.O., 539
Marcia, J.E., 93–94
Margolis, J., 241
Markman, E.M., 73
Marks, C., 294
Marland, S.P., Jr., 475
Marsh, H.W., 106, *119*
Marshall, S., 146, 148
Martin, J.F., 366, 539
Martin, W.R., 402, 403
Martinson, R.A., 478
Marx, R.W., 398
Masia, B.B., 394
Maslow, A.H., 318, 321
Mastropieri, M.A., 257
Matarazzo, J.D., 145–46
Matson, J.L., 202
Matthews, K.M., 537
Mayer, G.R., 184, 219, 220, *229*
Mayer, R.E., 278, 284, 285, 295, *307*, 574
Medley, D.M., 400, 421
Meeker, M.N., 304
Meichenbaum, D., 73, 157, 224, *229*
Melaragno, R.J., 190

Mendels, G.E., 331
Mercer, C., 466
Mercer, J.R., 453
Messer, S., 156
Messick, S., 511, 515
Metcalfe, B., 106
Meyer, B.J.F., 294
Meyers, P.I., 422
Mezynski, K.J., 252
Michelson, S., 142, 419
Miller, G.A., 235, 242, *267*
Miller, H.L., 6
Miller, P.H., 67; *81*
Miller, R.B., 390
Millett, G., 242
Millman, J., *519*
Moore, C.A., 155
Moos, B.S., 536
Moos, R.H., 536
Morgan, M., 223, 227
Morningstar, M., 565
Morris, C.G., 140, 321, 323
Morrison, C.R., 257
Morrow, L.M., 408
Moskowitz, G., 75, 77, 363
Mosokowitz, B.A., *81*
Munt, E.D., 221, 223
Murphy, D.A., *266*
Murphy, R.T., 570
Murray, H.G., 422, 424
Musgrave, G.R., 410, 411
Mussen, P., 49

N

Naremore, R., 533
Neimark, E., 65
Neisser, W., 135, *266*
Neisworth, J.T., 468
Nelson, K., 75
Newman, K., *29*
Nisbett, R., 226, 540
Norman, D.A., 237, 238, 250, 251, 256, *266*, 291
Nungester, R.J., 533
Nuttall, E.V., 130
Nuttall, R.L., 130

O

O'Connor, R.D., 185
O'Day, E.F., 188, 190
Ogden, J.E., 22, 24
Olds, S.W., 47
O'Leary, K.D., 200, 211, 212, 221, 222, 225, 226, *229*, 464, *483*
O'Leary, S.G., 200, 211, 212, 221, 225, 226, *229*
Olemich, C., 323

Ollendick, T.H., 185, 202
Olsen, J.B., 39
Olson, D.R., 574
O'Neil, H.F., 342
Oosthoek, H., 342
Opper, S., 53, 58
Orlansky, J., 570
Ornstein, A.C., 6, 9
Ortony, A., 247, *267*
Osborn, A.F., 151
O'Sullivan, J.T., 260

P

Page, E.B., 11, 15, *29*, 538
Paivio, A., 245
Palinscar, A.S., 262
Pallas, A.M., 146
Pancake, V., 90
Paolitto, D.P., 112, 116, *119*
Papalia, D.E., 47
Papert, S., 574, *576*
Park, O., 568
Parke, R.D., 129, 130
Pascal, R.A., 403, *413*
Pattison, P., 146
Pauk, W., 295, 296, *307*, 517, *519*
Paulman, R.G., 341, 342
Pavlov, I., 169–72
Pea, R.D., 574
Peeck, J., 236
Pelham, E.W., 241
Peper, R.J., 295
Pepper, F.C., 362, *377*
Perfetto, G.A., 252
Perkins, D.N., 302
Persampieri, M., 252
Peters, E.E., 257
Peterson, P., 146, 383, 398, 434, 436, *446*
Pfeffer, C.R., 130
Phillips, W., 156
Piaget, J., 50–71, *81*, 109, 116, 165, 281
Pidgeon, D.A., 336
Pilon, D., 321
Pippert, R.A., 332
Plager, E., 22
Poirot, J., 560
Poley, W., 125
Polit, D.E., 130
Polya, G., *307*
Popham, W.J., 389
Posner, M.I., 284
Postman, N., 14
Powers, D.E., 514
Prawat, R.S., 115, *119*
Premack, D., 203
Presse, D.P., 514
Pressley, M., 73, 257, 258, 260, *266*, *267*, *307*

Pribram, K.H., 235
Price, G., 221
Pring, R., 393
Prohaska, T., 41–43
Purkey, W.W., 106

Q

Quay, H.C., 463

R

Ragosta, M., 570
Ramey, C., 143, 144
Raudsepp, E., 287
Raugh, M.R., 257
Ravitch, D., 11, 15
Redfield, D.L., 399, *413*
Reed, S.K., 248
Reese, J.H.I., 454
Reid, D.K., 260, 464, 466, *483*
Reimer, J., 112, 116, *119*
Reis, S., 477
Renzulli, J., 474–75
Reschly, D.J., 514
Resnick, L.B., 236, 247, 285
Reynolds, W.M., 106
Richardson, W.M., 13
Rist, R.C., 335
Roberson, S.D., 11, 15, *29*
Roberts, M.D., 225
Roberts, N., 572, *576*
Robin, A.L., 191
Robinson, C.S., 285
Robinson, D.W., 14
Robinson, F.P., 292
Robinson, H.A., 292
Robinson, H.B., 114, 135, 468
Robinson, L., 285, 286
Robinson, N., 135, 468, *556*
Roedell, W.C., 114
Roemer, R., 21
Roethlisberger, F.J., 40
Rogers, D., 102
Rogoff, B., 71
Rohrkemper, M.M., *81*, 321
Rollins, H.A., 216
Romanczyk, R.G., 222
Rosch, E.H., 282
Rosen, L.A., 200
Rosen, R., 103
Rosenbaum, M.E., 535
Rosenberger, G., 20
Rosenfarb, I., 221, 223
Rosenshine, B., 5, 37, 353, 363, 401,
    403, 422–24, 426, 429–31, 438,
    440, 444, 445, *446*
Rosenthal, R., 40, 331, 336, 339
Rosman, B.L., 156

Ross, D., 113
Ross, S.A., 113
Ross, S.M., 568–70
Rothen, W., 568
Rotter, J., 316
Rousseau, E.W., 399, *413*
Rowe, M.B., 400, 401
Rubin, A., *119*
Rubin, L.J., *29*
Ruebush, B.H., 339
Rumelhart, D.E., 247, 260, *267*
Rushall, B.S., 223
Russell, D., 317
Rust, L.W., 324
Ryan, K., *29*
Ryans, D.C., 422, 424

S

Sadker, D., 98, *119*, 372, *377*, 399–
    401
Sadker, M., 98, *119*, 372, *377*, 399–
    401
Salili, F., 540
Sandefur, J.T., 15
Sanford, J.B., 356, 364, 366, 367,
    377, 421, 438, 439
Sanford, J.P., 356, 357, 364, *377*,
    421, 423
Santogrossi, D.A., 222
Sarason, S.B., 339
Sattler, J.M., 139, 142, 513
Savage, T.V., 15
Scarr, S., 143
Schab, F., 112
Schiedel, D., 93–94
Schlechty, P.C., 15
Schneider, W., 258
Schug, M., 10
Schunk, D.H., 317
Schwartzberg, N.S., 113
Schweinhart, L.J., 99, 144
Scruggs, T.E., 257
Seefeldt, C., 421
Seiber, J.E., 342
Self, J.A., 574
Seligman, C., 533
Seligman, M.E.P., 317
Selman, R., 100
Serralde De Scholz, H.C., 203
Seving, S.R., *446*
Shane, H.G., 561
Shantz, C., 107
Shantz, D.W., 114
Shapiro, B.B., 128
Shapiro, E.S., 185, 202
Shavelson, R., 106, 114, *119*, 426
Shaver, J.P., *519*
Shelley, M.F., 39
Sherman, J.A., 146, 214

Shiffrin, R.M., 236
Shostak, R., 401
Shuell, T.J., 152, 154, *159*, 279
Shultz, J., 354
Siegal, M.A., 565
Sigel, I.E., 152, 153, 156
Silberman, A., 203
Silberman, C., 3
Silberman, H.R., 190
Simon, D.P., 290, *307*
Simon, H.A., 285, *307*
Simon, T., 139
Simon, W., 534
Sinclair, H., 51
Singer, R.D., 113
Sipple, T.S., 66
Sirvis, B., 457
Skinner, B.F., 165, 175–76, 179, 187,
    189
Slaby, R.G., 114
Slavin, R.E., *29*, 149, 326, 327, 329,
    345, 353, 407
Smith, D., 422
Smith, E., 289, 291
Smith, F., 238, 254
Smith, L.R., 422
Smith, M., 142, 419
Smith, R.M., 468
Smith, S.M., 253
Snow, R.E., 149, *159*, 191, 331, 436–
    38, 535
Snowman, J., 295
Snyder, T.F.F., 572, *576*
Soar, R., 398, 424
Sokolove, S., 372
Solomon, G., 572
Solomon, R.L., 317
Soloway, E., 574
Soskin, R., 18
Sowell, E., *29*
Spearman, C., 136
Spielberger, C.D., 339
Spitalnik, R., 212
Sprafkin, J.N., 113
Spuhler, J.N., 126, 143
Sroufe, L.A., 90
Stallings, J.A., 398, 434, 439, 444
Stanley, J.C., 146
Stanton, G.C., 106, 114
Starch, D., 530
Starr, R.H., Jr., 133
Staudt, J., 65
Staybrook, N.G., 398
Stein, B.S., 252, *307*
Steinmetz, S.K., 133
Stenner, A.J., 421
Sternberg, C., 90
Sternberg, R.J., 137, 138, *159*, 283,
    290, *307*
Stevens, R.J., 106, 401, 429, 431,
    438

Stewart, J.R., 325, 539
Stipek, D.J., 437
Strathe, M.I., 8, 11, *29*
Straus, M.A., 133
String, J., 570
Strother, D.B., 132, 133
Sulzer-Azaroff, B., 184, 219, 220, *229*
Sund, R.B., *81*
Suppes, P., 561, 562, 565, 574
Swanson, R.A., 207
Swenson, E.J., 542
Swift, J., 401
Swing, S.R., 436
Switzer, E.B., 215

T

Tamburino, J.L., 285, 286
Tanner, J.M., 101
Taylor, J.B., 78
Taylor, R.P., 564
TenBrink, T.D., 385
Tennyson, R.D., 282, 350, 568
Terman, L.M., 510
Terwilliger, J.S., 546
Thomas, D.R., 22, 199, 205, 213
Thomas, E.L., 292
Thompson, M., 216
Thompson, S.A., 464
Thompson, T.J., 561
Thoresen, C.E., 176, 221
Thornburg, H., *119*
Thorndike, E.L., 139, 165, 174, 297
Thornton, A., 126
Thurstone, L.L., 136
Tiedt, I.M., 480
Tiedt, P.L., 480
Tikunoff, W.J., 400
Timpson, W.M., *446*
Tobias, S., 191, 341, 342, 384, 438
Tobin, D.N., *446*
Tokar, E., 350
Toolan, J.M., 465
Torrance, E.P., 150, 151
Travers, R.M.W., 239, 297
Trickett, E., 536
Trollip, S.R., 566, *576*
Tucker, G., 533
Tulving, E., 245
Tyler, L.E., 152

U

Uguroglu, M.E., 313
Ure, A., 305

V

Vaillant, C., 92
Vaillant, G., 92
Vance, V., 15
van den Bosch, A.B., 236
Van Mondrans, A.P., 39
Veenman, S., 12
Vernon, P.E., 143, *159*
Vidler, D.C., 325
Vilberg, W., 574
Vitello, S.J., 18
Vlandis, J.W., 535
Voydanoff, D.A., 114
Vye, N.J., 252
Vygotsky, L.S., 70–71

W

Wachs, H., 68
Wadsworth, B.J., 55, 70
Waite, R.R., 339
Walberg, H.J., 313, 403, *413*, 426
Walden, E.L., 464
Walker, D.F., *576*
Walker, H.M., *229*
Waller, T.G., 261, 278, 279
Walton, G., 476
Ward, B., 400
Ward, M.E., 460
Wati, D.H., 572, *576*
Watson, J.B., 165
Waxman, H.C., 426
Weaver, W.T., 15
Webb, N.M., 327, *345*
Wechsler, D., 136, 139–40
Weikart, D.P., 99, 144
Weiner, B., 316, 317, 534
Weiner, C., 572, *576*
Weinfeld, F.D., 418–19
Weinstein, C.S., 408, *413*
Weinstein, T., 403, *413*
Wellman, H.M., 73
Wertsch, J.V., 71
Wessells, M.G., 283, 287

Wessman, A., 536
West, C.K., 106
White, B.L., 128
White, E.M., 531
White, K.R., 126
White, M.A., 539
White, R.W., 315
Whitmer, S. 115
Wicks-Nelson, R., 101
Wigfield, A., 341, 342
Wiig, E. H., 461
Wiley, D.E., *519*
Wilkins, W.E., 331, 332
Willerman, L., 128, 145, 152, 153
Williams, D.D., 39
Williams, E.L., 356, 357, 364, 421, 423
Williams, J.P., 340
Wilson, C.W., 215
Winett, R.A., 217, 225
Winkler, R.C., 225
Winne, P.H., 398, 539
Winocur, S.L., 304
Winograd, P., 261
Witkin, H.A., 152, 155
Wittrock, M.C., 152, 234, 294, 342, *446*, *483*
Wlodkowski, R.J., 319–21
Wood, A.M., 419
Woodward, D.M., *483*
Woodyard, E.R., 297
Woolfolk, A.E., 36, 134, *229*, 336, 410, *483*
Woolfolk, R.L.A., 36, *229*
Worsham, M.E., 356, 357, 364, 366, 367, *377*, 421, 423, 438, 439
Wulfert, E., 221, 223

Y

York, R.L., 418–19
Young, T., 10
Youniss, J., 100
Ysseldyke, J.E., 454
Yussen, S.R., *81*

Z

Zettle, R.D., 221, 223
Zimmerman, D.W., 547

Subject Index

A

Ability(ies)
 differences, 437-39, 444
 grouping, 83, 148-49, 335-36
 matching strategies to, 67-70
 metacognitive, 258-64
 See also Creativity; Individual
  differences; Intelligence
Abstract, defined, 41
Abuse, child, 133
Academic abilities of teachers, 15
Academic self-concept, 106
Academic tasks, 426-29
Acceleration of the gifted, 477-78
Access to learning, 354-55
Accommodation, defined, 53
Accountability, 17-18
Achievement
 individual differences in, 550
 instructional objectives and,
  383-84
 needs and motivation, 321-24
 teaching high achievers, 440
 tests, 503-7, 520
Acronyms, 256
Action zone, 410
Active listening, 371-72, 415
Active teaching, 430-34
Adaptation, 52-53
Adaptive feedback, 401
Adjustment, physical problems
  and, 457
Adolescence, 64, 89, 92-95, 101-4,
  120. *See also* High school
  years
Advance organizers, 278-79
Affective domain, 394
Affective education, 114-17

Affective objectives, 394
Age
 effective teaching strategies by,
  435
 mental, 139
 mental abilities and, 147-48
 -related needs, 352-53
Aggression, 113-14, 464
Algorithm, 288, 289
Allocated time, 353
Alternate-form reliability, 499
American Association on Mental
  Deficiency (AAMD), 466
American Educational Research
  Association, 418
Analogical thinking, 289
Antecedents, 176, 181
Anticipatory set, 401
Anxiety, 171, 173, 339-43, 436-37,
  521
Anxiety-withdrawal disorder, 463
Aptitude, 435-40. *See also*
  Intelligence
Aptitude test, 508-10
Aptitude-treatment interactions
  (ATI), 436-37
Art curriculum, 484
Articulation disorders, 460-61
Assertive discipline, 372-74, 375
Assertiveness, 113
Assignment, oral, 195
Assignments, diversifying, 83
Assignment proposition, 284
Assimilation, 53
Associations, learning through,
  168-69
Attachment, trust and, 89-90
Attention, 71-72, 184, 187, 199-200,
  241-42

Attitude, 127, 272, 321
Attributes, 282-83
Attribution theory of motivation,
  316-18
Authoritarian parents, 129
Authoritative parents, 129
Autonomy v. shame and doubt, 89,
  90-91
Average student, overlooking, 160
Awareness, metalinguistic, 79-80
Awareness of others, development
  of, 107-8

B

Baby boom, 20
BASIC (Beginner's All-purpose
  Symbolic Instruction Code),
  572, 574
Basic skills, 430-34, 439
Beginning teachers, concerns of,
  12-13
Behavior
 disorders, 462-65
 observational learning of, 185-86
 teacher, student reactions and,
  335-39
Behavioral approaches, application
  of, 197-231
 classroom management
  programs, 213-20
 to cope with undesirable
  behavior, 108-15
 criticism of, 226-28
 to develop new behaviors, 204-8,
  209
 positive behavior, focus on, 114,
  198-204, 205

Behavioral approaches (cont.)
problems and issues in, 224-28
self-management, 221-24, 355
Behavioral views of learning, 165, 166
applying behavioral technology, 187-92
classical conditioning, 168-73
contiguity and, 167-68
observational learning, 182-87, 188
operant conditioning, 173-82
Behavioral views of motivation, 313-15
Behavior-content matrix, 396-98
Being needs, 318
Bias, 40, 98, 304-5, 347, 513-14
Bilingual education, 481
Bimodal distribution, 493
Birth order, 129-30
Birthrates, declining, 19-20
Black English, 77-78
Blind, educationally, 460
Bottom-up processing, 240
Brainstorming strategy, 151-52, 309
Branching programs, 189-90
Brookline Early Education Project, 100
Buckley Amendment, 554-55
Burnout, teacher, 10
Busywork, 8

C

Career, teaching, 8-11, 32
Cause-and-effect relationship, 24, 37
Central tendency, 492
Cerebral palsy, 457
Chain methods (memory), 257
Challenges, providing, 448-49
Change, learning and, 165
Cheating, 112-13
Child abuse, 133
Childhood and Society (Erikson), 87
Child-rearing practices, 128-29
Children, effects on adults of, 134
Chunking, 243
Circle seating arrangements, 410-11
Clarity effective teaching and, 422-24
Classical conditioning, 169-73, 174
Classification, 61
Classroom(s)
anxiety in, 339-43
characteristics of, 351-52
classical conditioning used in, 172-73
computers in, 564-71

creativity in, 151-52
ecology of, 351-53
evaluation and testing, 524-31, 532
observational learning used in, 185-87
positive emotional climate in, 326-28
seatwork, 403-5, 415
settings for achieving objectives, 408-12
Classroom management, 5, 22-23, 349-79
diagnosing problems, 370-71
encouraging student engagement, 363-64
during first weeks of class, 361-62
goals of, 353-55
maintaining effective, 363-68
need for communication and, 368-76
need for managers, 350-55
planning for good, 355-63, 378
praise, use of, 199-200, 201, 216
problem prevention, 364-68
research on, 23-24, 356
rules and procedures, 273, 357-62
special programs for, 213-20
Climate, positive emotional, 326-28
Cluster seating arrangements, 410-11
Coaching, 514-15, 521
Coding system, 274-76
Cognition, social, 107-8
Cognitive development
defined, 49
information processing theory of, 71-74
moral reasoning and, 111
Piaget's theory of, 50-71
criticisms of, 50-51
limitations and implications, 65-71
making sense of the world, 52-55
on readiness and thinking, 51-52
stages in, 55-65
speeding up, 70
zone of proximal development, 70-71
Cognitive domain, 393, 399
Cognitive learning theories, 165-66
Cognitive objectives, 393, 399
Cognitive perspective on learning, 233-69
elements of, 234-36
information processing model, 236-49
metacognitive abilities, 258-64

remembering and forgetting, 249-58
teaching practice and, 271-309
concepts, teaching, 280-83
discovery learning, 274-76, 277, 308
learning outcomes, 272-74
problem solving, 283-92, 303, 308, 309, 374-75
reception learning, 276-80
study skills, 292-97, 299
teaching thinking, 302-5
transfer, teaching for, 295-302, 309
Cognitive styles, 152-57
Cognitive views of motivation, 315-18
Commissions, 14
Communication, 369-76
beyond grades, 551-55
confrontation, 372-76
counseling, 6, 371-72
diagnosis of owner of problems, 370-71
disorders, 460-62
instructional objectives and, 384-85
metacommunication and, 369-70
paraphrasing, 370
student and parent conferences, 552-54
Comparative advance organizer, 278-79
Compensation, 61
Competence, development, of, 128
Competency tests, minimum, 17, 511-12
Competition, 326, 536
Components view of intelligence, 137-38
Comprehension, 247, 260-64, 284, 427. *See also* Learning
Computer-assisted instruction, (CAI), 565-71
Computer-assisted learning (CAL), 565-71
Computer-based education (CBE), 561-64
Computer-based instruction (CBI), 565-71
Computer managed instruction (CMI), 572
Computer(s), 18-19, 559-76
in classrooms, 564-71
future for, 574-75
as instructional tools, 571-72
literacy, 560-64
programming, 572-74
Concepts, 273, 281-83
Conceptual abilities, 140

Concrete operational stage, 55,
59-63, 91
Condition-action schemata, 290
Conditioned response (CR), 170
Conditioned stimulus (CS), 170
Conditioning, classical, 169-73, 174
Conditioning, operant, 173-82, 194
Conditioning, vicarious, 183
Conduct disorders, 463
Confederate, defined, 42
Confidence, 171, 173, 317
Confidence interval, 500-501, 506
Conflict, negotiations and, 374-76
Confrontation, 372-76
Consequences
    of breaking rules, 360
    controlling, 176-81
    defined, 176
    group, 214-16
    See also Reinforcement
Conservation, 58-61, 65, 73
Constructive criticism, 539
Constructive failure, 536-37
Context, remembering and, 253
Contiguity, 168-69
Contingency contract programs,
    218-20, 231
Continuous reinforcement
    schedule, 178
Contract system of grading, 548-49
Control, locus of, 316-17
Control group, 38, 40
Conventional moral reasoning, 109,
    111
Convergent questions, 398
Convergent thinking, 150
Cooperation, need for, 352
Cooperative goal structure, 326
Cooperative learning, 326-28, 407
Correlations, 23-24, 37, 135
Counseling students, 6, 371-72
Course objectives, 396-98
Creativity, 149-52, 153, 161
Crisis, developmental, 88
Criterion-referenced grading,
    542-43, 545
Criterion-referenced tests, 490-91
Critical thinking, 302-5
Criticism, constructive, 539
Criticism of schools, 14
Crystallized intelligence, 148
Cueing, 181, 204-7, 252
Cultural differences, 70, 112,
    126-28
Cultural reconstructions, 250-51
Culture, defined, 126
Culture-fair or culture-free tests,
    513
Cumulative records, 346-47
Curiosity, arousing, 324-25

Curriculum, 18-19, 114, 415, 484.
    See also Planning, teacher
Curriculum-based assessment, 518

D

Data-based instruction, 526
Data processing and data bases,
    571-72
Day care, impact of, 98-100
Debra P. v. Turlington, 512
Decentering, 59
Declarative knowledge, 290
Decoding, 261
Dedication, teacher, 30
Deductive reasoning, 277, 305
Deficiency needs, 318
Defining attributes, 282
Definitions, teaching concepts
    using, 82
Dependence, field, 152-55
Dependent variable, 38
Descriptive approach, 37-38
Descriptive-correlational-
    experimental loop, 421
Development
    general definition of, 48-49
    in infancy, 5, 88-90
    language, 74-80
    of mentally retarded, 469
    moral, 109-14
    physical, 49, 101-3, 104
    psychosocial, 87-96
    sex-role, 97-98, 99
    sexual maturation, 103
    See also Cognitive development;
        Personal and social
        development
Developmental crisis, 88
Deviation, standard, 493-95
Deviation IQ, 139
Diagnostic tests, 507-8, 525
Diagramming relationships,
    techniques for, 295
Dialects, 77-78
Diana v. State Board of Education,
    513-14
Differential Aptitude Test (DAT),
    510
Differential treatment of students,
    336-38
Diffusion, identity, 94
Dilemmas, moral, 109-11, 116-17
Direct instruction, 430-34
Direct method, 481
Direct observation, 35-36
Discipline, 129, 372-74, 375, 379
Discovery learning, 274-76, 277, 308
Discrimination, 171, 273

Discussion group, 402-3, 404
Disequilibrium, 69, 116
Disk drive, 563
Distraction, 342, 527
Distributed practice, 254
Distribution, bimodal, 493
Distribution, frequency, 492
Distribution, normal, 494-95, 497
Divergent questions, 398
Divergent thinking, 150
Divorce, 20, 130-32
Double negative, 77
Doubt and shame v. autonomy, 89,
    90-91
Down syndrome, 468
Downtime, 563
Drill-and-practice program, 565, 567
Dual marking system, 550-51

E

Early childhood, 56-59, 91. See also
    Elementary school years
Ecology of classrooms, 351-53
Education
    affective, 114-17
    defined, 21
    of effective teachers, 421-22
    hierarchy of needs and, 319
Educational Amendments Act
    (1974), 554-55
Educationally blind, 460
Educational psychology, role of,
    20-25
Education for All Handicapped
    Children Act (PL 94-142), 18,
    470-72, 514
Effect, law of, 175
Effective teaching, 417-46
    academic tasks for, 426-29
    characteristics of, 361-63, 421-26
    with different students, 434-40
    for different subjects, 429-34
    guidelines for, 425
    integrating ideas about, 440-45
    methods for studying, 420
    search for keys to success, 418-26
Effort, grading on, 550-51
Egocentrism, 59, 64
Eg-rule method, 275
Elaboration, 251-52
Elementary school years
    classroom management in, 352-53
    concrete operational stage in,
        59-63
    effective teaching in, 361-62
        440-43
    psychosocial development in, 89,
        91-92

Elementary school years (cont.)
rules for, 357-58, 361-62
Emotion, arousing, 187
Emotional climate, positive, 326-28
Emotional development, 111, 114-17. *See also* Personal and social development
Empathic listening, 371-72
Empathy, development of, 108-9, 371-72
Engaged time, 354, 448
Engagement, encouraging student, 363-64
English
black, 77-78
standard, 77-78
teaching methods for, 434
ENIAC (ELectronic Numerical Integrator and Calculator), 561
Enrichment, 477-78
Enthusiasm, teacher, 424-25
Environment, individual differences and, 126-33, 134
Environmental engineer, teacher as, 6. *See also* Classroom management
Environment-behavior research, 410
Epilepsy, 456-57
Episodic memory, 245
Equilibration, 54, 316
Errors, types of 366, 538
ESL students, 520
Essay testing, 527-31, 532
Ethical issues
with behavioral methods, 225-26
with standardized testing, 511
Evaluation
instructional objectives and, 385, 393, 394, 396
phase in self-management, 221-22
planning, 531-33
of problem solving results, 289-90
with testing, 488-91
See also Grades and grading; Measurement; Tests and testing
Examples, teaching concepts using, 283
Exceptional students, 451-85
defining, 452-55
gifted, the, 474-79
helping other sutdents accept, 484
with learning problems, 455-69
mainstreaming, 18, 469-74
multicultural and bilingual education, 479-81
Expectations
individual learning, 327-28, 550
labels and, 454

locus of control and, 317
student, effect of, 41-44
teacher, 331-39, 347, 534
Experience, learning and, 165
Experimental approach, 38-39
Experimentation, 24
Expert, problem solving by, 290-92
Expert teachers, 427
Explaining and lecturing format, 401-2
Explicit teaching, 430-34
Expository teaching, 276-80
Extinction, 172, 173
Extrinsic motivation, 313
Extrinsic reinforcement, 331

F

Faces of intellect, 136-37
Failure, 323, 536-37
Fairness in grading, 533-34
Family, changes in, 20, 31-32, 130-32. *See also* Parents
Family Education Rights and Privacy Act of 1974, 554-55
Fear, 171, 173. *See also* Anxiety
Feature analysis, 240
Feedback, 338, 365, 401, 537-38, 539. *See also* Communication; Grades and grading
Field dependence and independence, 152-55
Figure-ground concept, 239-40
Finger spelling, 485
Fixed-interval schedule, 179
Fixedness, functional, 287
Fixed-ratio schedule, 180
Flexibility, 150, 287
Floor plans, 409
Fluid intelligence, 147-48
Forgetting, 249-50. *See also* Memory
Formal operational stage, 55, 63-65
Formative measurement, 525
Formats for teaching, 398-408
group discussion, 402-3, 404
individualized instruction, 405-8
lecturing and explaining, 401-2
lesson, 363-64
recitation and questioning, 398-401
seatwork and homework, 231, 403-5, 415
Frames in programmed instruction, 189
"Free" schools, 445
Frequency distributions, 492
Friendships in childhood, 100-101
Frustration, teacher, 30
Functional fixedness, 287
Functional literacy test, 512

G

Game paddle, 564
Games, 68-69, 566
Gender, mental abilities and, 145-47
Gender identity, 97-98
Generalization in conditioning, 41, 171, 283
Generativity v. stagnation, 89, 96
Genetic differences, 125-26, 142, 143
Gestalt theory, 238-40
g factor, 136
Gifted, the, 414, 474-79, 485
Goal-directed actions, 56
Goal(s)
of classroom management, 353-55
ethics and selecting behavioral, 225
motivation and, 314-15
structure, 326, 328
See also Objectives for learning
Goal-setting phase, self-management, 221
Good Behavior game, 214
Grade, skipping a, 23, 485
Grade-equivalent scores, 496-97
Grades and grading, 535-55
communication beyond, 551-55
contract system, 548-49
criterion- v. norm-referenced, 542-44
effects on students, 535-42
on effort and improvement, 550-51
of essay tests, 531
fairness in, 533-34
mastery approach, 549-50
of multiple-choice tests, 527
percentage, 546-48
point system, 546
report cards, 544-46
See also Tests and testing
Gradual extinction, 173
Grand mal epilepsy, 456
"Grandma's rule," 203-4
Group achievement tests, 504
Group consequences, 214-16
Group discussion, 402-3, 404
Group focus, maintaining, 366-67
Grouping, ability, 83, 148-49, 335-36
Group IQ tests, 140, 148-49
Growth, emotional, education for, 114-17
Growth spurt, adolescent, 102. *See also* Development.
Guided discovery, 275
Guidelines
affective education programs, 117
anxiety, 343
children of divorce, 131

class discussions, 404
classical conditioning, 174
class procedures, 358-59
computer hardware and software selection, 573
concrete operations, 62
creativity, 153
developing new behaviors, 209
discovery learning, 277
effective teaching, 425
expository teaching, 276-80
formal operations, 66
gifted students, 478
grading systems, 541, 552-53
hearing-impaired students, 459
industry, 93
information processing theory, 248-49
initiative, 92
instructional objectives, 390
IQ score interpretation, 144
learning disabled students, 467
motivation theory applications, 332-33
objective test items, 528-29
observational learning, 188
operant conditioning, 182
organizing instruction, 442-43
parent-teacher conferences, 554
physical differences in classroom, 104
praise, appropriate use of, 201
preoperational children, 60
problem solving, 292
punishment, 214-15
research study evaluation, 43
retarded students, 470
self-management programs, 224
sex-role bias, 99
stressing the positive, 205
study skills and learning strategies, 299
stuttering students, 462
teacher expectations, 340-41
test reliability and validity, 503
test taking, 516-17
token reinforcement program, 218

H

Halo effect, 534
Handicaps. *See* Exceptional students
Hard copy, 564
Hardware, computer, 563-64, 570, 573
Hawthorne effect, 40
Hearing impairment, 457-58, 459
Helplessness, learned, 317
Hereditary factors, 125-26, 142, 143

Heritability ratio, 125
Heuristics, 288-89
Hierarchy of needs, 318-19
High achievers, teaching, 440
Higher-order interactions, 436-37
Higher-order rules, 273
High grades, effect of, 535
High-inference characteristics, 424-25
High school years, 63-65, 353
Histogram, 492, 493
Holophrases, 75
Homework, 231, 403
Hostile students, 368
Hostile teacher response, 373-74, 375
Humanistic approaches to motivation, 318-19
Hunter Mastery Teaching Program, 431-32
Hyperactivity, 464-65
Hypothesis, stating, 36

I

Identity
  achievement, 93-94
  defined, 61
  diffusion, 94
  foreclosure, 94
  formation, 92-95, 120
  gender, 97-98
  statuses, 93-94
  v. role confusion, 92-94
"I" messages, 372
Immaturity, 463-64
Improvement, grading on, 550-51
Impulsive cognitive style, 155-56
Incentives, learning, 331. *See also* Motivation
Independence, field, 152-55
Independent variable, 38, 39-40
Individual achievement tests, 504
Individual differences, 123-61
  in anxiety, 339-42
  aptitude-treatment interaction and, 436-37
  in cognitive style, 152-57
  in creativity, 149-52
  environment and, 126-33
  hereditary factors, 125-26, 142, 143
  in intelligence, 135-49
  origins of, 124-35
Individual intelligence tests, 140, 476
Individualistic goal structure, 326, 328
Individualized education program (IEP), 471

Individualized instruction, 405-8
Individual learning expectation (ILE), 327-28, 550
Inductive reasoning, 274-76, 304-5
Industry v. inferiority, 89, 91-92, 93
Infancy, development in 5, 88-90
Information processing
  defined, 71
  model of learning, 236-49
    attention, role of, 241-42
    long-term memory, 244-47
    perception, influence of, 238-41
    schemata, 247-49
    sensory register, 236-38, 242
    short-term memory, 242-44
  theory of cognitive development, 71-74
Inhibitions, 186-87
Initiative v. guilt, 89, 91
Insight, 287
Instruction
  data-based, 526
  direct, 430-34
  individualized, 405-8
  organization of, 442-43
  programmed, 188-91
  teacher-centered, 434
  See also Effective teaching; Learning; Planning, teacher; Teaching
Instructional application of computers (IAC), 565-71
Instructional expert, teacher as, 4
Instructional objectives, 383-90. *See also* Objectives for learning
Instructional tools, computers as, 571-72
Integrity v. despair, 89, 96
Intellectual skills, types of, 273
Intelligence
  age and, 147-48
  components view of, 137-38
  crystallized, 148
  day care and development of, 99-100
  defining, 135-38
  fluid, 147-48
  gender and, 145-47
  individual differences in, 135-49
    ability grouping and, 148
    age and, 147-48
    gender and, 145-47
    improving intelligence, 143-45
    measurement of, 138-42
    nature v. nurture and, 142-43
    tests, 140, 141, 476
Intelligence quotient (IQ), 140-42
  deviation, 139
  of the gifted, 474, 475, 477
  scores, 37, 139, 140-45, 509
  tests, 140, 148-49, 508-9, 513, 514

Interactions, teacher-student, 336-38
Interest-area classroom arrangements, 408-10
Interests, tapping students', 324-25
Interference, proactive and retroactive, 250, 295-96
Intermittent reinforcement schedule, 179
Internalization of action, 57
Intimacy v. isolation, 89, 95-96
Intrinsic motivation, 315
Intuitive thinking, 275
IQ. *See* Intelligence quotient (IQ)
Isolation, social, 212-13

J

Job market, future of, 19-20
Joy sticks 564
Junior high school, 63-65

K

Kamehameha Early Education Project (KEEP), 354
Keller Plan, 191-92
Keyword method (memory), 257
Kilobytes, 564
Knowledge, 183
  ability differences and prior, 437-38
  ability to apply new, 69
  clarity and, 422-23
  declarative and procedural, 290
  of effective teacher, 421-22
  novice, 291
  storage in schemata, 247-49
  structure in long-term memory, 245-47

L

Labels, use of with exceptional students, 453-54
Language
  computer, 572-74
  development of, 74-80
  dialects, 77-78
  disorders, oral, 461
  egocentrism in preoperational stage, 59
  meanings and, 79
  sign, 458
  teaching and, 78-80
Latchkey children, 20, 132-33
Law of effect, 175
Laws, defined, 25
Leader, teacher, as, 6

Learned behaviors, encouraging already, 185-86
Learned helplessness, 317
Learning, 163-95
  about concepts, 281-83
  access to, 354-55
  anxiety and, 341
  basic elements of, 165
  behavioral and cognitive views of, 165-67
  behavioral methods and interest in, 226-27
  behavioral technology applied to, 187-92
  classical conditioning and, 168-73
  contiguity and, 167-68
  cooperative, 326-28 407
  discovery, 274-76, 277, 308
  expectation, individual, 550
  field-dependent and -independent, 155
  general definition of, 163-68
  influences on motivation during, 319-31
  mastery, 549-50
  negative reinforcement to enhance, 209
  by observing others, 182-87
  operant conditioning and, 173-82
  outcomes, 272-74
  part, 254
  reception, 276-80
  time for, 353-54
  working for grades v. to learn, 539-41
  See also Behavioral views of learning; Cognitive perspective on learning; Objectives for learning
Learning problems, 455-69
  behavior disorders, 462-65
  communication disorders, 460-62
  impaired vision or hearing, 457-60
  mental retardation, 125, 466-69, 470
  physical and health problems, 456-57
  specific learning disabilities, 465-66, 467
Least restrictive placement, 470-71
Lecturing and explaining format, 401-2
Lessons, 363-64, 405-6, 414, 423, 438-39. *See also* Planning, teacher
Letter grades, 547
Levels of processing theory, 248
Linear programs, 189
Linguistic comprehension, 284
Listening, 371-72, 415

Literacy, computer, 560-61
Literacy test, functional, 512
Loci method (memory), 256
Locus of control, 316-17
Logic, one-way, 57
Logical mistakes, 538
Logic game, 566
LOGO, 574
Longitudinal studies, 147
Long-term memory, 244-47, 250
Low-ability class, lesson format for, 438-39
Low grades, effect of, 535-37
Low vision, 460

M

Mainstreaming, 18, 469-74
Management. *See* Classroom management
Manager, teacher as, 5
Marking system. *See* Grades and grading
Massed practice, 254
Mastery approach to learning, 549-50
Mastery of objectives, testing for, 491
Mastery orientation, 323
Mastery Teaching Program, 431-32
Match, problem of the, 67-70
Matching Familiar Figures test, 155, 156
Mathematics, 146, 432-33, 434
Maturation, 49, 52, 102-3
Meaningful lessons, 254-55, 268-69, 301
Meaningful verbal learning, 277
Means-ends analysis, 288-89
Measurement
  formative v. summative, 525
  program, planning a, 531-35
  standard error of, 500
  techniques in research, 35-36 40
  with testing, 138-42, 488-91
  See also Grades and grading
Median, 492-93
Memory, 72-74, 242-53
  forgetting, reasons for, 249-50
  long-term, 244-47, 250
  short-term, 242-44, 250
  strategies to help, 253-57, 268-69
  tasks, 427
Mental abilities. *See* Intelligence
Mental age, 139
Mental retardation, 125, 466-69, 470
Metacognition, 73-74, 258-64, 515
Metacommunication, 369-70
Metacomponents, 137-38
Metalinguistic awareness, 79-80

Microchip, 561
Microcomputers. *See* Computer(s)
Middle-class school culture, 513
Middle school years, 59-63, 89, 91-92
Mild retardation, 469
Minimal brain damage (MBD), 464
Minimum competency tests, 17, 511-12
Minority students, 479-81, 513-14
Missouri Mathematics Program, 432-33
Mnemonics, 255-57
Mode, 493
Modeling, 6, 183, 184, 188, 207
Modem, 564
Moderate retardation, 469
Moral development, 109-14
Moral dilemmas, 109-11
  in teaching, 116-17
Moral realism stage, 109
Moratorium, 94
Mothers at work, 132
Motivation, 4, 311-47
  achievement, 321, 323, 324
  anxiety in classroom and, 339-43
  behavioral views of, 313-15
  cognitive views of, 315-18
  defining, 312-19
  grading and, 540
  extrinsic, 313
  humanistic approaches to, 318-19
  influences on, 319-31
    attitudes toward learning, 321
    emotional climate, 326-28
    interest and curiosity, 324-26
    meeting achievement needs, 321-24
    sense of competence, 328-31
  intrinsic, 315
  to maintain effective classroom management, 363-64
  observational learning and, 185
  resultant, 322
  sources of, 314, 315
  teacher expectations and, 47, 331-41
Motor skills, acquisition of, 272-73
Mouse, computer, 564
Movement management, 367
Multicultural education, 479-80
Multiple-choice programming, 189-90
Multiple-choice tests, 526-27
"Multiple intelligences" theory, 137
Multisensory computer presentation, 568
Multistore view of memory, 248

N

National Commission on Excellence in Education (NCEE), 14

National Teachers' Examination, 15, 16
Nation at Risk, A, 511
Native-language approach, 481
Nature v. nurture, debate, 142-43
Needs
  achievement, 321-24
  age-related, 352-53
  defined, 318
  hierarchy of, 318-19
Negative behaviors, alternatives to, 200-201
Negative reinforcement, 177-78, 202, 209-10, 231
Negative transfer, 295-96
Negotiations, conflict and, 374-76
Neobehaviorists, 166
New behaviors, developing, 204-8, 209
No-lose method of conflict resolution, 374-75
Normal distribution, 494-95, 497
Norming sample, 492
Norm-referenced grading, 542, 543-44, 545
Norm-referenced tests, 489-90, 491, 504-7
Note taking, 294-97
Novice knowledge, 291

O

Obesity, 120-21
Objectives for learning, 383-90
  advantages of, 389-90
  criticisms of, 388-89
  in individualized instruction, 406
  letting students know, 414
  settings for achieving, 408-12
  sources and standards for, 414
  taxonomies of, 392-98
  testing mastery of, 491
  types of, 385-88
  value of, 383-85
Objective testing, 526-29, 532
Object permanence, 56
Observation, direct, 35-36
Observational learning, 182-87, 188
Observation as research method, 23
One-way logic, 57
Only children, 130
Open approaches, 445
Operant conditioning, 173-82, 194
  controlling antecedents and, 181
  controlling consequences and, 176-81
  defined, 175
  guidelines for using, 182
Operationalization of objectives, 386

Operation Head Start, 99
Operations, defined, 57
Opinion tasks, 427
Opportunities, teaching, 32
Oral assignments, 195
Oral feedback, 539
Oral language disorders, 461
Organization
  basic tendency toward, 52
  changes in, 52-53
  effective teaching and, 422-24
  of instruction, guidelines for, 442-43
  remembering and, 252-53
Organizers, advance, 278-79
Originality, 150, 161
Origins, 330
Orthopedic handicaps, 456-57
Outcomes, learning, 272-74
Overgeneralization, 75, 283
Overlapping, 366
Overlearning, 302
Overregularization, 76-77

P

Paperwork, 8
Paraphrasing, 370
Parents
  child abuse by, 133
  child-rearing practices, 128-29
  discipline styles, 129
  homework problems and, 231
  individual differences and, 134
  language development and, 74-75
  rights, 471-72, 554-55
  sex-role development and, 97
  See also Divorce
Parent-teacher conferences, 553-54
Partial retrieval of memory, 251
Participation structures, 354-55
Part learning, 254
Pascal (language), 572-74
Passive style of teacher response, 373, 375
Patience, shaping, 195
Patterns, recognizing, 290-91
Pawns, 330
Peer pressure, 216
Peer ratings, 36
Peer tutoring, 206-7
Peg-type mnemonics, 255-57
Percentage grading, 546-48
Percentile rank scores, 496, 497
Perception, 104-7, 227, 238-41, 317-18
Performance, reinforcement schedule and, 179-80
Peripherals for computers, 563
Permissive parents, 129

Personal and social development, 49
  day care and, 98-99
  education for, 114-17
  Erikson's theory of, 86-96
  moral development, 109-14
  self and others, 107-9
  of self-concept, 104-7
Personalization of computer instruction, 567-68
Personalized System of Instruction (PSI), 191-92
Personal territories, 410
"Person permanence," 107
Petit mal epilepsy, 456
Physical development, 49, 101-3, 104
Physical problems, 456-57
Piagetian theory, 50-71
  criticisms of, 50-51
  limitations and implications of, 65-71
  on making sense of the world, 52-55
  on readiness and thinking, 51-52
  stages of cognitive development, 55-56
PKU disease, 125
Placement, 468, 470-71
Planning, teacher, 382-415
  for classroom management, 355-63, 378
  formats for teaching, 231, 398-408, 415
  lesson, 414, 423
  of measurement program, 531-35
  research on, 382-83
  task analysis, 390-92
  See also Objectives for learning
Plato system, 562, 565
Plus-one matching, 116
Point grading system, 546, 547
Positive behavior, focusing on, 114, 198-204, 205
Positive emotional climate, 326-28
Positive practice, 202
Positive reinforcement, 176-77
Positive transfer, 295-96, 301-2
Postconventional moral reasoning, 109, 111
PQ4R, 292-94
Practice, 194, 195, 202, 254, 515
Prägnanz, 238
Praise, teacher, 199-200, 201, 216
Preconventional moral reasoning, 109, 110
Pregnancies, teenage, 20
Preliminary Report of the Commission on Behavior Modification, 225
Premack principle, 203-4

Preoperational stage, 55, 56-59, 60
Preschool child, 92, 98-100
Presentation punishment, 178
Pressure, peer, 216
Pretest, 525
Previewing, 293
Privacy rights, 554
Proactive interference, 250, 295
Problem of the match, 67-70
Problems, classroom, 364-68, 370-71
Problems, learning, See Learning problems
Problem solving, 283-92, 303
  defined, 283
  effective, 290-92, 309
  evaluating results, 289-90
  no-lose method of, 374-75
  selecting approach for, 288-89
  story problems, 286, 308
  understanding and representing problem, 283-87
Procedural knowledge, 290
Procedural tasks, 427
Procedures, classroom, 356-59, 361-62
Process simulations, 566
Profound retardation, 469
Programmed instruction, 188-91
Programming, computer, 572-74
Project Success Environment, 216-17
Prompting, 204-7
Proposition, assignment and relational, 284
Propositional network, 245-47
Prototype, 282
Proximal development, zone of, 70-71
Psychology,
  defined, 21
  educational, 20-25
  humanistic, 318
Psychomotor domain, 395-96
Psychomotor objectives, 395-96
Psychosocial development, 87-96
Puberty, 102. See also Adolescence
Public concern over schools, 14
Public Law 94-142, 18, 470-72, 514
Punishment, 178, 210, 211-13

Q

Quality, teacher, 14-17
Questions
  as part of teaching format, 398-401
  generating, 293, 415
  as part of teaching research, 34-39

R

Race, intelligence test scores and, 143
Random assignment of subjects, 24, 38, 39
Ratings, teacher and peer, 36
Readiness, thinking and, 51-52
Reading, 260-64, 292-94, 406, 458
Realism, moral, 109
"Reality shock," 12
Reasoning, 61, 63-64, 109-11, 146, 204-5, 274-76, 277
Reception learning, 276-80
Receptors, 236
Reciprocal teaching, 262-64
Reciting, 292, 398
Recording phase, self-management, 221-22
Records, cumulative, 346-47
Reflection, 155-56, 292
Rehearsal, 242
Reinforcement, 176-81
  behavioral approaches to motivation and, 313-14
  cognitive perspective on, 235
  extrinsic, 331
  group consequences, 214-16
  negative, 177-78, 202, 209-10, 231
  observational learning and, 185
  positive, 176-77
  schedules, 178-81
  self-, 223
  sense of competence from, 328-31
  shaping through, 208
  with teacher attention, 199-200
  teacher expectations and, 338
  timeout from, 212
  token, 216-18
Reinforcers, 202-4, 212
Relational proposition, 284
Relearning, 254
Reliability, test score, 499-500, 503
Remembering, 250-57, 268-69. See also Memory
Removal punishment, 178
Replication, 41
Report cards, 544-46
Representing problems in problem solving, 283-87
Repression of memory, 250
Reprimands, benefits, of, 211
Research, 33-45
  on classroom management, 23-24, 356
  on effective teaching, 420-21
  environment-behavior, 410
  guidelines for evaluating, 43
  hypothesis and approach, 36-39
  on individualized instruction, 407-8

questions, 34-39
sample study, 41-44
on teacher characteristics,
limitations of, 426
on teacher planning, 382-83
validity of, 39-41, 43-44
variables and measurement
techniques, 35-36, 38, 39-40
Resource rooms, 473-74
Response(s) in behavioral
approaches, 168, 169-82
cost, 212
patterns, reinforcement schedule
and, 179-80
set, 287
teacher, styles of, 373-74, 375
trying new, 173-82
Responsibility, encouraging
student, 365
Resultant motivation, 322
Retardation, mental, 125, 466-69,
470
Retention, observation and, 184
Retrieval cues, 252. See also
Memory
Retroactive interference, 250, 296
Reversible thinking, 57-58, 61
Revise option in contract system,
548-49
Rewards, 185, 194, 202-4, 214,
226-27
of teaching, 10-11
Rights, student and parent, 471-72,
554-55
Ripple effect, 186-87
Role playing, 308
Rote memorization, 254
Routine tasks, 427
Rule-eg method, 277
Rules, classroom, 273, 356-62

S

Salaries, teacher, 9, 15
Satiation, 210-11
Scaffolding, 71
Schedules of reinforcement, 178-81
Schemata, 247-49
Schema training, 285-86
Schemes, 53
Scholastic aptitude test, 508-9
School
  "free," 445
  middle-class culture of, 513
  public concern about, 14
  self-concept development and,
    106
  sex-role development and, 97-98
Scientific approach, need for, 22-25

Scientific reasoning, 63-64
Scores, test, 492-502
  basic concepts, 492-95
  interpreting, 498-502
  IQ, 37, 139, 140-45, 509
  norm-referenced achievement,
    505-7
  types of, 495-98
  See also Grades and grading
Seating, classroom, 410-12
Seatwork, 403-5, 415
Secondary school years, 7, 358-59,
  362-63, 367-68, 443-44
Segregated ability classes, 148-49
Selective attention, 241
Self-actualization, 318
Self-concept, 104-7, 334, 457
Self-efficacy, 314
Self-evaluation, 222
Self-fulfilling prophecy, 331, 332
Self-image of minority children, 480
Self-instruction, 156-57
Self-management, 221-24, 355
Self-pacing in computer instruction,
  567
Self-reinforcement, 223
Self-report method, 35
Self-worth, 323
Semantic memory, 245
Semantics, 75
Sensorimotor stage, 55, 56, 88, 90
Sensory register, 236-38, 242
Serial-position effect, 254
Seriation, 61
Set induction, 401
Severe retardation, 469
Sex, mental abilities and, 145-47
Sex roles, 97-98, 99, 120
Sexual maturation, 103
Sexual relations, 96
Shaping, 207-8
Short-term memory, 242-44, 250
Sign language, 458
Simulations, computer, 566, 569-70
Single-parent families, 32, 130-32
Skills
  basic, 430-34, 439
  study, 291-97
  verbal, 140, 146
Skinner boxes, 175-76
Skinnerian programming, 189
Skipping grades, 23, 485
Social cognition, 107-8
Social cognitive theory, 166, 183,
  185, 314-15
Social development. See Personal
  and social development;
  Psychosocial development
Social isolation, punishment with,
  212-13

Social issues affecting teachers,
  13-20
Socialized aggression, 464
Socioeconomic status (SES), 126,
  128, 142-43
Software, computer, 19, 570, 573,
  574-75
Spasticity, 457
Specific learning disabilities, 465-66,
  467
Specific objectives, 385-88
Specific transfer, 296-300
Speech impairments, 460-61
Speech reading, 458
Spelling, finger, 458
Split-half reliability, 500
Stack seating arrangement, 411
Stand-alone unit, 562-63
Standard deviation, 493-95
Standard error of measurement,
  500
Standardized tests, 492, 502-18
  achievement tests, 503-7, 520
  aptitude tests, 508-10
  current issues in, 510-18
  diagnostic tests, 507-8, 525
Standard scores, 497-98, 499
Standard speech, 77, 78
Stanford-Binet IQ test, 139
Stanford Program (CBE), 562
Stanine scores, 498
Statistical significance, 41, 44
Stereotypes, sex-role, 97-98
Stigmas, labels as, 453-54
Stimulus, 168, 169-73, 181
Story grammars, 260
Strengths, teaching to, 455
Stress, 9-10, 130
Structure, discovering, 274
Structure, need for, 342
Student(s)
  average, overlooking, 160
  differential treatment of, 336-38
  effective teaching of different,
    434-40
  expectations, effect of, 41-44
  grades and grading, effect of,
    535-42
  impact of behavioral methods on,
    227-28
  learning, academic tasks and,
    426-29
  minority, 479-81, 513-14
  needs, meeting, 319, 321-24
  obese, 120-21
  perceptions of rewards, 227
  responsibility, encouraging, 365
  rights, 471-72, 554-55
  secondary, special problems
    with, 367-68

Student(s) (cont.)
testing of new teachers, 230
See also Exceptional students
Student-teacher conferences, 552-53
Student-teacher interactions, 336-38
Student teachers, 415
Student Teams-Achievement
Divisions (STAD), 327-28
Study skills, 291-97
Stuttering, 461, 462
Subjectivity in testing, 530
Subjects, research, 36, 38, 39
Subsumer, 276
Success, motivation and sense of,
346
Success in life, IQ scores and, 142
Suicide, teenage, 465
Supervision, student involvement
without, 364
Sustaining expectation effect,
333-34

T

Target errors, 366
Task analysis, 390-92
Tasks, academic, 426-29
Taxonomies of objectives, 392-98
Teacher(s)
attention, reinforcement with,
199-200
burnout, 10
-centered instruction, 434
characteristics of effective, 361-63,
421-26
child abuse cases and, 133
classical conditioning use by, 170
cognitive styles, 154-55
conferences, student and parent,
552-54
development of empathy and, 109
discouraging aggression, 114
expectations, 331-39, 347, 534
getting student's attention,
241-42
identity formation and, 94-95
major concerns of beginning,
12-13
quality, 14-17
ratings, 36
roles of, 4-7
salaries, 9, 15
sex-role bias of, 98
social issues affecting, 13-20
-student interactions, 336-38
testing, 15-17, 32
training, 15, 31
See also Planning, teacher
Teaching
about concepts, 282-83

active, 430-34
as art v. science, 2-3
as a career, 8-11, 31
explicit, 430-34
expository, 276-80
formats for, 231, 398-408, 415
functions, 431
the gifted, 477-79
language and, 78-80
matching to students, 82-83
new behaviors, 185
reading comprehension, 262-64
reciprocal, 262-64
rewards of, 10-11
Skinner's guidelines for, 187-88
to strengths or weaknesses, 455
theories of, 24-25
thinking, 302-5
for transfer, 295-302, 309
See also Effective teaching
Team Assisted Individualization,
407
Technology. *See* Computers(s)
Technology, behavioral, 187-92
Teenage pregnancies, 20
Telegraphic speech, 75
Television, aggression and, 113-14
Territoriality, 408, 410
"Testing" behaviors, students', 230
Test-retest reliability, 499
Tests and testing, 487-521
anxiety and, 340-41, 342
classroom, 524-35
criterion-referenced, 490-91
essay, 527-31, 532
instructional objectives and, 385
intelligence, 140, 141, 476
IQ, 140, 148-49, 508-9, 513, 514
measurement and evaluation,
138-42
norm-referenced, 489-90, 491,
504-7
objective, 526-29, 532
role of, 511-12
scores, 37, 139, 140-45, 492-502,
505-7, 509
standardized, 492, 502-18
current issues in, 510-18
types of, 503-10, 520, 525
subjectivity in, 530
for teachers, 15-17, 32
on trial, 513-14
See also Grades and grading
Test taking, coaching and, 514-15,
521
Textbooks, 98, 294-97
Thinking
analogical, 289
convergent and divergent, 150
critical, 302-5

games, 68-68
intuitive, 275
original, 150, 161
Piaget's theory of changes in,
50-65
readiness and, 51-52
reversible, 57-58, 61
styles of, 152-57
teaching, 302-5
See also Cognitive development
Thought-provoking questions, 400
Time
cultural orientation toward, 127
engaged, 354, 448
for learning, 353-54
to think of answers, allowing,
400-401
Timeout from reinforcement, 212
Time-sharing system, 562
Timing errors, 366
Tip-of-the-tongue phenomenon,
251
Toddler stage, development in, 89,
90-91
Token reinforcement programs,
216-18
Top-down processing, 240
Training, teacher, 15, 31
Training in test-taking skills, 514-15
Transfer, teaching for, 295-302, 309
Translation and schema training,
285-86
True score, 500, 506
Trust v. mistrust, 88-90
Truth in testing, 512
T score, 498, 545-47
Tutorials, 565-66
Tutors, 206-7, 565-71

U

Unconditioned response (UR), 170
Unconditioned stimulus (US), 170
Undergeneralization, 283
Underlining, 294-97
Understanding of problem, 283-87

V

Validity, research, 39-41, 43-44
Validity, test score, 501-2, 503
Values, 121, 127, 511
Variable-interval reinforcement, 180
Variable-ratio schedules, 180
Variables, research, 35, 38, 39-40
Verbal information, types of, 273
Verbalization process, 289
Verbal learning, meaningful, 277
Verbal skills, 140, 146

Vicarious conditioning, 183
Violence
   in the classroom, 368
   on television, 113-14
Vocational tests, 509-10
Voice quality, grading and, 533
Voicing problems, 461

W

Weaknesses, teaching to, 455

Wechsler Scales (IQ), 139-40, 145-46
Whole-class rewards, 214
Within-class grouping, 149
Withitness, 364-66
"Word magic," 384
Word processing, 471
Workbooks, 82-83
Working-backward strategy, 289
Working mothers, 132
Written teacher comments, 538-39

Zone of proximal development, 70-71
z score, 498